WILDLIFE CONSERVATION
IN METROPOLITAN ENVIRONMENTS

Proceedings of a National Symposium on Urban Wildlife

11–14 November 1990
Cedar Rapids, Iowa

National Symposium on Urban Wildlife
Theme: Meeting Public and Resource Needs

Organized by:

National Institute for Urban Wildlife
Gomer E. Jones, President

Sponsors:

ARCO Foundation
Bureau of Land Management
Chevron U.S.A. Inc.
Edison Electric Institute
IE Industries
Iowa Department of Natural Resources

J.N. "Ding" Darling Foundation
Max McGraw Wildlife Foundation
National Institute for Urban Wildlife
National Park Service
U.S. Fish and Wildlife Service

In Cooperation With:

American Planning Association
American Society of Landscape Architects
Critter Control, Inc.
Iowa Chapter, The Wildlife Society
Iowa Power Company

Iowa Wildlife Federation
Natural Resources Management Program,
   University of Maryland, College Park
The Wildlife Society

Symposium Chairman:

Daniel L. Leedy
National Institute for Urban Wildlife

Program Committee:

Lowell W. Adams (Chairman), National Institute
   for Urban Wildlife
Thomas M. Franklin, The Wildlife Society
John E. Hench, Maryland National Capital Park
   and Planning Commission
Helene L. Kasser, American Planning
   Association
Tracy Kay, Rye Nature Center

Daniel L. Leedy, National Institute for Urban
   Wildlife
Jon Rodiek, Texas A & M University
William W. Shaw, University of Arizona
David L. Tylka, Missouri Department of
   Conservation
Larry W. VanDruff, State University of New York

Host Committee:

Lee Liu (Chairman), IE Industries

Local Arrangements:

Richard A. Patterson (Chairman), Indian Creek
   Nature Center

WILDLIFE CONSERVATION
IN METROPOLITAN ENVIRONMENTS

Edited by

Lowell W. Adams
and
Daniel L. Leedy

Published by
National Institute for Urban Wildlife
10921 Trotting Ridge Way
Columbia, Maryland 21044, USA

Production of this book was made possible
by a grant from Exxon Chemical Company.

ISBN 0-942015-03-7
Library of Congress Catalog Card Number: 91-60099

Published by the National Institute for Urban Wildlife, 10921 Trotting Ridge Way, Columbia, Maryland 21044, USA.

Typeset and printed in the United States of America by Automated Graphic Systems, White Plains, Md.

Contents

III.
PLANNING AND DESIGN

IV.
MANAGEMENT ISSUES AND SUCCESSES

V.
PUBLIC PARTICIPATION AND EDUCATION

VIII.
SYMPOSIUM SUMMARY

I.

Wildlife Conservation in Metropolitan Environments

Chair: Daniel L. Leedy, *Senior Scientist,*
National Institute for Urban Wildlife,
Columbia, Maryland

Welcome

GOMER E. JONES, *President, National Institute for Urban Wildlife, 10921 Trotting Ridge Way, Columbia, MD 21044*

On behalf of the officers, directors, members, and staff of the National Institute for Urban Wildlife, I extend a sincere welcome to you all. I especially want to thank our Symposium Chairman, Dr. Daniel Leedy; our Program Chairman, Dr. Lowell Adams; our Local Arrangements Chairman, Rich Patterson; our Host Committee Chairman, Lee Liu; and our session chairs and cochairs for all of the effort and expertise they have contributed. I believe their hard work will result in a most informative and inspirational meeting.

This conference would not have been possible without the support of our cosponsors: ARCO Foundation, Bureau of Land Management, Chevron U.S.A. Inc., Edison Electric Institute, IE Industries, Iowa Department of Natural Resources, J.N. "Ding" Darling Foundation, Max McGraw Wildlife Foundation, National Park Service, and U.S. Fish and Wildlife Service. In addition, the following symposium cooperators were instrumental in organizing and convening the meeting: American Planning Association, American Society of Landscape Architects; Critter Control, Inc.; Iowa Chapter, The Wildlife Society; Iowa Power Company; Iowa Wildlife Federation; Natural Resources Management Program, University of Maryland, College Park; and The Wildlife Society.

The theme for this opening session is "Wildlife Conservation in Metropolitan Environments: Meeting Public and Resource Needs." I believe the greatest threats to wildlife—indeed, to our environment—are our expanding population and the economy. There is a need, nationally and internationally, for a balanced commitment to both sustained economic development as well as responsible environmental and resource protection. The National Institute for Urban Wildlife believes that these are mutually dependent, not mutually exclusive.

The National Institute for Urban Wildlife was organized in 1973 as the only national scientific and educational organization concerned primarily with the enhancement of urban wildlife values and habitat for people in urban, suburban, and developing areas. We are concerned with the study of human-wildlife relationships and the natural environment where most of us live, work, and play.

The fact is humans have been affecting the environment since *Homo sapiens* first stood erect . . . and as our population grows, more and more green space is consumed. Wild animals are squeezed out of the habitat they need for survival as the habitat itself disappears under new development. But it is important to note that clean air, clean water, and the conservation of habitat are important not only to wildlife, but, more importantly, to people.

Where the developer's bulldozer meets nature there is a raw edge. It is the boundary between two worlds: the natural environment, studied by scientists and appreciated by many, and the manufactured environment, fabricated by those who know how to build homes, develop our natural resources, and make the products that stand between us and the elements, hunger, and disease. These two worlds vie to exclude each other. And, all too often, after the developer has gone, millions of people must live with less than what is attainable—a living environment in harmony with nature.

Considering the population projections for the United States alone, we know the growth of urbanization, agriculture, industry, and technology will require increasing volumes of land and resources. It is clear that we will continue to manipulate, urbanize, and utilize more and more of our natural resources. The challenge before us is to do this in ways that minimize adverse effects on wildlife and our environment.

The good news is that development and environmental protection can and do coexist well—that some of the best wildlife enhancements have been done by industry biologists.

Based on our work with government agencies and industry, through our studies of urban wildlife reserves and corridors, stormwater management for wildlife, wildlife compatibility studies of the petroleum, electric utilities, and coal surface mining industries, we have been impressed by the tremendous progress that has been made by industry in protecting the environment, controlling pollution, reducing waste, and enhancing wildlife habitat.

We see real estate developers planning in harmony with the land rather than dominating it; petroleum compa-

Wildlife Conservation in Metropolitan Environments. NIUW Symp. Ser. 2, L.W. Adams and D.L. Leedy, eds. Published by Natl. Inst. for Urban Wildl., 10921 Trotting Ridge Way, Columbia, MD 21044, USA, 1991.

nies spending millions of dollars on scientific research and planning to minimize the effects of their operations on the environment; utility companies managing their lands and rights-of-way for diverse habitat and corridors for wildlife; coal surface mining companies enhancing wildlife habitat on their lands both during operations and as a part of their reclamation; and I could go on and on.

Represented among the participants at this symposium are the disciplines that industry, government, and individual landowners must depend upon to help them protect the environment and enhance wildlife habitat. I congratulate all of you on your dedication, and I hope your participation in this conference will add new dimensions to your valuable expertise.

Opening Remarks

DANIEL L. LEEDY, *Senior Scientist, National Institute for Urban Wildlife, 10921 Trotting Ridge Way, Columbia, MD 21044*

I am pleased to join President Jones in welcoming you to this national symposium on urban wildlife. It is good to be in Iowa, a state that has produced many outstanding conservationists—Ding Darling and Ira Gabrielson to mention only two. I am listed in the program as Senior Scientist and Symposium Chairman. I may be senior in years, but I defer to Dr. Lowell Adams as the scientist who has done most of the work in organizing and developing the program.

As we discuss Wildlife Conservation in Metropolitan Environments during the next 3 days, we shall be doing what Professor Rudolf Bennitt, first president of The Wildlife Society, hoped might happen at a future wildlife conference. At the North American Wildlife Conference in 1946 when the emphasis in wildlife conservation still was largely on game and sport hunting, Professor Bennitt stated, ". . . I still look forward to the day when we shall hear men discuss the management of songbirds, wildflowers, and the biota of a city, a tropical rainforest, or the eroded wastelands of China . . . we shall not play our part if we concern ourselves only with sport and only with North America."

When I began my career in the wildlife conservation field as a graduate student studying pheasants in the 1930s, I was little concerned with urban wildlife. By the 1950s when I headed up research in the Fish and Wildlife Service and later in the Bureau of Outdoor Recreation, my interests had broadened a great deal. I tried without much success to obtain federal funds for research on endangered species, nongame, and, yes, for work on urban wildlife. We did make some headway and, I like to think, helped pave the way for my successors. Lack of adequate funding is still a major stumbling block, but progress is being made.

There is growing recognition among young people and others that we must alter our ways of living if we wish to maintain a high quality environment. At the polls November 6, the voters of Montgomery County, Maryland, where I live, apparently decided that progress does not necessarily mean more rapid development at the expense of the environment; so they did not re-elect some County Council members considered to be too development-oriented.

There are many competing interests in the use of our natural resources both in metropolitan and rural areas. Tough decisions have to be made, but I think our citizens are about ready to realize that they can't have their cake and eat it too. Development is necessary, but should be accomplished with minimal damage to the environment. That is one of the reasons we are here today.

Represented in this room are biologists, planners, landscape architects, industrialists, university professors, students and, I hope, builders, developers, and private citizens as well. You are the kinds of people who can provide leadership and, with the help of politicians and the support of the public, get sound programs of resource management underway.

Since our last symposium in Chevy Chase, Maryland in November 1986, several relevant meetings and happenings have taken place. There has been some follow-through on the suggested nationwide development of connecting greenways and vegetated corridors. An Urban Natural Areas Workshop was held in Calgary, Alberta, 24 January 1987. Proceedings of a national symposium entitled *Wildlife Conservation and New Residential Developments* held in Tucson, Arizona in January 1986 were published in 1987. A session on Perspectives in Urban Ecology was held at the Denver Museum of Natural History 18 March 1990. A promising new cooperative urban wildlife program has been initiated in Florida. The Wildlife Society's (TWS) Urban Wildlife Committee has published a report on urban research and education in North American Colleges and Universities. Also TWS and the Wildlife Management Institute have cooperated with the National Institute for Urban Wildlife in sponsoring annual Urban Wildlife Open Exchange sessions at the North American Wildlife and Natural Resources Conferences. The National Institute for Urban Wildlife has kept in touch with urban ecologists in England and elsewhere. We are honored to have two of these ecologists with us at this meeting—Mr. George Barker and Dr. David Goode. Dr. Lowell Adams participated in international urban ecology meetings in England and Holland in September 1987.

Recently, I read a 636-page book entitled *The Urban*

Wildlife Conservation in Metropolitan Environments. NIUW Symp. Ser. 2, L.W. Adams and D.L. Leedy, eds. Published by Natl. Inst. for Urban Wildl., 10921 Trotting Ridge Way, Columbia, MD 21044, USA, 1991.

Environment: A Sourcebook for the 1990s. This was compiled and published by the Center for Urban Ecology, Birmingham, England in conjunction with the Nature Conservancy Council and the World Wide Fund for Wildlife. This publication contains 1,768 abstracts of the work of over 2,000 people and it provides information from over 900 towns and cities from around the world. Ecologically oriented, many of the abstracts deal with air pollution, heat islands and urban forestry, but urban wildlife and various aspects of socioeconomics and community involvement are given their share of attention.

Many other new developments and challenges that have surfaced during the past 4 years will be brought out in the current meeting. I would urge you to be sure to attend the Poster Session in the Grand Ballroom this evening. This will give you an opportunity to discuss with the respective authors many highly relevant topics. I am sure you will be interested in what our speakers have to report this morning and I trust that within 4 years or so we can have another of these national meetings. Finally, before introducing our first speaker, I want to extend my personal thanks and appreciation to those sponsors and cooperators who made this symposium possible.

The Resource Enhancement and Protection Act—One Method of Meeting Our Public and Resource Needs

LARRY J. WILSON, *Director, Iowa Department of Natural Resources, Wallace State Office Building, Des Moines, IA 50319*

First of all, let me thank the National Institute for Urban Wildlife for the kind invitation to participate in this symposium. Second, I want to welcome you to Iowa and say that I hope your stay will be pleasant and productive. Iowa is a great state. We have at least one good football team here, fantastic scenery, the world's best agricultural lands, abundant fish and wildlife, and very little public land.

Being a native of Illinois but spending 21 years in Utah, including 5 years at Utah State University, I had, over time forgotten the importance of urban habitat and urban wildlife. In fact, the number one criterion my wife and I used in selecting a home in Iowa when we moved here from Utah in 1980 was that the trees had to be taller than the house! Western living, especially desert living, does not offer much in the way of city habitat and wildlife. It appears to me that most of the western states are more into the larger game species in the wide open spaces in contrast to smaller wildlife forms that do quite well in the city environment, at least in those areas where the trees are taller than the house! I acknowledge that some of the far west states and cities are not similar to the inter-mountain west, however. One of the benefits to city dwellers, at least in the Midwest and East, is the enjoyable opportunities to observe wildlife.

If you have seen much of our state, you will understand the comments that I hear occasionally from residents that the only wildlife to be seen is in the towns and cities. I also have heard that from a family in central Illinois, where large expanses of that former great prairie land are now intensively farmed. Simply put, there are many vast regions where the only habitat for wildlife is in the urban area, both large and small.

By about any measure you wish to use, Iowa ranks right close to the bottom in the category of public lands, either in total hectares or by percentage of the total. Although we have about 85 state parks and the same number of state preserves, several wildlife lands, and county and city parks, less than 2% of our state fits in the category of public land.

We rely very heavily on the private landowner to support many of our wildlife and outdoor recreation activities. One of our Natural Resource Commissioners remarked at a public meeting recently that one of the reasons we are so heavily into multiple use and multiple development is that we have so few areas and hectares to work with. We have to squeeze a lot of opportunities into very few places.

It is incumbent on directors of the state fish and wildlife agency to assure a place and support for an urban wildlife program, in my opinion. I realize that in some places there may be a different name of the responsible entity, but the message is, urban wildlife has a place in the overall program.

To help address the habitat-public land shortage, our state legislature in 1987 passed an Open Spaces bill that required a plan and goal of placing 10% of Iowa into public ownership or protection by the year 2000. Our agency, the Department of Natural Resources (DNR), was to prepare a plan, which we did, along with the suggestion that such a goal in 12 years was not realistic. A year later, our state legislature passed the Resource Enhancement and Protection Act (REAP), a broad purpose fund to benefit natural and cultural resources. This Act was established as one means to help fund the goals of the Open Spaces Act passed earlier. Further, REAP is probably one of the most important Iowa legislative acts in many years, comparable in importance to our 1987 Groundwater Protection Act.

In the first year of existence, $16 million was in the REAP fund. This current fiscal year we are receiving over $25 million, and the next fiscal years through the year 2000, $30 million a year will be in the fund. The Iowa lottery and the state general fund are the sources of money for the REAP fund.

Not all of the money in REAP goes to the DNR. The first $350,000 of each year's appropriation is allocated to a conservation education grant program administered by the Department of Education. One percent of the remaining goes to DNR for REAP administration. After these first two allocations, the remaining money is divided according to

Wildlife Conservation in Metropolitan Environments. NIUW Symp. Ser. 2, L.W. Adams and D.L. Leedy, eds. Published by Natl. Inst. for Urban Wildl., 10921 Trotting Ridge Way, Columbia, MD 21044, USA, 1991.

the programs and percentages listed in the legislation. The DNR receives 28% of the remainder for land acquisition and development. These funds are used for what is called open spaces purchase that includes cost sharing with private groups and purchase of special riverside lands. Twenty percent of the remainder goes into the county conservation board system, a unique county-level conservation program, for land acquisition and development; the Department of Agriculture and Land Stewardship receives 20% for soil and water enhancement programs; 15% is for city parks and open space grants; 5% goes to the State Historical Society for its Historic Resource Development grant program; 3% is allocated to the state Department of Transportation to beautify and more properly manage the state's roadsides; and the remaining 9% goes to the DNR for maintenance and expansion of existing state facilities.

Committees to judge grant applications, the method that cities, counties, and the private sector use to seek funds, are appointed by the DNR Director and score projects twice a year to distribute money.

Funds are eligible for use on park and recreation development, but at least 50% of the DNR's portion will be used on land purchases. City and county grants also score well if good land acquisitions are involved. To ensure public participation, the REAP Act requires 17 public assemblies across the state in even numbered years, to be followed by a congress meeting in Des Moines. The congress consists of 85 delegates, five elected from each of the 17 meetings. It met this past July (1990). The congress makes recommendations on REAP policy programs and funding to the Governor, Natural Resource Commission, and state legislature.

Not since the Land and Water Conservation Fund heyday and our state Open Spaces Fund have so many dollars been available for natural resource programs. The REAP Act enjoys very broad base support and is likely to remain intact. Because of this funding opportunity, new open spaces and habitats will be acquired, adding much needed growth to our publicly owned land base in Iowa.

One of our early nongame programs, which probably took very little time and effort but was appreciated by many, was the development of some bird feeding and watching stations at retirement and nursing homes. I am sure that over the years, countless hours have been spent by residents watching and enjoying the birds and other wildlife that used these stations. Our staff has developed urban wildlife plans for over 30 communities in Iowa. Bald Eagle Days along the Mississippi River are enjoyed by thousands of our citizens annually. Although not purely fitting the urban wildlife description, our staff has successfully managed the release of river otter (*Lutra canadensis*) back into former habitat, and the once plentiful barn owl (*Tyto alba*) again has new hope in some parts of our state. Most recently, and very exciting to me personally, has been the release of peregrine falcons (*Falco peregrinus*) in our second largest city. Our staff has aggressively worked with, and obtained support of, city officials for a potential introduction of this spectacular raptor in Des Moines in 1991.

And we have available to any Iowan, or anyone else for that matter, a wealth of printed information on what is the latest in nongame and urban wildlife programs. Our staff conducts numerous lectures to groups upon request, furthering their understanding of the importance and meaning of these species.

Earlier I stated my opinion of the wisdom to include urban wildlife in the planning and programming of the appropriate agency. As our rural population in Iowa declines and our city population increases, such programs will become more important. For many, even in Iowa, urban wildlife may be the only wildlife species they see and appreciate. City parks, and especially recreation trails, are becoming havens for small wildlife. Opportunities are plentiful for planners to include urban wildlife programs in the cities, and we should do just that.

Sanctuaries for birds and small wildlife, trails, small prairie plots, feeding stations next to retirement or nursing homes, and introduction of species that fit are just some of the possibilities for including wildlife species in our urban environment. Cities are full of people waiting to be enlightened with these important programs, and they are waiting for them to happen.

Thank you.

Life-styles and Outdoor Recreational Pursuits

WILLIE DANIEL, *Chair, Department of Health, Physical Education, and Recreation, P.O. Box 4244, Grambling State University, Grambling, LA 71245*

At Grambling State University, we are in the process of completing a study that deals with the life-styles and outdoor recreation pursuits of African-Americans. More specifically, we have attempted to learn something about the frequency and extent to which students in several freshman-level courses engage in outdoor recreation and other social activities in relation to age, sex, income, education, and other factors. We wanted to learn something, also, about the interest of the students in entering the fields of outdoor recreation, park management, and natural resources conservation on a professional basis.

Numbers were assigned to about 175 freshmen and, of these, 100 were selected at random. The students were shown a "Leisure behavior inventory" that listed 29 types of activities or variables. The students then were asked to reflect on what types of activities they had engaged in during their teenage years and report on their visitation frequency in the various categories or at the different sites. They were asked, also, to indicate what they thought they would do as adults.

In brief, the survey showed that, except for going to church, visiting neighbors, and fishing, these young folks did not participate very much in outdoor recreational pursuits. When asked what they would do as adults, a good percentage of the teenagers not visiting parks and other outdoor sites or engaging in outdoor leisure and recreation indicated they would do so later in life. The implication is that when these students mature and have families of their own there will be many more African-Americans utilizing parks and other recreation sites. They will be better educated and have more income as adults and perhaps have more leisure time.

In delving into why relatively few of the surveyed students visited outdoor recreation sites, we looked at demographic data. We found that a great many of the students were females and the largest number of students in the survey was from the South, followed by the North, then the East, and then the West. Not a lot of the respective family members were in college due in part, at least, to economics. Currently, in many cases the father, who may be less well educated, often earns more money than his spouse, who may have a college degree. Although more females get degrees, males get more advanced degrees. Reasons cited by the students for their low visitation rates to outdoor sites included: diverse interests within the family, family outings were not typical, disinterest, lack of funds, lack of time, other commitments, chores, lack of transportation, television viewing, family discord, other interests, and the fact that they did not like family outings.

We are optimistic that conditions will improve with education, including environmental education. Students coming out of school have been exposed to current issues and trends and are more oriented to outdoor recreation, leisure, and environmental quality values. Not only will there be more African-Americans involved in outdoor recreation as individual family members, but there will be more of them entering the wildlife, fishery, and other related fields professionally. Already at Grambling, some students have expressed interest in getting a degree in biology with a focus on park management. Money is being sought through a grant to develop several lakes and a health and fitness trail. Grambling is cooperating with federal and state agencies to advance outdoor and environmental programs. The institution is developing intern and placement programs to help students make intelligent decisions about their careers. With financial support and cooperation, Grambling can play an important role in producing manpower and information that will be required to meet the needs of increased numbers of people at parks, state historic sites, memorials, and the like.

Wildlife Conservation in Metropolitan Environments. NIUW Symp. Ser. 2, L.W. Adams and D.L. Leedy, eds. Published by Natl. Inst. for Urban Wildl., 10921 Trotting Ridge Way, Columbia, MD 21044, USA, 1991.

The National Park Service Experience with Urban Wildlife

F. EUGENE HESTER, *Associate Director, Natural Resources, National Park Service, U.S. Department of the Interior, P.O. Box 37127, Washington, DC 20013-7127*

The image of wildlife in national parks naturally runs to the big and impressive: grizzlies (*Ursus arctos*) in Denali, bighorn sheep (*Ovis canadensis*) in Rocky Mountain, the elk (*Cervus elaphus*) of Yellowstone. But in recent years the National Park Service (NPS) also has had to deal with such wildlife as gray squirrels (*Sciurus carolinensis*) near the White House and laughing gulls (*Larus atricilla*) at Kennedy Airport. Urban squirrels became part of our management portfolio when we assumed responsibility for the National Capital Parks. With the creation later of several national recreation areas at cities, the Service entered the urban park scene in an even bigger way. Now, after several decades of experience, I think we have made noteworthy strides in research, management, and interpretation of urban wildlife.

HISTORICAL BACKGROUND

The Park Service has been involved with city, county, and state parks in an advisory and technical capacity for many years. One example of this is our work to help develop greenways in urban areas—networks of linear open space connecting larger natural and recreational areas. This is an old idea that recently received a push from the President's Commission on Americans Outdoors. Emphasizing river and trail corridors, the Park Service is now assisting with greenway planning in Richmond and Loudoun County, Virginia; San Francisco; Chicago; and other urban (and rural) areas around the country.

The agency's direct management of urban natural areas began with transfer of the parks and monuments in Washington, D.C. to the Service in 1933. These included Rock Creek Park, which may be the largest natural area within a U.S. city, and smaller forested areas such as Glover-Archbold Park. More recent additions include Dyke Marsh and the forested Theodore Roosevelt Island. Donald McHenry, who was appointed the first Chief Naturalist for the National Capital Parks in 1936, energetically developed an interpretive program that reached schools as well as park visitors. Many of those walks, talks, and exhibits dealt with wildlife.

The work in the nation's capital, however, remained an anomalous adjunct to that in traditional national parks for more than three decades. Then, beginning in 1968 and running through the 1970s, a series of national recreation areas was established in or near other cities. These units included Gateway, at New York; Golden Gate, at San Francisco; Cuyahoga Valley, between Cleveland and Akron; Chattahootchee River, near Atlanta; and Santa Monica Mountains, near Los Angeles. Indiana Dunes National Lakeshore at Gary fulfilled much the same function, and Jean LaFitte National Historical Park, in and near New Orleans, included natural as well as historical areas.

This push for urban parks sprang from a desire by Presidents Johnson and Nixon and their Secretaries of the Interior, Stewart Udall and Walter Hickel, to improve life in the cities. The creation of NPS urban parks was championed at the agency level by Director George Hartzog. But support within the ranks was anything but universal. Traditionalists thought the Park Service had no business running natural parks in cities. To them it meant a lowering of standards.

There is no doubt that Park Service philosophy about natural areas receives a real test in urban areas. Obviously, you cannot have a Yellowstone or Yosemite in a city. But you **can** have natural areas in spite of all the urban influences. And these natural areas are invaluable in providing for city people a window on nature and a chance to experience naturalness. In addition to these green islands, any urban park, even if human-dominated or if established for its cultural values, still can offer worthwhile fragments of nature.

The National Park Service now manages areas in and near cities that range from Lafayette Park, a 3-ha square across from the White House in Washington, D.C., to such places as the Marin Headlands north of San Francisco, 2,400 ha of largely natural land where an occasional mountain lion (*Felis concolor*) wanders through. I think we have learned enough to make a few conclusions about managing and interpreting such areas.

MANAGING URBAN WILDLIFE AND HABITAT

We have found so far that in urban areas native ecosystems and their component species can be kept largely intact,

Wildlife Conservation in Metropolitan Environments. NIUW Symp. Ser. 2, L.W. Adams and D.L. Leedy, eds. Published by Natl. Inst. for Urban Wildl., 10921 Trotting Ridge Way, Columbia, MD 21044, USA, 1991.

and sometimes can be restored. Consider the case of Rock Creek Park in Washington, D.C. This 688-ha park, 85% of which is natural forest, is nearly surrounded by residential areas. Only narrow threads of parkway connect it to more rural land in Maryland to the north and to the Potomac River to the south. A heavily traveled road runs the length of the park, and numerous tributary roads branch off from this. Subject to urban run-off, Rock Creek is frequently scoured during storms and at times is loaded with sediment.

In spite of these impacts, the forest remains basically healthy, with good reproduction. Some 1,200 species of plants have been recorded in the park. The mammals include red (*Vulpes vulpes*) and gray (*Urocyon cinereoargenteus*) foxes and muskrats (*Ondatra zibethicus*). In recent years, white-tailed deer (*Odocoileus virginianus*) have increased and beaver (*Castor canadensis*) have recolonized the park. Among the birds are pileated woodpeckers (*Dryocopus pileatus*) and barred (*Strix varia*) and great horned (*Bubo virginianus*) owls. Some two dozen species of fish, including channel catfish (*Ictalurus punctatus*) and small-mouth bass (*Micropterus dolomieui*), manage to live in Rock Creek. Herrings (*Clupea harengus*) and a few white (*Morone americana*) and yellow (*Perca flavescens*) perch migrate up the stream in spring.

Inevitably, however, there have been losses. Skunks (Mephitinae), woodchucks (*Marmota monax*), and weasels (*Mustela* spp.) are no longer seen. A long-term bird census in a 26-ha tract revealed a gradual loss of black-and-white (*Mniotilta varia*), hooded (*Wilsonia citrina*), and Kentucky (*Oporornis formosus*) warblers and yellow-throated vireos (*Vireo flavifrons*), and a big decline of ovenbirds (*Seiurus aurocapillus*) and red-eyed vireos (*Vireo olivaceus*). Whether these losses are due to subtle changes in the Rock Creek habitat or problems elsewhere, such as loss of tropical forest winter habitat, is the subject of much debate. The larger snakes and the basking turtles are seldom seen. Amphibians are scarce because of lack of suitable breeding places.

To help maintain diversity, 23 small patches of meadow have been allowed to develop through restriction of mowing. Baseline inventories of various taxa were conducted in these meadows. Although follow-up surveys have not yet been conducted, butterflies appear to have increased.

The Park Service concept of naturalness is sharply illustrated in its approach to exotic species. These it defines as any species that reaches an area with human help, intentional or unintentional. The area can be as small as the portion of a stream above a waterfall. Exotics that threaten native species or the integrity of ecosystems are removed to the extent feasible. In Rock Creek Park, the exotic vines kudzu (*Pueraria thunbergiana*), Asian bittersweet (*Celastrus orbiculatus*), and porcelainberry (*Ameplopsis brevipedunculata*), which can smother and kill trees on the forest edge, are under management attack. Removal of exotic fish species, which constitute half of the fish fauna, probably will not be attempted because of the ease of reintroduction.

The increase of deer in Rock Creek Park is viewed by park managers with mixed emotions. Deer are an exciting, beautiful part of the original fauna, but there are few checks on their population growth. Hunting adjacent to the park is not possible, and direct reduction by NPS personnel would be highly unpopular with the public. Deer are a problem in many eastern parks, such as Gettysburg National Military Park and Fire Island National Seashore, where, besides putting pressure on park vegetation, they eat shrubs and garden plants of park neighbors. Such foraging could become a problem in Rock Creek; neighbors there already complain about "park" raccoons getting in their garbage or tearing up their mulch.

The fauna of Golden Gate National Recreation Area is probably still more intact than that of Rock Creek Park. It lacks primarily some of the larger carnivores. However, bobcats (*Lynx rufus*) are plentiful and the coyote (*Canis latrans*) is expected to become reestablished. Spread over a large area north and south of Golden Gate Bridge, the recreation area consists largely of a string of natural areas including rocky shore, grassland, coastal scrub, and coniferous forest. One 10,100-ha tract, long protected as a water supply area for San Francisco, has Douglas-firs (*Pseudotsuga menziesii*) 500 years old.

Convinced that these lands can be kept natural, the Golden Gate managers conduct an aggressive campaign against exotics. Volunteers and park staff pull up exotic plants every weekend, and a containment program for eucalyptus (*Eucalyptus* spp.) is underway, despite opposition from segments of the public that like this tree, exotic or not. Prescribed burning has been conducted for 5 years to maintain natural conditions. On Milagra Ridge, removal of exotic pampas grass (*Cortaderia selloána*) and planting of certain native species has benefited the endangered mission blue (*Icaricia icarioides missionensis*) and San Bruno elfin (*Callophrys mossii bayensis*) butterflies.

Restoration is the big story at Gateway National Recreation Area at New York. Only bits of salt marsh and beach and dune areas resemble the original ecosystems. The rest of the area consists of human-created landforms—land fill (some highly toxic) and dredge fill.

The ultimate goal on most of the area is to restore the native ecosystems, to the extent these can be determined from historical records. Salt marsh and dune grasses have been planted, and on Ruler's Bar Hassock, a dredge-fill island in the middle of Jamaica Bay, native reptiles and amphibians rescued from areas under development on the mainland have been released. Nest boxes have been put up for barn owls (*Tyto alba*), kestrels (*Falco sparverius*), and other birds. Freshwater ponds have been created.

At Floyd Bennett Field, once New York's municipal airport, 54 ha of grassland have been restored with the help of the New York City Audubon Society. With the Manhattan skyline as backdrop, meadowlarks (*Sturnella magna*) and grasshopper sparrows (*Ammodramus savannarum*) now nest here, and some 10 species of raptors have been observed. Other parts of Floyd Bennett Field are returning to shrubland and forest. Some planting of woody species once native to the area is contemplated to hasten this process.

At this stage, a somewhat relaxed attitude about exotics is necessary in a place so disturbed as Gateway. As one resource manager puts it, "Native is better than exotic, and exotic is better than concrete." The goal, however, remains native.

INTERPRETING URBAN WILDLIFE AND HABITAT

Tremendous numbers of people go to NPS urban parks, and because park-goers are traveling shorter distances and taking more, but shorter, vacations than they used to, urban park use is likely to increase faster than use of more distant parks. Golden Gate National Recreation Area recorded the most visits of any unit in the National Park System in 1989—over 16 million. Such numbers present a challenge to avoid damage to park resources, but they also create a huge opportunity for education of city people about wildlife and its environment.

Several of our urban parks have extensive environmental education programs for school children. At Indiana Dunes National Lakeshore, 3,000 programs will be given in 1990 for 50,000 to 70,000 children. Equal numbers are expected for the public programs. Of the 23 topics developed for grades K-12, nine focus specifically on wildlife. They range from puppet shows for first graders to a mock trial of a developer for threatening an endangered species—for high school students.

Park Service interpretation of wildlife, in both urban and more remote parks, does not dwell on the species alone but relates it to other species, its environment, and to local, regional, or global conservation issues. For instance, a butterfly walk designed for children in Rock Creek Park includes catching and identifying butterflies, but it also touches on butterfly biology, their role in nature, and butterfly conservation. On a snake walk at Jamaica Bay, the visitor not only sees snakes but learns about their habitats, the reptile restoration project there, and how urban development affects snakes.

The concept of a national park as a natural system functioning under natural processes is presented. The majority of urban visitors seem to understand and appreciate this idea when it is explained to them. Visitors to Cuyahoga Valley National Recreation Area from Cleveland and Akron, which have many landscaped parks, seem to like the idea and the difference of a totally natural park.

But many urban visitors have some fear of natural areas and what they might contain. This is strongest in inner city children. At Cuyahoga Valley, a wooded tract nestled between the adjoining cities, a Junior Ranger program introduces children from housing projects in Cleveland to the park's wildlife and habitats. They come with the belief that wolves and bears roam the park. They are afraid of snakes, bats, even frogs. The dark frightens them. A guided encounter with frogs usually dispels that fear, but other fears linger. One visit is not enough, and unfortunately that is all most of the inner city children get. I hope a way can be found to arrange repeat visits, here and elsewhere.

Interpreters at Indiana Dunes note a great difference in the responses of inner city and suburban children. Said one interpreter: "Some of the inner city kids, though harboring fear and no knowledge of wildlife, get really jazzed up about the animals. It's a new world to them. For suburban kids it's old hat."

Perhaps the most effective education in parks occurs through the hands-on activities of volunteers in resource management projects. Volunteers in Golden Gate band migrating raptors, inventory terrestrial vertebrates, and help restore native vegetation. In Gateway they have helped to create ponds, put up protective signs and fencing for piping plovers (*Charadrius melodus*), engaged in reptile and amphibian restoration, and participated in numerous other projects. Such volunteer work in parks calls to mind the two-way benefits of the Civilian Conservation Corps during the Depression.

One of our biggest interpretive challenges is to reach those people who, through ignorance of, or disdain for, national park values, abuse resources. Illegal taking of fish and shellfish, for example, is a problem in some NPS urban parks, and educational efforts are underway to address this.

In spite of the surroundings, some of our urban parks offer unusual wildlife viewing opportunities. Migrating waterbirds at Jamaica Bay attract many East Coast birders, as well as foreign nature tours and birdwatchers changing planes at John F. Kennedy Airport. Migrating waterfowl at Indiana Dunes and migrating hawks at Golden Gate are the subjects of special programs. Such places would be good candidates for inclusion in the networks of Watchable Wildlife sites now being developed in a number of states. This program identifies outstanding sites for viewing wildlife in a state, produces state guides to these sites, and promotes interpretation of wildlife and its needs at the sites. Inclusion of such sites in or near cities should be encouraged because of their accessibility for large numbers of people.

RESEARCH

Management and interpretation of urban wildlife requires continuous research. Urban wildlife biology is a relatively new field and many surprises undoubtedly await us. Places like Rock Creek Park are marvelous laboratories for studying the influences of urban activities on natural ecosystems and the behavior of animals in urban settings. Research in such places can not only help us manage urban parks better, but can forewarn us of problems to expect as development closes in on more remote parks.

In the National Park Service, we are fortunate to have the Center for Urban Ecology working on wildlife issues in the National Capital Region and scientists from within and outside the Service studying wildlife in our other urban parks. We consider it both a pleasure and a duty to share what we have learned in forums such as this symposium on urban wildlife.

CONCLUSIONS

I consider the National Park Service venture into urban areas a success. Although it is more difficult to try to achieve the Park Service ideal of fully natural native ecosystems near cities, the greatly expanded opportunity to bring enjoyment and understanding of the natural world into city people's lives more than compensates for any sacrifice of pristine park qualities.

Understanding, managing, and interpreting urban wildlife will continue to be an exciting, valuable adventure. The National Park Service is proud to be a part of it.

Wildlife in a Changing World: Urban Challenges for the Fish and Wildlife Service

BRUCE BLANCHARD, *Deputy Director, U.S. Fish and Wildlife Service, U.S. Department of the Interior, 18th and C Streets N.W., Washington, DC 20240*

I am privileged to be addressing this opening session of the National Symposium on Urban Wildlife. John Gottschalk, past Director of the U.S. Fish and Wildlife Service, presented the opening address at the 1968 Service-sponsored urban symposium, Man and Nature in the City (Gottschalk 1968). At that time, he discussed the rapid urbanization of America and the role of wildlife within that system. The points that he made are still relevant today as well as many of the challenges which past Director, Frank Dunkle, presented at the Institute's 1986 symposium in Chevy Chase, Maryland (Dunkle 1987). I intend, this morning, to continue that discourse and to highlight those directions in which I see the Service moving as we approach the year 2000—directions which I am hopeful that you, as wildlife professionals, will support and become involved in.

Having lived and worked in an urban area for some 20 years, I have developed an understanding of that environment and an appreciation for the wildlife that resides there. Over the years, I have witnessed the continuing migration of people into the Nation's Capital and have seen, first hand, the impacts of this seemingly endless influx of bureaucrats, executives, lobbyists, and upwardly mobile young people; as well as the homeless, the down-trodden, and those searching for a better quality of life.

I have watched the open spaces fill in and the wildlife of field and woodland depart for areas not so competitively sought. I ask myself, what will the City be like in another 30 years and what can we do to ensure that progress will not forever alter what those of us in this room hold valuable? I believe that groups like this come together in order to guarantee responsible action—action that will ensure adequate habitat and healthy populations of wildlife for future generations to enjoy.

As the leading Federal wildlife conservation agency in the world today, the Service is committed to its mission to conserve, protect, and enhance fish, wildlife, and their habitats for the continuing benefit of the American people. Given the state of our ever-changing world, this is a tall order to carry out, but one which the Service believes in and works to uphold. In addition to this statement of purpose that guides all activities within the Service, there are specific objectives which provide further guidance for programs and ventures involving Service participation.

In regard to urban wildlife, this guidance includes maintaining and enhancing desirable wildlife resources and appropriate habitat in existing and developing urban environments; minimizing negative interactions between urban wildlife and human populations in order to encourage public enjoyment and appropriate use of resources; and promoting understanding of wildlife management at all levels of society. Although attempts are made to serve all of these objectives, budget restraints and periodic shifts in national emphasis plague agencies and associated programs throughout the Federal system. Urban wildlife programs, as well as other resource programs, cannot be guaranteed immunity against these constraints.

In addition, it is important for you to understand that existing legislation and treaties dictate that the Service concern itself primarily with migratory, endangered, and interjurisdictional species. Also, the U.S. Department of Agriculture has responsibility for pest species and the states have primary responsibility for resident species. It is necessary to recognize these lines of authority because the misconception often exists that the Service is *directly* responsible for all wildlife.

As we near the end of this century, we can no longer afford to be complacent about urban wildlife or minimize its importance. Most Americans now live in cities and by the year 2000, it is estimated that 90% of all U.S. citizens will live in urban areas, particularly areas located near the coast. Compare this astounding figure to the fact that, in 1914, nearly 50% of the American people lived on farms. According to the 1980 Census, that figure is now less than 3% (U.S. Department of Commerce, Bureau of the Census 1983). We are currently witnessing third and fourth generations of people who have always lived in an urban atmo-

Wildlife Conservation in Metropolitan Environments. NIUW Symp. Ser. 2, L.W. Adams and D.L. Leedy, eds. Published by Natl. Inst. for Urban Wildl., 10921 Trotting Ridge Way, Columbia, MD 21044, USA, 1991.

sphere. Many are out of touch with the natural world and have a limited understanding of wildlife management concerns and concepts.

Based on attitudinal research, Kellert and Berry (1980) suppose that differences between urban and rural residents may represent one of the most difficult and important problems confronting the wildlife management field today. The Service is looking very seriously at what these differences will mean for wildlife, for resource managers, and to the quality of life as we know it.

As we look at this process of urbanization, we must examine what it means to our wildlife and habitat resources. Urbanization causes major changes in both the biological and physical components of existing ecosystems. Trees, shrubs, and other plants are largely removed and soil is covered with concrete and asphalt for buildings, roads, and parking lots. Unpaved soil is compacted by pedestrian traffic. Impermeable surfaces and wetland destruction create heavy rainwater runoff and the movement of wildlife is restricted due to roads, fences, and other obstructions. Urbanization results in increased temperatures, a decline in air and water quality, industrial contamination, and an increasing trend away from the natural world. In addition, urban development affects biodiversity, succession, energy and nutrient flow, and population dynamics and territoriality of species.

An ecological system so dramatically altered by "progress" must be managed very creatively to take advantage of every opportunity for enhancing habitat and stimulating wildlife populations. Through careful management, we can influence the types of wildlife in and near our cities. We can design urban areas to control undesirable species and encourage more preferable ones.

A recent shift toward non-consumptive wildlife activities was documented in the 1985 National Survey of Fishing, Hunting, and Wildlife-associated Recreation (U.S. Department of the Interior, Fish and Wildlife Service 1988). This shift is related to the altered perceptions, attitudes, and needs of urban residents created by urbanization. The survey reported that 110 million people, 61% of the population 12 years old and older, participated in non-consumptive wildlife activities during 1985, a 6% increase over 1980. The survey also identified urban dwellers to be the fastest growing group participating in non-consumptive wildlife-related activities. This group includes those people who have an active interest in wildlife around their homes and who engage in bird feeding, wildlife observation, and wildlife photography. This trend indicates that the Service, as well as other resource-related agencies and groups, must devote attention to the needs of this growing segment of our population.

As the urban sector of society increases, it will be important that the Service involve itself in an effective educational program designed to inform the public about wildlife and about conservation in general. This is necessary in order for people to develop an understanding that man-

aged use of resources is a part of the equation for maintaining well balanced populations of healthy wildlife. In this way, the Service will increase public understanding about the multiple values and benefits of managing wildlife resources. This will be an increasingly important task in the face of declining interest in traditional wildlife activities.

This brings me to a discussion of where I see the Service focusing its efforts, in regard to urban wildlife, during this decade. I feel confident in saying that our focus will be in the area of education, training, and cooperative ventures. This year, Director Turner established the Service's Office of Training and Education in Arlington, Virginia. This office is responsible for overseeing the development of a proposed training and education center to be located in Harpers Ferry, West Virginia. In addition, the office will oversee all training activities involving the Service's 7,000 employees and will direct and coordinate environmental education throughout the agency.

The Service already has a commitment to manage urban wildlife on National Wildlife Refuges (NWR) located in, or near, heavily populated areas of the country. Several of these refuges have active environmental education programs focused toward students, teachers, and, in some cases, the general public. San Francisco Bay NWR is one of the best examples. Located in an urban center of nearly seven million people and surrounded by industry and development, the refuge attracts 350,000 visitors each year. Fifteen thousand of these visits are attributed to students involved in hands-on environmental education in an outdoor classroom setting. An additional 200 visits are recorded annually by teachers who participate in workshops designed to familiarize them with wildlife habitats and with activities that they may later carry out with their students. Rick Coleman, the Refuge Manager, contends that the way to impact the environmental attitudes of adults is through kids. He and his staff are intent on doing their part to see that this transfer of knowledge takes place at San Francisco Bay NWR.

The Tinicum National Environmental Center, located adjacent to the airport in Philadelphia, Pennsylvania, is also part of the National Wildlife Refuge System. Established in 1972, the 364-ha refuge is located in the midst of six and one-half million people. Tinicum was established with environmental education as its primary objective, and since 1979, more than 800 teachers have been trained in one of four state-wide certified environmental workshops for teachers, designed by Tinicum staff.

Still another refuge leader in the field of urban wildlife education is the Minnesota Valley National Wildlife Refuge, located in the Minneapolis-St. Paul area. Established in 1976, the refuge opened the doors of its new multi-million dollar Wildlife Interpretation and Education Center in 1990. It is estimated that visitation will reach 250,000 during 1990 and that 12,000 students and teachers will utilize the refuge for environmental education annually. Surrounded by interstate highways, development, landfills, power plants, and an international airport, the topic of managing urban wildlife dramatically comes to life as refuge employees work with students, teachers, and the general public on this unique and challenging site.

In addition to these areas, urban issues are present at many other Service sites: Parker River and Great Meadows near Boston; New Jersey's Great Swamp located within the New York City metropolitan area; Back Bay and Mason Neck in Virginia; and at the recently established Bayou Sauvage in New Orleans. I guarantee that you will see an increased emphasis by the Service on urban areas such as these in the 1990s.

As the population becomes more urbanized, there will be an increasing need to provide the urban public with positive wildlife experiences—especially non-consumptive experiences. Kellert and Berry (1980) found that urban dwellers have a different orientation toward wildlife due to their lack of exposure to rural living and their less frequent contact with wildlife.

In the United States, an estimated 30% of urban populations are comprised of Americans under 18 years of age. In 1985, the Service funded a study on Youth and Wildlife that examined the attitudes of children toward wildlife (Westervelt and Llewellyn 1986). This study found that the perceptions of children toward wildlife were extremely diverse, although, like adults, the humanistic attitude toward animals exerted considerable influence over the views of these children. In addition, widespread concern about sport hunting among the children surveyed signifies a very real challenge for wildlife managers. These results were specifically aligned along gender and demographic lines with girls and urban children supporting the findings most strongly.

In addressing the attitudes of urban dwellers, one must also consider urban minorities. The 1980 Census stated that 85% of all black Americans live in urban areas. According to Kellert and Berry (1980), black Americans expressed significantly less knowledge and concern about wildlife and the natural environment than did white Americans. Dolin (1988) cited several theories as to why black Americans may express less interest in, or knowledge about, wildlife. These theories include the issues of socioeconomic status, personal priorities, and the lack of access to wildlife. The Service, in its efforts to increase emphasis on environmental education at urban sites, will attempt to provide more direct and positive opportunities for black Americans and other minorities to interact with wildlife and to become involved in the conservation field. Another very important area of emphasis for the Service is cooperative involvement with state and local governments, conservation organizations, and private industry, landowners, and interested individuals. So much of what needs to be accomplished in the area of urban wildlife and urban wildlife management cannot be accomplished by the federal government alone.

The success of the Service's new Wetlands Action Plan, aimed at stemming destruction of the Nation's vanishing wetlands, is a good example of an initiative that will require the participation of other federal agencies. Other examples of cooperative ventures are the North American Waterfowl Management Plan, which has become an innovative international partnership in wildlife conservation; Stewardship 2000—the Service's private lands initiative aimed at obtaining a net gain of fish and wildlife on private lands; and cooperative efforts between the Service and organizations such as the National Institute for Urban Wildlife, which provided printing for the Service's Teacher Pac series on Wildlife Habitat Conservation. This approach to conserving wildlife and wildlife habitat is the wave of the future. I invite and encourage everyone here today to investigate the many partnerships that are being formed within the conservation arena. Get involved!

Other efforts that promote citizen involvement are the Take Pride In America campaign and the many volunteer service programs found throughout government. Take Pride In America was developed to promote and recognize citizen involvement on public lands. This program particularly appeals to Boy Scouts and Girl Scouts, 4-H groups, and to local civic groups and non-profit organizations that are interested in community service projects. In recognition of these volunteer efforts, Secretary of the Interior, Manuel Lujan, and actress Linda Evans, presented 680 awards during the 1989 Take Pride in America National Awards Ceremony. In addition, the Service nationally recognized nearly 50 individuals and groups, during the same year, for their Take Pride In America efforts. For individuals or groups interested in continuous volunteer service, many refuges, hatcheries, and Service laboratories have a need for help.

In closing, I would like to thank you for your attention and ask that you reflect on the urban issues and possible solutions that I, and other speakers, bring to this podium today and throughout the week. Our Nation is experiencing a period of heightened environmental awareness. The time is ripe for establishing partnerships, for engaging the public in issues related to wildlife and the environment, and for renewing our own commitment to the world in which we live.

As professional wildlife managers, biologists, teachers, and naturalists, we must set an example through action and promote responsible stewardship for lands and wildlife. We live in an age of unrelenting pressures—a period when the urban environment, in particular, will require careful attention. As we leave this symposium at the end of the week, I challenge all of you to return to your respective homes and jobs and to consider what role *you* will play in our changing world. Urban responsibility belongs to us all; for what happens in the natural world will in turn happen to us.

Thank you.

REFERENCES CITED

Dolin, E.J. 1988. Black Americans' attitudes toward wildlife. J. Environ. Educ. 20:17–21.

Dunkle, F.H. 1987. Urban wildlife and the Fish and Wildlife Service: meeting a growing challenge. Pages 5–7 *in* L.W. Adams and D.L. Leedy, eds. Integrating man and nature in the metropolitan environment. Natl. Inst. for Urban Wildl., Columbia, Md.

Gottschalk, J.S. 1968. Opening remarks. Pages vii–viii *in* Man and nature in the city. Publ. No. 337-135-0-69, U.S. Gov. Printing Off., Washington, D.C.

Kellert, S.R., and J.K. Berry. 1980. Knowledge, affection and basic attitudes toward animals in American society. Publ. No. 024-010-00-625-1, U.S. Gov. Printing Off., Washington, D.C. 162 pp.

U.S. Department of Commerce, Bureau of Census. 1983. 1980 census of population—general population characteristics, United States summary. Publ. No. PC80-1-B1, U.S. Gov. Printing Off., Washington, D.C.

U.S. Department of the Interior, Fish and Wildlife Service. 1988. 1985 national survey of fishing, hunting, and wildlife associated recreation. U.S. Gov. Printing Off., Washington, D.C. 167 pp.

Westervelt, M.O., and L. G. Llewellyn. 1986. Youth and wildlife. Publ. No. 024-010-00-664-1, U.S. Gov. Printing Off., Washington, D.C. 78 pp.

Urban Wildlife: Industry Perspective

LEE LIU, *Chairman & Chief Executive Officer, IE Industries Inc., P.O. Box 351, Cedar Rapids, IA 52406*

I am pleased to have the opportunity to share some thoughts with this distinguished group attending the National Symposium on Urban Wildlife. We welcome you to Cedar Rapids. One of the most important reasons that energy companies such as IE Industries are involved with conservation and environmental protection is the corporate concern for quality of life in the communities we serve and the nation as a whole. This, I believe, is very much in line with the thinking of the conservation and environmental groups in this country. We do not see any conflict. We see a common goal that we must share together.

Energy companies such as ours have been much more proactive in recent years. We believe we must be part of a solution in environmental matters instead of being part of the problem. The solution requires our active participation. If we do not participate, then there is a genuine fear that emotion will win over facts and science will lose to perception. In the case of Iowa Electric and IE Industries, our commitment to environmental protection goes back quite some time. I would like to talk about three special projects that we have been instrumental in initiating and implementing.

The first project is Pleasant Creek Lake near our nuclear power plant. In that particular project, we provided the funding to create the approximate 162-ha lake, which eventually was developed into a state park. This lake has become a premium bass (*Micropterus* sp.) lake in this state used by thousands of Iowans every year.

Second is the cold water stream project. Our goal is to establish one or two pilot projects in the state to protect water quality and to enhance natural perpetuation of aquatic life. We started this project 2 years ago with the Department of Natural Resources and the Iowa Natural Heritage Foundation. I am happy the first of these projects is now completed and the second is in progress. This project has received a tremendous amount of support from the state government along with grassroots support from throughout Iowa.

The third project may be one of the most ambitious projects we have undertaken in recent years. This is the IE Branching Out project conducted in conjunction with the Iowa Natural Heritage Foundation and community groups in the state. The goal is to plant trees in Iowa in our service areas with a commitment of $500,000 in the next 5 years. In the first year, we received such enthusiastic support from the communities that we have now upgraded this project from $500,000 to $1 million. This decision was made only last week.

Clearly, IE Industries, along with many energy companies in this country, are committed to environmental protection. I want to assure you that we intend to work with the National Institute for Urban Wildlife and other environmental groups to protect the dwindling natural environment. Again, it is a pleasure to share with you some of my views regarding our participation in environmental matters. I look forward to further opportunities to work with this group and many others to enhance our quality of life.

Wildlife Conservation in Metropolitan Environments. NIUW Symp. Ser. 2, L.W. Adams and D.L. Leedy, eds. Published by Natl. Inst. for Urban Wildl., 10921 Trotting Ridge Way, Columbia, MD 21044, USA, 1991.

A New Era for Fish and Wildlife in the BLM

J. DAVID ALMAND, *Chief, Division of Wildlife and Fisheries, Bureau of Land Management, U. S. Department of the Interior, Washington, DC 20240*

Good morning ladies and gentlemen. On behalf of Director Jamison and our cadre of Bureau of Land Management (BLM) biologists and botanists, I want to thank you for the opportunity to participate in your meeting and for the chance to tell you about the new BLM—a BLM where, for the first time in its history, fish and wildlife are a top priority.

The first catalyst leading to this new era was *Fish and Wildlife 2000*, a strategic plan that provides a blueprint for managing fish and wildlife resources on BLM lands during the decade of the 1990s. This forward-looking plan also provides a foundation for BLM's stewardship of biological resources into the next century.

Implementation of *Fish and Wildlife 2000* is reshaping the way the BLM does business as it relates to fish and wildlife, the priorities placed upon these resources, and the way others perceive our management. Most importantly, it provides us with a means to influence and shape the future rather than being driven along in a knee jerk manner by ad hoc issues and events.

The second catalyst for this new era was the appointment of Cy Jamison as Director of BLM in 1989. It was then that implementation of *Fish and Wildlife 2000* was accelerated and made a top Bureau priority, along with recreation and riparian area restoration. It is the Director's belief that these programs represent the future for BLM and must be brought more on par with traditional programs such as minerals and rangeland management. Although he does not intend to diminish the importance of those programs, he does intend to bring fish and wildlife into equal footing. From a fish and wildlife resource standpoint, this new era is welcomed and long overdue.

The fish and wildlife resources on BLM's lands are among America's great treasures. More than 3,000 species make their homes on BLM lands, and no other federal or state agency manages more fish and wildlife habitat than BLM. For example:

- All native species of big game in North America can be found on BLM lands;
- Eighty percent of the remaining desert bighorn sheep (*Ovis canadensis mexicana*) reside on such lands;
- Some of the world's outstanding raptor habitat, perhaps the best in the world, is on BLM lands, including the renowned Snake River Birds of Prey Area in Idaho; and
- BLM lands have extensive habitat for salmon and trout (Salmonidae), and unusual desert fish species.

And the list could go on. The facts speak simply and clearly. There are no other lands like those managed by BLM, and the fish and wildlife of these public lands are equally distinct.

Fish and Wildlife 2000 has provided a picture and vision of where BLM stands, and should be headed, in the management of these resources. It has provided managers with direction and support, plus a better sense of where fish and wildlife fits with the other resources that BLM is legislatively mandated to manage.

Fish and Wildlife 2000 is bringing about changes where it counts most—on the ground. This is important for many reasons. One of these relates to the growing role BLM lands are playing now, and will play in the future, in meeting the mushrooming demand for fish and wildlife-related recreation.

Most of the 109 million ha administered by BLM are located in the West, an area that is becoming increasingly urbanized. For example, in Utah, 85% of the human population is already concentrated along the Watch Front in urban areas such as Salt Lake City, Provo, Ogden, and Logan. For the remainder of the 1990s, we will continue to see a strong shift in the United States population to the Western and Southern States. This will have greater impact on fish and wildlife habitats than otherwise would be expected. For example, we can expect increased growth and demand for consumptive and nonconsumptive recreational use of federal and state lands. Among other things, this means that greater pressure will be exerted on federal and state agencies to provide access to isolated lands. Sustained implementation of *Fish and Wildlife 2000* will enable BLM to be responsive to these changes in demographics and societal views and values.

Wildlife Conservation in Metropolitan Environments. NIUW Symp. Ser. 2, L.W. Adams and D.L. Leedy, eds. Published by Natl. Inst. for Urban Wildl., 10921 Trotting Ridge Way, Columbia, MD 21044, USA, 1991.

Doing is what *Fish and Wildlife 2000* is all about—doing more field projects; doing more with other agencies, conservation groups, outdoor organizations, and our other partners; doing more planning to help ensure that things up and down the organizational line turn out right; and, most importantly, doing more for the habitat on public lands. I would like to summarize a few of our accomplishments to give you a flavor of what we are doing.

WILDLIFE HABITAT MANAGEMENT

Under our wildlife habitat management component, we are doing many exciting things. For example, within our recreation program, we are implementing a Watchable Wildlife initiative jointly with the U.S. Forest Service, other federal and state agencies, and the Defenders of Wildlife. Good areas for viewing wildlife are identified and a state wildlife viewing guide is then published for the public. Viewing guides have recently been published in Oregon, Utah, Montana, and Idaho, with others in the planning stages. We believe that this will have considerable appeal to the urban segment of our society.

Animal Inn is another joint initiative with the Forest Service. This initiative is designed to help people realize the value of standing dead wood for wildlife and fish. BLM, the U.S. Forest Service, and conservation groups are working together on this innovative awareness program as a model for habitat conservation.

A third example relates to the Sikes Act. This Act requires BLM and the states to cooperate on conservation and rehabilitation of wildlife resources on public lands. We have a dynamic effort underway in New Mexico where a statewide Sikes Act stamp program was recently initiated. Revenues from the sale of public land management stamps are used to benefit fish and wildlife on BLM lands covered by the program. Montana is conducting a trial program and several other states are interested.

The desert bighorn is an example of a species that has benefitted from the guidance of *Fish and Wildlife 2000*. BLM administers some 3.6 million ha, or 80% of the habitat for this species. Approximately 10,000 desert bighorns occupy these lands. BLM has initiated a program of inventory, monitoring, and habitat management planning and improvement in a six-state area where this species lives. Through cooperative efforts with numerous state and private organizations and contributions of funds, labor, and materials from volunteers, BLM has successfully established viable populations in 92 of the 115 areas targeted for recovery. We will continue to implement this long-term management plan with emphasis on the remaining 23 areas.

In addition to desert bighorns, BLM manages over 83 million ha of big game habitat that includes habitats for all the major big game species of North America (deer, *Odocoileus hemionus, O. virginianus;* antelope, *Antilocapra americana;* elk, *Cervus elaphus;* moose, *Alces alces;* caribou, *Rangifer tarandus;* etc.). These species are also benefitting

from *Fish and Wildlife 2000,* as are upland game birds. In many parts of the country, BLM lands provide the only available habitat for some species. For example, 80% of all sage grouse (*Centrocercus urophasianus*) spend their entire life cycle on BLM lands, as do most desert quail species (e.g., *Callipepla* spp.). In total, BLM provides vital habitat for 23 species of upland birds. A strategy plan for managing BLM habitat for these species is nearing completion.

Enlisting the help of others is a top priority in BLM's efforts to improve the management of habitat for game birds. Cooperative projects with Pheasants Forever and Quail Unlimited and other interest groups are underway. BLM and the Idaho Department of Fish and Game also have embarked on a series of improvements, including coordinating habitat projects of mutual interest using funds generated from Idaho's upland game bird stamp.

BLM also manages more than 8.1 million ha of wetlands. A strategy plan in 1988 identified 225 key waterfowl areas on the public lands. We are working on several fronts to improve these areas. One is through an agreement with Ducks Unlimited (DU). Several joint habitat improvement projects are underway. In Montana and Alaska, we have completed 2 million ha of inventory work. Elsewhere we have completed several on-the-ground habitat improvement projects. We are in the final stages of establishing a position in DU's Sacramento office to help identify and coordinate projects. BLM also is working with the U. S. Fish and Wildlife Service and others to expand our role in wetlands protection and implementation of the North American Waterfowl Management Plan.

Raptors have been described as representing nature in the rough. There is no better place for nature to show them off than the canyons, cliffs, and open spaces managed by BLM. Our goal for raptors in *Fish and Wildlife 2000* is straightforward. It is to provide suitable habitat for birds of prey on public lands. A strategy plan approved by BLM in 1989 identified 223 key raptor areas encompassing 9.5 million ha of public land. These areas are widely scattered and contain a wide range of features. Protecting these special habitats through BLM's planning system will be a key to maintaining populations of the 45 raptor species found on public lands in the West. We also are concerned with maintaining populations of prey species; without the prey there soon could be no birds of prey. Managing all the components of raptor habitat is an essential step that we are taking.

Riparian areas—the bands of green near streams, springs, lakes, and other sources of water—are the most important lands managed by BLM. In some places, upwards of 80% of wildlife depend on riparian areas to supply water, food, shelter, and other life-giving needs. Healthy riparian areas usually mean healthy wildlife populations and fish habitat. They also mean improved soil stability, water quality, more recreation opportunities, and increased forage for livestock as well as wildlife.

These are facts recognized by BLM. In *Fish and Wildlife*

2000, the goal is to manage riparian areas for their long-term health and productivity. One of our specific objectives in *Fish and Wildlife 2000* is to bring 75% of our riparian areas into good or better ecological condition by 1997. We are making progress toward this end.

Each BLM office is developing at least one riparian showcase area where practices that benefit riparian areas are featured. The success of the effort was illustrated in 1988 when the American Fisheries Society's Western Division picked 20 BLM riparian improvement projects as winners in its "Riparian Excellence" program. Just one example of our on-the-ground work is in Idaho, where more than 200 riparian projects are in place. Livestock producers, conservationists, and others are working with us on these improvements.

FISH HABITAT MANAGEMENT

BLM boasts some pretty impressive numbers when it comes to fish habitat. We manage some 250,000 km of stream fish habitat, 1.6 million ha of lakes, and 77,760 ha of reservoirs. In the Pacific Northwest, 21,000 km of BLM-managed streams are vital to runs of salmon and trout, as are more than 160,000 km of stream in Alaska. In the Southwest, BLM waters feature species such as bass (Centrarchidae), catfish (Ictaluridae), and pupfish (Cyprinodontidae). And some of the small desert ponds and springs harbor populations of fish species found nowhere else in the world.

Fish and Wildlife 2000 targets working cooperatively with state and private interests, and identifying and improving habitats for high-value species as its main goals. Despite the funding and staffing shortages, we are making progress for both anadromous and resident fisheries on the public lands.

Our strategy plan for anadromous fish habitat management outlines an ambitious 12-year program that, if fully funded, will increase production of adult salmon (Salmonidae) and steelhead (*Oncorhynchus mykiss*) by about 172,000 fish annually in Idaho, Oregon, California and Alaska, with a return of $2.50 for every dollar invested.

There was a time when fish seemed to just take care of themselves. The anadromous runs always took place and the fishing hole always had a supply of hungry fish to take a look at a worm or fly. In most areas, that is no longer the case, and the actions taken by BLM over the next few years will be critical to the future of fish on the public lands.

THREATENED AND ENDANGERED SPECIES

Some 152 federally listed threatened or endangered species are found on BLM lands today. That number includes 99 animal species and 53 plant species. Another 876 plant species and 250 animals are candidates for listing. Our goals for threatened and endangered species are outlined clearly in *Fish and Wildlife 2000*. We are striving to

increase populations of these species to historic levels, consistent with BLM land use plans.

Available funds for threatened and endangered species management are spent on species that present special problems or seriously affect other resources. The desert tortoise (*Gopherus agassizii*) and northern spotted owl (*Strix occidentalis*) are two good examples.

We have some 900 species of special status plants on BLM lands and only a few botanists to deal with these species. These botanists spend much of their time inventorying and monitoring rare, threatened, endangered, and candidate plants, and providing information about actions that affect those species. An interdisciplinary team is producing a strategy plan for managing these species—no small task given the large number of plants in those categories.

We also manage habitat for 100 species of fish listed as threatened or endangered. A national strategy plan for managing these and candidate species also will be completed late in 1990.

CREATING PARTNERSHIPS

We obviously cannot do alone all the work outlined in *Fish and Wildlife 2000* and our associated state and national strategy plans. The work outlined is just too sweeping for us to achieve without outside help. So we have come to rely on others. And it seems to be working well. Since *Fish and Wildlife 2000* was approved, we have strengthened our traditional ties with state fish and wildlife agencies, other federal agencies, and opened the door to new organizations, inviting them in to lend a hand to a cause of mutual interest. National level agreements have been signed with a dozen organizations in the last 18 months. These agreements are fostering dozens of projects on-the-ground to improve habitat and to otherwise benefit fish and wildlife resource management.

We call all of this "partnerships." We are working with our partners in many ways. One of the best is a program called "challenge cost share," where we put up project money and other organizations donate matching funds or supply material or labor. It is a program that works. In 1986, Congress appropriated $300,000 for it. In 1990, the sum reached $2 million, to fund 60 of 208 proposed projects. In FY 1990, federal funds were matched by some $2.5 million by outside organizations. Our partnerships and team efforts toward improving wildlife and fish habitat may, in fact, be the most outstanding facet of *Fish and Wildlife 2000*.

Since *Fish and Wildlife 2000* was completed, the budget for the program increased from $16.3 million to $22.9 million. In FY 1990, that was 5.2% of the funds appropriated to BLM under the budget category called "Management of Lands and Resources." Of the $22.9 million allocated for fish and wildlife habitat management in FY 1990, $13.9 million was budgeted for wildlife and fish habitat management, with $4.1 million for threatened and endangered species.

Fish and Wildlife 2000 may be a vision, but it has its roots in reality. The plan does not come free. Our FY 1990 budget is about one-third what is needed annually to effectively implement the program. The commitment to make it work is in place. The timing is right. With the proper support, *Fish and Wildlife 2000 will* continue to make a difference.

With adequate funding, we can promise these results:

- Improved fishing, hunting, and wildlife viewing opportunities.
- Better access to public lands.
- Faster recovery of threatened and endangered species.
- Less need for listing of some candidate, threatened and endangered species through proactive management.
- Increased economic benefits to local communities.

- Sustained viability of recreationally important species.
- Enhanced recovery of riparian, stream, and wetland habitats.
- Expanded partnerships and contributions from outside sources.

A new era has indeed begun at BLM.

Fish and Wildlife 2000 has helped to usher a new attitude about these valuable resources and the way we manage them. And it is a tangible change. The dozens of plans and on-the-ground projects spawned by *Fish and Wildlife 2000* provide tangible evidence of this new era and our commitment to fish and wildlife. Achieving our goals will take our best effort, plus the support of Congress, organizations such as yours, and our other partners to make *Fish and Wildlife 2000* happen. We believe it will happen, for after all, this is an investment in the future of our great country, for the benefit of the American people.

II.

Ecology of Urban Wildlife

Chair: LARRY W. VANDRUFF, *Professor, State University of New York, Syracuse*

Cochair: CHARLES H. NILON, *Assistant Professor, University of Missouri, Columbia*

Ecology and Behavior of Free-ranging Cats in Brooklyn, New York

CAROL HASPEL[1] AND ROBERT E. CALHOON, *Department of Biology, Queens College, 65-30 Kissena Blvd., Flushing, NY 11367*

The urban environment is seldom considered a legitimate habitat for ecological inquiry because it is perceived to be artificial. There is an assumption that, because humans have modified nearly every feature of the landscape, any other organisms living in cities must be alien. The study of urban cats (*Felis catus*) is not a study of an organism alien to its environment. Rather, it is the study of a species in a unique ecosystem, one in which it has been reproductively successful for thousands of years (Beadle 1977). In addition, city lights permit observation of this nocturnal predator at night; studies in other environments have been limited to daylight hours (Kunz and Todd 1978, Oppenheimer 1980, Panaman 1981, Natoli 1985, and Konecny 1987). The purpose of the present study was to examine the activity, home range, and population size of free-ranging cats in Brooklyn, New York.

METHODS

Data Collection

A 33.2-ha study area was established based on a 1-year pilot project. The area consisted of two contiguous subhabitats (neighborhoods). Neighborhood AH was 16.4 ha and was characterized by large, multiple-dwelling rental apartment houses, voluminous garbage, and many abandoned buildings. Neighborhood PH, 16.8 ha, was characterized by privately-owned attached row houses, lidded garbage cans, and few abandoned buildings.

Cats were marked with color coded collars during 30 nights of trapping prior to each sampling season. Collars made the cats recognizable from 25 m. The cats were weighed, photographed, and their sex determined before collaring and releasing.

A transect was established in each neighborhood that permitted scan sampling (Altmann 1974) along the perimeter of each block-face. Sampling was conducted from 10:00 p.m. to 7:00 a.m. Each night from 9 September to 25 November 1981 (fall 1), 1 April to 18 June 1982 (spring), and 9 September to 7 December 1982 (fall 2), three 1-hour walks were conducted along one of the transects. While looking forward along the transect, all cats seen from the center of the road to the edge of the building line were recorded with regard to location, identity, date, and time. A student assistant accompanied the investigator during each hour walk and recorded garbage availability, number of people, and dogs. Air temperature and relative humidity also were recorded each hour. Six nights were necessary to complete one iteration in both neighborhoods. Ten iterations were conducted each season.

Prior to the fall 1982 sampling season, three feeding stations were established in AH. Sufficient commercial cat food was placed in each station to maintain from 12 to 30 cats nightly (Collier et al. 1978, Fitzgerald 1980). For more details about the sampling, trapping, and experimental procedures, see Calhoon and Haspel (1989) and Haspel and Calhoon (1989).

Subsequent to the field work, a telephone survey of the residents of the study area was conducted to ascertain the frequency, type, and quantity of food and shelter (as well as other resources) that humans provided for free-ranging cats. In addition, demographic data were collected for all respondents. Two hundred thirty randomly selected people were contacted for participation in the survey. For more information about the survey methods and questionnaire design, see Haspel and Calhoon (1990).

Data Analyses

Home range was estimated using the population utilization distribution method (Ford and Krumme 1979). As all data points were on the perimeter of blocks, the minimum convex polygon was deemed inappropriate (Ford and Myers 1981). Home range estimates were transformed to square-root and analyzed by one-way Anova with orthogonal contrasts; see Haspel and Calhoon (1989) for details.

Cat population size was estimated using the triple-

---

[1]Present address: Department of Natural and Applied Sciences, LaGuardia Community College, 31-10 Thomson Ave., Long Island City, NY 11101.

Wildlife Conservation in Metropolitan Environments. NIUW Symp. Ser. 2, L.W. Adams and D.L. Leedy, eds. Published by Natl. Inst. for Urban Wildl., 10921 Trotting Ridge Way, Columbia, MD 21044, USA, 1991.

capture-mark-recapture method developed by Jolly (1965); see Calhoon and Haspel (1989) for details.

Survey results were analyzed using the log-likelihood ratio test, which is chi-square distributed. Fifty-five different variables were tested in apriori contrasts (Haspel and Calhoon 1990). Estimates of the amount of energy available to cats were based upon our observations of open garbage receptacles, interviews with cat feeders, and published analyses of the nutritional value of garbage (Brunner 1984) and cat food (Anonymous 1982).

Activity patterns were analyzed using analyses of variance after Total-Cat frequency counts/hour were converted into square root and Collared-Cats frequency counts/hour were converted into arcsin-square-root-percent (Haspel and Calhoon, unpubl. data).

All analyses were calculated using the University Computer Center's IBM 6090 computer.

RESULTS

Habitat and cat population characteristics varied by neighborhood (Tables 1-2). There was no significant difference between neighborhoods in racial composition of humans (combined data showed 44% black, 22% white, and 34% other, mostly West Indian), however, residents of PH were more affluent than those of AH.

The available energy in PH was greater than in AH. This may be irrelevant as there was much more food (J/cat) than the population required in either neighborhood (4.5X in AH and 5.9X in PH) (Anonymous 1982).

Significant ($P \leq 0.05$) sex differences existed for number of cats seen/hour in PH (Table 2), and home range size and mean weight (Table 3).

Mean male home range size (Fig. 1, Table 3) was significantly larger ($P \leq 0.05$) than that of females, and males showed significantly greater ($P \leq 0.05$) variability of home range size and used the perimeter of their range more.

Hourly activity was consistent regardless of season or neighborhood. Peak activity occurred between 12:00 midnight and 2:00 a.m. and again near sunrise.

In fall, both males and females reduced their activity as winter approached; however, female activity declined significantly faster ($P \leq 0.05$). Male and female activity was similar in spring and significantly less than that in fall ($P \leq 0.05$).

A standardized partial regression analysis of cat activity by the measured environmental variables found that 30% of the variance in AH cat activity was accounted for by environmental variables, whereas these variables accounted for less than 15% of the variance in PH cat activity.

DISCUSSION

Behavior of the cats in Brooklyn, New York, was determined by biology and neighborhood. Behaviors such as a bimodal pattern of peak activity, reduced female activity in cold weather, clumping of the population near resources, and home range size were a function of biology. Cat visibility, sex ratio of visible cats, hourly and seasonal fluctuations in activity, and population size were a function of neighborhood.

It is difficult to ascertain which free-ranging cats are feral, stray, or pet unless they have some distinguishing feature (Childs 1990). However, human intervention is apparent from cat behavior. Cats living in AH exhibited greater fluctuations in hourly and seasonal activity than those in PH. In addition, the sex ratio of visible cats/hour in AH approached 1:1, whereas the ratio of females to males in PH was 1:1.9. Both of these observations reflected the difference in neighborhoods, and as such, the difference in cat status. We infer that cats in AH were feral and therefore vulnerable to seasonal and hourly weather conditions as exhibited by their activity patterns. Cats in PH were free-ranging pets. People were more reluctant to allow reproductively intact female pets to wander than male pets and owners determined the hour and conditions under which their cats were outside. These conclusions were supported by the standardized partial regression analysis, which showed that environmental variables accounted for more of the variability in cat activity in AH than in PH.

Neighborhood also had an effect on population size. There were almost 2.5 times as many cats in AH as in PH. The difference in population size was proportional to the difference in the amount of shelter available in the two neighborhoods (Calhoon and Haspel 1989, Table 1). Oppenheimer (1980) also found large populations of cats in apartment-house areas in Baltimore, Maryland. She attrib-

Table 1. Selected habitat characteristics in two neighborhoods in Brooklyn, New York, 1981–1982.

Neighborhood	Area (ha)	Floors of abandoned buildings	Available energy (J)	
			Garbage/cat/day	Handouts/cat/day
AH	16.44	62	3.6×10^6	7.36×10^5
PH	16.75	20	3.9×10^6	1.72×10^6

Table 2. Selected cat population characteristics in two neighborhoods in Brooklyn, New York, 1981–1982.

Neighborhood	Population size		Density (ha)			Cats seen (hr)								
						Male			Female			Combined sex		
	$\bar{x}$	SD	n	$\bar{x}$	SD	n	$\bar{x}$	SE	n	$\bar{x}$	SE	n	$\bar{x}$	SE
AH	80.3	6.9	134	4.88	0.81	69	2.62	0.13	65	2.25	0.13	134	2.43	0.09
PH	34.1	1.7	48	2.03	0.20	27	0.75	0.21	21	0.43	0.23	48	0.61	0.15

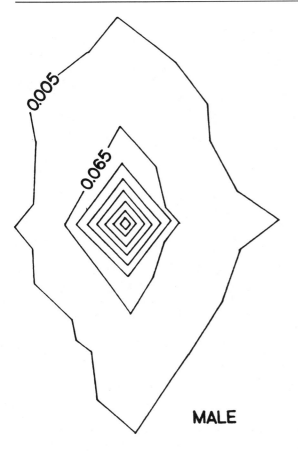

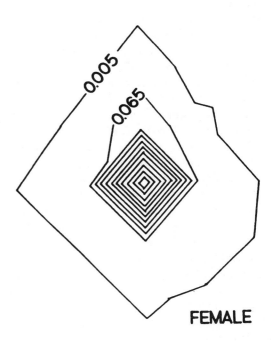

Fig. 1. Contour maps depicting the home range usage of male and female cats in Brooklyn, New York, 1981–1982. Each contour line represents the likelihood of cat sightings this far or farther from the center of their range. The closer the lines are the more concentrated is the land usage. The maps represent 99.5% confidence polygons. Scale: 1 cm = 32.3 m.

Table 3. Selected cat population characteristics by gender in Brooklyn, New York, 1981–1982.

Sex	Weight (kg)			Home range (ha)		
	n	$\bar{x}$	SD	n	$\bar{x}$	95% CI
Female	86	2.9	0.6	86	1.77	1.57–1.98
Male	96	4.1	0.8	96	2.62	2.38–2.87

uted this to large concentrations of food in the form of garbage in these neighborhoods. However, we found more food/cat in PH and food was far in excess of what the populations required in both neighborhoods. Therefore, we concluded that the differences in population size in the two neighborhoods could not be attributed to food availability.

Visibility of cats on the perimeter of the blocks also was a function of neighborhood. Four times as many cats (combined sexes) were seen/hour in AH as in PH (Table 2). Two factors, in addition to differences in population size, accounted for this behavior. People living in AH were more tolerant of free-ranging cats than were people in PH (Haspel and Calhoon 1990). Furthermore, food (from garbage cans) and entrances to shelter were often in front of buildings in AH. According to our survey, people in PH were significantly more likely than residents of AH to provide cats with shelter located in backyards. Cats tended to congregate near food and shelter.

The clumping of cats near resources also was apparent from the results of our supplementary feeding experiment. Increasing food availability in fall 2 did not alter cat population size, but it did increase cat visibility (Calhoon and Haspel 1989). The clumped dispersion pattern of cats occurred independently of neighborhood and could be seen in the congregations of cats near an area where resources were provided in either neighborhood. However, as our population study suggested, shelter must be available for the cats to establish the area as a center of activity.

Female cats showed this tendency more so than males. Also individual male home ranges encompassed those of many females. Other investigators have found similar behaviors for rural (Liberg 1980, Konecny 1987), farm (MacDonald and Apps 1978), and urban cats (Dards 1978, Tabor 1981). Natoli (1985) in Rome, Italy, found that female cats collectively occupied the area offering the best shelter and used it for rearing kittens. Those cats attacked strange male and female cats and all but one male of their own colony. By situating themselves near food and shelter, females reduced their energy expenditure and, as such, could be expected to enhance their reproductive success. Ghiglieri (1985) also explained a similar dispersion pattern among chimpanzees as a means of conserving energy for maternal chores.

Cat home range size in Brooklyn was not affected by neighborhood. Food for cats was in surplus and increasing food availability in fall 2 did not change home range size. Instead, home range size was dependent on body size (Haspel and Calhoon 1989) and sex (Table 3). We speculate that there may be a lower limit to which cat home range size shrinks as a result of increased food availability, but it probably remains proportional to body size (Lindstedt et al. 1986). Based on a review of other studies, there appears to be an inverse relationship between food availability (prey) and home range size. Cats in rural areas reportedly have larger home ranges (Liberg 1980, Warner 1985, Konecny 1987) than farm cats (George 1978, MacDonald and Apps 1978), which in turn have larger ranges than urban cats (Dards 1978, Tabor 1981). In the present study area, cats did not hunt for food and thus home range size was not influenced by the distribution of prey.

Females reduced their activity in fall more quickly than did males, regardless of neighborhood. The small size of females may have contributed to this behavior. Females had a significantly larger surface-to-volume ratio than did males and might be expected to be affected by cold weather more readily.

The bimodal peak activity of cats also was independent of neighborhood. Nocturnal predators often display such a pattern of activity, with peaks at sunset and sunrise (Brown 1962). We believe the sunset peak was delayed in the Brooklyn cats in order to avoid humans. Eguchi and Nakazone (1980) and Van Dyke (1986) found that red foxes and mountain lions, respectively, became more strictly nocturnal in proximity to humans. The plasticity of the endogenous hourly cat activity pattern reflected the adaptability that has permitted this species to live in a broad diversity of habitats from the tropics to the subantarctic islands (Brothers et al. 1985, Apps 1986).

REFERENCES CITED

Altmann, J. 1974. Observational study of behavior: sampling methods. Behaviour 49:227–267.

Anonymous. 1982. The inside story: a laboratory assessment of the chemical composition of Purina cat food products, and feeding guide. Ralston Purina Inc., Gray Summit, Mo.

Apps, P. 1986. Home ranges of feral cats on Dassen Island. J. Mammal. 67:199–200.

Beadle, M. 1977. The cat. Simon and Schuster, New York, N.Y. 251pp.

Brothers, N. P., I. J. Skira, and G. R. Copson. 1985. Biology of the feral cat, *Felis catus* (L.) on Macquarie Island. Aust. Wildl. Res. 12:425–436.

Brown, L. E. 1962. Home range in small mammal communities. Pages 131–171 *in* B. Glass, ed. Survey of biological progress 4. Academic Press, New York, N.Y.

Brunner, C. R. 1984. Incineration systems, selection and design. Van Nostrand Reinhold Co., New York, N.Y. 417pp.

Calhoon, R. E., and C. Haspel. 1989. Urban cat populations compared by season, subhabitat and supplemental feeding. J. Anim. Ecol. 58:321–328.

Childs, J. E. 1990. Urban cats: their demography, population density and owner characteristics in Baltimore, Maryland. Anthrozoos 3:234–244.

Collier, G., L. W. Kaufman, R. Kanarek, and J. Fagen. 1978. Optimization of time and energy constraints in the feeding behavior of cats: a laboratory simulation. Carnivore 1:34–41.

Dards, J. L. 1978. Home ranges of feral cats in Portsmouth Dockyard. Carnivore Genet. Newsl. 3:242–256.

Eguchi, K., and T. Nakazono. 1980. Activity studies of the Japanese red fox *Vulpes vulpes Japonica* Gray. Japanese J. Ecol. 30:9–17.

Fitzgerald, B. M. 1980. Feeding ecology of the feral house cat in New Zealand. Carnivore Genet. Newsl. 4:67–71.

Ford, R. G., and D. W. Krumme. 1979. The analysis of space use patterns. J.Theor. Biol. 76:125–155.

———, and J. P. Myers. 1981. An evaluation and comparison of techniques for estimating home range and territory size. Stud. Avian. Biol. 6:461–465.

George, W. G. 1978. Domestic cats as density independent hunters and "surplus killers." Carnivore Genet. Newsl. 8:282–287.

Ghiglieri, M. 1985. The social ecology of chimpanzees. Sci. Amer. 252:102–113.

Haspel, C., and R. E. Calhoon. 1989. Home ranges of free-ranging cats (*Felis catus*) in Brooklyn, New York. Can. J. Zool. 67:178–181.

———. 1990. The interdependence of humans and free-ranging cats in Brooklyn, New York. Anthrozoos 3:155–161.

Jolly, G. M. 1965. Explicit estimates from capture-recapture data with both death and immigration-stochastic model. Biometrika 52:225–247.

Konecny, M. J. 1987. Home range and activity patterns of feral house cats in the Galapogos Islands. Oikos 50:17–23.

Kunz, T. H., and N. B. Todd. 1978. Considerations in the design of gene frequency. Carnivore Genet. Newsl. 3:200–211.

Liberg, O. 1980. Spacing patterns in a population of rural free roaming domestic cats. Oikos 35:336–349.

Lindstedt, S. L., B. J. Miller, and S. W. Buskirk. 1986. Home range, time and body size in mammals. Ecology 67:413–418.

MacDonald, D., and P. Apps. 1978. The social behavior of semidependent farm cats. Carnivore Genet. Newsl. 3:256–261.

Natoli, E. 1985. Spacing pattern in a colony of urban stray cats (*Felis catus* L.) in the historic centre of Rome. Applied Anim. Behav. Sci. 14:289–304.

Oppenheimer, E. 1980. *Felis catus* population densities in an urban area. Carnivore Genet. Newsl. 4:72–80.

Panaman, R. 1981. Behaviour and ecology of free-ranging female farm cats (*Felis catus*). Z. Tierpsychol. 56:59–73.

Tabor, R. 1981. General biology of feral cats. Pages 5–11 *in* The ecology and control of feral cats: UFAW Symposium Proceedings, Royal Holloway College, Univ. London, Hertfordshire, U.K.

Van Dyke, F., et al. 1986. Reactions of mountain lions to logging and other human activity. J. Wildl. Manage. 50:95–102.

Warner, R. 1985. Demography and movements of free-ranging domestic cats in rural Illinois. J. Wildl. Manage. 49:340–346.

Ecology of Urban Skunks, Raccoons, and Foxes in Metropolitan Toronto[1]

RICHARD C. ROSATTE, MICHAEL J. POWER, AND CHARLES D. MACINNES, *Ontario Ministry of Natural Resources, Wildlife Research Section, P.O. Box 5000, Maple, Ontario, L6A 1S9, Canada*

INTRODUCTION

Wildlife is thriving in city areas of southern Ontario. Although industrial, residential, and commercial development does alter or destroy pristine habitats, it also creates or enhances opportunities for certain species. Populations of skunks (*Mephitis mephitis*), raccoons (*Procyon lotor*), and foxes (*Vulpes vulpes*) exist at higher densities within Toronto, Ontario, Canada, than in surrounding countryside. These higher densities elicit mixed reactions from the human population. On one hand, presence of wildlife provides reassurance about the state of the local environment, but these species can also become nuisances, and, in Toronto's case, contribute to a public health problem—rabies.

Southern Ontario annually reports more cases of animal rabies than any other area of comparable size in North America (MacInnes 1987). We also have to contend with that disease in certain carnivores in some cities of the region (MacInnes 1988, Rosatte et al. 1990). Toronto is one such city. Because skunks, raccoons, and foxes have been reported rabid in Toronto, the Ontario Ministry of Natural Resources initiated a rabies research program in 1984 that has continued to date (Rosatte and MacInnes 1987, Rosatte et al. 1987, Rosatte et al. 1990). In order to design the most feasible tactic to control rabies in those species, we have had to gain intimate knowledge of their biology and behaviors. This paper reports on some of our findings with respect to foxes, skunks, and raccoons in Toronto from 1984 to 1990.

STUDY AREA

These studies took place in the cities of Scarborough, North York, Etobicoke, York, Toronto, Mississauga, and the Borough of East York. This 800-km² urban complex, hereafter called Toronto for simplicity, is centered at latitude 43° 42'North, longitude 79° 25'West and has an approximate population of some 3 million people.

MATERIALS AND METHODS

A live-trapping and rabies vaccination program (Trap-Vaccinate-Release—TVR) was carried out at different sites throughout Toronto during 1984–1986. More intensive TVR studies were conducted from 1987 to 1990 in a 60-km² area of Scarborough, one of the constituent cities of Metropolitan Toronto. The materials and methods used in these studies were reported earlier (Rosatte et al. 1987, Rosatte and MacInnes 1989, Rosatte et al. 1990). During 1984–1986 and 1989–1990 animals also were tracked by radio transmitters. The materials and methods for the skunk and raccoon radio-telemetry programs were reported in Rosatte et al. (1987) and Rosatte and Kelly-Ward (1988). The same methodology was used for the fox telemetry program except transmitters were manufactured by Advanced Telemetry Systems, Minnesota, and by Lotek Engineering, Aurora, Ontario. Also, Lotek SRX-400 and Trackfinder 1000 receivers were used to monitor the movements and activities of foxes in Toronto. Age estimates were obtained by observing annual growth lines in thin sections of premolar teeth according to Johnston et al. (1987).

DATA ANALYSIS

Home range was estimated by the Minimum Area Method using a software package described by Voigt and Tinline (1980). Trapping effort significance was tested using Chi-square and an analysis of variance by ranks procedure according to Zar (1974). A modified Petersen index was employed for animal abundance estimations using capture-recapture data (Begon 1979). Skunk and raccoon mortality estimates were derived from population and percent cap-

[1]Ontario Ministry of Natural Resources, Wildlife Branch, Contribution No. 90–08.

tured estimates, as well as from recapture frequencies, including recapture of adults in succeeding years (Rosatte et al. 1990). Additional survival information was obtained from the fates of radio-collared individuals.

RESULTS AND DISCUSSION

During the skunk and raccoon live-trapping program in Toronto (1984–1989), 55,597 trap-nights produced 6,410 animal captures. That total included 730 different skunks captured 1,251 times and 1,723 different raccoons captured on 2,606 occasions. The radio-telemetry program provided additional information on 57 skunks, 36 raccoons, and 35 foxes. The following information on skunks, foxes, and raccoons was derived from the database produced from the above live-trapping and telemetry programs.

Life Cycle

Using information gained from our live-trapping and telemetry programs, we postulate that the life cycle of skunks and raccoons in Toronto includes a breeding period that is usually initiated during February and March. Following parturition in April, May, and June (and sometimes later), the young remain with the adult female at or near the maternity den usually until July. Dispersal of young away from the maternity den may occur from July through October-November. With the onset of inclement or cold weather, skunks and raccoons seek the protection of winter dens (either solitary or communal). Depending on the severity of the winter, denning may last from late November until February (when males seek breeding females).

Foxes in Toronto usually bear young during March and April, thus breeding must occur in January. The young stay with the parents at or near the maternal den until July–August when they may disperse from the maternal home range. Dispersal may occur as late as December or January because foxes in Toronto (and in rural Ontario) remain active year-round and do not den during the winter.

Reproduction

Skunks and raccoons in northern latitudes usually breed during February–March, whereas foxes may breed as early as January (Rosatte 1987, Sanderson 1987, Voigt 1987). We have recorded birth dates of early March and early April for Toronto raccoons (i.e., litters with eyes open were found on 17 March 1988, and 24 April 1986). Assuming an average gestation period of 63 days (Sanderson 1987), breeding must have taken place in early January and early February.

Productivity in city skunks and raccoons is probably high. Eighty-seven percent ($n = 23$) of adult female skunks from Toronto examined in June and July were lactating or had suckled young. In rural southern Ontario, 75% of the female skunks sampled had successfully bred (based on placental scar counts) (P. Bachmann, Ont. Min. Nat. Resour., unpubl. data). Seventy-three percent ($n = 15$) of adult rac-

coons examined in Toronto were lactating or had suckled young in June–July. This figure is considerably lower than the 94% observed for raccoons in rural areas of southern Ontario (Bachmann, Ont. Min. Nat. Resour., unpubl. data).

We have not collected a large enough sample of foxes in Toronto to determine reproductive success. However, in rural southern Ontario, 80–90% of the yearling and 95% of older vixens produced pups (Voigt and Macdonald 1984, Voigt 1987). We suspect success may be lower in Toronto than in rural Ontario, as two adult and two yearling females that were radio-collared had not suckled young during the summer of 1990.

Average litter sizes for foxes, skunks, and raccoons in rural southern Ontario are 8.0, 4.8, and 4.0, respectively (Voigt 1987; Bachmann, Ont. Min. Nat. Resour., unpubl. data; Craig and Buckingham, Ont. Min. Nat. Resour., unpubl. data). Although we have not had a large enough sample of road-killed animals for placental scar counts, we have viewed young at various maternal dens in Toronto. One skunk den in Toronto contained five young, and we have seen several raccoon litters containing three to four young. However, to date, we have only observed up to four fox pups per litter in Toronto. That figure is considerably lower than the mean of 8.0 for rural southern Ontario. (Observation of pups is not a very accurate way to estimate litter size as some may still be in the maternal den during observation times.)

Morphology and Weight Changes

Skunks, raccoons, and foxes were weighed and measured (Tables 1–2). Adults of all three species in Toronto averaged 1.0–1.5 kg heavier than their rural Ontario counter-parts (Bachmann, Ont. Min. Nat. Resour., unpubl. data; Craig and Buckingham, Ont. Min. Nat. Resour., unpubl. data; Voigt 1987). Fall body weights of juveniles were comparable between city and country samples. Body weights of skunks and raccoons indicated that individuals were in good condition, and able to put on ample weight during the summer and fall to allow survival over the winter (Figs. 1–2). We found that young raccoons doubled their weight through the summer and fall, then lost an average of 16% over the winter (Fig. 1). Adults lost more weight over winter (males 17%, females 24%) (Fig. 1).

Juvenile skunks tripled their weights between June and October but were 37–41% lighter when captured the following spring (Fig. 2). Adults lost the same amount over winter but regained the weight in the following summer. Individuals of both species which were recaptured several times lost as much as 55% of their maximum summer-fall body weight over the winter (Fig. 3).

The combination of increasing populations and high body weights suggests that conditions in Toronto are very favorable for all three species. Natural food resources are abundant and varied, ranging from excellent quantities of earthworms and insects on lawns and golf courses to a variety

Table 1. Body measurements (cm) and weights (kg) of skunks and raccoons in Toronto, 1985–1986.

Month	Age/sex	Number n	Weight $\bar{x}$ (SE)[a]	Total length $\bar{x}$ (SE)	Tail length $\bar{x}$ (SE)	Neck circumference $\bar{x}$ (SE)
Skunks						
June/	AM[b]	6	3.3(0.15)	63.6(4.1)	22.7(1.4)	16.4(0.68)
July	AF[c]	23	2.1(0.38)	57.6(3.2)	21.1(2.4)	13.6(1.1)
	JMF[d]	55	0.9(0.11)	49.1(3.1)	19.7(2.1)	11.3(0.9)
August/	AM	23	3.4(0.9)	62.7(2.4)	20.2(2.3)	16.7(1.9)
September	AF	8	2.4(0.35)	61.0(1.9)	21.0(2.1)	14.5(1.4)
	JMF	48	1.6(0.30)	57.6(3.3)	21.4(1.9)	13.6(1.1)
October/	AM	10	4.5(0.71)	60.9(3.4)	18.3(1.4)	18.9(1.9)
November	AF	8	3.3(0.44)	60.5(4.7)	18.4(2.6)	16.4(1.4)
	JMF	32	3.0(0.50)	60.9(4.2)	20.5(2.0)	15.8(1.0)
Raccoons						
June/	AM	38	7.5(1.2)	82.4(2.5)	23.9(2.9)	24.6(1.6)
July	AF	24	6.7(0.9)	81.5(3.4)	25.3(2.5)	22.7(1.9)
	JMF	45	2.2(0.6)	61.7(5.4)	19.9(2.2)	16.9(1.7)
August/	AM	40	7.8(1.4)	82.9(2.9)	22.3(3.1)	24.9(1.8)
September	AF	28	6.7(0.9)	79.4(3.1)	23.0(2.3)	23.7(1.9)
	JMF	109	3.4(0.9)	70.1(5.9)	22.6(1.9)	19.3(1.9)
October/	AM	2	8.1(0.4)	81.6(0.6)	21.8(0.8)	25.0(1.0)
November	AF	8	7.1(0.7)	78.4(3.0)	21.5(1.6)	24.1(2.0)
	JMF	26	5.8(1.3)	75.3(4.4)	22.5(1.7)	21.9(3.0)

[a] $\bar{x}$ = mean, SE = standard error; [b] adult male; [c] adult female; [d] juvenile male and female.

Table 2. Body measurements (cm) and weights (kg) of foxes in Toronto, 1989.

Month	Age/sex	Number n	Weight $\bar{x}$ (SE)[a]	Total length $\bar{x}$ (SE)	Tail length $\bar{x}$ (SE)	Neck circumference $\bar{x}$ (SE)
May/	AM[b]	3	5.4(0.47)	105.5(1.2)	37.0(1.1)	22.2(1.1)
June	AF[c]	2	5.3(0.7)	101.6(5.1)	36.0(4.5)	21.5(1.0)
	JMF[d]	2	3.4(0.2)	87.0(4.0)	31.1(2.6)	18.5(0.5)
July/	AM	8	5.6(0.5)	109.3(4.9)	39.7(1.3)	22.4(1.3)
August/	AF	5	5.0(0.5)	104.1(2.3)	38.4(3.1)	20.9(1.73)
September	JMF	22	3.8(0.72)	96.9(6.6)	35.7(3.4)	18.2(1.5)

[a] $\bar{x}$ = mean, SE = standard error; [b] adult male; [c] adult female; [d] juvenile male and female.

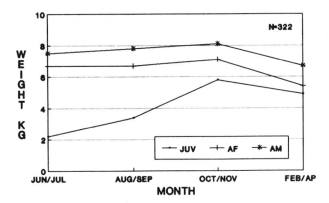

Fig. 1. Mean body weight of raccoons in Toronto, 1985–1986. N = sample size, JUV = juvenile, AF = adult female, AM = adult male.

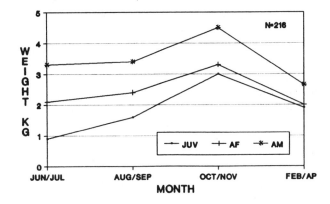

Fig. 2. Mean body weight of skunks in Toronto, 1985–1986. N = sample size, JUV = juvenile, AF = adult female, AM = adult male.

of bird and rodent species and their nests. Many city residents deliberately feed raccoons, skunks, and foxes. Skunks and raccoons frequently raid garbage containers in residential and commercial areas. In addition, the city individuals move around substantially less than their rural counterparts, and are therefore more conservative in their use of energy.

Age Ratios and Survival

During 1985, juveniles accounted for 62–67% of raccoons captured between July and November in Toronto (Fig. 4). We could find no significant change ($P > 0.05$) in the juvenile portion of the sample on a monthly basis. Within our 60-km² study area, juveniles accounted for 77%

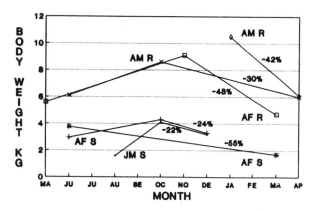

Fig. 3. Weight gain/loss of individual skunks and raccoons in Toronto, 1985–1986. AMR = adult male raccoon, AFR = adult female raccoon, AFS = adult female skunk, JMS = juvenile male skunk.

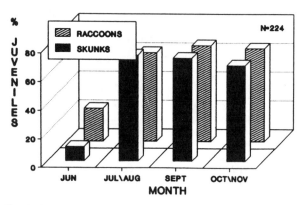

Fig. 4. Age structure of skunks and raccoons in three areas of Toronto, 1985. N = sample size.

(n = 193) of raccoons live-captured between July and November 1989 (Fig. 5). Twenty percent of the sampled animals were between 1.0–4.5 years and the remaining 3% were 5.0–7.5 years of age (Fig. 5). Juveniles accounted for 65%, 70%, and 81% of a sample of raccoons from three counties of rural southern Ontario (Craig and Buckingham, Ont. Min. Nat. Resour., unpubl. data).

Juveniles comprised 67–74% of skunks captured in Toronto during 1985 (Fig. 4). Again we could detect no

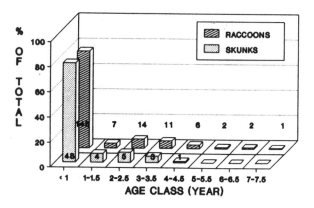

Fig. 5. Age structure of a sample of skunks and raccoons in Scarborough, July–October, 1989.

differences (P >0.05) among monthly ratios. Juveniles accounted for 79% (n = 61) of skunks in our 60-km^2 study area in 1989 (Fig. 5). Fifteen percent of the skunks were between 1.0–2.5 years and the remaining 6% were 3.0–4.5 years (Fig. 5). A sample of skunks trapped in rural southern Ontario consisted of 65% juveniles (Bachmann, unpubl. data).

Significant changes occurred in the proportion of juvenile and adult female skunks and raccoons captured between June and November in Toronto (Fig. 6). Assuming equal trapability, and equal sex ratio at birth, this suggests some degree of differential mortality or dispersal. Also, the high juvenile-to-adult ratio, coupled with apparently high survival of juveniles until late fall, indicated that populations were not limited by food resources or predators.

Population Density

Skunk and raccoon abundance in Toronto is habitat dependent. Where patches of forests-parklands are present, or in older residential areas with many large trees, exceptional numbers of raccoons and few skunks are present (Fig. 7). Conversely, fields usually support high numbers of skunks but few raccoons (Fig. 7).

As part of a rabies control program, we have been live-

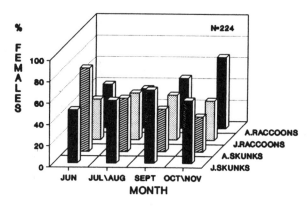

Fig. 6. Percent juvenile and adult female skunks and raccoons in three areas of Toronto, 1985. J. = juvenile, A. = adult.

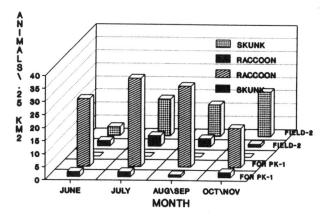

Fig. 7. Skunk and raccoon abundance in Toronto, 1985. FOR PK-1 = forest-park study area 1, FIELD-2 = field study area 2.

trapping skunks and raccoons in a 60-km² area of Scarborough since 1987 (Rosatte et al. 1990). Population densities in that area are also habitat dependent. Raccoon densities ranged from 56/km² to 4/km² going from forest-park to field, respectively. Skunk numbers ranged from a high of 36/km² in fields to 1/km² in forest-park. Both species were expanding their numbers and distribution during 1987–1989. Average densities in the 60-km² study area ranged from 2.6/km² and 7.9/km² in 1987, to 5.6/km² and 11.1/km² in 1989, for skunks and raccoons, respectively (Fig. 8).

The skunk population in the Scarborough study area increased by 120% between 1987 and 1989 (Fig. 8). That increase may be attributed to the fact that we vaccinated between 47 and 79% of the skunk population against rabies and were successful in our rabies control attempt (rabies has been prevalent in the study area since the early 1960's) (Rosatte et al. 1990). On the other hand, the population increase may be simply 'normal' recovery following a rabies outbreak during 1986 (Rosatte et al. 1990). However, rabies may play no major role in limiting the skunk population in our study area and other factors (e.g., road-kills) may have a greater controlling effect on the skunk population density.

The raccoon population in the Scarborough study area increased by about 40% between 1987 and 1989 (Fig. 8). As rabies is not very prevalent in Ontario raccoons (< 1% of annual diagnoses), it is doubtful that the disease will play any role in limiting raccoon population levels. Therefore, the population increase in our study area cannot be attributed to the fact that we may be controlling rabies through our vaccination program (Rosatte et al. 1990). However, another disease, canine distemper, may be a population density limiting factor. It is quite prevalent in Ontario raccoons (Cranfield et al. 1984, Wojcinski and Barker 1986).

We suspect that 1986 was a canine distemper outbreak year for raccoons in Toronto. We received numerous calls from the public noting rabies-like symptoms in raccoons. Animals subsequently submitted for diagnosis were negative for rabies. We also found numerous raccoon carcasses throughout Toronto (10 in one small park), although they were too decomposed to be tested for distemper or other diseases. Regardless, until we prove otherwise, we speculate that the 40% increase in raccoon numbers in our study area between 1987 and 1989 may be due to the natural rebuilding of the raccoon population following a distemper outbreak in 1986.

Our knowledge of fox densities is scanty. From our rabies case records, we suspect that the majority of Toronto foxes live in or along ravine systems. Golf courses, most of which are in ravines, all support foxes. In fact, during 1989, three litters composed of 15 different foxes were identified on one golf course. In May–June 1990, we managed to locate 44 different fox pup-rearing dens within Toronto. A preliminary estimate of the total Toronto population is 750–1000 foxes in 800 km² (1.0–1.25/km²).

Habitat Preference

When we initially started live-trapping skunks and raccoons throughout Toronto during 1985–1986, there was no question as to where high numbers of each species could be found. Most skunks were captured in fields ($P < 0.001$) and the majority of raccoons were taken in forest-park and residential areas ($0.001 < P < 0.025$) (Figs. 9–10). However, since we have been re-trapping the same 60-km² area continuously (July–November) from 1987 through 1989 (and continuing into 1990), a different picture is emerging. Other habitats are becoming more important with respect to capture success. During 1989, skunk capture success was highest in commercial and industrial areas as well as in field habitat ($0.001 < P < 0.05$) (Fig. 10). Raccoon capture

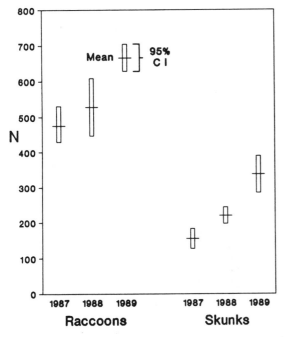

Fig. 8. Skunk and raccoon population estimates for a 60-km² area of Scarborough. CI = confidence interval.

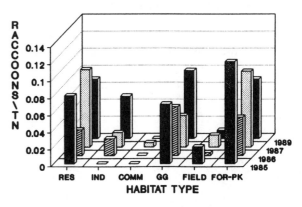

Fig. 9. Raccoon capture success in Toronto, 1985–1986; and in the Scarborough study area, 1987–1989. RES = residential, IND = industrial, COMM = commercial, GG = groomed grass, FOR PK = forest-park, TN = trap-night.

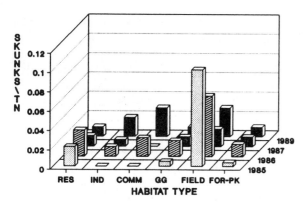

Fig. 10. Skunk capture success in Toronto, 1985–1986; and in the Scarborough study area, 1987–1989. RES = residential, IND = industrial, COMM = commercial, GG = groomed grass, FOR PK = forest-park, TN = trap-night.

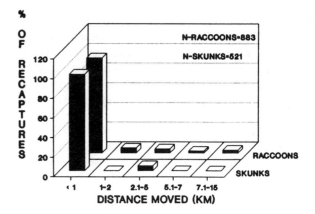

Fig. 11. Movements of recaptured skunks and raccoons in Toronto, 1984–1989. N = sample size.

success continued to be high in forest-park and residential areas; however, industrial and groomed grass habitats also produced significant numbers of raccoons (0.001< *P* <0.05) (Fig. 9). We suspect the change in habitat utilization is related to an increase in population density for both species.

Movements

Radio-telemetry indicated that home ranges and movements by all three species were generally very small (Table 3). Recapture data from the Scarborough study area also support that finding. Since 1984, 730 skunks and 1,723 raccoons have been live-captured, ear-tagged, vaccinated, and released as part of a rabies research and control program (Rosatte et al. 1990). About 40% of those animals were recaptured at some interval between 1 week and 2.5 years after the initial capture. Over 98% of skunks and 97% of raccoons were recaptured within 1 km of the original capture site (Fig. 11). Two raccoons moved 11 and 13 km, and only 2% of the skunks were recaptured 2–5 km from the initial capture location (Fig. 11).

Generally, movements and home ranges of our urban skunks, raccoons, and foxes were quite conservative when compared to other studies in rural areas (Schnell 1970, Sargeant et al. 1982, Rosatte and Gunson 1984, Voigt and Macdonald 1984, Zimen 1984). Our figures for skunks and raccoons, however, are comparable to findings by researchers in other urban areas (Hoffmann and Gottschang 1977, Hadidian and Manski, Natl. Park Serv., unpubl. data).

Movements of Toronto foxes are comparable in scale to those of rural foxes, although this may be, in part, due to the dispersion of fox habitat in Toronto. The ravine systems, including golf courses, are long and narrow. Thus, to cover a unit of area, the animals move considerable distances up or downstream. Some individuals have moved from one golf course to the next, traversing 30–40 km of apparently unsuitable habitat. We currently believe that they travel along railways while making such movements. These are preliminary observations from an ongoing study.

Mortality

Annual mortality for skunks in the Scarborough study area was 54 and 34% in 1987 and 1988, respectively (Fig. 12), based on tag-recapture data. For radio-collared skunks, mortality within the first year after collaring was 39% (Fig. 12). Comparable estimates for raccoons ranged between 50 and 60%, whereas seven of 10 radio-collared foxes died within the first 8 months of the study (Fig. 12).

Causes of death for urban skunks, foxes, and raccoons were highly variable, ranging from dogs, road-kills, and euthanasia by animal control agencies, to diseases such as rabies and canine distemper (Rosatte et al. 1987, 1990; Rosatte and MacInnes 1989). Road-kills were probably the

Table 3. Movements and home ranges of skunks, raccoons and foxes in Toronto, 1984–1989.

Species	*n*	Max. distance[a] km $\bar{x}$ (range)	Home range km[2] $\bar{x}$ (range)
Skunks	57	0.91 (0.3–2.7)	0.51 (0.05–1.88)
Raccoons	12	0.8 (0.3–1.8)	0.42 (0.07–1.37)
Foxes[b]	10	2.2 (0.6–6.5)	4.1 (1.3–12.9)

[a]Max. distance refers to the average distance moved from the point of release.
[b]A long distance dispersal of 30–40 km by three foxes was not included in the calculations.

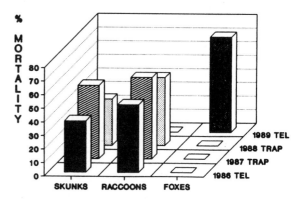

Fig. 12. Mortality estimates for skunks, raccoons, and foxes in Toronto during live-trapping (trap) and telemetry (tel) programs.

major cause of death, but because cause of death was determined for less than 50% of radio-collared animals, this could not be quantified. Road-killed skunks and raccoons were frequently seen in the Scarborough area. The highest frequency of deaths, and the period when most road-kills were observed, occurred in September–November. That is also the time when juveniles have left their parents and are dispersing.

Winter probably also results in mortality, but as winter-killed animals (due to disease, starvation, etc.) are in dens, they are almost impossible to find. There was no indication of winter-related mortality among our radio-collared animals.

Diseases

The most notable disease of skunks and foxes in cities of southern Ontario is rabies. Those urban areas account for about 10% of the skunk and about 3% of the fox diagnoses in Ontario each year (Rosatte et al. 1990). Toronto accounts for about 40% of the urban rabies cases in Ontario (Fig. 13). Raccoons, on the other hand, are seldom reported with rabies in urban Ontario. In fact, only five cases were reported in Toronto between 1980–1989.

Canine distemper (CDV) is suspected of being quite prevalent in Ontario raccoons (Cranfield et al. 1984, Wojcinski and Barker 1986), and the species also has been found to be quite susceptible to feline panleukopenia virus (FPL) (Barker et al. 1983). Although we are not certain of the prevalence of these and other pathogens, we do suspect that several pathogens exist in the Toronto skunk and raccoon populations. Sixty-four and 71% of raccoon sera were positive for antibody against CDV and FPL, respectively, in Toronto (Fig. 14). Skunk sera samples also had a high prevalence for antibody against CDV (60%) and FPL (25%) (Fig. 14). More samples from adult males were positive for FPL antibody than any other age/sex class ($P < 0.01$), and males also dominated the samples positive for CDV antibody ($P < 0.05$)(Fig. 15). In addition, some skunk samples (7.5%, 5.0%) were positive for antibody against infectious canine hepatitis and canine adenovirus, respectively (Fig. 14), but both skunk and raccoon sera samples were negative

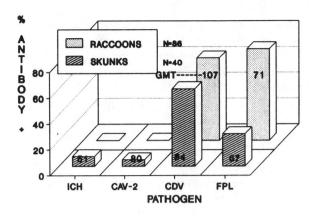

Fig. 14. Prevalence of antibodies in sera from Toronto skunks and raccoons, 1985. GMT = geometric mean titer (reciprocal of dilution), ICH = infectious canine hepatitis, CAV-2 = canine adenovirus, CDV = canine distemper, FPL = feline panleucopenia, N = sample size.

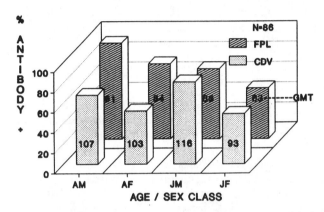

Fig. 15. Prevalence of canine distemper and feline panleucopenia antibodies in sera from raccoons in Toronto, 1985. FPL = feline panleucopenia, CDV = canine distemper, GMT = geometric mean titer (reciprocal of dilution), AM = adult male, AF = adult female, JM = juvenile male, JF = juvenile female, N = sample size.

for canine parainfluenza, feline rhinotrachaetis, and feline calicivirus.

During our TVR program in Toronto, 45% (n = 122) of the skunks examined were positive for ticks (Ixodidae). However, only 2% (n = 322) of the raccoons had ticks (*Ixodes texanus*). It is unlikely that ticks severely affected the physical condition of skunks and raccoons in Toronto; however, we do not yet know the role, if any, that ticks play with respect to transmission of diseases to urban skunks, raccoons, and foxes.

CONCLUSION

All indications from these studies are that disease is the most likely limiting factor for skunks and raccoons (and probably foxes) living in Toronto. Weight, population, and movement data all indicated that neither food nor habitat seemed to be limiting. Both species were still increasing in number, and spreading through a greater variety of habitats, after 4 years of study. We are aware of rabies and distemper

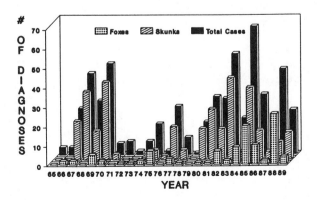

Fig. 13. Rabies cases in Toronto, 1965–1989.

outbreaks in Toronto in past years, but we have not observed either during the period of intensive study.

Acknowledgments.—Numerous people provided input to the Urban Rabies Program, without whose support, the program would not exist. They include: D.H. Johnston, D.R. Voigt, P. Bachmann, F. McKay, D. Joachim, G. Smith, S. Smith, M. Pedde, B. Derych, M. Allan, C. Adkins, P. Stott, B. Pond, C. Heydon, M. Ronda, P. Kelly-Ward, B. Wilkinson, W. Sinclair, C. Nunan, S. Fraser, J. Topping, I. Grillo, R. Warren, E. Eaves, B. Korell, D. Miller, K. Donn, G. Pacitto, A. Fattore, J. Arnosti, R. Meerveld, C. Hogenkamp, J. Sirois, D. Rodrigues, L. Virgin, E. Brolly, C. Murphy, D. Stephenson, H. Miller, J. Brown, D. Briggs, M. Garscadden, S. Slavec, J. Campbell, K. Lawson, K. Charlton, A. Wandeler, J. Lotimer, S. Strathern, B. Heron, W. Davenport, T. Berman, A. Chui, and many others. E. Addison identified the raccoon ticks and I. Barker assayed the skunk and raccoon sera for antibody against selected pathogens. The program is supported by the Rabies Advisory Committee.

REFERENCES CITED

Barker, I.K., R. Povey, and D.R. Voigt. 1983. Response of mink, skunk, red fox, and raccoon to inoculation with mink virus enteritis, feline panleukopenia, and canine parvovirus, and prevalence of antibody to parvovirus in wild carnivores in Ontario. Can. J. Comp. Med. 47:188–197.

Begon, M. 1979. Investigating animal abundance: capture-recapture for biologists. Univ. Park Press, Baltimore, Md. 97pp.

Cranfield, M.R., I. K. Barker, K.G. Mehren, and W.A. Rapley. 1984. Canine distemper in wild raccoons (*Procyon lotor*) at the Metropolitan Toronto Zoo. Can. Vet. J. 25:63–66.

Hoffmann, C.O., and J.L. Gottschang. 1977. Numbers, distribution, and movements of a raccoon population in a suburban residential community. J. Mammal. 58:623–636.

Johnston, D.H. et al. 1987. Aging furbearers using tooth structure and biomarkers. Pages 228–243 in M. Novak, J.A. Baker, M.E. Obbard, and B. Malloch, eds. Wild furbearer management and conservation in North America. Ontario Trappers Assoc., North Bay, Ontario.

MacInnes, C.D. 1987. Rabies. Pages 910–929 in M. Novak, J.A. Baker, M.E. Obbard, and B. Malloch, eds. Wild furbearer management and conservation in North America. Ontario Trappers Assoc., North Bay, Ontario.

——. 1988. Control of wildlife rabies: The Americas. Pages 381–406 in J.B. Campbell, and K.M. Charlton, eds. Rabies. Kluwer Academic Publishers, Boston, Mass.

Rosatte, R.C. 1987. Striped, spotted, hooded, and hog-nosed skunk. Pages 599–613 in M. Novak, J.A. Baker, M.E. Obbard, and B. Malloch, eds. Wild furbearer management and conservation in North America. Ontario Trappers Assoc., North Bay, Ontario.

——, and J.R. Gunson. 1984. Dispersal and home range of striped skunks, *Mephitis mephitis*, in an area of population reduction in southern Alberta. Can. Field Nat. 98:315–319.

——, and P.M. Kelly-Ward. 1988. A surgical procedure for implanting radio transmitters in striped skunks (*Mephitis mephitis*). Can. Field Nat. 102: 713–715.

——, ——, and C.D. MacInnes. 1987. A strategy for controlling rabies in urban skunks and raccoons. Pages 161–167 in L.W. Adams, and D.L. Leedy, eds. Integrating man and nature in the metropolitan environment. Natl. Inst. for Urban Wildl., Columbia, Md.

——, and C.D. MacInnes. 1987. A tactic to control rabies in urban wildlife. Trans. NE Sect. Wildl. Soc. 44:77–79.

——, and ——. 1989. Relocation of city raccoons. Pages 87–92 in Proc. 9th Great Plains Wildl. Damage Control Workshop, Fort Collins, Colorado. Great Plains Agric. Counc. Publ. 127.

——, M.J. Power, C.D. MacInnes, and K.F. Lawson. 1990. Rabies control for urban foxes, skunks and raccoons. In L.R. Davis, ed. Proc. 14th Vert. Pest. Conf., Univ. of California, Davis. 24pp.

Sanderson, G.C. 1987. Raccoon. Pages 487–499 in M. Novak, J.A. Baker, M.E. Obbard, and B. Malloch, eds. Wild furbearer management and conservation in North America. Ontario Trappers Assoc., North Bay, Ontario.

Sargeant, A.B., R.J. Greenwood, J.L. Piewl, and W.B. Bicknell. 1982. Recurrence, mortality, and dispersal of prairie striped skunks, *Mephitis mephitis*, and implications to rabies epizootiology. Can. Field Nat. 96:312–316.

Schnell, J.H. 1970. Rest site selection by radio-tagged raccoons. Minn. Acad. of Sci. 36:83–88.

Voigt, D.R. 1987. Red fox. Pages 379–392 in M. Novak, J. Baker, M. Obbard, and B. Malloch, eds. Wild furbearer management and conservation in North America. Ontario Trappers Association, North Bay, Ontario.

——, and D.W. Macdonald. 1984. Variation in the spatial and social behaviour of the red fox, *Vulpes vulpes*. Acta Zool. Fennica 171:261–265.

——, and R.L. Tinline. 1980. Strategies for analysing radio-tracking data. Pages 387–404 in C.J. Amlaner, and D.W. Macdonald, eds. A handbook on biotelemetry and radiotracking. Oxford, U.K.

Wojcinski, Z.W., and I.K. Barker. 1986. Tyzzer's disease as a complication of canine distemper in a raccoon. J. Wildl. Dis. 22:55–59.

Zar, J.H. 1974. Biostatistical analysis. Prentice-Hall Inc., Englewood Cliffs, N.J. 620 pp.

Zimen, E. 1984. Long range movements of the red fox, *Vulpes vulpes* L. Acta Zool. Fennica 171:267–270.

Daytime Resting Site Selection in an Urban Raccoon Population

JOHN HADIDIAN, *National Park Service, Center for Urban Ecology, 1100 Ohio Dr., S.W., Washington, DC 20242*

DAVID A. MANSKI, *National Park Service, Cape Cod National Seashore, South Wellfleet, MA 02663*

SETH RILEY, *National Park Service, Center for Urban Ecology, 1100 Ohio Dr., S.W., Washington, DC 20242*[1]

INTRODUCTION

The raccoon (*Procyon lotor*) is one native North American mammal that has benefited from contact with humans. Historically it has extended its former range and occupied a variety of new habitats created by humans (Sutton 1964, Lynch 1971, Kaufmann 1982). This adaptability has led to the successful exploitation of urban and suburban areas where raccoons often become nuisance animals and may be regarded as threats to the public health through the transmission of diseases such as rabies (Jenkins and Winkler 1987, Rosatte et al. 1987).

Although some information exists regarding such factors as the home range and population density of urban raccoons (Schinner and Cauley 1973, Hoffmann and Gottschang 1977, Sherfy and Chapman 1980), much less is known about daytime resting site selection. The potential for human-raccoon conflicts identified above as well as the need for basic information regarding native animal populations within the National Park Service (NPS 1988) provide us with a strong incentive for collecting information regarding all aspects of urban raccoon ecology and habitat utilization. The present study documented the daytime resting habits of adult raccoons in an urban National Park and its adjacent residential neighborhoods. It was part of a long-term research project on raccoon ecology and behavior conducted to address issues relevant to the management of natural resources in urban parks.

STUDY AREA

The study was conducted in Rock Creek Park (ROCR), a 710-ha urban National Park located entirely within the confines of metropolitan Washington, D.C. Established in

1890 by an Act of Congress, and administered by the National Park Service since 1933, approximately 85% of ROCR is zoned as a natural area, where wildlife and other natural resources are managed to maintain natural processes.

Data were collected in two study areas referred to as Piney Branch and Bingham (Fig. 1). The predominant overstory vegetation in both study areas was mature deciduous hardwood forest, dominated by oak (*Quercus spp.*), tulip

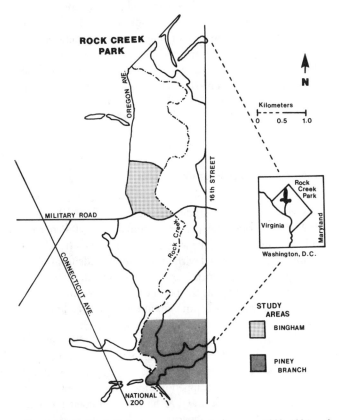

Fig. 1. Rock Creek Park raccoon project study areas, 1983–1984 and 1989–1990.

[1]Present Address: Department of Environmental Studies, University of California, Davis, CA 95616.

Wildlife Conservation in Metropolitan Environments. NIUW Symp. Ser. 2, L.W. Adams and D.L. Leedy, eds. Published by Natl. Inst. for Urban Wildl., 10921 Trotting Ridge Way, Columbia, MD 21044, USA, 1991.

poplar (*Liriodendron tulipifera*), and beech (*Fagus grandiflora*). The Piney Branch study area encompassed the older, less disturbed vegetative community. The Bingham area included an old Civil War fort as well as a currently occupied Park Police horse stable, a community vegetable garden plot, and the abandoned site of a 1930s Civilian Conservation Corps camp. Black locust (*Robina pseudoacacia*) was common in the Bingham study area, mostly as older groves in the process of being replaced by other hardwoods. In several places, these old locust groves were associated with dense ground thickets of greenbriar (*Smilax spp.*) and other viney plants. Such thickets were not found in the Piney Branch study area.

Rock Creek Park was surrounded almost entirely by residential neighborhoods. Two neighborhood subdivisions occurred in the Piney Branch study area. Mount Pleasant consisted mostly of multiple family dwellings and row houses, with few large street trees. In 1980, Mt. Pleasant had, per hectare, 135.2 housing units, an average population density of 238.6 people, and 3.04 vacant housing units. The Crestwood residential subdivision was a relatively old suburban-like community, with mature street and yard trees, remnant woodlots, and large single family homes. Crestwood had, per hectare, an average of 13.8 housing units, a population density of 32.5 people, and 0.77 vacant housing units in 1980. The neighborhoods adjacent to the Bingham study site consisted mostly of single family residences, but also included an apartment complex and a high school. In 1980, per hectare, there were 95.2 housing units and an average population density of 231.7 people in the residential subdivision adjacent to the Bingham study area.

METHODS

Trapping and Handling Procedures

Raccoons were caught in live-traps set at various locations throughout the study areas during 1983–1984 and 1989–1990. Following capture, animals were taken to a workup facility where they were anesthetized, given physical examinations, and fitted with radio-collars made from commercially available transmitters (Hadidian et al. 1989). All animals were released at the point of capture within 8 hours of workup. Traps were set in pairs at each trapsite. Trapping was conducted both on and off park property in Piney Branch, with a trapsite density of 1/6 ha and 1/40 ha inside and outside the park boundary, respectively. In Bingham, traps were set only within the park, at a trapsite density of 1/6 ha. The total area trapped in Piney Branch consisted of roughly 60 ha of park and 170 ha in the residential area, whereas 56 ha were trapped in the Bingham study area. Radio-collars were put on Piney Branch animals until our supply was exhausted. In the Bingham study area, we collared all live-trapped adult females and two adult males. In both study areas subadults were radio-collared as well as adults, but observations on these animals are not covered

in this report. The criteria used to classify animals as adult were a fully extrudable baculum measuring 95 mm or more for males (Sanderson 1950, 1961) and teats of 5 mm or longer for females (Stuewer 1943).

Radio Telemetry

Daytime resting locations were determined by walking directly to den sites. Dens were usually located a minimum of three times each week, with some locations taken immediately following nighttime radio-tracking sessions. Individual sites in which animals rested were usually accessible, except in neighborhood areas where denning on private property occurred. Whenever a resting site could not be precisely located, a minimum of two and usually three compass bearings were taken and an "area" location assigned by triangulation. All other den sites were given unique numbers and their exact locations were plotted on maps (1:2000) of the study area.

Four types of dens were recognized: trees, buildings, ground dens, and ground rests. Ground rests occurred where raccoons made surface beds within dense thickets of vegetation. Seasonal data were represented by samples of no fewer than 18 radio-collared raccoons in each of four defined annual periods: spring (April–June), summer (July–September), fall (October–December), and winter (January–March).

Data Analysis

We analyzed data on raccoon daytime resting sites to characterize the population as a whole as well as to compare results between study areas and by sex. Relative frequencies, usually expressed in percentage of total use, were employed to adjust for sampling differences. Habitat distinctions were drawn between the park (natural) and residential areas outside it. Some finer distinctions were implicitly recognized in the classification of different types of dens, such as the differentiation between raccoon use of buildings and trees in residential areas. Student's *t*-test was used to compare means after variances were tested for equality (Rosner 1986). Because of the known lack of independence between observations, which occurred both as a result of the repeated sampling of the same individuals and through the potential positive or negative influences that animals may have exerted on one another in den site selection, we have attempted to apply such inferential tests with restraint.

Den site availability was not determined. We determined a *den reuse* index for the average number of times an animal was located in a den by dividing the number of locations on it by the number of individual, unique sites chosen. Den co-occupancy, as employed here, refers to the use of a given den by more than one animal, which may or may not have been simultaneous.

RESULTS

Site Selection

Nine adult males and eighteen adult females were followed for periods ranging from 3 to 24 months and were located in dens a total of 3,914 times (Table 1). Trees accounted for the majority (69%) of all daytime resting sites located in both study areas (Table 2). Residences (15%) and ground dens (11%) received about equal use, whereas ground rests (1%) represented the smallest proportion of sites used. Four percent of all daytime resting sites could not be verified and were classified as undetermined. The majority (95%) of the latter resulted from animals denning on private property inaccessible to us.

Although animal locations in trees could not always be exactly determined, branch or trunk cavities were usually found on trees that received repeated use. In good weather, animals were occasionally observed resting on limbs or in the crotch formed by the union of two or more trunk branches.

The majority (90%) of all locations of raccoons in buildings occurred in houses occupied year-round by humans. Although we did not systematically survey locations within buildings, our observations suggest that chimneys and attics were most frequently used, whereas basements, porch crawl spaces, and other locations received only occasional use. Of the 575 times raccoons used buildings, only two cases involved a building other than a residence. In both instances, a male denned in a detached garage.

Slightly more than half (56%) of all ground den use occurred in association with storm sewer systems. On some occasions, animals may have rested on ledges within sewers, but use even during heavy rains suggested the raccoons had access to locations leading away from the main drainage tunnels that were secure from flooding. Almost all other use of ground dens occurred where man-made cavities had been created, such as among riprap material along stream banks or at sites where building materials had been dumped and partially buried. Raccoons were not found to use fox (*Vulpes*

vulpes) dens, even when these appeared to have been abandoned for some time. Woodchucks (*Marmota monax*) are absent from ROCR and their burrows, known elsewhere to be used as daytime refuges by raccoons (Butterfield 1954), were unavailable.

No marked shift occurred seasonally in the type of den sites chosen except for the increased use of trees in spring and ground rests in summer (Table 2), both of which we attribute to activities by adult females related to birth and the raising of young. We did note that certain individual trees and residences received repeated use during extreme cold weather, and these may have been selected because of extra protection they provided. Males and females differed primarily in the greater use of ground dens by males (23% as opposed to 4%) and trees by females (72% v. 62%). Twenty percent of all den sites chosen in the summer by adult males in the Piney Branch area were ground dens. This was the highest use of dens of this type by any group, and may have occurred because the ground dens chosen were cooler than other sites. Building use, by both males and females and between study areas, was consistent throughout the year.

The relative use of trees and ground dens was highly comparable between Piney Branch and Bingham. One noteworthy difference between study areas was the greater use of buildings by Piney Branch study animals, where these comprised 21% of all dens occupied as compared to only 3% in Bingham. However, we found that three of the fifteen animals in Piney Branch were responsible for the bulk (76%) of the use of residences. When these animals were excluded, the use of buildings in Piney Branch by the remaining 12 raccoons accounted for only 5% of all den use. A second noticeable difference between study areas was that no ground rest use occurred at all in Piney Branch. Although only 4% of total den use in the Bingham study area was of ground rests, nine of the 10 adult females radio-tracked there used these locations at some time.

Habitat Use

Seventy-seven percent of occupied dens were located within ROCR, a greater use ($t = 6.03$, df = 25, $P < 0.05$) than was made of dens in neighborhoods. There was no difference ($P > 0.05$) between males and females or between study areas in regard to the use of ROCR and residential areas. The variation among individuals was great enough, however, to suggest that the majority favored either one or the other in which to den. Eighteen of the 27 animals used ROCR for 80% or more of their denning, and 10 had all of their dens within park boundaries. Only three animals, all from Piney Branch, used the residential areas outside ROCR for 80% or more of their denning, and one of these was the only animal followed that denned exclusively in residential areas.

If the use of different types of dens in ROCR and adjacent residential areas is examined relative to the total use of sites in each, the significance of trees as resting sites

Table 1. Raccoon radio-telemetry observations on Piney Branch males ($n = 7$) and females ($n = 8$), and Bingham males ($n = 2$) and females ($n = 10$), Rock Creek Park, 1983–1984 and 1989–1990.

Sex Observation	Piney Branch		Bingham		Combined	
	$\bar{x}$	SE	$\bar{x}$	SE	$\bar{x}$	SE
Males						
Months observed	15	1.93	7	1.41	13	1.96
No. locations	175	23.02	105	46.52	159	21.82
Females						
Months observed	14	2.02	9	1.14	11	1.25
No. locations	168	19.23	113	15.32	138	13.43

Table 2. Frequency (%) of raccoon den site selection, Rock Creek Park, Washington, D.C., 1983–1984 and 1989–1990.

Den site	Season				
	Spring	Summer	Fall	Winter	Combined
Trees	78	60	65	65	69
Buildings	13	12	16	19	15
Ground dens	6	16	13	11	11
Ground rests	1	5	1	0[a]	1
Undetermined	2	7	5	5	4
Total	100	100	100	100	100

[a]<0.01%

within the park is immediately apparent (Table 3). This was not the case in residential areas, where buildings (Piney Branch) and ground dens (Bingham) were more frequently occupied. However, the use of trees in neighborhoods was undoubtedly underestimated. We suspect that many undetermined locations actually involved animals denning in trees in back yards or woodlots on private property.

Ground dens in the Piney Branch study area were used primarily within park boundaries, where there were three preferred locations. Of these, one was associated with riprap used for bank stabilization along a stream, whereas two others were in storm sewers along park roads. Thus, human-modified habitat features were utilized even within the relatively natural setting of the park. Although there was a horse stable on park property in the Bingham study area, it was never found to be occupied by study animals. There were no buildings on park property in the Piney Branch study area.

Den Site Use and Average Occupancy

A total of 534 individual den sites was used by 27 radio-collared animals, with more than half of those in each type being used two or more times (Table 4). A few individual dens were extensively used in both study areas. In Piney Branch, the three most frequently used of the 181 active den trees accounted for 27% of all tree use. In Bingham, with 215 trees identified as denning sites, the three most used accounted for only 11% of all use. Certain ground dens were heavily used also. In each study area, the three most

frequently occupied ground dens accounted for 71% of all observed use.

The fewest different dens that any animal used was nine; the most was 54. However, the animal using nine dens was located only 33 times, whereas the one with 54 was found 202 times. Thus, the *average* number of times each raccoon occupied a den before being found in a new and previously unused (for that animal) site was about 3.7. The *den reuse* index was estimated for both study populations as the value expressed by dividing the total number of locations for an animal by the number of individual and unique den sites which that animal occupied.

Because higher index values represented relatively greater reuse or fidelity to dens than did lower values, the higher ($t = 3.20$, $df = 25$, $P < 0.05$) average for Piney Branch ($\bar{x} = 6.8$) than for Bingham ($\bar{x} = 3.9$) suggested that suitable sites might be more limited at Piney Branch. However, the basis for this difference was observed to lie in the repeated use of buildings and ground dens in Piney Branch and not in the use of trees, for which no difference ($P > 0.05$) was found between study areas (Table 5). Animals continued to use "new" sites (i.e., ones in which they had not been previously found) throughout all periods of observation. For example, one adult female was tracked for 24 months and used 28 different trees in which we located her a total of 233 times. In the last 6 months during which she was followed, this female added six trees to the 22 in which she had previously been found.

Co-occupancy of Dens

We found animals denning together as well as using the same dens at different times. Although the majority (73%) of dens were associated with only one user, sites were found in each den category that received use by more than one animal (Table 6). The maximum number of users over the duration of both studies was seven for one tree in the Bingham study area. Two trees in Piney Branch were used by six different animals. Only one ground den received use by more than three radio-collared animals, and the maximum number of animals found using the same building was three.

DISCUSSION

That the raccoon is an opportunistic and highly adaptable species is evidenced in many aspects of its behavior, including the selection and use of daytime resting or refuge sites. As we also observed, trees are often preferred for denning (Stuewer 1943, Johnson 1970, Allsbrooks and Kennedy 1987). However, other types of sites may receive comparable or even greater use in certain areas (Giles 1942, Shirer and Fitch 1970, Rabinowitz 1981). Urban (1970), for example, reported that 89% of the dens used by raccoons on a managed waterfowl marsh were in muskrat houses, which indicates the adaptability these animals have in making use of what is available to them. Fritzell (1978a) found

Table 3. Relative use (%) of den sites by raccoons within and outside park boundaries, Rock Creek Park, Washington, D.C., 1983–1984 and 1989–1990.

	Den site location			
	Within park		Outside park	
Den site	Piney Branch	Bingham	Piney Branch	Bingham
Trees	85	93	3	19
Buildings	0	0	74	13
Ground dens	14	1	6	46
Ground rests	0	5	0	0
Undetermined	1	1	17	22
Total	100	100	100	100

Table 4. Frequency (%) of den use by raccoons, Rock Creek Park, Washington, D.C., 1983–1984 and 1989–1990.

Area No. times used	Trees	Buildings	Ground dens	Ground rests	Undetermined
Piney Branch					
1	35	40	35	0	26
2–4	37	14	30	0	32
5+	28	46	35	0	42
Total percent	100	100	100	—	100
Total dens	181	48	29	0	19
Bingham					
1	47	38	24	12	22
2–4	30	50	52	38	67
5+	23	12	24	50	11
Total percent	100	100	100	100	100
Total no. dens	215	8	17	8	9

Table 5. Raccoon den reuse index, Rock Creek Park, Washington, D.C., 1983–1984 and 1989–1990.[a]

	Piney Branch						Bingham					
	Male			Female			Male			Female		
Den site	n	$\bar{x}$	SE	n	$\bar{x}$	SE	n	$\bar{x}$	SE	n	$\bar{x}$	SE
Trees	7	5.5	1.3	8	5.4	1.1	2	2.9	0.8	10	4.0	0.5
Buildings	2	4.2	1.1	4	17.3	7.7	2	2.0	0.0	3	4.8	2.7
Ground dens	7	13.9	2.7	2	3.3	2.3	2	2.4	1.4	5	5.1	2.3
Ground rests	0	—	—	0	—	—	0	—	—	9	2.7	0.6
Undetermined	4	3.1	0.7	3	4.8	3.6	2	2.5	0.5	5	5.7	3.1

[a]See text for description of index.

Table 6. Frequency (%) of den use by different raccoons, Rock Creek Park, Washington, D.C., 1983–1984 and 1989–1990.

Area No. users	Trees	Buildings	Ground dens	Ground rests	Undetermined
Piney Branch					
1	69	77	69	0	74
2–3	23	23	28	0	21
4+	8	0	3	0	5
Total percent	100	100	100	—	100
Total dens	181	48	29	0	19
Bingham					
1	79	88	76	50	67
2–3	18	12	24	50	33
4+	3	0	0	0	0
Total percent	100	100	100	100	100
Total no. dens	215	8	17	8	9

[a]Use may or may not have been simultaneous.

44% of all diurnal locations of raccoons in the prairie pothole region of North Dakota to be in buildings, a considerably higher figure than we found in our urban area, and one that reflects the likely limitations of den sites in Fritzell's study area.

The choice by an animal of a particular site as a den or daytime refuge undoubtedly depends on many factors, such as availability, competition for access with other species or conspecifics, individual preferences, site suitability (especially in protection from environmental extremes), and security for the raising of young. Furthermore, social factors may influence site selection and use, and much remains to be learned regarding the attraction or aversion associated with the presence of other animals, or their odor, at a given den site.

The data from this study indicate that park natural areas were heavily utilized by raccoons in selecting daytime resting sites and that mature trees with hollow trunks or other cavities were much more frequently occupied than other types of dens. Of the four types of dens identified, only trees were used by all of the animals we studied. Ground dens and buildings were used extensively by some animals, whereas ground rests were used only by adult females and only in the Bingham study area. We believe the failure of Piney Branch animals to use ground rests is explained by the absence of dense thickets of vegetation that are apparently necessary for this activity to take place. Schneider et al. (1971) reported ground rest use in Minnesota raccoons as primarily involving family groups that used these sites during the summer after the young had been weaned and moved from natal dens.

We have attempted to avoid suggesting that tree dens are preferred by raccoons because we lack knowledge of exactly what choices our animals had available to them. Den site availability can be estimated through indices that make adjustments for den use as a function of abundance. However, such indices probably should be restricted to approximations based on examination of entire habitat areas (e.g., Fritzell 1978a) rather than specific types of dens. In Central Iowa, Cabalka et al. (1953) monitored 68 trees during the spring and fall that had been picked by investigators as suitable for denning by raccoons. Of these, only one-third proved to be actually occupied, which appears to indicate the inability of human observers to determine exactly what are suitable den sites for raccoons.

Individual animals varied considerably in den selection and habitat use patterns, but we have deferred interpreting these data until the larger movement and activity patterns of which denning is a part are examined. In Piney Branch, the larger trapping area that extended into the neighborhoods favored the capture of animals whose home ranges included more residential area than park. Two adult females, caught at a distance of 0.3 km from the nearest park boundary, almost exclusively used residential areas for denning, and influenced the higher total use of buildings as dens in the Piney Branch population. Whether this indicates individual preferences for denning in residential areas or exclusion from park areas because of home range limits remains to be determined. One adult male, that also frequently denned in residential areas, was known to frequently forage in the park, and may have denned outside it as a matter of preference. Finally, although we hypothesized that raccoons might shift to greater use of residential areas and buildings during the winter than at other times of the year, no marked preference for such use was found in either study population. This could suggest that, for this area, no one type of den possessed any particular seasonal advantage.

Although it is often reported in the literature that raccoons frequently shift daytime resting sites (Mech et al. 1966, Schnell 1970, Shirer and Fitch 1970, Lehman 1984, Allsbrooks and Kennedy 1987), little information is available to indicate whether animals return to and reuse the same sites. Rabinowitz and Pelton (1986) reported that 46% of 327 daytime resting sites of raccoons in Tennessee were used more than once. In the present study, we found that raccoons reused 61% of 534 sites. Rabinowitz and Pelton

(1986) also reported the extensive reuse of a few select sites, a phenomenon which we encountered as well. In fact, a few of our sites received such extensive reuse by so many animals that they might be considered as *communal* dens. Mech and Turkowski (1966) reported a large assemblage of raccoons at a single denning site in winter which Fritzell (1978b) suggested indicates animals have greater tolerance for each other during that time than during spring or summer. Whatever the cause, such special and frequently used sites are deserving of further study.

In addition to the reuse of den sites, we also found dens that were used by as many as seven individuals, although not necessarily at the same time. Because all of our study animals were adult when caught, we have no knowledge of relatedness among them. The users of dens may have been related, may have occupied different and individually 'owned' den sites within the same tree, ground den, or residence, or may have been unrelated animals who simply were expressing mutual tolerance and perhaps even attraction to one another. Our data for the reuse of dens and the average number of users are known to be underestimates because many uncollared resident animals were known from our mark-recapture studies in both study areas, and because we have excluded all associations of family groups from this report. Our own observations, as well as information provided from long-term residents in neighborhoods adjacent to the park, suggest that raccoons will utilize the same trees and houses for many years, as long as den sites within them are available. One resident in the Mount Pleasant area reported to us in 1985 that raccoons had been continuous occupants of her attic since 1957.

Shirer and Fitch (1970) and Lehman (1984) recorded shifts in den site location and expressed an "average occupancy rate" for raccoons in Kansas and Indiana. These rates may either be taken to represent shifts between novel den sites or shifts between den sites that receive use again at some later time. In either case, the derived rates should closely depend on sampling protocols. Animals that are checked every day are likely to show quite different occupancy rates than those checked on a weekly basis. In attempting to minimize this kind of bias, we have used a similar estimate, but based it on the quotient derived from dividing the total number of locations on an animal by the number of individual den sites it used. Our data indicate that frequent shifts between trees occur, but that ground dens and dens in buildings are changed less frequently. Again, this may indicate either that raccoons were more limited in the selection of these sites or that the sites themselves were preferred and reused frequently because they possessed characteristics that attracted the animals to them.

Whatever the reasons for animals utilizing a variety of den sites, the benefits of such behavior are obvious. For raccoons, dens may provide direct security from predators and environmental extremes, and indirect benefits like avoidance of repeated exposure to ectoparasites. Having alternative den sites also may allow an animal to increase its foraging efficiency by positioning itself near seasonally localized food resources. We also have observed the loss of den sites from time to time, as trees were felled during storms and chimneys on residences capped after homeowners apparently became aware of raccoons denning there. Certainly an important benefit a raccoon derives from having alternative den sites is the ability to relocate when a den becomes unavailable.

One practical conclusion that may be derived from these data concerns the planning of management strategies for raccoons that become nuisance animals. Given that dens are often occupied by different animals, it is obvious that only the exclusion of animals from places where they are not wanted is likely to be an effective, long-term method of control. Given, too, that no animal seems dependent on any single den site as its only refuge, we recommend the use of repellents and aversive stimuli to encourage site abandonment followed by mandatory structural repairs or modifications, such as chimney capping, to permanently exclude animals from further access. Such practices should be undertaken outside the birth season.

Acknowledgments.—We would like to thank the past and current Park Superintendents, Georgia Ellard and Roland Swain, for support in conducting these studies and permission to conduct this work in Rock Creek Park. The Natural Resource Manager for Rock Creek Park, Bob Ford, has encouraged and assisted us through all the many phases of raccoon research. The 1983–1984 study was supported, in part, by the Washington Biologists' Field Club and conducted in cooperation with the Centers for Disease Control, Atlanta, Ga., the District of Columbia's Department of Human Services, the University of the District of Columbia, and the National Zoological Park. The 1989–1990 study was sponsored by grants from the Geraldine R. Dodge Foundation and the Humane Society of the United States.

REFERENCES CITED

Allsbrooks, D.W., and M.L. Kennedy. 1987. Movement patterns of raccoons (*Procyon lotor*) in western Tennessee. J. Tenn. Acad. Sci. 62:15–19.

Butterfield, R.T. 1954. Some raccoon and groundhog relationships. J. Wildl. Manage. 18:433–437.

Cabalka, J.L., R.R. Costa, and G.O. Hendrickson. 1953. Ecology of the raccoon in central Iowa. Iowa Acad. Sci. 60:616–620.

Fritzell, E. K. 1978a. Habitat use by prairie raccoons during the waterfowl breeding season. J. Wildl. Manage. 42:118–127.

———. 1978b. Aspects of raccoon (*Procyon lotor*) social organization. Can J. Zool. 56:260–271.

Giles, L.W. 1942. Utilization of rock exposures for den and escape cover by raccoons. Am. Midl. Nat. 27:171–176.

Hadidian, J., S.R. Jenkins, D.H. Johnston, P.J. Savarie, V.F. Nettles, D.M. Manski, and G.M. Baer. 1989. Acceptance of simulated oral rabies vaccine baits by urban raccoons. J. Wildl. Dis. 25:1–9.

Hoffmann, C.O., and J.L. Gottschang. 1977. Numbers, distribution, and movements of a raccoon population in a suburban residential community. J. Mammal. 58:623–636.

Jenkins, S.R., and W.G. Winkler. 1987. Descriptive epidemiology from an epizootic of raccoon rabies in the Middle Atlantic States, 1982–1983. Am. J. Epidem. 126:429–437.

Johnson, A.S. 1970. Biology of the raccoon (*Procyon lotor varius*, Nelson and Goldman) in Alabama. Bull. 402. Agric. Exp. Sta., Auburn Univ. 148pp.

Kaufmann, J.H. 1982. Raccoons and allies. Pages 567–585 *in* J.A. Chapman and G.A. Feldhammer, eds. Wild mammals of North America. Johns Hopkins Univ. Press, Baltimore, Md.

Lehman, L.E. 1984. Raccoon density, home range, and habitat use on South-Central Indiana farmland. Pittman-Robertson Bull. No. 15. Indiana Dep. Nat. Resour., Div. Fish and Wildl., 66pp.

Lynch, G.M. 1971. Raccoons increasing in Manitoba. J. Mammal. 52:621–622.

Mech, L.D., J.R. Tester, and D.W. Warner. 1966. Fall daytime resting habits of raccoons as determined by telemetry. J. Mammal. 47:450–466.

———, and F.J. Turkowski. 1966. Twenty-three raccoons in one winter den. J. Mammal. 47:529–530.

NPS. 1988. Management policies. U.S.D.I., National Park Service, Washington, D.C.

Rabinowitz, A.R. 1981. The ecology of the raccoon (*Procyon lotor*) in Cades Cove, Great Smoky Mountains National Park. Ph.D. Thesis, Univ. Tenn., Knoxville. 133pp.

———, and M.R. Pelton. 1986. Day-bed use by raccoons. J. Mammal. 67:766–769.

Rosatte, R.C., P.M. Kelly-Ward, and C.D. MacInnes. 1987. A strategy for controlling rabies in urban skunks and raccoons. Pages 54–60 *in* L.W. Adams and D.L. Leedy, eds. Integrating man and nature in the metropolitan environment. Natl. Inst. for Urban Wildl., Columbia, Md.

Rosner, B. 1986 Fundamentals of biostatistics. Duxbury Press, Boston, Mass. 584pp.

Sanderson, G.C. 1950. Methods of measuring productivity in raccoons. J. Wildl. Manage. 14:389–402.

———. 1961. Techniques for determining age of raccoons. Ill. Nat. Hist. Surv. Biol. Notes 45:1–16.

Schinner, J.R., and D.L. Cauley. 1973. The ecology of urban raccoons in Cincinnati, Ohio. Pages 125–130 *in* J.H. Noyes and D.R. Progulske, eds. Wildlife in an urbanizing environment. Planning and Resour. Dev. Ser. No. 28, Holdsworth Nat. Resour. Cent., Amherst, Mass.

Schneider, D.G., L.D. Mech., and J.R. Tester. 1971. Movements of female raccoons and their young as determined by radio-tracking. Anim. Behav. Monogr. 4:1–43.

Schnell, J.H. 1970. Rest site selection by radio-tagged raccoons. Minn. Acad. Sci. 36:83–88.

Sherfy, F. C., and J.A. Chapman. 1980. Seasonal home range and habitat utilization of raccoons in Maryland. Carnivore III:8–18.

Shirer, H.W., and H.S. Fitch. 1970. Comparison from radio-tracking of movements and denning habits of the raccoon, striped skunk, and opossum in northeastern Kansas. J. Mammal. 51:491–503.

Stuewer, F.W. 1943. Raccoons: their habits and management in Michigan. Ecol. Monogr. 13:203–257.

Sutton, R.W. 1964. Range extension of raccoon in Manitoba. J. Mammal. 45:311–312.

Urban, D. 1970. Raccoon populations, movement patterns, and predation on a managed waterfowl marsh. J. Wildl. Manage. 34:372–382.

Distribution and Habitat Associations of Coyotes in Seattle, Washington[1]

TIMOTHY QUINN, *College of Forest Resources, AR-10, University of Washington, Seattle, WA 98195*

INTRODUCTION

The coyote (*Canis latrans*) is perhaps the most controversial mammal that frequently inhabits urban areas in the United States. For some, the coyote is a welcome and exciting part of urban living (Froman 1961), but to others the animal is a threat to personal property and safety (Gill 1965, Gill and Bonnett 1973). The presence of coyotes in urban environments raises several concerns. There have been a number of reported coyote attacks on humans in urban areas (Howell 1982). Like other urban mammals, the coyote is a potential vector for the spread of human disease including rabies. Coyotes may also prey upon small domestic pets (MacCracken 1982, Shargo 1988).

Since the end of the second world war, American cities have rapidly expanded into traditional wildlife habitat causing the displacement or extinction of many species, particularly carnivores. Urbanization causes widespread changes in habitat that generally result in the dispersion of food sources, a reduction in the quality and quantity of natural vegetation and an increase in many forms of pollution. Typically it is the dietary and habitat specialists that are least able to cope with these changes (Gavareski 1976, Harris 1984).

Major metropolitan areas consist of a mosaic of distinct habitat types, many of which represent very disturbed environments (Schlauch 1978). Not surprisingly, urban mammals are most frequently associated with the relatively undisturbed areas such as parks or cemeteries. However, it is often unclear exactly what role these areas play in maintenance of urban wildlife populations (Jones 1958, Harris 1977). The objectives of the present study were to (1) determine the distribution of coyotes in Seattle, Washington, (2) characterize the important urban habitat features related to the presence of coyotes in the city, and (3) evaluate the role these habitats play in maintaining coyotes in Seattle.

[1]Supplemental paper not presented at the symposium.

STUDY AREA

The City of Seattle makes up the core of the Greater Seattle Metropolitan Area in King County, Washington. Seattle lies in the Puget Sound Basin and is bordered on the west by Puget Sound and on the east by Lake Washington. The city is divided by an east-west human-made ship canal. The north and south Seattle land masses are approximately 8,340 and 13,664 ha, respectively. In 1990, the population of the city was 512,094, with an average density of 23 people per hectare.

METHODS

Two independent methods were used to identify the distribution of coyotes within the Seattle city limits.

Telephone Survey of Selected Individuals

All city and county parks, cemeteries, golf courses, college campuses, and other relatively large, undeveloped tracts of land within Seattle were identified. Persons responsible for these properties, including park naturalists, grounds keepers, or others knowledgeable about wildlife, were interviewed by phone. Coyotes were recorded "present" if they had been seen at any time in the last 2 years.

Telephone Hotline

A local "Seattle Coyote Hotline" telephone number was established whereby people could report Seattle coyote sightings. The hotline number and an accompanying story requesting public help were published in the two major metropolitan newspapers, all Seattle community newspapers, and broadcast by two local television stations and three local radio stations.

People who called the hotline were asked to give their name and phone number; the time, date and location of the sighting; the number of animals seen; and what the animal was doing. Calls were either handled personally or recorded. All respondents who left recorded messages were later contacted to assess their ability to correctly identify coyotes.

Wildlife Conservation in Metropolitan Environments. NIUW Symp. Ser. 2, L.W. Adams and D.L. Leedy, eds. Published by Natl. Inst. for Urban Wildl., 10921 Trotting Ridge Way, Columbia, MD 21044, USA, 1991.

Seattle coyote sightings that occurred from 1988 to the present were plotted directly on 1:25,000 U.S. Geological Survey topographic maps, and Universal Transverse Mercator coordinates were established for each. All analyses of hotline sightings were conducted in the Geographical Resources Analysis Support System (GRASS ver. 3.1, developed by the U.S. Army Corps of Engineers). The base map for GRASS came from a landsat photograph taken in August, 1985. The landsat scene was classified into 27 wildlife habitat types (cell resolution, 812.25 m²) using aerial photos and extensive verification in the field by personnel at the University of Washington Remote Sensing Laboratory.

A proximity analysis was performed on forest and shrub habitat types in Seattle. Each proximity analysis generated a map layer with one habitat type at the center of concentric 114-m zones. A proximity layer could then be combined with other map layers to determine the number of hotline sightings and the area per concentric zone.

Proximity analysis generated zones around all fragments of a chosen habitat type, which may have been as small as 812.25 m² (cell resolution of the base map). Thus, extreme fragmentation could have the same effect on proximity analyses as increasing the absolute amount of that habitat type. To estimate some of the effects of fragmentation, another proximity analysis was conducted on forest habitat after small, isolated fragments were removed. Isolated habitat fragments were removed in a procedure that compared each cell's habitat type in the base map with the habitat types in the surrounding eight cells. The center cell was then given the most frequently occurring habitat type in the block of nine cells. All coyote sightings that occurred in the habitat type, around which proximities were calculated, were included in the first proximity zone.

A final proximity analysis was carried out on north Seattle hotline sightings to determine the area of each habitat per proximity zone. Differences in actual and expected sightings or areas were analyzed by chi-square.

RESULTS

Classification of the landsat image indicated that Seattle could be represented using 12 distinct habitat types. After open fresh water habitats were removed and similar habitats grouped into single types, both north and south Seattle were represented with seven distinct habitat types (Table 1, see Appendix A for definitions).

Table 1. Classified habitat types (ha) for Seattle, Washington, 1985.

Habitat type	North Seattle	South Seattle
Tidal mudflat	2.0	70.4
Forest	187.4	447.2
Shrub	510.7	904.5
Shadow	6.2	11.8
Urban, high cover	906.7	1,494.4
Urban, medium cover	3,982.3	4,911.4
Urban, low cover	2,737.1	5,824.6
Total	8,332.4	13,664.3

Of 28 relatively undeveloped large tracts of land in Seattle, coyotes were seen on 12, including 10 in north Seattle (Fig. 1). I received a total of 108 calls on the Seattle Coyote Hotline in a 2-month period. When asked, 107 callers said they felt sure about their ability to correctly identify coyotes. The one unsure caller was reporting a sighting in the heart of downtown Seattle.

Except for one animal seen in shadow habitat, the greatest number of coyote sightings, by area of habitat type, was in forest followed by shrub types (Table 2). Hotline sightings were more abundant in north Seattle than south Seattle (86 and 22, respectively) despite the fact that there was both a greater amount and a greater percentage by area of forest and shrub habitats in south Seattle (Table 1).

Proximity analysis indicated that there were significantly more coyote sightings in the first two proximity zones around forest habitat than would be expected on the basis of area alone (Fig. 2). This was also the case when small, isolated forest fragments were removed from the analysis (Fig. 3), although coyote sightings tended to be slightly farther away from forest habitat as a result.

Proximity analysis also indicated that coyote sightings were closer to shrub habitat than expected (Fig. 4). However, the distributions of forest and shrub habitat were not independent. Significantly more shrub habitat occurred in the first proximity zone around forest than would be expected on the basis of area alone ($\chi^2_1 = 37.28$, $P <$

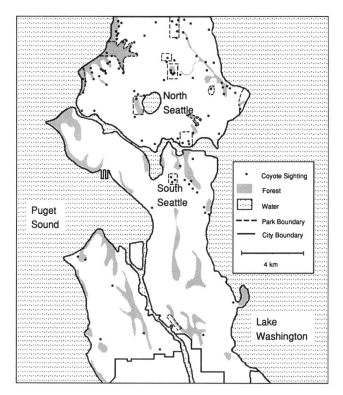

Fig. 1. The distribution of coyote sightings in relation to forest habitat in Seattle, Washington, 1990. Forest patches are drawn slightly larger than scale for illustrative purposes. Only parks where coyotes were reported by park personnel are included on this map.

Table 2. Coyote sightings by habitat type in Seattle, Washington, 1988–1990.

Location within city	Tidal mudflat	Forest	Shrub	Shadow	Urban cover			Total
					High	Medium	Low	
North Seattle								
Animals seen	0	10	13	1	8	33	21	86
Sightings/100 ha	0	5.3	2.5	16.2	0.9	0.8	0.8	
South Seattle								
Animals seen	0	3	7	0	3	5	4	22
Sightings/100 ha	0	0.7	0.8	0	0.2	0.1	0.1	

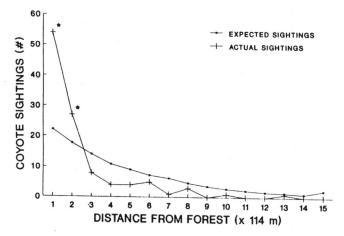

Fig. 2. Distance of coyotes from forest habitat in Seattle. Asterisks signify significant differences between expected and actual sightings ($P < 0.05$).

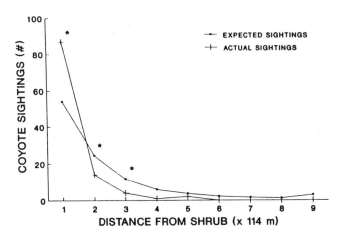

Fig. 4. Distance of coyotes from shrub habitat in Seattle. Asterisks signify significant differences between expected and actual sightings ($P < 0.05$).

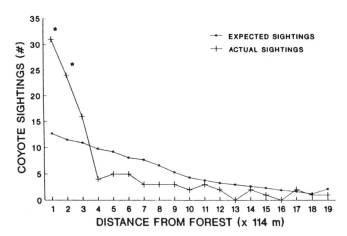

Fig. 3. Distance of coyotes from forest habitat in Seattle after small, isolated forest fragments were removed from the analysis. Asterisks signify significant differences between expected and actual sightings ($P < 0.05$).

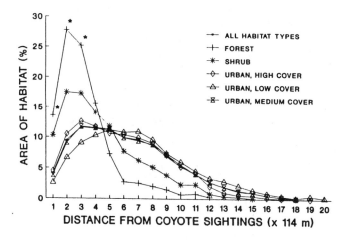

Fig. 5. Distance of habitat types to coyotes sighted in north Seattle. Asterisks signify significant differences between expected and actual areas ($P < 0.05$).

0.001). Coyotes were preferentially clustered near forest patches even in areas where shrub was the most abundant habitat type (Fig. 5).

DISCUSSION

Much of the remaining forest habitat in Seattle occurs in discrete patches, many of which are within the boundaries of parks. There also are some long, narrow strips of forest that border creeks flowing through steep ravines, particularly in north Seattle. Coyote sightings were closely associated with these patches, despite the fact that sightings were probably biased towards residential areas where people were more concentrated. In fact, the greatest number of sightings, relative to area, came from forest habitat where vision should have been most restricted. The association between coyote sightings and forest would probably have been even stronger (because of the nature of GRASS proximity analysis) had there been opportunities to see coyotes on either side of parks that border water.

Shrub and forest habitat tended to occur together with

nearly 80% of all shrub occurring within two proximity zones of forest. Shrub habitat probably occurred most often in the transition areas between forest and other types of habitat.

The proximity analysis around coyote sightings was meaningful only if the distribution described by hotline reports was an accurate reflection of the real coyote distribution and if coyotes were using all suitable habitat within the study area at the time of the survey. Although it is impossible to know for certain whether these conditions were met, north Seattle probably was a better candidate than south Seattle judging from the distribution and number of coyote sightings.

Almost all home range estimates for coyotes, covering a vast variety of habitat types, are larger than the area of Seattle's parks (Laundre and Keller 1984). Coyotes are probably moving between forest patches or are including areas other than forest habitats in their home range. Shargo (1988) found that Los Angeles urban coyotes that foraged in residential areas had relatively small home ranges, and suggested that this was indicative of the relatively large and diverse assortment of foods in urban areas. Increase in both the abundance of food and overgrown building lots may be why there has been a recent increase in the number of foxes (*Vulpes vulpes*) in British cities (MacDonald and Newdick 1982). Urban environments may consist of enough different types of habitat that food becomes less variable in space and time (Andelt and Mahan 1977). This is one reason why coyotes that are unable to live within cities may come to forage there. Gill and Bonnett (1973) documented a case where coyotes traveled from rural areas into more urbanized areas along a fenced causeway, presumably in search of food. Foxes in Britain frequently move in and out of cities, although it is unclear if these movements are related to food gathering.

The pattern of coyote sightings in this study suggested that if coyotes do forage in residential areas, they probably remain only in those areas that are immediately adjacent to forest cover. If urban areas provide abundant food sources for coyotes, then forest habitats, which probably provide the majority of cover and thus denning sites (Gier 1968), may limit the coyote population in north Seattle.

The ship canal that divides Seattle seems to prevent north Seattle coyotes from moving to south Seattle with one possible exception. The fact that coyotes occupy both sides near the east border of the city suggests that coyotes have recently crossed the bridge linking these two areas.

At present it is not entirely clear why north Seattle seems to have more coyotes relative to the amount of forest habitat than south Seattle, although I suspect a number of factors. North Seattle is mainly residential and was urbanized later than south Seattle. The northwest corner of Seattle has a number of steep wooded ravines that until recently have been unsuitable for building. Finally, the area immedi-ately north of the city bordering Puget Sound is mostly vegetated, has very low housing density, and may ultimately act as a source of coyotes to more isolated urban populations. Gill and Bonnett (1973) described a similar combination of factors that were important in maintaining coyotes in urban areas of Los Angeles. In Los Angeles, coyotes are most often associated with areas of low housing density that abut more remote areas such as the Santa Monica Mountains. Coyotes use the steep undeveloped ravines adjacent to residential areas that, in some cases, stretch into the Los Angeles metropolitan area.

Acknowledgments.—The study was supported by the Washington Department of Wildlife and the College of Forest Resources, University of Washington. Success of the study was attributed to the input of many people including L. Heggen, Dr. S. West, J. P. Quinn, L. Scheman, W. Sauer, T. Kuter, and D. Fox.

REFERENCES CITED

Andelt, W.F., and B.R. Mahan. 1977. Ecology of an urban coyote. Proc. Nebr. Acad. Sci. 87:5. (abstract.)

Froman, R. 1961. The nerve of some animals. J.B. Lippincott Co., Philadelphia, Pa. 268 pp.

Gavareski, C.A. 1976. Relation of park size and vegetation to urban bird populations in Seattle, Washington. Condor 78:375–382.

Gier, H.T. 1968. Coyotes in Kansas. Kansas Agric. Exp. Sta. Bull. 393.

Gill, D.A. 1965. Coyote and urban man: a geographical analysis of the relationship between coyote and man in Los Angeles. M.S. Thesis. Univ. of Calif., Los Angeles. 110 pp.

————, and P. Bonnett. 1973. Nature in the urban landscape: a study of city ecosystems. York Press, Baltimore, Md. 209 pp.

Harris, L.D. 1984. The fragmented forest: island biogeography theory and the preservation of biotic diversity. Univ. of Chicago Press, Chicago. 176 pp.

Harris, S. 1977. Distribution, habitat utilization and age structure of a suburban fox (*Vulpes vulpes*) population. Mamm. Rev. 7:25–39.

Howell, R.G. 1982. The urban coyote problem in Los Angeles County. Proc. Vertebr. Pest Conf. 10:21–22.

Jones, J.C. 1958. How to control wildlife pests in suburban developments. Pest Control 26:9–20.

Laundre, J.W., and B.L. Keller. 1984. Home-range size of coyotes: a critical review. J. Wildl. Manage. 48:127–139.

MacCracken, J.G. 1982. Coyote food in a southern California suburb. Wildl. Soc. Bull. 10:280–281.

MacDonald, D.W., and M.T. Newdick. 1982. The distribution and ecology of foxes, *Vulpes vulpes* (L.), in urban areas. Pages 123–135 *in* R. Bornkamm, J.A. Lee, and M.R.D. Seaward, eds. Urban ecology. Blackwell Sci. Publ., Oxford, U.K.

Schlauch, F.C. 1978. Urban geographical ecology of the amphibians and reptiles of Long Island. Pages 25–41 *in* C.M. Kirkpatrick, ed. Wildlife and people. Purdue Res. Found., West Lafayette, Ind.

Shargo, E.S. 1988. Home range, movement and activity patterns of coyotes (*Canis latrans*) in a Los Angeles suburb. Ph.D. Dissertation, Univ. of Calif., Los Angeles. 113 pp.

APPENDIX A
Definitions of the seven habitat types used to represent Seattle, Washington.

Tidal Mudflat—gently sloping, intertidal saltwater areas.

Forest—areas dominated (> 60% cover) by trees over 6 m in height.

Shrub—areas dominated (> 50% cover) by shrubs or trees from 1 to 6 m in height.

Shadow—areas that are otherwise impossible to classify because they occur in regions shaded by some other feature of the landscape. This habitat type is usually associated with tall trees.

Urban, High Cover—areas that are dominated (> 70%) by any combination of vegetation including grasses, shrubs and forest. No more than 50% of the total ground area is covered with grass and at least 50% of the total plant cover is comprised of nonnative species.

Urban, Medium Cover—areas in which any combination of vegetation types comprise 30 to 70% of total ground cover. At least 50% of the total plant cover is comprised of nonnative species and no more than 70% of the total ground area can be covered by structures and impervious surfaces.

Urban, Low Cover—areas in which any combination of vegetation types comprise less than 30% of the total ground cover. No more than 90% of the total ground area can be covered by structures and impervious surfaces.

Movement and Mortality Patterns of Resident and Translocated Suburban White-tailed Deer

BEVERLY K. BRYANT, *Department of Biological Sciences, P.O. Box 413, University of Wisconsin-Milwaukee, Milwaukee, WI 53201*

WILLIAM ISHMAEL, *Bureau of Wildlife Management, Department of Natural Resources, P.O. Box 7921, Madison, WI 53707-7921*

INTRODUCTION

During the past decade, the white-tailed deer (*Odocoileus virginianus*) has become North America's most delightful and controversial species of urban wildlife. Expanding human communities and the deer's adaptable nature have led to urban deer populations in cities throughout the eastern and midwestern United States (Shoesmith and Koonz 1977, Ashley 1982, Decker and Gavin 1987, Sillings 1987, Witham and Jones 1987, Ishmael 1989). Low to moderate deer densities are viewed positively by residents because of the white-tail's high aesthetic value (Decker and Gavin 1987). However, when deer-vehicle collisions and damage to gardens and natural vegetation increase, residents turn to wildlife managers to solve the "urban deer problem" (Ishmael 1989).

Management of an urban deer herd is a complex issue, often made more difficult by public reaction to proposed management options (Witham and Jones 1987). Control techniques are rarely implemented before the herd size has grown to damaging levels and the controversy that surrounds urban deer management further delays action (Ishmael 1989). The first management techniques suggested are usually public hunting or shooting by marksmen, but, because of safety concerns and public sentiment against killing deer, these techniques are often not implemented (Diehl 1988). As an alternative, many communities turn to live capture and translocation as a humane, publicly acceptable method of reducing the size of their urban deer herd (O'Bryan and McCullough 1985, Witham and Jones 1987, Diehl 1988).

White-tailed deer are abundant in the Milwaukee metropolitan area and herd management has become a hotly debated issue in many local communities. One suburb, the Village of River Hills, has experienced a steady increase in deer numbers during the past 10 years and has attracted considerable media attention because of its efforts to control herd size. Like other communities, River Hills strongly considered a shooting program but public opinion and legal concerns led to initiation of a trapping and translocation program in 1987–1988. In 1989, a research program was begun by the Wisconsin Department of Natural Resources, University of Wisconsin-Milwaukee, and the Village of River Hills to evaluate the success of the translocation program by monitoring the resident deer population and following the movements and survival of deer removed from the Village. This paper presents data collected during 1.5 years of monitoring radio-tagged and ear-tagged deer.

STUDY AREA

The Village of River Hills (43° 10′ N; 88° 56′ W) is a 14.3-km² community of estate size properties located in northern Milwaukee County. Seventy-five percent of River Hills is zoned for a 2-ha minimum lot size and larger lots are common. Natural vegetation covers at least half of most properties, offering deer ample cover and food. In addition, many residents stock deer feeders throughout the year.

Deer were translocated to four different state managed wildlife areas in southeastern Wisconsin (Fig. 1). These areas were considered good deer habitat and supported deer densities of between 5.8–7.7 deer/km² prior to release of translocated animals. Hunting pressure was heavy on all four of the areas.

METHODS

Trapping and Translocation

Live trapping was conducted by River Hills Department of Public Works employees from December–March 1987–1988, 1988–1989, and 1989–1990. Deer were captured in modified Stephenson traps baited with corn and

Wildlife Conservation in Metropolitan Environments. NIUW Symp. Ser. 2, L.W. Adams and D.L. Leedy, eds. Published by Natl. Inst. for Urban Wildl., 10921 Trotting Ridge Way, Columbia, MD 21044, USA, 1991.

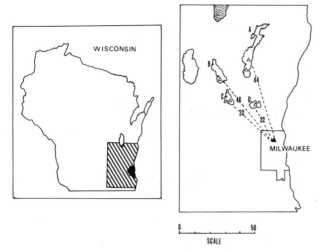

Fig. 1. Map of study area. Numbers refer to distances (in kilometers) between deer capture and release sites. A = Kettle Morraine, B = Theresa Marsh, C = Allentown Marsh, D = Jackson Marsh. Scale is in kilometers.

apples and transferred to travel crates for transport to a release site. Sex and approximate age were recorded (Table 1) and each deer was marked with a colored numbered eartag. Data on mortality and movements of ear-tagged deer were obtained from tag returns.

Radio-Telemetry

To supplement tag return data, 12 of the 121 translocated deer in 1989 (4 male, 8 female) and 13 of the 120 translocated deer in 1990 (6 male, 7 female) were fitted with solar-powered ear-tag transmitters (Telemetry Systems, Mequon, Wis.) or battery-powered radio-collars (Advanced Telemetry Systems, Bethel, Minn.). In addition, 12 River Hills deer (6 male, 6 female) were tranqualized with succinylcholine chloride (Anectine brand) using a dart gun, radio-tagged, and re-released at the point of capture. All deer were monitored for at least a year after tagging to evaluate survival and movements. Deer were tracked from a vehicle, airplane, or on foot bi-weekly (for resident deer) or monthly (for translocated deer). Telemetry locations were determined by triangulation or by sighting the animal.

Data Analysis

Travel distances for translocated deer were calculated as the maximum straight line distance from release site to point of death or location of permanent range. Movements of resident deer were measured as the maximum observed distances from the location of capture. Minimum convex polygon home ranges were calculated for resident deer with the program MCPAAL (Smithsonian Institution, Washington, D.C.). A two sample t-test was used to compare the movements of resident and translocated deer, movements of males and females, and the numbers of days resident and translocated deer remained alive. Mortality rates of native deer were calculated from records of hunter and road kills for the deer management units encompassing the release sites. Mortality rates were compared using Chi-square analysis. Survivorship curves were determined using the method outlined by Pollock et al. (1989).

RESULTS

Movements of Translocated Deer

Translocated deer tended to stay near the release areas, although there was large variation between individuals ($\bar{x} = 16.08$ km, range = 0.53–67.0, $n=58$). Fifty-six percent of the 58 ear-tagged deer that died in 1989 did so within 8 km of their release points. However, 26% of the deer traveled over 24 km and as many as five deer traveled as far as 50–60 km. Radioed animals exhibited a similar range of movements (0.91–32.4 km, $n=12$) (Table 2). There was no significant difference between males and females for either the ear-tagged ($t =1.32$, $P >0.19$) or radio-tagged sample ($t= 0.552$, $P>0.59$).

Translocated deer showed little tendency to home. Only one animal is known to have returned to River Hills. This individual was an adult female that traveled from the Kettle Morraine release site (44 km) in a maximum of 240 days.

Movement Patterns of Radio-tagged Deer. — Movements of radio-tagged deer showed strong seasonal influence. All radio-tagged deer ($n=12$) released in mid-January to early March 1989 remained within 3.2 km of their release site during the first month after release. In fact, these deer remained within 8 km of the release point until April–May. By this time, three animals had died, three remained within

Table 1. Live trapped and translocated white-tailed deer in River Hills, Wisconsin, 1987–1990.[a]

| | | Deer captured | | | | |
| | | Male | | Female | | |
Year	No. of traps	Fawn	Adult	Fawn	Adult	Total
1987–1988	4	9	6	11	18	44
1988–1989	10	35	6	31	49	121
1989–1990	20	39	17	26	38	120
Total	—	83	29	68	105	285

[a]Source: K. Fredrickson, 1987–1990, Unpubl. reports to Wis. Dep. of Nat. Resour.

Table 2. Average distances (km) traveled by translocated and resident deer, 1988–1989.

| | | | Distance traveled (km) | | |
Deer	Sex	n	$\bar{x}$	SE	Range
Translocated					
Radio-tagged	Male	4	10.15	5.4	1.17–23.7
	Female	8	11.39	4.0	0.91–32.4
	Combined	12	10.98	3.1	0.91–32.4
Ear-tagged	Male	28	18.80	4.1	0.94–67.0
	Female	30	12.31	2.9	0.53–48.1
	Combined	58	16.08	2.4	0.53–67.0
Resident					
Radio-tagged	Male	6	1.93	0.64	0.75–4.2
	Female	5	0.62	0.19	0.34–1.34
	Combined	11	1.34	1.3	0.34–4.2

8 km of the release site, and six animals had dispersed away from the area. Five of the dispersing deer had established stable ranges by June. One adult doe continued to move throughout the summer, but settled in an area 22.6 km from her release point by late August. Deer that survived the first 1.5 years after release are still occupying the same range they established in May 1989.

Location of New Home Ranges.— Of the nine deer radio-tagged in 1989 that survived over 2 months, six established home ranges in or within 1.6 km of a residential or developed area. Five animals established home ranges in low density residential-farmland areas adjacent to small towns (<24,000 pop.). One juvenile doe (B2038) settled within a resort community along Lake Michigan where she lives in residents' yards. Of the 1990 sample, two does are known to have established home ranges within developed areas. One adult doe occupies a range within the same resort community as B2038. The other deer was living in a city park until she was killed by a car.

Movements of Deer

Radio-tagged translocated deer moved significantly greater distances away from the point of release than did resident deer ($t = 3.11$, $P<.01$) (Table 2). The mean distance moved for radioed translocated deer was 10.98 km (0.91–32.4) versus 1.34 km (0.34–4.2) for resident deer. Only 10 resident deer had sufficient data to calculate home range size due to mortality (1), and transmitter failure (1). All 10 deer had stable home ranges during the year of monitoring. Mean home range size for females was 0.413 km^2 (0.17–0.75 km^2) and 2.66 km^2 (0.90–4.8 km^2) for males.

Mortality Rates

Translocated deer experienced high mortality. Ten of the radio-tagged deer (83%) were dead within an average of 185 (2–321) days after release. Ear-tag returns revealed 42% mortality, significantly ($\chi^2 = 6.78$, $P< 0.01$) lower than that estimated by telemetry. It is likely that tag returns underestimate mortality due to the potentially large number of unreported hunter kills, and animals that die from capture stress and vehicle collisions that are never found.

Mortality rates of radio-tagged translocated deer were greater than those for deer native to the release areas. Based on car kill reports and hunter harvest, native deer in these areas were estimated to have 59% mortality in 1989.

Deer that remained in River Hills lived significantly longer ($t = 3.6$, $P< 0.005$) than animals removed from the Village (Fig. 2). Resident deer survived a mean of 448 (81–513) days after capture, with a 17% mortality rate. Translocated deer showed significant mortality within the first 3 months following release. In addition, survivorship dropped sharply due to hunting pressure in November (Fig. 2). Resident deer, on the other hand, exhibited a more uniform curve indicative of the low mortality rate, including the lack of hunting.

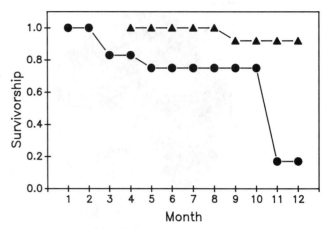

Fig. 2. Survivorship of resident (▲) and translocated (●) suburban white-tailed deer, southeastern Wisconsin, 1989.

Cause of Death

Sources of mortality for translocated deer were vehicle collisions, hunters, stress and injury due to trapping, and unknown causes. The percentage of translocated deer dying from vehicles and hunters was similar to that of deer native to the release areas in 1989 (Fig. 3). The higher mortality rate for translocated deer would therefore appear to be due to deaths caused by translocation. During the 3 years of trapping, eight deer died or were euthanized because of injuries sustained while in the trap. In addition, at least five died from capture-related stress soon after release. Animals that died within a week of release and had no other apparent injuries were classified as victims of capture-related stress. This figure is undoubtedly an underestimate due to the number of deer that die within a week of release and are found months later, when cause of death cannot be determined, or are never found at all. It is likely, therefore, that the 20% trap-related mortality reported for radio-tagged deer is a more accurate estimate than the 4% based on ear-tag returns.

The only source of mortality for resident deer that could be assessed was vehicles. In recent years, some 35 deer have died a year on River Hills roads. Figure 4 shows the percentage of the annual roadkills that occurred each month in 1989 for River Hills and translocated deer, based on Village police records and ear-tag returns. In 1989, the peak in Village road kills occurred in November. This corresponds to increased deer movements during the seasonal rut. Translocated deer suffered equal mortality to cars in January and November, and also had peaks in April and May, although differences between the two populations were not significant. These peaks correspond with the peaks in movement noted for radio-tagged deer.

DISCUSSION

Live-trapping and translocation has been successful in controlling herd size in River Hills. Annual aerial censuses made in 4 of the past 5 years (Table 3) indicated that the

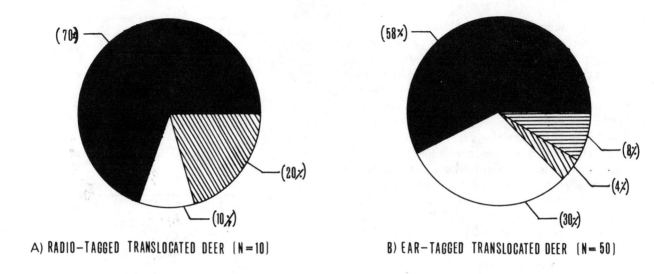

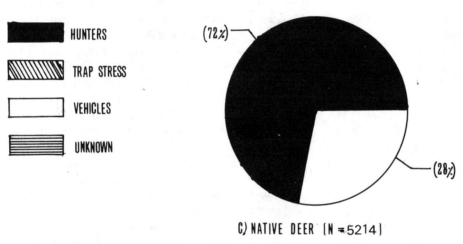

A) RADIO-TAGGED TRANSLOCATED DEER (N=10)

B) EAR-TAGGED TRANSLOCATED DEER (N=50)

■ HUNTERS

▨ TRAP STRESS

☐ VEHICLES

▤ UNKNOWN

C) NATIVE DEER (N=5214)

Fig. 3. Sources of mortality for translocated and native deer, southeastern Wisconsin, 1989.

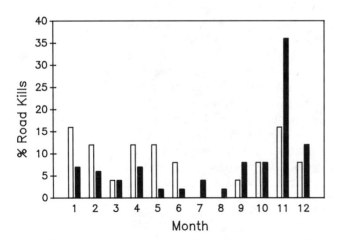

Fig. 4. Percent of annual vehicle-caused mortality by month for River Hills resident (solid bars) and translocated (open bars) deer, southeastern Wisconsin, 1989.

Table 3. Aerial censuses of deer and pre-fawning population sizes, River Hills, Wisconsin, 1986–1990.

Census technique	Year			
	1986	1988[a]	1989[a]	1990[a]
Aerial count	159	227	248	171
Pre-fawning[b]	159	216	159	128

[a]Trapping year.
[b]Pre-fawning figures represent the population size in April and were calculated by subtracting the number of deer translocated and roadkilled from the winter aerial counts.

deer population has decreased during the 3 years of trapping, although such counts yield only minimum population figures (Witham and Jones 1990a). Despite this success, the population remains well above the recommended size of 100 deer (6–8 deer/km^2) and road kills have increased annually. The cost of removing deer from River Hills has increased each year from $17,600 in 1987–1988 to $32,760 in 1990. The price per deer removed, however, has dropped from $400 to $273.

Live-trapping and translocation is advocated in many communities despite its costs because residents feel that removal is in the best interest of the animals (Diehl 1988). However, our results, and those of other studies, indicate that translocated deer do not lead idealized lives (Hawkins and Montgomery 1969, O'Bryan and McCullough 1985, Witham and Jones 1990b). Translocated deer have significantly lower survival than their resident suburban counterparts and it appears that they are more susceptible to mortality sources than deer born in a non-urban environment. Suburban deer are habituated to people and, when transplanted to rural areas, fail to react adequately to the threat of hunting and feral dogs (O'Bryan and McCullough 1985). The process of capture, transport, and release into an unfamiliar area is stressful to deer. Frightened animals occasionally try to force their way out of the trap and injure themselves severely. This can be minimized by frequent trap checks and prompt release, however, little can be done to eliminate the stress an animal experiences after being introduced into an unfamiliar landscape.

White-tailed deer are social animals, living in small family or bachelor groups, and utilizing the same home range throughout most of their lives (Marchinton and Hirth 1984). Translocating deer removes them from both their familiar habitat and social groups. Once they are released, animals must establish a new range and integrate into the existing herd. This may be particularly difficult for young, inexperienced animals. The major victims of trap-related stress in our radio-tagged sample were fawns.

White-tailed deer generally have small home ranges and most live out their lives within 2.6 km of the area they were born (Ishmael 1989). In the present study, movements and home range sizes of resident deer were typical of southeastern Wisconsin deer (Larson et al. 1978). Translocated deer, on the other hand, moved relatively long distances from their release areas. It is still unclear why some translocated animals remained within a kilometer of the release area, while others ranged as far as 67 km. Variability in movement may be related to an individual's success at establishing a new range. Radio-tagged deer that moved significant distances away from the release sites did so in April and May. This is a period when juvenile and subordinate animals are driven away by females that are securing areas for fawning (Marchinton and Hirth 1984). This increase in aggression between deer, along with the newly available forage, probably triggers deer movements and they continue to travel until they find an acceptable new range.

Although translocated deer did not "home" back to River Hills (with one exception), some did settle in familiar suburban habitats, and most retained their urban habits. We do not know whether these deer preferred this kind of habitat over less developed areas. It is clear, however, that many translocated deer continued the habits that made them nuisance animals in River Hills. There have been numerous reports from residents throughout the release areas of tagged deer browsing shrubs and gardens, eating at bird feeders, and causing traffic hazards. One radio-collared doe has caused so much damage to gardens near the Kettle Morraine release area that the local game warden has requested to shoot her.

High mortality rates of translocated deer, combined with the manner in which many of these animals die, make it difficult to justify translocation as a humane alternative to harvest methods. Further, our data indicate that, by translocating suburban deer, nuisance animal problems are being created in other communities. As the number of communities with urban herds continues to grow, translocation will become a less viable option. Many states already prohibit the release of deer onto public land because deer populations are currently at desired capacity. Wildlife managers, together with local officials and citizens, must begin to address the issue of herd control using a multi-faceted approach, including culling programs as well as education on damage control techniques.

Acknowledgments.—Funding for telemetry equipment and radio-tracking time and travel was provided by Whitetails Unlimited, Inc. and the Safari Club International. Phillip Dorn assisted in tagging animals and did the early telemetry work. Many thanks go to Kurt Fredrickson, the River Hills Department of Public Works, and the River Hills Police Department for providing support and sharing their files. R. Selvakumar prepared the figures and provided invaluable comments. Charles M. Weise provided key insights throughout the project.

REFERENCES CITED

Ashley, R.F. 1982. Milwaukee's dear deer. Wis. Nat. Resour. 6:6–11.

Decker, D.J., and T.A. Gavin. 1987. Public attitudes toward a suburban deer herd. Wildl. Soc. Bull. 15:173–180.

Diehl, S.R. 1988. Selective removal as an alternative in deer management. Pages 1–10 in L. Nielson and R.D. Brown, eds. Translocation of wild animals. Wis. Humane Soc., Milwaukee.

Hawkins, R.E., and G.G. Montgomery. 1969. Movements of translocated deer as determined by telemetry. J. Wildl. Manage. 33:196–203.

Ishmael, W. 1989. In a rut. Wis. Nat. Resour. 10:22–28.

Larson, T.J., O.J. Rongstad, and F.W. Terbilcox. 1978. Movement and habitat use of white-tailed deer in southcentral Wisconsin. J. Wildl. Manage. 42:113–117.

Marchinton, R.L., and D.H. Hirth. 1984. Behavior. Pages 129–168 in L.K. Halls, ed. White-tailed deer: ecology and management. Stackpole Books, Harrisburg, Pa.

O'Bryan, M.K., and D.R. McCullough. 1985. Survival of blacktailed deer following relocation in California. J. Wildl. Manage. 49:115–119.

Pollock, K.H., S. Winterstein, C.M. Bunick, and P. Curtis. 1989. Survival analysis in telemetry studies: the staggered entry design. J. Wildl. Manage. 53:7–15.

Shoesmith, M.W., and W.H. Koonz. 1977. The maintenance of

an urban deer herd in Winnipeg, Manitoba. Trans. North Am. Wildl. and Nat. Resour. Conf. 42:278–285.

Sillings, J.L. 1987. White-tailed deer studies in a suburban community: ground counts, impacts on natural vegetation, and electric fencing to control browsing. M.Sc. Thesis, The Univ. of Minnesota, St. Paul. 84 pp.

Witham, J.H., and J.M. Jones. 1987. Deer-human interactions and research in the Chicago metropolitan area. Pages 155–159 *in* L.W. Adams and D.L. Leedy, eds. Integrating man and nature in the metropolitan environment. Natl. Inst. for Urban Wildl., Columbia, Md.

_____ , and _____ . 1990a. White-tailed deer abundance on metropolitan forest preserves during winter in northeastern Illinois. Wildl. Soc. Bull. 18:13–16.

_____ , and _____ . 1990b. Post-translocation survival and movements of metropolitan white-tailed deer. Wildl. Soc. Bull. 18:434–441.

Control of White-tailed Deer in Non-hunted Reserves and Urban Fringe Areas[1]

CATHERINE C. BRUSH[2] AND DAVID W. EHRENFELD, *Department of Environmental Resources, Cook College, Rutgers—The State University of New Jersey, New Brunswick, NJ 08903*

INTRODUCTION

New challenges face nature reserve and game managers in controlling white-tailed deer (*Odocoileus virginianus*) populations to limit the damage they cause to ecological communities, property, and even human life. This is especially challenging in places where, for ethical or safety reasons, regulated hunting is not allowed or feasible. The purpose of this paper is to review and assess methods of controlling deer populations in such cases and to indicate workable strategies for managers of nature reserves and wildlife in urban fringe areas.

CAUSES AND EFFECTS OF DEER OVERABUNDANCE

An animal population may be too numerous relative to ecological standards, people's perceptions, or both. Deer are called overabundant if they damage human life, property, or species preferred by people, or if deer condition is less than optimal; whether these conditions result from ecological imbalance or not.

Deer populations in the United States have undergone dramatic changes in overall abundance. Destruction of forests and unregulated hunting caused deer numbers to reach a low by the end of the Nineteenth Century. Since the early 1900's, white-tails have increased to an all time high in response to forest rejuvenation and game management techniques (Halls 1978). Currently, other than hunting, the primary regulation of deer populations is food availability, with cover being an interactive factor. The role of predation in regulation has been debated, and in most areas major predators have been extirpated (Peek 1980).

At subsistence density deer natality is balanced by mortality. Deer primarily subsist on staple forage species that are able to withstand continual browsing pressure. A deer population at, or even below, this density may be perceived as being overabundant simply because landowners notice the negative impacts of living in close association with deer. This occurs especially in exurban areas where excellent deer habitat coexists with housing developments. Also, at subsistence density deer health and productivity are less than maximal.

The population may increase above subsistence density in some cases. This generally is a reaction to a substantial, relatively sudden change in food abundance causing the deer population growth to overshoot food production. This change in food abundance may be from loss of habitat or disturbances in forest succession. Historically such changes were produced by natural events; however, currently, human development of the landscape is the primary controlling factor.

As a deer population increases above subsistence density, deer browse more heavily on all edible forage and become less healthy. Eventually the deer population outstrips its resources and a population crash is imminent. At high browsing pressure, plant species abundance can be altered, and in the extreme cases plant populations extirpated, and forest profiles altered (Ross et al. 1970, Bratton 1979, Reynolds 1980, Alverson et al. 1988, and Tilghman 1989). Other dependent resident plant and animal species, for example birds (Baird 1990), may thus be affected and the total community altered by high deer populations.

MANAGEMENT DECISION MAKING IN NATURE RESERVES

The nature reserves we discuss are essentially contiguous properties with distinct management boundaries set aside for conservation and public enjoyment of nature. We focus on those that are or would be primarily wooded if allowed to mature. They are rarely over 5000 ha in size and typically under 1000 ha. For the purpose of this paper we

---

[1]Supplemental paper not presented at the symposium.
[2]Present address: 900 McKee Dr., Edinburg, TX 78539.

---

assume the resource manager is faced with a no-hunt situation.

Before management decisions are made, a thorough analysis of the problem is necessary. Deer-related community trends, such as damage to vegetation, should be determined (methods summarized in Riney 1982, Harlow 1984) and related to the objectives of the reserve management. These objectives typically include the maintenance of ecological diversity and sample ecosystems in a natural state as well as the provision of natural resources for education and recreation (Riney 1982). Each reserve must take into account the management form on its surrounding lands. This will help determine the reserve's role in the regional conservation of species (Harris 1984). It is also important to obtain the cooperation of neighboring landowners in applying management decisions that may affect them. Once the most appropriate method of deer control is found, continued monitoring of the reserve is critical in judging its success and in detecting further deer problems (Jewell et al. 1981, Riney 1982).

PASSIVE MANAGEMENT RESPONSE

One way to deal with deer overabundance is to do nothing to alleviate the problem and rely on natural mechanisms of population regulation to take their course. This option assumes willingness to accept the present and potential damage. In some reserves, intrusive management may be against reserve policy, subsistence density of deer may be acceptable, or tolerance to deer damage may be high. Indeed, "damage," if it is caused by a natural agent, may not be regarded as damage at all. In these cases, it is reasonable that the passive management choice would be made. Caughley (1976) suggested that only population fluctuations greater than 30% justify the effort of intrusive management procedures. Also, theoretically, in even the worst case of overpopulation, an irruption, the population will eventually return to lower levels.

There are, however, several complicating factors. Deer population size and damage may increase beyond the tolerance limits of the reserve and attainment of lower, more stable population sizes may be indefinitely delayed. Thus, in foregoing active management to control the deer population, the reserve is accomplishing the goal of "naturalness," but is risking major changes in the community, including disturbance of rarer habitats and loss of plant species originally present.

Despite this caveat, it is unlikely that the community will be degraded completely because of deer overpopulation, given the evolutionary coexistence of forest vegetation and white-tailed deer—a history in which deer population fluctuations must have occurred (Dasmann 1971). If the reserve manager is willing to cope with the ecological uncertainty and the public relations minefield, the reserve's deer problem could serve as an ecological experiment. In most cases, management control is imposed before density-dependent self-regulation of the deer population has had a chance to occur (Jewell et al. 1981).

DIRECT CONTROL OF POPULATION SIZE

The amount of deer damage on the reserve can be kept within tolerable limits by reducing the number of deer. The number of deer needed to be removed, or births to be prevented, can be determined in ways similar to the ways hunting quotas are designed. The emphasis will be on reducing the number of does or their fecundity. Control must be continued indefinitely if the desired deer density is below the ecological carrying capacity of the reserve. If subsistence density is tolerable, then control can be used as needed to lower a burgeoning population to this level and to arrest future irruptions (Caughley 1976).

Capture and Transfer

Capture and transfer of deer is a method commonly suggested for reducing deer populations in areas closed to hunting. There are many variations of box traps for capturing individual deer. Groups of deer can be baited or driven into a corral or drive trap. Netting deer as individuals or groups is another alternative. Snares and capturing newborn fawns are not viable options. Chemical sedation by remote injection or oral administration is an alternative to traps. Methods and devices are discussed in Day et al. (1980), and Rongstad and McCabe (1984).

The efficiency of trapping devices is discussed in Hawkins et al. (1967), Palmer et al. (1980), Day et al. (1980), Ishmael and Rongstad (1984), and Conner et al. (1987). Corral and box traps seem to be the most efficient methods reported, but trapping success varies with habitat and seasonal factors. For example, the effectiveness of baiting is inversely related to the quality and quantity of naturally-occurring foods. Devices other than box traps may not require the use of bait, but it is suggested to increase their efficiency.

An average mortality rate of 3–5% for traps is reduced with increased cost (Rempel and Bertram 1975, Rongstad and McCabe 1984). Most box traps, except the Clover trap, are difficult to move, which limits the number of deer coming into contact with them.

Chemical sedation by remote injection has been done successfully (Ashley 1982). However, it is costly and is subject to malfunctioning equipment, poor placement of darts, and improper dosages, all causing variable success rates (Halls 1978). Drugs used in feed must have a wide safety margin, be fast-acting, and not injurious to other animals that may consume the drugged food—requirements that most available drugs do not fulfill (Day et al. 1980). Administration of drugs may require special permits and the supervision of a veterinarian.

The relocation of the deer is a major deterrent for a capture and transfer program. The new location for the deer should be able to sustain them and be far enough away (at least 32 km) to prevent the return of transported deer (Halls 1978, Harrison 1983). Such habitat is usually lacking, especially for a large scale removal program. Also, mortality of transferred deer can be high (Rongstad and McCabe 1984, and Bryant and Ishmael in this volume).

Despite all the limitations, for a small nature reserve with low numbers of deer, a translocation program may be a feasible, though costly, option for limiting the population (Ashley 1982, Harrison 1983). A suitable relocation site(s) may be found and costs to the reserve can be reduced significantly through the use of volunteers and donations.

Reproductive Control

Most research on the control of deer reproduction has been on chemosterilants for females. Diethylstilbestrol (DES), a synthetic estrogen, and melengestrol acetate (MGA), a synthetic progestin, have been most widely studied. Both have been administered orally through drug-laced feed, by intramuscular injections, and subcutaneous implants.

Oral applications of chemosterilants have limited efficacy primarily because of the lack of control of dosage especially in free-ranging herds (Matschke 1977, Roughton 1979). Oral chemosterilants combined with a removal program may be effective in controlling enclosed populations (Harder and Peterle 1974).

Intramuscular injections of DES during pregnancy significantly decreased the fetal rate of a population (Harder and Peterle 1974). Subcutaneous chemosterilant implants have been tested for effectiveness using DES, MGA, and DRC-6246, a synthetic progestin. Implants are effective in preventing pregnancy for 2 years following insertion (Matschke 1980).

Remote injection of microencapsulated steroids (microTP) has been successfully used on feral horses (Turner and Kirkpatrick 1982). A formal study of this alternative has not been done with cervids. Remote injection of long-acting chemosterilants is a desirable form of wildlife population control. However the techniques need to be researched and perfected for each species (Kirkpatrick and Turner 1985).

A mechanical device placed in does that was designed to prohibit penetration by bucks was found to be ineffective (Matschke 1976). Surgical sterilization of female elk was completed successfully in Yellowstone National Park (Greer et al. 1968) and has been suggested for population control of white-tailed deer (Roughton 1979).

There has been little research on the control of reproduction in bucks. Chemical or physical castration alters buck appearance and behavior (Paulsen 1977, Lincoln and Kay 1979). No studies of male sterilants or vasectomies for controlling deer populations have been done. The absence of harem formation and strong territoriality in white-tailed deer, and the difficulty of capturing bucks in woodland habitat, are factors limiting the effectiveness of these methods.

The most effective birth control methods are chemical or surgical sterilization of does. The latter has an advantage in that it yields a permanent effect for each capture, immobilization, and operation. However, the need to capture and handle individual deer is a key limitation for all of the currently available reproduction control technologies for free ranging deer. This need escalates the cost in dollars and labor hours and reduces the overall effectiveness of the program (see Botti 1985, for an example). Remote injection of long-lasting sterilants eliminates the need to capture deer, and thus, if perfected, may be the preferred method.

Control of reproduction may be preferred over capture and transfer for two reasons. One is that there is no need to find a suitable habitat for translocated deer. Also, competition for resources will be maintained by sterilized animals, preventing a compensatory increase in birth rates for any unsterilized does. Ultimately the cost and effectiveness of reproduction control is strongly influenced by the technology and expertise available to the reserve. With the increasing need to control deer numbers other than by hunting, this avenue of control, especially remote injection techniques, should be more vigorously explored.

Regulated Sharpshooting

Although the purpose of this paper is to discuss non-hunting solutions to deer overabundance, regulated sharpshooting should be mentioned as an option for some reserves. In one case, charitable contributions of the deer meat met with public acceptance (Witham and Jones 1987). Sharpshooting is not a "quick fix" solution in that the strongly held reasons against hunting on the property would have to be met, public resistance overcome, and the hunt by experts strictly regulated.

INDIRECT MANIPULATION OF POPULATION DENSITY

Population density is greater in high-quality habitat, by definition. An indirect way to lower deer density is to lower the habitat quality for deer. Thus far, only food availability, occasionally interactive with cover in severe winter conditions, has been shown to limit deer populations where there is no hunting and low predation pressure (Giles 1978).

The amount of forage varies through succession. There is an increase in food abundance through early to mid-succession with a decrease as dense canopy cover develops, and a slight increase in mature forest due to light gaps (Dasmann 1971, Harlow 1984). Selective cuts and small openings in second growth forest increase browse production (Halls and Alcaniz 1968). Extensive forest areas supply consistent but limited food (Crawford 1984). For deer, the needs of cover and forage throughout the year are best met by interspersion of dissimilar habitats or seral stages, especially field and forest (Giles 1978, Riney 1982).

Habitat quality can be reduced by making specific desirable elements unavailable or by altering the overall habitat by allowing it to return to contiguous mature forest over as large an area as possible. The former is a more immediate habitat manipulation. The latter involves long-term, large scale redesigning of the reserve's ecological structure. Both options are discussed here in a general way, but it should be remembered that each reserve is ecologically unique.

Reducing the Availability of Specific Habitat Elements

The main methods discussed in the wildlife literature for preventing deer use of existing desirable food are repellents and fencing. A third way is to remove specific key resources.

Repellents.— Lights, loud sounds, and visual devices have been used as deterrents with little effect. Noise devices used at night (Bashore and Bellis 1982) or at irregular intervals (Hawthorne 1980) have shown some success. Scare tactics are a short-term solution that can be used until deer become accustomed to the stimulus, or in conjunction with other measures (Matschke et al. 1984). All sound and visual deterrents also may have adverse effects on other animal species and on human visitors.

Taste and odor repellents (reviewed by Harris et al. 1983, Palmer et al. 1983, Conover 1984, and Matschke et al. 1984) also have limited effectiveness. Those containing putrescent egg solids have been found best in reducing, not eliminating, deer damage. Treatment with repellents, even of commercial crops, is typically not cost effective because chemicals must by reapplied during the growing season. Also, they provide little protection under intense browsing pressure or over large areas.

Fencing.— The only sure way to eliminate deer damage is by fencing. There are many designs of fences that have varying ability to exclude wildlife from an area (reviewed by Craven 1983, and Matschke et al. 1984). When there is high deer pressure, the non-electric 2.4- to 3-m woven-wire and the electric fences are recommended.

The 2.4- to 3-m woven-wire fence is higher than deer can jump (McAninch and Winchcombe 1982). Such fencing is very expensive and is cost-effective only when valuable crops, such as orchards, are protected (Caslick and Decker 1979). Electric fences require more maintenance but are much less expensive to build. They have proven to be effective under high deer pressure (Craven 1983, Hygnstrom and Craven 1988, Palmer et al. 1985).

Removal of Key Habitat Elements.— Removal of specific resources from the reserve prevents their use by deer. Removal of key habitat elements includes: (1) mowing of midsuccessional, shrubby areas, (2) cutting of shelter groves, and (3) removing hardwood forage from traditional yarding sites. These methods all require regular removal of new plant growth.

The effectiveness of repellents, fencing, or removal of key sites in reducing deer density depends on how much the habitat quality has been reduced. To accomplish them

thoroughly enough to significantly decrease the habitat quality would be difficult, especially in larger reserves.

If protection or alteration of a specific habitat element is achieved, the deer will usually shift their activity and their damage to an adjacent area within or outside of the reserve. If deer do not or cannot shift their activity, ill health of the deer dependent on those resources will result.

Repellents and fencing can be useful in protecting valuable plants such as rare species. Repellents may reduce damage until a long-term solution becomes effective. Individual plants can be protected by poultry wire, plastic netting, or tubes (DeYoe and Schaap 1983, Matschke et al. 1984). Fencing protection may be needed permanently for vegetation that is both preferred forage for deer and especially important to conservationists. Even if lower deer densities are achieved, browsing levels may remain unacceptably high on these species.

Deer will not be the only species affected by these efforts. Repellents may deter other animals from using food resources. Removal of vegetation will disturb its associated animals. Fencing can be designed either to allow or prohibit small animal passage (McAninch and Winchcombe 1982). Finally, any lack of aesthetic appeal of these techniques should be considered.

Manipulation of Succession and Habitat Interspersion

Another way of reducing deer density is to alter the vegetation structure of the entire reserve so that it is less suitable for deer. Intermingling of different seral stages should be reduced and large areas of mature contiguous forest be promoted. This management approach is aided by natural successional processes and also will promote the preservation of late successional forest species, which are commonly threatened by loss of habitat. The management objective is to promote and maintain habitat supporting a low-density population.

Natural successional processes may be enough to regenerate forest. Early successional fields often contain established trees of later, forested stages within 10 years of abandonment (Niering and Goodwin 1974). Studies of clearcuts indicate that successful commercial regeneration occurs despite deer browsing in 50–60% of unmanaged cuts and 90% of cuts with advanced regeneration (Marquis 1974). However, many studies of cut areas show deer browsing can reduce height growth of saplings of several tree species, reduce shrub cover, and increase herbaceous density (Curtis and Rushmore 1958, Tierson et al. 1966, Reynolds 1980). Dense shrub and ground cover resists tree seedling invasion, often delaying succession by decades (Niering and Goodwin 1974, Marquis and Brenneman 1981). Thus, the state of succession in a field and the intensity of browsing by deer will determine if active management is necessary to ensure or hasten forest regeneration.

Succession can be hastened by releasing desired species from competition. Release of selected species can be done by herbicide treatments, cutting, or burning competing species

(Yoakum et al. 1980, Boyd 1987). Fertilizing desired species will stimulate their rapid growth (Marquis and Brenneman 1981, Garver 1987) but also may increase the palatability of the forage to deer (Yoakum et al. 1980). Browsing pressure can be reduced by fencing an area or individual trees until vegetation is tall enough to be out of reach of deer. Plantings of young trees about 2 m in height will require less protection than will seedlings from deer (Matschke et al. 1984). Repellents or supplemental planting of special crops to draw deer away from growing trees are not recommended, being both costly and ineffective.

Another method of hastening succession is to propagate tree species of later seral stages. Native species that are unpalatable to deer, have rapid growth, and are tolerant of deer browsing are preferred. Regional studies are the best source of such information. The methodology and literature of propagation and restoration is reviewed in Yoakum et al. (1980) and Morrison (1987). There is no question that natural regeneration of native species is less costly. When possible, management should maintain and improve existing natural growth and assist the closure of gaps in the forest canopy.

Deer density will eventually decrease as forest area increases, assuming that the resulting forest interior is large relative to edge. The first effect of this management is likely to be an exacerbation of deer damage and, perhaps, increased deer mortality, as forage declines during succession. The extent of the population response depends on the initial deer density relative to carrying capacity and the extent of the habitat change.

After adjustment to the change in vegetation structure, deer density in the forest interior will be low, with high activity levels at the forest edges. If these edges coincide with the reserve boundary, deer damage to neighboring property will remain the same or increase. Also, during the hunting season, there may be increased use of the reserve as a refuge by deer with home ranges overlapping the reserve (Root et al. 1988).

The major resource necessary for the application of this management approach is time and patience while forest regeneration occurs. The approach does not offer immediate relief of deer overpopulation. Reserves that are suffering intolerable amounts of damage or that do not wish to change their vegetation structure will need to use other methods. The "succession" approach can be, however, a long-term solution that, once in effect, will require minimal management.

Changes in species diversity and composition will occur. Decreasing the density of deer by promoting mature forest and decreasing interspersion (and therefore edge) will not maximize species diversity in the reserve. However, edge can no longer be assumed to be beneficial to all wildlife communities (Harris 1988, Yahner 1988). Also, regional species diversity may be increased by the presence of a reserve that is all or mostly forest. The size of an existing reserve may limit how many forest species it alone can

preserve (Anderson and Robbins 1981). Even so, the presence of uninterrupted forest will support some species not favored by most land use practices. These species are the ones likely to be considered valuable by conservationists and the public.

If openings are desired in the reserve, it is critical that they be few in number and minimize the interruption of forest vegetation. This may mean siting openings at the reserve boundary rather than in the interior portion. The opening design most apt to discourage deer use is a large, circular or square lawn-like one with an abrupt edge (Giles 1978). Conservatively, openings should be at least 8 ha, if possible, and forage should be at least 250–300 m away from the edge (McCaffery and Creed 1969, Harlow 1984).

Construction of grass-dominated openings involves clearing, leveling and disking, removing roots and seedlings, and the seeding of desired species (McCaffery et al. 1981, Crawford 1984). This is cost and labor intensive, so existing openings should be used if possible. Another, sometimes less costly, approach to reducing deer use of openings is to fence the perimeter. This is the most ecologically equitable approach in that natural vegetation can remain in the clearing and small mammals and birds can still have access to the clearing and its edge. Also, maintaining vegetative complexity at edges has been indicated to reduce foraging efficiency of predators taking advantage of edge ecological traps (Yahner 1988).

RESERVE LOCATION AND COMBINING METHODS

The size and surroundings of the reserve determine how much control the reserve manager has over the resident deer and their habitat. For reserves in urban-suburban areas, as density of the human population in the surrounding areas increases, the deer on the reserve are more under the control of the reserve manager. In the extreme case of a reserve in a dense urban area, the deer are restricted to the reserve, although control measures may be needed for neighboring open areas, such as airports (Bashore and Bellis 1982).

In exurban, rural areas, as wooded and open area patchiness increases, there will be a higher deer population. These areas may or may not be hunted, according to local laws and landowner preference. A small reserve (under 300 ha) in such areas does not have control over the total homeranges of its resident deer. Population density is controlled by the surrounding landowners more than by the reserve manager. The reserve can try to shift the activity center of deer away from the reserve or its sensitive areas by fencing, repellents, or habitat change.

Surrounding areas with good deer habitat will serve as a source of deer for the reserve. Direct population control measures undertaken by the reserve would have to negate this influx regularly. The amount and frequency of removals/reproduction control will determine their feasibility. Often, such long-term programs will not be a realistic alternative.

In this case, reducing overall deer density must be done in cooperation with the local landowners. Because promoting widespread habitat reversion to forest is not typically feasible, direct population control measures (which may include hunting on non-reserve land) will be needed. The program of choice will have to be continued indefinitely if the desired density is less than subsistence carrying capacity.

For reserves of 500 to several thousand hectares, no single management approach for reducing deer density is likely to be satisfactory. The cost of direct control measures is proportional to the size of the reserve and number of deer. Indirect control may cause short-term exacerbations of deer damage and sustained deer activity at the boundaries of reserves in rural or suburban areas. Combining methods can remedy some of these problems. Deer damage and mortality could be reduced by using direct control methods while habitat alteration is underway. This results in a gradual lowering to a smaller population in a reserve with a lower carrying capacity. One specific combination could be to sterilize deer prior to and during the use of fencing to restrict their access to openings. The vegetation of these openings can then be allowed to revert to forest. Once deer density has been reduced and succession has proceeded to stages less favorable to deer, birth control and fencing will no longer be necessary. Non-hunted adjacent lands with good deer habitat may be a source of young deer dispersing into the reserve, necessitating periodic direct control measures. Management will aim to maintain low deer carrying capacity and control any damage occurring at the reserve's boundary. Ecological monitoring of the reserve will reveal whether another problem is beginning and more intensive management will again be required.

MANAGEMENT RESPONSES TO OVERABUNDANCE IN URBAN FRINGE AREAS

Deer interactions with people in suburban areas are on the increase. Surveys of suburbanites in the New York area reveal that they enjoy deer but are concerned about deer-vehicle collisions and Lyme disease. Damage to ornamental plants is costly but tolerated. There is no consensus as to whether deer populations should be increased, maintained at their current level, or reduced. Most respondents recognized the need for population management, but few were in favor of recreational hunting (Decker and Connelly 1989).

Control of deer populations where deer coexist with people in urban fringe areas is difficult and solutions are less than satisfactory. Control of deer numbers through habitat changes is not feasible and direct control methods have limited application because of the large area and number of deer involved.

Damage prevention is the main recourse for suburban landowners. Damage to gardens and ornamentals can be prevented by fencing, or reduced, to a variable extent, by repellents or by planting less-preferred species (Conover and Kania 1988). Damage resulting from deer-vehicle collisions is of more concern because of the possibility of human injury or death (Hansen 1983, Witham and Jones 1987). Light and sound tactics have been employed, with mixed to little success, in an attempt to keep deer off the road as a vehicle approaches. Roadsides can be made less attractive to deer by decreasing palatable forage, using repellents, interceptive feeding, or nonsalt deicers (Feldhamer et al. 1986, Wood and Wolfe 1988). Fencing, 2.4- to 2.7-m high, currently remains the most effective alternative, although it will be a sound economic investment only if there are many deer-vehicle accidents along the length of road in question before the fence is erected (Reed et al. 1982).

Deer-vehicle collisions generally occur at predictable times and places (Bashore et al. 1985). For rural and suburban areas with relatively low-speed traffic, a combination of increased public awareness of high risk locations and fencing along critical sections of road should reduce accident frequency.

CONCLUSIONS

A literature review did not reveal any single, completely adequate method of limiting white-tailed deer populations in nature reserves and urban fringe areas that are not hunted. The absence of active management in the face of deer overpopulation may lead to an increase in deer damage, and to changes in plant and animal community structure and species composition. The currently available nonhunting methods to directly reduce a deer population, e.g., capture and transfer, and reproductive control, require treatment of individual deer, and are therefore costly and labor intensive. Until new technologies, such as remote injection of chemosterilants, are perfected, these methods are best used as short-term means of deer population reduction. Deer density also can be reduced by lowering the land's carrying capacity primarily by promoting the growth of contiguous mature forest. This measure is slow to take effect and until then deer damage may be exacerbated. However, the results are more permanent, making this approach cost-effective in the long run. A side benefit can be an increase in the number and population densities of species of plants and animals that depend on mature forest.

Large reserves can combine methods of direct control and habitat alteration to moderate the negative consequences of each. Direct control measures can be used until habitat alterations take effect. Small reserves in other than dense urban areas have limited capacity to control their resident deer because the reserve represents a small portion of the total deer habitat. Management may shift deer activity away from the reserve or its sensitive areas, but direct control of deer numbers will be especially difficult if the reserve is surrounded by good deer habitat.

Damage to human property and life caused by deer in exurban areas may be lessened, but not eliminated, by using repellents and fencing. However, controlling deer numbers in exurban areas is unlikely with currently available non-hunting techniques.

Acknowledgments.—We thank Drs. A. Katz, J. Kuser, C. Leck, and L. Wolgast for their advice and cooperation. This work was supported in part by a generous grant from Friends of Animals, Inc., which, however, is not responsible for the findings and recommendations contained in the paper.

REFERENCES CITED

Alverson, W.S., D.M. Waller, and S.L. Solheim. 1988. Forests too deer: edge effects in northern Wisconsin. Conserv. Biol. 2:348–358.

Anderson, S.H., and C.S. Robbins. 1981. Habitat size and bird community management. Trans. North Am. Wildl. and Nat. Resour. Conf. 46:511–519.

Ashley, R.F. 1982. Milwaukee's dear deer. Wis. Nat. Resour. 6:6–11.

Baird, T.H. 1990. Changes in breeding bird populations. Bull. No. 477, New York State Museum, State Educ. Dep., Albany, N.Y. 41pp.

Bashore, T.L., and E.D. Bellis. 1982. Deer on Pennsylvania airfields: problems and means of control. Wildl. Soc. Bull. 10:386–388.

———, W.M. Tzilkowski, and E.D. Bellis. 1985. Analysis of deer-vehicle collision sites in Pennsylvania. J. Wildl. Manage. 49:769–774.

Botti, F.L. 1985. Chemosterilants as a management option for deer on Angel Island: lessons learned. California-Nevada Wildl. Trans., pages 61–65.

Boyd, R.J. 1987. Vegetation management and animal damage. Pages 55–57 *in* D.M. Baumartner et al., eds. Animal damage management in Pacific northwest forests. Washington State Univ., Pullman.

Bratton, S.P. 1979. Impacts of white-tailed deer on the vegetation of Cades Cove, Great Smoky Mountain National Park. Proc. Conf. Southeast. Assoc. Game and Fish Comm. 33:305–312.

Caslick, J.W., and D.J. Decker. 1979. Economic feasibility of deer-proof fence for apple orchards. Wildl. Soc. Bull. 7:173–175.

Caughley, G. 1976. Wildlife management and the dynamics of ungulate populations. Pages 183–246 *in* T.H. Croaker, ed. Applied Biology, Vol. 1. Academic Press, New York, N.Y.

Conner, M.C., E.C. Soutiere, and R.A. Lancia. 1987. Drop-netting deer: costs and incidence of capture myopathy. Wildl. Soc. Bull. 15:434–438.

Conover, M.R. 1984. Effectiveness of repellents in reducing deer damage in nurseries. Wildl. Soc. Bull. 12:399–404.

———, and G.S. Kania. 1988. Browsing preference of white-tailed deer for different ornamental species. Wildl. Soc. Bull. 16:175–179.

Craven, S.R. 1983. Deer. In R.M. Timm, ed. Prevention and control of wildlife damage. Great Plains Agric. Counc. Wildl. Resour. Committee, and Nebr. Coop. Ext. Serv., Univ. of Nebraska, Lincoln.

Crawford, H.S. 1984. Habitat management. Pages 629–646 *in* L.K. Halls, ed. White-tailed deer: ecology and management. Stackpole Books, Harrisburg, Pa.

Curtis, R.O., and F.M. Rushmore. 1958. Some effects of stand density and deer browsing on reproduction in an Adirondack hardwood stand. J. For. 56:116–121.

Dasmann, W.P. 1971. If deer are to survive. Stackpole Books, Harrisburg, Pa. 128pp.

Day, G.I., S.D. Schemnitz, and R.D. Taber. 1980. Capturing and marking wild animals. Pages 61–88 *in* S.D. Schemnitz, ed. Wildlife management techniques manual. The Wildl. Soc., Washington, D.C.

Decker, D.J., and N.A. Connelly. 1989. Deer in suburbia-pleasures and pests. The Conservationist, March–April, pages 47–49.

DeYoe, D.R., and W. Schaap. 1983. Comparison of eight physical barriers used for protecting Douglas-fir seedlings from deer browse. Pages 77–93 *in* D.J. Decker, ed. First eastern wildlife damage control confer. proc. Coop. Ext., Dep. of Nat. Resour., Cornell Univ., Ithaca, N.Y.

Feldhamer, G.A., et al. 1986. Effects of interstate highway fencing on white-tailed deer activity. J. Wildl. Manage. 50:497–503.

Garver, J.W. 1987. Using chemicals and fertilizer to increase productivity and manage animal damage to plantation seedlings. Pages 59–60 *in* D.M. Baumartner et al., eds. Animal damage management in Pacific Northwest forests. Washington State Univ., Pullman.

Giles, R.H. 1978. Wildlife management. W.H. Freeman, San Francisco, Calif. 416pp.

Greer, K.R., W.W. Hawkins, and J.E. Catlin. 1968. Experimental studies of controlled reproduction in elk (wapiti). J. Wildl. Manage. 32:368–376.

Halls, L.K. 1978. White-tailed deer. Pages 43–65 *in* J.L. Schmidt and D.L. Gilbert, eds. Big game of North America. Stackpole Books, Harrisburg, Pa.

———, and R. Alcaniz. 1968. Browse plants yield best in forest openings. J. Wildl. Manage. 32:185–186.

Hansen, C.S. 1983. Costs of deer-vehicle accidents in Michigan. Wildl. Soc. Bull. 11:161–164.

Harder, J.D., and T.J. Peterle. 1974. Effect of diethylstilbestrol on reproductive performance of white-tailed deer. J. Wildl. Manage. 38:183–196.

Harlow, R.F. 1984. Habitat evaluation. Pages 601–628 *in* L.K. Halls, ed. White-tailed deer: ecology and management. Stackpole Books, Harrisburg, Pa.

Harris, L.D. 1984. The fragmented forest. Univ. of Chicago Press, Chicago, Ill. 211pp.

———. 1988. Edge effects and conservation of biotic diversity. Conserv. Biol. 2:330–332.

Harris, M.T., W.L. Palmer, and J.L. George. 1983. Preliminary screening of white-tailed deer repellents. J. Wildl. Manage. 47:516–519.

Harrison, G.H. 1983. Wildlife: coping with excess white-tailed deer on a suburban nature center. Audubon Mag. 85:128–129.

Hawkins, R.E., D.C. Autry, and W.D. Klimstra. 1967. Comparison of methods used to capture white-tailed deer. J. Wildl. Manage. 31:460–464.

Hawthorne, D.W. 1980. Wildlife damage and control techniques. Pages 411–439 *in* S.D. Schemnitz, ed. Wildlife management techniques manual. The Wildl. Soc., Washington, D.C.

Hygnstrom, S.E., and S.R. Craven. 1988. Electric fences and commercial repellents for reducing deer damage in cornfields. Wildl. Soc. Bull. 16:291–296.

Ishmael, W.E., and O.J. Rongstad. 1984. Economics of an urban deer-removal program. Wildl. Soc. Bull. 12:394–398.

Jewell, P.A., S. Holt, and D. Hart, eds. 1981. Workshop report. *In* Problems in management of locally abundant wild mammals. Academic Press, New York, N.Y.

Kirkpatrick, J.F., and J.W. Turner, Jr. 1985. Chemical fertility control and wildlife management. BioScience 35:485–491.

Lincoln, G.A., and R.N.B. Kay. 1979. Effects of season on the secretion of LH and testosterone in intact and castrated red deer stags (*Cervus elaphus*). J. Reprod. Fertil. 55:75–80.

Marquis, D.A. 1974. The impact of deer browsing on Allegheny hardwood regeneration. USDA For. Serv. Res. Pap. NE–308. 8pp.

_____, and R. Brenneman. 1981. The impact of deer on forest vegetation in Pennsylvania. USDA For. Serv. Gen. Tech. Rep. NE-65. 7pp.

Matschke, G.H. 1976. Nonefficacy of mechanical birth control devices for white-tailed deer. J. Wildl. Manage. 40:792–795.

_____, D.S. deCalesta, and J.D. Harder. 1984. Crop damage and control. Pages 647–654 *in* L.K. Halls, ed. White-tailed deer: ecology and management. Stackpole Books, Harrisburg, Pa.

_____. 1977. Microencapsulated diethylstilbestrol as an oral contraceptive in white-tailed deer. J. Wildl. Manage. 41:87–91.

_____. 1980. Efficacy of steroid implants in preventing pregnancy in white-tailed deer. J. Wildl. Manage. 44:756–758.

McAninch, J.B., and R.J. Winchcombe. 1982. Deer damage control in orchards and vineyards in New York. New York State Dep. of Agric. and Markets and The New York Botanical Garden Cary Arboretum, Millbrook, N.Y. 16pp.

McCaffery, K.R., J.E. Ashbrenner, and J.C. Moulton. 1981. Forest opening construction and impacts in northern Wisconsin. Wis. Dep. Nat. Resour. Tech. Bull. 120, Madison, Wis. 41pp.

_____, and W.A. Creed. 1969. Significance of forest openings to deer in northern Wisconsin. Wis. Dep. Nat. Resour. Tech. Bull. 44, Madison, Wis.

Morrison, D. 1987. Landscape restoration in response to previous disturbance. Pages 159–172 *in* M.G. Turner, ed. Landscape heterogeneity and disturbance. Ecological Studies, vol. 64, Springer-Verlag, New York, N.Y.

Niering, W.A., and R.H. Goodwin. 1974. Creation of relatively small shrublands with herbicides: arresting "successions" on rights-of-way and pastureland. Ecology 55:784–795.

Palmer, D.T., D.A. Andrews, R.O. Winters, and J.W. Francis. 1980. Removal techniques to control an enclosed deer herd. Wildl. Soc. Bull. 8:29–33.

Palmer, W.L., R.G. Wingard, and J.L. George. 1983. Evaluation of white-tailed deer repellents. Wildl. Soc. Bull. 11:164–166.

_____, J.M. Payne, R.G. Wingard, and J.L. George. 1985. A practical fence to reduce deer damage. Wildl. Soc. Bull. 13:240–245.

Paulsen, C.A. 1977. Regulation of male fertility. Pages 458–465 *in* R.O. Greep and M.A. Koblinsky, eds. Frontiers in reproduction and fertility control. MIT Press, Cambridge, Mass.

Peek, J.M. 1980. Natural regulation of ungulates (What constitutes a real wilderness?). Wildl. Soc. Bull. 8:217–227.

Reed, D.F., T.D.I. Beck, and T.N. Woodard. 1982. Methods of reducing deer-vehicle accidents: benefit-cost analysis. Wildl. Soc. Bull. 10:349–354.

Rempel, R.D., and R.C. Bertram. 1975. The Stewart modified corral trap. Calif. Fish & Game 61:237–239.

Reynolds, A.K. 1980. Effects of deer on old field succession at the Great Swamp National Wildlife Refuge, New Jersey. Ph.D. dissertation, Rutgers, the State University of New Jersey, New Brunswick. 114pp.

Riney, T. 1982. Study and management of large mammals. John Wiley, Chichester, U.K. 552pp.

Rongstad, O.J., and R.A. McCabe. 1984. Capture techniques. Pages 655–676 *in* L.K. Halls, ed. White-tailed deer: ecology and management. Stackpole Books, Harrisburg, Pa.

Root, B.G., E.K. Fritcell, and N.F. Giessman. 1988. Effects of intensive hunting on white-tailed deer movement. Wildl. Soc. Bull. 16:145–151.

Ross, B.A., J.R. Bray, and W.H. Marshall. 1970. Effects of long-term deer exclusion on a *Pinus resinosa* forest in north-central Minnesota. Ecology 51:1088–1093.

Roughton, R.D. 1979. Effects of oral melengestrol acetate on reproduction in captive white-tailed deer. J. Wildl. Manage. 43:428–436.

Tierson, W.C., E.F. Patric, and D.F. Behrend. 1966. Influence of white-tailed deer on the logged northern hardwood forest. J. For. 64:801–805.

Tilghman, N.G. 1989. Impacts of white-tailed deer on forest regeneration in northwestern Pennsylvania. J. Wildl. Manage. 53:524–532.

Turner, J.W., Jr., and J.F. Kirkpatrick. 1982. Androgens, behaviour and fertility control in feral stallions. J. Fertil. Suppl. 32:79–87.

Witham, J.H., and J.M. Jones. 1987. Chicago urban deer study. Ill. Nat. Hist. Surv. Rep., No. 265, Ill. Dep. of Energy and Nat. Resour., Champaign, Ill. 4pp.

Wood, P., and M.L. Wolfe. 1988. Intercept feeding as a means of reducing deer-vehicle collisions. Wildl. Soc. Bull. 16:376–380.

Yahner, R.H. 1988. Changes in wildlife communities near edges. Conserv. Biol. 2:333–339.

Yoakum, J., W.P. Dasmann, H.R. Sanderson, C.M. Nixon, and H.S. Crawford. 1980. Habitat improvement techniques. Pages 329–403 *in* S.D. Schemnitz, ed. Wildlife management techniques manual. The Wildl. Soc., Washington, D.C.

Effects of Urbanization on Foraging Strategy of Woodpeckers

CYNTHIA A. MOULTON,[1] Marine-Estuarine-Environmental Science Program, University of Maryland, College Park, MD 20742

LOWELL W. ADAMS, National Institute for Urban Wildlife, 10921 Trotting Ridge Way, Columbia, MD 21044; and Natural Resources Management Program, University of Maryland, College Park, MD 20742

INTRODUCTION

Six species of woodpeckers coexist in the Washington, D.C. metropolitan area. Although omnivorous, these woodpeckers are generally insectivorous (Beal 1911), so competition for food resources may exist. Theoretically, two species cannot coexist indefinitely over time using limited resources in identical ways because one eventually replaces the other (Hutchinson 1958, Green 1971, Schoener 1974, and others). This principle of competitive exclusion was developed independently by Gause (1934) and Volterra (1926), and both authors implied that niche overlap indicates competition.

Competition may be reduced or avoided, however, through partitioning of resources whereby each species occupies a distinct niche (Darlington 1972). Partitioning occurs if species use: (1) different resources; (2) the same resource in different places; or (3) the same resource at different times (MacArthur 1958, Bull et al. 1986). Crombie (1947) and Weatherley (1963) found that competition acted as a selective pressure to reduce the niche overlap among species when a particular resource was in limited supply. In an urban environment, many niches are eliminated, others are altered, and some new niches are created. As urban development intensifies, resources become more limited and competition for those resources increases. How does this affect closely related coexisting species of woodpecker? Are some species at competitive disadvantages as resources become more limited? If so, will they be lost from the bird community with increased urban development? Can management efforts be implemented to keep this from happening? These are important questions currently lacking suitable answers.

Many field studies have indicated that a decrease in niche overlap occurs when resources become less abundant,

and when demand for a resource is greater than the supply (Crombie 1947, Hartley 1953, Weatherley 1963, Zaret and Rand 1971, May and MacArthur 1972, Baker and Baker 1973, and Weins 1976). Partitioning of food resources among woodpecker species has been observed for downy (Picoides pubesens), hairy (P. villosus), red-bellied (Melanerpes carolinus), red-headed (M. erythocephalus), pileated (Dryocopus pileatus), northern three-toed (P. tridactylus), white-headed (P. albolarvatus), and black-backed (P. arcticus) woodpeckers and the yellow-bellied (Sphyrapicus varius) and Williamson's (S. thyroideus) sapsuckers (Stallcup 1968, Willson 1970, Kisiel 1972, Morse 1972, Reller 1972, Williams 1975, Jackson 1976, Conner 1977, Raphael 1980, Raphael and White 1984, and Bull et al. 1986). None of these investigators studied effects of urban development on woodpeckers. The objective of the present study was to determine the effect of urbanization on the foraging behavior of woodpeckers in central Maryland.

DESCRIPTION OF STUDY AREA

The study was conducted in Montgomery and Prince George's Counties, Maryland, on three distinct study sites: (1) an undisturbed woodland, (2) a managed parkland, and (3) a woodland residential neighborhood. Each site was approximately 25 ha and included a river, pond, or stream as a water source.

The woodland site was located at Patuxent Wildlife Research Center (PWRC), in Laurel. This mainly bottomland forest area consisted of a complete vertical profile with mixed hardwoods of various age classes, shrubbery, and an intact leaf litter. The area has been relatively undisturbed since logging in the mid 1800's and human impact was minimal.

The managed parkland site was located at the University of Maryland Golf Course (GC), in College Park. This area was characterized by lawns and greens; fairway woods

---

[1]Present Address: Environmental Protection Agency, H7507C, 401 M St., SW, Washington, D.C. 20460.

Wildlife Conservation in Metropolitan Environments. NIUW Symp. Ser. 2, L.W. Adams and D.L. Leedy, eds. Published by Natl. Inst. for Urban Wildl., 10921 Trotting Ridge Way, Columbia, MD 21044, USA, 1991.

(mature trees dispersed on manicured lawns); and forest fragments of dense mixed hardwoods and pines with a shrub layer and intact leaf litter. There were a few small, well maintained trails, roads, and buildings. Human impact was moderate.

The woodland residential neighborhood site was located at Quaint Acres (QA), in Silver Spring, abutting the Northwest Branch Park of the Anacostia River. The area was predominately mixed hardwoods with some conifers and a complete vertical profile. It remained relatively undisturbed in parts. Clearings had been made for the houses and small lawns, and there were paved roads and driveways leading to the homes. Many residents kept seed feeders and five suet feeders were located within the study site. Human impact was moderate.

METHODS

Field Methodology

Observations of woodpecker (downy; hairy; northern flicker, *Colaptes auratus*; pileated; red-bellied; and the yellow-bellied sapsucker) feeding activity on each of the sites were made at least once each week from August, 1989 to May, 1990. Each 3-hour observation period took place within 6 hours of sunrise or sunset in order to include periods of intense feeding activity. The focal point sampling technique (Altmann 1974) was used at 10-second intervals for a maximum of 5 minutes per individual. A tape recorder indicating 10-second time frames was used instead of a stop watch to monitor intervals. This allowed the observer to maintain visual contact with the bird and record data efficiently. The activity of the bird was recorded at the sounding of each interval. At the end of 5 minutes, the tape was rewound for the next bird sighting.

Foraging behavior and habitat characteristics were recorded at each feeding site for each bird observed. Habitat characteristics included feeding substrate (tree, snag, stump, log, or ground) and tree species and size, among others (for a complete list, see Moulton 1990). The location of birds on trees and snags was identified as trunk, branch, or stub. A tree with leaves or leafbuds on less than 10% of its branches was classified as a snag. A stump was less than 1 m high and a snag was greater than 1 m high. A dead branch on a live tree was considered a stub. Foraging techniques were classified as: pecking, scaling, excavating, gleaning, ground foraging, and feeder activity (the latter subclassified as suet or seed feeder). Each is a distinct method of finding and securing food.

Pecking, also described as percussion, refers to the motion of rapid continuous blows as the woodpecker moves along a limb, trunk or log. Kilham (1965) suggested that the birds locate their prey through auditory cues when they cause it to move or when a differential is detected in reverberations between insect-tunneled and solid wood.

Scaling, as described by Bull et al. (1986), is the activity of prying bark layers off trees to get at insects below.

Excavating refers to the woodpecker actually digging into the wood with its bill to retrieve insects. This action may follow pecking in some cases or may involve a site familiar to the woodpecker, such as an ant infested log.

Gleaning includes a variety of actions. It is a technique whereby the woodpecker typically moves up a tree or along a limb peering and poking into fissures, junctions of branches, foliage, or any other place that might yield food. This category is distinguished by the superficial gleaning of food items from surfaces. It includes fruits and berries as well as insects.

Ground foraging refers to the technique of gleaning off the leaf litter on the ground or actually digging in the soil for insects.

Feeder activity refers to birds using supplemental seed or suet bird feeders placed outdoors by people.

To obtain an indication of relative abundance of the woodpeckers on each site, the point count technique was used with a modification of the Indices Pontuel d'Abondance (IPA) method (Blondel et al. 1970, Ferry 1974; see Whitcomb et al. 1981 and Robbins et al. 1989, for modifications). A single point was established near the center of the plots. The points were sampled three times, one time each in January, March, and May, 1990, between 7:00–8:00 a.m. On each visit, all woodpeckers detected during a 20-minute period were recorded. The highest number recorded at each site was used as an estimate of relative abundance of the bird for that site.

To obtain a measure of available habitat, the point center quarter method was used at 50 random points within each study site (Cottam and Curtis 1956). At each point, the closest tree (or snag) in each direction (NW, NE, SW, SE) was identified to species; its distance to the point was recorded along with its diameter at breast height (dbh). From this information, tree species diversity, abundance, and dominance were obtained for each study site.

Data Analysis

Simple statistics, including means and standard deviations, were calculated from the random habitat sample to obtain site characteristics, average dbh, and relative dominance of individual tree species within each site. Chi-square analysis was performed on the IPA woodpecker data to test for differences in abundance of individuals among and within sites, as well as for differences in the total number of woodpeckers among sites.

A comprehensive multivariate statistical analysis was completed on the foraging technique and primary substrate variables, using contingency tables to test up to three dimensions of interaction. A statistical unit was defined as one 10-second interval of observation for each individual. Therefore, if a bird was observed for 60 seconds (30 seconds of pecking and 30 seconds of gleaning), that was equivalent to six units (three pecking and three gleaning). The 10-second time frame was consistent with other woodpecker behavioral research (Bull et al. 1986). Each 10-second interval appeared to be independent of every other interval. Thus, at any one time, the foraging method or location of the bird was not dependent on what the bird was doing 10 seconds earlier. The procedures used to analyze contingency table data were the Pearson Chi-square (and P value) and the Likelihood Ratio Chi-square (and P value). In all tests, the chi-squares were in agreement. For variables recorded in the present study, contingency tables were most appropriate as they could be used to evaluate foraging behavior in relation to habitat. Williams (1975) also used contingency table analysis to make comparisons of yellow-bellied sapsuckers and red-headed, downy, and red-bellied woodpeckers in Illinois. He focused on lowland vs. upland forested habitat as well as interspecific comparison.

RESULTS AND DISCUSSION

Relative Abundance of Woodpeckers

There were no significant differences ($P>0.05$) between the number of individual woodpeckers among or within sites and the total number of woodpeckers among sites.

Resource Partitioning within Sites

Patuxent Wildlife Research Center.—The percent time each woodpecker spent using a specific foraging technique was calculated and compared (Fig. 1). At PWRC, gleaning was the most important method used by the woodpeckers, except for the northern flicker, which predominantly foraged on the ground. The downy, hairy, and red-bellied woodpeckers relied almost entirely on gleaning, whereas the yellow-bellied sapsucker excavated almost as much as it

gleaned. The most uniform foraging strategy was employed by the pileated woodpecker; it gleaned most of the time but it pecked, scaled, and excavated frequently. The pileated, red-bellied, and sapsucker utilized pecking as a foraging technique more so than the other three species.

Analysis of a three-way interaction contingency table examining foraging techniques of all woodpeckers on trees and snags (Table 1) showed that the behavior of species was significantly different ($P<0.05$) on each substrate. Downies and flickers used trees and snags with smaller average dbh's (Fig. 4). Furthermore, the downy and hairy foraged predominantly on trunks, whereas the red-bellied and sapsucker primarily used branches, and the pileated and flicker foraged almost equally on both trunks and branches (Fig. 5). The flicker, when foraging on woody substrate, only used snags, whereas the other woodpeckers only foraged on them occasionally. The sapsucker preferred white birch (*Betula alba*) and red maple (*Acer rubrum*) trees, and the other woodpeckers were sighted on white oak (*Quercus alba*), American beech (*Fagus grandifolia*), tuliptree (*Liriodendron tulipifera*), and red maple. During this study, observations of the woodpeckers on stumps and logs at PWRC were too few to include in the analysis.

University of Maryland Golf Course.—Foraging techniques of woodpeckers at GC were tabulated, converted into percentages, and compared (Fig. 2). As at PWRC, gleaning was the most employed technique. The time spent pecking was greater at GC and was highest for the pileated woodpecker and sapsucker. The northern flicker gleaned much more than at PWRC and this large amount of gleaning has not been identified in previous research. Although insecticides were not applied to turf, there were fertilizer and herbicide applications, which may have affected ground foraging by the flicker. Usually golfers were not present on the fairways during the hours of observation. They often drove carts when they were present, as did the groundskeepers, which also may have disrupted ground foraging activity by flickers. Further research is needed to clarify the factors responsible for altered feeding behavior of flickers on the golf course.

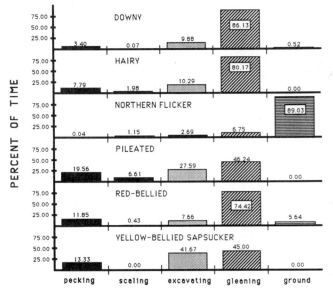

Fig. 1. Foraging techniques used by six species of woodpeckers at Patuxent Wildlife Research Center, Laurel, Md., 1989–1990. Numbers represent frequency of use in percent. Total observations on which frequencies were calculated were: downy, 1545; hairy, 648; northern flicker, 1313; pileated, 738; red-bellied, 695; and yellow-bellied sapsucker, 600.

Table 1. Foraging behavior of woodpeckers at Patuxent Wildlife Research Center, Laurel, Md., 1989–1990. Numbers represent total observations.

Substrate Species	Feeding techniques			
	Gleaning	Excavating	Pecking	Scaling
Trees				
Downy	1304	30	34	0
Hairy	469	0	31	10
Pileated	357	45	105	50
Red-bellied	455	0	64	2
Sapsucker	270	250	80	0
Snags				
Downy	26	71	8	1
Hairy	15	20	20	3
N. Flicker	42	35	5	15
Pileated	0	50	12	1
Red-bellied	60	53	18	1

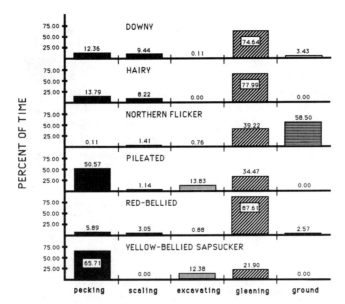

Fig. 2. Foraging techniques used by six species of woodpeckers at the University of Maryland Golf Course, College Park, Md., 1989–1990. Numbers represent frequency of use in percent. Total observations on which frequencies were calculated were: downy, 1747; hairy, 720; northern flicker, 902; pileated, 528; red-bellied, 1,477; and yellow-bellied sapsucker, 210.

A two-way interaction contingency table was calculated with trees only for the substrate (Table 2). The foraging techniques each woodpecker used on trees were significantly different (P<0.05). The average dbh of foraging substrate was lowest for the downy and sapsucker (around 48 cm for both), whereas the average dbh's of substrate used by the other four species were higher, ranging between 56 and 58 cm (Fig. 4). The flicker, sapsucker, and red-bellied woodpeckers predominantly foraged on branches, whereas the downy and hairy mainly foraged on trunks (as they did at PWRC), and the pileated used trunks, branches, and stubs (Fig. 5). Except for the sapsucker, which preferred red maple, all woodpeckers preferred white oak. The downy and hairy also used Virginia pine (*Pinus virginiana*). Snags, logs, and stumps were not used sufficiently enough by the woodpeckers to include in the statistical analysis.

Quaint Acres.—The northern flicker foraged on the ground extensively and occasionally gleaned and used suet feeders. For other woodpeckers, gleaning was the most used

technique, as it was at GC and PWRC (Fig. 3). However, the second most common foraging method was feeding on suet. All species shifted foraging strategies to make use of the suet feeders (minimally by the flicker), but none used suet exclusively. Pecking was important for the pileated and red-bellied, but not for the other species.

Two two-way contingency tables were created for techniques used by all birds at QA, one for trees and one for snags (Table 3). The tables were analyzed separately because there were enough observations to include both, but the number of observations on trees was much greater than on snags for all woodpeckers. Both tests rejected the null hypothesis (P<0.05), therefore the proportions of time each technique was used by the birds was significantly different on each substrate. Differences in the average dbh's of foraging substrate were greatest at QA for the hairy, red-bellied, and

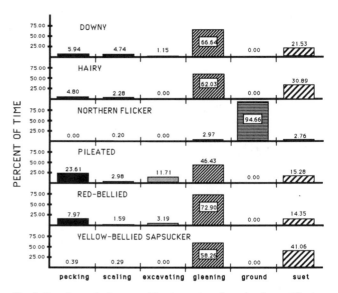

Fig. 3. Foraging techniques used by six species of woodpeckers at Quaint Acres, Silver Spring, Md., 1989–1990. Numbers represent frequency of use in percent. Total observations on which frequencies were calculated were: downy, 2980; hairy, 1,756; northern flicker, 1,512; pileated, 591; red-bellied, 1,639; and yellow-bellied sapsucker, 1,795.

Table 2. Foraging behavior of woodpeckers on trees at the University of Maryland Golf Course, College Park, Md., 1989–1990. Numbers represent total observations.

Species	Feeding techniques			
	Gleaning	Excavating	Pecking	Scaling
Downy	1304	0	213	165
Hairy	560	0	99	59
N. Flicker	283	0	0	3
Pileated	181	68	242	6
Red-bellied	1250	8	12	33
Sapsucker	46	26	138	0

Table 3. Foraging behavior of woodpeckers at Quaint Acres, Silver Spring, Md., 1989–1990. Numbers represent total observations.[a]

Substrate Species	Feeding techniques			
	Gleaning	Excavating	Pecking	Scaling
Trees				
Downy	1546	27	133	93
Hairy	726	0	49	15
N. flicker	44	0	0	3
Pileated	226	50	89	15
Red-bellied	1006	14	84	21
Sapsucker	603	0	4	3
Snags				
Downy	14	[b]	6	18
Hairy	37		10	13
Pileated	8		30	0
Red-bellied	46		31	2

[a]Does not include use of suet feeders, see Fig. 3.
[b]Excavation of snags was not observed.

pileated woodpeckers (Fig. 4). The average dbh's for all species at QA were more discrete than at the other sites as well. Furthermore, the pileated, red-bellied, and flicker foraged mainly on branches, and the downy, hairy, and sapsucker mainly used trunks (Fig. 5).

Intraspecific Foraging Strategy Among Sites

Among sites, one point that stands out is that the pileated woodpecker made the greatest use of all techniques. At all sites, the species pecked, scaled, excavated, and gleaned, and used suet feeders at QA. It used a wide range of substrates, including trees and snags, with occasional use of stumps and logs. Furthermore, the pileated woodpecker used stubs, branches, and trunks for foraging at all sites.

The red-bellied woodpecker had the least variation in its foraging strategy among sites. In all cases, gleaning was the most used technique, with pecking next (except at QA).

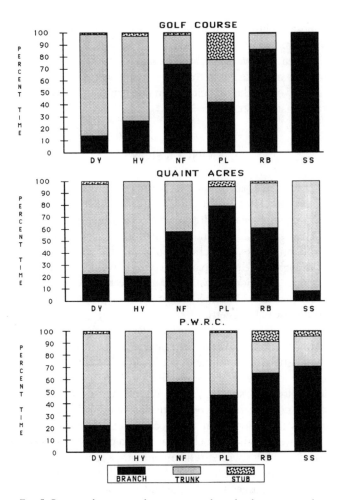

Fig. 5. Percent of time spent by six species of woodpeckers on secondary foraging substrates at Patuxent Wildlife Research Center, Laurel, Md.; University of Maryland Golf Course, College Park, Md.; and Quaint Acres, Silver Spring, Md.; 1989–1990.

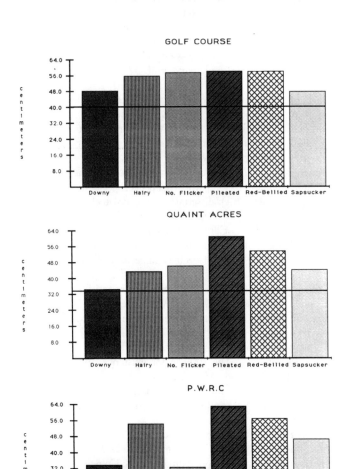

Fig. 4. The average dbh of woodpecker foraging substrates (trees and snags) at Patuxent Wildlife Research Center, Laurel, Md.; University of Maryland Golf Course, College Park, Md.; and Quaint Acres, Silver Spring, Md.; 1989–1990. Solid lines indicate the average dbh of 200 random trees and snags from each site.

The dbh of substrates used was consistently around 56 cm. The red-bellied mainly foraged on branches, but fed on trunks and stubs occasionally.

The downy and hairy were most similar to each other but were flexible among sites. Hairies used substrates with a larger average dbh than downies, but both birds fluctuated among the three sites. They mainly used trunks to forage, branches occasionally; the downy used stubs at all sites and the hairy used stubs only at GC.

The northern flicker had the most unique foraging strategy by ground feeding extensively (except at GC where it gleaned on snags almost 40% of the time). Flickers did not winter at any of the sites.

The yellow-bellied sapsucker had broad behavioral plasticity among the three sites in terms of foraging techniques and secondary substrates utilized. The sapsucker used live trees only at PWRC and GC, and foraged mainly on the branches. Foraging techniques included pecking, excavating, and gleaning, which varied in proportions at the two sites. At QA, sapsuckers used snags and live trees (predominantly the trunks), and foraging techniques were almost exclusively gleaning and suet feeder activity. It is important to note that sapsuckers were winter residents of this area. The variation seen in sapsucker foraging strategy may have resulted from the bird entering a previously established woodpecker foraging guild and being forced to adapt to available resources.

CONCLUSIONS

Resource partitioning by woodpeckers occurred on all three study sites by the birds (1) using different foraging techniques on each substrate type, (2) using substrates of varying sizes (dbh's), and (3) differing the amount of time spent on trunks, branches, and stubs of trees and snags. Although niche overlap appeared to be avoided at all sites, resource partitioning was most intense at QA (the most urbanized site), intermediate at GC, and least at PWRC (the most natural setting).

The degree of urbanization affected foraging behavior of woodpeckers. However, the birds exhibited enough foraging plasticity to continue to coexist in about the same relative abundance on the most urbanized site (QA) as on the least disturbed site (PWRC). We do not know at what degree of urbanization competitive pressures will force some species to be lost from the woodpecker community. We speculate that the sapsucker may be at a competitive disadvantage as it is a winter resident only, thus does not interact with the other species and the local environment year-round. Perhaps, as a result, the bird would not be as capable as resident species of adjusting to local environmental changes resulting from increased development. However, it is encouraging that the species exhibited a capability of altering its foraging behavior among sites. A rigid and narrow feeding strategy would be more worrisome. The northern flicker is also a migrating species, but has the advantage of a unique woodpecker foraging strategy. However, we caution that increased use of lawn pesticides in residential areas may disrupt the feeding behavior of flickers and other ground foraging species. Pileated woodpeckers were least abundant at all sites. They used larger trees and diverse substrates (trees, snags, logs, and stumps where available). Because of their need for larger trees for foraging and their larger territory requirements, loss or reduction of large wooded tracts and large trees are likely to impact the species. It is encouraging that the bird exhibited broad feeding behavior, including use of suet feeders at QA.

Feeding on suet was a significant part of the foraging behavior of all species (except the flicker) at QA. We do not know to what extent supplemental suet feeding will help to retain woodpecker species as urbanization intensifies. Further research of this question is needed. Also, research into survival rates of woodpeckers using suet as a supplemental feeding source would provide more insight into the question of niche overlap and intraspecific niche differences. Finally, as urbanization intensifies, competition for nesting cavities also will increase. Further research of nesting behavior is needed.

Acknowledgments. —Special appreciation is extended to Brendan Nerney for his time, patience, and assistance in preparing the figures for this paper. Many thanks also go to Grey Pendleton for his expert statistical advice and to Mary E. (Cherry) Keller for her input during the design of this project. We express sincere thanks to all the residents of Quaint Acres who allowed access to their property, especially Beverly and Vagn Flyger and Beatrice Barnard. Drs. Vagn Flyger and Robert Ridky reviewed early drafts of the manuscript. We are grateful to all.

REFERENCES CITED

Altmann, J. 1974. Observational study of behavior: sampling methods. Behaviour 49:227–267.

Baker, M. C., and A.E.M. Baker. 1973. Niche relationship among six species of shore birds on their wintering and breeding ranges. Ecol. Monogr. 43:193–212.

Beal, F. E. L. 1911. Food of the woodpeckers of the United States. U.S. Dep. Agric. Biol. Surv. Bull. 37. 64pp.

Blondel, J., C. Ferry, and B. Frochot. 1970. La methode des indices ponctuels d'abondance (IPA) ou des releves d'avifaune par "station d'ecoute". Alauda 38:55–71.

Bull, E. L., S. R. Peterson, and J. W. Thomas. 1986. Resource partitioning among woodpeckers in northeastern Oregon. U.S. Dep. Agric. PNW-444.

Conner, R. N. 1977. Seasonal changes in the foraging methods, and habitats of six sympatric woodpecker species in southwestern Virginia. Ph.D. dissertation, Va. Polytechnic Inst. and State Univ., Blacksburg.

Cottam, G., and J. T. Curtis. 1956. The use of distance measures in phytosociologist sampling. Ecology 37:451–460.

Crombie, A. C. 1947. Interspecific competition. J. Animal Ecol. 16:44–73.

Darlington, P. J., Jr. 1972. Competition, competitive repulsion, and coexistence. Proc. Natl. Acad. Sci. 69:3151–3155.

Ferry, C. 1974. Comparison between breeding bird communities in an oak forest and a beech forest censused by the IPA method. Acta Ornithol. 14:302–309.

Gause, G. F. 1934. The struggle for existence. Williams and Wilkins, Baltimore, Md. 163pp.

Green, R. H. 1971. A multivariate approach to the Hutchinsonian niche: bivalve molluscs of central Canada. Ecology 52:543–556.

Hartley, P. H. T. 1953. An ecological study of the feeding habits of the English titmice. J. Animal Ecol. 22:261–288.

Hutchinson, G. E. 1958. Concluding remarks. Cold Spring Harbor Symp. Quart. Biol. 22:415–427.

Jackson, J. A. 1976. A comparison of some aspects of the breeding ecology of red-headed and red-bellied woodpeckers in Kansas. Condor 78:67–76.

Kilham, L. 1965. Differences in feeding behavior of male and female hairy woodpeckers. Wilson Bull. 77:134–145.

Kisiel, D. S. 1972. Foraging behavior of *Dendrocopus villosus* and *D. pubescens* in eastern New York State. Condor 74:15–24.

MacArthur, R. H. 1958. Population ecology of some warblers of northeastern coniferous forests. Ecology 39:599–617.

May, R. M., and R. H. MacArthur. 1972. Niche overlap as a function of environmental variability. Proc. Natl. Acad. Sci. 69:1109–1113.

Morse, D.H. 1972. Habitat utilization of the red-cockaded woodpecker during the winter. Auk 89:429–435.

Moulton, C. A. 1990. Effects of urbanization on foraging behavior of six coexisting woodpeckers. M.Sc. Thesis, Univ. of Maryland, College Park. 100pp.

Raphael, M. G. 1980. Utilization of standing dead trees by breeding birds at Sagehen Creek, California. Ph.D. Dissertation, Univ. of Calif., Berkeley. 195pp.

———, and M. White. 1984. Use of snags by cavity nesting birds in the Sierra Nevada. Wildl. Monogr. 86. The Wildlife Society, Washington, D.C. 66pp.

Reller, A. W. 1972. Aspects of behavioral ecology of red-headed and red-bellied woodpeckers. Am. Midl. Nat. 88:270–290.

Robbins, C. S., D.K. Dawson, and B.A. Dowell. 1989. Habitat area requirements of breeding forest birds of the middle Atlantic states. Wildl. Monogr. 103. The Wildlife Society, Washington, D.C. 34pp.

Schoener, T. W. 1974. Resource partitioning in ecological communities. Science 185:27–37.

Stallcup, P. L. 1968. Spatio-temporal relationships of nuthatches and woodpeckers in ponderosa pine forests of Colorado. Ecology 49:831–843.

Volterra, B. 1926. Vartazioni e fluttuazioni del numero d'individui in specie animali conviventi. Mem. R. accad. Lincei Ser. 6:1–36.

Weatherley, A. H. 1963. Notions of niche and competition among animals, with special reference to freshwater fish. Nature 197:14–17.

Weins, J. A. 1976. Review of "Competition and the structure of bird communities" by M. L. Cody. Auk 93:396–400.

Whitcomb, R. F., C. S. Robbins, J. F. Lynch, B. L. Whitcomb, M. K. Klimkiewicz, and D. Bystrak. 1981. Effects of forest fragmentation on avifauna of the eastern deciduous forest. Pages 125–206 *in* R.L. Burgess and D. M. Sharpe, eds. Forest island dynamics in man-dominated landscapes. Springer-Verlag, New York, N.Y.

Williams, J. B. 1975. Habitat utilization by four species of woodpeckers in a central Illinois woodland. Am. Midl. Nat. 93:353–367.

Willson, M. F. 1970. Foraging behavior of some winter birds of deciduous woods. Condor 72:169–174.

Zaret, T. M., and A. S. Rand. 1971. Competition in tropical stream fishes: support for the competitive exclusion principle. Ecology 52:336–342.

Correlations Between Birds and Vegetation in Cheyenne, Wyoming

ADAM R. SEARS AND STANLEY H. ANDERSON, *Wyoming Cooperative Fish and Wildlife Research Unit, University of Wyoming, Box 3166, University Station, Laramie, WY 82071*

INTRODUCTION

Cheyenne, Wyoming offers a diversity of wildlife habitat that is not found in the adjacent short grass prairie. This diversity of vegetation in the urban area may be important habitat for migrating and resident birds. In order for the Wyoming Game and Fish Department to suggest methods of attracting birds in this urban setting, it needs to gain knowledge about the vegetation and structural characteristics important to the birds. Some birds are generalists and can be found in an array of habitat types, whereas others are specialists and select specific habitat types. For example, DeGraaf (1986) found that black-capped chickadees (*Parus atricapillus*) were significantly correlated with coniferous tree crown volumes in the 1.5-3 m and 7.6–9.1 m height ranges.

Many cities displace native trees and shrubs as urban areas expand, thus lowering insectivorous bird species diversity (DeGraaf and Wentworth 1986). However, Cheyenne developed in the middle of a short grass prairie with little vegetation diversity. Development in similar habitats with little vegetation, such as deserts, shrublands, or steppes, has increased vegetation cover with artificially watered trees and shrubs, resulting in an increase in the numbers of insectivorous birds (Guthrie 1973, Emlen 1974).

Objectives

This study was designed to:

(1) Describe the vegetation characteristics of four age zones of a city.
(2) Compare bird species diversity and composition among the four zones.
(3) Determine bird species diversity for each species of tree.
(4) Determine which trees and shrubs were selected by birds.
(5) Determine relationships between certain species of birds and certain species of trees.

STUDY AREA AND METHODS

The study was conducted in Cheyenne, Wyoming, located at 41° 07′30″ longitude and 104° 47′30″ latitude. The city is surrounded by short grass prairie, which begins at the base of the east side of the Laramie Range. Cheyenne is a typical western city with the old commercial area concentrated in the center and residential areas growing concentrically outward. The population is just under 50,000 people.

Site Selection

The city was divided into four age zones:

Commercial Zone.—This area was in the center of the city and has been developed for more than 75 years. Newer outlying commercial developments were not included in order to maintain consistency in surveys and measurements. This zone was dominated by buildings and asphalt parking lots. The buildings varied in height and size but most were taller than the average home. There was little vegetation except for some isolated trees along the streets. About 20% of the area consisted of lawn. Human disturbance was high in this area from traffic and people.

Old Residential Zone.—This was a transition area from the commercial zone to the outlying newer residential areas. This zone consisted of residential neighborhoods more than 50 years old. It was located mostly on the northern side of the commercial area because there was a large railroad complex bordering the south side of the commercial area. Large mature cottonwood (*Populus* spp.), Siberian elm (*Ulmus pumila*), single-leaf ash (*Fraxinus anomala*) and Colorado spruce trees (*Picea pungens*) were dominant here. The cottonwoods were found mostly along the streets. There were many shrubs and a few younger trees that created a layering of the vegetation. Two-story houses were common and were located 6–8 m from the roadside.

Medium Age Residential Zone.—This area ranged from 25 to 50 years old. This zone, which was larger than the other three, completely surrounded the old residential and commercial areas. Some portions of this zone bordered the open prairie. There were fewer cottonwood trees lining the streets and many of the trees had not yet reached mature size. Spruce trees were more common in this area than in

Wildlife Conservation in Metropolitan Environments. NIUW Symp. Ser. 2, L.W. Adams and D.L. Leedy, eds. Published by Natl. Inst. for Urban Wildl., 10921 Trotting Ridge Way, Columbia, MD 21044, USA, 1991.

the old residential zone. House size was similar but the designs were more modern.

New Residential Zone.—This area consisted of developments less than 25 years old. Houses were similar to the medium age zone, however, the area was bordered by the open prairie. Very little vegetation was found in this zone. Most sites were dominated by lawns with a few young trees and shrubs, almost all less than 6.1 m tall.

Boundaries of these zones were subjectively selected using habitat characteristics that appeared to differ between each area. To determine the age of the residential areas, old engineering maps were used from the Wyoming Archives Museum and Historical Department. Eighty study sites were selected randomly throughout the city, 20 in each zone. A grid was overlain on a map of the city and an X, Y coordinate in 0.5-mm increments was selected randomly. The coordinate was placed on the grid, and the street that the point fell closest to was a candidate for selection as a site. We tried to select sites typical of the residential or commercial area. The residential sites did not contain any commercial buildings, only homes. The site boundaries were defined by an intersecting street at either end of one side of a block. Each site was restricted to either the north or west side of the street to minimize sun glare and maximize visibility of the birds.

Bird Surveys

Bird surveys were conducted in 1989 and 1990 for 2 hours beginning at sunrise. Eleven surveys were performed each year—two each summer, fall, and winter, and five surveys each spring. Bird surveys were conducted by walking a transect along the sidewalk starting at the east or south end of the site. Every 20 paces a bird count was performed for 2 minutes. Birds were identified and recorded that were seen or heard within 10 paces on either side of the transect, or as far back as the alley. The vegetation or structure, and its height, where the bird was seen also was recorded.

Habitat Analysis

Sketches were made to quantify the structural and vegetation characteristics of each bird count point in all 80 sites. Each sketch represented a 20-pace cross section of a transect with the survey point in the middle. The drawings were performed by starting at one edge of a section and working toward the other edge while sketching the trees, shrubs, houses, and other features. The heights of structures and vegetation were estimated with a clinometer and the widths were estimated by the number of paces the object covered along the cross section. Distances to the variables were estimated.

The sketches then were divided into three vertical strata: < 1.5 m, 1.5–6.1 m, and > 6.1 m. These divisions were the approximate heights to separate ground cover-low shrubs, large shrubs-small trees, and large trees. Light-lined graph paper was used for the sketches so precise measurements could be made in the field. To quantify percent cover for each variable, a grid was traced onto a transparent sheet of plastic so quick and precise estimates could be made for each height stratum. The transparency was placed over the sketch and the coverage was estimated from the number of squares filled in the grid.

Data Analysis

Statistical tests were performed using the program SOLO (BMDP Statistical Software Inc., 1988). Differences among zones and height strata were determined using the vegetation and structural variables as discriminating factors tested by one-way analysis of variance (ANOVA). If the ANOVA indicated a difference, Duncan's multiple-range test was used to determine differences in vegetation and structural variables between zone and height strata.

Bird species diversities for zones and tree species were calculated using the Shannon diversity index in an Ecological Measures program (Kotila 1984). To test for significant differences between two diversity indices, Hutcheson's *t*-test equations were used on the Shannon index (Zar 1984).

The Bonferroni method was used to calculate 95% simultaneous confidence intervals to determine a selectivity index for each species of tree used by birds (Byers et al. 1984). The values were both positive if a species of tree was used in greater proportion than its availability (i.e., the tree was selected for). One value was positive and one was negative if a species of tree was used in proportion to its availability. If both values were negative, a species of tree was used less than its proportion of availability (i.e., the tree was selected against).

Histograms were drawn to show percent use of height strata of certain species of trees by certain species of birds.

RESULTS

Habitat Descriptions

Commercial and new residential areas were very similar with regard to tree and shrub cover (Table 1). Old residential and medium-aged residential areas had similar tree and shrub cover in the first height stratum, but the old residential stratum had more cover in the second and third height strata (Table 1).

Bird Diversity and Area

There was a near linear relationship for the number of bird species among the four development zones, with the commercial area containing the fewest species and the old residential area the most (Table 2). The Shannon diversity indices (H') seemed to follow this same trend.

Bird Diversity and Tree Species

A Shannon diversity index was calculated for bird use of dominant species of trees in the city (Table 3). There were seven vegetation variables with a bird diversity index over 0.60. Cottonwood trees had the highest diversity index

Table 1. Percent cover for habitat variables in commercial and residential zones of different ages (1 = commercial, 2 = < 25 yrs., 3 = 25–50 yrs., 4 = > 50 yrs.) and height strata (1 = < 1.5 m, 2 = 1.5–6.1 m, 3 = > 6.1 m) in Cheyenne, Wyoming, 1989–1990. Numbers within a row showing the same letter are not significantly different (P > 0.05) based on Duncan's multiple range test.[a]

Variable	Zone (height strata combined)				Height strata for each zone											
					Stratum 1				Stratum 2				Stratum 3			
	1	2	3	4	1	2	3	4	1	2	3	4	1	2	3	4
Deciduous trees	4a	4a	17	25	3	7ab	9b	8a	8a	7a	33	41	1a	.1a	9	26
Coniferous trees	3a	2a	6	7	4a	4a	8b	7b	4a	2a	12	8	1ab	0a	2b	3
Deciduous shrubs	1a	2a	6	8	4a	5a	10	13	.01a	1a	2a	3	0a	0a	0a	0a
Coniferous shrubs	1a	2a	4b	3b	4a	5b	9a	7ab	1a	.2b	2a	2ab	0a	0a	.01a	.02a
Houses	29a	32	29a	29a	45a	60b	57bc	51ac	35ab	38b	30a	34ab	7	.07a	.04a	.7a
Lawn	21	78a	83a	81a												

[a]Percent cover was estimated for each variable independent of overlap so percentages may total less than or greater than 100% for each column. Columns under height strata for each zone total the values under zone.

Table 2. Bird species diversity in commercial and residential areas of Cheyenne, Wyoming, 1989–1990.

Area	Diversity index (H')	Evenness (J')	Number of Species	Number of Birds
Commercial	0.541[a]	0.640	7	316
New residential	0.662[a]	0.577	14	277
Medium-aged residential	0.749[a]	0.518	28	915
Old residential	0.854[a]	0.540	38	930
Combined areas	0.787	0.482	43	2438

[a]Significant at P < 0.05.

Table 3. Bird species diversity in dominant trees of Cheyenne, Wyoming, 1989–1990.

Tree	Diversity index (H')	Evenness (J')	Number of Species	Number of Birds
Cottonwood	1.041	0.727	27	173
Ash	0.842	0.780	12	62
Black locust	0.783	0.821	9	28
Siberian elm	0.770	0.672	14	120
Russian olive	0.721	0.927	6	12
Other coniferous	0.649	0.928	5	8
Maple	0.578	0.827	5	14
Aspen	0.570	0.732	6	28
Willow	0.555	0.921	4	7
Spruce	0.550	0.447	17	590
Box elder	0.519	0.614	7	27
Crab apple	0.385	0.546	6	81
Birch	0.338	0.483	5	20
Limber pine	0.299	0.497	4	29

Table 4. Selection for specific trees by birds in the combined commercial and residential areas (80 sites) and for each height stratum (80 sites) using the simultaneous confidence intervals in Cheyenne, Wyoming, 1989–1990.

Species	No. times used	Cover avail.	% used	% avail	Selectivity index
Spruce	591	6415	48.5	17.3	+0.312
Birch	20	771	1.6	2.1	−0.004[a]
Other dec. tree	22	812	1.8	2.2	−0.004[a]
Russian olive	12	456	1.0	1.2	−0.002[a]
Other conif. trees	8	352	1.0	1.0	−0.004
Limber pine	29	1233	2.4	3.3	−0.010
Crab	81	3122	6.6	8.4	−0.018
Maple	14	868	1.1	2.3	−0.012
Austrian pine	1	743	0.1	2.0	−0.019
Locust	30	1692	2.5	4.6	−0.021
Elder	27	1622	2.2	4.4	−0.021
Aspen	28	1756	2.3	4.7	−0.024
Ash	62	3354	5.1	9.0	−0.040
Elm	120	6664	9.8	18.0	−0.082
Cottonwood	174	7231	14.3	19.5	−0.052
Total	1219	37092	100.3	93.7	

[a]used in equal proportion to availability at the 95% confidence interval, + used in greater proportion to availability, − used in less proportion to availability.

(1.04) and an evenness value of 0.73. Spruce trees, the most frequently used tree, had a diversity index of 0.55 and an evenness value of 0.45. The number of sightings of birds per species of tree varied from seven sightings in willows to 590 sightings in spruce trees.

Vegetation Selection and Availability

Spruce was the only species of tree selected by birds, with 95% confidence intervals between 0.336 and 0.288 (Table 4). Cottonwood, Siberian elm, ash, locust, elder, crab apple, aspen, maple (*Acer spp.*), limber pine and Austrian pines (*Pinus nigra*) were selected against, and the others were used in proportion to their availability.

Mourning doves (*Zenaida macroura*) were seen in more kinds of trees, but cottonwood was the most frequently used

(Fig. 1A). These birds were seen primarily in the second and third height strata, with only 2.5% in the first stratum.

Blue Jays (*Cyanocitta cristata*) were seen in a variety of trees, including cottonwoods, elm, ash, locust, and spruce (Fig. 1B). They were always seen in the second and third height strata.

Yellow warblers (*Dendroica petechia*) also were seen in a variety of trees (Fig. 1C), with most use occurring in the second height stratum of aspen. For all trees combined, 80% were seen in the second height stratum.

Willow flycatchers (*Empidonax traillii*) were seen in only four kinds of trees, with more birds found in cottonwoods than in other trees (Fig. 1D). All height strata were used by the willow flycatcher, although some preference was shown for the third stratum.

Mountain chickadees (*Parus gambeli*), warbling vireos (*Vireo gilvus*), western kingbirds (*Tyrannus verticalis*), and dark-eyed juncos (*Junco hyemalis*) varied in use of tree species (Fig. 2). Chickadees were seen in spruce trees, with 82% observed in the second height stratum. Vireos were seen 90% of the time in the tops of cottonwoods and the rest of the time in the tops of elms. Kingbirds were seen in the tops

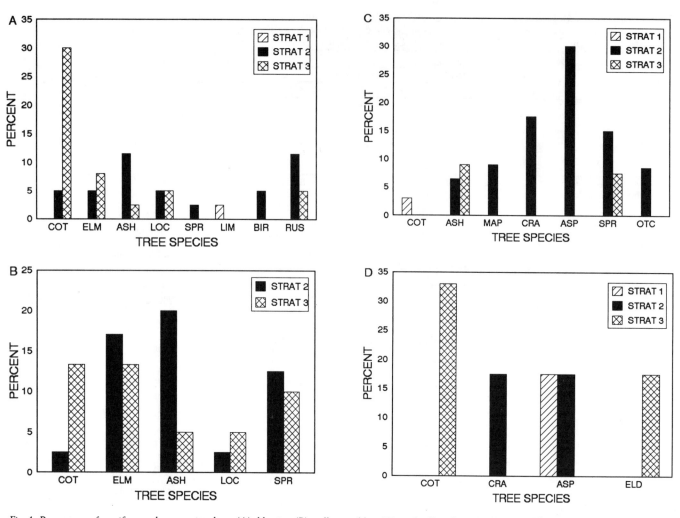

Fig. 1. Percent use of specific trees by mourning doves (A), blue jays (B), yellow warblers (C), and willow flycatchers (D) in Cheyenne, Wyoming, 1989–1990. Use was determined for three height strata of trees (Strat 1 = <1.5 m, Strat 2 = 1.5–6.1 m, Strat 3 = >6.1 m). COT = cottonwood, ASH = ash, MAP = maple, CRA = crab apple, ASP = aspen, SPR = spruce, OTC = other coniferous tree, ELD = box elder.

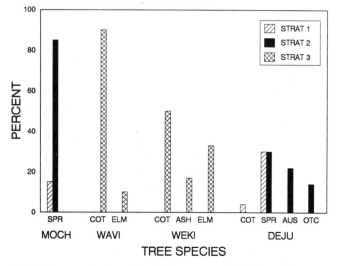

Fig. 2. Percent use of specific trees by mountain chickadees (MOCH), warbling vireos (WAVI), western kingbirds (WEKI), and dark-eyed juncos (DEJU) in Cheyenne, Wyoming, 1989–1990. Use was determined for three height strata of trees (Strat 1 = <1.5 m, Strat 2 = 1.5–6.1 m, Strat 3 = >6.1 m). ASH = ash, AUS = Austrian pine, COT = cottonwood, ELM = Siberian elm, SPR = Spruce.

of three kinds of deciduous trees. Cottonwoods were the most frequently used trees (50%), but ash and elms were used also. Juncos were seen only in the first and second height strata of cottonwood, spruce, Austrian pine, and other coniferous trees. Ninety-three percent of the sightings of dark-eyed juncos were in coniferous trees.

DISCUSSION

The commercial and new residential areas were not significantly different except for percent cover of lawn and houses, with the new residential area having more of both. The new residential area had a larger bird diversity than the commercial area (Table 2). Height Stratum 1 in the new residential area had greater percent cover of deciduous trees, coniferous shrubs, houses, and lawns. This may have contributed to the larger bird diversity found in the new residential area. Height Stratum 2 had more coniferous shrubs in the commercial area and more houses in the third height stratum (Table 1). These differences were small and may not have had a strong influence on the bird diversity. The commercial area also had more human disturbance with cars and concentrated numbers of people along the streets, which may have reduced the number and bird species found in this area, although this was not quantified. Large numbers of buildings have been found to reduce the number of birds and the diversity of bird species (Tilghman 1987). The commercial area had only seven species of birds, all of which were generalists that adapt well to human disturbance. The Shannon evenness value was higher for the commercial area than the new residential area. There was a larger number of house sparrows (*Passer domesticus*) and house finches (*Carpodacus mexicanas*) in proportion to the overall number of birds in the new residential area. Starlings (*Sturnus vulgaris*) and rock doves (*Columba livia*) made up a large proportion of the commercial bird population. The new residential zone contained specialists such as the western meadowlark (*Sturnella neglecta*) and the barn swallow (*Hirundo rustica*), which were seen only in sites bordering the prairie. Several of the less common birds were seen in small numbers in the new residential zone, which lowered the evenness value but not the diversity index.

There was more vegetation in the old and medium-aged residential areas than in the commercial and new residential areas. The old residential area had much more tree cover in the third height stratum than the medium-aged residential area. The Swainson's hawk (*Buteo swainsoni*) and sharp-shinned hawk (*Accipiter striatus*) were seen only in the tops of deciduous trees in the old residential area. Western kingbirds and warbling vireos were more abundant in the old residential area, and only found in the tops of the large deciduous trees. Because of the greater quantity of vegetation in the old residential zone, there was more habitat available. This area had a larger abundance and diversity of birds than the medium age zone because it had more cover. Evenness values were similar for the two areas.

Species diversity of birds followed the same trend as the proportion of species seen and percent cover of vegetation among the four development zones. The more vegetative cover and lawn space available, the higher the species diversity and the greater the abundance of birds.

Cottonwood, spruce, elm, and ash were the trees most frequently used by birds. Spruce was used by birds over three times as much as cottonwood, but it had only half the diversity of birds with a very low evenness value (Table 3). Spruce trees were frequented most by house sparrows and house finches for nesting and perch sites. This was particularly true in the medium-aged residential area where spruce trees were often the tallest trees. The low diversity value does not mean the tree is not important in the urban habitat, because some birds, like the mountain chickadee, red crossbill (*Loxia curvirostra*), and dark-eyed junco were seen most frequently in the spruce. These birds are found in local mountain habitats and probably are present in the urban habitat only because of the presence of the spruce.

Cottonwoods had a very high diversity index and a high evenness value. Cottonwoods are native to this region and are frequently found in riparian areas. Many native birds, such as hawks, western kingbirds, warbling vireos, and willow flycatchers were seen using this tree. Southwood (1961) found that non-native trees supported fewer species of insects than native trees. Insects are important food for the western kingbird, warbling vireo, and willow flycatcher, and may explain these birds' frequent presence in the cottonwood trees. Several birds considered gleaners, such as the downy woodpecker (*Picoides pubescens*), northern flicker (*Colaptes auratus*), red-breasted nuthatch (*Sitta canadensis*), and brown creeper (*Certhia americana*) also were seen using this tree.

Elm trees had a high diversity of bird species and a relatively high evenness value (Table 3). Because this tree grows as tall as the cottonwood, it is an important perching tree for birds like the warbling vireo, western kingbird, and Swainson's hawk. This tree is not native to Cheyenne and is not used as frequently by these birds as cottonwood. It was used often by starlings and common grackles (*Quiscalus quiscula*) during the fall for perching sites while flocking.

Ash trees were used by birds in a similar fashion to elms. The diversity index was fairly high for this tree as was the evenness value (Table 3). This tree does not grow as tall as the cottonwood and elm trees, but it is similar in morphology.

Blue jays, mourning doves, yellow warblers, and willow flycatchers were generalists in their use of urban habitat, although they were seen most frequently in areas with dense vegetation. Yellow warblers are found in shrubby riparian areas in their natural habitat, yet here they were seen in a variety of trees in the early spring and late fall during migration. They may have been using a variety of vegetation for resting sites and not selecting vegetation normally used in their native habitat.

There was a greater use of native trees by native birds. Except for spruce, trees not native to this area were not selected to a high degree by birds. It was the generalist species of birds, such as house sparrows, house finches, starlings, and American robins (*Turdus migratorius*) that used both exotic and native trees. Many of the specialist birds, such as mountain chickadees, warbling vireos, western kingbirds, and dark-eyed juncos, used native trees. Landscaping with native vegetation will attract native birds from surrounding habitats and maintain a high diversity of birds.

REFERENCES CITED

BMDP Statistical Software, Inc. 1988. Solo user's guide. Version 2 ed. BMDP Stat. Software., Inc., Los Angeles, Calif. 286pp.

Byers, C.R., R.K. Steinhorts, and P.R. Krausman. 1984. Classification of a technique for analysis of utilization-availability data. J. Wildl. Manage. 18:1050–1053.

DeGraaf, R.M. 1986. Urban bird habitat relationships: application to landscape design. Trans. North Am. Wildl. and Nat. Resour. Conf. 51:232–248.

———, and J.M. Wentworth. 1986. Avian guild structure and habitat associations in suburban bird communities. Urban Ecol. 9:399–412.

Emlen, J.T. 1974. An urban bird community in Tucson, Arizona: derivation, structure, regulation. Condor 76:184–197.

Guthrie, D.A. 1973. Suburban bird populations in southern California. Am. Midl. Nat. 92:461–466.

Kotila, P.M. 1984. Ecological measures. Computer software. Phoenix Software Associates LTD, Phoenix, Ariz.

Southwood, T.R.E. 1961. The number of species of insect associated with various trees. J. Anim. Ecol. 30:1–8.

Tilghman, N.G. 1987. Characteristics of urban woodlands affecting breeding bird diversity and abundance. Landscape and Urban Planning 14:481–495.

Zar, J.H. 1984. Biostatistical analysis. Second ed. Prentice-Hall, Inc., Englewood Cliffs, N.J. 718pp.

III.
Planning and Design

Chair: JON RODIEK, Professor, Texas A&M University, College Station

Cochair: HELENE L. KASSER, Environmental Planner, Greenhorne & O'Mara, Inc., Greenbelt, Maryland

Human Predation on Isolated Nature Reserves

KERRY J. DAWSON, *Department of Environmental Design, University of California, Davis, CA 95616*

INTRODUCTION

The problems of theft and other depreciative behavior on public lands has been repeatedly addressed in recreation literature (Miner 1988). Unfortunately, attempts to fully derive a theory of causation for social predation have not been as successful as theoretical attempts in biogeography (Samdahl et al. 1982). This situation has left voids for both fields in that there are factors of biogeography which significantly affect causation and there are factors of causation which can be very significant for biogeography.

Social predation can be the most important factor in nature reserve biogeography if use is intense and management is weak. If we heed the words of Brian Wilkes (1977) that everyone is a consumptive user of public lands, then it is only the type and degree of use that needs to be measured. The difficulty is that the current state of knowledge about the type and degree of use is inadequate for the theoretical underpinnings that social impacts on biogeography must have, if we are to fully address the management needs of nature reserves.

Predation on valued resources is much more intense than on other resources (Pittman 1989). Therefore, the intensity of management after the acquisition of a nature reserve with valued resources must match the intensity of aberrant behavior that is evident during its purchase (Sutter 1986). In field work at Fuchs Hammock Nature Reserve in Florida, there were 17 species of orchids identified throughout a 20-year survey period. Of those, six have been extirpated from the reserve due to human activity. The unavoidable conclusion is that the primary extinction factor within Fuchs Hammock has been human predation, not ecological factors.

FUCHS HAMMOCK

Land Use

In 1970, The Nature Conservancy arranged the purchase of a natural area in South Florida meant to conserve a representative sampling of the West Indian hammock communities still sprinkled across western Dade County near Everglades National Park. Known as Fuchs Hammock, the purchase area covered only 10.1 ha, making it a relatively small reserve (Fix 1969). As is the desirable practice in most Nature Conservancy purchases, a cooperative public agency responsible for future management existed and gradual transfer of the property to the Metropolitan Miami-Dade Parks and Recreation Department occurred. Landscape architects on the planning and design staff developed conservation and management plans to establish one of Dade County's first nature reserves, and administrators were satisfied that the cause of native landscape conservation had been served. Unfortunately, the fight for the conservation of Fuchs Hammock had only begun.

When the value of the property was first recognized in the late 1940's, hammocks were still common in private ownership in South Florida. Agriculture was well established on drained marl soils previously occupied by wetlands, but a large proportion of the pinelands and hammocks had been by-passed. That was ended by the post World War II housing boom that focused on the by-passed woodlands.

As with other hammocks associated with Florida's everglades, Fuchs Hammock is a mixed hardwood sub-tropical forest. A third of the reserve is disturbed scrubland from previous limestone mining operations; the remainder has an oak overstory to the south and west and a mixed pine overstory to the northeast. The canopy is a closed dome at roughly 20 m with shading at 75–90%. Hammocks are considered to be the climax community of South Florida for uplands without fire.

In the early 1900's, the pinelands and glades surrounding Fuchs Hammock covered several thousand hectares but orchard development on the north and south had reduced the contiguous area to 40.5 ha by 1950. A housing project on the east was well established by 1960 and to the west, gradual estate development steadily continued. The most recent addition is an estate further separating the main hammock from western segments (Fig. 1).

Predation Survey

From 1968 through 1988, Fuchs Hammock was studied for impacts on its most commercial resources: epiphytic

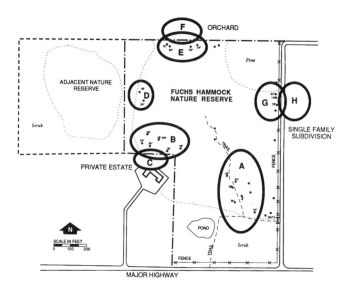

Fig. 1. Land use map and transect plot distributions (labeled A–H) at Fuchs Hammock, South Florida.

orchids, ferns, and bromeliads. Surrounding land use was monitored and sample plots established to determine the relationship between predation on these commercial resources and reserve size, boundaries, adjacent land use, and facility design (Fig. 1). Complete inventories of all vegetation were made early in the monitored period, with sample plots randomly selected on host branches that were 3.7 m long and a minimum 15.2 cm diameter. Host trees were randomly selected from clusters related to eight land use categories. Recordings of land use change, police records, facility changes, and impacts on sample plot populations occurred periodically throughout the monitoring period.

The intent of the survey was to determine the relationship between adjacent land use and the intensity of human predation on the epiphytic plants. Generally, after an initial increase in plants due to suspected stocking, a serious decline in indicator plants occurred as the reserve was publicized in the press during the acquisition years from 1968 to 1978 (Fig. 2). The trend ended in the late 1970's when the

reserve was fenced and police patrols became more frequent (Fig. 3).

Tree branches overhanging the estate boundary faced heavy predation during the acquisition years but, by 1988, had fully recovered from predation (Fig. 2). Stocking was suspected. Trees bordering an adjacent natural area fared very well during the survey period as did the trees adjacent to the estate. This was attributable to buffering and remoteness. Trees adjacent to neighboring agriculture had lessened impact as the edge thickened. The central trail showed the most improvement after the reserve was fenced, but was still a popular destination for poachers. Trees adjacent to a subdivision also improved greatly after fencing, but remained popular to poachers. Branches overhanging neighboring agricultural fields had a steady decline in numbers of epiphytes because of accessibility; the branches overhanging the subdivision had over 60% of the surveyed plants removed.

The purchase of Fuchs Hammock brought the area to the attention of the public for the first time. Human predation began to increase with establishment of the County Nature Reserve, subsequent opening of the area to guided tours, and featured articles in the print media. Theft of flora and fauna was both swift and relentless. Letters of complaint from The Nature Conservancy to the county were well received and ordinances, signages, and reduction of access ensued. Short of stationing a ranger on the site, the county gave increasing attention to the property. Unfortunately, problems of theft and vandalism have continued to increase. A follow-up letter from the Conservancy in 1982 reached receptive, but increasingly puzzled, administrators. Although education reaches most people, and ordinances and signs reach additional individuals, for the intolerant species of a small reserve to survive in the human occupied environment, buffers or proximity to other landscape reserves is vitally important.

Interruption of Ecological Process

In addition to the direct predation seen at Fuchs Hammock, increasing development can indirectly endanger even the largest reserves if supporting ecological processes of an area are interrupted. Such has been the case with the Everglades region of South Florida where the hydrologic cycle of the wetlands has been drastically altered by flood control

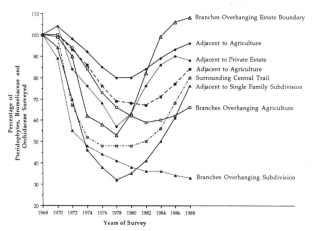

Fig. 2. Yearly percentage increase or decrease in indicator plants relative to each of eight land use categories, Fuchs Hammock, South Florida.

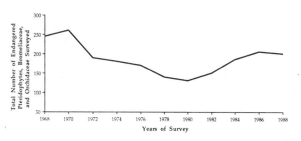

Fig. 3. Changes in total numbers of endangered orchids, ferns, and bromeliads in Fuchs Hammock, South Florida.

and water supply improvements. Although Big Cypress National Preserve has enlarged political boundaries of the Everglades to the northwest, the leveed impoundment of the landscape as a water conservation measure has, by altering water flow, had the most dramatic effect on the ecosystem.

The plight of nesting wading bird populations due to surface water flow alterations is a good example of problems that native fauna are having in the Everglades. A researcher with Everglades National Park has documented diminishing populations and traced the impacts to hydrologic interference (Kushlan 1979). Numbering between 2 and 5 million in 1870 (Robertson 1965), wading bird populations were reduced to 130,000 by 1975 (Kushlan and White 1977).

Sadly, native flora seems to be having an equally difficult time. Australian pines (*Casuarina equisetifolia* and *C. leidpolphloia*) and melaleuca (*M. quinquenervia*) are rapidly replacing South Florida's evolutionarily young and noncompetitive natives. As they envelop the drained wetlands between the east coast urban area and the park, the list of additional invading exotics relying on altered surface water flow also includes Brazilian pepper (*Schinus terebinthefolius*), Asian tamarind (*Tamarindus indica*), and the guava (*Psidium guajava*).

Examples of threats to the ecological integrity of reserves are numerous. Many directly affecting the quality of national parks were publicized by United States Congressional hearings on HR 5552, a bill introduced to authorize the Secretary of the Interior to control activities on adjacent lands that degrade park resources. The bill stems from a "State of the Parks" report (U.S. Natl. Park Serv. 1980), which found that 50% of park threats arise outside the system boundaries. The threats include altered flow and reduced quality of waters passing through parks, geothermal tapping of pools shared by park geysers, acid rain, waste dumping near parks, interference in cross-boundary wildlife migrations by land use as well as poaching, and pesticide and herbicide damage through atmospheric drift and the food chain.

Many of these issues are extremely complex and far exceed the authority of land use plans. However, land use planning is the realm of the landscape architect-environmental planner and efforts that we make to integrate reserves into the planning of neighboring property will certainly help solve some problems.

ISLAND BIOGEOGRAPHY AND THE ISOLATED NATURE RESERVE

The equilibrium theory of island biogeography as outlined by MacArthur and Wilson (1967) basically states that species richness is lower on small islands than on continents. Most of the basis for the theory has come from research studies on island ecology in the Atlantic and Pacific Oceans (Diamond 1975). Numbers and diversity of species are being examined in relation to the fundamental processes of community biogeography: dispersal, invasion-colonization, competition-predation, adaptation, and extinction. Variables being studied that affect these processes include: geographic isolation; habitat structure, productivity, and diversity; area; configuration; elevation; and climate (MacArthur 1972). However, Sullivan and Shaffer (1975) believed that area and distance (geographic isolation) are the two most important influences on island species numbers.

Distance is the factor most affecting colonization. Dispersal and subsequent invasion or reintroduction of species depends heavily on the difficulty of bridging distances between reserves. Together, immigration, exportation, and extinction rates determine species richness in a reserve at equilibrium and, because these rates are so dependent on sources of colonization, total isolation can be hazardous (Pickett and Thompson 1978). The only way to truly avoid the problem of species extinction in a reserve is to include enough habitat to ensure internal recolonization sources.

One of the most difficult concepts in individual species biogeography is the creation of community. Because of interrelationships among individuals that are crucial to survival, community formations become the focus of attention. Unfortunately, the difficulty in defining communities for study is that individual species intergrade with other species on a continuous basis. The chances of finding the same exact community at different locations are very small. The environmental variables of geology, hydrology, soils, and microclimate are enough to alter most of the processes.

It is recognized that the smallest of habitat islands can be valuable because large quantities of lower life forms can survive with minimal range requirements and small habitats offer the preservation of unique microhabitats. Small areas also can serve as "stepping stones" between larger reserves and small areas provide multiple open space and education benefits (Whitcomb et al. 1976). However, large reserves are favored by most researchers in biogeography because the maximum area requirements to avoid species extinction are more exclusive even though short-term minimum area requirements for an individual species may be well known. Basically, as Diamond (1976) pointed out, species most in need of refuge are doomed in a system of small, isolated islands.

The reason for attention to island biogeography research in the design and planning for nature reserves lies in recognition of isolation as increasing among continental reserves caused by land use encroachment and subsequent alienation from ecological systems. In the instance of oceanic islands, isolation is a given that is controlled by distance at sea. On continents, causes of isolation frequently are intensively occupied human environments that can be just as deadly to dispersal as sea distance, with problems such as barriers to movement (buildings, roads, fences, canals, etc.), lack of cover, and trophic barrenness. As reserves and nature parks become more island-like and less representative of larger areas, the attention to island biogeography should increase.

The point of the small reserve argument is that if we are forced by economics and/or resource availability to select only certain areas for reserve status, a series of small habitat reserves may be better than one large reserve if the large reserve is less diverse or more vulnerable. But, to include this point in the design of nature reserves, one cannot overlook depredation on small reserves as discussed earlier for Fuchs Hammock. The need is for a means to buffer the reserve area, thus allowing forest-interior species the range they require.

Zoning to Provide Buffers

Zoning and recreational use deployment within nature parks has been cited frequently in park master plans and in the literature (Forster 1973, Crossen 1979). Intensive recreation is recommended for development on the periphery of the park with the core or adjacent land protected from development (Fig. 4). This approach provides for buffering of species with little tolerance for human contact,

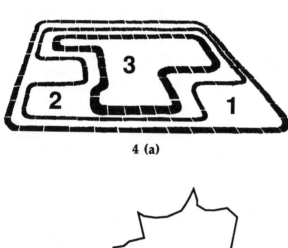

4 (a)

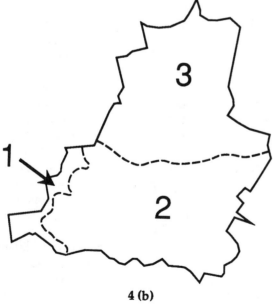

4 (b)

Fig. 4.   Schematic examples that limit intensive recreation to the periphery (Zone 1) of conservation reserves. Declining development and access are reduced in Zone 2, and Zone 3 is intended for maximum conservation. [4(a) was adapted from Forster (1973) and illustrates a park with extremities penetrating adjacent conservation areas; 4(b) was adapted from Crossen (1979).]

prevents loss of habitat to trampling, concentrates use for improved management, and allows the natural qualities of the site (for which the original park probably was created) to continue.

In the instance of nature reserve versus nature park, if the area is a closed access preserve, the issue of interior zoning is moot. The issue becomes exterior zoning and the relationship of the reserve to surrounding landscape. Although species other than man cannot identify with political boundaries, they are tenants of human civilization. As practiced in most regions of the United States, conservation zoning of land use is the most readily available means to reduce isolation short of fee title land ownership.

Connective Corridors

Landscape corridors are areas that either presently connect or could be restored to connect reserves in danger of problematic isolation. At present, large corridors still exist in some areas and several studies have identified statewide systems (Lewis 1964, Dawson 1976). Corridor areas generally tend toward linear patterns along floodplains and ridges. Interpreted broadly, floodplain refers to all wetlands from rivers to lakes and coastal wetlands, whereas ridge refers principally to areas of steep slope and poor soils. Basically, these are the areas by-passed by human occupation due to hazards or low productivity.

In most regions of the world, large corridors still exist, but the needs of a resource-starved society are taking their toll. Still, corridors often are larger than the existing reserves they connect and compared to the agricultural and urbanized landscape they pass through, few would question their value. To quote Sullivan and Shaffer (1976, p. 16):

> "A corridor would permit greater interchange between taxa for which the corridor is functional—large mammals for example. . . Being within the interactive field of two planned reserves, the corridor, of whatever surface area, will function as a preserve to a greater extent than an equivalent quantity of land outside the interactive field."

The questions of diminishing value for corridors arise solely around size and configuration. A corridor with a width dimension less than the two connected reserves would be less desirable for forest-interior species. Ecologically disjunct corridors such as hedgerows or cross-country forest fragments (areas that may be linear because of sociopolitical reasons) suffer from the disadvantage of separation from basic landscape patterns occupied by natural corridors. Even these forest fragment corridors, however, have some value as "stepping stones" for species with high dispersal potential, like most vegetative species, or for those with the ability to traverse barriers, such as most avian species (MacClintock et al. 1977).

Clustering to Increase Reserve Concentrations

Simberloff and Abele (1976) and Simberloff (1982) argued that size and configuration of nature reserves are secondary to habitat considerations. These authors believed that a single reserve would have to be very large and/or extraordinarily located to contain the same habitat diversity as could be found in smaller, clustered reserves. Further, they stated that several small scattered reserves (with separate populations) would be less vulnerable to inbreeding depression, collective destruction by fire, and the repeated introduction of disease. Several reserves would contain more edge (a traditional area of species diversity) and could allow the survival of mutually exclusive competitors if isolation were continued and habitat diversity maintained.

A successful approach may be the clustering of reserves to attain a high percentage of surface area in reserve status. This can encourage compatible land use through example and preserve a rural flavor, which may inhibit urbanization. If the distance between reserve segments is not too great and the level of disturbance of the separating landscape not severe, a series of small reserves could avoid predation simply by volume. Such an area is the Ogeechee Wildlife Management Area in the central Piedmont of Georgia (Fig. 5). There are 10 segments of the management area ranging in size from 16.2 ha to 5,184 ha. The management area has the most edge per volume of any wildlife management area in the southeastern United States and has determined surrounding land use through the pervasive quality of the boundary configuration. Through the intertwining effect of the segments, the surrounding landscape has become heavily wooded and acts to connect some segments and to enlarge

others while still allowing some separation of segments if fire, disease, or competitors become problems. Human activity in the area largely is recreational and the rural atmosphere is sought and encouraged rather than altered.

There is a simple explanation for the origins of the Ogeechee Wildlife Management Area boundaries. The eastern Piedmont of Georgia was historically one of the first areas settled and land ownership tracts have become small and choppy. With increasing acquisition costs and demands on the landscape, diminishing tract size may well be the dominant future trend for rural areas.

CONCLUSION

Size, configuration, and habitat conditions are recognized generally as the primary design determinants of landscape reserves. Considering the pressure that human society places on small isolated reserves, it seems imperative that reserves be large enough to contain representative habitat and internal sources of colonization; be buffered by land use zoning, connected by landscape corridors; or clustered in an area where a high percentage of the surrounding land is zoned for conservation and can act as a medium of exchange between reserves.

Small, isolated reserves with separate populations may be necessary because of economics or to avoid inbreeding, wildfire, and disease. If so, such areas must still be buffered and protected in some way. The most appropriate means is the police power of local government to zone land surrounding the reserve for conservation. Zoning for levels of activity, from management for renewable natural resources to light agriculture, has to be considered on a case by case basis. However, tough restrictions on permanent intensive human occupation of land surrounding reserves have to be enforced. Some people have argued that humans should be viewed as an integral part of nature; therefore, the recreational use of, and close proximity to, nature reserves are not problems. This is an interesting philosophy and the study of humans as animal life in nature is surely a needed area of research. But, we have to realize that vandalism (especially against species not well represented in the justice system), predation, and development are increasing steadily and, for the time being, the more land buffering human activity from nature reserves, the better for both in the long run. Because most reserve boundaries are determined administratively rather than ecologically, modeling of perimeter social influences must become as important as modeling perimeter ecological influences (Schonewald-Cox 1988).

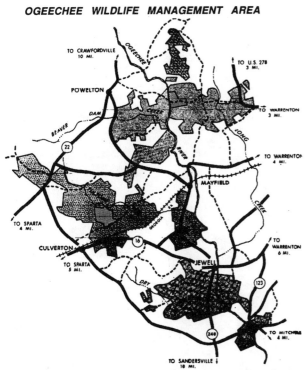

OGEECHEE WILDLIFE MANAGEMENT AREA

Fig. 5. The concept of clustering small reserves to avoid total isolation of the separate tracts is illustrated in the central Piedmont of Georgia. Some tracts connect small watersheds to the Ogeechee River floodplain, while others enclose diverse upland habitat.

REFERENCES CITED

Crossen, T. I. 1979. A new concept in park design and management. Biol. Conserv. 15:105–126.

Dawson, K. J. 1976. Environmental corridor study. Georgia Dep.

of Nat. Resour., Office of Planning and Research, Atlanta. 370 pp.

Diamond, J. M. 1975. The island dilemma: lessons of modern biogeographic studies for the design of natural reserves. Biol. Conserv. 7:129–146.

———. 1976. Island biogeography and conservation: strategy and limitations—a series of position papers. Science, Vol. 193.

Fix, J. 1969. Unique hammock preserved. Fla. Wildl. 11:20–21.

Forster, R. R. 1973. Planning for man and nature in national parks: reconciling perpetuation and use. Int. Union for Conserv. of Nat. and Nat. Resour., New Series Publication #26, Morges, Switzerland. 85 pp.

Kushlan, J. A. 1979. Design and management of continental wildlife reserves: lessons from the Everglades. Biol. Conserv. 15:281–290.

———, and D. A. White. 1977. Nesting wading bird populations in southern Florida. Fla. Sci. 40:65–72.

Lewis, P. H., Jr. 1964. Quality corridors for Wisconsin. Landscape Architecture Magazine 54:100–107.

MacArthur, R. H. 1972. Geographical ecology: patterns in the distribution of species. Harper & Row Publishers, New York, N.Y. 269 pp.

———, and E. O. Wilson. 1967. The theory of island biogeography. Princeton Univ. Press, Princeton, N.J. 203 pp.

MacClintock, L., R. F. Whitcomb, and B. L. Whitcomb. 1977. Evidence for the value of corridors and minimization of isolation in preservation of biotic diversity. Am. Birds 31:6–16.

Miner, C. 1988. Understanding vandalism helps prevent it. For. Res. West, USDA 11:7–10.

Pickett, S. T. A., and J. N. Thompson. 1978. Patch dynamics and the design of nature reserves. Biol. Conserv. 13:27–37.

Pittman, C. 1989. Foiling raiders of lost orchids. Santa Rosa Press Democrat, pp. D2, July 22.

Robertson, W. B., Jr. 1965. Inside the Everglades. Audubon 67:274–279.

Samdahl, D., H. Christensen, and R. Clark. 1982. Prevention and control of depreciative behavior in recreation areas: managerial concerns and research needs. Pages 52–54 *in* Forest and river recreation. Misc. Publ. 18–1982. Univ. of Minnesota Agric. Exp. Sta., St. Paul.

Schonewald-Cox, C. 1988. Boundaries in the protection of nature reserves. BioScience 38:470–486.

Simberloff, D. S. 1982. Big advantages of small refuges. Nat. Hist. 91:6–15.

———, and L. G. Abele. 1976. Island biogeography and conservation: strategy and limitations—a series of position papers. Science, Vol. 193.

Sullivan, A. L., and M. L. Shaffer. 1975. Biogeography of the megazoo: biogeographic studies suggest organizing principles for a future system of wild lands. Science 189:13–17.

Sutter, R. D. 1986. Monitoring rare plant species and natural areas: ensuring the protection of our investment. Nat. Areas J. 6:3–5.

U. S. National Park Service. 1980. State of national parks: a report to Congress. Natl. Park Serv. Off. of Sci. and Tech., U. S. Dep. of the Inter., Washington, D.C. 57 pp.

Whitcomb, R. F., J. F. Lynch, P. A. Opler, and S. R. Chandler. 1976. Island biogeography and conservation: strategy and limitations—a series of position papers. Science, Vol. 193.

Wilkes, B. 1977. The myth of the non-consumptive user. The Can. Field-Nat. 91:343–349.

The Environmental Resource Overlay Zone—An Approach to Protecting Riparian Habitat in Tucson, Arizona

GRACE L. EVANS, *City of Tucson Planning Department, P. O. Box 27210, Tucson, AZ 85726*

INTRODUCTION

The City of Tucson, situated in the eastern third of Pima County's 23,932 km², has been losing a valuable resource as development occurs on the outer fringes of its 40l-km² corporate limits. That resource is the riparian vegetation found along the network of desert washes which meander into the Tucson basin from the nearby foothills of the Tucson, Rincon, and Catalina Mountains.

Riparian vegetation provides valuable habitat for a wide variety of native wildlife species (Murphy 1988), including javelina, coyotes, bobcats, gray foxes, vermilion flycatchers, Gambel's quail, northern cardinals, roadrunners, and many other birds and animals that have called the Sonoran desert home for many more years than its human inhabitants.

Although Tucson is fortunate to have both topographic variety as well as substantial biological diversity of species, it has been estimated that the City already has lost 90% of its riparian vegetation (Shaw et al. 1986). This loss occurs largely through grading, bank protection, and channelization of washes.

STATEMENT OF PROBLEM

Of particular concern is the impact that habitat loss has on the nearby Saguaro National Monument. Several experts have discussed the disappearance of native species from national parks and forests (Quammen 1988). Saguaro National Monument includes 25,293 ha in the Rincon Mountains to the east of the City and 8,560 ha located in the Tucson Mountains west of the City limits. The natural washes that emanate from the Monument, as well as those in proximity to the Monument, have served to provide food, shelter, and nesting habitat, and migratory networks for wildlife between the east and west Monument units and the Coronado National Forest, north of the City in the Catalina Mountains.

Private land in unincorporated Pima County that is adjacent to Saguaro National Monument has been under special development guidelines for the past 30 years. References were made to a "low density buffer" or "one-mile buffer" around Saguaro National Monument East in the 1959 Pima County *Rincon Area Plan*. The 1979 *Tucson Mountain Plan* and the more recent update of that plan also contain a "buffer" area designation around Saguaro Monument West. This buffer area may be related to what the curator of Birds and Animals at the Arizona Sonora Desert Museum refers to as the "suburban ecotone" (Siminski 1989).

Although the City limits do not touch the boundaries of either unit of the Monument, Tucson has recognized the need to protect this internationally-known plant and wildlife preserve from the impacts of urbanization.

In addition to the impact of human activities (noise, air pollution, and domestic pets), there is another concern for wildlife managers. This is the loss of biological diversity that may occur where natural preserves are physically cut off from one another; one result is loss of migration routes necessary for gene pool interaction (Murphy 1988, Quammen 1988).

Finally, there is the problem of wildlife straying from the boundaries of the Monument or preserve in times of drought. In the case of the Tucson basin, many animals will forage in the desert washes that emanate from the nearby mountain ranges and continue beyond park boundaries. Clearly at times like these, there will be conflicts with human residents of these areas (Stone 1989).

REGULATORY APPROACHES TO HABITAT CONSERVATION

Questions often are raised about the legality of regulations that go beyond the immediate public purpose of health and safety. However, there is public purpose behind regulations that protect riparian habitat, whether wetlands or ephemeral streams, so long as there is a balance between the public interest and a landowner's ability to make reasonable use of property (Thurow et al. 1975).

Wildlife Conservation in Metropolitan Environments. NIUW Symp. Ser. 2, L.W. Adams and D.L. Leedy, eds. Published by Natl. Inst. for Urban Wildl., 10921 Trotting Ridge Way, Columbia, MD 21044, USA, 1991.

Pima County

In response to these issues, which focused largely on Saguaro National Monument, Pima County planning staff drafted land use regulations in 1987 designed to minimize development impacts adjacent to public lands. To many citizens, a buffer ordinance simply meant large lot, low density development near the Monument. However, the County regulations went beyond that, incorporating a number of design controls for new development within a 1.6-km radius of the Monument or other public preserve, as well as mandatory preservation of a certain amount of designated critical riparian habitat. This approach is considered to be far more effective than density limitations.

The areas of critical riparian habitat were based on the work carried out by Dr. William Shaw and his colleagues of the University of Arizona. This work identified various types of plant communities, including the mesquite (*Prosopis* sp.) bosques, which frequently include the blue paloverde (*Cercidium floridum*), catclaw acacia (*Acacia greggii*), wolfberry (*Lycium* sp.), and brittlebush (*Encelia farinosa*) association, among other plant types (Shaw et al. 1986). Although these washes are dry most of the year, they are exceptionally diverse in terms of plant communities and are therefore able to sustain a wide variety of wildlife.

The regulations drafted in Pima County were known as the buffer ordinance (or unhappily by its acronym, "BOZO"). The regulations were drafted with the help of a citizens' committee made up of developers, environmentalists, and wildlife experts.

The final ordinance adopted by the Pima County Board of Supervisors applies to projects that are: (1) located within 1.6 km of a public preserve, (2) greater than 32 ha in land

area, and (3) being rezoned or developed under the County specific plan ordinance. The final ordinance pleased some small landowners, but few in the Tucson environmental community (Stone 1989).

City of Tucson

After the Pima County ordinance was adopted in 1988, the Mayor of the City of Tucson urged preparation of a City "buffer" ordinance as soon as possible. The only guidelines given were that the regulations would be resource based, have some positive effect on the National Monument, and be tougher than the County regulations.

Charged with preparation of this ordinance, City of Tucson Planning staff held a number of discussions with Dr. Shaw, Mr. William Paleck, Superintendent of Saguaro National Monument, and other professionals in wildlife and resource conservation. As a result of these discussions, it was determined that the "resource" to be preserved was the natural vegetation that provided wildlife habitat along the washes originating within, or in proximity to, Saguaro National Monument (east and west units) and Tucson Mountain Park.

CITY ORDINANCE

Study Area

Many of the important washes that maintain vegetative cover and provide habitat for native wildlife had been designated in Dr. Shaw's work as critical riparian habitat (Fig. 1). The need to maintain the natural vegetation in place was understood because it had been documented that revegetation does not compensate for the loss of the original

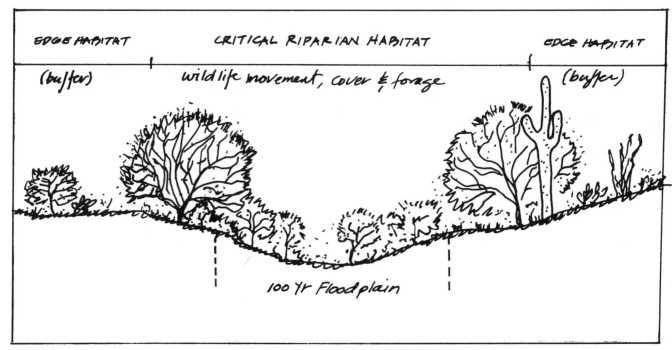

Fig. 1.   Critical habitat resource corridor concept to protect riparian habitat in and near Tucson, Arizona.

structural complexity and spatial diversity of plant life (Camp Dresser & McKee and Lloyd 1987).

Fourteen washes (eight on the west side of the City and six on the east) were finally selected by Planning staff for designation under the proposed City ordinance. These washes were picked for their relatively undisturbed character (ample natural vegetation), length, connection or close proximity to a major park or natural area, and their relationship with either the east or western units of Saguaro National Monument (Fig. 2). Regional watercourses that had been channelized or developed with major bikeways or equestrian trails were not included (except for one segment of the west branch of the Santa Cruz River), due to their general lack of vegetation.

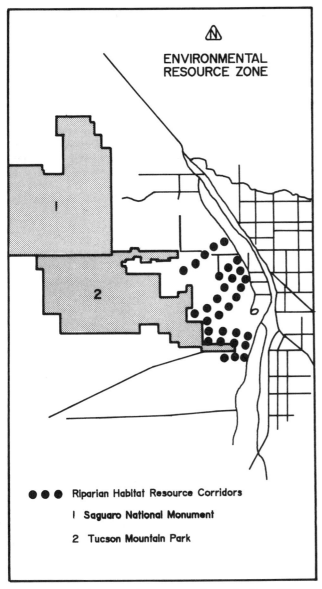

Fig. 2. Westside locations of resource corridors in the City of Tucson, Arizona, related to major public preserves.

Mapping Technique

The washes were evaluated using 1990 aerial photographs at a scale of 1:4800. Over the aerial photograph, a transparency was mounted at the same scale that showed all parcels of land in proximity to the designated washes. The transparency was used to determine both the specific land area affected by the proposed ordinance and which property owners would require notification of the required public hearings.

The vegetation, or riparian habitat, appeared as a darker area adjacent to the channel on the aerial photos. The wash and its area of habitat on both sides of the bank were defined as the resource corridor for purposes of the ordinance. Corridors were of variable width, ranging from 46 m to 213 m, with an average of 76 m. In terms of land use, many of the corridors had existing adjacent development that was generally residential at suburban densities. There was considerable vacant land adjacent to these washes as well.

The aerial photography technique used for this project has been employed successfully in Tucson for several other wildlife-related projects, including the work of Dr. Shaw and Camp Dresser & McKee.

Ordinance Objectives

The ordinance drafted for the City of Tucson was geared toward allowing development to occur that was compatible with the presence of wildlife. This would be accomplished by restricting development so that the area of habitat adjacent to the wash was left alone. Revegetation would be required in those instances where certain types of encroachment were allowed.

The approach to the ordinance was to work with the resource so that wildlife would not be driven away as development occurred in more sensitive areas. In keeping with that objective, the regulations would apply to requests for all types of construction permit applications, rather than being restricted to rezoning requests and new subdivisions as is the case with the Pima County ordinance.

After public discussion and hearings, the final ordinance adopted by the Mayor and Council included two items not originally presented in the staff draft. The first was the application of the regulations to all land, regardless of size. The staff proposal was to apply the regulations to parcels > 2 ha. However, the Mayor and Council felt that to not apply the regulations to all property was to "checkerboard" the resource and diminish its value.

The second change was to provide the landowner with an option so that it was not mandatory to conduct a study of the riparian resource on site. The option was for the owner to stay outside the 100-year floodplain (no bank protection) with any development. The Mayor and Council concluded that the majority of the habitat was in fact located within the 100-year floodplain and to simply leave the wash alone would substantially achieve the ordinance objectives.

Results and Outcomes

The ordinance has been in place since 1 August 1990; no permits that would trigger Environmental Resource Zone (ERZ) provisions have been requested to date. However, there was considerable discussion during the public hearings over the issue of protecting "urban" washes. The Planning Department felt strongly that the integrity of this particular ordinance depended on the fact that the 14 washes and their adjacent vegetative cover truly represented a resource for wildlife.

The Planning Department was aware that, in the more densely developed area of the City, wildlife was less of an issue than was the public dislike for bank protection and channelization (with the resultant loss of vegetation). It was after agreement by staff to work on another ordinance to protect urban washes from channelization that the community's environmental groups gave reluctant support to the ERZ.

Because of the Mayor and Council's commitment to the objectives of this ordinance, the regulations apply to all City projects as well as to private projects. As a result of the adoption of this ordinance, the Tucson water utility will drill no more wells within 1.6 km of the designated washes of the ERZ.

The Planning Department considers the application of these regulations to City activities a major milestone because much of the destruction of riparian vegetation and habitat can be traced to actions of local government.

In summary, it should be noted that people prefer to live in communities in which wildlife is integrated. The effect of urbanization on wildlife makes it even more important to plan for natural areas so that the presence of wildlife can be maintained (Leedy et al. 1978).

REFERENCES CITED

Camp Dresser & McKee, Inc., and W.B. Lloyd. 1987. Houghton East basin management plan for the City of Tucson Department of Transportation. Tucson, Ariz. 179pp.

Leedy, D.L., R.M. Maestro, and T.M. Franklin. 1978. Planning for wildlife in cities and suburbs. Rep. No. FWS/OBS-77/66, U.S. Fish and Wildl. Serv., Washington, D.C. 64pp.

Murphy, D.D. 1988. Challenges to biological diversity in urban areas. Pages 71–76 in E.O. Wilson, ed. Biodiversity. Natl. Acad. Press, Washington, D.C.

Quammen, D. 1988. The Newmark warning: why our national parks are resembling desert isles. Outside Magazine 13:31–36.

Shaw, W.W., J.M. Burns, and K. Stenberg. 1986. Wildlife habitats in Tucson: a strategy for conservation. School of Renewable Nat. Resour., Univ. of Arizona, Tucson. 17pp.

Siminski, P. 1989. Wildlife in the suburban ecotone. Sonorensis (Tucson, Ariz.) 9:3–6.

Stone, R.D. 1989. National parks and adjacent lands. Conserv. Found. Letter No. 3, The Conserv. Found., Washington, D.C.

Thurow, C., W. Toner, and D. Erley. 1975. Performance controls for sensitive lands. Planning Advisory Serv. Rep. Nos. 307 and 308, U. S. Environ. Prot. Agency, Washington, D.C. 156pp.

Hypothetical Mammalian Habitat Potential in Syracuse, New York

EDMUND N. HILLIARD, *Division of Landscape Architecture, University of Oklahoma, 830 Van Vleet Oval, Norman, OK 73019*

INTRODUCTION

The "imbalance and disruption," or entropy, of our urban ecosystems has long been a fact. One way to redress the balance and stabilize the system may be to encourage a more natural environment—one that contains communities of plants and animals valued purely for their aesthetic and psychological value. For if man can educate himself in his day-to-day life to the ways of nature, then he may feel more a part of the world he lives in.

The presence of wildlife and the opportunity to observe it depend on the existence of suitable habitats. This discussion concentrates on mammals because their habitat at present is limited, and accessibility to open space almost impossible as the automobile replaces natural predators in the city.

There are some 52 species of mammals in Onondaga County, New York (Alexander 1969). Of these, it is estimated that approximately 30 species might be expected to enter the city and the majority could become permanent residents. Among the permanent residents are "nuisance" species, such as the Norway rat (*Rattus norvegicus*) and house mouse (*Mus musculus*). These mammals are introduced species and depend on man's waste material and poor design for their habitat. It is hoped that by creating a variety of habitats in a more balanced system and by careful disposal of waste, these nuisance species can be designed out of the central urban areas. Domestic pets also can sometimes be a nuisance. If native wildlife is to be observed, existing laws must be more efficiently enforced. Educational programs must be initiated so that the general public is prepared to chain the dog, bell the cat, and build a fence. At present, wildlife is at the mercy of our own top carnivore pets.

The purpose of this paper is to assist in the reestablishment of "natural" areas within the City of Syracuse by serving as a guide to estimating the potential mammal populations, their habitats, and associated plant species that would support them. This work has been prepared to assist in the planning and design of urban public land. The paper will not attempt to indicate locations for specific habitats, as these can be created in the future. It will look at the overall potential for mammalian habitats.

STUDY AREA

Syracuse represents a unique opportunity for the future development of areas for urban wildlife. It has a relatively small human population for the amount of available open space within its boundaries. Twenty percent of the city's area (1320 ha) is open, undeveloped, and represents a resource for the future. This establishes a situation where high density human populations are adjacent to large tracts of potentially "natural" land with good accessibility for people and wildlife. The city's habitat potential is therefore great and varied.

PLANNING FOR URBAN WILDLIFE

Leedy et al. (1978) stated (p. 13), "Planners, landscape architects, biologists, and ecologists need to work together to promote environmental conditions close at home that are desirable for people and wildlife alike." Urban wildlife management is primarily *habitat management,* just as it is in wild areas away from the city. There should be as much interest in what species *might* appear as there is in species already observed. It may be desirable to discourage some species present in abundance. Species not adapted to residing with man are more likely to limit their home ranges to those habitats created for them, provided situations of stress or overpopulation can be managed.

Wildlife must have food, water, cover, and habitat space. The food and cover can be provided by careful use of vegetation plantings, especially for those omnivorous and herbivorous "desirable" species that we may wish to promote. Each species has preferred food and staple food and plants used primarily as cover (Fig. 1). Each species also has a specific home range or habitat space requirement. Current information can act as a guide to what specific species under normal conditions one would expect to find on tracts of land of a particular size.

Access to water is often a limiting factor for many species. Unfortunately, our society still promotes the channelizing, culverting, and filling in of water courses and

COMMON NAME	GENERA	Oposssum	Eastern Cottontail	Woodchuck	Chipmunk-Eastern	Squirrel - Gray	Red	Flying	Beaver	Mouse (spp.)	Vole (spp.)	Muskrat	Porcupine	Raccoon	Skunk - Striped	Deer - Whitetail	Plants Used as Cover
Maple	Acer spp.		X		X	X	X	X		O	O			X	O		X	
Chokeberry	Aronia spp.		O								O					O	●
Barberry	Berberis spp.		O													X	●
Birch	Betula spp.		O					O						O		O	
Bittersweet	Celastrus spp.		X			X	O	O								O	●
Hackberry	Celtis spp.	O					O	O						O	O		
Dogwood	Cornus spp.	O	X	O	O	O	O			O	O			O	O	X	●
Hawthorn	Crataegus spp.		O							O	O			O	O	X	●
Ash	Fraxinus spp.						X	O					O			O	
Witch-Hazel	Hamamelis spp.		O		X	O	O	O								X	
Honeysuckle	Lonicera spp.		O	O							O					X	●
Crabapple	Malus spp.	O	X		X	O	O			O			O	O	O	X	●
Mulberry	Morus spp.	O	O		O									O			●
Tupelo	Nyssa spp.	O												O		O	
Spruce	Picea spp.		O		O	O							O		O		●
Creeper	Parthenocissus spp.		O												O		●
Poplar	Populus spp.		O				X						O		O		
Oak	Quercus spp.	O	O		X	X	X	X	O	O			O	X		X	
Buckthorn	Rhamnus spp.		O											O			●
Sumac	Rhus spp.		X		O	O	O	O								X	
Currant	Ribes spp.		O	O	O	O					O			O	O		●
Rose	Rosa spp.	O	O	O	O	O	O	O	O		O			O	X		●
Raspberry	Rubus spp.	O	X		O	X	O							O	X		●
Elderberry	Sambucus spp.	O	O	O	O		O							O	O	X	●
Mountain-Ash	Sorbus spp.		O													X	
Snow/Coralberry	Symphoricarpos spp.		O													O	●
Yew	Taxus spp.		O			O	O	O								X	●
Linden	Tilia spp.				X						O					O	
Arborvitae	Thuja spp.					O		O					O			X	●
Hemlock	Tsuga spp.		O			O		O		O	O		O			X	●
Elm	Ulmus spp.		O			O	O			O		O				O	
Blueberry	Vaccinium spp.	O	X		O	O	O			O				O	O	X	●
Viburnum	Viburnum spp.		X	O	O	O	O	O							O	X	●
Grape	Vitis spp.	O	O		O									O	O	O	●

Fig. 1.   Simple matrix of some common mammals and associated plants that provide food and cover. O = present in diet, X = greater than 10% of diet. Adapted from Martin et al. (1951), Myers (1965), Thomas et al. (1972), Gill and Healy (1974), and Dawson and Decker (1978).

wetland areas. Wherever possible, this trend should be reversed—open up water, stop it, pond it, and use it for contemplation, recreation, and the creation of habitats. The large open areas in today's cities have room for more use of water and those areas could easily support the wildlife that open water will promote. Perhaps the regulations for wetlands and flood control will help accomplish the necessary change.

Accessibility of wildlife to urban green spaces is another problem. At present only those open areas lying directly on the city boundary provide access to wildlife from wild areas and these are really not "urban." Those "green corridors" that do penetrate the city are functional geographic units following water courses, railway lines and highways, and they are not ideal in their present form as wildlife corridors.

These areas must be considered as part of the whole, for the lack of connective habitat will certainly limit wildlife. Experiments with culverts, land bridges over roads, and planted strips should be promoted to discover the extent to which wildlife will move through and inhabit the city.

The applied ecology of urban wildlife management involves a collaboration of expertise. At present, there is much we do not understand about wildlife use of urban systems. However, there is sufficient information available to promote the revegetation of our urban "green spaces," not just for aesthetic or recreational reasons, but for the deliberate purpose of promoting urban wildlife. What may be unsuitable habitat at present could well be adapted to accommodate the "preferred" species by careful design and planning.

The Mammalian Resource

This section is based on research of others trained and experienced in zoology rather than on my own professional experience.

A starting place for deciding what mammals might be observed in the City of Syracuse are the publications *Vertebrates of Onondaga County, New York* (Alexander 1969) and the *Preliminary Annotated List of the Wild Terrestrial Mammals of New York State* (New York State Department of Public Service, Office of Environmental Planning, unpubl. draft rep.). Both of these works list many more mammals than would be likely to venture over the city boundary. However, by process of elimination, using regional habitats and range data, a preliminary list has been prepared (Table 1). The mammals are arranged as they appear in Dr. Alexander's paper. Also listed for each species is the home range, habits, diet, and a description of habitat preference (Burt and Grossenheider 1976).

The home range is the area where most time is spent by the animal. It must contain food, water, and cover, and is literally the habitat space requirement for that species provided all necessities are readily available.

The habits listed in Table 1 are a summary of physiological patterns observed for the various species. They are expected behavior and must be subject to cautious interpretation. The mere observation of the species listed is a particularly challenging problem. Not only are most of the more "significant" species nocturnal but they are also shy. There would appear to be an inverse relationship between frequency of observation and the desire to see the animal. Thus, the more common species are frequently less exciting. In some cases, just the observation of habitat or "home" of the species may be of sufficient interest—the woodchuck hole, the hollow tree, and so on. These experiences may be very educational, but certainly are not as exciting as observing the animal itself.

The majority of the species listed in Table 1 are active year-round. The others "winter sleep" during periods of extreme cold or hibernate most of the winter. There is, however, considerable activity in the winter, and the obser-

Table 1. Preliminary list, and some requirements, of mammals that might inhabit Syracuse, New York.[a]

Species	Home range[b] (ha)	Habits[c]			Diet[d]	HABITAT
Opossum (*Didelphis marsupialis*)	8–16	WS	P	N	H	Mixed woods, agriculture, lowlands
Shrew—Masked (*Sorex cinereus*)	0.1	A	P	D/N	I	Moist mixed woods, thicket, wetland
Shorttail (*Blarina brevicauda*)	0.8	A	P	D/N	I	Unrestricted woods and fields
Mole—Starnose (*Condylura cristata*)	?	A	P	D/N	I	Thicket, wetland, stream & pond
Bat—Little Brown (*Myotis spp.*)	3K	WS	M	N	I	Unrestricted, roosts in buildings
Northern Brown (*Pipistrellus spp.*)	?	H	PM	N	I	Woods near water, roosts in bldg. & trees
Rabbit—Eastern Cottontail (*Sylvilagus floridanus*)	1.2–8	A	P	N/D	H	Thicket, brush, agriculture
Woodchuck (*Marmota monax*)	0.4–16	H	P	D	H	Meadow, agriculture, uplands
Chipmunk—Eastern (*Tamias striatus*)	0.8	H	P	D	H	Open Woods, stone work, uplands
Squirrel—Gray (*Sciurus carolinensis*)	2.8	A	PM	D	H	Open deciduous woods
Red (*Tamiasciurus hudsonicus*)	2.8	A	P	D	H	Mixed Woods
Flying (*Glaucomys spp.*) (2 spp.)	1.6	A	P	N	H	Mixed to Open woods
Beaver (*Castor canadensis*)	2–6	A	PM	N/D	H	Brush, wetland, stream & pond
Mouse—Deer (*Peromyscus maniculatus*)	1.2	A	P	N	H	Moist Mixed Woods
White-footed (*Peromyscus leucopus*)	0.6	A	P	N	H	Open woods, brush, meadow
Vole—Redbacked (*Clethrionomys spp.*)	0.2	A	P	D/N	H	Moist Mixed woods, cool
Meadow (*Microtus pennsylvanicus*)	0.4	A	P	D/N	H	Meadow, wetland, agriculture
Pine (*Pitymys pinetorum*)	0.2	A	P	D/N	H	Deciduous woods
Muskrat (*Ondatra zibethicus*)	0.8–2.8	A	PM	?	H	Wetlands, stream & pond
Mouse—Meadow Jumping (*Zapus hudsonius*)	0.8	H	P	N	H	Brush, meadow, wetland
Woodland Jumping (*Napaeozapus insignis*)	0.8	H	P	N	H	Deciduous woods, brush
Porcupine (*Erethizon dorsatum*)	1.2	A	PM	N/D	H	Mixed Woods
Fox—Red (*Vulpes vulpes*)	259–518	A	P	N/D	C	Mixed woods, brush, agriculture
Raccoon (*Procyon lotor*)	3K	WS	PW	N/D	O	Mixed woods, wetlands, agriculture
Weasel—Shorttail (*Mustela erminea*)	12–16	A	P	N	C	Mixed woods, brush, wetland, agriculture
Longtail (*Mustela frenata*)	12–16	A	P	N	C	Mixed woods, meadows, wetland, agriculture
Mink (*Mustela vision*)	12–32	A	P	N	C	Wetland, stream & pond, lowlands
Skunk—Striped (*Mephitis mephitis*)	0.8 K	WS	PW	N	O	Mixed woods, brush, wetland, agriculture
Deer—Whitetailed (*Odocoileus virginianus*)	259	A	PM	D	H	Mixed woods, brush, wetland, agriculture

[a]Sources: Alexander (1969), Burt and Grossenheider (1976), New York State Dep. of Public Serv. (unpubl. draft rep.).
[b]The little brown bat, raccoon, and skunk are considered "corridor species" and home ranges are given in kilometers.
[c]A = active all seasons, H = true hibernation, WS = winter sleep (intermittent), P = permanent resident, PM = permanent but travels seasonally, PW = permanent but extensive travel outside home range, M = migratory, N = nocturnal, D = diurnal, D/N = primarily diurnal, N/D = primarily nocturnal.
[d]H = herbivore, I = insectivore, C = carnivore, O = omnivore.

vation of wildlife activity at this time is rewarding due to the many tracks left in the snow and easily seen animals above the snow foraging for food or escaping a predator.

Fig. 2 summarizes current knowledge about home range size for different groups of mammals. Home range is a concept that can serve as a guide to area requirements for various species and various habitats appropriate to those species. However, it must be recognized that home ranges vary seasonally and annually and are influenced greatly by available food, water, and cover.

Habitats, as shown in Fig. 2, are placed in a generalized continuum from forest land to agricultural land. This description of habitat is hypothetical. It is, therefore, difficult to describe habitat scale as it relates to intensity of use by individual species. However, by proper management of designed, maintained habitats, the home range overlap may be intensified to an artificial state provided territoriality remains discrete and the density of individuals does not

remove the food and cover put there deliberately for support of the species of interest.

As one compares habitat to home range size, it is possible to postulate on the identification of the urban wildlife population. The hypothesis is that those species having broader tolerance of various habitats and smaller home range size, such as the shorttail shrew, are most likely to be present in the city's open spaces. Conversely, those species with a narrow habitat tolerance requiring a large home range, such as the mink, are very unlikely to appear in the city. The major exception to this line of reasoning is the accidental provision of narrow habitat in large quantities, such as cemeteries. It is possible to rate the likelihood of an animal's presence in the city from Fig. 2 while recognizing the exceptions.

Plants For Mammals

As this section deals with our ability to create habitats through the use of plants as food and cover, the list of

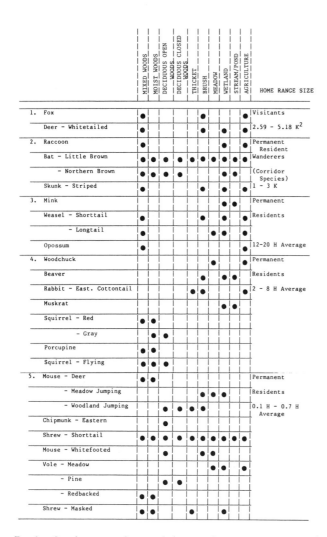

Fig. 2. Simple matrix of various habitats and some common mammals listed by size of home range. Adapted from Alexander (1969), Burt and Grossenheider (1976), and New York State Department of Public Service (unpubl. draft rep.). K = kilometers, K² = square kilometers, H = hectares.

mammals in Fig. 1 is shortened from Table 1 to include only those species that are omnivorous or herbivorous. This is not to say that the carnivorous varieties will not be present, or indeed that they will not utilize the plant materials as cover.

Fig. 1 is a summary of research and a degree of personal professional experience. The plant genera selected are from a longer list suitable for "city conditions." Such conditions are variable from city to city but relate to a plant's tolerance of such factors as air pollution, soil compaction and disturbance, poor drainage, salt pollution, and modified climate; all of which may be experienced in our urban areas. Also, and more importantly, in the context of this paper, the plants listed are those genera that provide food and cover for mammals.

The ability of certain plants to support wildlife is well documented. However, it is not always clear in the literature just how a plant is utilized, or indeed if it has any nutritional value. In the present paper, I have attempted to indicate those plants that appear to constitute more than 10% of the animals' diet as a way of evaluating importance. Fig. 1 also indicates those plants useful as cover. The plants are listed to genus due to insufficient dietary data, and there is at present a discrepancy between those plants available commercially and those most useful to wildlife. Also, given an urban wildlife population artificially supported at certain times of the year, perhaps with an unregulated population growth, the diet will no doubt be expanded to include things not normally eaten.

FROM PLANNING TO PRACTICE

Although Syracuse has a large area of habitat potential, the actual habitat is limited. A great deal will have to be done to promote a greater ecological diversity by improving vegetation mix of food and cover for wildlife. Those areas that have by accident gone "wild" or "natural" may have limited potential because of their temporary nature due to a lack of planning and the ability to control plant succession. The City of Syracuse, Department of Parks and Recreation has considered ways of "designing" natural areas not necessarily to promote wildlife, but principally to reduce the maintenance load. The deliberate creation of such areas will, if allowed to mature, promote wildlife habitat and if open space corridors connect these habitats, then the potential for wildlife should be greatly increased.

Having identified the potential mammalian community—those species most likely to appear in the city—and the genera of plants most likely to survive our urban conditions to provide food and cover to these mammals, it is possible to make certain hypothetical projections. If financial support is available to proceed with revegetation, then the principal concerns would be water and habitat space. The map shown in Fig. 3 illustrates a simplified pattern of urban hydrology and available open space. The drainage pattern is under constant modification, but the open space remains relatively constant. By combining the mammalian groups identified in Fig. 2 with the theoretical mammalian species occupation patterns shown in Fig. 3, it is possible to project what mammals might appear in specific areas according to available space. The assumption is that space will be the critical limiting factor because the habitat can be modified.

The theoretical pattern of urban wildlife occupation by various species can be generalized in order to predict where various species may occur. The wide ranging visitors are not likely to venture as far into the open space system as the "corridor" species. Other permanent residents may settle in successively smaller areas according to home range sizes.

The major physical deterrent against potential mammalian habitation shown in Fig. 3 is road traffic. At present, roads create barriers, which could be modified to facilitate

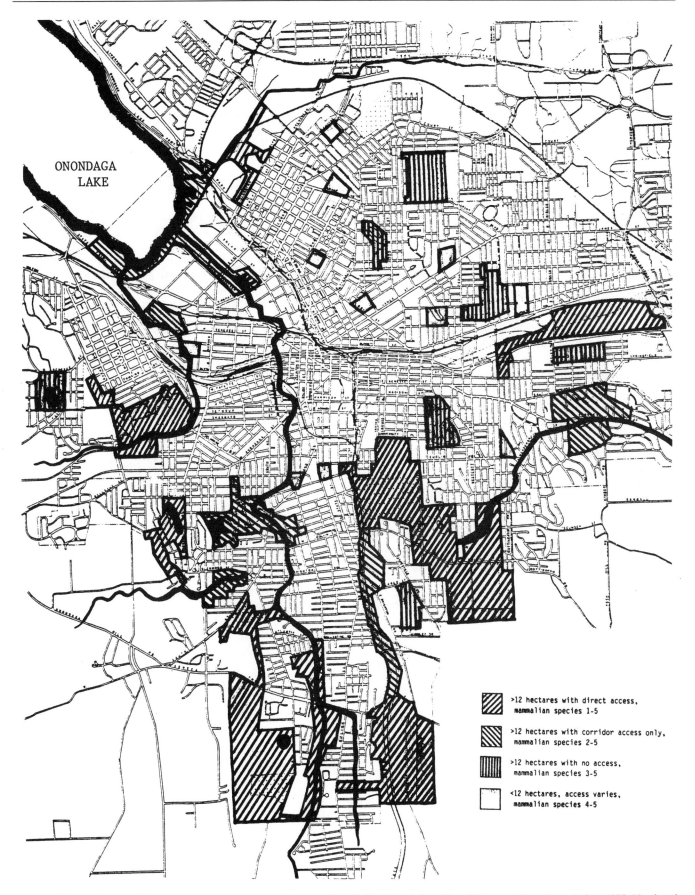

>12 hectares with direct access, mammalian species 1-5

>12 hectares with corridor access only, mammalian species 2-5

>12 hectares with no access, mammalian species 3-5

<12 hectares, access varies, mammalian species 4-5

ONONDAGA LAKE

Fig. 3. Theoretical mammalian species occupation patterns, Syracuse, New York. Adapted from City of Syracuse, Open Space Index, 1975. Numbered mammalian species are from Fig. 2.

wildlife use of the city. Open spaces following water courses or abandoned railways are already barrier free and these are well documented as places of urban wildlife. This limited network could be extended to provide free passage of wildlife, thereby minimizing the conflicts as wildlife moves in its own system independent of our traffic patterns. Animals tend to avoid danger, and provided man has not created a conflict of food with no access, most wildlife will choose a secretive route away from headlights and noise. Theoretically, the species of mammals entering particular urban areas can be predicted, provided for, and to some extent controlled.

DISCUSSION

Urban wildlife requires habitat. Situations in which site configuration, vegetation, hydrology, and food supply lend themselves to the provision of specific wildlife requirements are needed to support such wildlife. In order to provide potential habitat for appropriate species, decisions must be made concerning the size of home range needed, and what varieties of plants will encourage those mammalian species to be accommodated. At the time of writing, the diversity of mammals in the City of Syracuse had not been established accurately. Habitat potential is also inadequately understood and there is no clear idea of what diversity or extent of habitat already exists in Syracuse. However, the ability to improve habitat and thereby increase the diversity of wildlife within the existing urban open space system remains a desirable objective.

In summary, the "theoretical mammalian species occupation patterns" mapped in Fig. 3 indicate those species in Fig. 2 that are most likely to occur in the Syracuse urban area. Fig. 2 illustrates the habitat types that will most likely accommodate certain mammalian species. The plants listed in Fig. 1 can be used to select the appropriate plant communities that can provide food and cover for appropriate mammalian species. With this information, the urban planner can theoretically "design" the available open space for particular species of mammals thought to be beneficial to the urban ecological system.

REFERENCES CITED

Alexander, M.M. 1969. Vertebrates of Onondaga County, New York, with notes on other major taxa. Third ed. Dep. of For. Zoo., State Univ. of New York, College of Environ. Sci. and For., Syracuse. 32 pp.

Burt, W.H., and R.P. Grossenheider. 1976. A field guide to the mammals. The Peterson Field Guide Ser. Third ed. Houghton Mifflin Co., Boston, Mass. 289 pp.

Dawson, C.P., and D.J. Decker. 1978. Plants for improving wildlife habitat around your home. Conserv. Circ., Vol. 16, No. 7. Dep. of Nat. Resour., New York State College of Agric. and Life Sci., Cornell Univ., Ithaca. 8 pp.

Gill, J.D., and W.M. Healy. 1974. Shrubs and vines for northeastern wildlife. U.S.D.A., For. Serv. Gen. Tech. Rep. NE-9. 180 pp.

Leedy, D.L., R.M. Maestro, and T.M. Franklin. 1978. Planning for wildlife in cities and suburbs. Rep. No. FWS/OBS-77/66, U.S. Fish and Wildl. Serv., Washington, D.C. 64 pp.

Martin, A.C., H.S. Zim, and A.L. Nelson. 1951. American wildlife and plants. McGraw-Hill Book Co., Inc., New York, N.Y. 500 pp.

Myers, R.E. 1965. Wild plants and their value to upland wildlife. U.S.D.A. Soil Conserv. Serv., Information Sheet NY—59. 4 pp.

Thomas, J.W., R.O. Brush, and R.M. DeGraaf. 1972–73. Invite wildlife to your backyard. The Conservationist, Dec.–Jan. New York State, Dep. of Environ. Conserv. 12 pp.

Glass and Bird Kills: An Overview and Suggested Planning and Design Methods of Preventing a Fatal Hazard

Daniel Klem, Jr., *Department of Biology, Muhlenberg College, 2400 Chew Street, Allentown, PA 18104-5586*

INTRODUCTION

Small sheets of glass existed as window panes as long ago as 290 A.D. (Phillips 1941:8). Glass permits a view from protected enclosures, admitting light and warmth into human dwellings. In the Middle Ages, tinted and clear panes were lavishly incorporated into cathedrals of Europe and then into the domestic homes of the rich, especially Tudor England (Anonymous 1967). Large sheets of glass were first produced about 1903 and are commonplace today in structures throughout much of the modern world. Many modern buildings are surfaced entirely with glass, and often human dwellings contain large picture windows. Thus, it appears that window glass has enriched man's aesthetic, cultural, physiological, and psychological well-being for at least 16 centuries.

Glass panes, as a source of avian mortality, probably are as ancient and progressive as their use, but confirmations of bird fatalities do not appear in the literature until well after 1800 with the development of modern ornithology in Europe and North America (Nuttall 1832:88, Baird et al. 1874:417, Townsend 1931). The literature now contains accounts of window-kills from most of the world's continents (Weir 1976, Klem 1979, Avery et al. 1980, Klem 1989).

Available evidence suggests that all free flying birds are potentially vulnerable to glass (Klem 1979, 1989, 1990a). My extensive observational data and experiments indicate that, with the possible exception of hunting mortality, glass kills more birds than any other man-caused avian mortality factor, including the higher image catastrophes resulting from oil spills, pesticide poisoning, and collisions with vehicles, tall towers, and buildings (Table 1). With few exceptions, a willingness to modify or incorporate alterations to building and landscape designs can save millions of birds. Protecting our birds promotes sound environmental practices by conserving a group of animals that are used regularly to monitor the overall health of the environment, and provides an immeasurable source of human enjoyment through a variety of recreational activities (Temple and Wiens 1989). Although I have reported on this subject

Table 1. Estimates of annual man-caused avian mortality in the United States.[a]

Mortality factor	Number of individuals killed	Percentage of total kill
Hunting	120,539,500	41.53
Depredation control	2,000,000	0.69
Scientific research and propagation	894,010	0.31
Other direct sources[b]	3,500,000	1.21
Pollution and poisoning[c]	3,815,000	1.31
Vehicle collisions	57,179,300	19.70
Tall structure collisions (towers, stacks, buildings)	1,250,000	0.43
Plate glass collisions[d]	97,563,626	33.61
Other indirect sources[e]	3,510,000	1.21
Total	290,251,436	100.00

[a]Modified from Banks (1979) and Klem (1990a).
[b]Includes casualties related to falconry and attempts to raise young wild birds, illegal shooting, and vandalism.
[c]Includes deaths related to the upper estimate (300,000) of one annual oil spill having the same effect as the 1989 Exxon Valdez spill in Alaska (Piatt et al. 1990).
[d]Lower estimate of 97,563,626 to 975,636,260 range (Klem 1990a). If the upper estimate of the range is used, glass would dominate all other man-caused mortality factors by representing 84% of the 1,168,324,070 total kill.
[e]Includes deaths due to bird banding, electrocution by power lines and fences, fish net and line entanglement, birds trapped in buildings, domestic pets such as cats, mammal traps, and other factors described by Lincoln (1931).

elsewhere in the scientific literature (Klem 1989; 1990a,b), my objectives in this paper are to: (1) briefly review existing knowledge, (2) further emphasize the magnitude, significance, and human perception of the problem, and (3) formally present site-specific alternative solutions to architectural and landscape professionals and their allies.

THE PROBLEM

Backyard birds, such as the American robin (*Turdus migratorius*) and northern cardinal (*Cardinalis cardinalis*), that repeatedly bang into and flutter against windows in the spring and summer are little harmed by such activity. These occurrences are often of concern to humans (and an annoyance to some), but, except for an occasional bloodied face, they are harmless to birds. Strikes of this type result from

Wildlife Conservation in Metropolitan Environments. NIUW Symp. Ser. 2, L.W. Adams and D.L. Leedy, eds. Published by Natl. Inst. for Urban Wildl., 10921 Trotting Ridge Way, Columbia, MD 21044, USA, 1991.

male birds defending their territories against their reflected image.

By contrast, birds are frequently killed when they strike windows as if unaware of the presence of these structures. These collisions can be a problem for birds and humans. As the human population and the dwellings in which we live and work increase, windows may contribute to significant declines of select species and the persistent and increasing losses may affect bird populations in general. Window-kills are a serious problem to a growing number of people who experience remorse, guilt, and anxiety when they discover, or are made aware, that the glass in their homes, work places, and the commercial buildings they frequent are unintentionally killing the birds they enjoy or appreciate as part of their environment.

Evidence from documented collisions and controlled experiments clearly indicates that birds are not able to recognize glass as a potentially lethal obstacle. Glass is simply invisible to birds. Other animals such as insects, fish, and mammals like dogs, deer, and humans strike stationary windows, but the momentum at which they impact usually does not cause serious injury. Alternatively, even the smallest flying birds can reach speeds that result in fatal collisions.

No birds appear to be immune to the hazard. Approximately 25% (225/917) of all avian species in the United States and Canada have been documented striking windows. The species not recorded as window-kills are those that usually do not occur near human dwellings, such as most waterbirds, soaring hawks, and terrestrial species occupying unpopulated or sparsely populated desert, grassland, and forest. Sex, age, and resident status have little influence on vulnerability to collisions. There is no season or time of day, and almost no weather conditions during which birds elude glass. Transparent or reflective windows of various colors are equally lethal to birds. Strikes occur at windows of various size, height, and orientation in urban, suburban, and rural environments, but birds are more vulnerable to large ($>2m^2$ panes near ground level and at heights above 3 m in suburban and rural areas.

Strike rates at specific sites are unique and require attention to a combination of contributing factors. Overall, the magnitude of the kill at any one site is directly related to avian, dwelling, or environmental features that increase the density of birds near windows. From extensive analyses of bird strike accounts, a survey of window-killed specimens, and a series of experiments, I found that collisions and their resultant fatalities are possible wherever birds and windows coexist (Klem 1989).

The significance of this type of man-caused mortality is unknown, but I suggest that enough evidence exists to indicate it may be substantial for some species and for birds in general (Table 1). The widespread, persistent, and increasing loss due to windows contrasts sharply with the relatively meager losses from higher image catastrophes resulting from oil spills, pesticide poisoning, and collisions with vehicles, tall towers, and buildings. If my 100 million

toll is accepted as a relative order of magnitude (Table 1), an equal number of victims would require approximately 333 Exxon Valdez oil spills. The Exxon Valdez released 260,000 barrels of crude oil into Alaska's Prince William Sound on 24 March 1989, and the spill was estimated to have killed from 100,000 to 300,000 marine birds (Piatt et al. 1990). Of course, to keep the disaster in perspective, the Valdez oil spill harmed numerous species other than birds and also affected the fishing-based economy and general ecology of the region.

These seemingly dramatic figures only have biological relevance if windows affect the survival of birds as a whole or local breeding populations that contribute uniquely to the genetic diversity of a species. If relevant, the problem demands serious attention by all professionals acting in an environmentally responsible manner and dedicated or sympathetic to conservation, management, and the preservation of biodiversity. In my view, enough evidence already exists to suggest that unless preventive measures are enacted, glass will become an ever increasing threat to select species and birds in general. There appears to be no avian trait that has evolved to permit individuals to recognize and avoid man-made sheet glass. Potential victims are the fit and unfit of abundant as well as rare, threatened, and endangered species. My estimates of 98 to 976 million annual window-kills represent 0.5 to 5.0% of the estimated continental U.S. bird population after the breeding season (Klem 1990a); 10 billion are estimated at the start of the breeding season (American Ornithologists' Union 1975). These seemingly low percentage rates mask the impact on select species, and potential increasing tolls on all birds, as more construction places more windows in avian breeding and non-breeding habitats and across their migratory routes.

Specific cases support a serious cause for concern. At one European building, 54 birds were killed in a 2-month period (Morzer Bruijns and Stwerka 1961). Another European site was abandoned by a local breeding colony of swallows (*Hirundo rustica*) after the population suffered critical declines due to window-kills at a nearby glass corridor (Lohrl 1962). Through continuous and systematic monitoring of two single houses in the United States, I found annual kills of 33 and 26 birds, respectively (Klem 1990a). Collisions at one of these houses in the same 4-month period (September to December) resulted in 26 (1975) and 15 (1976) fatalities. For both homes, one out of every two strikes was lethal, and small (hummingbird to sparrow) and large (cardinal to bobwhite) species were equally vulnerable.

Specific accounts also document window deaths for endangered or other species of special concern. A Kirtland's warbler (*Dendroica kirtlandii*) was killed on migration (Walkinshaw 1976), and peregrine falcons (*Falco peregrinus*) have died crashing into the windows of buildings near their urban reintroduction sites. A survey of North American window-kills suggested a greater vulnerability for those species whose activities occur on or near the ground, such as several species of thrushes, wood warblers, and finches (Klem 1979,

1990a). These same data revealed that most neotropical migrants—North American species that travel to Central or South America during non-breeding periods—are known to be killed at windows. Windows will continue to exact a non-selective toll on these particular migrants, already suspected of population declines due to tropical forest destruction and temperate forest fragmentation (Robbins et al. 1989a). One neotropical migrant, the ovenbird (*Seiurus aurocapillus*), was a bird reported most often as a window-kill in my survey and a species under intense study due to suspected population declines resulting from habitat fragmentation.

Representing an ever increasing threat to birds are human population trends that show a return to rural areas in the United States (Long and DeAre 1982), and world-wide development of farmland, forest fragments, and previously undisturbed large tracts of habitat (Robbins et al. 1989a, Robbins et al. 1989b).

The actual cause of death resulting from window strikes is almost always described by the uninformed as a "broken neck." This explanation is wrong in every known case. Detailed internal and external examinations and x-rays of over 500 victims revealed that birds died from head injuries (Klem 1990b, Veltri and Klem, in prep.). The sustained injuries are similar to those occurring in fatal human accidents involving head collisions. Additionally, documented accounts record birds succumbing to injuries after leaving the collision site and seemingly recovering completely (Klem 1990b). Initially recovered individuals are generally debilitated for varying periods, or they dramatically exhibit increasing paralysis over time (Klem 1990b). In either case, while attempting to recuperate, they are in a weakened condition to face the pressures of a demanding climate, predators, scavangers, and other environmental forces.

Humans are affected most often by the realization that windows have fatal consequences for birds, and to a lesser extent by the damage that some birds pose to windows. Although accounts of window breakage by large birds are documented (Blain 1948, Giller 1960, Dawson and Dalby 1973), it is a rare event; most windows are unaffected by bird strikes.

To my knowledge, the earliest attempt to inform architects of the problem of window-killed birds was made by Lohrl (1962). He justified a plea to eliminate transparent glass in new buildings, especially in schools where students regularly found victims beneath glass panes, by stating that such action would set an example for our children by protecting birds and demonstrating a respect for nature.

Ironically, many local, state, and federal park visitor centers are literally covered with glass, and these buildings regularly kill some of the birds that the public comes to see. Even more ironically, many conservationists and conservation groups who directly or indirectly criticize the collecting of specimens for scientific study own homes or buildings that regularly kill birds. In two instances, complaints from employees that the windows of their work places in New York and Maryland were killing birds prompted corporate architects to seek advice to address the concerns. As more attention is given to the extent of mortality and debilitating injury resulting from window strikes, similar concerns for the safety of birds, especially at higher image structures, may be expressed by all conservation-minded individuals and groups.

Developers, architects, landscape planners, or other associated professionals may become involved in litigation as attention and concern for this man-caused lethal hazard for birds increases. In the past 5 years, advice was sought for two possible court cases in Connecticut and California. The Connecticut case dealt with the construction of a large glass-covered building adjacent to a wildlife refuge. The California case dealt with a series of glass-covered buildings proposed for construction on a university campus. Overall, I believe the concern about window-kills and their significance to birds and humans will pose demands and expectations for responsible action from the glass industry and associated professionals as well as the conservation community in general. To date, the sheet glass industry and its commercial allies appear to be unaware of, or have chosen to ignore, the problem. Almost equal ignorance and concern have been expressed by individuals and groups whose interests focus on birds. Most textbooks and encyclopedia treatments of ornithology, as well as articles addressing man-caused avian mortality in professional and popular periodicals, present little, if any, description of the fatal hazards that windows pose to birds. Exceptions include two current textbooks that introduce the problem to students of ornithology (Gill 1990) and wildlife management (Robinson and Bolen 1989).

One might very well ask: Why has this subject not received more attention? Some concerned individuals often have the impression that window-kills are rare or the consequence of some abnormal trait or disease. I suspect that most people are simply unaware of the regularity and extent of the kill. Although window bumps occur while occupants are home, these sounds are often forgotten or dismissed as having an unknown origin. Because of practices of placing foundation plantings beneath and around windows, after a collision, bird victims are often hidden when they fall into adjacent vegetation, and the injured or weak seek out nearby concealed perches. Also, predators and scavengers learn that the dead and dying are readily available prey beneath or in the vicinity of windows (Klem 1981). Even seemingly unlikely scavengers, such as the eastern gray squirrel (*Sciurus carolinensis*), take advantage of available victims. One squirrel on the Muhlenberg College campus collected a window-killed adult male rose-breasted grosbeak (*Pheucticus ludovicianus*), opened its skull, and was observed feeding on the brain. To remove the offending or unsightly dead and dying birds from some commercial sites, such as the large plate glass windows of motels and hotels along the gulf coast of Texas, owners hire personnel to make early morning collections of window-kills that lie beneath their picture windows.

SOLUTIONS AND MANAGEMENT

Solutions at various problem sites will require varying financial investment and structural modifications that may influence the aesthetic appearance of houses, and commercial and other buildings. Some solutions at some sites will be cost prohibitive, and some designers will find any modification of their designs unacceptable. My hope is that such conditions or intolerant attitudes will be rare, and environmentally responsible solutions will be enacted at most, if not all, existing or potential collision sites.

At most sites, realistic solutions will have to maintain the functional and aesthetic qualities of glass. Successful solutions at any one site will require compromises that consider visual alterations and an acceptable level of bird protection.

To prevent collisions with existing windows, birds must recognize that the area glass covers is a space to be avoided. Collisions can be completely eliminated by covering windows with netting that prevents birds from ever reaching the unyielding surface. This solution is acceptable for small to medium-sized plate glass, but netting is cost prohibitive for large or continuous sheets forming glass walls.

Covering all or parts of the external glass surface with opaque or translucent curtains also can completely eliminate bird strikes. Proper external coverings disrupt the transparent or reflective image enough to direct flying birds away from the glass area. Partially covering the outside of windows is as effective as complete covering if individual elements of varying sizes and shapes uniformly cover the entire glass surface and are separated by 5 to 10 cm. Interestingly, if covering elements are individual strips as narrow as 2.5 cm and oriented either horizontally or vertically like venetian blinds, the strips must be separated by 5 cm horizontally but can be as much as 10 cm apart when placed vertically.

My test results of the effectiveness of partially covered windows in reducing bird kills suggest the potential for a new conservation product to prevent bird strikes at individual windows (Klem 1990a). I suggest the development and manufacture of an external roll up window covering that completely or partially covers the glass surface and consists of various creative designs. Coverings could be made with one of several different patterns, such as hawk silhouettes or pleasing geometric figures, or a combination of different patterns. Depending on technical production, requests for custom patterns also could be accommodated. If not in place at all times, coverings could be lowered when occupants were away from their windows such as at night, during the early morning hours when birds might be more active, or when away from their dwellings for extended periods.

Single objects such as falcon silhouettes or owl decals, large eye patterns, various other pattern designs, and decoys do not reduce strike rates to a statistically significant level (Klem 1990a). Many such items are commercially available, sold by conservation groups and garden clubs, or illustrated and described as solutions in landscaping publications (Henderson 1987). However, these objects fail to prevent most strikes because they cover only one part of the glass and are not applied in sufficient number to alert the birds to the glass barrier. These objects, like any others, must uniformly cover the glass surface and be separated by 5 to 10 cm to be effective.

New developments and resultant new products from the glass industry may eventually offer the best solutions for reducing bird kills at windows. Non-reflective tinted glass would uniformly transform windows into visible obstacles for birds. Alternatively, glass with non-reflective or interference zones containing patterns that uniformly alter the surface by the 5 to 10 cm criterion is expected to be as effective as analogous external coverings. However, to my knowledge, such products are not currently available, and they may be technically impossible to manufacture given the physical structure of glass.

For new or remodeled buildings, architects and allied professional designers are encouraged to install windows at an angle so that the pane reflects an image of uninviting ground instead of an illusion of safe passage through habitat or into the sky. The angle at which glass is offset from its conventional vertical position will vary depending on the position of the structure relative to the surrounding terrain. The effective angle will require knowledge of the point at which the pane reflects a complete image of the ground and knowledge of the stress applied to panes of varying size and thickness. My research group is currently collecting observational data and designing various experiments to further quantify the effectiveness of window angling.

Placement of bird attractants such as feeders, watering areas, and nutritious and aesthetic vegetation in front of windows increases the hazard of bird strikes. Eliminating bird attractants near conventional windows will reduce or completely prevent strikes by reducing the number of birds near the hazard. However, using preventive techniques such as netting or partial but uniform external coverings will permit the use of attractants and retain the enjoyment of viewing birds up close without the worry of exposing them to injury or luring them to their deaths. If attractants are used without preventive strike measures, attempt to place feeders or other resources within 0.3 m of the glass surface. Birds will be drawn to the attractant upon arrival, but due to the close proximity of the attractant to the window, they will not build up enough momentum to sustain serious injury if they hit the glass upon departure.

CONCLUSIONS

Windows are non-selective killers of birds, and this particular man-caused mortality factor may be contributing to population declines of select species and birds in general. Windows also are important and valuable components of human dwellings, and a solution at any one problem site most likely will have to maintain the functional and aesthetic qualities of glass. Because transparent and reflective plate glass is invisible to birds, various current and potential future solutions require altering windows so that birds functionally recognize them as barriers. Problem sites generally are unique, and acceptable solutions will require creative planning and design for new or remodeled man-made structures. Whatever solution or management practice is enacted at a particular site, it is likely that humans will have to sacrifice some aesthetic appearance to their dwellings. The birds will have to sacrifice some lives.

Acknowledgments.—I thank Irvin R. Schmoyer and James R. Vaughan for helpful comments on earlier drafts of the manuscript. I am especially grateful to Lowell W. Adams and Daniel L. Leedy for their editorial suggestions that markedly improved the manuscript.

REFERENCES CITED

American Ornithologists' Union. 1975. Report of the ad hoc committee on scientific and educational use of wild birds. Auk 92(Suppl.):1A-27A.

Anonymous 1967. Mississippi handbook. Mimeographed, 54pp.

Avery, M. L., P. F. Springer, and N. S. Daily. 1980. Avian mortality at man-made structures: an annotated bibliography (Revised). U.S. Fish and Wildl. Serv., Washington, D.C. 152pp.

Baird, S. F., T. M. Brewer, and R. Ridgway. 1874. A history of North American birds: land birds. Volume I. Little, Brown and Co., Boston, Mass. 596pp.

Banks, R. C. 1979. Human related mortality of birds in the United States. Spec. Sci. Rep. 215, U.S. Fish and Wildl. Serv., Washington, D.C. 16pp.

Blain, A. W. 1948. On the accidental death of wild birds. Jack-Pine Warbler 26:59-60.

Dawson, G. A., and P. L. Dalby. 1973. A goshawk-thermopane encounter. Jack-Pine Warbler 51:128.

Gill, F. B. 1990. Ornithology. W. H. Freeman and Co., New York, N.Y. 606pp.

Giller, F. 1960. Eine moderne "Vogelfalle." Ornithologische Mitteilungen 12:152-153.

Henderson, C. L. 1987. Landscaping for wildlife. Dep. of Nat. Resour., St. Paul, Minn. 145pp.

Klem, D., Jr. 1979. Biology of collisions between birds and windows. Ph.D. Dissertation, Southern Illinois Univ., Carbondale. 256pp.

_____ . 1981. Avian predators hunting birds near windows. Proc. Pa. Acad. Sci. 55:90-92.

_____ . 1989. Bird-window collisions. Wilson Bull. 101:606-620.

_____ . 1990a. Collisions between birds and windows: mortality and prevention. J. Field Ornithol. 61:120-128.

_____ . 1990b. Bird injuries, cause of death, and recuperation from collisions with windows. J. Field Ornithol. 61:115-119.

Lincoln, F. C. 1931. Some causes of mortality among birds. Auk 48:538-546.

Lohrl, H. 1962. Vogelvernichtung durch moderne glaswande. Kosmos 5:191-194.

Long, L., and D. DeAre. 1982. Repopulating the countryside: a 1980 census trend. Science 217:1111-1116.

Morzer Bruijns, M. D., and L. J. Stwerka. 1961. Het doodvliegen van vogels tegen ramen. De Levende Natuur 64:253-257.

Nuttall, T. 1832. A manual of the ornithology of the United States and of Canada. Volume I. Hilliard and Brown, Cambridge, Mass. 683pp.

Phillips, C. J. 1941. Glass: the miracle maker. Pitman Publ. Corp., New York, N.Y. 424pp.

Piatt, J. F., C. J. Lensink, W. Butler, M. Kendziorek, and D. R. Nysewander. 1990. Immediate impact of the 'Exxon Valdez' oil spill on marine birds. Auk 107:387-397.

Robbins, C. S., J. R. Sauer, R. S. Greenberg, and S. Droege. 1989a. Population declines in North American birds that migrate to the neotropics. Proc. Natl. Acad. Sci. 86:7658-7662.

_____ , D. K. Dawson, and B. A. Dowell. 1989b. Habitat area requirements of breeding forest birds of the Middle Atlantic States. Wildl. Monogr. No. 103. 34pp.

Robinson, W. L., and E. G. Bolen. 1989. Wildlife ecology and management, 2nd ed., Macmillan Publ. Co., New York, N.Y. 574pp.

Temple, S. A., and J. A. Wiens. 1989. Bird populations and environmental changes: can birds be bio-indicators? Am. Birds 43:260-270.

Townsend, C. W. 1931. Tragedies among Yellow-billed Cuckoos. Auk 48:602.

Walkinshaw, L. R. 1976. A Kirtland's warbler life history. Am. Birds 30:773.

Weir, R. D. 1976. Annotated bibliography of bird kills at man-made obstacles: a review of the state of art and solutions. Dep. Fish and Environ., Can. Wildl. Serv., Ottawa, Ont. 85pp.

Ecological Corridors in Urban Southern California

JOHN LYLE, *Landscape Architecture Department, California State Polytechnic University, 3801 W. Temple Avenue, Pomona, CA 91768*

RONALD D. QUINN, *Department of Biological Sciences, California State Polytechnic University, 3801 W. Temple Avenue, Pomona, CA 91768*

Since the early years of the Industrial Revolution, cities have been growing and spreading in patterns that lead to the formation of urban regions that destroy or modify wildlife habitat over large areas of land. This trend first became obvious in the mid-19th century in the industrialized region that grew up near the center of England around Manchester and Birmingham. Somewhat later, similar patterns appeared in the Ruhr Valley of Germany, along the northeast coast of the United States, and in other areas of early industrialization.

It was the Scottish biologist Patrick Geddes who first recognized urban regions as something new in the history of cities. He called them "conurbations" and pointed out rather forcefully the social ills that accompanied them (Geddes 1915). He also proposed regional analysis and planning as the means for guiding urban growth into more suitable patterns.

Although regional planning has developed rapidly as a discipline since Geddes' proposal, it has had little discernible effect on the form of conurbations. Such areas have continued to grow with little effective control, especially since World War II. They have spread to virtually every habitable corner of the world.

URBAN PARKS AND PARK SYSTEMS

The urban parks movement first appeared in mid-19th century England as a means of introducing some small taste of the countryside, which was perceived as beautiful and healthy, into the confines of the growing and industrializing city that was perceived as monotonous, ugly, and unhealthy. The movement struggled to establish rather modest green spaces within the dense gray confines of conurbations.

It soon became apparent that such modest places were too small to establish the benign qualities of the countryside within the city. Park advocates and planners expanded their ambitions and began to envision whole systems of parks that would knit the parts of cities together in green networks.

Frederick Law Olmsted brought the urban park movement to the United States and introduced it in grand fashion with his design for Central Park in New York City in 1858. In the years after that, Olmsted designed large parks for a number of other American cities. At the same time, he became increasingly interested in urban park systems as integrating networks. His notion of a park system seems to have been a group of small parks spotted through the city and interconnected by a system of tree-lined boulevards. This is similar to the park system of Paris that came into being during roughly the same period.

Olmsted designed such park systems for several cities, usually as extensions of a large park that was the main purpose of his commission. The parks-connected-by-boulevards concept is still clearly visible in some of his surviving work, most notably in Brooklyn, New York, where the Ocean and Eastern Parkways form connections between Prospect Park and other parts of the city.

With the park system he designed for Boston, Massachusetts, which came to be called the Emerald Necklace, Olmsted's concept of a park system reached well beyond this basic notion, to encompass the city's hydrological system. He shaped a portion of Back Bay into a large retention basin to absorb flood waters and extended this approach to Muddy River as an alternative to the underground drainage pipe that had been proposed. Thus, the park system also became a flood control system without pipes or concrete. Altogether, about a third of its area was devoted primarily to this purpose (Spirn 1984).

Among the other park systems, or partial systems, designed by Olmsted were those for San Francisco, Buffalo, Montreal, and Chicago. But none of these matched the Boston design in breadth of vision.

GREENBELTS AND OPEN SPACE SYSTEMS

At the turn of the century, British reformer Ebenezer Howard proposed to deal with the conurbation plague by

Wildlife Conservation in Metropolitan Environments. NIUW Symp. Ser. 2, L.W. Adams and D.L. Leedy, eds. Published by Natl. Inst. for Urban Wildl., 10921 Trotting Ridge Way, Columbia, MD 21044, USA, 1991.

building carefully planned new towns with limited populations, which he called "garden cities." Within his idealized garden city was a highly organized system of parks and boulevards. Most prominent among these was a Grand Avenue ". . . 420 feet wide, and forming a belt of green upwards of three miles long . . . It really constitutes an additional park of 115 acres—a park which is within 240 yards of the furthest removed inhabitant" (Howard 1965). Surrounding the garden city on its outskirts was a much wider belt of agricultural land that contained the city's growth and provided its citizens access to openness and greenery.

After Howard, greenbelts or open space systems were adopted by the city planning and regional planning movements and became a standard part of the planning vocabulary. Most comprehensive plans include what have come to be called open space systems of some sort. Although they are rarely fully implemented, such systems usually take shape to some degree, if only by default. Even without a plan, there is a great deal of de facto open space, left over for various reasons, within most urban regions. In his well-known study of the conurbation that extends along the Atlantic Coast from Washington to Boston, Jean Gottman found well over half of the land in farms and woodlands. He also believed that wildlife existed within the urbanized region in both large numbers of individuals and greater species richness than in the wild state (Gottman 1960). Thus, the raw materials for an interconnecting open space system were still there.

ECOLOGICAL FUNCTIONS OF URBAN GREEN SPACE

Through the rather brief history of urban open space systems, perceptions of their services to urban populations have expanded considerably: from their origins in concern for the health of urban dwellers to desire for places for games and sport, to visual amenity, to circulation routes and urban hydrology. But even among planning professionals, the potential ecological importance of open space is not widely understood. The term "open space" itself is a reflection of this, with its implication that there is nothing there. In fact, the complexity of activities and processes occurring within even a small area of green landscape in an urban area is far greater than that in the surrounding city. For this reason, in the remaining sections of this paper, the term green space will be used in preference to the term open space.

Early park proponents recognized that green areas cleansed the air, but they could not have understood the vital roles of plants in providing oxygen, absorbing carbon dioxide, and filtering particulates. The effects of green space in microclimate control have also been understood for only a few years. Temperatures in heavily urbanized areas are often 10 to 20 degrees warmer than in green landscapes, and it has been well established that green space within cities can contribute in a major way to lowering overall urban temperatures and thus reduce energy consumption and air pollution (Bryson and Ross 1972). For example, the Santa Monica Mountains have been called the "lungs of Los Angeles" because they allow clean air from the Pacific Ocean to move toward the core of that smoggy city. In this case, prevailing winds pass across a nonurbanized landscape that adds little pollution to the moving airmass. The slopes of the mountain range are mostly covered by native vegetation, and much of it will be maintained in a natural condition within the boundaries of the Santa Monica Mountains National Recreation Area and other parks.

As Olmsted's plan for Boston demonstrated, green space systems can become the framework for drainage and flood control systems that are more effective than those constructed of concrete. They also can become the media for management and recycling of water. In some places, such systems can filter water into underground storage, and they can serve to absorb other urban waste materials and recycle them through ecological processes (606 Studio 1988a).

Closely related to all of these functions and most germane to the purpose of this paper are the potentials of green space systems to provide wildlife habitat within urban areas. In the writings of the early advocates of urban parks and park systems, there is no mention of wildlife habitat. This is not so surprising when we consider the human-centered attitudes of that time, and when we realize that the ecological understanding of the complex roles of other species had hardly begun to emerge by the end of the 19th century. Nevertheless, when we look at a typical plan for urban regional green space (Fig. 1), it can easily be envisioned as a system of larger habitat areas, patches, and reserves, with connecting corridors. This suggests that such systems can serve as wildlife habitat in addition to fulfilling other ecological and social functions.

If this is the case, then urban green space systems might partially counterbalance the enormous loss of wildlife habitat brought about by the growth of urban regions. They might also bring humans into closer contact with other species. But at the present time, we have insufficient data to make detailed and accurate judgments about the value to wildlife of such systems. Interest concerning the effectiveness of urban green space systems as wildlife habitat is growing, as evidenced by this and other recent volumes (Adams and Leedy 1987, Adams and Dove 1989).

Green Space Corridors

In this paper, we deal primarily with corridors of green space—long and narrow stretches of wildlife habitat that run between larger patches of habitat. These corridors provide ecological connections between animals and plants living in the larger patches. Ideally corridors knit together all pieces so that inhabitants of any part of the system are members of unified populations. Members of these populations can move freely from one patch to another and are afforded the full range of social and genetic interactions

Fig. 1.   Olmsted Brothers' park and parkway plan for the County of Los Angeles, California, 1930.

that characterize natural populations living in continuous habitat.

Corridors can compensate to some degree for habitat fragmentation, which is the division of wildlife habitat into patches separated from one another by distance. To illustrate, Fig. 2A shows contiguous habitat, with the exception of five small patches that have been urbanized. In this case, organisms can move in a straight line from any habitat location to another, with little likelihood of encountering an urbanized patch, so Fig. 2A is said to have high connectivity. The term "connectivity," which has its origin in mathematics, is frequently used in this way by landscape ecologists (Forman and Godron 1986). Fig. 2B represents five patches of habitat, joined by four corridors. The corridors provide connectivity between patches, but the only route for an animal to move from the center patch to that in the lower left corner, without leaving its habitat, is less direct than in continuous habitat. The connectivity of Fig. 2B is higher than it would be with any corridor removed, but less than Fig. 2A, where habitat is more continuous. Corridors can achieve the goal of improving connectivity between patches, but their effectiveness may depend on variables such as length, width, number, or the pattern of patches they serve to connect.

Although the desirability of corridors has been widely accepted, there is limited evidence of their effectiveness as tools of urban wildlife management (Simberloff and Cox 1987, Adams and Dove 1989). There are numerous questions that need further research before corridors can be planned to optimize ecological and cost effectiveness. A given corridor will not serve the same purposes for small, sedentary species as it would for large, mobile species (Soulé et al. 1988). For example, a corridor 20 m wide could contain entire home ranges of some species of rodents and snakes, but might function only as a route between bigger patches for a large mammal. The corridors proposed for the Florida panther (*Felis concolor coryi*) would be 50–130 km in length, and "extremely broad" (Simberloff and Cox 1987). In contrast, Fahrig and Merriam (1985) concluded

that fencerows no wider than a few meters between otherwise isolated woodlots would reduce the probability of extinction within patches for populations of white-footed mice (*Peromyscus leucopus*) occupying the woodlots. The edges of corridors will be influenced more strongly by the surrounding landscape than parts nearer to its center, so that effective corridor width may be less than its actual width. A narrow corridor may have its habitat quality altered due to edge effects, or due to heavy human disturbance (Hoehne 1981, Levenson 1981). Species of birds and mammals that favor edges may increase in numbers along narrow corridors, whereas birds of forest interiors and wilderness species of mammals may not use them at all. In this respect, narrow corridors may have some of the habitat qualities of small patches. Wildlife corridors in urban areas, if not planned and managed carefully, may lose their effectiveness if they attract heavy use by humans, feral cats, or unleashed dogs.

Despite the above points, extremely narrow wildlife corridors can function quite well for some species. In Southern California chaparral, Soulé and coworkers (1988) observed wrentits (*Chamaea fasciata*) and rufous-sided towhees (*Pipilo erythrophthalmus*) using habitat strips 1 m wide; three other species of chaparral birds used strips of habitat 10 m across. These investigators concluded that corridors of well developed chaparral no wider than 5 m, running between habitat patches, would be the most economical and effective way to reduce local extinctions of birds with low mobility that occupy isolated patches. Wildlife corridors do not necessarily have to be perfectly continuous in order to be effective, as long as the species using them are capable and willing to cross corridor breaks, and can safely do so.

THE LOS ANGELES URBAN REGION

For several reasons, the Los Angeles conurbation presents a good setting for research and development of urban green space systems as wildlife habitat. Its topographic complexity results in a diverse range of habitat types. The largest of the region's several mountain systems, the chain formed by the Santa Monica, San Gabriel and San Bernardino Mountains, extends from the Pacific Ocean inland over 300 km to the east and reaches upward over 3500 m at one point. The portion of this chain that crosses Los Angeles County can be seen across the upper portion of Fig. 1. It is almost entirely in public ownership, including two national forests and a national recreation area, and functions as a large reservoir for most species of animals found in the region prior to settlement by Europeans.

Stretching out between mountain ranges are several broad, flat valleys with clusters of low-lying hills jutting up here and there. A series of rivers emerges from canyon mouths at the feet of the mountains to flow across the valleys and eventually empty through small estuarine wetlands into the Pacific Ocean.

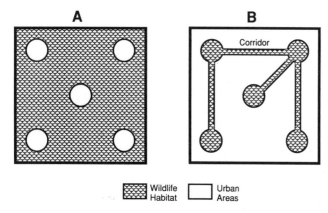

Fig. 2. Schematic relationships between wildlife habitat patches and habitat corridors. Landscape A has almost complete connectivity, and Landscape B has partial connectivity by corridors.

Urban sprawl came to Southern California in the 1880s shortly after the railroads arrived and several decades after the early conurbations in England and the Eastern United States had taken shape. Since then, urban growth has been rapid and almost uninterrupted (Fig. 3). At the turn of the century, there were slightly more than 100,000 people living in the City of Los Angeles and less than 200,000 in the entire region. Today there are over 3.4 million in Los Angeles and more than 15 million in the region. By 1975, Southern California's major valleys (the San Fernando and San Gabriel), and the coastal plains of Los Angeles and Orange County to the south, were almost entirely covered by urbanization.

THE OLMSTED BROTHERS PLAN

By 1927, it had become obvious that urban growth was swallowing up the wild, open landscape that had attracted many of Los Angeles' residents to settle here. That year, Los Angeles Chamber of Commerce formed the Citizen's Committee on Parks, Playgrounds and Beaches to survey recreation lands in Los Angeles County and make recommendations as to how they should be expanded. The Committee hired the Olmsted Brothers, Landscape Architects, and Bartholomew and Associates, City Planners, to carry out the work. The two firms completed the work in 1930.

The Olmsted Brothers firm was successor to Frederick Law Olmsted and operated by his sons. The lineage is obvious in their report, *Parks, Playgrounds and Beaches for the Los Angeles Region*. It included an inventory of existing beaches and parks and an analysis which showed these to be inadequate to serve even the population that then existed. Following this were detailed recommendations for acquiring additional beaches, parks and playgrounds, along with strong arguments for making the acquisitions quickly. The last and largest section of the report laid out detailed plans for a system of "pleasureway parks or parkways and related

large parks." The authors of the report argued that ". . . one of the most urgent park needs of the Los Angeles Region (is) the need for a system of interconnected pleasureway parks, regional in scope" (Olmsted Brothers et al. 1930, p.12).

The proposed system encompassed the entirety of Los Angeles County, and in it are clearly visible the Olmsteds' notions of a park system updated for the automobile age. The principal argument for the system centered on automobile circulation; the system is ". . . so designed that, having reached any part of it, one may drive within the system for pleasure, for many miles under thoroughly agreeable conditions and in pleasant surroundings" (ibid, p.13). Also included within the system, as in the senior Olmsted's later work, were stream channels and floodways. The report argued for ". . . parks along natural drainage lines on lands relatively cheap, and extensive enough for recreation purposes." Even at this relatively recent date, there was still no mention of wildlife or of any ecological function other than hydrological.

As presented in the report (Fig. 1), the proposed system included a dispersed array of large parks interconnected by linear elements called chains. The chains followed four types of physiographic lines: (1) The Coast Chain, which included all of the county's ocean beaches and coastal lagoons; (2) The Mountain Chain, which extended along the foothills at the base of the San Gabriel Mountains; (3) The Hilltop Chain, which included several clusters of hills along an east-west line between the Santa Monica Mountains and the City of Pomona; and (4) Several River Chains along river courses and drainageways, generally extending from the bases of the mountains across the valleys to the ocean.

Although wildlife concerns had no part in selecting these areas, it is strikingly apparent that if one were laying out a system of wildlife habitat areas and corridors for this region, regardless of urban development patterns, it would probably look very much like this. Large habitat patches are dispersed rather evenly throughout the area, and most are located in estuaries along the coast, around bodies of water in the valleys, and at the mouths of canyons emerging from the expanse of mountains to the north. The variety of habitats, including those associated with water, provides the potential for a rich array of wildlife species. The corridors that trend from northeast to southwest are watercourses, whereas most corridors that go east-west are ridge tops. Even now, 60 years after the Olmsteds prepared this plan, most of the ridgetop corridors are free, to one degree or another, from urbanization. With some exceptions, the watercourses have lost most of their value for wildlife habitat and for recreation, as they have been narrowed to flood control channels lined with concrete. In a later section, we describe a plan to restore one of these watercourses, and the function of a ridge top corridor that continues to support wildlife despite substantial urbanization.

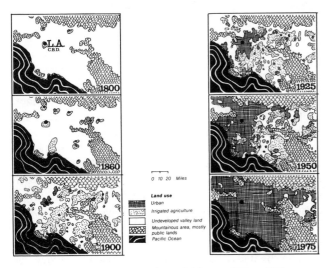

Fig. 3. Land use change in Southern California, 1800 to 1975.

The Parkway System and Wildlife Corridors

The pattern of parks and greenways suggested by the Olmsteds, connecting large non-urbanized areas with corridors, is dictated by the interactions of earth forms and urban needs. The large natural parks of Southern California, with mostly intact native biota, tend to occupy mountains and hills. They escaped the earlier phases of urbanization because of the physical difficulties of development—it was easier to build in the valleys. Later, when it became apparent that there was value in leaving some lands in the conurbation in their natural state, primarily for reasons of watershed protection and public safety, these mountainous areas were purchased or retained in public ownership. Some areas followed by watercourses also remained nonurbanized and unchanneled, and continue to carry seasonal runoff. Thus, in Southern California, as in Boston, the location of surface waters and watercourses provided the framework for a system of green space corridors.

In 1930, only a few small parts of the Olmsteds' network were actually in the region's park system. A number of the proposed areas have since become part of the system, including the Santa Fe, Whittier Narrows, and Tujunga floodways; the Santa Monica Mountains State Parks and National Recreation Areas; and a number of beaches. The Rim-of-the-Valley Corridor, recently adopted by the State of California (606 Studio 1984), is an updated version of a portion of the Olmsted system as is the Mulholland Corridor (606 Studio 1981), now being implemented by the City of Los Angeles. Recently, California State legislators and the City of Los Angeles began examining the possibility of restoring natural vegetation along portions of the Los Angeles River, which is now a 100-km concrete-lined flood control channel. This too was part of the Olmsteds' system.

Although a general understanding of wildlife habitat suggests that this greenway system of hills and river courses also is an effective system of wildlife corridors, much remains to be learned about which species will actually use it and what kind of ecosystem it might actually become. Two efforts in which we are currently involved begin to provide some answers to these questions. The first is a plan to reestablish the native riparian and floodplain ecosystems within a floodway corridor, and the second is an ongoing study of wildlife populations within a hilltop corridor.

THE LOWER ARROYO SECO

The Arroyo Seco is a canyon of varying width that extends 18 km from the base of the San Gabriel Mountains through the City of Pasadena into the northern part of the City of Los Angeles. In the Olmsteds' plan, it is designated as a major "chain" and was one of the few that was already functioning as a park.

In 1930, although it had been a recreational place for some years, the native plant and animal community of the

Arroyo Seco was still essentially intact (Fig. 4A). Within the following decade, two construction projects changed the situation radically. First came a concrete flood control channel built as a Works Progress Administration project. This destroyed most of the riparian community that had existed alongside the stream (Fig. 4B). Over time, the meadow community that had covered most of the canyon floor outside the riparian zone was deprived of water and disappeared also. Exotic turf and trees, mostly *Eucalyptus*, were planted to replace these communities and in some areas the Arroyo began to look like a conventional English park.

The second event was the Los Angeles area's first freeway, the second in the United States, which was built along the edge of the Arroyo Seco in its southerly part. This is one of a very few of the parkway drives proposed by the Olmsted Brothers that actually came about, and it bears out their contention that these would be very pleasant places for automobile travel. Elsewhere, the routes of the famous Los Angeles freeways cut through urban areas, concerned only with moving efficiently from one place to another, not with the pleasure of the experience.

The Plan for the Arroyo

Recently, the 606 Studio group of the California State Polytechnic University developed for the City of Pasadena a new plan for the portion of the Arroyo Seco lying within that city (606 Studio 1988b). The plan (Figs. 5–6) called for removal of the concrete channel in a portion of the Arroyo where hydrological analysis showed it to be unnecessary for flood control. This will make possible the reestablishment of the riparian and meadow communities. Although non-native species of plants cover most of the canyon floor, there are still remnant stands of three of the five native communities of the Arroyo (see Fig. 4B): coastal sage, oak-sycamore woodland, and the riparian woodland that still exists alongside small unchannelized portions of the streambed. Only a few species of plants from the chaparral community remain, and the meadow community has entirely disappeared. However, there are intact examples of these communities nearby.

Establishing a Functioning Ecosystem

The first step called for in the plan is reestablishment of the streambed in an approximation of its natural state. Water will then be diverted from the channel into the stream and the channel filled in. Once the stream is functioning, exotic vegetation will be removed, probably by a combination of burning, covering to exclude light, and manual grubbing. After that, native plant communities will be reestablished in a pattern approximating that which existed before the channel was built (Figs. 6–7). This will be accomplished by a combination of hydroseeding and manual seeding techniques.

As the native plant communities begin to regrow, we can expect a more complete representation of native animal

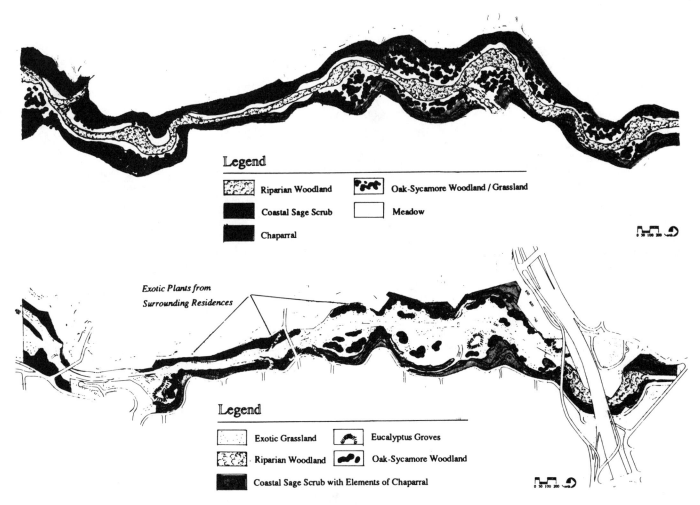

Fig. 4.   A comparison of the vegetation pattern in the Arroyo Seco of Southern California in 1930 (upper panel, 4A) and 1990 (lower panel, 4B).

species to return as well. As with the plant communities, many of the native species of mammals are still present, although in reduced numbers. This is especially true for the smaller ones. The vertebrate species now most common tend to be habitat generalists that do well in disturbed ecosystems. Common mammals include deer mice (*Peromyscus* sp.), pocket gophers (*Thomomys bottae*), and California ground squirrels (*Spermophilus beecheyi*). Avian species include city birds such as house finches (*Carpodacus mexicanus*) and rock doves (*Columba livia*), and species tolerant of disturbed conditions like scrub jays (*Aphelocoma coerulescens*), mourning doves (*Zenaida macroura*) and the northern mockingbird (*Mimus polyglottos*). The predators observed are adaptable to many habitats and widespread in the region, such as the barn owl (*Tyto alba*), red-tailed hawk (*Buteo jamaicensis*), and coyote (*Canis latrans*). The presence of feral and domestic dogs, and quite probably feral house cats, may account for the apparent rarity of snakes, desert cottontails (*Sylvilagus audubonii*), and complete absence of bobcats (*Lynx rufus*), long-tailed weasels (*Mustela frenata*), and gray foxes (*Urocyon cinereoargenteus*). Soulé et al. (1988) pointed out that domestic cats and dogs can be "subsidized" predators. Because the majority of their food is

supplied by humans, domestic carnivores can afford, in their leisure time, to hunt prey species to extinction in green spaces near residences. The presence of domestic predators, the absence of cover, and uncontrolled use by large numbers of people could all contribute to the total absence of mule deer (*Odocoileus hemionus*). In other places in southern California, deer do exist on patches of wildlands as small as a few hectares, but these patches contain cover and refugia that are more remote from human activities.

Once the native communities have been reestablished, recreational use of the lower Arroyo Seco will still be possible, but will have to be managed in relation to the requirements for an effective natural area. A system of use intensity zones will provide the means for accomplishing this (Fig. 8). Human use will be excluded entirely from the canyon's sloping walls and a small portion of the floor along their edges. At the other extreme, a small area will be devoted to intensive recreational use, including an interpretive center. Other areas, including the stream banks, will be available for limited and quiet human use. The planners hope to prohibit dogs from all parts of the Lower Arroyo Seco, but this is controversial.

In addition to restoration of the original species compo-

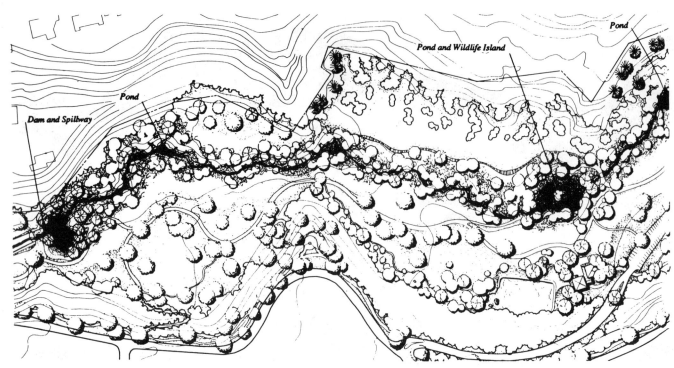

Fig. 5. Stream environment planned for the Arroyo Seco, Southern California.

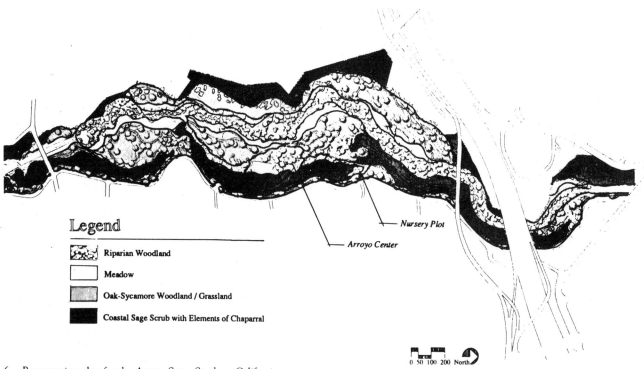

Legend

- ▨ Riparian Woodland
- ☐ Meadow
- ▧ Oak-Sycamore Woodland / Grassland
- ■ Coastal Sage Scrub with Elements of Chaparral

0 50 100 200 North

Fig. 6. Revegetation plan for the Arroyo Seco, Southern California.

sition and structure of the plant community, and separation of wildlife zones from areas of concentrated human use, the restoration of a free flowing stream is of enormous importance to wildlife. In the Mediterranean climate of Southern California, canyons with surface water support a large num-

ber of invertebrate and vertebrate species that are absent from otherwise comparable habitats that lack water. Many species must frequently drink, especially in the hot and dry summer. Other wildlife resources that are concentrated in watered canyons include gallery forests with several layers

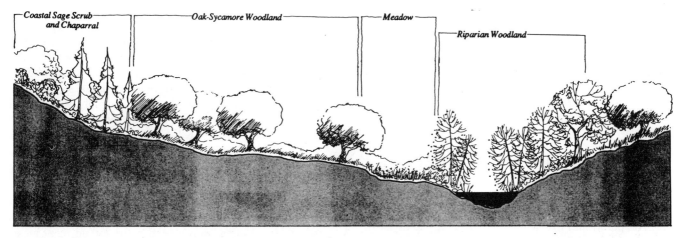

Fig. 7. Section through the Arroyo Seco of Southern California showing the revegetation plan.

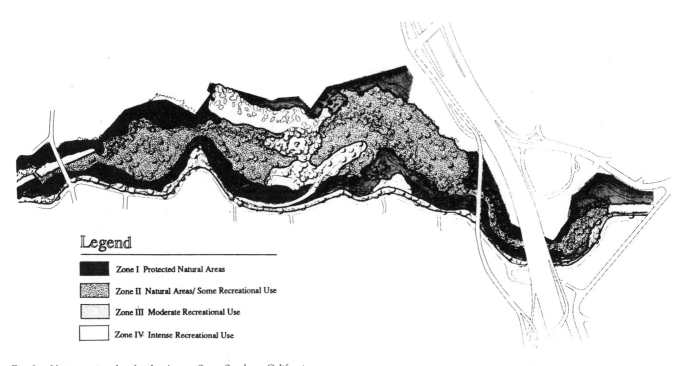

Legend

▣ Zone I Protected Natural Areas

▣ Zone II Natural Areas/ Some Recreational Use

▢ Zone III Moderate Recreational Use

▢ Zone IV Intense Recreational Use

Fig. 8. Use intensity plan for the Arroyo Seco, Southern California.

of vegetation, a large number and variety of insect prey, a thick layer of organic ground litter that remains moist and decomposing in all seasons, sand and mud, boulders, and steep, rocky slopes.

Given the fact that all of the species now missing in the Lower Arroyo Seco are present in the nearby San Gabriel Mountains, to which the Arroyo corridor connects, we believe that after the plan has been implemented the species richness of the animal community in the Lower Arroyo Seco will approach that which existed prior to 1930. The corridor to the mountains is quite important in this respect. Soulé et al. (1988) showed that, for sedentary species of birds in the shrublands of Southern California, connection between patches is the most important feature for maintaining species diversity. The same could be true for reptiles and amphibi-

ans, for some mammalian species, and for species of invertebrates that are not good dispersers. Present plans for the Arroyo include monitoring the process of ecosystem recovery as well as future interactions between humans and wildlife. It is possible that the boundaries between wildlife zones and zones of intensive human use may need modification, depending on how well the original design functions. Because the array of plant communities will be artificial, in the sense that most of it will be planted according to a plan, this too will require monitoring and ongoing management. Key plant species for wildlife may be missing, or fail to thrive. Maintaining the proper mix and composition of plant species in the chaparral and coastal sage areas will probably call for prescribed fires after the first decade. Seasonal closure of some areas to human use may be needed according to the needs of breeding birds. The snags called for to support cavity nesting birds could become safety hazards to people. All of these variables and others will have to be taken into account as part of an ongoing management program, which fine tunes the restoration of the Lower Arroyo Seco in accordance to the original goals and the changing needs of the human community.

THE SAN JOSE HILLS

General Description

The San Jose Hills are 18 km long, 6 km wide at the broadest point, and rise at the highest point 420 m above the San Gabriel Valley of eastern Los Angeles County. They are loosely connected with two more mountain systems, the Puente Hills to the west and south, and the Chino Hills to the south. On the Olmsteds' map (Fig. 1), they are shown at the lower right to be open land, although already surrounded by low density urbanization and agriculture. Grasslands are one of the common plant communities across the more gentle slopes of these hills, and cattle and sheep have continuously grazed there since the Spanish arrived in 1771. Over the past 60 years, the valleys around the hills have been gradually urbanized. More recently, residential subdivisions have been built upon substantial portions of the hills. Green spaces in and around the hills include a large public park with expanses of natural vegetation, approximately a dozen small municipal parks, four golf courses, a large, private cemetery, two landfills, a community college, and the California State Polytechnic University. Both the university and adjacent college have agricultural programs that maintain extensive hilly areas on the campuses that are managed as rangelands. These campus hills contain mixtures of annual grasslands, native shrublands, and woodlands and forests of native tree species.

Few of these green spaces have preservation or enhancement of wildlife habitat as explicit management goals, but hillsides that are steep and remote from existing roads and utilities tend to be left in their natural condition. Consequently the San Jose Hills matrix contains patches of wildlife habitat, and its central backbone serves as an irregularly shaped and somewhat discontinuous corridor uniting these patches.

State University Campus

With a complex mixture of intensely urban, agricultural, and natural lands, we view the campus and surroundings of the California State Polytechnic University as a model for corridors and patches of wildlife habitat within the Southern California conurbation. Less than one-half of the 600-ha campus is urbanized; the remainder is agricultural fields, hillside rangelands, and natural areas. One portion of the hillsides contains a 9-ha ecological reserve, and another part is occupied by a 210-ha research area called LandLab. About half of LandLab is an active regional land-

fill, and the remainder is dedicated to the development of sustainable dwellings, agriculture, and wildlife habitat. The campus is partially bounded by a pair of 8-lane interstate highways, and a transcontinental railroad. It is adjacent to several industrial parks, and residential and commercial areas. The region is growing extremely rapidly, so that most of the privately held green space near the campus either has recently been, or soon will be, intensively urbanized with residential, industrial, and commercial development. In the past decade, the two cities that bound the university have increased their populations by 132% and 39%, and almost all of these new residences are in the hills.

For the past 4 years, we have studied the biota of the natural areas of the university campus and adjacent areas, with particular emphasis on the interactions between wildlife and rapid urbanization at the urban-wildland interface. The flora (Clark 1990), avifauna (Stanton 1986, Moriarty et al. 1985), and ecological organization (Quinn et al. 1988) were described elsewhere. Here we describe movements and habitat utilization by coyotes and raccoons (*Procyon lotor*) as determined by radiotelemetry and fecal analysis (coyotes only).

Raccoons.—The adult raccoons studied are best described as suburban animals; they spent all of their time in close association with human developments. They drank from artificial ponds and leaky irrigation pipes, slept in and around buildings, and fed on orchard fruits and from garbage bins. Raccoons did use wildland corridors for movement, but also moved directly through residential neighborhoods. They occupied subterranean tunnels and drainage pipes, both for movement and for resting places. The route chosen for movement seemed to be determined by the destination, and not by a preference for natural vegetation or pathways created by humans. The mean range length of four males was 1.63 km (± 1.06), and for three females was 1.00 km (± 0.10). Of 10 animals tracked for periods of 5 to 24 months, only one individual, a male, showed a range shift. His move of 6.75 km required that he cross an eight lane freeway. He left the San Jose Hills and moved to a residential neighborhood with no natural green spaces, but with an extensive storm drainage system. All of these observations are consistent with behavior reported for raccoons in other urban locations (Hoffmann and Gottschang 1977, Manski and Hadidian 1985).

A number of raccoons have been removed from the university campus as pests, because they tear up lawns in search of insect larvae, overturn potted plants, and move inside buildings. The removal program, directed at problem individuals, has had no observable effect on the size or distribution of the campus population. The dense vegetation of backyards and urban green spaces, connected by urban pathways below and above the ground, is sufficient to keep raccoons living in the suburbs and feeding on garbage, pet foods, and orchard fruits. They are commensal with humans in the Southern California conurbation, and we see little evidence that green spaces or wildlife corridors are required for their continued existence.

Coyotes.—Of 12 adult coyotes captured in the San Jose Hills and studied by radio-tracking, half (two males and four females) spent all their time in relatively small patches of natural habitat within the urban matrix. The eight males studied had range lengths of 1.36 to 3.58 km, excluding range shifts. Four females had range lengths of 0.91 to 2.81 km. All six males tracked for periods greater than 1 year were found to make long distance moves outside of their previously observed home ranges. These moves varied in length from 5.0 to 16 km. One male returned 15 km to the point of original capture 1 year after departing, and another returned 8.4 km after an absence of 10 months.

The coyotes we studied were not generally associated closely with humans, although they often came close enough to buildings and backyards to be easily seen. We observed animals moving along the backbone of the San Jose Hills, canyons and washes, fence lines, roadsides, railroad tracks, and storm drains. They tended to rest in dense natural vegetation, particularly in canyons.

Three male coyotes moved over long distances, and we have tracked them closely to determine how they used corridors. One individual spent the first year of his adult life around two centers of activity in a pair of canyons 2.72 km apart, and moved frequently between the two along the ridge top corridor. After 8 months of this pattern, he moved 6.1 km to the Puente Hills, where he now uses a home range 0.83 km across. Some of his nocturnal foraging is done on a golf course. Most of this move probably occurred along the San Jose Hills ridge top corridor, but he must have crossed an urbanized valley to reach his destination. Another male, which was quite old, made the same move 2 years earlier. A third young male occupied a hillside home range 2.34 km wide for 10 months, where he was observed to occasionally venture into suburban backyards. He then moved 12.65 km to the Puente Hills, where he regularly moved distances of 7.3 km foraging in weedy fields adjacent to industrial buildings, on hillsides and in canyons with natural vegetation, and on a golf course. During daylight hours, he frequently rested in a small area surrounded on three sides by homes, where he was seen regularly by the residents. In these frequent moves, he used hill ridges, canyons, backyard fence lines, a culvert beneath an interstate highway, and an industrial railroad track with no vegetation whatsoever. He has moved along this track 5.4 km in 45 minutes. He recently returned to his original home range, and forages in an area being graded for a residential subdivision. Although the outside points of 36 days of this animal's recent activity enclosed a triangle of 24 km^2, all of his foraging and resting time was spent in a few specific locations that were connected by natural and anthropogenic corridors. The movements of these three coyotes demonstrate that green spaces connected by corridors are important. The natural corridors associated with the hills are discontinuous, but these highly adaptable animals are able to connect natural corridor fragments by moving through urban areas along other pathways such as a railroad track or a culvert beneath a busy freeway. This illustrates that the effectiveness of a green space corridor must be evaluated against the biology of the species it is designed to serve.

Urban coyotes do most of their foraging in green spaces with natural vegetation; much hunting time is spent in grasslands and fields, where they catch rodents, rabbits, and large insects. Some individuals do enter suburban backyards, where they consume garbage, fruit, and an occasional domestic cat. We have observed coyotes to be attracted to construction areas. We hypothesize that these sites are particularly fruitful places to hunt because the disturbance of building displaces their natural prey and removes potential cover, and there are no humans or dogs present at night. Analysis of scats collected from a nearby population of urban coyotes showed that only one of seven items (domestic fruit) found in more than 10% of 892 samples collected over a 32-month period was anthropogenic in nature (Quinn et al. 1989). From their behavior and diet, we conclude that this population of urban coyotes subsists on natural foods gathered for the most part in natural areas and urban green spaces.

CONCLUSION

The concept of urban park systems that developed through the 19th century has expanded to include a broad range of ecological processes. Such green space networks have the potential to become a key component of future urban ecosystems. The studies and plans presented here suggest that these urban ecosystems can include habitat for communities of wildlife and that the connecting greenways can function as wildlife corridors. The cases presented here illustrate how ecologically degraded wildlife corridors can be restored, and how informal, fragmented corridors can continue to connect green spaces for some species. We still have a great deal to learn about the ecological functioning of corridors, and the nature of their utilization by wildlife. Nevertheless, enough is now known to say that they are effective, at least to some degree, and to justify incorporating them into the planning of cities.

Acknowledgments.—No particular significance should be attached to the order of authorship. Co-principal investigator for the Arroyo Seco project was Jeffrey Olson. The project team included professors Francis Dean and Arthur Jokela, and graduate students Allyson Aultfather, Kevin Talma, and Patricia Trapp. We thank the Board of Directors and the Park and Recreation Commission of the City of Pasadena for their enlightened support and commitment to implementing the plan. Many years of research in the Arroyo Seco by professor Roland Ross also was most useful. Co-principal investigator for the mammal project was Glenn Stewart. The project team included professor W. O. Wirtz, and students Gerald Braden, Chris Brady, Nichole Chain, Lydia Gonzales, Karen Jensen, Kelly Middleton, and

Michele Tesitor. Mammal research was supported by Land-Lab Research grants from the Kellogg Foundation of California State Polytechnic University.

REFERENCES CITED

Adams, L. W., and D. L. Leedy, eds. 1987. Integrating man and nature in the metropolitan environment. Natl. Inst. for Urban Wildl., Columbia, Md. 249pp.

——— , and L. E. Dove. 1989. Wildlife reserves and corridors in the urban environment: a guide to ecological landscape planning and resource conservation. Natl. Inst. for Urban Wildl., Columbia, Md. 91pp.

Bryson, R., and J. Ross. 1972. The climate of the city. Pages 52–76 *in* T. Detwyler and M. Marens, eds. Urbanization and environment. Duxbury Press, Belmont, Calif.

Clark, C. 1990. Vascular plants of the undeveloped areas of California State Polytechnic University, Pomona. Crossosoma 16:1–7.

Fahrig, L., and G. Merriam. 1985. Habitat patch connectivity and population survival. Ecology 66:1762–1768.

Forman, R. T., and M. Godron. 1986. Landscape ecology. John Wiley & Sons, New York, N.Y. 620pp.

Geddes, P. 1915. Cities in evolution: an introduction to the town planning movement and to the study of civics. Ernest Benn Ltd., London, U.K. 409pp.

Gottman, J. 1960. Megalopolis: the urbanized northeastern seaboard of the United States. The MIT Press, Cambridge, Mass. 810pp.

Hoehne, L. M. 1981. The groundlayer vegetation of forest islands in an urban-suburban matrix. Pages 47-54 *in* R. L. Burgess and D. M. Sharpe, eds. Forest island dynamics in man-dominated landscapes. Springer-Verlag, New York, N.Y.

Hoffmann, C. O., and J. L. Gottschang. 1977. Numbers, distribution, and movements of a raccoon population in a suburban residential community. J. Mammal. 58:623–636.

Howard, E. 1965. Garden cities of tomorrow. The MIT Press, Cambridge, Mass. 810pp.

Levenson, J. B. 1981. Woodlots as biogeographic islands in southeastern Wisconsin. Pages 13-39 *in* R. L. Burgess and D. M. Sharpe, eds. Forest island dynamics in man-dominated landscapes. Springer-Verlag, New York, N.Y.

Manski, D., and J. Hadidian. 1985. Rock Creek raccoons: movements and resource utilization in an urban environment. Natl. Park Serv., Prog. Rep., Washington, D.C. 40pp.

Moriarty, D. J., R. E. Farris, D. K. Noda, and P. A. Stanton. 1985. Effects of fire on a coastal sage scrub bird community. Southwestern Nat. 30:452–453.

Olmsted Brothers and Bartholomew and Associates. 1930. Parks, playgrounds and beaches for the Los Angeles Region. Los Angeles, Calif. 178pp.

Quinn, R. D., P. A. Stanton, and G. R. Stewart. 1988. Vertebrates. Coord. by P. C. Catling. Pages 116–121 *in* R. L. Specht, ed. Mediterranean-type Ecosystems. Kluwer Acad. Publishers, The Netherlands.

——— , K. Middleton, and W. O. Wirtz. 1989. Habitat utilization by coyotes (*Canis latrans*) and raccoons (*Procyon lotor*) in urban Southern California. Abstracts of the National Meetings of the Am. Soc. of Mammal. Fairbanks, Alas.

Simberloff, D., and J. Cox. 1987. Consequences and costs of conservation corridors. Conserv. Biol. 1:63–71.

Soulé, M. E., D. T. Bolger, A. C. Roberts, J. Wright, M. Sorice, and S. Hill. 1988. Reconstructed dynamics of rapid extinctions of chaparral-requiring birds in urban habitat islands. Conserv. Biol. 2:75–92.

Stanton, P. 1986. Comparison of avian community dynamics of burned and unburned coastal sage scrub. The Condor 88:285–289.

Spirn, A. 1984. The granite garden. Basic Books, New York, N.Y. 334pp.

606 Studio. 1981. Santa Monica Mountains trail system. California State Polytechnic Univ., Pomona. 117pp.

——— . 1984. Rim-of-the-Valley trail corridor. California State Polytechnic Univ., Pomona. 108pp.

——— . 1988a. Regeneration of degraded landscapes utilizing composted organic waste. California State Polytechnic Univ., Pomona. 123pp.

——— . 1988b. Master plan for the Lower Arroyo Seco. California State Polytechnic Univ., Pomona. 94pp.

The Roanoke River: Enhancement of an Urban Corridor for People and Wildlife

ELISABETH B. LARDNER, *Lardner/Klein Landscape Architects, P.C., 1426 Dairy Road, Charlottesville, VA 22903*

INTRODUCTION

The City of Roanoke, located in mountainous southwestern Virginia, is bisected by an attractive and benign river—except following periods of heavy rain when the swollen Roanoke River may rise out of its banks by more than 6 m. Lardner/Klein Landscape Architects was hired by the city to review the U.S. Army Corps of Engineers (ACOE) Flood Reduction proposal for the 16.1-km stretch of the river that flows within the city's boundary. This paper concerns our work in developing a long-term plan for conservation and enhancement of wildlife habitat within the urban corridor as a part of the ACOE Flood Reduction Project.

History of the Project

Roanoke, Virginia was established in a large basin of marshland surrounding a segment of the Roanoke River. As urban development intensified, these flood-absorptive lands were destroyed and the city was, and still is, frequently inundated with raging floods. The 1985 flood caused an estimated $200 million in damage and buildings were submerged under 1.8–2.4 m of water (Turner 1988). Floods such as these affect one-quarter of the city's tax base (Roanoke Times & World-News 1989) and given Virginia's laws regarding annexation, no source of vacant, dry replacement land exists (Turner 1988).

The ACOE has been proposing to channel the river in one form or another since the early 1960s, to protect life and reduce property damages. Because the city is dependent on the tax base generated by industries along the river, it has continued to work with the ACOE to develop a viable project, unlike other adjacent communities. Many of these flood-threatened businesses have several disaster loans and could not financially recover from another flood. The current ACOE project, and one that has been granted bonding authority by the voters of Roanoke City consists of:

(1) bench channel and training wall construction for flood stage reductions and protection of low-lying areas,
(2) nonstructural floodproofing of the Sewage Treatment Plant,
(3) nonstructural automated flood warning system, and
(4) a recreation trail (U.S. Army Corps of Engineers 1988).

Roanoke River Resources

Today, the Roanoke River is a hidden and often unappreciated resource. In some areas, its banks are lined with a mixture of mature deciduous trees and saplings, and numerous bird, mammal, and fish species occupy its shores and channel. In other areas, it is a forgotten and ignored place, a dump where car tires and old refrigerators are thrown. The Roanoke River Drainage has the richest and most unique fauna of any drainage on the Atlantic slope (Jenkins et al. 1972) and a thin band of riparian vegetation lines much of the Roanoke River's banks within the city. But, as described by the Citizens Environmental Council in an editorial supporting the ACOE project and our work (Gray et al. 1989), "The Roanoke River is not a pristine resource like a wilderness area. It runs through an urban, industrial corridor. Some of it is lovely, other parts are not. Some areas along the river are suspected of being illegal hazardous-waste sites. The river is a resource which has been neglected and ignored."

Although the river is not pristine, potential exists to enhance the river corridor and to link it with surrounding natural areas. Within the city is a 216-ha forested park; the Blue Ridge Parkway is within 4.8 km of the river and is flanked by a ribbon of protected and managed lands on either side; and the National Park Service is proposing the Roanoke River Parkway, which would link the City of Roanoke and its section of river with the Blue Ridge Parkway. In addition, the city has a series of both developed and undeveloped parks along the river.

Wildlife Conservation in Metropolitan Environments. NIUW Symp. Ser. 2, L.W. Adams and D.L. Leedy, eds. Published by Natl. Inst. for Urban Wildl., 10921 Trotting Ridge Way, Columbia, MD 21044, USA, 1991.

PREVIOUS STUDIES AND INVENTORIES

Past Studies

Two types of river studies have been made over the years: local, those within the City of Roanoke that focused on the creation of a linear system of parks; and regional, those proposals for greenways and parkway connections throughout the valley. As early as 1907, a report called for the preservation of the most available and beautiful of the natural landscape features of the neighborhoods to serve as a basis for a system of parks, parkways, and reservations (Nolen 1929). In 1928, the Comprehensive Plan recommended that much of the river's edge be committed to park use, although at that time park use was envisioned as a manicured environment with playgrounds, rather than managed for wildlife (Nolen 1929). In 1975, the Fifth Planning District identified critical environmental areas for preservation (Fifth Planning Dist. Comm., Parks and Open Space, 1975). The National Park Service (1987) surveyed 64 km of the Roanoke River corridor in anticipation of the construction of a parkway. The corridor was subdivided into segments and natural and cultural resource data were collected and evaluated. A subsequent master plan identified conservation areas and recommended further study of their potential (Jones & Jones Architects and Landscape Architects for the River Foundation, Roanoke River Greenway Master Plan Draft, 1987). Furthermore, the greenway plan advocated excavating bypass channels in several locations to create a series of islands that would preserve existing riparian habitat and improve the appearance of the flood damage reduction project in lieu of the ACOE channel-widening proposal.

Previous Inventories

Previous inventory and assessments by public agencies were extremely valuable in the preparation of the Roanoke River Corridor Plan, and their use offers insight in how wildlife professionals and designers can work together. Landscape architects, although exposed to these issues, do not have the knowledge or training that these experts do. However, landscape architects do have the ability to translate the technical information so that a lay audience in a public meeting, or the decision-makers in city government can comprehend it, and then together apply their knowledge to physical planning and policy recommendations.

The U.S. Fish and Wildlife Service (FWS) (1984) and the Commonwealth of Virginia's Department of Game and Inland Fisheries (1988) were involved in reviewing the ACOE work. Agreements were made between the ACOE and other agencies prior to our involvement: the ACOE would limit its work to one bank to the greatest extent possible, equipment crossing of the river would be kept to a minimum, no disturbance of the river channel would be made for bench cuts, a construction time period was agreed to, and efforts would be made to reduce erosion and siltation. As a part of this process, FWS staff members had been to the river and identified areas where several threatened and endangered fish species were likely to be found.

THE ROANOKE RIVER CORRIDOR PLAN

The Roanoke River Corridor Plan is to be used by the City of Roanoke as a means of accomplishing two primary goals: (1) maintaining the long-term integrity of the Roanoke River corridor, and (2) reducing the risk of flood hazard through measures that support and extend the U.S. Army Corps of Engineers Flood Reduction Project.

Based upon agreements between the City of Roanoke and the ACOE, we put together a concept plan for the 16.1-km river corridor and developed site specific designs for five areas along the river. The existing character of the river is recognized within the plan, the upper reaches within the city being inaccessible to the general public and surrounded by industrial land uses. Due to space limitations, the ACOE recreation trail will not run parallel to the river in this section until, or if, Norfolk Southern's "belt line" is abandoned and donated to the city. Therefore, this area was designated as a conservation zone. Downstream, which includes most of the established parks, was designated as an active recreation zone (Fig. 1).

This emphasis on active recreation does not mean that wildlife enhancement has been disregarded. Members of the Roanoke Valley Bird Club and the Blue Ridge Chapter of the Virginia Wildflower Society suggested that islands of native plant materials be planted in the more open and traditional city parks to provide wildlife food and cover. Important habitat areas for birds and mammals were identified along the entire 16.1-km stretch of river. Habitat lands were defined as areas that included water, low lying vegetation such as shrubs and grasses, and a mixture of saplings and mature trees. Snag trees, or dead and dying trees necessary for bird and mammal habitat were also noted.

To achieve this plan, our effort included the following three activities.

(1) The landscape architect directed river tours and the ACOE project engineer served as interpreter, so that the disparate groups in attendance were able to understand what the lines on paper really

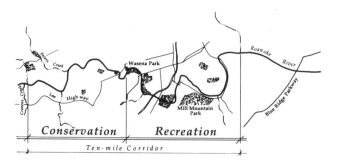

Fig. 1. Location map of the Roanoke River Corridor Plan, southwestern Virginia.

meant. Would this tree be cut down? Would this river bank be removed? A single plan, on one sheet of paper 1.2 m long summarized the ACOE collection of 116 blueprints. The plan identified the location of bench cut, tree removal, concrete retaining walls, etc.

(2) City-wide public forums were held to provide citizens with an opportunity to physically locate areas of conservation interest.

(3) An internal city workshop was convened to air the ideas, concerns, and needs of city staff, city officials, and business leaders in relation to the long-term project benefits and costs, including maintenance, zoning administration, economic development, and recreation. (This workshop resulted in the recognition that many key city staff supported an environmentally-conscious approach to the project. Economic development would benefit from the opportunity of marketing an environmentally-sensitive community with attractive recreational features.)

ACOE Agreements

A number of general principles and guidelines were agreed to by the ACOE. These are to be incorporated in the final Flood Reduction Project construction documents, yet to be released. The River Corridor Plan, which we prepared, extends these six actions as presented below.

(1) Plant materials will be used that were recommended by the U.S. Fish & Wildlife Service (Soil Conservation Service 1983) and representatives from the environmental community (Ellington and James 1989).

(2) A formula that related the linear footage of bench cut to the number of shrubs to be added was used for determining the total number of shrubs to be planted in the project. The figure for numbers of shrubs per linear footage of bench cut was based on a spacing pattern of one shrub per 1.5 m. This number was then translated into the figure of 625 shrubs per km of bench cut. Originally, the ACOE Project called for 120 shrubs, primarily hybrid azaleas, for the entire 16.1-km corridor (U.S. Army Corps of Engineers 1988).

(3) Low shrubs and groundcovers will be planted within the riprap. These materials will grow in and over the riprap, eventually covering it, making it less visually prominent and providing cover for small birds, mammals, and amphibians. Two techniques can be used for such plantings. The first is to plant rows of shrubs and groundcovers at the top of the slope. As the plants grow, they can trail down over the riprap. Over time, the crevices between the rocks that make up the riprap will fill with soil both from river flooding and wind

deposits, and the plants can establish a foothold as they cascade down the riprap's surface. The second technique, which will give a more immediate "finished" appearance, is to use sleeves when initially placing the riprap on the slope. The sleeves could be made from concrete pipe sections. Willow whips could then be planted directly in the underlying soil throughout the riprapped slope.

(4) Many trees along the river's edge will be pruned rather than completely removed. Mature trees that will not incur root disturbance during the construction of the grass bench will be allowed to remain along the river's edge. The lower branches may be pruned to conform with the ACOE design template for the Flood Reduction Project. (Originally, all trees were to be removed during the construction of the bench.)

(5) Wildflowers and "seed" grasses will be planted on the grass bench cuts.

(6) Much of the vegetation found on islands within the river will be left intact.

City of Roanoke Agreements

The City of Roanoke agreed to be responsible for the following six actions during and following the Flood Reduction Project construction period.

(1) The city will cable the dead and dying trees to maintain as snags. Of great concern to the birders and naturalists in the community was the status of dead and dying trees (Hamel et al. 1982, U.S. Fish and Wildlife Service 1982–1987). With the understanding that these trees provide valuable habitat for birds in particular, the City of Roanoke agreed to cable the trees to keep them from washing against any obstructions such as bridge abutments during floods. The selection of trees to be cabled will be made in conjunction with the Roanoke Valley Bird Club.

(2) Conservation zones will be established. The establishment of habitat and conservation areas that are clearly set aside and protected is one of the exciting developments to emerge from the Corridor study. Although recognizing that much of the river corridor has served as an industrial corridor for the last 100 years and therefore is not as pristine as what is found in more remote undeveloped corridors, there are a number of sites that can be enhanced to provide better habitat and riparian vegetation stands. The areas at the tributaries' junctures with the river are biologically the most important areas to protect and enhance. With good management practices, the city can serve a number of needs with a few actions. The tributaries' role in flooding is being studied, and their potential as recreation trail links from neighborhoods to the river recre-

ation trail could add to a city-wide recreational network.

(3) "Green" or recreation space will receive the highest priority for future land use within the Roanoke River floodway. These and industrial development are the only viable land uses within the Roanoke River's 100-year floodplain. Residential and commercial land uses are unsuitable.

(4) Existing residential structures within the Roanoke River's floodplain will be acquired and/or removed.

(5) An emphasis will be placed on conservation actions upstream of Wasena Park and public access and recreation actions downstream of Wasena Park.

(6) A tree planting program will be established along the river to supplement those trees provided by the ACOE. The trees should be interplanted with the existing river parks' trees and also planted to screen industry from the river users' view.

Site Specific Designs

The five site specific plans reflected the concerns raised with the ACOE regarding conservation actions. Three of those sites are described: Wasena Park; Craven's Creek; and a Prototypical Industrial and Conservation site.

Wasena Park was carefully examined. The ACOE proposed to remove the majority of the mature deciduous trees along the river's edge and replace them with a channel bench cut (Fig. 2). As an alternative, the ACOE was asked to determine the economic and hydrologic feasibility of replacing the bench cut with a by-pass channel through the park (Fig. 3). Two plans were prepared, one for each option. Alternative A's program is oriented more towards active recreation. Alternative B's program is oriented more towards conservation, placing a priority on the retention of the large mature trees along the river. A by-pass channel essentially moves the grass bench cut inside the park, saving all of the existing trees along the river's edge (Fig. 3).

The Craven's Creek site is part of the Blue Ridge Industrial Center, but is at a lower elevation and much of it falls within the 100-year floodplain. This proposal incorporates industrial land use with conservation, interpretive, and educational use of the river's edge. The design proposal (Fig. 4) builds upon the access point and small parking lot provided by the ACOE as a part of the Flood Reduction Project. By creating a destination park as an anchor to the ACOE river access point and the extended recreation trail, the city can enhance its existing parkland investment, create a buildable industrial site, and provide additional park land for the section of the city identified in the Comprehensive Plan as being underserved. Unlike some of the other parks in Roanoke, this would be a relatively undeveloped park, with the primary development investment made in site grading. The soils removed to create the pond and wetland area could be placed to create a building

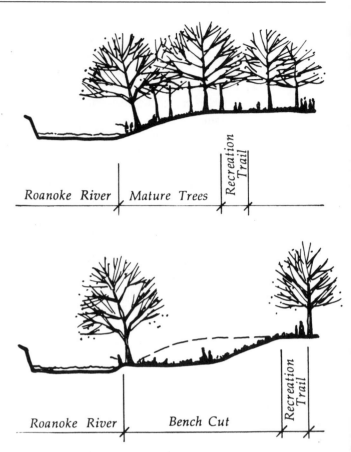

Fig. 2. Existing (top) and ACOE proposed (bottom) river bank conditions in the Roanoke River corridor project area of southwestern Virginia.

Fig. 3. Wasena Park by-pass proposal for the Roanoke River corridor project in southwestern Virginia.

pad above the 100-year floodplain at the new industrial site shown on the plan.

The proposed park is in a relatively isolated area, which is important for wildlife habitat. The pond could be ringed with a trail and boardwalk and a small viewing shelter could be constructed for wildlife observation. The pond also is adjacent to a large open meadow and picnic shelter, making the site ideal for family picnics and school field trips. Connections with the Science Museum, Mill Mountain Zoo,

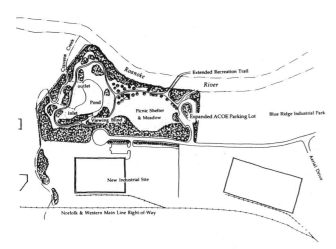

Fig. 4. Craven's Creek Conservation Park proposal for the Roanoke River corridor project in southwestern Virginia.

and area schools could also be made to establish an environmental education program at Craven's Creek. The site could serve as a laboratory to teach visitors about the number of different water systems and their inhabitants found on the site: the creek, a new pond, new wetlands, and the river, all linked together.

A site that demonstrates the importance of the juncture of the river and its tributaries, and the compatibility of industrial land use and conservation actions, is located at the confluence of Peter's Creek with the Roanoke River. Guidelines for habitat enhancement with conservation zones should be incorporated in the Zoning Code's Floodway Overlay Zone. Using the floodway line as a boundary line, an additional 4.6-m planted setback from the floodway line should provide adequate space for food, cover, and shelter for wildlife (Fig. 5). The habitat enhancement and conservation zones at the various creek confluences may require different management practices—some creek confluences may require minimal monitoring to ensure that vegetation is not removed, and that litter is; others may require more intense clean-up efforts and replanting, especially at a conservation zone's perimeter.

Legislative Actions

One of the key requirements to ensure success of the Roanoke River Corridor Plan is to gain a protected buffer along the Roanoke River, publicly accessible on at least one side of the corridor. The City of Roanoke is obtaining construction easements from adjacent property owners for

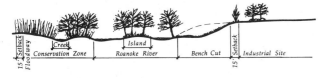

Fig. 5. Tributary Conservation Zone in the Roanoke River corridor project area of southwestern Virginia.

the ACOE project. These will cover the lands adjacent to the river where the ACOE work such as the bench cut, training wall, and riprap are to occur. Because approximately 60% of the river corridor will not be part of the project, alternative means for protecting the river's edge must be explored.

Virginia has established several different easement programs for the conservation of open space and scenic lands. These vary from easements given to the state or other acceptable body in perpetuity and administered by the Virginia Outdoor Foundation, to the set aside program of agriculture and forestal lands also administered by the Commonwealth of Virginia, which have a set time period but can be renewed. However, these programs and the scenic river program are designed for rural lands. No state programs per se exist for urban lands or reclaimed industrial river corridors.

Most of the easement options offered by the Commonwealth of Virginia also depend upon tax incentives for the enticement of a property owner's participation. Because protection and retention of the tax base within the river corridor is important, it is more sensible to select a method of river buffer protection that does not rely upon local tax abatements.

Four programs may be combined to establish a protected riparian buffer along the Roanoke River and its tributaries:

(1) Solicitation of additional easements may be made for a *Conservation Easement or Setback*, preferably donated, to continue public access along one side of the river upstream of Wasena Park. This is the most important tool in conserving the river's resources and achieving the successful implementation of the Corridor Plan. The easement or setback should include a floodway and tributary conservation zone that would support and strengthen the existing zoning ordinance on floodways and floodplains. This will create a ribbon of green along the river and its tributaries, achieving one of the city's long-standing goals, and also will support the ACOE project by managing land uses within the floodway.

(2) *More rigorous enforcement of the existing floodplain ordinance should ensue*, particularly in regard to the floodway requirements. The city has already started on this through additional training of engineering and planning staff. Workshops held with the Board of Zoning Appeals, the Planning Commission, and the planning, engineering, and zoning departments would do much to ensure that the city has a single approach to interpretation and enforcement of the ordinance regulations.

(3) *An overlay district for environmental protection and erosion control* (similar to that used to conserve the historic district in Southwest Roanoke) could be

established for the Roanoke River and its tributaries. Such a program could spell out additional standards for stream protection as well as standards for maintenance and management of adjacent vegetation and habitat. A filter strip of vegetation along the river's edge and its tributaries' edges will reduce siltation in the river and protect the investment made in flood reduction. (Siltation raises flood levels!)

(4) *A tree protection ordinance should be established.* The 1989 Reconvened Virginia General Assembly passed enabling legislation for tree conservation (Code of Virginia 10.1—1127.1) and tree replacement (Code of Virginia 15.1—14.2). The governing body of any city may adopt a tree conservation ordinance regulating the preservation and removal of heritage, specimen, memorial, and street trees.

These actions, in combination with donated easements obtained for the construction of the U.S. Army Corps of Engineers Flood Reduction Project, provide for realistic and reasonable alternatives to a tax incentive easement program for the City of Roanoke.

CONCLUSION

The long-held dream of a linear park system for the City of Roanoke, Virginia will finally be achieved. We hope that the citizens of Roanoke will gain not only some reduction in flooding and therefore a safer community, but also the enhancement and reclamation of what is a tremendous natural resource to the citizens and other inhabitants of the Roanoke Valley.

There must be an on-going effort to monitor the ACOE and the City of Roanoke's implementation of these modifications to the Flood Reduction Project. Much of what we proposed requires continuing education of citizens and city staff regarding the folly of building or repairing residential structures within the floodplain; the importance of being stewards of the creeks, drainageways, and river resources, and not using them for trash disposal; and the value to the community from the enhancement of the corridor for both people and wildlife.

REFERENCES CITED

Commonwealth of Virginia Department of Game and Inland Fisheries. 1988. Correspondence regarding wildlife fauna of the Roanoke River Corridor within the City of Roanoke, Virginia, August.

Ellington, S., and P. James. 1989. Recommended plant list for the Roanoke river corridor. Virginia Wildflower Society, Roanoke.

Gray, J., J. Loesel, and J. P. Cone, Jr. 1989. Roanoke flood-control plan would be a good beginning. Roanoke Times & World-News, Roanoke, Va., 3 April.

Hamel, P. B., H. E. LeGrand, Jr., M. R. Lennartz, and S. A. Gauthreaux, Jr. 1982. Bird-habitat relationships on Southeastern forest lands. Gen. Tech. Rep. SE-22, USDA For. Serv., Southeast For. Exp. Sta., Ashville, N.C. 417pp.

Jenkins, R.E., E.A. Lachner, and F.J. Schwartz. 1972. Fishes of the Central Appalachian Drainages: their distribution and dispersal. Pages 43–117 *in* P. C. Holt, ed. The distributional history of the biota of the Southern Appalachians. Part III: Vertebrates. Res. Div. Monogr. 4, Virginia Polytechnic Inst. and State Univ., Blacksburg.

National Park Service. 1987. Reconnaissance survey of the Roanoke river parkway corridor. 2 vols. Denver Serv. Cent., Denver, Colo.

Nolen, J. 1929. Comprehensive city plan Roanoke, Virginia. 1928. The Stone Printing and Mfg. Co., Roanoke.

Roanoke Times & World-News. 1989. Editorial. Roanoke Times & World-News, Roanoke, Va., 5 April, p. A10.

Soil Conservation Service. 1983. Sources of planting stock and seed of conservation plants used in the Northeast 1983–1985. U.S. Dep. Agric., Soil Conserv. Serv., Northeast Tech. Serv. Cent., Broomall, Pa.

Turner, J. 1988. Why millions can't stop floods. Roanoke Times & World-News, Roanoke, Va., 17 April.

U.S. Army Corps of Engineers. 1988. Preliminary general design memorandum Roanoke river flood reduction project, Wilmington, N.C., July.

U.S. Fish and Wildlife Service. 1982–1987. Habitat suitability index models for great blue heron, July 1985; belted kingfisher, August 1985; wood duck, July 1983; yellow warbler, July 1982; black-capped chickadee, April 1983; gray squirrel, July 1982; eastern cottontail, July 1984; muskrat, June 1984; green-backed heron (draft); pileated woodpecker, April 1983; hairy woodpecker, September 1987; field sparrow, December 1983; downy woodpecker, April 1983. U.S. Dep. Inter., Fish and Wildl. Serv., Washington, D.C.

——— . 1984. Final fish and wildlife coordination act report for upper Roanoke river basin study. U.S. Dep. Inter., Fish and Wildl. Serv., Div. of Ecol. Serv., Annapolis, Md.

Use of Habitat Conservation Plans Under the Federal Endangered Species Act

TIMOTHY BEATLEY, *School of Architecture, University of Virginia, Charlottesville, VA 22903*

INTRODUCTION

Increasingly, urban growth and development are bumping directly up against the habitat needs of endangered species. As the number of species listed under the Endangered Species Act (ESA)—the cornerstone of the federal effort to protect biodiversity—continues to rise, and as areas available for development diminish over time, conflicts between development and species conservation seem almost inevitable. The ESA, enacted by Congress in 1973, is a strong law and prohibits, under Section 9, the "taking" of any federally-listed species. "Take" is defined quite broadly to include harassing, harming, trapping, and killing. (For a review of the major provisions of the ESA, see Yaffee 1986, and Tobin 1990.) Section 9 of the Act has been particularly problematic for developers and owners of habitat areas who wish to modify the natural environment in major ways. Activities such as grading, land clearance, and housing construction would clearly often lead to the take of listed species.

To provide some degree of flexibility under ESA, the law was amended in 1982 to allow the U.S. Fish and Wildlife Service (USFWS) to issue incidental take permits, under Section 10(a) of the Act, in situations where developers and landowners have prepared satisfactory "habitat conservation plans" (commonly referred to as "HCPs"). This paper describes the concept of the HCP and how it has been used to date, and briefly discusses nine of the more prominent examples of its use. These profiles tend to capture the types of biological, economic, and political issues confronted in preparing HCPs. Following these profiles, the paper briefly discusses the success of the HCP mechanism to-date. Although the mechanism is still in its infancy, some tentative thoughts can be provided about its effectiveness and desirability. A number of basic policy questions emerge from an examination of HCPs, including insights about the most appropriate and effective approaches to protecting biodiversity, and these are identified and discussed.

BACKGROUND

The idea of the HCP came out of a unique planning effort in San Bruno Mountain, California in the late 1970's and early 1980's, where development was halted because of its potential impact on several species of butterfly, including the federally-listed mission blue butterfly (*Icaricia icarioides missionensis*). A special planning process was undertaken, involving both environmental and development communities, and eventually a special management plan was prepared that allowed some take of butterflies, but which also set aside large portions of the mountain as protected habitat. The plan also incorporated provisions for long-term habitat management and restoration, and a continuous funding source (Marsh and Thornton 1987). The plan itself was preceded by a series of biological studies that identified certain habitat types on the mountain necessary to the survival of the butterflies. Although the plan was experimental, USFWS gave its approval, and on the merits of the San Bruno experience, ESA was amended to officially permit the use of this mechanism in other similar circumstances.

The habitat conservation plan idea is clearly still in its infancy and USFWS has so far issued few Section 10(a) permits. Approximately 30 HCPs have been prepared or are in preparation (the majority in the latter category). The information to follow is primarily the result of extensive personal interviews I conducted with key participants involved in a number of HCPs. Because so few HCPs have been completed, and because most of the on-going HCPs are "moving targets," what is presented here must be considered work-in-progress. It is far too early to reach any definitive conclusions about how well the HCP mechanism is working.

An initial distinction of some importance is made between HCPs that are prepared for individual private projects and properties, and those that can be considered "regional" in nature (i.e., which involve multiple property owners and parcels, and usually multiple governmental units). These regional plans have been my primary research focus, and have been completed or are in progress in a

Wildlife Conservation in Metropolitan Environments. NIUW Symp. Ser. 2, L.W. Adams and D.L. Leedy, eds. Published by Natl. Inst. for Urban Wildl., 10921 Trotting Ridge Way, Columbia, MD 21044, USA, 1991.

number of locations around the country (see case studies below).

The ESA established certain basic requirements for the preparation of HCPs and certain standards that plans must satisfy before USFWS can issue a Section 10(a) permit. Plans must, at a minimum, specify the following: (1) the impact that will result from the taking, (2) the steps that will be taken to minimize and mitigate such impacts and the funding that will be available to implement these steps, (3) the alternative actions to the taking considered by the applicant and the reasons why such alternatives were not chosen, and (4) such other measures that the Secretary of the Interior may require as being necessary or appropriate for the purposes of the plan (ESA, Section 10(a)(2)(A)). A Section 10(a) incidental-take permit can only be issued if the following conditions are satisfied: (1) the taking will be incidental to an otherwise lawful activity; (2) the applicant will, to the maximum extent practicable, minimize and mitigate the impacts of such a taking; (3) the applicant will ensure that adequate funding for the plan will be provided; and (4) the taking will not appreciably reduce the likelihood of the survival and recovery of the species in the wild (ESA, Section 10(a)(2)(A); see also U.S. Fish and Wildlife Service 1990).

Most HCPs have followed fairly similar processes and most have involved the appointment of a steering committee to oversee the preparation of the plan. The committee is usually comprised of representatives of the major stakeholder groups in the community or region (e.g., developers, environmentalists, local officials, representatives of federal and state resource management agencies, etc.) and is frequently chaired by a more neutral party, such as The Nature Conservancy. A biological or technical committee also is frequently convened to guide the preparation of necessary background studies and to offer advice on technical and biological issues. Usually a private consultant is hired to actually prepare the plan and any necessary background studies.

Most HCPs entail the setting-aside of a certain amount of habitat in the form of one or more habitat preserves (Beatley forthcoming, Beatley 1990). Preserve areas are generally secured either through fee-simple purchase or through land dedication by major landowners involved in the process. In addition to preserve acquisition, HCPs typically include a variety of other management techniques, including: habitat restoration, predator control, and land use controls, among others. Sources of funding, both for the initial preparation of the plan and its implementation (e.g., land acquisition) have been varied, but have generally involved a combination of federal, state, and local government funding, as well as some private funding (e.g., The Nature Conservancy). Most HCPs impose, through participating local governments, a mitigation fee on new development occurring in or near habitat areas (e.g., fees ranging from about $620 to $4,800 per ha are typical). Beyond these common features, there is considerable variation among the HCPs, including differences in the type and number of species addressed, the threats posed to species, the size of planning areas, the specific implementation and management techniques, and the specific funding combinations, among others. For a full discussion of the similarities and differences between HCPs, see Beatley (forthcoming).

PROFILES OF SELECTED HABITAT CONSERVATION PLANS

Coachella Valley Fringe-Toed Lizard HCP

Coachella Valley, located approximately 145 km east of Los Angeles, California, is home to such fast-growing resort communities as Palm Springs, Rancho Mirage, and Palm Desert. Heavy development pressures in recent years have resulted in the loss and degradation of natural desert habitat—the dunes and sandy plains—located over much of the valley floor. This "blowsand" habitat is home to the Coachella Valley fringe-toed lizard (*Uma inornata*), federally listed as a threatened species in 1980. The lizard is uniquely adapted to its desert environment in a number of ways. In addition to its "fringe-toes," which provide traction and allow it to "skate" along the sand, the lizard has other adaptations, including: a wedged-shaped snout that facilitates diving into the sand, double-sealed eyelids, a U-shaped nasal passage (which traps sand and allows it to be easily blown out), and a special flap of skin that covers the lizard's ears when sand-diving. Its behavior also has been specially adapted to the harsh desert environment (see Beatley 1990 for a more extensive discussion).

Conflict between development and species protection came to a head in 1983 when a proposed country club development threatened to destroy approximately 162 ha of potential lizard habitat. Local environmentalists demanded that the project mitigate for this habitat destruction by buying and protecting an equal land area elsewhere in the Valley. The developer balked at this proposal and threatened to initiate legal action. The impasse was overcome when the developer, along with local environmentalists, agreed to participate in the preparation of an HCP for the lizard. A working group was convened, representing major interests in the Valley, including local governments and resource agencies, in addition to development and environmental interests. Specifically, the following groups participated in the development of the plan: The Coachella Valley Association of Governments, Bureau of Land Management (BLM), California Department of Fish and Game, USFWS, Coachella Valley Water District, Riverside County Planning Department, Coachella Valley Ecological Reserve Foundation, Sunrise Development Company, Aqua Caliente Indian Tribe, and the California Nature Conservancy. A consultant was hired to assemble land use and biological data and to prepare the actual plan. The California Nature Conservancy played an influential role in overseeing the preparation of the plan and in securing, early-on, necessary lizard habitat. The plan was completed in 1985, and USFWS issued a 30-year 10(a) permit in April of 1986. The Coachella Valley HCP was only the second HCP, after the San Bruno Mountain plan, to gain approval by USFWS (Coachella Valley HCP Steering Committee 1985).

The major conservation strategy of the plan was establishment of a system of three preserves for the lizard. Together, the preserves contain nearly 6,885 ha (the largest being the Coachella Valley Preserve containing about 5,265 ha), of which 3,240 ha is lizard habitat. The amount of habitat protected in the preserves represents approximately 10% of the potentially-occupiable habitat that existed at the time the plan was prepared. Each of the preserves includes its own sand source. In addition to the preserve lands, some additional public lands were to be managed so as to protect lizard habitat. When these lands are taken into account, protected habitat comprises about 15% of existing habitat. Total acquisition costs have been estimated at approximately $25 million (Table 1). Funding for acquisition has come from a number of sources, with the lion's share ($15 million) obtained from the federal Land and Water Conservation Fund, and through BLM land trades. The California Department of Fish and Game and The Nature Conservancy each contributed funds, and a substantial portion of the funds are generated through mitigation fees charged on development occurring in habitat areas (about $1,500/ha). (See Fig. 1 for the mitigation fee zone.)

The California Nature Conservancy took the lead in acquiring preserves and secured options for much of the land in the largest of the preserves (the Coachella Valley Preserve) even before the plan had been completed. Securing the Coachella Valley Preserve was made easier by the fact that the majority of the desired land was under single ownership. The vast majority of the preserve habitat has now been acquired and a management agreement has been signed by The Nature Conservancy, California Fish and Game, BLM, and USFWS. Various habitat restoration activities have been undertaken, as well as a biological research program. Whether the preserves, together, are large enough to ensure the long-term survival of the lizard is still uncertain. In recent years, lizard counts taken on the preserves have shown dramatic population swings—changes that are not well understood but which are apparently closely tied to rainfall trends (and in turn to the availability of vegetation and insects).

Table 1. Projected funding sources for Coachella Valley fringe-toed lizard preserves (in millions).

Funding source	Amount
Federal Land and Water Conservation Fund	$10.0
BLM land exchange (cash value)	5.0
State wildlife conservation board	1.0
The Nature Conservancy	2.0
Developer mitigation fees	7.0
Total	$25.0

Source: Coachella Valley Fringe-Toed Lizard Habitat Conservation Plan, June 1985.

North Key Largo HCP

North Key Largo, a barrier island in the northern Florida keys, is home to a diversity of plant and animal species. An HCP has been prepared for a 19.3-km segment of the island, intended to protect four federally-listed species: The American crocodile (*Crocodylus acutus*), the Schaus swallowtail butterfly (*Heraclides aristodemus ponceanus*), the Key Largo woodrat (*Neotoma floridana smalli*) and the Key Largo cottonmouse (*Peromyscus gossypinus allapaticola*). The HCP was precipitated by two lawsuits claiming that projects planned in the area (the installation of a federally-funded aquaduct and a large resort housing project) were in violation of the federal ESA.

At the request of several of the largest landowners, an HCP process was initiated with special funding provided by the Governor's Office. Additional funds to finance biological studies were provided by landowners. The preparation of the HCP roughly coincided with the updating of the county's comprehensive plan, and was eventually to become part of the overall county plan. The outside planning consultant preparing the county's comprehensive plan also staffed the North Key Largo HCP. An HCP steering committee was established, including representatives of major landowners, the Florida Audubon Society, and state and federal agencies, among others.

The resulting plan proposed the designation of 84% of the existing hardwood hammock as "conserved habitat," in which future land development would be prohibited under the county zoning ordinance (North Key Largo HCP Steering Committee 1986). Future development, then, would be allowed to destroy up to 16% of the hardwood hammock habitat and would be clustered into five designated development nodes. Although owners of land in the conserved habitat would not be able to build on-site under the plan, they would be able to transfer this unused development density to parcels within the development nodes, or to other development sites in the county. A maximum of 3500 dwelling units would be permitted in the development nodes, with this maximum density achievable only through transfer of density from the conserved habitat. Under the plan, it was agreed that any attempt to develop in the nodes would be delayed for a period of 2 years, to give the state legislature the opportunity to provide funds to purchase these lands. (Complete acquisition of the North Key Largo habitat was deemed the preferable approach by groups like Florida Audubon.)

In addition to land use controls and land acquisition, the HCP set forth a series of other actions that will be undertaken to promote recovery of the species. These included: actions to control and remove exotic plants, and domestic pets; controls on the use of insecticides; restoration of natural habitat, including the removal of roads and bridges to restore historic water regimes; introduction of host species (e.g., periodic burns to promote torchwood (*Amyris elemifera*) and wild lime (*Zanthoxylum fagara*), plants upon

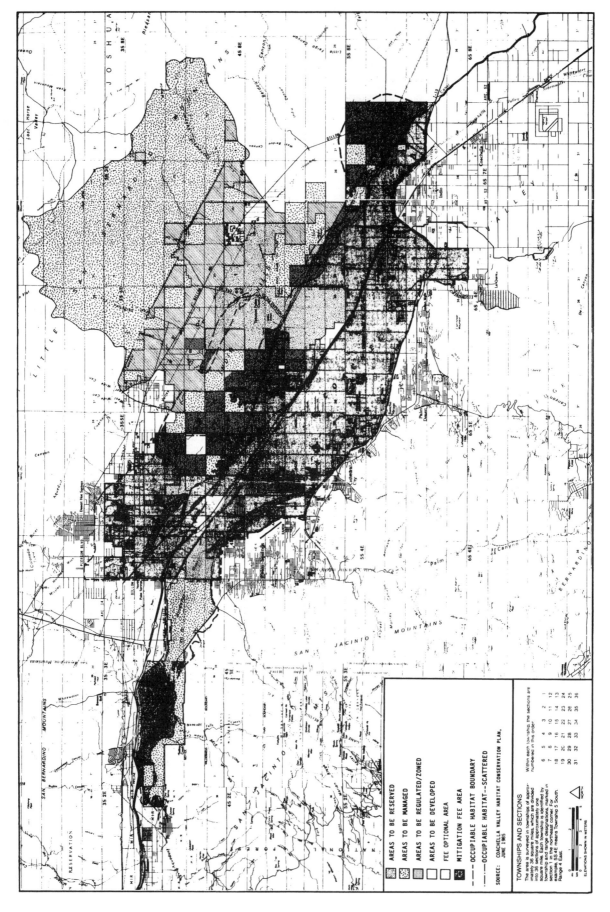

Fig. 1.   Habitat conservation plan for the Coachella Valley fringe-toed lizard in southern California, 1985. (From Coachella Valley HCP Steering Committee 1985.)

which the female swallowtail lays her eggs); modification of canal banks to provide nesting sites and habitat for the American crocodile; trapping and relocation of endangered woodrats and cottonmice prior to development; captive breeding and reintroduction; education programs; and research and monitoring activities. The plan also envisioned that on-going habitat management would be funded through both a one-time development fee ($2500 per dwelling unit) and an annual mitigation fee ($2.00 per overnight accommodation unit per night, or $2.00 per week for residential units).

The original HCP was never officially adopted by the county or approved by the USFWS, and the county is still considering several more recent versions of the HCP. The plan can be considered a success, however, in that it has resulted in the acquisition, primarily by the state's Conservation and Recreations Lands (CARL) program, of much of the habitat. Efforts at acquisition continue, though a number of smaller landholdings remain. It is not clear if an HCP will be adopted to address these remaining private parcels.

Least Bell's Vireo HCP

The least Bell's vireo (*Vireo bellii*), a small grayish migratory songbird, once inhabited much of Southern California. The species has experienced tremendous reductions in population and range, primarily as a result of the gradual conversion of its natural riparian habitat (streamside willow woodlands) to urban and agricultural uses. The expansion of the range and numbers of the brown-headed cowbird (*Molothrus ater*), a competitor and parasitic species, has also been responsible for shrinking numbers. It is believed that the California population of least Bell's vireos has dropped to about 350 pairs. As a result of these dramatic declines, the vireo was placed on the California endangered species list in 1980, and on the federal list in 1986 (Regional Environmental Consultants 1989.)

Since 1986, the San Diego Association of Governments has coordinated an ambitious effort to prepare a regional HCP for the vireo. Unlike most of the other HCPs profiled here, the primary threat to vireo habitat comes now from public improvements, such as highways, dams, and flood-control projects. The San Diego program is also organizationally more complicated than the other HCPs profiled. A two-level approach has been taken. To address conservation of the species on a rangewide basis, a Comprehensive Species Management Plan (CSMP) has been prepared (Regional Environmental Consultants 1989). Among other things, the CSMP examines data on the existing number of vireo pairs and the extent of existing habitat in each riparian area, and sets quantitative targets for each specific river basin. Biological studies conducted as part of the CSMP have included field surveys, nest counts, cowbird studies, and limited vireo banding. The CSMP sets a goal of 5,000 breeding pairs of vireos (as recommended in the

USFWS recovery plan), and at least 3,645 ha of vireo habitat (6,075 to 8,100 ha of riparian habitat overall).

Another level of planning is being undertaken at the river basin level. More detailed HCPs have been under preparation for four river basins: the San Luis Rey River, the San Diego River, the Sweetwater River and the Santa Ana River. The HCPs for the Santa Ana and San Luis Rey Rivers have been completed, and plans for the San Diego and Sweetwater Rivers are nearing completion. These river basin HCPs are intended to contain more specific plans for acquiring, regulating, and managing habitat areas. Two other important river basins in the area were not included in the study because they are primarily under the control of the federal government (the Santa Margarita River, which flows through Camp Pendleton Marine Corps Base; and the Santa Ynez River, which is under the jurisdiction of the U.S. Forest Service). Because of strong landowner opposition to the San Luis Rey River HCP, plans to apply for a Section 10(a) permit for this river have been dropped. The Santa Ana River HCP will also probably not lead to a Section 10(a) permit application, but will be adopted as a policy document by the local governments involved.

Administratively, two sets of steering committees have been functioning. A large 30-member task force oversees the entire program and directs the preparation of the CSMP. Each of the individual river basins has its own separate advisory committee guiding and overseeing the preparation of each of the more detailed HCPs. Because the landownership patterns and development threats, as well as the status of the vireo, are somewhat different in each of the river basins, the content of the individual HCPs tends to be somewhat different as well. Funding for the program has been obtained from the state legislature on a matching share basis. The bulk of the funds have been used to pay consultants to conduct the necessary biological studies, and to prepare the draft CSMP and HCPs.

Some have argued that an HCP in the case of the least Bell's vireo was simply not needed because virtually all projects in riparian areas must go through a Section 7 consultation with the USFWS anyway (as a result of the need to obtain a Section 404 federal wetlands permit). In reply to this, supporters of the HCP process point to the value of taking a regional view, and of evaluating specific project-level proposals within the context of the broader rangewide needs of the species. The regional planning effort has already been influential in the design and review of several highway and bridge projects (including an extension of State Highway 52, which will cross the San Diego River).

Many of the key implementation issues in this HCP have yet to be resolved, including how the plan will be funded. A number of alternatives are being considered, including the creation of special riparian assessment districts. Unlike Coachella Valley and most of the other HCPs, little emphasis is being given to fee-simple habitat acquisition. Rather, the assumption appears to be that much of the implementation of the HCPs will largely continue through project-by-project mitigation (e.g., replacement of habitat lost with new habitat). The San Diego program has experienced significant opposition from some landowners, particularly farmers along the San Luis Rey who fear that the HCP may result in restrictions on their ability to extract water from the river (i.e., because of the potential impacts on streamside willows). It is because of this type of landowner opposition that the San Luis Rey River has been dropped from the regional plan.

Stephens' Kangaroo Rat HCP

The Stephens' kangaroo rat (*Dipodomys stephensi*), like other kangaroo rats, has a large head, external cheek pouches, small front legs, and long rear legs. It is native to the arid, low-lying grasslands of western Riverside County, California. The major threat to the kangaroo rat has been the loss of habitat from the disking of grasslands for agricultural and livestock uses, and the grading and clearance of land for urban development. The USFWS declared the Stephens' kangaroo rat endangered on 31 October 1988.

Planning for the species began almost immediately following its listing. A Stephens' kangaroo rat technical advisory committee was established initially and the county enacted an emergency mitigation fee ordinance in mid-November, which imposed a $4,818/ha impact fee for all development occurring in rat habitat areas. These funds have been used to hire consultants to undertake the necessary biological and land use studies. A formal HCP steering committee was formed in the spring of 1989, meeting for the first time in March of that year. The committee is chaired by the attorney who represented Sunrise Development Company in the Coachella Valley case, and consists of representatives of developers and builders, members of environmental groups, local government representatives, and representatives of state and federal resource agencies.

The initial efforts of the steering committee were focused on the preparation and submittal to the USFWS of an interim or short-term HCP. The central idea was to devise a way to make available for development large portions of the county where few, if any, rats were likely to be located, while protecting those areas where rat habitat and populations were concentrated, and where the studies and management activities of the long-term HCP would focus. A final, revised interim HCP was prepared and submitted to USFWS in March, 1990 (Regional Environmental Consultants 1990a) and an interim Section 10(a) permit was recently issued. Under the interim plan, 10 kangaroo rat study areas have been identified and designated, including nearly 8,100 ha of rat habitat, or what is estimated to be approximately 80% of the habitat in the County (Fig. 2). Under the provisions of the interim 10(a) permit, the USFWS will allow incidental take of kangaroo rats only in areas outside of the designated study areas. This short-term permit will be in effect only for a period of 2 years. During this period, the preparation of a thorough HCP will proceed for the study areas, including extensive biological and field

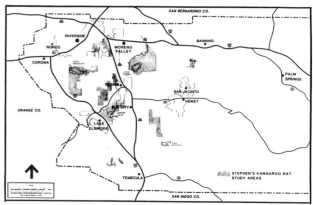

Fig. 2. Stephens' kangaroo rat habitat in western Riverside County, California, 1990. (From Regional Environmental Consultants 1990a.)

studies of the rat's habitat, land use compatibility studies, and the development of an appropriate long-term protection strategy. Over the course of preparing the long-term HCP, the boundaries of rat habitat may be modified substantially as new and more detailed biological and land use information is generated (probably substantially reducing the boundaries). Under the long-term HCP, a special subcommittee will be appointed to oversee the work for each of the 10 study areas.

It should be noted that although the Section 10(a) permit does not apply to land in the study areas, the local governments have taken no actions to protect these lands from development (e.g., by perhaps placing moratoria on development). To develop these areas, however, a landowner or developer will still have to confront the endangered species issue and perhaps secure a 10(a) permit on his own.

Although it is too early to tell what the final HCP will call for, most involved in the process seem to envision a large system of acquired preserves, which may eventually cost between $50 and $250 million. The Stephens' kangaroo rat controversy has been treated in the media as a conflict between a rat—albeit a "cute" rat—and affordable housing. Western Riverside County has been characterized as one of the last remaining areas of affordable housing in the Los Angeles region, with the median price of homes at about $113,000. This compares to approximately $231,000 in Orange County, and $191,200 in Los Angeles.

Metropolitan Bakersfield HCP

An HCP is currently being prepared for the Bakersfield, California, metropolitan area. The area encompassed includes the 1,050-km² Metropolitan Bakersfield 2010 Plan, and the HCP is primarily focused on conservation of the federally-listed San Joaquin kit fox (*Vulpes macrotis*) and its necessary habitat. Other animal species of concern addressed by the HCP are the endangered blunt-nosed leopard lizard (*Gambelia silus*), the Tipton kangaroo rat (*Dipodomys nitratoides nitratoides*), the giant kangaroo rat (*Dipodomys ingens*), and the San Joaquin antelope squirrel (*Ammospermophilus nelsoni*). Several plants are also addressed, including the Bakersfield cactus (*Opuntia treleasei*) and the California jewel flower (*Caulanthus californicus*).

The endangered species issue emerged in Bakersfield in 1986 when environmentalists charged that the proposed Sand Creek Golf Course along the Kern River would have resulted in take of the federally-listed San Joaquin kit fox. Local environmentalists were instrumental in bringing these potential threats to the attention of USFWS, which began to scrutinize development projects in the area more carefully. As a result, the Sand Creek Golf Course (on city-owned land) was scrapped and several development projects were placed on hold. The need to find a solution to the local species problem led to the city initiating an HCP.

A steering committee, consisting of developers, environmentalists, and city officials, has been meeting since 1986. The city and county have both adopted an interim mitigation fee requirement for all development occurring in the metro area while the HCP is being prepared (with the exception of urban infill areas that are clearly not habitat). Like the Coachella Valley case, USFWS has tacitly approved this temporary arrangement even though it is undoubtedly leading to some take of endangered species. The temporary mitigation fee is $1,680 per gross ha. A temporary moratorium in prime habitat areas was considered but discarded because these are the fastest growing areas in the region (the southwest and northeast quadrants). The USFWS has issued a strongly worded special notice to developers requiring that potential kit fox dens found on site be hand-excavated prior to development (allowing any kit foxes present to "escape unhindered"). Most developers in habitat areas appear to be adhering to this requirement.

A draft HCP was issued in September 1990. Its main strategy is a combination of habitat acquisition and restoration. More specifically, the plan calls for: the acquisition and management of between 202 and 405 ha in the northeast portion of the study area primarily to preserve the Bakersfield cactus; the acquisition and management of between 2,023 and 4,047 ha of land adjacent to the Kern County Water Bank project; and cooperative agreements for restoring and enhancing between 1,214 and 4,856 ha of land within the Kern County Water Bank project (Metropolitan Bakersfield HCP Steering Committee 1990). Dovetailing the HCP's habitat acquisition-enhancement efforts with the Water Bank project is a major component of the Metro-Bakersfield strategy. Under this project, the State Department of Water Resources has recently purchased some 8,100 ha of farmland southwest of the city to become the Kern County Water Bank. (These are areas to be used by the state to replenish regional groundwater supplies.)

The proposed plan calls for the issuance of a 10(a) permit for a 20-year period, which would allow take in areas outside of the primary floodplain of the Kern River (which is an important kit fox movement corridor connecting populations in the northeast foothills and valley to the southwest), and lands within the Kern Water Bank. The Section 10(a) permit will cover development activities, but will not cover oil extraction or agricultural activities in natural habitat lands. The Bakersfield plan takes a "pay-as-you-go" approach, with yearly mitigation intended to stay ahead of take. The amount of mitigation called for in the draft plan is to be directly proportional to the amount of habitat destroyed. A distinction is made in the plan between open lands (agricultural lands primarily) and natural lands (which provide superior habitat). Under the plan, each hectare of natural land lost to development will be mitigated by the enhancement of three hectares elsewhere. (For open lands the mitigation ratio is one-for-one.)

Funding to implement the plan will come primarily from development mitigation fees (proposed to be increased to $2,471/ha), and supplemented as necessary with federal and state funds. Responsibility for administration of the plan will be given to a specially-created Implementation Trust. Each year, the Implementation Trust will monitor and report the cumulative status of take and enhancement to USFWS.

Kern County, in which Bakersfield is located, has initiated its own Habitat Conservation Planning Process, as part of its land use plan update. The HCP will specifically encompass the approximately 8,024-km² valley floor portion of Kern County (the southern end of the San Joaquin Valley). Federally-listed species to be addressed in the HCP include: the San Joaquin kit fox, the giant kangaroo rat, the blunt-nosed leopard lizard, and the Buena Vista lake shrew (*Sorex ornatus*). In addition to the HCP, the county is also preparing an Endangered Species Element of its General Plan. The endangered species element will also include other species that have not yet been federally listed, and will serve as the umbrella policy document for the more-specific HCPs. In addition to such species as the San Joaquin kit fox and the blunt-nosed leopard lizard, other species of concern in the county include: the San Joaquin antelope squirrel, the short-nosed kangaroo rat (*Dipodomys nitratoides*), and the Tipton kangaroo rat, among others. Endangered plant species will also be included.

For approximately 3 years, the county has convened a Threatened and Endangered Species work group, consisting of representatives from state and federal resource agencies, private conservation groups, private land developers, the oil and gas industry, and agriculture. This group oversees the preparation of the valley floor HCP and the endangered species element, and generally advises the county on endangered species issues. The objectives of the Kern County program are "(1) to develop a cooperative program among public agencies with permit authority over threatened and endangered species of concern which will ensure that activities or private parties comply with applicable laws and regulations concerning species of concern in Kern County and; (2) assure the long term protection of species of concern while allowing for the continued economic growth of Kern County." (Kern County, California 1989.) A memorandum of understanding has been entered into among USFWS, the

U.S. Bureau of Land Management, California Department of Fish and Game, California Energy Commission, California Department of Conservation (Division of Oil and Gas), and Kern County. A consulting firm has been hired to prepare the HCP, the endangered species element, implementing agreements, and related environmental documentation (e.g., the necessary environmental impact reports). A large portion of the money to fund the HCP and endangered species element ($350,000) has been obtained from a grant from the State Division of Oil and Gas.

At this point in time, the consultant has assembled a series of habitat maps and other necessary background biological information for the plan. The county work group has been exploring alternative mitigation strategies with different key interest groups in the county (e.g., farming, oil interests). Although a variety of different strategies may ultimately be utilized, some form of habitat protection will be central (including fee-simple acquisition, easements, etc.). A mitigation fee has not yet been imposed (outside of the Metro-Bakersfield area), but county officials see this as a likely major source of the HCP's long-term funding.

Sand City HCP

Sand City, California, is a small scenic coastal town located north of Monterey. It has, for several years, been in the process of preparing an HCP for the federal-listed Smith's blue butterfly (*Euphilotes enoptes Smithi*). A major portion of the city's remaining undeveloped dune area is prime habitat for the butterfly and its primary host plant, the buckwheat. A steering committee has been appointed by the city council to oversee the HCP process. The committee includes representatives of developers and landowners, USFWS, California Department of Fish and Game, Caltrans, and environmental interests such as the Sierra Club and Native Plants Society. A consultant has been hired to prepare the HCP and background biological studies. Funding for the plan has been split between landowner contributions and the California Coastal Conservancy, with each providing $50,000.

The prime butterfly habitat in the city is located in dune areas seaward of the coastal highway (Highway 101). The largest remaining block of habitat is in an area known as the "East Dunes." Much of the steering committee's discussion has centered on what to do with this area. To developers and city officials, prohibiting all development in the area would be unreasonable in that it comprises such a large percentage of the remaining buildable land in the city (the city is very small to begin with). In addition, this area is already heavily parcelized—with some 250 existing lots. Buying these lands would be extremely expensive, as small lots, even without public facilities, are selling for as much as $25,000 each. A number of alternative development concepts have been considered, including clustering development in the center of the area, with large areas of conserved habitat around the edges. Even under this type of arrangement, it is unclear to city officials how the problem

of existing lots will be addressed and how acquisition of the conserved habitat (if acquired outright) will be paid for. The steering committee has also been considering the establishment of a butterfly corridor to run adjacent to Highway 101.

Local officials have expressed considerable frustration about the HCP process. Despite repeated attempts to learn from USFWS what an acceptable habitat conservation scheme would consist of, they feel that they have been given little or no direction. Rather, they feel USFWS has adopted the attitude that "once we see the plan we'll tell you whether or not it's adequate." Officials have also been critical about the lack of federal or state funds to pay for habitat acquisition. In their case, the habitat in question is very expensive and represents such a large percentage of the city's remaining potentially-buildable land. Thus, there is no large development base over which to distribute the costs of conservation (e.g., by way of a mitigation fee), as there was in Coachella Valley and many of the other HCPs. Also, because areas such as the East Dunes are some of the few last remaining areas to develop, the city's ability to expand its tax base is in jeopardy. City officials have also expressed concern that these are the last potential areas for affordable housing (at least relative to development in the Monterey region as a whole).

Marina Dunes HCP

The City of Marina, California, is a coastal jurisdiction north of Monterey. The primary endangered species of concern here is also the endangered Smith's blue butterfly. Marina is jointly preparing an HCP for the butterfly and a new local coastal plan ("LCP"), together generally referred to as the Marine Dunes plan. Funding for the plans has been split between local landowners and the California Coastal Conservancy, each putting up $60,000. The process was originally initiated as a result of a lawsuit filed by the Sierra Club. A steering committee, consisting of the landowners involved, environmentalists, resource agency representatives, and local officials, has been meeting since 1986. Because of the joint HCP/LCP effort, the Marina Committee has been considering a much larger set of management issues than just the butterfly, including such things as shoreline erosion, view protection, and public beach access. One consultant has been involved in preparing both of these components.

The primary butterfly habitat in Marina is located along a 223-ha continuous tract of beachfront, beginning just north of the Marina Point State Park. The Marina Dunes HCP has been made easier by existing landownership patterns (in contrast to Sand City). The habitat areas are essentially owned by three landowners: Lonestar Company, Granite Rock, and Monterey Sand. All three companies currently use the land as part of sand mining operations. The Lonestar Company is the largest of the three, owning about 162 ha of the habitat. In contrast to the experience of Sand City, the Marina steering committee has had an easier time reaching general consensus about what the management strategy should be. The consultant has done detailed analyses of the extent of land and vegetation disturbance, and the committee has made the general assumption that any future development should occur in areas owned by these companies. The committee has agreed that future development should be restricted to designated "bubbles," which will allow substantial density, but also large remaining areas to be set aside as conserved habitat. Of the 223 ha in the area, development is planned for about 50 ha, leaving the remainder as conserved habitat. It does not appear that any land acquisition will be needed, as the conserved habitat will simply be protected by deed restrictions on the land, preventing any future development.

Although there appears to be general agreement on the conservation strategy, a number of specific implementation issues have not yet been resolved. It is not clear who will be given management responsibilities for the conserved habitat areas once they are set aside. Among the alternative management entities that have been under consideration are the regional park authority, the California Department of Parks and Recreation, and USFWS. At this point, it is probable that the regional park authority will take over these management responsibilities. Extensive funding does not appear to be necessary in the case of Marina. Each landowner will be responsible for undertaking certain initial habitat restoration activities (until conserved habitat areas achieve certain restoration standards), after which management responsibilities for conserved habitat areas will be turned over to the regional park authority or other designated agency. At that point, developments will be charged an annual contribution necessary to maintain habitat areas (these funds will likely, in turn, be generated through a room tax).

At this point in time (1990), an administrative draft of the LCP/HCP has been prepared and will soon be presented to the City Council for approval. It is estimated that the additional environmental review documentation will take another 18 to 24 months to complete. To local participants, a distressing aspect of the Marina Dunes process has been the length of time it has taken—nearly 5 years already.

Desert Tortoise HCP

The Mojave desert tortoise (*Gopherus agassizii*) has, in recent years, experienced precipitous declines over much of its western range. These sharp declines are due to a number of factors, including: direct loss of habitat as a result of land development; habitat degradation; and tortoise deaths due to off-road vehicle use, shooting and other forms of vandalism, predation from ravens (a species whose numbers have risen dramatically in many desert areas as result of the extension of telephone and power lines, the existence of dumps and landfills, and other results of a greater human presence in the desert), and disease. The latter, a respiratory ailment, has had a particularly significant impact on desert tortoise populations in the wild, and was formerly thought only to exist in captive tortoises.

Because of the sharp reduction in desert tortoise populations, the species was emergency listed in August of 1989. Very shortly after this, Clark County, Nevada (the Las Vegas area) initiated a habitat conservation plan for the tortoise. Much of the county's undeveloped land is potential habitat and the desert tortoise was viewed a major obstacle to future development and growth of the area. A steering committee was established to oversee the preparation of the HCP, and consists of: representatives of Clark County and each of the five municipalities located in the county; development and real estate interests (the Summa Corporation, a major developer in the region; the Southern Nevada Homebuilders Association; and the Board of Realtors); representatives from the environmental community, including the Desert Tortoise Council, Defenders of Wildlife, Environmental Defense Fund, and The Nature Conservancy; the Nevada Department of Wildlife; the Nevada Department of Transportation; the Nevada Department of Agriculture; USFWS; BLM; the Southern Nevada Zoological Park; the Nevada Cattlemens Association; the Southern Nevada Miners Association; representatives of off-road vehicle groups; and representatives of the state's congressional delegation, among others. This committee met on a weekly basis for the first 2 months or so of its existence and now holds monthly meetings. The Nature Conservancy has been given the responsibility of directing the biological and other necessary technical studies and preparing the actual HCP (which has been sub-contracted out to an environmental consulting firm in San Diego). In addition to the steering committee, a technical advisory committee, consisting of biologists and scientific experts, was formed to oversee and advise on the preparation of the plan.

In October of 1989, the county and each of the five municipalities adopted a desert tortoise development ordinance that imposes a $618 per gross ha mitigation fee on all development in the county. These monies are placed in a special fund and are to be used to pay for the costs of preparing the HCP and for acquiring future habitat areas, among other things. As of spring 1990, these fees have generated about $750,000, a portion of which has been used to pay the plan consultants. The fee requirement applies to virtually all undeveloped land in the county. Payment of the mitigation fee, however, does not permit species take. Developers are also required to undertake biological assessments of their property to determine whether there are tortoises or evidence of tortoises present on the site (e.g., burrows, trails). If the latter are found, then development is considered to be prohibited without a 10(a) permit. The desert tortoise fund is administered by the Clark County Board of Supervisors, consistent with the recommendation and guidance of the steering committee.

One of the key issues in the Clark County HCP process has been finding a way to allow some degree of development to proceed in tortoise habitat while the longer-term HCP was being prepared. The steering committee examined a number of different options and decided finally on preparing a short-term HCP that would allow "take" within Las Vegas Valley (which includes the City of Las Vegas and most of the development pressures) for a 3-year period, in exchange for certain short-term habitat conservation measures, primarily in the form of removing certain BLM habitat areas from livestock, mining, and off-road vehicle uses. The priority conservation areas have been identified (Fig. 3) and short-term habitat protection will be focused here (Regional Environmental Consultants 1990b.)

Maximum take of tortoises over the 3-year permit period will not exceed 3700, with the following habitat conservation compliance thresholds (Regional Environmental Consultants 1990b:ix): "1) At least 100,000 acres [40,500 ha] will be conserved within either of two priority areas before any take is allowed. . . ; 2) At least 200,000 acres [81,000 ha] will be conserved by the end of the fourth quarter after take is allowed; 3) At least 300,000 acres [121,500 ha] will be conserved before take exceeds 2,000 tortoises or habitat loss exceeds 13,000 acres [5,265 ha]; 4) Before the 3-year permit expires, at least 400,000 acres [162,000 ha] will be conserved, with at least 200,000 acres [81,000 ha] in either of the two priority areas, before take exceeds 3,500 tortoises or habitat loss exceeds 18,000 acres [7,290 ha]." The 10(a) permit would cover approximately 162,000 ha in the Las Vegas Valley. Habitat would be conserved through several different types of land use controls, including the acquisition of grazing rights, additional restrictions on off-road vehicle use of habitat areas, and review of mining claims on BLM lands. As well, a tortoise research and relocation program would be initiated (to study, for instance, the effects of livestock grazing on tortoises). Any proposed development would have to prepare a tortoise survey for the site and any tortoises found would be relocated (to be used for research, education, etc.). A $1,359/ha mitigation fee would also be imposed (the $618/ha fee would still apply to areas outside of the permit zone).

Balcones Canyonlands HCP

The Balcones Canyonlands is a region located in the Hill Country and Edwards Plateau to the west of Austin, Texas. Its steep canyons, ridgetops, and plateaus are home to two species of endangered migratory songbirds—the black-capped vireo (*Vireo atricapillus*), and the golden-cheeked warbler (*Dendroica chrysoparia*). The limestone geology has resulted in a series of subterranean caves, sinkholes, and fissures that are home to a diversity of unique and rare invertebrates. Five cave-adapted invertebrates have been federally-listed, including a spider, two types of beetles, a pseudo-scorpion, and a daddy longlegs. Several species of rare plants are also found in the area (Austin Regional Habitat Conservation Plan 1990).

In recent years, this rich habitat has come under considerable development pressures as the Austin metropolitan area has expanded. The conflict between endangered species and development came to a head in 1988 when a number of public and private projects threatening black-capped vireo

habitat were halted. Public awareness about the problem of habitat destruction in the Austin area was facilitated by the actions of the radical environmental group Earth First! staging a variety of public protests, receiving national as well as local coverage. Among other things, members of the group chained themselves to bulldozers in vireo habitat and occupied, for a 2-week period, a series of Karst caves threatened by a proposed shopping center. Earth First! has also played an important role in closely monitoring habitat destruction and alteration and alerting USFWS to these activities. (See Beatley et al., forthcoming.)

An HCP for the Austin area was initiated in 1988 through a joint proposal of the Texas Nature Conservancy and the City of Austin's Department of Environmental Protection (now called the Environmental and Conservation Services Department). An executive committee was formed to oversee the preparation of the plan and was chaired by the Director of the Texas Nature Conservancy. The committee includes representatives of the development community (attorneys for local developers), as well as representatives of the environmental community (Audubon Society and Sierra Club). Several local governments are also represented on the committee, as are relevant state agencies (e.g., Texas Parks and Wildlife Department, and the Texas General Land Office). In addition to the executive committee, a Biological Advisory Team ("BAT") was also appointed and consists of some 20 leading scientists and biologists from the area (e.g., from the University of Texas, and the City of Austin). Consultants were hired to collect land use and other necessary data, and to prepare the plan itself.

The process of biological assessment began with BAT reviewing a list of endangered and threatened species identified by one or more public and private conservation groups (e.g., USFWS, Texas Parks and Wildlife Department, Texas Natural Heritage Program) as species of concern. Species were targeted for inclusion in the plan based on whether there was a significant population in the area, the extent of the threat to the species, and the extent to which the HCP would be effective in protecting or conserving the species (Austin Regional Habitat Conservation Plan 1990). Several biological background studies were conducted, including specific studies of the biology and habitat requirements of the migratory songbirds, botanical studies, and studies of the underground cave ecosystems. The overall findings of BAT are contained in a comprehensive biological assessment issued in January 1990. The assessment contains specific recommendations about the necessary size and characteristics of habitat preserves. A series of habitat maps also has been generated by the planning consultant and BAT, based in part on remote sensing.

The main strategy of the Balcones Canyonlands HCP is to set aside large contiguous tracts of habitat. An "overlay" approach has been used to identify habitat areas already under public ownership (e.g., The Norma Long City Park) and areas that would not be buildable under the city's Com-

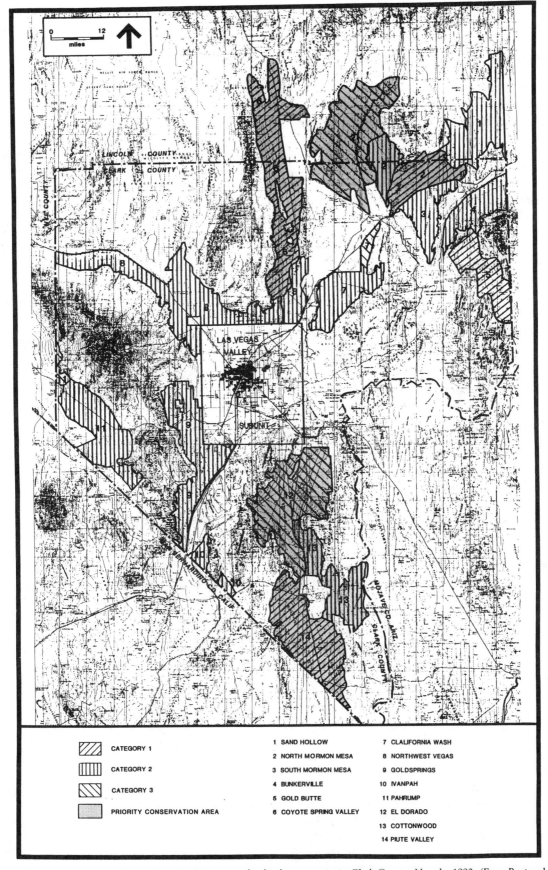

Fig. 3.   Potential management areas and priority conservation areas for the desert tortoise in Clark County, Nevada, 1990. (From Regional Environmental Consultants 1990b.)

prehensive Watersheds Ordinance. Two macrosites have been identified where acquisition will be focused: the Post Oak Ridge site and the west Austin site. Between these two sites, the proposed HCP envisions acquiring between 24,300 and 32,400 ha of habitat. Acquisition will not occur all at once, but will proceed over a 10-year period. The Texas Nature Conservancy has already obtained options to buy 7,290 ha of habitat in the Post Oak Macrosite. There is a high likelihood that the Post Oak Ridge macrosite will become a National Wildlife Refuge and USFWS has recently allocated $2 million for its acquisition. In addition, because considerable amounts of habitat in the Austin area are now owned by the Resolution Trust Corporation and FDIC (as a result of savings and loan failures), efforts are being made to secure some of these lands through donation or at bargain prices. In addition to land acquisition, land use regulations are also under consideration. In particular, a 152.5-m habitat buffer is being discussed that would curtail development and habitat alteration in areas adjacent to preserve lands.

The biggest uncertainty with the Balcones Canyon-lands HCP is where the necessary funding will come from. It is estimated that over the 10-year acquisition period, funding needs may exceed $100 million. The Executive Committee has been examining a number of different sources of revenue, including the federal Land and Water Conservation Fund ($2 million already secured), the State Parks and Wildlife Fund, and a variety of potential local sources (e.g., impact fees, real estate transfer taxes, a special habitat taxing district, a percentage add-on to capital improvement projects, and general obligation bonds). Impact fees are currently being considered at the rate of $750 per living unit, or $370/ha for commercial and industrial development.

The plan has not yet been officially adopted by the local governments and it is not at all clear that the coalition between the development and environmental communities will remain intact. Those in the development community are beginning to express concerns that the acquisition plan is too ambitious and too costly, while those in certain environmental circles (especially Earth First!) are concerned that not enough habitat will be protected and are threatening to sue.

EVALUATING THE HCP CONCEPT

Although the Habitat Conservation Plan is still a relatively new tool under the Endangered Species Act, there is sufficient experience to date to offer some tentative observations about its effectiveness and desirability. So far, there has been a wide range of reaction to the HCP concept, from those in the development community who see it as a badly-needed vehicle for flexibility, to some in the environmental community who view it skeptically as simply a way of circumventing the otherwise tough restrictions of ESA. In this section, I will briefly identify key implementation issues and discuss the prospects for the success of the HCP approach.

The experiences to date provide a mixed review for the HCP mechanism. On the one hand, it has indeed offered an alternative to the traditional confrontation and litigation that often arise in endangered species-development conflicts. The HCPs so far completed or underway generally reflect an amazing willingness on the part of typically-warring parties to sit down at the same table and to compromise on certain issues. Moreover, the HCP mechanism does seem to have provided a sort of pressure release valve under ESA, allowing some degree of flexibility and deflecting some of the potential political opposition and criticism of ESA that might otherwise have resulted in gutting or loosening the law.

The tangible accomplishments of HCPs are also already quite impressive. In the case of the San Bruno Mountain HCP, some 1,100 ha of habitat have been protected. In the case of the Coachella Valley HCP, close to 6,900 ha of desert habitat (3,240 ha of habitat for the fringe-toed lizard) have been protected in perpetuity. Even in the case of North Key Largo, where an HCP has never officially been adopted, the planning efforts have clearly resulted in the acquisition of considerable amounts of hardwood hammock habitat (primarily by the state). Habitat Conservation Plans also have provided a mechanism for generating funds, such as through development mitigation fees, which are being used for a variety of acquisition, restoration, research, and management activities; funds that would not otherwise be available. And, in some cases, the species of concern would clearly be worse off had an HCP not been prepared. In the case of San Bruno Mountain, for instance, butterfly habitat was gradually declining as native grasslands continued to be replaced by non-native vegetation. The San Bruno Mountain HCP is resulting in the gradual restoration of native grasslands (San Bruno Mountain HCP Steering Committee 1982, Marsh and Thornton 1987). Similar restorative activities are components of other HCPs, for instance cowbird trapping will be a significant part of the strategy of the Balcones Canyonlands HCP.

On the other hand, the HCP experiences to date suggest a number of concerns about the use of this mechanism and its potential for protecting species and their habitat over the long term. The major concerns or issues that arise in reviewing the HCPs as a whole are briefly listed and discussed below, and are considered in much greater detail elsewhere (see Beatley, forthcoming).

The Adequacy of Conservation Measures

Although significant acquisition and protection of species habitat has and will continue to occur, there are serious concerns about the adequacy of the conservation measures contained in many HCPs. Recall that a Section 10(a) permit cannot be issued unless the Secretary of the Interior finds that the take will not appreciably reduce the likelihood of the "survival or recovery" of the species. Almost by definition, the HCPs involve the loss of habitat to development and in some cases the loss can be substantial. The Coachella Valley HCP, for example, will protect only about 15% of the existing potentially occupiable habitat of fringe-toed lizards (less than 10% is protected in the preserves). And, even though much of the habitat outside of the preserves has undergone degradation (e.g., through sand-shielding), the HCP results in the opening-up of substantial habitat areas to new development. This type of result has led one environmentalist to recently charge that HCPs amount to "little more than a developer paying for the right to turn an ecosystem into an intensely managed open zoo" (Johnson 1990:22).

It is not at all clear that protected habitat areas will remain ecologically-viable over the long run. Many will amount to little more than small habitat "postage stamps," eventually surrounded by urban development and intense human activities. It is also interesting to note that not a single HCP has explicitly considered the potential impacts of global warming, which could potentially negate habitat conservation efforts and which might suggest special preserve acquisition and design strategies (Peters 1988).

The Extent of Biological Knowledge

Disturbing also is the often low level of biological knowledge about the species of concern and their habitat requirements. The extensive biological and scientific study and research ideally needed to understand conservation needs of species of concern is typically in direct conflict with the perceived need to move quickly by those in the development community (i.e., "time is money"). The limits of our biological understanding are well illustrated by the Balcones Canyonlands HCP. Here, ecology of the underground karst habitat is very poorly understood, and some 30 previously-unknown cave-adapted invertebrates have been discovered in recent months (and have yet even to be scientifically named). A thorough understanding of this biologically-rich ecosystem might take many years, and would require development delays that would be politically intolerable.

The Failure to Consider Larger Patterns of Biodiversity

Many of the HCPs have assumed a relatively narrow focus on the habitat needs of a single species, or a few species, with little attention to protecting larger regional patterns of biodiversity. This is perhaps not surprising given the fact that the HCP mechanism is legally-driven by the requirements of ESA and tends to encourage a species-by-species view. Habitat conservation efforts to be truly effective will require a multi-species and a broader ecological approach. Consideration must be given not just to federally-listed species, but to candidate species and other species of concern, as well as to larger patterns of flora and fauna (species that might become threatened and endangered) and to the basic ecological processes and conditions upon which they rely (e.g., taking a watershed view).

Some of the more recent HCPs are indeed considering multiple species and are identifying important ecological processes that must be protected. This is encouraging. The Balcones Canyonlands HCP is a case in point. It is regional in geographic focus, and seeks to address simultaneously the habitat needs of seven listed species. Furthermore, it explicitly takes a watershed orientation, acknowledging that for long-term species survival the fundamental integrity of the larger ecosystem must be maintained. Even the Balcones Canyonlands HCP, however, fails to explicitly consider all species of concern and does not consider larger regional and state patterns of biodiversity.

Habitat Conservation and Land Use Planning

In reviewing current habitat conservation efforts, it is apparent that HCPs are, in large part, reactive attempts to correct for previous habitat loss and other land use impacts on flora and fauna. In many of the localities where HCPs are under preparation, a major part of the problem is the fact that few efforts have been made early-on to incorporate biodiversity considerations into land use and growth management plans.

The Balcones Canyonlands HCP illustrates, to a considerable extent, the problems associated with failure to integrate species conservation into land use planning and growth management. In the 1970s, the City of Austin adopted an impressive comprehensive plan, called Austin Tomorrow, intended to funnel most of the city's future growth into an urban corridor running from the southwest to the northeast, and in turn, to avoid the region's most environmentally-sensitive areas (City of Austin 1980). For a variety of reasons, this plan was never effectively implemented and much of the growth in recent years has occurred in precisely the most environmentally-damaging locations (to the west and northwest in the Balcones Canyonlands area). Had the city possessed the legal authority and political will to effectuate the Austin Tomorrow plan, the development pressures on the Balcones Canyonlands ecosystem would be substantially reduced. It is encouraging that some of the more recent HCPs, such as those in preparation in Kern County, California, (Bakersfield), are seeking better integration and coordination with local planning and land use policy. Kern County, as already mentioned, is currently preparing an endangered species element of its general plan.

Problems of Cost

One of the most significant issues emerging in the continued use of the HCP mechanism is the high cost of such plans, particularly the habitat acquisition components. Because of the typical threat from urban growth and development in HCP localities, natural habitat lands often have very high fair market values. As an example of the increasingly high price of habitat in metropolitan areas, a recent survey of land prices for Stephens' kangaroo rat habitat in eastern Riverside County found land selling for as much as $988,400/ha. Future habitat acquisition under the Stephens' kangaroo rat HCP may ultimately cost between $50 and $250 million. Even in a depressed land market like Austin, Texas, the costs of habitat acquisition (over a 10-year period) may exceed $100 million.

Moreover, few solutions have been put forth on how to satisfy the long-term funding needs for the many HCPs that will be undertaken in the future. Most HCPs have relied, or are planning to rely, heavily on federal funding. In the case of the Coachella Valley fringe-toed lizard HCP, approximately 60% of the cost was assumed by the federal government. Although virtually all HCPs are utilizing some local funding (primarily development mitigation fees), the level is usually inadequate to cover the major costs associated with an HCP. States and localities may be required to assume greater levels of funding in the future and will need to explore a variety of alternative revenue-raising tools and sources. There are, as well, important equity questions concerning who should be asked to bear the burden for habitat acquisition needs. It is a commonly heard argument that the federal government should bear the lion's share because it is a *federal* law that is requiring HCPs to be prepared in the first place. Others believe that, because land development is threatening species extinction, the majority of the cost should be borne by new development (i.e., through development impact fees). These funding and cost distribution issues are clearly yet to be settled.

Need for Interim Conservation

Another important issue yet to be fully resolved is the question of appropriate interim conservation measures—actions that should be taken while an HCP is being prepared. Preparation of an HCP, as the previous case studies illustrate, can take a number of years. From the point of view of developers, landowners, and local officials it is unreasonable to expect all development in habitat areas to stop while an HCP is being prepared. Different approaches to the interim conservation question have been taken by different HCPs. In the case of Coachella Valley, for instance, USFWS allowed take to occur while the plan was being prepared. In other HCPs, efforts have been taken to adopt temporary or short-term HCPs while the full HCP is being prepared. The Stephens' kangaroo rat and Clark County desert tortoise HCPs offer interesting examples of how to address the interim conservation problem. In the case of the Stephens' kangaroo rat, an interim HCP was prepared to cover only a 2-year period. A Section 10(a) permit was issued only for areas outside of the 10 designated study areas where the bulk of the rat population is believed to be located. In this way, development is allowed to proceed with little impact on the kangaroo rat. The longer-term HCP focuses on those portions of the county which represent critical habitat. The USFWS has validated this approach, to some extent, by issuing the 2-year 10(a) permit. As noted, a similar approach is being taken in Clark County, Nevada. Here a short-term HCP has been prepared that would allow take for a 3-year period in the Las Vegas

Valley (an area of low quality tortoise habitat) in exchange for undertaking certain minimum habitat conservation measures. For example, certain BLM land will be taken out of grazing and mining use, and new restrictions will be placed on off-road vehicle uses (Regional Environmental Consultants 1990b).

CONCLUSIONS

Although it is too early to offer definitive conclusions about the effectiveness and benefits of the HCP mechanism, a number of preliminary observations about it can be made. Clearly, the preparation of HCPs is on the rise and will likely continue as urban development and growth increasingly threaten important species and their habitats. Early experiences with HCPs suggest mixed results. On the one hand, HCPs have already resulted in the protection of large amounts of habitat (e.g., nearly 6,900 ha of land in the case of the Coachella Valley HCP) and have generated resources necessary for undertaking important habitat restoration and management activities (e.g., restoration of native grasslands in the case of the San Bruno Mountain HCP). On the other hand, it could be argued that HCPs, and the issuance of Section 10(a) permits, have resulted in significant loss of species and habitat, and in this sense are contrary to the otherwise-stringent provisions of the federal ESA. The preparation of HCPs will likely continue to open up significant amounts of habitat for development that would otherwise have been off-limits under ESA.

This paper has summarized the current status of a number of the larger and more important HCPs and has identified several of the more important policy dilemmas that emerge from these efforts. In particular, concerns have been raised about the adequacy of habitat conservation measures, the extent and level of biological knowledge, the failure to address multi-species and broader patterns of biodiversity, the failure to adequately integrate species conservation and land use planning, the problem of the high cost of habitat conservation, and the issue of appropriate interim conservation. There is a need for USFWS and others to concentrate attention on these issues in the future, and to explicitly evaluate the merits and effectiveness of the HCP as a mechanism for balancing the needs of urban growth and species protection.

REFERENCES CITED

Austin Regional Habitat Conservation Plan. 1990. Comprehensive report of the Biological Advisory Team. Austin Div., Austin, Tex. 68 pp.

Beatley, T. Forthcoming. Preserving biodiversity through the use of habitat conservation plans. The Urban Land Inst., Washington, D.C.

———. 1990. Land development and protection of endangered species: a case study of the Coachella Valley habitat conservation plan. Natl. Fish and Wildl. Found., Washington, D.C. 58 pp.

_____, R. Bernard, and D. Braun. Forthcoming. The Balcones Canyonlands habitat conservation plan: a regional, multi-species approach. The Urban Land Inst., Washington, D.C.

City of Austin. 1980. Austin Tomorrow comprehensive plan. Dep. of Planning, Austin, Tex. 176 pp.

Coachella Valley HCP Steering Committee. 1985. Coachella Valley fringe-toed lizard habitat conservation plan. Riverside County Planning Dep., Riverside, Calif. 141 pp.

Johnson, S. 1990. Gambling with another kind of greenback: Las Vegas' growth means desert tortoise demise. E. Magazine 1:20–22.

Kern County, California. 1989. Request for proposals to prepare an endangered species element of the Kern County general plan and a habitat conservation plan. Dep. of Planning and Dev. Serv., Kern Co., Calif. 7 pp.

Marsh, L. L., and R. D. Thornton. 1987. San Bruno Mountain habitat conservation plan. Pages 114–139 *in* D. Brower and D. Carol, eds. Managing land use conflicts: case studies in special area management. Duke Univ. Press, Durham, N.C.

Metropolitan Bakersfield HCP Steering Committee. 1990. Metropolitan Bakersfield habitat conservation plan and environmental impact report. Draft Summary. Bakersfield Planning Dep., Bakersfield, Calif.

North Key Largo HCP Study Committee. 1986. Habitat conservation plan and final report. Monroe Co. Planning Dep., Key West, Fla. 102 pp.

Peters, R. L., II. 1988. The effect of global climatic change on natural communities. Pages 450–461 *in* E. O. Wilson, ed. Biodiversity. Natl. Academy Press, Washington, D.C.

Regional Environmental Consultants. 1989. Comprehensive species management plan for the least Bell's vireo. Reg. Environ. Consultants, San Diego, Calif. 212 pp.

_____. 1990a. Interim habitat conservation plan for the Stephens' Kangaroo Rat. Reg. Environ. Consultants, San Diego, Calif. 105 pp.

_____. 1990b. Short term habitat conservation plan for the desert tortoise in Las Vegas valley, Clark County, Nevada. Reg. Environ. Consultants, San Diego, Calif.

San Bruno Mountain HCP Steering Committee. 1982. San Bruno Mountain area habitat conservation plan. Vol. I., San Mateo Co. Planning Div., Redwood City, Calif. 80 pp.

Tobin, R. 1990. The expendable future: U.S. politics and the protection of biological diversity. Duke Univ. Press, Durham, N.C. 325 pp.

U.S. Fish and Wildlife Service. 1990. Draft conservation planning guidelines. U.S. Fish and Wildl. Serv., Sacramento, Calif. 40 pp.

Yaffee, S. L. 1986. Prohibitive policy: implementing the federal endangered species act. MIT Press, Cambridge, Mass. 237 pp.

Landscape Planning and Wildlife: Methods and Motives[1]

KENNETH F. LANE, *Department of Landscape Architecture, 146 College of Design, Iowa State University, Ames, IA 50011*

INTRODUCTION

Landscape architects often play an influential role in land development projects. They advise on the placement of buildings and roads, offer recommendations on the reshaping of ground surfaces to accommodate stormwater runoff, and suggest plantings to augment or replace vegetation on the site. In these ways, landscape architects, as partners in the land development process, also have an impact on wildlife habitat. They can play either a constructive or destructive role in this process, depending on a variety of factors. One critical factor is the landscape architect's education.

The training of landscape architects as land planners and site planners has had a strong ecological basis since the 1960s due largely to the influence of landscape architects Phil Lewis (of the University of Wisconsin) and Ian McHarg (of the University of Pennsylvania). However, concern for landscape ecology has been manifested at the regional scale rather than site scale of landscape design.

In opposition to this concern is a strong contingent of design educators who consider landscape architecture an art form that should be expressed through the "language" of the painter and sculptor. This language includes concerns for texture, color, space, unity, and variety. Although plants are used by these landscape architects in their compositions, the ecological role of plants is largely ignored in favor of the visual qualities of the plants. The form (shape), texture, and color of the plant are the main considerations used in this kind of artistic design. The ecological role the plant plays in a living community (which includes animals) is ignored. Landscape architects trained in this manner are generally insensitive to animals, and their designs tend to show little concern for animal habitat.

This paper presents planning methods for integrating wildlife considerations into landscape architecture design projects and reviews results of a survey of landscape architecture design firms about design projects in which wildlife

played a key role. The nature and motives of these projects are discussed, along with their implications.

LANDSCAPE PLANNING AND WILDLIFE

About 10 years ago, I introduced the course "Landscape Planning and Wildlife" in the Landscape Architecture program at Iowa State University. This course began as an experimental one and became popular enough to win acceptance as a regular elective course in the curriculum. Emphasizing the use of plants in site planning from the standpoint of habitat rather than as visual materials of artistic composition, the course's objectives are to provide information about the habitat needs of animals and to show how to use this information in site design. The course explains basic habitat needs of animals in general and stresses the importance of plants. Lists of local birds and mammals are provided along with their habitat and food needs. Several site planning projects are undertaken to illustrate how the habitat needs of these animals should be accommodated. Local sites are used, and birds and small mammals acceptable— and appealing—to suburban residents are selected as target species.

The students electing this course are in their fourth or fifth year (landscape architecture is a 5-year program). They are interested in wildlife, concerned about habitat preservation, usually very knowledgeable about native plants, but unfamiliar with native animals.

Course Objectives and Techniques

The major objectives of this wildlife-oriented course are to demonstrate, through skillful site planning methods, how humans and wildlife can co-exist on a site (or how to develop land for human use while considering the needs of wildlife). Students are taught that one effective way to manage (or impact) wildlife is to manage or impact vegetation of an area, and that a change in vegetation equates with a change in animals. Landscape architects are involved in "transitioning" land from an undeveloped to a developed stage. This transitioning can be accomplished without a

---

[1]Supplemental paper not presented at the symposium.

Wildlife Conservation in Metropolitan Environments. NIUW Symp. Ser. 2, L.W. Adams and D.L. Leedy, eds. Published by Natl. Inst. for Urban Wildl., 10921 Trotting Ridge Way, Columbia, MD 21044, USA, 1991.

large impact on vegetation (and wildlife) depending on several factors, one being the skill of the site planner to minimize this impact. Other general guidelines suggested in the course include:

1. Preserve wooded areas whenever possible. Riparian areas are especially important. Streams and rivers of the upper Midwest often contain the only wooded areas available to wildlife, except for towns.
2. Preserve wetlands. They add diversity and contrast with uplands, filter runoff contaminants, and help to recharge underground aquifers.
3. Design residential areas using cluster housing to reduce the impact on woodlands or wetlands within the housing project site.
4. Maximize the number and variety of plants present on a site—the greater the amount and variety, the higher the potential for a wide variety of animals to exist on the site.
5. Introduce plants that provide nesting sites and food for wildlife. The selection and arrangement of woody plants in particular will have a significant effect on whether or not certain animals will recolonize the area.
6. Prescribe vegetation management procedures that do not conflict with the needs of wildlife species attracted to the site. The prescription of appropriate vegetation management techniques may be as important to the continued presence of wildlife as the choice of plants.

Two general techniques for creating habitat attractive to animals are also introduced in the course. One is termed the "shotgun" approach; the second, the "target species" approach.

The "shotgun" approach assumes that if all basic needs of wildlife are met (food, cover, water, and adequate space), wildlife will occupy a site. All the site planner has to do to attract wildlife, according to this technique, is to make sure there is a wide variety of plants available for food and cover and that water is available on site or within 0.4 km. An advantage of this approach is that it requires little special knowledge of wildlife, but the planner must persuade the client to accept a wilder, less tidy-looking landscape effect for the project to be truly effective.

The "target species" approach contains the following steps:

1. Make attracting wildlife a goal of the project at the outset.
2. Select for attraction species common to the locale of the site.
3. Make a list of the habitat requirements for these "target" species.
4. Examine the site for the presence (or absence) of the habitat items needed by each species.

5. Provide for all missing habitat items needed by the target species on the proposed site plan.
6. Provide for preservation on site of all existing habitat needed by the target species. (If endangered species are involved, this may include nesting or denning and foraging areas.)

An advantage of using the target species approach is that the designer is more likely to be effective in attracting desired wildlife to the site. He knows which species are nearby and has provided the necessary habitat items to attract those species. One disadvantage of this method is that it takes more time to determine the species present in the locale of the site and their habitat needs. If the designer continues to work in the same region, however, this time investment pays off over and over again. Because the animals and their habitat needs stay the same in a given region, the designer does not have to repeat the research process a second or third time if his projects stay within that region.

Selected Course Projects

The projects selected for the course in which the shotgun and target species approaches are applied include housing projects (both complete, planned-unit developments and individual residential grounds), small city parks, college campus areas, and corporate headquarters areas. In addition to these traditional site planning projects, the course introduces students to city-wide habitat concerns, such as identification of unique wetland areas or extensive forest tracts, potential corridors such as stream valleys, or abandoned railroad rights-of-way that can be used to link isolated habitat areas together. Multiple use (where habitat is combined with recreation, aquifer recharge, or stormwater retention) is encouraged as a concept.

SURVEY OF DESIGN FIRMS

Landscape architects today may be surprised to find their clients favorably inclined to consider needs of wildlife and to incorporate wildlife habitat enhancement and preservation in a development project. A survey in progress of professional landscape architects is revealing why this is so.

Survey Technique

Approximately 330 professional site planning firms were contacted throughout the United States regarding landscape design projects in which wildlife was a major influence. Materials received included site photographs, plans and drawings, and written documents. These materials provide examples of the various types of projects in which wildlife habitat has been considered, the motives for this emphasis, and the methods used to mitigate the project's various impacts on wildlife.

Results

A wide range of projects, varying in size from < 1 to hundreds of ha, has incorporated wildlife considerations. Projects include:

1. large planned-unit residential development,
2. housing developments for the elderly,
3. wildlife preserves,
4. stream valley revegetation projects (wildlife habitat master plan),
5. off-road vehicle impact study on wildlife, and
6. stormwater retention and runoff areas.

Housing projects were the most prevalent among the examples received and impacted the largest land areas.

Approximately 11% of the firms indicated involvement in projects in which wildlife is a major consideration. The materials the author has already received, plus informal phone conversations with the persons involved with these projects, provide insights into the motivation for, and planning methods used in, protecting wildlife in the projects. The motives include the following:

1. The proposed development project would impact an endangered species, protected by law, and development plans had to include accommodations for that species or the project could not proceed.
2. The clients were aware that incorporating wildlife preserves into their housing developments would be considered favorably by prospective home buyers and the public in general.
3. Establishment of a wildlife preserve as part of corporate headquarters reduces grounds maintenance costs and brings wildlife within viewing range of employees.
4. The developer of a large subdivision in a western state was aware that habitat of large game animals must be protected within the proposed development area. (His state is protective of large game habitat because it receives large amounts of income from non-resident hunters seeking these animals.)
5. The proposed project would impact a riparian area, wetland, or upland habitat protected by state law. The proposed development plans must protect the wetland or the project could not proceed (as in No. 1, the emphasis is mandatory).
6. Wildlife habitat is included for beautification as part of a stormwater retention pond required by a municipal ordinance. Carefully selected plantings are used to make an attractive area from an otherwise utilitarian one.

Laws protecting habitat and endangered species appear to be the biggest single motivation for habitat protection in site-planning projects. Our class projects are representative of the types of projects experienced by professional landscape architectural firms as revealed by this survey. An overview of environmental laws (state and federal) protecting wildlife species and habitat has not been presented in the class, however, and needs to be covered in the future.

CONCLUSIONS

The materials collected in this survey have not been detailed enough to describe the precise methods used in each of the projects for habitat protection and preservation. Informal phone conversations with designers of the projects revealed some commonalities concerning the methods used. In projects where public image was of greater concern than protection of specific animals, the method used was analogous to the "shotgun" approach described earlier. In these projects, it was sufficient to protect wetlands, woodlands, or prairie areas within the project; to specify nest boxes of various types; to select trees and shrubs known to provide small fruits and seeds attractive to wildlife; and in one case to recommend mowing times for meadow areas and to conserve snags in mature woodlands within the project.

The target species approach was used in the projects involving endangered species. These projects required the professional expertise of scientists to determine exact habitat needs of the species and to recommend how development of the project was to proceed to avoid impact on the target species.

The planning method most often used incorporated wildlife data at the beginning of the planning process with the following steps:

1. Habitat (or target species) preservation was made an objective of the project.
2. The project site was surveyed (before any planning began) to inventory wildlife species and habitat present on the site. These data were recorded on maps.
3. The proposed development program was analyzed to make a rough determination of area needed for the development.
4. The potential impacts of the proposed development on wildlife and habitat areas recorded in Step 2 were analyzed.

After these steps, the site planner integrated other site factors (such as slopes and soils) and then developed a conceptual master plan. This plan indicates where proposed facilities are to be located and identifies the habitat areas to be protected or enhanced.

The dichotomy between the ecological approach in landscape architectural design and the visually based design mode need not be an either/or situation; they can work together. A concern for wildlife, if expressed in a garden's design, need not negate visual design principles. A garden designed for visual delight can also be attractive to wildlife. The impact of suburban development and the impacts of urban expansion on wildlife can be minimized if wildlife habitat is considered a factor in the planning process. Until a broader concern for wildlife is evidenced by planners and other citizens, the implementation of laws protecting habitat is necessary. Laws protecting species and general habitats such as wetlands appear to be the strongest motive for site planners and landscape architects to be concerned about wildlife.

IV.

Management Issues and Successes

Chair: WILLIAM W. SHAW, Professor, University of Arizona, Tucson

Cochair: DAVID L. TYLKA, Urban Biologist, Missouri Department of Conservation, St. Louis

A Natural Resources Management and Protection Plan for the Econlockhatchee River Basin

JOE SCHAEFER, *Department of Wildlife and Range Sciences, University of Florida, Gainesville, FL 32611-0304*

MARK T. BROWN, *Center for Wetlands, University of Florida, Gainesville, FL 32611*

RICHARD HAMANN AND JOHN TUCKER, *Center for Governmental Responsibility, University of Florida, Gainesville, FL 32611*

INTRODUCTION

The Econlockhatchee River Basin (725 km²) is one of the few intact, relatively unaltered river systems remaining in peninsular Florida. However, the future of the basin's natural integrity has become the focus of intense scrutiny because of rapid urban sprawl occurring in, and planned for, East Orlando. The annual projected population growth rate for the Orlando area through 1992 is 38,670 (West 1989). In August 1989, the St. Johns River Water Management District contracted with the University of Florida to develop a management plan to protect the natural resources of this basin from Orlando's urban sprawl.

We conducted a 5-month study to determine the status of the water and wildlife resources, and the regulatory framework of the Econ Basin. Based on this information, we prepared a Critical Areas Management and Protection Plan that provided suggestions for management, regulation, and acquisition strategies. The goal of the plan is to ensure no net loss of water quality, quantity, or ecological functions of the systems in the basin.

DESCRIPTION OF STUDY AREA

The Big Econ River flows 57.3 km north and east through three counties (Osceola, Orange, and Seminole) to the St. Johns River. The Little Econ originates on the eastern edge of the Orlando metropolitan area and flows eastward 23.7 km to the confluence with the Big Econ.

Climate

The climate of this region is characterized as subtropical; the average annual temperature is 22 C (Knockenmus 1975). Average annual rainfall is a little over 129 cm (Jenab et al. 1986). More than 50% of the rainfall usually occurs during a 4-month period, June through September.

Landscape

The Econlockhatchee River Basin is relatively flat. Ground elevations range from about 1.5 m above mean sea level (amsl) near the northeastern end to about 21.3 m amsl in the headwater marshes to the extreme south. Elevations increase from east to west.

The predominant landscape association in the basin is pine flatwoods. The width of swamps and hydric hammocks that follow river and stream channels averages about 170 m from the edge of the river landward. Because of the low relief and poorly drained soils, many isolated wetlands are interspersed throughout the flatwoods. Several small patches of scrub habitat also can be found in some of the higher elevations.

STATUS OF NATURAL RESOURCES

Water

The water table is very close to the ground surface for much of the year (Tibbals 1976). Characteristic of this type of landscape, the water resources in the isolated and flowing wetlands are affected to a large degree by alterations of surface water flow rates and groundwater table levels in the surrounding terrain. The water table has been lowered by drainage ditches in many urban and agricultural areas (Tibbals 1976). Depending on the average amount of rainfall, topographic relief, and soil structure and composition, water control structures can cause wetland water levels to drop as much as 1.5 m when constructed between 25 to 180 m from a wetland (Table 1, Brown et al. 1990).

The Big Econ River, flowing through a relatively undeveloped area from its origins in large headwater swamps,

Wildlife Conservation in Metropolitan Environments. NIUW Symp. Ser. 2, L.W. Adams and D.L. Leedy, eds. Published by Natl. Inst. for Urban Wildl., 10921 Trotting Ridge Way, Columbia, MD 21044, USA, 1991.

Table 1. Wetland buffers (meters from wetland-upland edge) required to minimize effects of water table drawdown on landscape associations in the Econlockhatchee River Basin, Florida.

| Drawdown at structure (m)[a] | Landscape association[b] | | |
| | Flatwoods | | Swamps |
	(1% slope)	(2% slope)	(2% slope)
0.5	50	25	25
1.0	100	50	50
1.5	180	80	80

[a]At the present time, the St. Johns River Water Management District allows a maximum 1.5-m groundwater drawdown at any one point within project boundaries and an overall average drawdown of 1 m.
[b]The slopes given are estimates of the slope of the surficial aquifer characteristic of each association based on averages of topographic relief of the various associations. Where more than one slope is given, variation of topographic relief within associations was sufficient to require listing several slopes.

runs clear, with few, if any, water quality problems. The majority of activities in the Upper Big Econ, up to the 1970s, had been grazing and some citrus groves. In the early 1970s, a major drainage project was constructed encompassing over 2,400 ha.

The Little Econ, for years impacted by sewage outfalls from 11 sewage treatment plants, is channelized through much of its headwaters and receives stormwater runoff from a relatively urbanized watershed. Heavy nutrient loading and resulting fish kills had been recorded for the Little Econ through the 1970s. Considerable improvement in average water quality was observed following the completion of two major sewage treatment plants (Hand et al. 1986).

Some construction and land-clearing activities have caused soil erosion in uplands and sediment deposition in adjacent wetlands. The result is a conversion of wetlands into drier uplands. Water quality also has been degraded by suspended silt eroded into the water from adjacent upland soils. Depending on the soil type, vegetated buffers ranging from about 23 to 137 m in width adjacent to wetlands have been recommended to minimize sedimentation in wetlands and to control turbidity in open waters (Table 2, Brown et al. 1990).

Wildlife

The Econlockhatchee River Basin has become the focal point of a regionwide wildlands network. To the east of the basin are the wildland resources of the St. Johns River floodplain, Tossohatchee State Wildlife Area, and the Orlando Wilderness Park; to the south are the lands of the Desseret Ranch containing large areas of wetlands; and to

Table 2. Wetland buffers required to minimize sedimentation in wetlands and to control turbidity in adjacent open waters in east central Florida.

USDA soil type	Buffer requirements
Clay	Sedimentation and turbidity control cannot be met with buffer requirements alone.
Silt	137.2 m measured from open water-wetland boundary through the wetlands to the upland.
Fine sand	61 m from wetland-upland boundary.
Coarse sand	22.9 m from the wetland-upland boundary.

the north and west are the wildlands associated with the Wekiva River system. Because of its location, central to these important regional resources, the Econ River system is a critical link in a regional network of wildlands that preserve biotic diversity and ensure access to a wilderness experience for all Eastcentral Floridians.

Of the 706 native, vertebrate wildlife species (excluding fish) that occur in Florida, 214 (30%) can be found in the Econ Basin. About 44 fish species occur in the aquatic environments. Although all vegetation communities support large numbers of wildlife, flatwoods and hardwood hammocks have the greatest species richness (Table 3).

Some species occur almost exclusively in only wetlands or uplands (Table 4). However, more than half of the wildlife found in the basin need access to both wetlands and uplands in order to satisfy their life-sustaining requirements.

As a result of the diverse landscape in this system, 27 species and subspecies occur here but not outside of the state (Muller et al. 1989, Table 5). At least 15 endemics are found in each habitat type.

Table 3. Number of wildlife species associated with various habitats within the Econlockhatchee River Basin, Florida.

| Habitat type | Taxa | | | | |
	Amphibians	Reptiles	Birds	Mammals	Total
Xeric scrub	9	33	45	24	111
Flatwoods	14	39	79	26	158
Hardwood hammock	15	40	71	25	151
Cypress swamp	23	27	49	20	119
Swamp hardwoods	23	31	52	20	126
Freshwater marsh and river	17	21	41	16	95
Total[a]	26	50	104	34	214

[a]Total number of species. Some species occur in more than one habitat type, therefore, columns do not sum to these figures.

Table 4. Number of wildlife species that occur almost exclusively in wetlands, in both wetlands and uplands, or in upland habitats within the Econlockhatchee River Basin, Florida.

| Habitat type | Taxa | | | | Total | |
	Amphibians	Reptiles	Birds	Mammals	No.	%
Wetlands	7	4	20	4	35	16
Wetlands and uplands	19	30	51	19	119	56
Uplands	0	16	33	11	60	28
Total	26	50	104	34	214	100

Table 5. Number of endemic species and subspecies associated with various habitats within the Econlockhatchee River Basin, Florida.[a]

| Habitat type | Taxa | | | | |
	Amphibians	Reptiles	Birds	Mammals	Total
Xeric scrub	1	12	2	3	18
Flatwoods	1	12	1	3	17
Hardwood hammock	2	12	—	1	15
Cypress swamp	5	10	—	1	16
Swamp hardwoods	4	10	—	1	15
Freshwater marsh and river	4	9	2	1	16
Total[b]	5	15	3	4	27

[a]Endemic species and subspecies have distributions that occur entirely or almost entirely within the state of Florida.
[b]Total number of species. Some species occur in more than one habitat type, therefore, columns do not sum to these figures.

Of all the species that occur in the basin, 21 are listed by either the U.S. Fish and Wildlife Service or the Florida Game and Fresh Water Fish Commission as endangered, threatened, or species of special concern (Table 6). Flatwoods contain the largest number of listed species.

Based on literature data, home range needs of wildlife found in this basin range from 0.018 ha for species such as the green anole (*Anolis carolinensis*) to 1,322 ha for red fox (*Vulpes vulpes*). We used the diameter of an assumedly circular home range and other spatial requirement data such as minimum distance from humans tolerated before taking flight, distance between captures of the same individual, diameter of smallest isolated forest patch in which species was found, and maximum distance a semi-aquatic species was found from water to determine the width of habitat adjacent to the river needed to provide sufficient area for various species. We also applied a guilding technique to categorize species according to which vertical strata they use to obtain feeding and nesting resources. If spatial data were not found for a species, we assigned values from species that are closely related, similar-sized, found in comparable habitats, and occupying similar guilds.

According to these data, the range of habitat widths required by those species that use the wetlands almost exclusively was 15 to 213 m (Fig. 1). About 25% of the species

Table 6. Number of state and federally listed species associated with various habitats within the Econlockhatchee River Basin, Florida.[a]

Habitat type	Taxa				
	Amphibians	Reptiles	Birds	Mammals	Total
Xeric scrub	1	4	6	2	13
Flatwoods	1	4	10	2	17
Hardwood hammock	—	4	6	—	10
Cypress swamp	1	1	6	—	8
Swamp hardwoods	—	2	6	—	8
Freshwater marsh and river	—	1	8	—	10
Total[b]	1	5	13	2	21

[a]Listed species: endangered, threatened, and special concern species.
[b]Total number of species. Some species occur in more than one habitat type, therefore, columns do not sum to these figures.

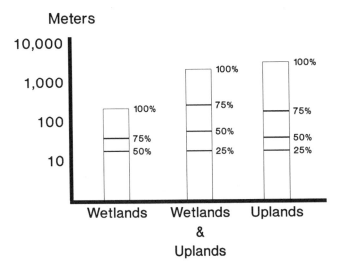

Fig. 1. Habitat widths (in meters) required for those species that use 1) wetlands almost exclusively ($n = 35$), 2) both wetlands and uplands ($n = 119$), and 3) uplands almost exclusively ($n = 60$). See text for details.

that use both wetlands and uplands, and 25% of those that use only uplands needed a width of more than 450 and 350 m, respectively.

REGULATORY FRAMEWORK

As part of the study, we examined the existing planning and regulatory mechanisms in the Econ River and evaluated whether they are adequate to protect the water, wetland, and wildlife resources of the basin.

Local Government Land Use Planning and Regulations

Florida law requires that local governments adopt comprehensive plans and land development regulations to guide and control existing and future development (Florida Statutes 1989, Section 163). Comprehensive plans must include future land use, conservation, and recreation and open space elements that are consistent with state criteria. Land development regulations must implement the goals and policies of the comprehensive plans (Florida Statutes 1989, Section 163.3202(1)), and typically include ordinances regulating wetlands, flood plains, shorelines, stormwater, and dredge and fill.

We found that existing local government plans and regulations did not adequately protect the natural resource values of the Econ Basin because they did not provide for protection of upland habitat adjacent to watercourses and wetlands. In addition, local governments did not protect small isolated wetlands.

Environmental Regulations

A complex array of regional, state, and federal regulations pertain to natural resource values in the Econ Basin. However, existing environmental regulations were inadequate to protect the natural resource values of the Econ Basin. The regulations did not provide for protection of upland habitat or adequate consideration of wildlife values. Current regulations routinely allowed destruction of small isolated wetlands—essential habitat for certain wildlife species. In addition, the regulations did not adequately protect water quality and quantity within the basin. Surface water management regulations allowed harmful groundwater drawdowns that reduced the base flow of the river system. Stormwater regulations permitted inadequate treatment systems and depended on a nutrient standard that was difficult to enforce.

Significant Development Structures and Activities

The Econ Basin lies within one of the most rapidly growing areas in the nation and is under intense development pressure. At least 40 major developments, involving over 13,600 ha, have recently been approved within the Econ Basin. Many proposed developments straddle or are adjacent to the Big Econ River, which currently is relatively undeveloped. Two such development proposals involve over 6,400 ha and 32,000 dwelling units. The Little Econ

River, which is near the eastern edge of Orlando, provides a good example of what may happen to the Big Econ River if additional regulations are not adopted soon. Much of the land adjacent to the Little Econ River has been intensely developed, thereby destroying many of the recreational and natural resource values of the river ecosystem.

RESOURCE ISSUES AND PROBLEMS

Water

Channelization of streams, rivers, and tributaries of the Econ Basin have lowered average water table levels, decreased the residence time of stormwaters within the system, and decreased flooding of natural wetlands. Stormwater management systems consisting of open water ponds and straight connecting ditches maximize runoff and do not allow for adequate filtering of nutrients and pollutants.

An upland buffer of natural vegetation has been removed along most of the Little Econ and some areas of the Big Econ. These buffers are needed to filter out nonpoint source pollution and sediments that are carried by surface water flows.

Wildlife

Many habitats in the basin already have been fragmented by encroaching land uses and highways. The relatively unaltered, native habitat has been compressed into four somewhat disjunct corridors along the Big Econ.

One of the reasons for the great richness of wildlife in the Econ Basin is its historic linkages with vast flatwoods to the east and the sandhills to the west. Several current land use practices have severed these connections that are essential for recolonization and the maintenance of genetic variation in viable populations.

Conversion of natural habitats into improved pastures and management of these man-made systems have benefitted open-canopy species such as brown-headed cowbirds (*Molothrus ater*) and red-tailed hawks (*Buteo jamaicensis*) that parasitize and compete with remaining forest-associated species. Silvicultural activities have reduced the age of the forests and altered the vegetation composition. Development has brought with it free-ranging cat and dog pets, and noise that exert additional unnatural pressures on wildlife in adjacent natural areas.

Very narrow token strips of vegetation are commonly used in landscaping to provide visual screening and are mistakenly sold as wildlife corridors or conservation areas. These strips support very few, it any, wildlife species that are sensitive to development and in greater need of conservation.

SOLUTIONS AND MANAGEMENT PLAN

The overall goal of the management plan is to ensure no net loss of water quality, quantity, or ecological functions of systems through acquisition, management, and land use regulations. The more specific objectives are:

1. Improve water quality in the Little Econ River.
2. Maintain water quality in the Big Econ.
3. Approximate natural surface and groundwater table hydrologic regimes.
4. Protect significant ecological communities in the basin.
5. Maintain viable populations of all existing wildlife species.

We first identified the following Critical Areas that, because of their location, ecological function, or sensitive nature, were worthy of special attention. We then proposed management and development guidelines for each area.

A. Urbanized portions of the Little Econ.
   1. Dechannelize and reestablish old floodplain wetlands wherever practicable.
   2. Establish and revegetate native plants along the channelway wherever possible.
B. Headwaters of the Big Econ.
   1. Require management of stormwaters from any proposed developments so that pre-development and post-development runoffs are similar in quantity, quality, rate, and timing.
   2. Restrict agricultural and silvicultural operations, including harvesting in wetlands.
   3. Require upland buffers for all isolated wetlands and tributaries that are the greater of: 15 m measured toward the upland from the wetland-upland edge, or, sufficient uplands to provide a habitat area with a minimum of 168 m centered across the smallest axis.
   4. Minimize further fragmentation of the headwaters by locating any additional highway and utility corridors within existing corridors.
C. Xeric Scrub Communities.
   1. Development activities should be prohibited within remaining scrub communities unless they do not alter essential habitat components.
   2. Establish linkages with other habitat types so the scrub communities do not become isolated islands in developed landscapes.
D. River Corridor of Big Econ and Unurbanized Portions of the Little Econ.
   1. Establish a Conservation Zone along both sides of the main stem measuring 335 m from the landward edge of the river channel toward the upland.
   2. Limit development activities within the Conservation Zone to those that do not permanently alter vegetation.
   3. Prohibit new agricultural and silvicultural operations within the Conservation Zone that have adverse effects on wildlife or water quality, or that lower ground water tables.

4. Control passive recreation by locating nature trails along either edge of the Conservation Zone. Pavilions, nature centers, parking lots, or other structures should be prohibited.
5. Prohibit further highway and utility crossings.
6. All cleared and previously altered lands should be revegetated with native ecological communities.
7. Free-ranging domestic animals should be prohibited in the Conservation Zone.
8. Design and operate surface water management systems so as to prevent alteration of the hydrological regime within the floodplain wetlands.
9. Prohibit all gasoline-powered water craft.
E. Wildlands Corridors.
1. Institute an overlay zoning category called "wildlands corridor" and develop performance criteria and incentives for uses of lands that are consistent with wildlife corridor functions.
F. Several key parcels that could not be adequately protected through regulations were recommended for acquisition.
G. Outside of Critical Areas.
Several activities, because of their intensity or because they are ubiquitous in their effect, can impact a Critical Area even if removed some distance from the area in question. To address this, management guidelines also were suggested for areas outside of the specific Critical Areas. These included:
1. Develop prescribed burning programs in areas adjacent to Critical Areas to protect them against wildfires.
2. Develop standards for stormwater retention basins that include the use of native emergent vegetation, littoral zones, and native vegetation along the shore so that developed lakes and ponds will provide aquatic and wetland wildlife habitat values.
3. A maximum drawdown of 1 m from the average wet season water table level should be established throughout the Big Econ and unurbanized portions of the Little Econ.
4. Encourage the construction of forested or herbaceous wetland detention systems.

PROCESSES FOR IMPLEMENTING THE PLAN

We conducted the study for the St. Johns River Water Management District (WMD), a regional agency charged with regulating the water resources within its jurisdiction, which includes the Econ Basin. The WMD assisted the study by providing valuable insight into permitting programs and treatment methodologies. In addition to receiving continual review by the WMD, our study was evaluated by the Econ River Task Force, a committee with representatives from many interest groups such as county commissioners, developers, environmentalists, Florida Division of Forestry, and Florida Department of Natural Resources. The WMD

and the Task Force endorsed most of our recommendations, although they condensed the recommendations and modified some of the more controversial provisions.

We recommended that Econ protection provisions be implemented through existing WMD regulatory programs and local government planning and land development regulation programs. Specifically, the WMD should amend its management and storage of surface water and stormwater regulations to prevent activities that would adversely affect the natural resources of the Econ Basin. The WMD rules should be amended to preserve riverine wetlands, establish 168-m protection zones along each side of the river to protect water quality and aquatic and wetland-dependent species, limit groundwater drawdowns, strengthen stormwater permitting criteria, and provide for protection zones adjacent to isolated wetlands. We recommended that local governments implement additional protection measures including an additional 168-m protection zone to protect upland species. We also recommended that state environmental and growth management agencies take additional actions to protect the river, such as lowering the threshold for state and regional review of "developments of regional impact" (Florida Statutes 1989, Section 380.06) and classifying the Econ River as an "Outstanding Florida Water" (Florida Statutes 1989, Section 403.061(27)(a)).

STATUS OF RECOMMENDATIONS

In the spring of 1990, a bill was introduced in the Florida Legislature that directed the WMD, other agencies, and local governments to adopt measures to implement many of the recommendations of our study. The WMD, at the direction of its Governing Board, commenced preliminary rule making. Although the bill died in committee hearings, the WMD Governing Board recently directed its staff to continue rule development. The draft rules contain many of the recommendations from our report. Although there is strong developer opposition to imposition of the protective buffers, it appears likely that the WMD will adopt rules to protect the Econ River within the year.

Local governments also have begun to act. Orange County is considering developing an ordinance that would protect an additional 168 m along each side of the river. Seminole County plans to amend its comprehensive plan to provide additional protection for the Econ River, but this process may take several years. Osceola County adopted a temporary moratorium on the issuance of development permits within the headwaters area of the Econ River but has taken no action toward long-term protection of the resource. Ultimately, successful protection of the Econ Basin depends on rapid action by all involved regulatory entities.

REFERENCES CITED

Brown, M. T., J. M. Schaefer, and K. H. Brant. 1990. Buffer zones for water, wetlands and wildlife in East Central Florida.

Final rep. (Fla. Agric. Exp. Sta. J. Ser. No. T-00061) to the East Central Fla. Reg. Plan. Counc., Winter Park. 71 + pp.

Florida Statutes. 1989. Chapter 163, Part II; Chapters 380 and 403.

Hand, J., V. Tauxe, and J. Watts. 1986. Florida water quality assessment 305(b) technical report. Florida Dep. of Environ. Regul., Water Quality Monit. and Quality Assurance Sect., Tallahassee. 47 pp.

Jenab, S. A., D. V. Rao, and D. Clapp. 1986. Rainfall analysis for Northeast Florida. Part II: summary of monthly and annual rainfall data. Tech. publ. SJ 86-4, St. Johns River Water Manage. Dist., Palatka, Fla. 32 pp.

Knockenmus, D. D. 1975. Hydrologic concepts of artificially recharging the Floridan Aquifer in eastern Orange County, Florida—A feasibility study. Rep. of Invest. No. 72, Florida Dep. of Nat. Resour., Div. of Resour. Manage., Bur. of Geol., Tallahassee. 128 pp.

Muller, J. W., E. D. Hardin, D. R. Jackson, S. E. Gatewood, and N. Caire. 1989. Summary report on the vascular plants, animals and plant communities endemic to Florida. Tech. Rep. No. 7, Florida Game and Fresh Water Fish Comm., Nongame Wildl. Program, Tallahassee. 113 pp.

Tibbals, C. H. 1976. Availability of groundwater in Seminole County and vicinity, Florida. U.S. Geol. Surv., Tallahassee, Fla.

West, C. T. 1989. Forecast summary: Florida economy. The Florida Outlook, Third Quarter, pp. 9–30.

Interagency Cooperation in Restoring Freshwater Wetlands in an Urban National Recreation Area[1]

MICHAEL J. MATTHEWS, *New York State Department of Environmental Conservation, Delmar, NY 12054*

ROBERT P. COOK AND JOHN T. TANACREDI, *Gateway National Recreation Area, Brooklyn, NY 11231*

JOSEPH J. PANE, *New York State Department of Environmental Conservation, Long Island City, NY 11101*

INTRODUCTION

Gateway National Recreation Area consists of 10,522 ha located within and adjacent to New York City, New York and New Jersey (Fig. 1). The area is divided into four separate units: Jamaica Bay, Sandy Hook, Staten Island, and Breezy Point. Gateway lands range from relatively intact natural landforms to heavily disturbed land (i.e., former landfills). Some of Gateway's facilities lie on filled marshlands. Since its establishment in 1972, the National Park Service (NPS) has been working to restore and enhance these altered and once degraded habitats. The NPS's goal, within the park, is to restore as much native habitat and wildlife as possible within such an urbanized environment, and to provide urban residents access to these natural habitats.

STUDY AREA

In early April, 1983, the "North 40" of Floyd Bennett Field (Fig. 2), so entitled due to its isolation from visitor use, had a fire encompassing about 16.2 ha (40 acres). Common reed (*Phragmites communis*), the predominant plant that burned, left bare the old landfilled surface of undeveloped Floyd Bennett Field. Within 2 days of the fire, a torrential downpour occurred, filling several large depressions with water.

This new source of water and the lingering summer heat that year contributed to a dramatic increase in the number of many resident bird species using the area. The "ponds" attracted numerous waterfowl and shorebirds, so the thought occurred to us, "why not make permanent ponds there?"

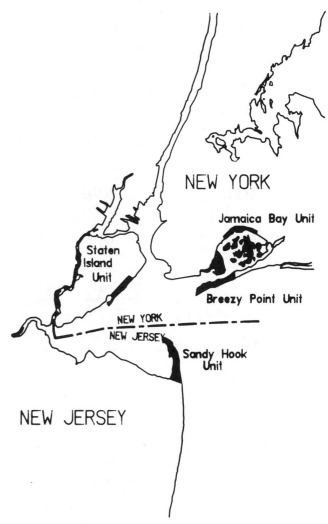

Fig. 1. The four units of Gateway National Recreation Area, New York and New Jersey.

[1]Due to unavoidable circumstances, paper was not presented at the symposium.

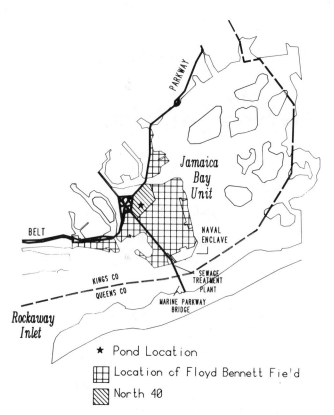

Fig. 2. Floyd Bennett Field and the "North 40" of Gateway National Recreation Area, New York.

MATERIALS AND METHODS

From April to September, the site was surveyed and photographed. Tests were made to determine soil consistency and presence of chemical contaminants. Estimates of equipment, funding, staffing, and maintenance needs were projected for creation of a 0.4-ha freshwater pond and nature trail. Sources of year-round freshwater were identified. Abandoned electric, water, and sewer lines were plotted so that none were within the boundaries of potential pond excavation. A nature trail theme and concept were identified.

All of this was documented, reviewed, and approved in-house by late September, 1983. However, due to fiscal restraints, funding was not available for implementation; cuts in staffing meant no long-term maintenance.

In early 1984, it was learned that projects could be funded under the New York State "Return a Gift to Wildlife" program. Under this program, taxpayers may contribute part of their refund or make a tax deductible contribution on their New York State Income Tax Returns. Monies are placed within the State's Conservation Fund for the preservation, protection, and enhancement of wildlife; information and education material; habitat restoration; and wildlife management demonstration projects. The New York State Department of Environmental Conservation (DEC) administers this program through a variety of competitively sought project proposals. It appeared somewhat incongruous for a federal government entity to seek "State monies" to conduct a habitat restoration project. However, there was no stipulation excluding the NPS from seeking funding as long as the project met standards established by DEC. For the proposal, general criteria were necessary, such as long-term maintenance, security, and dedication to sound wildlife management activities.

DEC entered into a Memorandum of Understanding with the NPS to establish and manage a portion of Gateway's Floyd Bennett Field as a demonstration area on urban wildlife management. The plan called for the creation of a freshwater pond and the construction of an interpretive hiking trail around the pond. Along the trail a number of wildlife management techniques, such as erection of nest boxes and establishment of food and cover plantings, would be demonstrated and interpreted for the public via signage and NPS ranger interpretive programs.

MULTI-USE CAPACITY

Floyd Bennett Field is dedicated to a variety of recreational and educational uses. In order to determine carrying capacities for wildlife, assessments must be made on both the macro and micro level. Variety in habitat components is essential for food, shelter, and visitor perceptions of wildlife. Planning for wildlife habitat enhancement must be multidisciplinary in approach and recognize that man is a biological component in the system under study (Tanacredi 1987).

Considering the human use capacities of parcels of space within an overall Floyd Bennett Field unit poses problems, such as overuse, that directly affect natural systems. For example, vegetation to support wildlife should provide more than just food—it should include suitable habitat. This involves escape cover, nesting space, alternative species (floral and faunal) interactions, continuity of habitat, and potential nuisance problems to and from man. Wildlife does not recognize legal boundaries or jurisdictional lines. Few animals consistently remain within small home ranges or territories. Contiguous systems, not isolated sites within an entire district, must be maintained and monitored.

Traditionally, urban parks have emphasized lawn areas, and areas that contain only mature trees. Yet, other area types are important; shrubs, saplings, and a tall herbaceous ground cover will be productive to a variety of wildlife. Grey and Deneke (1978) noted several benefits of urban forests, such as weather amelioration (temperature modification in cities, which are generally 0.5 to 1.5 C warmer during the day than the countryside), wind protection, water runoff control, noise and air pollution abatement, and aesthetics.

Fragmented ecosystems affect migratory species, many of which have been characteristically dependent upon large tracts of forests. Long-distant migrant populations decrease when large tracts of land are broken into smaller tracts and isolated from a source of repopulation. Floyd Bennett Field and Jamaica Bay Refuge are two of the few remnant tracts of remaining coastal estuarine systems in New York City that can support a variety of species. Extirpated wildlife species now find the approximate 6,900 ha of Jamaica Bay their last outpost (Cook and Pinnock 1987).

It has been shown (Franklin 1981) that provision of freshwater habitat directly influences the variety of wildlife. Several activities have been suggested that can improve habitat conditions in urban areas:

1. Maintaining wetland habitat,
2. Creating additional impoundments where practical,
3. Erecting various types of nesting boxes, and
4. Providing brush (cut for road and trail maintenance) near woodland borders as valuable habitat for species ranging from bacterial decomposers, to fungi, wood-boring insects, amphibians, reptiles, birds, and mammals.

Without implementing long-term monitoring of carrying capacities in a multi-use area, detection of alterations and their prime causes is extremely difficult. Comprehensive monitoring programs covering habitat management activities must be in place prior to implementation of any planning scenarios (Gregg 1980). Critical thresholds of visitor demands must be acknowledged prior to placing ecosystems under their stress. In urban areas where systems are presently in danger of being irreversibly lost or irreparably damaged, biological carrying capacities must be compatible with visitor demand levels so that natural regenerative capacities of systems can work unchecked to restore or maintain equilibrium conditions for that ecosystem.

On 16 May 1986, DEC announced the transfer of $20,000 through the Return a Gift program to a special account to be utilized for the establishment of an urban wildlife management area in the National Park Service-Gateway Floyd Bennett Field "North 40."

The selection criteria noted below consolidated the mandates of our respective agencies. Progress in areas such as increasing potential habitat for wildlife with commensurate increases in biodiversity in urban stressed ecosystems could be accomplished. In addition, the site had an active constituency using the Field for interpretative-education programs through NPS cooperative agreements with the New York City Board of Education, New York City Chapter of the National Audubon Society, Cornell Cooperative Extension, and New York State Office of Parks, Recreation and Historic Preservation. The site was accessible to visitors of Gateway National Recreation Area. In addition, it was one where a long-term commitment would be made for maintenance and upkeep, and there would be only a one-time cost to establish the area.

In July 1986, a Site Development Plan was prepared, which built on the Park's General Management Plan. Both plans discussed "environmental zones" for research, education, and wildlife preservation. The Action Plan for the "North 40" called for the establishment of designated trails, closing off random vehicle or human access, initiating inter-

pretive programs, and a number of wildlife enhancement projects. Both the NPS and DEC staff (Miller and Matthews 1978) had extensive experience in pond restoration and management, and designing trails and interpretive programs for urban areas.

Creation of the approximately 0.4-ha freshwater pond was central to the plan. Proximity of the pond to the waters of Jamaica Bay would encourage birds seeking fresh water to use this pond. After excavation, revegetation of spoil berms around the pond would involve use of plants with wildlife support capability or wind erosion control.

In the pond itself, an assortment of freshwater species ranging from deep-water submergents to shallow water emergents would be planted. Sago pondweed (*Potamogeton pectinatus*), arrowhead (*Sagittaria latifolia*), and smartweed (*Polygonum pennsylvanicum*) were major components. On the berms, ground cover such as wild millet (*Echinochloa crusgalli*) and birdsfoot trefoil (*Lotus corniculatus*) would be utilized from cuttings and seeds started in the Park's greenhouse/nursery. Nest boxes, native animal releases, and plantings to attract insects were all part of the "North 40 Pond Action Plan."

The Memorandum of Understanding was officially signed by both DEC and NPS in February 1988. On 16 March 1989, a bulldozer began the excavation. It took only 2 weeks to complete the pond. On 31 August 1989, an official ribbon cutting took place. By September 1989, the pond had bird-blinds completed by the New York City Telephone Pioneers, a volunteer group of retired New York Telephone Company employees. Also, the trail (over 2.4 km) had been cut by NPS maintenance crews (and trail signs purchased), and berm plants were established through joint efforts by an NPS agronomist, Cornell University, New York City Board of Education, New York City Chapter—National Audubon Society, and NPS Jamaica Bay District interpreters.

HABITAT IMPROVEMENTS AND COMMUNITY RECREATION

Floyd Bennett Field lacks the herpetofaunal diversity that once existed locally prior to urbanization. In recognition of this paucity, and the continuing urbanization pressures on nearby unprotected populations, a program of transplants was formulated by NPS for Floyd Bennett Field. The program is modelled after an older, ongoing program at Gateway's Jamaica Bay Wildlife Refuge that seeks to recreate a herpetofaunal community resembling, as closely as possible, that which formerly occurred on the now urbanized lands adjacent to the park (Cook and Pinnock 1987). This is consistent with NPS goals and policies for native species restoration and protection at Gateway (USNPS 1979) and could help preserve local gene pools threatened by urbanization. Similar programs had been proposed in theory by Campbell (1974) and used in Great Britain to protect endangered populations of *Bufo calamita* (Beebee 1973).

The success of the program at Jamaica Bay Wildlife Refuge (Cook and Pinnock 1987) suggested that a parallel program at Floyd Bennett Field would also meet with success.

Because so many species of amphibians and reptiles are dependent on aquatic habitats, the restoration of freshwater wetlands was a key step in recreating the native herpetofauna on Floyd Bennett Field. Other improvements, such as enhancing micro-habitats by placing piles of boards, logs, leaves, and woodchips, benefit both aquatic and terrestrial species. Criteria for candidate species for transplanting, and collection techniques, followed those of Cook and Pinnock (1987). Candidate species were restricted to local, Long Island populations.

Working under permits granted by DEC, transplants began in 1989 and continue. Different species were collected at different life stages, and some species (e.g., spring peeper) were collected at more than one life stage. All reptiles released were marked for future identification (Woodbury 1956).

To date, individuals of 12 species have been released at Floyd Bennett Field. Six of these species are wetland dependent for all or part of their life cycle, and were released into Return-A-Gift Pond (Table 1). Monitoring records indicate that survival and reproduction are occurring, and short-generation-time species, such as spring peeper, are already established. For longer-lived species, such as spotted salamander and painted turtle, several more years of monitoring will be necessary to determine their status. Encouraged by these results, NPS is exploring the possibility of releasing additional native species.

Wildlife use of the pond began immediately after excavation, and continues to expand. Muskrats (*Ondatra zibethicus*) have moved in and established a lodge, and spring

Table 1. Population status of amphibians and reptiles released at Return-A-Gift Pond, Floyd Bennett Field, Gateway National Recreation Area, New York, 1989–91.

Species released	Number of individuals	Overwinter survival	Breeding records	Established
Spotted salamander (*Ambystoma maculatum*)	8,000 eggs 71 larvae	*	*	*
Spring peeper (*Hyla crucifer*)	2,600 larvae 10 adults	yes	many	yes
Grey treefrog (*Hyla versicolor*)	1,500 larvae	*	*	*
Green frog (*Rana clamitans*)	132 metamorphs 8 adults	yes	*	*
Fowler's toad (*Bufo woodhousii*)	700 larvae 31 adults	yes	many	yes
Painted turtle (*Chrysemys picta*)	20 hatchling 62 adults	yes	2 nesting females	*

* = insufficient elapsed time or data to determine.

Table 2. Bird species using the "North 40 Pond" at Floyd Bennett Field, New York City.

Common Name	Scientific Name
Great blue heron	*Ardea herodias*
Great egret	*Casmerodius albus*
Snowy egret	*Egretta thula*
Cattle egret	*Bubulcus ibis*
Black-crowned night-heron	*Nycticorax nycticorax*
Glossy ibis	*Plegadis falcinellus*
American black duck	*Anas rubripes*
Mallard	*Anas platyrhynchos*
Common moorhen	*Gallinula chloropus*
Spotted sandpiper	*Actitis macularia*
Herring gull	*Larus argentatus*
Great black-backed gull	*Larus marinus*

peepers transplanted as larvae in 1989 were breeding in 1990. A variety of bird species uses the pond (Table 2). Although all of these species have been observed at Floyd Bennett Field, the common moorhen listed in the table constitutes the first record of this species for the site.

What was also remarkable were the number of pioneer plant species that appeared in and around the pond, such as common cattail (*Typha latifolia*) and duckweed (*Lemna minor*). These species appeared as uninvited, although welcomed, additions to the plant community of the "North 40" trail system. Use of the site by the general public and school groups has increased as a result of ongoing publicity, and the program continues to result in the establishment of additional native wildlife species.

All the objectives for this project were met: habitat alteration was successful, and wildlife use of the area increased in terms of transplanted animals and resident animal populations. The project has demonstrated that wildlife populations can thrive when habitat restoration is undertaken, even in highly disturbed environments. An additional benefit is that individuals who contributed to the Return a Gift program can see the results of their contribution as money well spent! The "North 40" pond and trail system serves as a model outdoor laboratory to show the public how habitat enhancement and restoration efforts can work. Similar projects can be undertaken not only for the benefits of habitat restoration but also for the educational benefits such restoration efforts can bring to urban areas.

Acknowledgments.—We wish to thank the following people, units, and companies. Maps were produced by the Habitat Inventory Unit of DEC, in particular by K. Barnes, G. Rasmussen, W. Richter, and J. Davis. Staff of DEC's Bureau of Construction and Maintenance, A. Niles and M. Malinoski provided engineering support and technical assistance. Telephone Pioneers of America constructed the blinds. Finally, the O'Connor Contracting Corp. built the pond.

REFERENCES CITED

Beebee, T.J.C. 1973. Observations concerning the decline of the British amphibia. Biol. Conserv. 5:20–24.

Campbell, C.A. 1974. Survival of reptiles and amphibians in urban environments. Pages 61–66 *in* J.H. Noyes and D.R. Progulske, eds. Wildlife in an urbanizing environment. Univ. of Mass., Coop. Ext. Serv., Amherst.

Cook, R. P., and C.A. Pinnock. 1987. Recreating a herpetofaunal community at Gateway National Recreation Area, New York. Pages 151–154 *in* L. W. Adams and D.L. Leedy, eds. Integrating man and nature in the metropolitan environment. Natl. Inst. Urban Wildl., Columbia, Md.

Franklin, T. M. 1981. Wildlife in city parks. Trends in Urban For. 18:14–18.

Gregg, W.P. 1980. Development alternative: new directions. Pages 43–53 *in* Barrier island forum and workshop proc., Cape Cod Natl. Seashore, May.

Grey, G. W., and F. J. Deneke. 1978. Urban forestry. John Wiley Press, New York, N.Y.

Miller, R. L., and M. J. Matthews. 1978. Tivoli lakes management plan. New York State Dep. Environ. Conserv., Wildl. Resour. Cent., Delmar. 67 pp. Multilith.

Tanacredi, J.T. 1987. Natural resource management policy constraints and tradeoffs in an urban national recreational area. Pages 221–227 *in* L. W. Adams and D.L. Leedy, eds. Integrating man and nature in the metropolitan environment. Natl. Inst. Urban Wildl., Columbia, Md.

USNPS. 1979. General management plan, Gateway National Recreational area. USDI Natl. Park Serv., Washington DC. 180 pp.

Woodbury, A.M. 1956. Uses of marking animals in ecological studies: marking amphibians and reptiles. Ecology 37:670–674.

Wildlife Habitat Analysis for Alcatraz Island, Golden Gate National Recreation Area, California

JUDD A. HOWELL AND TANIA POLLAK, *National Park Service, Golden Gate NRA, Fort Mason, Bldg. 201, San Francisco, CA 94123*

INTRODUCTION

As urban development continues to replace natural wildlife habitat in response to human population and economic growth, the need to recognize the value of alternative habitats becomes critical. In 1989, the San Francisco Bay encompassed 1,419 km². Historically, fill and development have reduced the bay by 30%, with proportional loss of wetlands and wildlife habitats. As this trend continues, parks, historical sites, and other protected areas become more important for maintaining populations of native species in the urban context. Better understanding of the relationships of factors such as area size, habitat fragmentation, preserve design as formulated in conservation biology (Soulé 1986), and the basic principles of island biogeography (MacArthur and Wilson 1967) will improve our abilities to manage these sites for wildlife.

Alcatraz Island is a dynamic ecological system altered through its history by human use. The plant community has been modified by the introduction of horticultural species, providing habitats that were not present historically. Habitat structure is quite different from what was probably a mixture of sparse grassland and coastal scrub influenced by guano deposits.

In 1988, the National Park Service in cooperation with the Golden Gate National Park Association organized a series of planning workshops to examine the transformation of Alcatraz from a prison to a park, implementing the park's General Management Plan (National Park Service 1980). A noted landscape architect facilitated the effort. The resultant design plan called for numerous amenities to provide for visitor use. An element of the overall plan was proposed for implementation that would rehabilitate a trail through the closed portion of the island and open it for public use. The proposed trail extends around the southeastern perimeter of the island. Since this area remained in disuse from the early 1970s, it became important for nesting and roosting, contributing to the avian diversity of the island. Although considerable effort was expended on planning

for Alcatraz, the focus tended to remain on the cultural landscape and human use of the island.

Once the planning phase was completed, a series of meetings, reviews, and an environmental assessment were begun to determine the value of, and impacts to, wildlife on the island. First, the assessment of development on western gulls (*Larus occidentalis*) was examined, resulting in the belief that little impact would occur to the species. Next, black-crowned night-herons (*Nycticorax nycticorax*) were examined, resulting in a different position because they were thought to be sensitive to disturbance. The Alcatraz population became a focus of interest as the U.S. Fish and Wildlife Service began to study night-herons as biological indicators of environmental poisoning (Custer et al. 1983, Hoffman et al. 1986, Ohlendorf et al. 1988, Ohlendorf and Fleming 1988). In the Bay Area, the night-herons have lost much of their original habitat to development (Alvarez and Thomas 1989). Western gulls and night-herons on Alcatraz constitute approximately 15% and 10% of their Bay Area populations, 450 and 100 nesting pairs, respectively (D.A. Bell, Golden Gate Natl. Rec. Area; R. Hothem, U.S. Fish and Wildl. Serv.; and P. Woodin, San Francisco Bay Bird Observatory; pers. commun.).

The cultural history of Alcatraz Island was well documented (Thompson 1972), but wildlife history prior to the island's transfer to the National Park Service on 22 May 1973 was anecdotal, speculative, or non-existent. Throughout the 1980s, several wildlife studies and inventories were conducted intermittently in response to specific management questions or the specific interests of individual investigators (Howell 1983, Howell et al. 1983, Thompson 1988, Boarman 1989, Annett and Pierotti 1989, Bell 1990). Previous studies highlighted single species on the island, reflecting information for them but little information for the remaining species.

The purpose of the present study was to develop a detailed wildlife habitat analysis of a heavily visited cultural site, Alcatraz Island. The analysis would be used by park

Wildlife Conservation in Metropolitan Environments. NIUW Symp. Ser. 2, L.W. Adams and D.L. Leedy, eds. Published by Natl. Inst. for Urban Wildl., 10921 Trotting Ridge Way, Columbia, MD 21044, USA, 1991.

management to evaluate impacts related to proposals for opening areas of the island for public visitation. Through the analysis of wildlife habitat on Alcatraz, we planned to demonstrate the value of geographic information system (GIS) methodology as an analytical tool for micro site analysis. Finally, we wanted to formulate a rationale for protecting cultural landscapes as viable habitats for native wildlife.

STUDY AREA

Alcatraz Island encompasses 9.1 ha in the middle of San Francisco Bay, California. It rests 1.8 km north of the city of San Francisco (UTM: 550,800 E; 4,186,600 N). The island is a National Historic Landmark, managed by the National Park Service as part of the 3,036-ha Golden Gate National Recreation Area (Fig. 1). Alcatraz became a popular tourist attraction after its days as a military fortification, military prison, and an infamous federal penitentiary. Visitor use patterns changed in the mid-1980s from regular ranger led walks to an open trails policy over the central third of the island. Annual visitation increased from 350,000 in the mid-1980s to approximately 950,000 visitors by 1990.

The long axis of Alcatraz Island lies in a northwest-southeast orientation. Although much of the island is concrete, Alcatraz has distinct areas of habitat, which we separated into sublocations. Cliffs, which rise to 23 m around the island, are generally barren of vegetation. The northeastern shore has an extensive grassy area above the cliffs; the western cliffs extend from the northern end of Alcatraz to midway along the western shore; and the southern cliffs extend from midway along the western shore to the southern end. Tidepools lie at the base of these cliffs. The southern tip of the island is covered with agave (*Agave shawii*) and eucalyptus (*Eucalyptus globulus*). North of the eucalyptus grove is the launch landing area where visitors disembark and staff maintain offices, a museum, and a visitor center. The central upland of the island is primarily concrete and buildings, including the former prison industries area, cellhouse, and parade ground. A grassy bluff, the cistern, lies

between the industries and cellhouse on the northwestern end. The west side of the island, below the cellhouse, supports historic gardens and shrubs, mainly mirrorbush (*Coprosma baueri*) and blackberry (*Rubus vitifolius*). Large rubble piles, with some shrubs, border the parade grounds on the southern end of Alcatraz. To the east of the cellhouse are historic ruins, covered with mirrorbush, blackberry, eucalyptus, and Monterey cypress (*Cupressus macrocarpa*). Interspersed among the horticultural plants are areas of grass and native coyote bush (*Baccharis pilularis*).

MATERIALS AND METHODS

Database Analysis

Existing wildlife information from Alcatraz was derived from two sources and entered into separate databases. The first data set came from incidental observations by Alcatraz staff. These data were recorded in a log book or on wildlife observation cards from 1980 to 1990. The second data set came from systematic surveys of the island. Surveys included distribution and abundance data that were recorded on maps from 1981 to 1985, and from 1989 to 1990. Additional information was derived from summaries of literature about each species and the effects of human disturbance on wildlife. Specific surveys were conducted for black-crowned night-heron, western gull, deer mouse (*Peromyscus maniculatus*), and California slender salamander (*Batrachoseps attenuatus*).

Modelling

Maps of Alcatraz were entered into a GIS by digitizing overlays using GRASS software (Westervelt et al. 1986). Digitized themes included topography, wildlife habitats mapped in 1985 (R. Crabb, Natl. Park Serv., pers. commun.), land use, and island sublocations. An index of avian activity was derived using total observations per unit area, which standardized values for island sublocations. Species richness was derived using the number of species within an island sublocation. Location themes were reclassified to reflect the rank of these values and to reflect species specific use by black-crowned night-herons, western gulls, and deer mice.

Compiled information was used to develop simple models to analyze the effects of four buffers at 7.6-m intervals on wildlife habitats. In GIS terminology, buffers are defined as incremental extensions from a mapped feature of interest permitting calculation of area within the buffer. The 7.6-m interval was derived as an approximation for disturbance effects. The underlying assumptions were that animals would tend to avoid habitat within 7.6 m of the trail, and that animals were uniformly distributed throughout the sublocations.

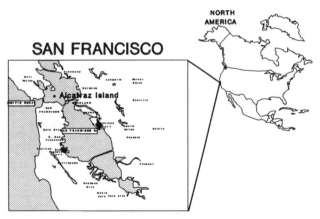

Fig. 1. Alcatraz Island in San Francisco Bay, California.

RESULTS

Database Analysis

The incidental observation database had 1,015 records and the locational database had 2,339 records of wildlife observations. A total of 108 bird species was observed on Alcatraz from 1980 to 1990. These observations were grouped into four categories: (1) seven known breeders (Table 1), (2) eight possible breeders, (3) 20 frequent users, and (4) 73 infrequent users. Individual bird species with 10 or more observations were placed in the frequent category, and species with less than 10 observations were placed in the infrequent category. One amphibian (the California slender salamander) and one mammal (the deer mouse) maintain populations on the island.

Seasonal use was examined for the seven known breeders using the pooled databases (Fig. 2). January through July represents the active breeding period with all seven species present simultaneously during March, April, and May. Activity diminished in August with three of the breeding species present. September through December had three to five of the breeders present.

The 15 sublocations identified on Alcatraz were ranked using the bird activity index (Fig. 3). Seven areas tended to cumulatively rank higher; parade ground (PRG), eucalyptus grove (EUC), ruins (RUN), southern cliffs (SCL), agave cliff (AGV), western cliffs (WCL), and rubble piles (RUB). Eight areas tended to have secondary cumulative ranks;

Table 1. Confirmed breeding populations of birds on Alcatraz Island, California, 1980–1990.[a]

Common name	Scientific name
Pigeon guillemot	*Cephhus columba*
Mallard	*Anas platyrhynchos*
Western gull	*Larus occidentalis*
Black-crowned night-heron	*Nycticorax nycticorax*
Raven	*Corvus corax*
White-crowned sparrow	*Zonotrichia leucophyrs*
Song sparrow	*Melospiza melodia*

[a]For a complete vertebrate species list for the island, please contact the authors.

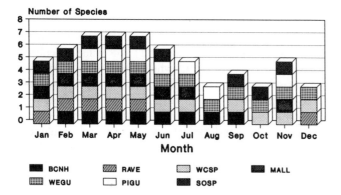

Fig. 2. Seasonal use by seven breeding bird species of Alcatraz Island, California, 1980–1990. BCNH = black-crowned night-heron, RAVE = raven, WCSP = white-crowned sparrow, MALL = mallard, WEGU = western gull, PIGU = pigeon guillemot, SOSP = song sparrow.

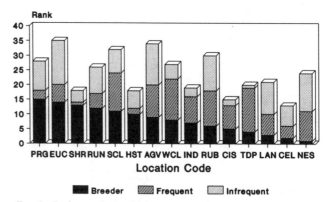

Fig. 3. Bird use of 15 sublocations on Alcatraz Island, California, 1980–1990. Use was ranked by the activity index. Breeder = known and possible breeding birds. Frequent = species for which 10 or more observations were recorded. Infrequent = species for which fewer than 10 observations were recorded. (See text for description of the activity index and sublocation codes.)

the shrub-historic garden (SHR), historic gardens (HST), industries (IND), cistern (CIS), tidepools (TDP), launch landing (LAN), cellhouse (CEL), and northeast shore (NES). Habitats for black-crowned night-herons were ranked based upon number of nests in each location (Fig. 4).

Modelling

From the 1985 wildlife habitat map, 39% (3.55 ha) of the island was classified as concrete. The 15 sublocations identified on the island comprised 6.81 ha of habitat. The current trail covers 0.73 ha, 8% of the island surface. Existing land use was mapped and buffered with four 7.6-m intervals out to 30.5 m to approximate different levels of disturbance. The buffering assumed diminishing impact with greater distance from the existing trail system. The current trail with the first 7.6-m buffer affected 1.22 ha, 13% of the island surface (the innermost solid black area of Fig. 5). The first 7.6-m buffer was partially based on the fact that black-crowned night-herons utilized shrub cover for nesting that averaged 6.9 m (n = 6) from the current trail.

The proposed trail covered 0.45 ha, 5% of the island

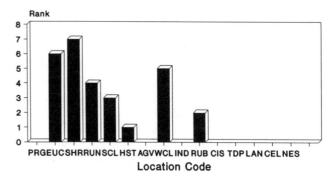

Fig. 4. Black-crowned night-heron use of seven sublocations on Alcatraz Island, California, 1980–1990. Use was ranked by number of nests in each location.

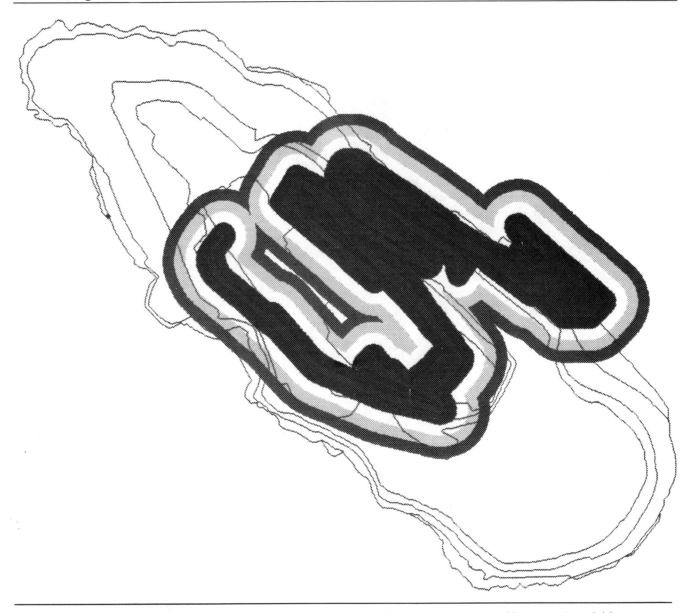

Fig. 5. Existing trail footprint surrounded by four incremental 7.6-m buffers, Alcatraz Island, Golden Gate National Recreation Area, California.

surface. The proposed trail was mapped and buffered with four 7.6-m intervals out to 30.5 m. The first 7.6-m buffer affected 1.17 ha, 13% of the island surface (the innermost solid black area of Fig. 6). The combined effect of old and new trails (considering one buffer width) would influence over 26% of the island (the innermost solid black area of Fig. 7). The same procedure was used to mask habitat for species activity and richness resulting in a 17% potential reduction of existing habitat (Table 2). Three areas tended to rank higher for black-crowned night-heron habitat; euca-lyptus, shrubs and western cliffs (Fig. 4). The first 7.6-m buffer was masked over black-crowned night-heron habitat to determine the amount of potential loss. The proposed trail reduced black-crowned night-heron habitat by 0.68 ha, which was 8.4% of the island surface but 22% of existing heron habitat (Fig. 8).

DISCUSSION

This study examined two issues that arose from the matter of wildlife on Alcatraz: (1) the value of cultural landscapes as wildlife habitat when alternative natural habi-tats were becoming less available, and (2) appropriateness of a community approach to planning for the long-term conservation of wildlife on the island. Immigration rates, extinction rates, and genetic changes of island populations strongly influence the faunal composition of an island (Mac-Arthur and Wilson 1967). Island biogeography remains a powerful unifying theory that must be applied for maintain-ing the dynamics and composition of faunal communities like the one found on Alcatraz. This requires a community ecology approach rather than concentrating on single spe-cies as in previous work.

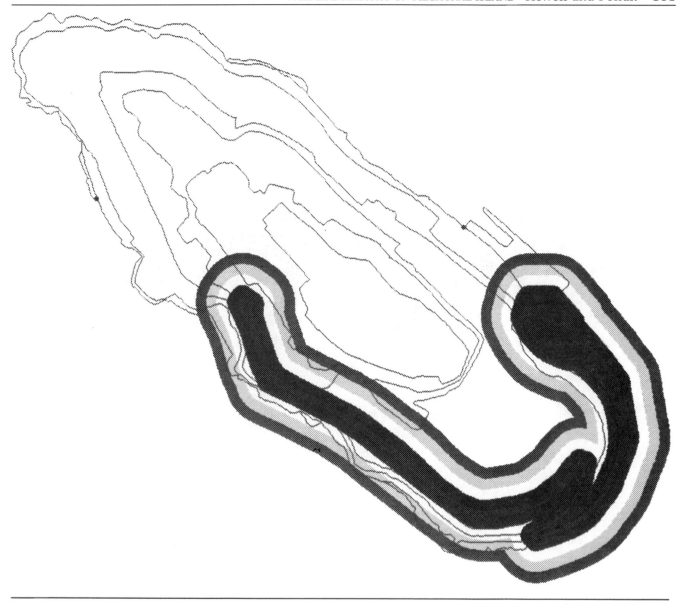

Fig. 6. Proposed trail footprint surrounded by four incremental 7.6-m buffers, Alcatraz Island, Golden Gate National Recreation Area, California.

The results of this study indicate that Alcatraz is similar to other small islands having a depauperate fauna. Species richness included nine vertebrates breeding on the island with an additional eight bird species as possible breeders. Visitation to the island by birds was frequent because of proximity to the mainland and large island points within a 2.4-km radius. The island was used as roosting habitat for species such as Brandt's cormorant (*Phalacrocorax penicillatus*) and Heermann's gull (*Larus heermanni*), and may be of value as a storm refuge from the outer coast. Marine mammals also use the island beaches and tidepools intermittently for resting. Two records of colonization attempts by breeders were documented in the last decade, Heermann's gull (Howell et al. 1983) and raven. The raven successfully fledged young; the Heermann's gull did not.

Because of historic development and current management, the effective size of the island for wildlife is approxi-

mately 6.8 ha, 75.0% of the island's total area. Presently two thirds of the island remains closed to visitors. This reduced size sets the limit for the number of species the island can accommodate. The current trail had an 8% footprint (actual trail surface area) and affected 13% of the island with a single 7.6-m buffer. The proposed trail had a 5% footprint and affected 13% of the island with a 7.6-m buffer. Because of the linearity of the proposed trail, it potentially has a proportionately greater impact than the existing switchback trail. The proposed trail could affect up to an additional 17% of the island habitat for frequent and infrequent users based on the simple assumptions of our model. Although these simplifying assumptions affect the accuracy of our predictions, we think this process represents a reasonable estimate for orders of magnitude related to impact.

For potential and actual breeding species, human intru-

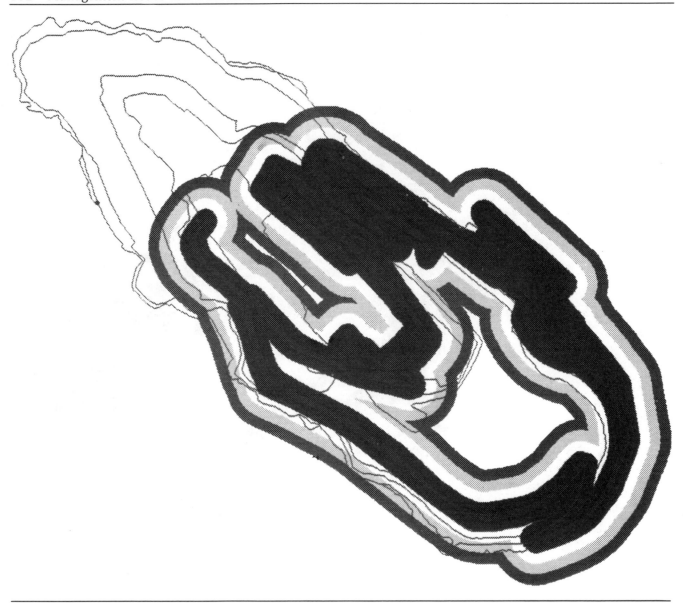

Fig. 7. Total footprint of existing and proposed trail system (Fig. 5 and Fig. 6 combined), Golden Gate National Recreation Area, California.

sion during the breeding season will reduce productivity for black-crowned night-herons (Tremblay and Ellison 1979, Parsons and Burger 1982), western gulls (Hand 1980), and other species (Ellison and Cleary 1978, Anderson and Keith 1980, Erwin 1989). From this study, the most sensitive breeding period was determined to be from January through July. That interval includes territory establishment, courtship, copulation, nesting, and fledging for the seven breeding species.

MANAGEMENT RECOMMENDATIONS

Alcatraz provides a unique setting in the San Francisco Bay, sheltered yet near the Golden Gate, the bay's opening to the Pacific Ocean. Although the island has been extensively altered, much of it currently remains relatively undisturbed by human use. Undisturbed areas provide habitat for

a variety of species. Species such as the black-crowned night-heron, which experienced a drastic loss of habitat on the mainland, have been given greater value because of their role as bioindicators of ecosystem condition. All these factors must be incorporated in development plans to provide effective wildlife management strategies for the island.

Several management approaches may be pursued: (1) maintain current use patterns, (2) abandon human use of the island, (3) provide complete human access, or (4) modify current use with intensive habitat management. Alternatives one through three seem unlikely. Maintenance of current use patterns is doubtful, given management's desire to provide more varied visitor experiences on the island. If alternative two were pursued, part of our culture would be lost. If alternative three were pursued, part of our wildlife heritage would be lost. Alternative four requires planning and commitment.

Table 2. Potential loss of ranked habitats for wildlife if a proposed trail is opened on Alcatraz Island, Golden Gate National Recreation Area, California.

Location[a]	Habitat Rank[b]			Area (Ha)	Potential Loss	
	I	II	III		Ha	%
Parade ground	1	13	0	0.70	0.07	9.5
Eucalyptus grove	2	10	2	0.28	0.17	60.0
Shrub-historic garden	3	15	1	0.60	0.19	32.0
Ruins-tree	4	11	4	0.44	0.00	0.0
Southern cliffs	5	3	5	0.48	0.17	35.5
Historic garden	6	14	7	0.22	<0.01	0.9
Agave cliff	7	5	0	0.20	0.18	86.7
Western cliffs	8	2	3	0.62	0.00	0.0
Industries	9	7	0	0.65	0.00	0.0
Rubble piles	10	4	6	0.46	0.16	34.2
Cistern	11	8	0	0.33	0.00	0.0
Tidepools	12	1	0	0.08	<0.01	3.8
Launch landing	13	9	0	0.80	0.24	29.6
Cellhouse	14	12	0	0.77	0.00	0.0
Northeast shore	15	6	0	0.19	0.00	0.0
Total				6.81	1.17	17.1

[a]See text for description.
[b]Ranked for breeding birds (I), frequent birds (II), and black-crowned night-herons (III). (See text for description.)

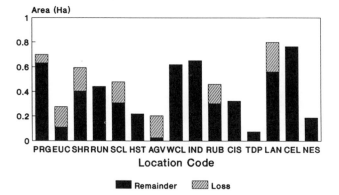

Fig. 8. Potential black-crowned night-heron habitat loss if a proposed trail is opened on Alcatraz Island, Golden Gate National Recreation Area, California. Calculations were based on one 7.6-m buffer surrounding the proposed trail.

To manage Alcatraz for wildlife and accommodate greater human use, we recommend the following: (1) identify areas for restoration to suitable habitats; (2) establish habitat elements, such as shrub planting for nesting substrate, cover, and screening; (3) close trails seasonally to prevent disturbance to established nesters and potential colonizers; (4) maintain undisturbed areas exclusively for wildlife; (5) provide educational opportunities for visitors to observe wildlife without intruding into sensitive habitats; and (6) explain the role of islands in our understanding of ecological and evolutionary processes. Any management actions will affect wildlife diversity on the island, and must be monitored.

Because the area of potential habitat loss through future development on the island can be measured fairly accurately, there will be some opportunity to mitigate habitat impacts. Restoration of habitats using native vegetation would contribute to the island's biological conservation. It is important to manage the island as a dynamic system with an ever changing species composition and to not preclude, through management actions, the natural colonizations and extinctions that would occur on the island. However, total size of the island, effective size, and carrying capacity will remain the major constraints to wildlife diversity on Alcatraz.

Human population growth is not likely to stop. The demand for housing, commerce, and industrial and recreational sites will continue to encroach on wildlife habitat. Disturbance will play a major role in limiting species richness. Some species will colonize alternative or secondary habitats. As they do so, parks and preserves must be in a position to respond with planned management actions to protect wildlife species in these alternative habitats.

Acknowledgments.—This study was supported in part by a grant from the Golden Gate National Park Association in cooperation with the National Park Service. The authors want to thank the numerous individuals who contributed to our understanding of Alcatraz as a site for wildlife, especially Roxi Farwell, Allen Fish, Doug Bell, Roger Hothem, and Peg Woodin. The manuscript benefitted greatly from review by Allen Fish, Nancy Hornor, and Doug Nadeau. We also want to thank Ken Gardels and Dr. Robert Twiss for the use of the Geographic Information Laboratory, Department of Landscape Architecture, University of California, Berkeley. Without their assistance, patience, and forbearance we could not have completed this analysis.

REFERENCES CITED

Alvarez, M., and T. Thomas. 1989. 1989 nesting status—the black-crowned night-heron in the San Francisco bay area. Unpubl. ms., Golden Gate Natl. Rec. Area, San Francisco, Calif. 7 pp.

Anderson, D. W., and J. O. Keith. 1980. Human influence on seabird nesting success: conservation implications. Biol. Conserv. 18:65–80.

Annett, C., and R. Pierotti. 1989. Chick hatching as a trigger for dietary switching in the western gull. Colonial Waterbirds 12:4–11.

Bell, D. A. 1990. Alcatraz island western gull nest survey. Unpubl. ms., Golden Gate Natl. Rec. Area, San Francisco, Calif. 15 pp.

Boarman, W.I. 1989. The breeding birds of Alcatraz Island: life on the Rock. Western Birds 20:19–24.

Custer, T., G. Hensler, and T. E. Kaiser. 1983. Clutch size, reproductive success, and organochlorine contaminants in Atlantic coast black-crowned herons. Auk 100:699–710.

Ellison, L., and L. Cleary. 1978. Effects of human disturbance on breeding of double-crested cormorants. Auk 95:510–517.

Erwin, M. R. 1989. Responses to human intruders by birds nesting in colonies: experimental results and management guidelines. Colonial Waterbirds 12:104–108.

Hand, J. L. 1980. Human disturbances in western gull (*Larus occidentalis livens*) colonies and possible amplification by intraspecific predation. Biol. Conserv. 18:59–63.

Hoffman, D., B. Rattner, C. Bunck, A. Krynitsky, H. Ohlendorf, and R. Lowe. 1986. Association between PCBs and lower embryonic weight in black-crowned night herons in San Francisco Bay. J. of Toxicol. and Environ. Health 19:383–391.

Howell, J.A. 1983. Heermann's gull (*Larus heermanni*) on Alcatraz Island in Golden Gate National Recreation Area, California. Pages 230–233 *in* C. van Riper et al., eds. First biennial conference of research in California national parks. Natl. Park Serv. Coop. Parks Study Unit, Davis, Calif.

———, D. Laclerque, S. Paris, W. Boarman, A. DeGange, and L. Binford. 1983. First nests of Heermann's gull in the United States. Western Birds 14:39–46.

MacArthur, R.H., and E.O. Wilson. 1967. The theory of island biogeography. Princeton Univ. Press, Princeton, N.J. 203 pp.

National Park Service. 1980. General management plan, environmental analysis, Golden Gate National Recreation Area/Point Reyes National Seashore, California. U.S. Dep. Inter., Natl. Park Serv., San Francisco, Calif. 279 pp.

Ohlendorf, H., and J. Fleming. 1988. Birds and environmental contaminants in San Francisco and Chesapeake Bays. Mar. Pollut. Bull. 19:487–495.

———, T. W. Custer, R. W. Lowe, M. Rigney, and E. Cromartie. 1988. Organochlorines and mercury in eggs of coastal terns and herons in California, USA. Colonial Waterbirds 11:85–94.

Parsons, K., and J. Burger. 1982. Human disturbance and nesting behavior in black-crowned night herons. Condor 84:184–187.

Soulé, M.E., ed. 1986. Conservation biology: the science of scarcity and diversity. Sinauer Assoc., Inc., Sunderland, Mass. 584 pp.

Thompson, E.N. 1972. The rock: a history of Alcatraz Island 1847–1972. Historic Resour. Study, Historic Preservation Div., Natl. Park Serv., Denver, Colo. 637 pp.

Thompson, R.L. 1988. *Peromyscus maniculatus* on Alcatraz Island with a new coat-color variant. Unpubl. ms., Golden Gate Natl. Rec. Area, San Francisco, Calif. 11 pp.

Tremblay, J., and L.N. Ellison. 1979. Effects of human disturbance on breeding of black-crowned night-herons. Auk 96:364–369.

Westervelt, J., W. Goram, and M. Shaprio. 1986. Design and development of GRASS: the geographical resources analysis support system. U.S. Army Construction Eng. Res. Lab., Champaign, Ill. 13 pp.

Influence of Urban Wildlife Habitats on the Value of Residential Properties

DAVID A. KING, JODY L. WHITE, AND WILLIAM W. SHAW, *School of Renewable Natural Resources, University of Arizona, Tucson, AZ 85721*

INTRODUCTION

Many communities are confronting the issue of preserving wildlife habitat as well as other open space. Decisions to preserve and protect urban wildlife habitat will depend, to an important degree, upon demonstration of its social and private values.

A purpose of our study was to estimate the influence of proximity to wildlife habitat on the value of single family residential properties in the Tucson, Arizona urban area. We used the property value approach to estimate what people actually pay for such areas, a measure of private value. If the influence of wildlife habitat is positive, then values to the community may accrue through positive impacts on the property tax base.

CONCEPTUAL FRAMEWORK

In purchasing a home, a family chooses from among a range of houses having different bundles of characteristics. The choice is based on relative preferences for the characteristics available and the family's budget. Some characteristics may add to the value of a house and some may subtract.

When this scenario is played out in a housing market, the relationship between the housing prices that result and the characteristics of the housing may be used to estimate the values of the characteristics (Rosen 1974, Freeman 1979a). The approach, an application of hedonic price theory, has been used to estimate the values of clean air (Harrison and Rubinfeld 1978), quiet (McMillan et al. 1980), and multiple amenities (Blomquist et al. 1988).

METHODS

The Hedonic Technique

The hedonic technique consists of two stages. We are reporting results of the first stage from which the value of small changes in quantities of the characteristics can be estimated. The second stage combines results from the first stage with socioeconomic data gathered from property buyers to estimate demand functions for the characteristics.

In the first stage, a hedonic or implicit price function is estimated by regressing the prices of residential properties on the characteristics of the properties. A generalized implicit price function is shown below:

$$P_h = f(Z_s, Z_n, Z_e) \qquad (1)$$

Three general categories of characteristics affecting the price of a house (P_h) are included: structural (Z_s), neighborhood (Z_n), and environmental (Z_e). Structural characteristics include such things as lot size, area of living space, number of bathrooms and bedrooms, age of house, type of construction, and presence of fireplace. Neighborhood characteristics include distance to central business district or nearest major employment center, zoning density, and distance to nearest shopping mall. The environmental characteristics include, of course, the habitat and open space variables of particular interest in this study and others thought to influence housing prices.

Partial differentiation of the estimated implicit price function with respect to a particular characteristic results in a marginal implicit price function. This differential function can be used to estimate the change in the price of a property resulting from a one unit change in the quantity of the characteristic, the marginal implicit price of the characteristic. A generalized form of a marginal implicit price function for characteristic Z_i is:

$$p_{zi} = \frac{\partial P_h}{\partial Z_i} \qquad (2)$$

The marginal implicit price of Z_i can be calculated by substitution of the appropriate values for P_h and Z_i in Equation 2 and solving for p_{zi}.

Data Collection

Sample.—Market segmentation is a concern in the analysis of housing markets. Segmentation can occur when

Wildlife Conservation in Metropolitan Environments. NIUW Symp. Ser. 2, L.W. Adams and D.L. Leedy, eds. Published by Natl. Inst. for Urban Wildl., 10921 Trotting Ridge Way, Columbia, MD 21044, USA, 1991.

there are differences in the structure of supply and demand in different parts of an urban area. These differences can result from racial barriers, desire to maintain ethnic communities, and different preferences for housing. If segmentation exists, a single implicit price function cannot be a valid representation of the market forces at work.

To account for potential market segmentation, the Tucson urban area was divided into five strata (Fig. 1). Secondary socioeconomic data (Tucson Trends 1986) and our knowledge of the urban area were used to identify the strata. The sample frame comprised all single family homes sold in 1986 as reported by the Multiple Listing Service of Tucson. A random start was taken within each stratum and then every 10th listing was selected, resulting in a sample of 575 homes. Sixty-eight townhouses were dropped from the analysis because they made up less than 10% of the sample in four of the five strata. The final sample size was 507 homes.

Structural and Neighborhood Variables.—The variables measured for each property are shown in Table 1. It was hypothesized that the structural variables would be positively related to selling price. Among the neighborhood variables, it was hypothesized that proximity to employment centers and regional shopping malls would also be positively related to selling price. A negative relationship between zoned density and price was expected.

Formal Open Space Variables.—Evidence in the literature is mixed concerning the impact on property values of proximity to designated park and recreation areas. Weicher and Zerbst (1973) found that parks with recreational facilities such as playground equipment and lighted playing fields lowered the value of adjacent homes. Another study reported a positive relationship (Hammer et al. 1974), and a third was inconclusive (Allen et al. 1986). In Tucson, most of the neighborhood, district, and regional parks are designed and managed to provide for active recreation and team sports. Natural vegetation and habitat are minimal or nonexistent in these areas.

Distance to publicly-owned golf courses was not used

Table 1. Independent variables measured for each house sold and used in the analysis.

Structural variables
  HAREA—Interior living area (sq. ft.)
  LAREA—Area of lot (sq. ft.)
  BEDROOMS—Number of bedrooms
  BATHROOM—Number of bathrooms
  AGE—Age of house (years)
  Presence of: (0,1)
    FP—Fireplace   GH—Guest house   GA—Garage
    SP—Swimming pool PA—Patio

Neighborhood variables
  Distance to nearest: (miles)
    EMP—employment center
    MALL—regional mall
  DEN—Density   0 = low ($\geq$ 1 acre per dwelling)
                 1 = high ($<$ 1 acre per dwelling)

Open space variables
  Distance to nearest: (miles)
    NEIGHPK—Neighborhood park
    DISTPK—District park
    REGPK—Regional park
    PRIVGOLF—Private golf course
    BIG—Tucson Mtn. Park, Coronado National Forest, or Saguaro National Monument
    HABI—Wildlife habitat I
    HABII—Wildlife habitat II
    OTHOP—Other natural open space

in the analysis because all of these courses are located next to or within regional parks. Distance to private golf courses was included because they are built as complements to large, upper-middle and upper income developments. Some of these courses are open to the public, but at much higher fees than those charged at publicly-owned courses. Construction of publicly-owned golf courses tends to follow, rather than precede or be congruent with residential development, and their location is more highly dependent on land cost than is the case for private courses. A positive relationship between proximity to private golf courses and selling price was expected.

Natural Open Space Variables.—Four categories of lands were considered to be natural open space in our analysis. The Tucson basin is bounded on three sides by large protected natural areas. On the west side are Tucson Mountain County Park and Saguaro National Monument West. The Santa Catalina District of the Coronado National Forest borders the northern and northeastern portions of the basin. On the east side is Saguaro National Monument East. These three areas existed before the bulk of urban development in the basin. Because of the similarity of the characteristics of these areas (large, natural, and mountainous), the distance to the nearest of the four was used in the analysis. It was hypothesized that selling price would be positively related with proximity to these areas.

Two categories of natural open space occur within the metropolitan area that are important as wildlife habitats. Definitions of these habitats were taken from a study of critical and sensitive wildlife habitats by Shaw et al. (1986) that identified and located two classes of wildlife habitat. Class I habitats were defined as "habitats that are exceptionally important for wildlife and which are scarce and declining in supply" (Shaw et al. 1986, p. 3). Specific types of

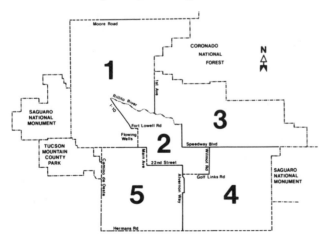

Fig. 1. Map of Tucson urban area with location of strata and large protected areas.

areas falling into this class include: 1) deciduous riparian woodlands; 2) mesquite bosques; 3) lakes, ponds, and wetlands; and, 4) major extensions of riparian habitat from protected areas. Class II habitats were defined as "areas important to wildlife because they support a diversity of species and large numbers of individuals" (Shaw et al. 1986, p. 7). They include: 1) major segments of riparian habitat not linked with protected areas; 2) the Paloverde-Saguaro Sonoran Desert Community; and 3) the Ironwood Plant Community. Note that these habitats were defined and located for the purpose of assisting land use planning in the basin. These definitions express an area's potential to contribute to the maintenance and enhancement of viable and diverse wildlife populations, not its attractiveness to humans.

The fourth category of natural open space was defined to account for areas not formally designated as public or private open space or identified as wildlife habitat. This category was defined to include units of land 2 ha or larger in area, without visible human disturbance, and not categorized as Wildlife Habitats I or II. These areas tended to be tracts of undeveloped upland.

Data Analysis

Multiple regression was used to estimate the implicit price function. Specification of the equation was complicated by the high multicollinearity among both the structural and the neighborhood independent variables. The problem was resolved by selecting one variable from each of the two categories. To make this selection, regressions were run in each of the two categories between each variable as the dependent variable and all of the other variables in the category (Kelejian and Oates 1989, p. 209). The variables chosen in each category were those most highly correlated with the others as measured by the coefficient of multiple determination, R^2. The results led to the selection of living area (HAREA) to represent the structural variables and distance to nearest employment center (EMP) to represent the neighborhood variables. Age of the house (AGE) and zoned density (DEN) were also included in the specification. Age was included as an indicator of condition and as a measure of the time of neighborhood development. Density was used to account for differences in private open space associated with the properties. Potential market segmentation was accounted for by entering the geographic strata in the regression as dummy variables. The remaining independent variables were the environmental variables listed in Table 1.

A double, natural logarithmic functional form of the continuous variables was used to allow the marginal implicit prices of the characteristics to vary with the levels of other characteristics (Freeman 1979b). The one-tailed t test was used to test significance of the regression coefficients.

RESULTS

The Implicit Price Equation

The implicit price equation is shown in Table 2. For the distance variables, a negative sign indicates a positive influence of proximity on the dependent variable, price.

As a group, the coefficients on the strata variables are significantly different from zero ($P < 0.05$), indicating that the geographical strata were appropriate zones of market segmentation.

Formal Open Space.—The natural logarithmic form of the variables measuring distance to urban public parks (LNEIGHPK, LDISTPK, & LREGPK) all have positive signs, indicating a negative effect of proximity to them on the price of residential properties. The one-tail probabilities indicate that the coefficients on neighborhood parks and district parks are significantly greater than zero at the 5% level and the coefficient on regional parks is significant at the 10% level. The coefficient on the natural logarithm of distance to private golf courses (LPRIVGOLF) has a negative sign, indicating proximity to them has a positive effect on price, and is significantly less than zero at the 1% level.

Natural Open Space.—The natural logarithm of distance to the nearest large protected area (LBIG) has a negative sign and is significantly different from zero at the 10% level. Surprisingly, the natural logarithm of distance to other open space (LOTHOP) has a positive sign on its coefficient and is also significant at the 10% level.

As hypothesized, the natural logarithm of distance to the two classes of wildlife habitat (LHABI and LHABII) have coefficients with negative signs, but only the coefficient on LHABII is significantly less than zero ($P < 0.05$).

Marginal Implicit Prices

The marginal implicit prices for the open space variables and area of living space are presented in Table 3. Marginal prices vary with the price of the home and distance

Table 2. Implicit price regression equation for single family residential properties, Tucson, Arizona, 1986.[a]

Variable	Coefficient	SE	t	P[b]
Constant	5.392	0.302	17.838	0.000
LHAREA	0.859	0.036	23.874	0.000
LEMP	−0.111	0.041	2.732	0.004
LAGE	−0.095	0.016	5.731	0.000
DEN	−0.134	0.035	3.790	0.000
LNEIGHPK	0.063	0.032	1.976	0.025
LDISTPK	0.066	0.030	2.154	0.016
LREGPK	0.046	0.029	1.597	0.056
LPRIVGOLF	−0.087	0.031	2.808	0.003
LBIG	−0.067	0.042	1.598	0.056
LHABI	−0.011	0.039	0.279	0.390
LHABII	−0.090	0.040	−2.273	0.012
LOTHOP	0.073	0.046	1.574	0.058
STRATA1	0.080	0.058	1.380	0.084
STRATA2	0.141	0.051	2.746	0.003
STRATA3	0.196	0.057	3.420	0.001
STRATA4	0.093	0.055	1.685	0.046

[a]double, natural logarithmic form. R^2_{adj} = 0.819, F(16,490) = 144.02, $P < 0.001$.
[b]one-tail probabilities.

from a particular open space. Hence, the prices shown in the table were calculated at the means of the home prices and distances for each strata.

For example, given the mathematical form of the regression equation and the regression coefficient on LHABII of 0.090, the marginal implicit price function for HABII is:

$$p_{HABII} = \frac{(0.09) \cdot (P_h)}{(HABII)} \qquad (3)$$

For Stratum 5, substituting its mean value for HABII of 1.596 miles (2.568 km) and its mean home price of $53,707 into Equation 3 and solving, gives a price for HABII of $3,029 per mile ($1,882/km).

The prices in Table 3 are expressed in terms of proximity, not distance, to the open spaces. Hence, their signs are the opposite of the signs of the equivalent regression coefficients. The positive prices of proximity to Class II wildlife habitat are higher than those of private golf courses. Class II wildlife habitat prices are highest in the three strata that abut the Coronado National Forest and Saguaro Monument East (Strata 1, 3, 4).

DISCUSSION

The geographic stratification used was effective and indicates the presence of market segmentation. This segmentation means that the prices of the characteristics vary across the metropolitan area, other things being equal.

Distance from three of the four categories of natural open space, (BIG, HABI, and HABII) are negatively correlated with price indicating that proximity to these areas is positively related to price of housing. However, the level of significance on these relationships is low.

Proximity to areas in the other natural open space category (OTHOP) has a negative influence on the price of housing at the 10% level of significance. We think this result may stem from the fact that these are the natural open spaces remaining after all other natural open space has been categorized. They are lumped into a residual category and

simply may not be as attractive (to people as well as wildlife) as the other kinds of natural open space (BIG, HABI, and HABII).

A possible cause of the low level of statistical significance for three of the four natural open space variables (BIG, HABII, and OTHOP), and lack of significance for the fourth (HABI), is multicollinearity. The six simple correlation coefficients between each pair of the natural logarithmic forms of the four variables range from 0.360 to 0.601 with a mean of 0.528. Multicollinearity reduces the precision of the estimates of the regression coefficients, resulting in higher standard errors and lower t values for the coefficients.

As a simple test for the effects of multicollinearity, we ran a regression without the natural logarithm of distance to the large public areas (LBIG) but with all of the other variables included. The regression coefficient on the natural logarithm of distance to wildlife habitat Class I (LHABI) rose in absolute terms to -0.034 with a P of 0.17 rather than 0.39, still statistically insignificant. We then did the opposite, dropping LHABI from the regression analysis while keeping LBIG and the other variables. The coefficient on LBIG changed by 0.001, but its P level changed to 0.034. Neither of these alternative specifications made any difference to the significance of the coefficients on other open space (LOTHOP) or on wildlife habitat of Class II, (LHABII). It appears that the correlation between distance to one of the large public areas and to wildlife habitat of Class I may be the cause for lack of precision of the estimates of their respective regression coefficients.

Recall that one of the types of habitats in Class I was "major extensions of riparian habitat from protected areas." The large public areas (BIG) in this study are those "protected areas." The probability that a particular Class I wildlife habitat is such an extension depends upon which strata it is in. For example, that probability is much lower for Strata 2 and 5, than it is for Strata 1, 3, and 4. Based on this reasoning and the results of the additional regressions described above, we intend to extend the analysis (as a future project) to include interaction terms between the strata and the natural open space variables.

A better understanding of how humans perceive urban wildlife habitats, and behave in relation to them, would help improve definitions of habitats for valuation efforts such as reported in the present paper. As noted above, the wildlife habitats were defined in terms of their potential wildlife productivity. They do, however, provide other benefits of direct interest to humans. A study of public values of urban riparian areas in Tucson suggested that these areas are perceived by the public in terms of scenic beauty, freedom of activity, buffers, naturalness, and vegetative diversity, as well as wildlife (Simcox and Zube 1989). The estimated marginal prices, then, measure more than wildlife benefits. The results presented here must be viewed in the context of the Tucson metropolitan area. Residential land use densities are light compared to cities in the United

Table 3. Marginal implicit prices of living area and of various types of open space for single family residential properties by strata, Tucson, Arizona, 1986.[a]

Characteristic	Strata				
	1	2	3	4	5
Living area	$44	$41	$54	$39	$39
Neighborhood park	−$1,486	−$1,770	−$1,734	−$2,283	−$1,073
District park	−$1,294	−$1,901	−$2,852	−$2,148	−$1,624
Regional park	−$1,294	−$892	−$1,576	−$1,209	−$699
Private golf course	$2,808	$1,075	$4,172	$2,537	$483
Large natural public area	$1,346	$574	$2,235	$712	$775
Wildlife habitat II	$5,612	$2,363	$8,602	$3,271	$3,029
Other natural	−$4,951	−$1,404	−$6,440	−$2,888	−$2,479

[a]Prices are expressed as $/sq. ft. for living area and $/mile for open space characteristics.

States that developed earlier. Furthermore, heated battles are fought over proposals for developments that will occupy or impinge upon natural open space. The result is that such areas still do exist to a larger extent in Tucson than in many other cities.

For a second phase of this study, a survey was conducted of the owners of the homes in the sample. These data, which include socioeconomic characteristics, attitudes, and market search information, will be used with estimates of the marginal implicit prices to estimate demand functions for the various types of open spaces.

CONCLUSIONS

It is obviously difficult to parcel out the effects of any single characteristic upon the value of residential properties. Nevertheless, this study presents evidence of a positive influence of natural open space and some kinds of wildlife habitats on property values. The low level of statistical significance of some of the estimates could result from two factors: 1) interaction effects, specifically with regard to the geographical strata, and 2) definitions of wildlife habitat that were inappropriate in terms of human benefits. In further analysis, we will include interaction effects. Studies to address the issue of what urban wildlife habitats mean to people are underway.

Acknowledgments.—This research was supported under McIntire-Stennis Forestry Research Project ARZT 139030 and Western Regional Research Project (W-133) ARZT 137030. The authors acknowledge the full measure of assistance provided by M. Briggs and S. Ritter.

REFERENCES CITED

Allen, P.G., T.H. Stevens, G. Yocker, and T. Moore. 1986. The benefits and costs of urban forest parks. Res. Bull. No. 709. Dep. of Agric. and Resour. Econ., Univ. of Massachusetts, Amherst.

Blomquist, G.C., M.C. Berger, and J.P. Hoehn. 1988. New estimates of quality of life in urban areas. Am. Econ. Rev. 78:89–107.

Freeman, A.M., III. 1979a. Hedonic prices, property values and measuring environmental benefits: a survey of the issues. Scandinavian J. of Econ. 81:154–173.

———. 1979b. The benefits of environmental improvement: theory and practice. The Johns Hopkins Univ. Press, Baltimore, Md. 272pp.

Hammer, T.R., R. Coughlin, and R. Horn. 1974. The effect of a large urban park on real estate value. J. Am. Inst. Plan. 40:274–277.

Harrison, D., Jr., and D.L. Rubinfeld. 1978. Hedonic housing prices and the demand for clean air. J. Environ. Econ. and Manage. 5:81–102.

Kelejian, H., and W. Oates. 1989. Introduction to econometrics. Harper and Rowe Publ., New York, N.Y. 367pp.

McMillan, M.L., B.G. Reid, and D.W. Gillen. 1980. An extension of the hedonic approach for estimating the value of quiet. Land Econ. 56:315–328.

Rosen, S. 1974. Hedonic prices and implicit markets: product differentiation in pure competition. J. Political Econ. 82:34–55.

Shaw, W.W., J.M. Burns, and K. Stenberg. 1986. Wildlife habitats in Tucson: a strategy for conservation. School of Renewable Nat. Resour., Univ. of Arizona, Tucson. 17pp.

Simcox, D.E., and E.H. Zube. 1989. Public value orientations towards urban riparian landscapes. Soc. and Nat. Resour. 2:229–239.

Tucson Trends. 1986. Tucson Newspapers, Inc. and Valley National Bank of America. Tucson, Ariz. 96pp.

Weicher, J., and R. Zerbst. 1973. The externalities of neighborhood parks: an empirical investigation. Land Econ. 49:99–105.

Managing People and Wildlife on Urban Wildlife Areas

LISA A. DEBRUYCKERE AND JAMES E. GARR, *Missouri Department of Conservation, August A. Busch Memorial Wildlife Area, 2360 Highway D, St. Charles, MO 63304*

INTRODUCTION

By the year 2000, four out of every five Americans will live in urban areas. As urban centers expand into rural communities, it is becoming increasingly evident that we must manage resource lands with people as a prime consideration. Management of the resource and management of people are not mutually exclusive, and finding the appropriate balance between the two is one of the greatest and most rewarding challenges managers face. In fact, the extent to which we nurture the conservation interest of urbanites will measure how successful we are as resource professionals.

I [LAD] am employed as a Wildlife District Supervisor by the Missouri Department of Conservation in the St. Louis Wildlife District. The five wildlife areas for which I oversee management comprise 7,290 ha of land within 20 minutes of downtown St. Louis, the largest metropolitan area in the state with 2.5 million people. All five areas are managed to provide habitat for fish and wildlife species while furnishing the public with a variety of recreational opportunities. Today, I will discuss how our district has responded to increased urban development by implementing proactive strategies to satisfy the public while maintaining healthy, harvestable populations of wildlife. I will focus primarily on our two largest wildlife areas as they receive the most public visitation, thus present us with the greatest challenges.

The August A. Busch Memorial Wildlife Area totals 2,830 ha, receives 800,000 to 1,000,000 visitors annually, and is the most intensively managed of our wildlife areas. The Busch Area has gently rolling topography, 32 lakes, 60 small ponds, 113 km of roads, and shooting and archery ranges. It is surrounded on the north and west by subdivisions, on the east by Interstate 40, and on the south by Highway 94 and a federal training area. We have one entrance to the area, which opens and closes by an electronic gate.

The Weldon Spring Wildlife Area comprises 2,979 ha and receives 46,000 to 76,000 visitors annually. The area is moderately hilly and forested with 9.6 km of bluffs along the Missouri River. It has one lake and several small ponds. The Weldon Spring Area is surrounded on the north by Highway 94 and the federal training area, on the east by a subdivision and Interstate 40, on the south by the Missouri River, and on the west by private lands.

Individuals, as well as organized and very vocal special interest groups, use our areas for many activities that include, but are not limited to: hiking, biking, mushroom and berry picking, fishing, picnicking, sightseeing, hunting, field trialing, dog training, bird watching, cross country skiing, nature photography, outdoor education classes, and target shooting. In the past, we have had good estimates of the number of anglers and hunters using our areas because they are required to purchase a daily tag. However, of the remaining 80% of the people entering and exiting our areas annually, we had little idea "who" they were, what they did on our areas, how much time they spent visiting, etc.—but they did leave signs they had been there. To answer these and several other questions, Dan Witter, Edd Brown, and Steve Sheriff of our Planning and Research Sections designed and implemented a Public Use Survey from April of 1989 through April of 1990. Users exiting our areas were asked 13 questions, including primary activity on the area, secondary activity, time spent on the area, wildlife species harvested, residence, age, and sex. The preliminary results of the Weldon Spring study are in; however, the Busch Area results are incomplete at this time.

On the Weldon Spring Wildlife Area, results indicated 59% of area users were nonconsumptive, 25% were anglers, and 16% were hunters. Of the nonconsumptive users, 36% were hikers, 25% were boaters, 13% were bicyclists, and 11% were sightseers. Dog trainers, sunbathers, joggers, and people scouting deer each composed 1% of the total. Other uses totalled less than 1% and are not included here.

Of the hunters, 25% were bow hunters, 19% were squirrel hunters, 15% were rabbit hunters, 14% were gun deer hunters, 9% were dove hunters; quail and turkey hunters each comprised 6%. The remaining 6% consisted of uses that each comprised less than 1% of the total.

These results were somewhat surprising to us because

Wildlife Conservation in Metropolitan Environments. NIUW Symp. Ser. 2, L.W. Adams and D.L. Leedy, eds. Published by Natl. Inst. for Urban Wildl., 10921 Trotting Ridge Way, Columbia, MD 21044, USA, 1991.

the Weldon Spring Area has been thought of as the more "traditional" area of the two areas I have discussed, yet hunting and angling activities were dwarfed by the number of users participating in nonconsumptive activities. We anticipate Busch Area results will reflect a greater disparity in consumptive vs. nonconsumptive user numbers because we know from past records only about 100,000 of our 1 million annual visitors there are hunters or anglers.

As managers, we were faced with these results, along with realizations that our visiting public was not completely satisfied and that tremendous pressures were being placed on our wildlife resources. We concluded that immediate changes had to be made if our programs and our district were going to be successful. Realistically, passive management could not efficiently allocate area resources and satisfy our expanding urban population. As a result, we made changes in the following programs: area maintenance, area regulations, habitat manipulation, harvest strategies, information and education, public programs, public input opportunities, and public participation.

PROGRAM CHANGES

Area Maintenance

The largest and most expensive program in our district is area maintenance, which accounts for 37% of our operating budget. Our maintenance program changed by incorporating an "urban perspective." Urbanites have a somewhat different view of how "wild" a wildlife area should be. As a result, our lakes and walk-in ponds now are mowed 5–10 times throughout the growing season, signing is extensive and explicit, restrooms and buildings are maintained in an exceptionally clean appearance, woody growth along roadsides is kept to a minimum for sightseeing opportunities, and all roads can accommodate two wheel drive traffic throughout the year.

Area Regulations

Our proximity to the largest population center in the state required that we incorporate more restrictive regulations to protect and fairly allocate resources.

Generally, hunting and fishing seasons on our areas, particularly on Busch, are more restrictive than on statewide regulation areas because of the large number of people who participate in hunting and angling and because of potential user group conflicts. However, we make it a point to explain to the public that restrictive regulations mean more quality recreational experiences for the user.

All of our areas have closing hours, which enable us to curtail illegitimate, undesirable activities. Open hours are maximized to enable legal activities to be accomplished at their own prime time. For example, area open hours are expanded into the late evening for 1 month in the winter for furbearer hunters. We take special requests from conservation-oriented groups who choose to use our areas beyond

closing hours. The flexibility to regulate hours for special user groups has been a popular and very successful management strategy.

No shooting zones have been designated on our areas to reduce conflicts with user groups. A neighboring subdivision that borders the Weldon Spring tract has been the target for stray bullets from hunters and/or illegal target shooting, which prompted us to designate a "No Shooting Zone" and incorporate a shotshell only area surrounding the subdivision. We have a "No Shooting Zone" on a 32.4-ha popular birding area and a 9.6-km hiking-biking trail.

Habitat Manipulation

We made changes in habitat manipulation to disperse hunters and provide an array of recreational opportunities for all users. Sunflower fields and other food plots are planted throughout the district in zones to disperse hunter pressure and reduce chances of a hunting accident. Agricultural fields in the fallow period of rotation are strip-mowed for field trialers and dog trainers to provide more edge and a better view of their dogs. These mowed areas also provide wildlife with sunning areas, travel lanes, and a diversity of cover. Our two 2.4-ha shorebird pools are now managed for both the spring and fall migrations. Seven area lakes have drawdown capabilities, which also are managed for migratory waterbirds.

Harvest Strategies

We disperse user numbers, provide quality hunts, and provide resources for nonconsumptive users by changing our harvest strategies. We currently have 12 managed hunts for archery, primitive weapons, and modern firearms deer hunters. In 1989, we provided opportunities for 2,700 deer hunters. Plans for 1991 include expansion of the managed hunts to include a spring turkey season on Busch. We have lengthened our squirrel, rabbit, and dove seasons to provide more hunting opportunities.

Fishing programs will be expanded in 1991 by having pre-Busch opener bass and crappie seasons to better manage Busch lakes and provide more fishing opportunity.

Information and Education

To inform the public about available information and education programs, we publish a monthly bulletin with a calendar. The Busch Bulletin describes our programs and the activities of district and area management staff. The public can subscribe to the bulletin for free and can sign up for it in our area office. We also have a calendar of events board outside our office that informs the public of monthly programs and wildlife activities.

We interact with radio, television, and newspaper reporters throughout the year. However, we feel we need to go one step further and be proactive in terms of dealing with the media by submitting our own material for publication. Therefore, we submit newspaper articles to local newspapers highlighting all programs. These articles are a great way to introduce readers to the district, advertise our programs, and educate.

When we have special programs that may be sensitive in terms of the public's perception of land management, such as timber cutting, we go out of our way to educate our constituents. For example, when the public noticed we were marking trees on a portion of the Busch Area for timber stand improvement, they feared we were going to clearcut the area and were quite vocal in their opinions. We presented an audiovisual program and invited concerned citizens to Busch to explain the reasons for, and benefits of, the timber cuts. We also drafted a short explanation on timber harvesting to give to the public. By being proactive, we informed and educated the public and will likely carry out our timber management program with minimal resistance, and hopefully support.

Information and education efforts are closely tied to expanded programs. In cooperation with the Soil Conservation Service, Department of Conservation staff and our area manager compiled a Neighbor-to-Neighbor informational brochure that explains different land use practices to prevent soil erosion and provide wildlife habitat. The difference between this and other Neighbor-to-Neighbor programs you may have heard about is that this one is geared towards the small urban landowner.

Public Programs

We have expanded the hours of operation at our shooting range 1 October through 30 November from 5 days a week, 4 hours a day, to 7 days a week, 8 hours a day. During the other 10 months of the year, the range is open 7–8 hours/day, 5 days a week. In addition, we are planning for six general audience instructional range programs annually. Our 5-year area plan calls for expansion of the shooting range to add more shooting points and concrete pathways for disabled users. We also plan to construct two firing points for muzzleloader shooters because the popularity of muzzleloader hunting is increasing in the St. Louis area.

Our office is staffed 7 days a week to field questions, process hunters and anglers, and help the public with any problem.

We offer more and more hiking trails for nonconsumptive and consumptive users, and brochures or interpretive signing to educate and inform area users about each trail's theme.

We host four major events in our district annually (Hunter Education Day, Family Fishing Fair, Kids Fishing Day, and Day On The Marsh). These programs attract from 800 to 1,000 people and each one requires 30–50 instructors and Department personnel. Special programs like these are exceptionally popular, informative, well attended, and desired by the public.

Upland and wetland viewing blinds and walkways for the disabled to visit our lakes and ponds are other ways we have responded to demands for more public recreation. Strategically placed, these facilities can provide interested

users with excellent recreational opportunities while not interfering with other user activities.

We now have two naturalists employed at the Busch Area who provide 11 monthly general audience programs for the public and talks to local school, scout, elderly, and disabled groups. Our general audience programs educate people about our natural resources, particularly near urban centers. Owl prowls, how animals prepare for winter, and talks on backyard bird feeding are examples of popular naturalist programs. In 1989, we provided programs to 14,629 people and contacted 1,227% more individuals in general audience programs than in 1988. Group programs increased 44% in 1989 from 1988.

Small projects at minimal cost go a long way towards gaining public support. A butterfly garden, a chalkboard where birders can document birds they see on the area, and walking trails with bird feeders are small projects we have implemented that act as catalysts for people to become involved in our other programs and activities.

Public Input

Public input is the key to success in managing people and wildlife on urban areas. Urban people, in general, lack the land ethic described by Aldo Leopold in *A Sand County Almanac*. Many urbanites do not have close ties to the land and lack an understanding of traditional consumptive activities, such as hunting and trapping. This is not to say urbanites are not strong supporters of sound land management once they are given the education and information to make decisions; in fact, by offering educational programs, the opposite can be true.

Because of intense interest in our areas and our management programs, we regularly meet with birding groups, archery clubs, field trialers, and other organized groups. We explain our programs and they provide input that has saved us a great deal of time and money.

Public Participation

We have taken public participation one step further in our district by allowing the public to become involved in our programs through volunteer efforts. One reason we were able to increase general audience naturalist programs in 1989 was because of our new volunteer naturalist program. Citizens contribute a minimum of 10 hours per month giving programs, working on hiking-biking trails, and assisting our two permanent naturalists.

Our Adopt-A-Lake program, an idea stemming from the Highway Department's Adopt-A-Highway program, has been a tremendous success on our areas. Local groups can adopt any one of our lakes and walk-in ponds for litter control and beautification. These groups sign a contract to pick up litter around the lakes once a week or once every 2 weeks. This has helped to reduce our litter problem tremendously and allows our employees to perform other management-oriented job duties.

We have expanded the "Adoption" program to include

our field archery range. Each of the four courses and practice range has been adopted for litter control and maintenance projects by local St. Louis groups.

We have also become involved in working with the St. Charles County Office of Employment and Training. In that program, we hire local inner city youths for the summer to work at no cost to our agency. This is an excellent program in that it allows city youths to become familiar with conservation, allows us to increase our work output with no increase in personnel costs, and is a great public relations tool.

Our area manager has worked with local field trialers to build brush piles and plant food plots, while our fisheries biologist has worked with local bass fishing groups to cut and place cedars on the lakes in the winter for fish habitat. When groups come to us requesting projects and programs, we ask, "How are you going to help us give you what you want?"

CONCLUSIONS

Our wildlife areas are used by both nonconsumptive and consumptive users and by wildlife that is losing its habitat to neighboring subdivisions. Changes in programs from area maintenance to public participation were necessary to fairly allocate existing resources and encourage sound use by people and wildlife. The challenges we face in maintaining healthy, harvestable populations of wildlife and traditional hunting and fishing programs, while catering to an urban public that participates extensively in nonconsumptive activities, test our skills as managers of people and wildlife. The key to success in managing urban people and resources is being proactive, reaching out to the different user groups, and listening to what our constituents want. The challenges are constant, but there is no greater reward in the resource field than making management decisions that ultimately benefit both people and wildlife in urban areas.

Thank you.

Canada Goose Management at the Minneapolis-St. Paul International Airport

JAMES A. COOPER, *Department of Fisheries and Wildlife, College of Natural Resources, University of Minnesota, St. Paul, MN 55108*

INTRODUCTION

Bird strikes are a significant aircraft hazard (Murton and Wright 1968, Blokpoel 1976). Because birds fly below the cruising altitudes of most commercial airplanes, the maximum strike likelihood occurs during take-off and early climb, and approach and landing at or near airports (Burger 1983). The most serious collisions have involved large (>1 kg), flocking species, and jet-powered planes (Staples and New 1968).

Although the Canada goose (*Branta canadensis*) may have nested in the area in presettlement times, recent nesting on the Minneapolis-St. Paul International Airport was first recorded in 1975 when a 2-year-old female, banded at the Hyland Park Reserve in Bloomington, hatched young on Mother Lake (J. A. Cooper, Univ. Minn., unpubl. data). By 1981, an estimated 100–150 geese were using sites on or near the airport (U.S. Fish and Wildlife Service 1981). The birds reached peak numbers in late summer and fall, fed and roosted on or near the airport grounds, and made frequent low altitude flights through the aircraft landing and take-off paths (operations airspace). The Twin Cities Metropolitan Airports Commission (MAC) deemed, "the presence of geese near active runways as undesirable due to possible bird strike accidents," and requested advice from the U.S. Fish and Wildlife Service (USFWS) on methods to reduce the number of geese on or near the airport (U.S. Fish and Wildlife Service 1981).

Because a bird-proof aircraft capable of flight has not been developed (Blokpoel 1976:89) and bird-avoidance maneuvers are limited during take-off and landing, hazard reduction must focus on bird management. Hazard bird reduction techniques suggested for the Minneapolis-St. Paul International Airport included habitat modification to make the airport less attractive to geese, visual or acoustical harassment, and translocating or killing of the birds.

Habitat modification was deemed unfeasible. The geese prefer the short, mowed-grass on the runway borders, adjacent golf course greens and fairways, and nearby city parks over the longer vegetation present in unmowed areas (U.S. Fish and Wildlife Service 1981). The short grass reduces the airport fire hazard and is essential to parks and golf course management (U.S. Fish and Wildlife Service 1981). Harassment, when employed at the airport, was ineffective because "when chased by airport vehicles they [the geese] merely fly to the other side of the runway or to the nearby golf course" (U.S. Fish and Wildlife Service 1981). Harassment also had the disadvantage of additional goose flights, thus increasing the potential for a strike. Intensive, long-term goose shooting on the airport property was discussed as an alternative if an effective, but less drastic procedure was not found. The most promising but untested procedure remaining was bird capture and shipment of the birds to distant sites, i.e., translocation.

The biologic and cost effectiveness of a translocation program depends on whether the geese use a site selectively or randomly, and the number of breeding groups associated with the specific area. Recent research suggested that selective use would likely be the case. Koerner (1973) reported that Canada geese in southwestern Lake Erie were observed in the same locations annually. Zicus (1981a) suggested that Canada geese maintain distinct social groups and that these units were established on brood-rearing marshes. Zicus further speculated that the individual groups had predictable flight patterns and repeatedly used specific feeding and roosting areas throughout summer and fall. Schultz (1983) (see Schultz et al. 1988) found that geese from specific brood-rearing sites not only remained together, but that the birds did not readily abandon the summer and fall flight patterns or feeding sites when hunted. Thus, from these studies, it was surmised that: 1) a limited set of locally breeding geese were likely to be using the airport and nearly areas, and 2) these birds, if removed, would not be replaced quickly by others.

This 4-year (1984–1987) study was designed to test the hypothesis that if the geese using the airport could be identified and reduced, there would be a corresponding

Wildlife Conservation in Metropolitan Environments. NIUW Symp. Ser. 2, L.W. Adams and D.L. Leedy, eds. Published by Natl. Inst. for Urban Wildl., 10921 Trotting Ridge Way, Columbia, MD 21044, USA, 1991.

reduction in the number of geese and goose flights at the airport. By default, the study also was a test of the existence of non-random summer-fall movement and site use behavior described by Zicus (1981a) and Schultz et al. (1988). The primary goal of the present study, however, was to reduce goose numbers and flights through the airport operations airspace as much as possible. Late summer and fall (August-November) were targeted for study because this was the time of maximum goose numbers and flights (U.S. Fish and Wildlife Service 1981).

STUDY AREA

The 1,174-ha Minneapolis-St. Paul International Airport is located in Hennepin County, 16.2 km southwest of downtown St. Paul and 14.6 km southeast of Minneapolis. Minnesota State Highway 62 and military and residential housing border the airport on the north. Fort Snelling State Park, the Mississippi River, and the Minnesota River comprise the eastern border. The southern border consists of U.S. Interstate Highway 494. The Rich Acres Golf Course lies along the western fenceline of the airport (Fig. 1).

The airport is the largest in the five-state region (Iowa, Minnesota, North Dakota, South Dakota, and Wisconsin) and 19th largest in the conterminous United States. Combined with six MAC-owned reliever airports in the Twin

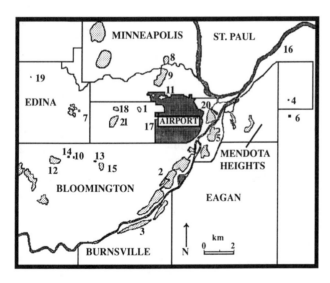

1.	Apple Lake	12.	Normandale Lake
2.	Bass Ponds	13.	N.W. Clinic
3.	Blackdog Lake	14.	Pauley's Pond
4.	Dodge Nature Center	15.	Penn Lake
5.	Gun Club Lake	16.	Pickeral Lake
6.	Hwy. 110 and Delaware	17.	Rich Acres G.C.
7.	Lake Cornelia	18.	Richfield Lake
8.	Lake Hiawatha	19.	Schaefer Road
9.	Lake Nokomis	20.	Snelling Lake
10.	Miller's Playlot	21.	Wood Lake
11.	Mother Lake		

Fig. 1.   The location of the Minneapolis-St. Paul International Airport study area and banding sites, Minnesota.

Cities Metropolitan Area, the system is the third busiest in the world (T.B. Haberkorn, MAC, pers. commun.). During this study, the International Airport averaged 900 aircraft operations per weekday; peak daily averages occurred at 12:00–12:30 p.m. (67 operations), 5:00–5:30 p.m. (59 operations), 8:00–8:30 a.m. (43 operations), and 8:00–8:30 p.m. (42 operations).

The study area encompassed Canada goose brood-rearing sites within 10 km of the airport, plus intensively monitored feeding and roosting sites on and near the airport. Goose brood-rearing sites occurred in the cities of Bloomington, Burnsville, Edina, Minneapolis, Mendota Heights, Richfield, and West St. Paul. These areas included city parks, golf courses, Fort Snelling State Park, the Minnesota River Valley National Wildlife Refuge, unaltered wetlands and lakes, and two nature centers (Fig. 1). The airport study area (ASA) consisted of goose concentration locations adjacent to, or on, the airport (Mother Lake, Rich Acres Golf Course, and Fort Snelling National Cemetery), and, based on 1984 observations, sites where goose flights through the operations airspace typically originated or terminated (Apple Lake, Lake Hiawatha, Lake Nokomis, and Snelling Lake).

METHODS

This study consisted of five steps: 1) the identification of brood-rearing locations for Canada geese that potentially could be using the airport, adjacent parks, golf courses, and wetlands, 2) the marking of geese at these sites, 3) the pre-removal measurement of marked goose occurrence and goose populations in the ASA, and the intensity of flights through the operations airspace as a baseline for evaluating the removal effectiveness, 4) reduction of goose groups found to be using the airport by capture and translocation, and 5) estimation of program effectiveness by monitoring of post-removal airport goose use, populations, and operations airspace flight levels.

Field Work

Potential Canada goose brood-rearing areas were surveyed within a 10-km radius of the airport in the spring (May-June) of 1984 by University of Minnesota and USFWS personnel (Table 1). Goose groups, consisting of flightless families and non-breeding (not associated with a family group) individuals, were drive-trapped and banded during mid-June and early July 1984. Captured geese were sexed, aged, and legbanded with USFWS aluminum legbands. Adult birds were neckbanded with markers similar to those described by Sherwood (1968), but with routed-symbols and sealed with a pop-rivet. In 1984, a subsample of adult geese was fitted with radio transmitters (Dwyer 1972) to determine daily flight time budgets. Geese on Gun Club Lake, Snelling Lake, and Mother Lake were not trapped and banded because these areas were assumed to be human safety hazards due to their close proximity to the

Table 1. Study area locations by city, distance to the Minneapolis-St. Paul International Airport, size, wetland type class, and use by geese, 1984–1987.

Location	City	Distance[a] (km)	Size (ha)	Wetland type[b]	Use[c]
Apple Lake	Richfield	1.7	2.9	V	A,F,R
Bass Ponds, (Minnesota River Valley NWR)	Bloomington	2.4	1.6	V	B
			8.5	V	B
			1.2	V	B
Blackdog Lake	Burnsville	6.8	261.9	V	B,F,R
Dodge Nature Center	West St. Paul	9.2	1.6	V	B,F,R
Gun Club Lake	Mendota Heights	1.1	210.1	V	B,R
Hwy. 110 and Delaware	Mendota Heights	7.1	44.0	V	B
Lake Cornelia Wetland Complex	Edina	7.1	19.4	V	B,F,R
			1.2	V	B,F,R
			1.8	V	B,F,R
			2.0	V	B,F,R
			2.4	V	B,F,R
Lake Hiawatha	Minneapolis	2.6	21.9	V	A,F
Lake Nokomis	Minneapolis	1.2	80.6	V	A,B,F
Miller's Playlot	Bloomington	6.8	6.9	V	B,F
Mother Lake	Minneapolis	0.0	125.5	V	A,B
Normandale Lake	Bloomington	8.8	44.9	V	B,F
N.W. Chiro Clinic	Bloomington	5.4	2.8	V	F
Pauley's Pond	Bloomington	6.6	2.8	V	B,F
Penn Lake	Bloomington	4.9	19.0	V	B,F
Pickeral Lake	St. Paul	6.2	10.0	V	B
Rich Acres G. C.	Richfield	0.0	<1.0	IV	A,F
Richfield Lake	Richfield	3.7	62.8	IV	B,R
Schaefer Road	Edina	11.1	2.5	V	B,R
Snelling Lake	Minneapolis	0.5	44.5	V	A,B
Wood Lake	Richfield	3.7	66.8	IV	B,R

[a]Distance from middle of water area to nearest airport boundary.
[b]See Cowardin et al. (1979).
[c]Use codes are: A = airport study area, B = Banding site, F = feeding and resting site, R = removal site.

airport. Additional banding was done at Blackdog Lake in 1985, Normandale Lake in 1986 and 1987, and at Miller's Playlot in 1987 to maintain marked-goose numbers. In 1985, banding was done at a wetland on Schaefer Road in Edina (11 km from the airport) to determine if birds from this area of concentrated breeding were using the airport area. Similarly, birds from a newly established brood-rearing group on Pickerel Lake in St. Paul (6 km from the airport) were banded to ascertain if they used the ASA.

Goose use of the ASA was ascertained from 1 August until the geese left the area in late November or December, 1984 and 1985. Because only one flight was observed in August, 1984 and 1985, observations and counts were delayed until 1 September in 1986 and 1987. Population counts and neckband readings were conducted 4–5 times per week within the ASA and weekly at the other feeding and resting locations. Neckband codes, location, time, number of geese present, and pertinent comments were recorded in the field using a portable lap computer. The highest daily population count per week at each site was used in the analysis.

Brood-rearing groups were arbitrarily assigned "hazard" or "non-hazard" status based on repeated ASA neckband sightings. ASA use indices were calculated by dividing the total number of neckband sightings per banding site by the number of marked geese in that group on 1 August each year. Due to removal, too few neckbanded geese remained from control locations in 1986 and 1987 for meaningful estimates and the 1984–1985 hazard classifications were

used. Groups with an observation rate of one or more per neckband were assigned to the "hazard" category. The exception to this was the Bass Pond geese. Although no marked geese from this small (<20) group were seen in the airport area in 1984, a Bass Pond-banded male, associated with the Wood Lake birds in 1985 and 1986, was frequently found at the airport. As a result, the Bass Pond geese were not classified as hazards in spite of an observation index of 9 and 6.5 in 1985 and 1986, respectively. Hazard status groups were drive-trapped during the molt (June-July 1985–1987), and the adults translocated to Oklahoma and the immatures to Minnesota locations (Cooper 1987).

Because all groups of geese encountered in the ASA contained markers, the influx of migrant geese was detected by the occurrence of flocks without markers.

Radio-marked geese were monitored from dawn to dark 1 day/week during August and September 1984 to determine daily flight activity. Groups of geese containing radio-marked individuals were constantly observed from the time they flew into the ASA in the morning until they left at night. If a group divided, the one with the most radio transmitters was followed. When possible, all radio-marked birds were located. However, interference from the airport air traffic control tower and other radio transmissions prevented consistent radio relocation and required frequent visual confirmation.

Goose flights through the airport operations airspace were monitored at the peak goose flight times, five times/ week from the air traffic control tower. The tower, located near the western border of the airport, stands 55 m high. Based on radio tracking, peak flight activity occurred 30 minutes before and after sunrise and 30 minutes before and after sunset. Observations were made at these times except when fog, rain, or snow obscured portions of the operations airspace. The airspace monitored consisted of that over the airport and within 4 km of the runway ends and below 100 m. Although somewhat arbitrary, this space constituted the zone of highest hazard for the ascent and descent paths of aircraft (T.B. Haberkorn, MAC, pers. commun.). The number of goose flights per session, time, estimated altitude, direction, and birds per flight, and weather conditions (temperature, wind speed, and cloud cover) were recorded for an observation period. Direction was estimated as one of the eight ordinal directions and altitude classified at or below 100 m or above 100 m based on known heights of nearby towers and buildings. Weather data were provided by the air traffic controllers. Tower observations started 1 August 1984–1985 and 1 September 1986–1987, and ended 30 November each year.

Because dense cattail (*Typha* spp.) at Wood Lake and Mother Lake reduced 1986 drive-trapping efficiency, an alternative method of goose removal was developed. Nests were located by searching on foot and from a canoe during April, 1986 and 1987. A mini-rocket system was used to trap incubating females. The trap consisted of two remotely fired rockets and a 5 by 14 m gill net. When placed within 2 m of an active nest, the rocket propelled the net over the incubating bird. Once captured the females were translocated.

The efficiency of shooting small numbers of geese during the last 2 weeks of July and the first 2 weeks of August was evaluated in 1987. Birds were collected opportunistically on the airport with a shotgun.

Data Analysis

Paired *t*-tests were used to test for differences in the highest weekly 1984 ASA goose population, number of flights, and geese per flight with those following removals in 1985, 1986, and 1987. This test also was done for the number of geese in an unmanipulated area (Miller's Playlot, Normandale Lake, and Northwestern Clinic ponds in Bloomington) to ascertain the effects of natural fluctuation on the ASA geese. Cross-classified categorical data analysis was used to evaluate the effects of weather on airspace goose flight intensity.

RESULTS

Three hundred-seventeen flightless geese at 11 sites were located and captured in June 1984. One hundred twenty-seven adults were neckbanded and 190 immatures legbanded. Fifty-one geese were caught at two sites in June 1985; 19 adults were neckbanded and 34 goslings legbanded. In

1987, in addition to data presented in Table 2, 126 adults were drive-trapped and legbanded and 199 young legbanded at two Bloomington locations. Six adults were fitted with radio transmitters in 1984 (Table 2).

Neckbanded geese from seven of the 11 banding sites were observed in the ASA in 1984, six of 11 in 1985 and six of 10 in 1986, and two of 9 in 1987 (Table 3). The use rates declined over the study due to removal, but followed a similar pattern. Most marked geese seen in the airport study were captured at the Wood Lake Nature Interpretive Center. These geese comprised 90, 70, 53, and 56% of the observations in 1984–1987, respectively. Certain banded geese, e.g., Wood Lake Nature Interpretive Center and Lake Nokomis birds, were observed in the ASA repeatedly, whereas other groups such as Normandale and Miller's Playlot geese were infrequently found in the ASA. These results support the subpopulation concept strongly. However, there were exceptions. Geese banded at Penn Lake were not seen in the ASA in 1984 but were observed an average of 9 times/neckband in 1985, and were translocated in 1986 and 1987. The Schaefer Road birds, not observed in the airport in 1985, were seen an average of 3.3 times/neckband in 1986 when they used Lake Hiawatha exclusively while in the ASA. This group was caught in 1987 and translocated.

Thirty-six of the 37 neckbanded geese from the Wood Lake brood-rearing area were seen in the ASA from 1 August until the birds left the area on 20 December 1984. However, not all birds were encountered with the same intensity. In 1984, 10 geese were observed 0-25% of the sampling period, eight geese 26-50%, 10 geese 51-75%, and nine geese 75% or more. Eleven of the 14 Wood Lake neckbanded birds, known to be alive on 1 August 1985, were observed in the ASA in 1985. Three geese were observed 0-25% of the sampling period, three geese 26-50%, five geese 51-75%, and no geese were observed more than 75%. Four out of the five geese observed most frequently in 1984 also were observed most frequently in 1985. Thus, some birds used the airport more than others and the intensity of use was similar between years. To further

Table 2. Number of breeding adult Canada geese neckbanded in the vicinity of the Minneapolis-St. Paul International Airport, 1984–1987.

Location	Year			
	1984	1985	1986	1987
Bass Ponds	3	0	0	0
Blackdog Lake	2	10	0	0
Dodge Nature Center	3	0	0	0
Hwy. 110 and Delaware	3	0	0	0
Lake Cornelia	21	0	0	0
Lake Nokomis	2	0	0	0
Miller's Playlot	24	0	0	29
Normandale Lake	23(2)[a]	0	25	64
Penn Lake	7	0	0	0
Pickerel Lake	0	0	0	3
Richfield Lake	1	0	0	0
Schaefer Road	0	9	0	0
Wood Lake	38(4)	0	0	0
Total	127(6)	19	25	93

[a]Number of radio-marked individuals in parentheses.

Table 3. Banding location, number of neckbanded Canada geese, reobservation of neckbanded individuals, and observation per neckband in the airport study area, 1984–1987.

Banding location	Neckbanded geese[a]				Number of observations				Observation/ neckband			
	'84	'85	'86	'87	'84	'85	'86	'87	'84	'85	'86	'87
Bass Ponds	3	2	2	1	0	18	13	0	0.0	9.0	6.5	0.0
Blackdog Lake	1	11	8	3	0	15	3	0	0.0	1.4	0.4	0.0
Dodge Nature Center	3	3	1	1	2	0	0	0	0.7	0.0	0.0	0.0
Hwy. 110 and Delaware	3	2	0	0	0	0	0	0	0.0	0.0		
Lake Cornelia	18	4	2	1	33	0	0	0	1.8	0.0	0.0	0.0
Lake Nokomis	2	2	1	0	118	98	35	0	59.0	49.0	35.0	
Miller's Playlot	22	17	8	29	2	9	0	0	0.1	0.5	0.0	0.0
Normandale Lake	23	19	30	64	11	0	7	19	0.5	0.0	0.2	0.3
Penn Lake	7	2	1	0	1	18	0	0	0.1	9.0	0.0	
Pickeral Lake	0	0	0	3	0	0	0	0				0.0
Richfield Lake	1	0	0	0	0	0	0	0	0.0			
Schaefer Road	0	7	6	1	0	0	20	0		0.0	3.3	0.0
Wood Lake	37	14	7	4	1529	368	87	24	41.3	26.3	12.4	6.0
Combined areas	120	83	66	107	1696	526	165	43	14.2	6.3	2.5	0.4

[a]Neckbanded geese known to be alive on 1 August.

evaluate repeated use, observations/sampling day for Wood Lake birds were computed for 1984 and 1985 and regressed. The fit was highly significant ($P < 0.01$, Fig. 2).

Based on 1984 repeated observations in the ASA, brood-rearing groups with a use rate greater than one and geese breeding or molting within the ASA were deemed "hazards" and slated for removal. One hundred ninety-two geese from six sites were captured and translocated in June, 1985, 71 from five sites in 1986, and 141 from seven locations in 1987 (Table 4). Based on 1985–1987 pre-trapping counts, 93, 82, and 86% of the flightless geese present at hazard group sites were removed in the respective years. Adult and immature geese were banded and shipped by truck; the adults to Oklahoma and immatures to Minnesota wetlands at distances ranging from 50 to 300 km from the ASA. Recapture of translocated geese indicated that 10% of the 1985 translocated adults returned while no immatures were encountered in 1986 or 1987. All adults caught in 1986 and 1987 were pinioned (rendered permanently flightless) and moved to a captive rearing facility at the Red Lake Indian Reservation in northern Minnesota.

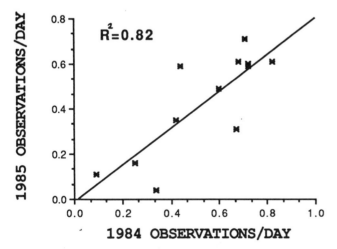

Fig. 2.   Regression of 1984 and 1985 airport study area sighting frequency (sightings/observation day) for Canada geese neckbanded at the Wood Lake Interpretive Nature Center, Richfield, Minnesota.

Nest trapping of breeding females at Mother Lake and Wood Lake proved moderately effective (9 of 16 females captured). Drawbacks of the technique centered on the net and rocket positioning. With modifications, the technique should be highly effective, permitting capture and removal of incubating geese from wetlands where dense cattail hampers drive-trapping.

The shooting of flying or sitting birds on the airport property from 1 July to 15 August 1987 proved inefficient. A month of labor was expended and seven birds were shot from a population of 23. Once exposed to shooting, the geese shifted to nearby public use parks and golf courses and were rarely found where they could be safely collected.

The pattern of change in the ASA population was similar each year, but with an increasing decline in the number of birds seen in August, September, and October (Fig. 3). Goose numbers were lowest from August until the third week of September. They then increased slightly, probably because of the returning molt-migration birds (see Zicus 1981b). Migrant geese were first seen in the area in late October. From this time until the second week in November, the populations fluctuated but steadily increased, peaking in late November or early December. Snow and freezing weather stimulated departure and all birds left the ASA by early December.

Weekly airport area populations declined significantly ($P < 0.001$) in August 1985, in September 1985–1987, and October 1986–1987. The rate of decline increased by year (Fig. 4) and averaged 75% for these months from 1984 to 1987. Population levels after 1 November, when migrant geese were present, were not significantly different ($P > 0.05$) between 1985, 1986, or 1987, but overall levels for the entire study period were significantly lower than 1984 in all years ($P < 0.05$). The biweekly 1984 and weekly 1985 through 1987 Bloomington population counts were more variable compared to the ASA numbers, but did not differ significantly ($P > 0.05$) between years (Fig. 4). Thus, while the airport population declined in all months but November, there was no concurrent decline in the uncontrolled Bloomington concentration.

Table 4. Canada geese removed in June, 1985–1987 by location, age, and percent of pre-removal population, Minneapolis-St. Paul International Airport study area.

	1985				1986				1987			
Location	Ad.	Im.	Total	%	Ad.	Im.	Total	%	Ad.	Im.	Total	%
Apple Lake	2	4	6	100	0	0	0		0	0	0	
Gun Club Lake	5	10	15	94	0	0	0		4	15	19	66
Lake Cornelia	23	6	29	94	4	8	12	80	4	7	11	100
Lake Nokomis	2	6	8	100	0	0	0		0	0	0	
Mothers Lake	0	0	0		b	b	b	b	6	11	17	100
Penn Lake	a	a	a	a	17	19	36	97	1	5	6	86
Richfield Lake	2	4	6	100	3	10	13	93	2	8	10	83
Schaefer Road	a	a	a	a	a	a	a	a	10	29	39	80
Wood Lake	35	80	115	92	b	b	b	b	6	33	39	74
Combined areas	69	110	192	93	24	37	71	82	33	108	141	86

[a]Not trapped.
[b]Breeding females rocket netted at nest and birds and eggs removed.

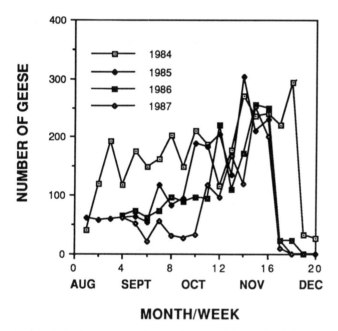

Fig. 3. Weekly maximum Minneapolis-St. Paul International Airport study area Canada goose population counts, August to December, 1984 and 1985; and September to December, 1986 and 1987.

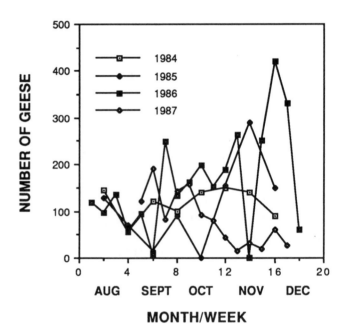

Fig. 4. Weekly maximum Bloomington area Canada goose population counts, August to December, 1984 and 1985; and September to December, 1986 and 1987.

The number of goose flights and the number of geese observed from the control tower decreased significantly ($P < 0.001$, Fig. 5). There were 87 flights in 1984, and 42, 39, and 15 in 1985, 1986, and 1987, respectively. After 3 years of removal, flights were 83% below 1984 levels. The decrease in numbers of geese observed in the airspace between 1984 and 1987 was even lower at 85% (1,476 vs. 222). The greatest number of flights occurred in October until 1987, when proportionately more flights were in September.

Tower observation data suggested that there was a relationship between flight intensity and weather. Goodness-of-fit tests conducted between temperature and wind speed, and flights observed (Fig. 6) were significant ($P < 0.005$, $G^2 = 13.37$, df = 3; and $P < 0.005$, $G^2 = 15.17$, df = 3, respectively). The effects of cloud cover could not be determined because flights could not be seen during heavy fog or rain. A three-way classification of temperature, wind, and flights indicated the best fit included all three factors and that the wind speed and temperature interaction was significant ($P < 0.005$, $G^2 = 4.24$, df = 9). Four categories of temperature, cloud cover, and wind speed description were used in the analysis. The greatest proportion of flights was associated with low temperatures (-12.2 to -1.7 C), and high winds (34+ km/hr).

DISCUSSION

The results of this study demonstrate that, by identifying the origins of local breeding geese using an airport and removing them, the bird-aircraft strike hazard can be reduced dramatically. The repeated use of the ASA by some geese and not others supports the rigid summer-fall movement described by Zicus (1981a) and corroborated by

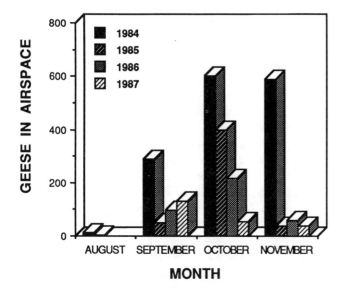

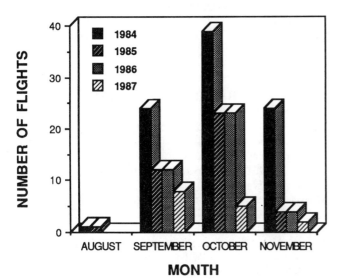

Fig. 5.   Canada goose flights and total number of geese observed through Minneapolis-St. Paul International Airport operations airspace by month, 1984–1987.

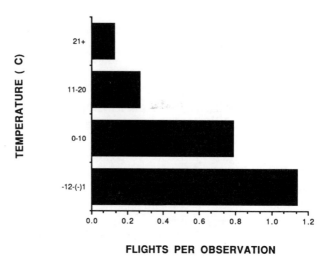

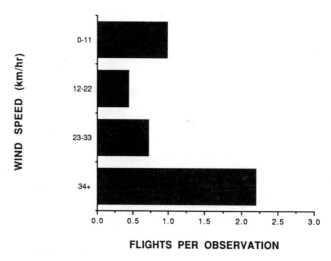

Fig. 6.   Classification of Minneapolis-St. Paul International Airport Canada goose flights by air temperature and wind speed categories, 1984 and 1985 combined.

Schultz et al. (1988). The same geese were consistently observed in ASA in both 1984 and 1985. The frequency at which individual geese from Wood Lake Nature Interpretive Center were observed in 1984 and 1985 (Fig. 3) suggests that goose movement patterns in summer and fall are consistent for at least a 2-year period. Neckbanded geese from Wood Lake Nature Interpretive Center and Lake Nokomis used the airport area during the summer and fall and at a far greater intensity than geese from the other brood-rearing marshes, and the individual geese had similar patterns between years. Koerner et al. (1974), Zicus (1981a), and Schultz et al. (1988) also observed that the majority of individual geese used the same general locations day after day, and in some cases, the same individuals were observed in the same locations as long as the food supply remained. The success of goose removal from specific brood-rearing areas in reducing goose numbers at the airport supports our

assumption that subflocks also existed. For example, Penn Lake birds used the airport, whereas nearby Miller's Playlot birds did not. Because local subflocks exhibited these patterns in a predictable manner during the summer and fall, "hazard" birds from distinct brood-rearing areas can be identified, and selective rather than blanket control measures used.

Individual geese varied in their use of the ASA. Not all birds from a specific brood-rearing marsh followed identical patterns, but the patterns were consistent from year to year. This variability could allow managers to work on an even finer level than that of the subflock. For example, Wood Lake pairs that were not resighted in the ASA could be left, and the pairs with a high percentage of reobservations at the airport removed. This would provide the nature center with geese for public enjoyment and lessen the hazard at the airport.

Removal and translocation is an effective and efficient

method for reducing local subflocks of Canada geese. The removal of the airport's "problem birds" significantly reduced the population of local geese and decreased the number of goose flights through the airport operations airspace. In other urban locations such as golf courses, city parks, and residential neighborhoods removal could provide an immediate reduction in the number of geese, whereas, other control options such as adult sterilization or egg removal-destruction will reduce the population in the first year, but at a reduced rate compared with removal and translocation. Sterilization and egg removal affect offspring produced that year, whereas bird removal in June and July reduces the number of offspring in addition to the breeding adults. Any non-breeding birds molting in the control area can also be removed.

Unfortunately, removal and translocation have drawbacks. Cooper (1987) found that translocation was not as effective at some sites within the Twin Cities compared to that reported in Michigan by Martz et al. (1983), and in New York and Connecticut by Converse (1985). Cooper (1987) reported that adult birds translocated to Oklahoma returned at an average annual rate of 21% (range 12-28%), and that 50% of the breeding females captured at Lake of the Isles and other sites in the Twin Cities area in 1985 were translocated birds. Ten percent of the birds captured in this study returned from Oklahoma in 1985. Because of the importance of population reduction at the airport, all adult geese caught at control locations were rendered permanently flightless after 1984. The major limitation of translocation is that ultimately it will be self-limiting as managers using translocated geese for restoration programs meet their goals.

The rate at which new geese will begin using the airport is unknown and needs to be studied. The restricted subflock movement that limited the use of the airport is not so fixed that no new geese used the ASA. For example, geese from Penn Lake in Bloomington did not use the ASA in 1984 but did so in 1985. This could have resulted from variation in the fall movement patterns or from the reduction in competing groups of geese in ASA in 1985. It is important that additional monitoring be done to ascertain the longer-term (5-10 years) effectiveness of selective removal.

Migrant geese, present in the ASA from late October until the end of November or mid-December, are a potential problem that cannot be controlled by brood-rearing removal and translocation. Decoy flocks of captive geese attracted migrant geese during reintroduction programs at Crex Meadows, Wisconsin (Kooiker 1982), Michigan, Minnesota, Missouri, and Ohio (Nelson 1962). Local breeding flocks may function similarly. Thus, a decrease in the local goose numbers could lead to a decline in migrant geese using a site. The results of this study do not support this logic; migrant use of the ASA continued after a substantial reduction of local geese. Alternative techniques such as intensive harassment of migrant flocks, rocket-netting and removal, or special hunts where possible, are needed to control the number of migrants at the airport.

Acknowledgments.—I thank Tim Anderson and Arlis Olson, Metropolitan Airports Commission, and Oren Burckhardt and Les Case, Federal Aviation Administration for their coordination of funding and providing access to the airport facilities. Roger Johnson, Lloyd Knudson, Jon Parker, Tim Wallace, and others with the Minnesota Department of Natural Resources provided invaluable assistance, as did Nancy Burgstahler and Mary Mitchell, U.S. Fish and Wildlife Service, and Richard Wetzel, U.S. Department of Agriculture. Ann Sigford, Tim Anderson, and volunteers from the Wood Lake Nature Interpretive Center assisted with a public information meeting, goose capture, and surveys. Mari Smaby, Wayne Winkleman, Terry Birkenstock, Lori Hawkins, Tom Roster, Judi Mikolai, Llew Wright, Tom Buhl, Caroline Yineman, and Mike Palanuk, University of Minnesota, cheerfully assisted with banding, population surveys, tower observations, translocation, and data processing. Norma Essex typed and proof-read the manuscript.

REFERENCES CITED

Blokpoel, H. 1976. Bird hazards to aircraft: problems and prevention of bird/aircraft collisions. Clark, Irwin, and Co., Ottawa, Ont. 236pp.

Burger, J. 1983. Bird control at airports. Environ. Conserv. 10:115–124.

Converse, K. A. 1985. A study of resident nuisance Canada geese in Connecticut and New York. Ph.D. Thesis, Univ. Massachusetts, Amherst, 84pp.

Cooper, J. A. 1987. The effectiveness of translocation control of Minneapolis-St. Paul Canada goose populations. Pages 169–172 *in* L. W. Adams and D. L. Leedy, eds. Integrating man and nature in the metropolitan environment. Natl. Inst. for Urban Wildl., Columbia, Md.

Cowardin, L. M., V. Carter, F. C. Golet, and E. T. LaRue. 1979. Classification of wetlands and deepwater habitats of the United States. U.S. Dep. Inter., Fish and Wildl. Serv., Office Biol. Serv., Washington D.C. 103pp.

Dwyer, T. J. 1972. An adjustable radio package for ducks. Bird Banding 43:282–289.

Koerner, J. W. 1973. Fall movements of Canada geese near southwestern Lake Erie. M. S. Thesis, Ohio State Univ., Columbus. 150pp.

———, T. A. Bookhout, and K. E. Bednarik. 1974. Movements of Canada geese color-marked near southwestern Lake Erie. J. Wildl. Manage. 38:275–289.

Kooiker, P. 1982. Giant Canada goose restoration at Crex Meadows, Wisconsin. Pages 48–49 *in* M. A. Johnson, ed. Transactions of the Canada goose symposium. North Dakota Chap. of The Wildl. Soc., Bismarck.

Martz, J., L. Pospichal, and E. Tucker. 1983. Giant Canada geese in Michigan: experiences with translocations and nuisance management. Pages 57–59 *in* M. A. Johnson, ed. Transactions of the Canada goose symposium. North Dakota Chap. of The Wildl. Soc., Bismarck.

Murton, R. K., and E. N. Wright, eds. 1968. The problems of birds as pests. Academic Press, New York, N.Y. 254pp.

Nelson, H. K. 1962. Restoration of breeding Canada goose flocks in the north central states. Trans. North Am. Wildl. and Nat. Resour. Conf. 28:133–148.

Schultz, D. F. 1983. Fall flock behavior and harvest of Canada geese in the vicinity of the Talcot Lake Wildlife Management Area in southwest Minnesota. M.S. Thesis, Univ. Minnesota., St. Paul. 72pp.

———, J. A. Cooper, and M. C. Zicus. 1988. Fall flock behavior and harvest of Canada geese. J. Wildl. Manage. 52:679–688.

Sherwood, G. A. 1968. Factors limiting production and expansion of local populations of Canada geese. Pages 73–85 in R. L. Hine and C. Schoenfeld, eds. Canada goose management. Dembar, Madison, Wis. 195pp.

Staples, E. R., and N. D. New. 1968. Birds and aircraft: the problems. Pages 3–16 in R. K. Murton and E. N. Wright, eds. The problems of birds as pests. Academic Press, New York, N.Y.

U.S. Fish and Wildlife Service. 1981. An ecological study of the Minneapolis/St. Paul International Airport, Twin Cities, Minnesota, with recommendations to alleviate bird hazards. Wildl. Assistance Off., St. Paul. 13pp.

Zicus, M. C. 1981a. Flock behavior and vulnerability to hunting of Canada geese nesting at Crex Meadows, Wisconsin. J. Wildl. Manage. 45:830–841.

———. 1981b. Molt migration of Canada geese from Crex Meadows, Wisconsin. J. Wildl. Manage. 45:54–63.

Effects of Winter Bird Feeding on Wild Birds

MARGARET C. BRITTINGHAM, *The Pennsylvania State University, School of Forest Resources, Ferguson Building, University Park, PA 16802*

On a national basis, over 82 million people feed birds during the winter and dispense over 454 million kg of seed annually (U. S. Fish and Wildl. Serv. 1988). Feeding birds on such a massive scale is a relatively new phenomenon. Over time, the number of people feeding birds has increased, and the reasons for feeding and concerns about feeding have changed.

In the late 1800s, naturalists in New England fed birds to attract them in for study. In the early 1900s, as interest in conservation matters grew, bird feeding was promoted as a way to help wildlife. It was not until the 1960s–1970s that bird feeding grew to the scale we see it today, and feeders and seed began to be sold commercially at a number of stores. During the 1980s, the popularity of bird feeding boomed, and specialty shops devoted exclusively to birds and bird-feeding products sprang up around the nation. Numerous books and articles provided information on how to feed birds, types of feeders and seeds, and the food preferences of different species (e.g., Arbib and Soper 1971, Geis 1980, Mahnken 1983, McElroy 1985, Dennis 1986). However, there was very little information on the effects this practice actually had on the birds themselves.

POTENTIAL EFFECTS OF BIRD FEEDING

As the popularity of bird feeding continues to soar, some nagging concerns about the actual benefits and risks of bird feeding have surfaced. Is bird feeding actually helping birds? Can this practice harm them?

Because such a massive amount of seed is distributed over such a large geographic area, the potential effects of this practice are great. Potential positive effects of bird feeding include better physical condition, higher overwinter survival rates, and higher reproductive rates during the spring following feeding (Table 1). Potential negative effects of bird feeding include increased risks of disease and predation as birds are concentrated into small areas, lower overwinter survival rates, and a change in the ecological balance favoring species that use feeders over those that do not. Bird feeding also may influence the dispersion pattern of individuals and the winter ranges of species (Table 1). In this paper, I synthesize the available data on how supplemental feeding affects wild birds.

Physical Condition

Winter bird feeders provide a concentrated source of high energy food during a time of year when energy requirements are high. As a result, birds with access to feeders may be in better physical condition particularly during periods of extreme cold or inclement weather when natural food may be difficult to obtain. On the other hand, there has been concern that birds with access to feeders may experience dietary deficiencies, particularly if they obtain almost all of their energy needs from this one food source.

The effect that bird feeding has on the physical condition of an individual will depend largely upon how important this source of food is in the overall diet of the bird. If feeder users are obtaining the majority of their energy requirements from the feeder and if the food offered at feeders is lacking in certain necessary nutrients, dietary deficiencies might occur. However, if this food source is only a minor part of an individual's diet or if it provides a balanced diet, dietary deficiencies would be less likely to occur.

One researcher (A.D. Geis, pers. commun.) banded approximately 5,000 birds that were using feeders at his Maryland study area. He measured the amount of seed consumed per day and found that given the number of individuals present and the amount of seed consumed, this food source was only a minor portion of their diet. He concluded that these individuals were feeding primarily on natural foods. In Wisconsin, Brittingham and Temple (Univ. of Wisconsin, unpubl. data) banded black-capped chickadees (*Parus atricapillus*) and calculated the number of seeds individual birds were removing from a feeder and the percentage of the chickadees' diet that was obtained from the bird feeder. On average, most individuals obtained less than 25% of their energy requirements from the bird feeder. The birds were depending primarily on the natural food supply and were merely supplementing this otherwise natural diet with

Table 1. Potential effects of bird feeding on wild birds.

Factor influenced	Potential effect	
	Positive	Negative
1. Physical condition (body weight, fat, etc.)	Better physical condition because of abundant food supply.	Poor physical condition because of dietary deficiencies.
2. Disease	Less risk of disease because individuals are in better physical condition.	Increased risk of disease because of concentration of many individuals in a small area.
3. Predation	Reduced risk of predation because individuals are able to fulfill energy needs in a shorter period of time and can then spend more time watching for predators.	Increased risk of predation by domestic (cats) and wild (hawks) predators attracted to concentration of birds.
4. Accidents	None	Higher rates of accidents such as flying into windows near feeders.
5. Survival rates	Higher survival rates because of additional food supply.	Lower survival rates because of higher rates of disease, predation, and accidents.
6. Reproduction	Breeding occurs earlier and more young are produced per female because of better physical condition.	None
7. Dispersion pattern (Distribution of individuals)	Birds are able to persist in areas that may no longer have sufficient natural food to support them.	Individuals are clumped together where food is abundant. Vacant, yet suitable habitat is not used.
8. Range expansion or change in migratory behavior	Higher species diversity over winter as some birds that previously wintered in the south remain in northern areas.	Birds remain in northern areas during winter where other factors may be less suitable for survival.
9. Ecological balance among species	None	Feeding favors certain species over others and may result in selection against species that do not use feeders.

seed from feeders. Results from these two studies suggest that birds would be unlikely to suffer dietary deficiencies as a result of using bird feeders.

Brittingham and Temple (1988) compared body weights of chickadees that used feeders with chickadees in similar habitats that depended totally on the natural food supply. Chickadees with access to feeders weighed approximately 0.13g more than birds without access to feeders. Although the difference in weight was small, at −18C, the additional weight would enable a roosting chickadee to survive an extra 1.8–2.0 hours without foraging. In Holland, great tits (*Parus major*) with access to feeders increased in weight by an average of 1g during cold weather while birds that did not have access to this food source lost 0.4g (Kluijver 1952). On the other hand, in Germany, supplemental feeding had no influence on body weights of great tits (Schmidt and Wolff 1985). The effect of bird feeding on physical condition probably varies among species, with ambient temperature, and with the local abundance of natural food. If natural food is abundant and temperatures are mild, feeders will probably have little or no effect on physical condition. In any case, I was unable to locate any studies showing that birds which used feeders were in poorer physical condition than non-feeder users.

Disease

At bird feeders, large numbers of birds often feed together in a very small area. Because of the close contact between birds at feeders, one sick individual can potentially infect a number of susceptible ones. In addition, there is often a build up of fecal material in and around the feeder that may contaminate the food and increase the risk of disease spread. On the other hand, bird feeding could poten-

tially reduce the risk of disease if birds that use feeders are in better physical condition and therefore less susceptible to disease.

Every year there are reports of birds dying at feeders and occasionally these involve large numbers of individuals. The primary disease reported at winter bird feeders is salmonellosis (Hudson and Tudor 1957, Wilson and Macdonald 1967, Macdonald et al. 1968, Macdonald and Cornelius 1969, Locke et al. 1973, Hurvell et al. 1974, Nesbitt and White 1974, Fichtel 1978); a bacterial disease that causes an intestinal infection. Infected birds have diarrhea and become weak, listless, dehydrated, and emaciated. Fecal contamination builds up near the feeder and increases the risk of infection to other susceptible individuals (Macdonald et al. 1968, Macdonald and Cornelius 1969, Fichtel 1978, Terres 1981). Other diseases that have been associated with bird feeders or crowded feeding conditions include trichomoniasis (Rosen 1961), coccidiosis (Todd and Hammond 1971), aspergillosis (Terres 1981), avian pox (Bergstrom 1952), and avian mange.

In order to determine how frequently problems with disease occur at feeders and to identify factors associated with outbreaks of disease, Brittingham and Temple (1986) surveyed 624 individuals who fed birds. Problems with disease occurred approximately once in every 21.5 feeder years. Problems with disease did not occur randomly; instead the probability of disease was related to a number of factors including the species using the feeder, the number of individuals using the feeder, and the type of feeder in use. Risk of disease was highest at feeder sites that were visited by mourning doves (*Zenaida macroura*), European starlings (*Sturnus vulgaris*), house sparrows (*Passer domesticus*), American goldfinches (*Carduelis tristis*), and American tree sparrows (*Spizella arborea*). All of these species are highly gregarious, a trait that facilitates disease transmission. Similarly, the risk of disease was highest at sites where large numbers of individuals were present and where platform feeders were used. Fecal contamination, the primary way salmonellosis is spread, builds up as large numbers of birds congregate at feeders. In addition, bird seed is more likely to become contaminated when open platform feeders are used. This suggests that bird feeding may facilitate the transmission of disease between susceptible and infected individuals, particularly at sites where large numbers of birds are present and where fecal contamination of the seed is likely to occur.

Although bird feeding may facilitate the transmission of disease, there are no data on how frequently songbirds die of disease when they are away from feeders or in areas where feeders are not present. As a result, it is not possible to compare rates of disease-caused deaths between populations that use feeders and those that feed on more dispersed natural foods.

Predation

Bird feeders may influence predation rates in a number of ways. During the winter, birds are faced with high energy requirements because of cold winter temperatures. At the same time, the number of hours of daylight when a bird can search for food is reduced. To survive, many birds spend the majority of the daylight hours searching for food and reduce the time spent on other activities such as preening and watching out for predators. For example, in winter, European tits (*Parus* spp.) spend up to 90 % of the daylight hours searching for food (Gibb 1954, 1960). Bird feeders provide a concentrated and abundant supply of food. If this supplemental food source enables an individual to obtain its required energy needs in a shorter period of time, it may be able to spend more time scanning for predators. This could translate into lower predation rates. On the other hand, the large concentration of birds at feeders often attracts both wild predators, like sharp-shinned hawks (*Accipiter striatus*) and Cooper's hawks (*Accipiter cooperii*), as well as domestic predators like cats.

Determining how rates of predation at feeders compare with rates in the wild is difficult and similar to the problem of comparing rates of disease-caused deaths in the wild and at feeders. One study in Europe compared predation rates on tits in areas where feeders were present and where they were absent (Jansson et al. 1981). At feeder sites, individuals were able to obtain their food in a shorter amount of time and spend more time scanning for predators. As a result, predation rates were lower for birds that used feeders than for those that did not. This may not be the case in the United States where sharp-shinned hawks and Cooper's hawks are frequently reported near feeders. However, I am unaware of any studies comparing rates between the two groups.

People who feed birds are concerned primarily about predation by domestic cats. Most researchers report that the main prey diet of both domestic and feral cats is composed of rabbits and small mammals with birds making up a very small percentage of the diet (Eberhard 1954, Coman and Brunner 1972, Liberg 1984). These results may underestimate the actual amount of cat predation on birds, however, if birds are killed but not consumed. Laboratory studies have shown that cats will continue to kill available prey even when they are currently feeding on preferred food items, suggesting that surplus killing may also occur in the wild (Adamec 1976). In any case, local situations may occur where a particular cat kills excessively at feeders. In these situations, feeding should be discontinued.

Accidents

Because bird feeders usually are placed near windows, there is the risk that birds will unwittingly fly into these windows. The number of bird-window collisions is a function of the type of window, the size and placement of the window, and the number of birds near the window (Klem 1989). Large picture windows with clear or reflective glass are particularly hazardous to birds. Seeing the reflection of sky and trees, birds fly into them and are stunned or killed. Feeding birds increases the probability of bird strikes by concentrating birds near windows (Klem 1989). The number of birds killed annually in this manner and the overall effect of this cause of mortality on populations is unknown, but in local situations it may be a significant cause of mortality.

Survival Rates

The ultimate test of whether bird feeding is beneficial or harmful is how it affects survival rates. In Wisconsin, a comparison was made over three winters between three populations of chickadees that had access to feeders and two that did not and depended totally on the natural food supply. The overwinter survival rate of birds with access to feeders (0.69 ± 0.20) was significantly higher ($t = 3.48$, df = 13, $P<0.01$) than the survival rate of those without access to feeders (0.37 ± 0.12) (Brittingham and Temple 1988). In that study, the overall effect of winter bird feeding was clearly positive. Survival of birds with access to feeders was almost twice as high as that for birds without access to feeders.

Although the overall effect of bird feeding was positive in the Wisconsin study, it did not have a strong positive effect during all winters or all months (Brittingham and Temple 1988). During mild or average winter months, feeding had almost no influence on survival rates. Monthly survival rates were above 0.90 for both groups. It was during months with extended periods of very cold temperatures that the positive effects of feeding were observed. During these months, birds that could get to feeders maintained a high survival rate (0.93 ± 0.08) while survival of chickadees without access to feeders (0.67 ± 0.13) dropped precipitously.

Additional evidence of the positive effects of bird feeding during periods of extreme cold occurred in Illinois. During an unusually cold winter, Graber and Graber (1979) noted that populations of many species of birds, including chickadees, woodpeckers, and titmice, virtually disappeared from rural wooded areas, whereas their counterparts in suburban areas survived much better. This difference could have been due to slightly higher temperatures in suburban areas in conjunction with the greater availability of food. The positive effect of bird feeders during periods of extreme cold is probably most pronounced for small birds that may have difficulty obtaining needed energy requirements during extremely cold days. Larger birds have lower metabolic rates and require proportionately less food. In addition, they are able to store more body fat, so they can survive for longer periods of time when feeding is not possible.

Reproduction

Within limits, breeding dates and clutch size for birds are dependent on the condition of the female and the availability of food. Because of this relationship, it has been suggested that bird feeding may enable birds to begin breeding earlier and to lay more eggs. Researchers have provided birds with extra food and tested whether this in fact occurred (Perrins 1979, Drent and Daan 1980). The results have been mixed. In some cases, the females bred earlier, in others they did not. The number of eggs laid, however, rarely changed when extra food was provided.

The influence of supplemental feeding on timing of breeding seems to be dependent largely upon the type of food provided. Many species, such as chickadees, virtually stop visiting bird feeders in spring and switch to a high protein diet of insects. As a result, providing sunflower seeds did not induce chickadees to breed earlier (Brittingham and Temple, University of Wisconsin, unpubl. data). In contrast, great tits provided with meal worms began laying earlier than a control group (Kallander 1974). Because most people provide seed at their feeders, and many species reduce feeder use in spring, bird feeding probably has little effect on timing of breeding. However, this relationship needs to be studied in a species such as the house finch (*Carpodacus mexicanus*), which uses feeders continuously throughout the spring and summer.

Distribution of Individuals

Bird feeding probably attains its greatest effect by influencing where individuals are found during the winter. In fact, this is the primary reason people feed birds. By putting food out, we are able to attract birds to specific locations where we can enjoy them. Researchers studying songbirds and woodpeckers in winter have found the greatest concentrations near feeders (e.g., Winter and George 1981), and it is not uncommon for one who has looked for birds during the winter to search the woods for birds only to find them all at home by the feeder. Proponents of bird feeding suggest that, because of this supplemental food source, birds are able to persist in areas that may no longer

have a sufficient supply of natural food to support them. Critics argue that the feeders draw birds away from higher quality habitat where chances of survival would be better because of other factors. In addition, because feeders draw birds into areas where much of the natural habitat has been altered, the detrimental effects of habitat loss are masked giving a false sense of well being (Deis 1982).

The effect that bird feeding has on distribution patterns depends to a large extent on the social system of the species in question. Some species maintain territories or home ranges during the winter. Within these areas, they obtain the majority of their food requirements, have roost sites, and often breed on or near these areas during the following spring. Species that fit into this category include many of the woodpeckers, nuthatches, and chickadees. When feeders are available, these individuals maintain their home areas and commute to feeders. Densities are higher at the feeder, but the overall area does not appear to support more individuals.

The finches, including the goldfinch, pine siskin (*Carduelis pinus*), and evening grosbeak (*Coccothraustes vespertinus*) have a different social strategy. They do not maintain home ranges or territories during the winter. Instead, they are found in large flocks and move over extensive areas looking for abundant patches of food. When food is located, they settle in the area until the food is consumed. Once it is gone, they travel to a new area. For example, in Montana, Swenson et al. (1988) found that color banded rosy finches (*Leucosticte arctoa*) traveled over 40 km between feeders. Bird feeders represent abundant food patches and attract these species to specific locations where they would not normally be found. It is with species such as these that feeders probably have the greatest impact on where individuals are found.

Does the fact that birds congregate at feeders where they are highly visible mask the detrimental impacts of habitat loss? To the casual observer, this may be the case because the density of birds is often highest in urban areas where loss of habitat is greatest. The more knowledgeable bird watcher, however, would note that although the number of birds present may be greater, the types of species found are fewer and different from ones found in more natural areas. Bird feeders do not and can not take the place of natural habitat.

Range Expansion or Change in Migratory Behavior

The northern cardinal (*Cardinalis cardinalis*), tufted titmouse (*Parus bicolor*), American goldfinch, blue jay (*Cyanocitta cristata*), and mourning dove are examples of species that have been expanding their ranges northward (Boyd 1962, Beddall 1963, Alison 1976, Bock and Lepthien 1976, Middleton 1977). The range expansions have been attributed to a number of factors, including milder winters, habitat changes, and winter bird feeding. It is difficult to separate the potential causes because an increase in suburbanization, an increase in bird feeding, and milder winters all occurred simultaneously. However, for those species whose northern range limit is determined by availability and abundance of food, supplemental feeding should enable them to winter farther north.

A closely related issue is whether bird feeding causes birds to change their migratory behavior. The ultimate reason that birds migrate is to avoid food shortage during a northern winter. If an abundant food supply is available, many of these species may change their migratory behavior over time. Migratory behavior has evolved over thousands of years, so though this is a possibility, it is doubtful that changes would occur during the relatively short period of time that bird feeding has been occurring. The proximate clue most birds use to time migration is change in day length or photoperiod and not the availability of food (Welty 1975). In fact, the peak of migration occurs in late summer or early fall when natural foods are plentiful. As a result, supplemental feeding probably does not alter the timing of migration.

Ecological Balance Among Species

By improving the survival of some species over others, bird feeding could result in changes in competitive interactions among species, tipping the balance in favor of one species over another. Concern about this has occurred primarily in two areas. Blue jays have increased in abundance during recent decades and the increase has been attributed, at least in part, to winter bird feeders (Bock and Lepthien 1976). The increased abundance of blue jays is of concern because increased nest predation by jays has been hypothesized as a factor responsible for declining populations of neotropical migrants (Wilcove 1985, Terborgh 1989).

The second area of concern is that bird feeding may support large numbers of introduced species like house sparrows and starlings that would not be able to survive without human handouts. As numbers of these birds build up, they compete with native species like cavity nesting eastern bluebirds (*Sialia sialis*) and purple martins (*Progne subis*). This is difficult to control. Urban and agricultural areas are the two places where these pest species really build up. In both of these areas, there are excessive amounts of food in the form of garbage, livestock feed, and other human-produced or related food products. Bird feeders are just one part of a massive amount of human-associated foods.

THE OVERALL EFFECT OF BIRD FEEDING

In certain local situations, bird feeders may be associated with higher risks of disease, predation, and accidents. Anyone who feeds birds should take precautions to minimize these risks or cease feeding. At sites where disease, accidents, and predation are rare, supplemental feeding benefits individual birds by enabling them to survive during times of the year when weather conditions are harsh and energy demands are high. As a result, the population size of many "feeder-species" apparently has increased and some may

have expanded their ranges northward. Supplemental feeding indirectly may harm species that do not use feeders by tipping the ecological balance in favor of feeder users.

The benefits of bird feeding to people are numerous and well known. It is the primary way the majority of the public interacts with wildlife. As our society becomes more urbanized, feeding and observing birds fulfills a need to have some contact with wild animals. The sounds and sights of wild birds around our homes is educational, entertaining, and brightens a bleak winter landscape. Through feeding birds and gaining knowledge about ecology of familiar birds at the feeder, people become more aware of, and more interested in, learning about wildlife. As awareness, interest, and knowledge increase, people are more likely to participate in, and contribute to, programs that involve and benefit all wildlife.

REFERENCES CITED

Adamec, R. E. 1976. The interaction of hunger and preying in the domestic cat (*Felis catus*): an adaptive hierarchy? Behav. Biol. 18:263–272.

Alison, R. M. 1976. Mourning doves wintering in Ontario. Canadian Field-Nat. 90:174–176.

Arbib, R., and T. Soper. 1971. The hungry bird book. Taplinger Publ. Co., New York, N.Y. 126pp.

Beddall, B. G. 1963. Range expansion of the cardinal and other birds in the northeastern states. Wilson Bull. 75:140–158.

Bergstrom, E. A. 1952. Foot pox in passerines. Bird-Banding 23:169–171.

Bock, C. E., and L. W. Lepthien. 1976. Changing winter distribution and abundance of the blue jay, 1962–1971. Am. Midl. Nat. 96:232–236.

Boyd, E. 1962. A half-century's changes in the bird-life around Springfield, Massachusetts. Bird-Banding 33:137–148.

Brittingham, M. C., and S.A. Temple. 1986. A survey of avian mortality at winter feeders. Wildl. Soc. Bull. 14:445–450.

——— , and ——— . 1988. Impacts of supplemental feeding on survival rates of black-capped chickadees. Ecology 69:581–589.

Coman, B. J., and H. Brunner. 1972. Food habits of the feral house cat in Victoria. J. Wildl. Manage. 36:848–853.

Deis, R. D. 1982. Is bird feeding a no no? Defenders of Wildl. 57:17–18.

Dennis, J. V. 1986. A complete guide to bird feeding. Alfred A. Knopf, New York, N.Y. 288pp.

Drent, R. H., and S. Daan. 1980. The prudent parent: energetic adjustments in avian breeding. Ardea 68:225–252.

Eberhard, T. 1954. Food habits of Pennsylvania house cats. J. Wildl. Manage. 18:284–286.

Fichtel, C. C. 1978. A salmonella outbreak in wild songbirds. North Am. Bird Bander 3:146–148.

Geis, A. D. 1980. Relative attractiveness of different foods at wild bird feeders. Fish and Wildl. Serv. Spec. Wildl. Rep. 233. U. S. Fish and Wildl. Serv., Dep. of the Inter., Washington, D.C.

Gibb, J. A. 1954. The feeding ecology of tits, with notes on the treecreeper and goldcrest. Ibis 96:513–543.

———. 1960. Populations of tits and goldcrests and their food supply in pine plantations. Ibis 102:163–208.

Graber, J. W., and R. R. Graber. 1979. Severe winter weather and bird populations in southern Illinois. Wilson Bull. 91:88–103.

Hudson, C. B., and D. C. Tudor. 1957. *Salmonella typhimurium* infection in feral birds. Cornell Vet. 47:394.

Hurvell, B., K. Borg, A. Gunnarsson, and J. Jevring. 1974. Studies on *Salmonella typhimurium* infections in passerine birds in Sweden. Int. Congr. Game Biol. 11:493–497.

Jansson, C., J. Ekman, and A. Von Bromssen. 1981. Winter mortality and food supply in tits *Parus* spp. Oikos 37:313–322.

Kallander, H. 1974. Advancement of laying of Great Tits by the provision of food. Ibis 116:365–367.

Klem, D., Jr. 1989. Bird-window collisions. Wilson Bull. 101:606–620.

Kluijver, H. N. 1952. Notes on body weight and time of breeding in the Great tit, *Parus m. major* L. Ardea 40:123–141.

Liberg, O. 1984. Food habits and prey impact by feral and house-based domestic cats in a rural area in southern Sweden. J. Mammal. 65:424–432.

Locke, L. N., R. Schillinger, and T. Jareed. 1973. Salmonellosis in passerine birds in Maryland and West Virginia. J. Wildl. Dis. 9:144–145.

MacDonald, J. W., and L. W. Cornelius. 1969. Salmonellosis in wild birds. Br. Birds 62:28–30.

———, M. J. Everett, and M. Maule. 1968. Blackbirds with salmonellosis. Br. Birds 61:85–87.

Mahnken, J. 1983. Feeding the birds. Storey Commun., Inc., Pownal, Vt. 186pp.

McElroy, T. P., Jr. 1985. The new handbook of attracting birds. W. W. Norton and Co., New York, N.Y. 258pp.

Middleton, A. L. A. 1977. Increase in overwintering by the American goldfinch, *Carduelis tristis*, in Ontario. Canadian Field-Nat. 91:165–172.

Nesbitt, S. A., and F. H. White. 1974. A *Salmonella typhimurium* outbreak at a bird feeding station. Fla. Field-Nat. 2:46–47.

Perrins, C. M. 1979. British Tits. Collins, London, England. 304pp.

Rosen, M. N. 1961. Trichomoniasis or canker in doves. Calif. Dep. Fish and Game, Game Manage. Leaf. 2. 11pp.

Schmidt, K. H., and S. Wolff. 1985. Has feeding during winter any influence on bodyweight and survival of great tits (*Parus major*)? (In German. Translated by S. Postupalsky). J. Fur Ornithologie 126:175–180.

Swenson, J. E., K. C. Jensen, and J. E. Toepfer. 1988. Winter movements by rosy finches in Montana. J. Field Ornithol. 59:157–160.

Terborgh, J. 1989. Where have all the birds gone? Princeton Univ. Press, Princeton, N.J. 207pp.

Terres, J. K. 1981. Diseases of birds—how and why some birds die. Am. Birds 35:255–260.

Todd, K. S. Jr., and D. M. Hammond. 1971. Coccidia of Anseriformes, Galliformes, and Passeriformes. Pages 234–281 *in* J. W. Davis, R. C. Anderson, L. Karstad, and D. O. Trainer, eds. Infectious and parasitic diseases of wild birds. Iowa State Univ. Press, Ames.

U. S. Fish and Wildlife Service. 1988. 1985 national survey of hunting, fishing, and wildlife-associated recreation. U. S. Gov. Print. Off., Washington, D.C. 167pp.

Welty, J. C. 1975. The life of birds. W. B. Saunders Co., Philadelphia, Pa. 623pp.

Wilcove, D. S. 1985. Nest predation in forest tracts and the decline of migratory songbirds. Ecology 66:1211–1214.

Wilson, J. E., and J. W. MacDonald. 1967. Salmonella infection in wild birds. Br. Vet. J. 123:212–219.

Winter, W. R., and J. L. George. 1981. The role of feeding stations in managing nongame bird habitat in urban and suburban areas. Trans. North Am. Wildl. and Nat. Resour. Conf. 46:414–423.

V.

Public Participation and Education

Chair: TRACY KAY, Director, Rye Nature Center, Rye, New York

Cochair: JOAN M. GALLI, Nongame Wildlife Specialist, Minnesota Department of Natural Resources, St. Paul

Public Participation in Urban Nature Conservation in Britain

DAVID A. GOODE, *London Ecology Unit, Bedford House, 125 Camden High Street, London NW1 7JR, U.K.*

INTRODUCTION

The past 10 years have seen a remarkable shift in attitudes towards nature conservation in towns and cities throughout Britain. Radical changes have been made in conservation practice and a new philosophy has been established. At the heart of this movement is the acceptance that wildlife in towns and cities is of considerable value to the increasing number of people who live and work in urban areas. Public participation is an integral part of this newly developing philosophy.

Urban nature conservation differs in a number of ways from more traditional approaches. Although the importance of rare or endangered species or habitats is recognized, considerable weight also is given to the value of ordinary wildlife. Completely new criteria for conservation have been established and accepted as part of the planning system. These criteria include social factors, and an acceptance that quite unassuming habitats can be of great importance to local residents. Many of these habitats have developed relatively recently on derelict or disused land. The value of such "artificial" habitats has now become firmly established.

But there is a great deal more to urban nature conservation than simply the protection of these areas. Essentially one is dealing with opportunities for wildlife in the broadest sense. The whole approach involves imagination and creativity. Enhancement of existing habitats and creation of completely new ones are a normal part of the job. This applies within the whole urban fabric, including the built environment. Many aspects of urban conservation involve a positive approach to urban design in which ecological knowledge is used as part of the creative process.

Perhaps the most fundamental difference from more traditional approaches is the role of local communities, local authorities, and local politics, all of which are crucial factors in urban nature conservation. I have described it as a grass roots movement of the dispossessed (Goode 1987a). Certainly people who feel dispossessed of nature are taking action to protect places that they value, or to encourage more wildlife in their neighborhood. Many of these people have little or no specialist knowledge of wildlife, but they care passionately about their local environment. Urban nature conservation is as much, if not more, concerned with the needs of such people as it is with protection of rare or diminishing habitats of high intrinsic value; though clearly the two are often intertwined.

Many local authorities in towns and cities have now developed programs for nature conservation which emphasize that wildlife should be accessible for people to enjoy. These new initiatives include detailed policies for nature conservation in planning, new approaches to open space management, and the creation of new wildlife habitats often in close cooperation with local communities. Numerous partnerships have been forged with voluntary bodies as part of this process. Increasingly there is an awareness among local government politicians that there are votes in the environment, and we are seeing some very significant results.

Individually these various developments may not seem very different from traditional approaches to conservation, but together they comprise something altogether new. They provide a new impetus and a new philosophy which is fundamentally different. I believe that the philosophy and practice of *urban* wildlife conservation is the most significant change affecting nature conservation in Britain in the past 30 years.

THE ROLE OF LOCAL AUTHORITIES

Adoption of strategies for nature conservation by many local authorities—especially those in metropolitan areas—has been an important step. Published strategies for London (Greater London Council 1984, 1985), Greater Manchester (Greater Manchester Council 1986), Tyne and Wear (Nature Conservancy Council 1988), and the West Midlands (West Midlands County Council 1984) have not only been significant locally, but have provided models for use elsewhere. These examples have certain features in common. All recognize the need for protection of habitats of value, enhancement of existing open land for wildlife, the creation of new habitats in areas of particular need, and provision of an ecological database for planners. In addition,

Wildlife Conservation in Metropolitan Environments. NIUW Symp. Ser. 2, L.W. Adams and D.L. Leedy, eds. Published by Natl. Inst. for Urban Wildl., 10921 Trotting Ridge Way, Columbia, MD 21044, USA, 1991.

these strategies all place considerable emphasis on the local value of nature to residents of urban areas. For further details see Goode (1989).

Nature conservation policies for London were first described in a popular handbook (Greater London Council 1984). At that time, few local plans in London contained specific policies for nature conservation. The GLC's proposals included a requirement for local plans to identify and make provision for the protection of sites of nature conservation value, and for ecological factors to be taken into account in considering proposed new developments. They also recognized the need to cater more positively for wildlife in new developments, and to encourage greater ecological diversity by appropriate design and management of open spaces, especially in urban areas deficient in wildlife. The need to create new habitats in such areas was accepted. In emphasizing the value of nature to people, it was argued that priorities for conserving sites should be based on both intrinsic biological features and their value as a source of inspiration and enjoyment for the local community. This was the first recognition by a local authority in Britain that people's enjoyment of nature should be catered for in local planning.

The subsequent inclusion of these, or similar, policies in many of London's Local Plans was instrumental in ensuring that nature conservation became an integral part of planning in the capital. Since 1986, the London Ecology Unit has produced detailed strategies for 12 of the boroughs. Several hundred sites have been identified as worthy of protection, right down to the local level, and areas of wildlife deficiency also have been defined. In producing these strategies, the London Ecology Unit undertakes several phases of public consultation to ensure that people with local knowledge have a say in the final product. Some of these strategies have been adopted in local plans. The Ecology Unit also has provided model policies for newly developing plans (Pape 1989) and it seems likely that most boroughs will include detailed strategies for nature conservation in their new plans. Policies for London's open spaces are contained in a recent joint report by the main conservation organizations (Countryside Commission 1991).

So, significant progress is being made in the implementation of nature conservation strategies. London is only one of the many places where this is occurring. Most metropolitan areas and many smaller towns and cities now have well developed programs for nature conservation promoted by local authorities. Leicester, Nottingham, Norwich, Newport, Bristol, and Edinburgh are all good examples. Some district councils have produced detailed strategies too. The small town of St. Helens has identified 97 sites of wildlife interest in its policy for nature (St. Helens Borough Council 1986). Adoption of such strategies was encouraged by the Nature Conservancy Council (NCC) in its national guidance to local authorities on the content of local plans (Nature Conservancy Council 1987). The Department of the Environment also recognized their value in its circular on nature conservation (Department of the Environment 1987).

Some towns and cities have gone further by adopting a "Green Plan" or "Environmental Charter" addressing wider environmental issues including pollution, recycling, and energy conservation. There is currently considerable impetus for adoption of such charters by local authorities, and the Association of Metropolitan Authorities has provided a valuable lead through its policy recommendations in "Action for the Future" (Association of Metropolitan Authorities 1989) and its guidance on good environmental practice (Association of County Councils et al. 1990). Many cities recognize that nature conservation is a component of the quality of life and it has high priority in such charters. Examples include Leicester, the UK's first 'Environment City'; also Norwich, Bristol, and parts of London, notably the London Borough of Sutton. Further details are contained in Elkin et al. (1991).

The adoption of strategies for nature conservation has provided an official framework for action within which public participation can have effect at many levels. One way in which local authorities are facilitating this involvement of local people is through the formation of council subcommittees specifically for ecology or nature conservation. In London, there has been a proliferation of such committees during the past 5 years, which has had considerable effect. Many local politicians are now closely involved. They take pride in what is happening and ensure that the strategies are implemented. But just as important is the surge of activity on the part of local communities which has been facilitated by this official recognition of nature conservation. The official framework provides a means by which grassroots action can have real effect, either by ensuring that important habitats are protected or providing volunteer labor for their management.

HABITAT CREATION AND URBAN DESIGN

Another distinctive feature of urban nature conservation is the central role of habitat creation. Over the past 10 years, there has been an enormous shift in people's attitudes on the subject. Although there are, no doubt, still some traditional conservationists who abhor the idea of introductions, nevertheless, in the urban environment, the creation of habitats is now widely accepted. This is particularly so in inner city areas where least wildlife habitat survives. It also applies in many other places within the urban fabric where opportunities for habitat creation frequently occur in association with new developments.

Much effort in urban nature conservation is devoted to protecting surviving remnants of habitats that are under increasing pressure for development. In the densely built-up parts of inner cities, local groups regularly campaign to save particular plots simply because they are the only places in the neighborhood where anything resembling the natural world can still be seen. Such places may be poor examples of natural habitats when judged by traditional criteria for evaluating intrinsic biological interest; but their value to people in cities is not in doubt. The need for conservation of such sites has been clearly demonstrated on many occasions. However, most of these habitats have only survived until now by chance, not by design. If we were to design cities to include nature, the picture could be very different.

To a large extent, the techniques are already available. Landscape designers, ecologists, and horticulturalists together hold the necessary skills to create new habitats. Let me make it clear that I am not talking about creating the equivalent of old growth forest or long-established prairie ecosystems. It must be understood that, once destroyed, ancient habitats such as these cannot be recreated; but many other kinds of naturalistic vegetation can be created very effectively.

Technical information is now widely available in Britain and enormous progress has been made in both theory and practice since the NCC published its guide for "creating attractive grasslands" (Wells et al. 1981). Practical handbooks now exist for a wide variety of habitats and the compendium published by the Ecological Parks Trust provides a wealth of practical information for promoting nature in cities and towns (Emery 1986). The GLC's guide to habitat creation (Baines and Smart 1984) was another milestone in urban nature conservation, providing detailed advice in a palatable form for local authorities. It proved to be exceedingly popular as a guide for local people to create new wildlife habitats, and was reprinted in 1991 as a pocket guide.

Apart from new towns, such as Warrington and Milton Keynes, most habitat creation schemes in urban areas of Britain have been at the modest scale of ecology parks. The William Curtis Ecological Park, which existed near Tower Bridge from 1978 to 1985, was a fine example of what could be achieved in an inner-city area. It was remarkably successful, not only in the range of habitats and species that it supported, but also in catering for local schoolchildren who otherwise had little or no contact with nature. Sadly, the land was only available on a temporary lease and the site is now part of the London Bridge development. Ironically, the ecological park has been replaced by a paved open space with "lollipop trees." It was, however, an important pioneer venture that has been emulated in many other towns and cities. More recently constructed examples include Benwell in Newcastle upon Tyne, Norman Street Park in Birmingham, and Camley Street Nature Park near King's Cross in London. Others in London include Tump 53 Nature Park in Thamesmead, and Lavender Pond and Stave Hill nature parks in the Surrey Docks. All have dual roles, providing for formal education and enjoyment by local people (Goode 1987b).

It is, of course, possible for ecological approaches to be used on a much larger scale. The Amsterdam Bos is a superb example. These woodlands planted in the suburbs of Amsterdam in the 1930s have provided a stimulus for many landscape designers. Dutch experience has formed the basis of several examples of naturalistic planting in Britain, of which Warrington New Town is probably the best known (Scott et al. 1986). A most attractive wooded town-scape has been created, a town which is now characterized by an abundance of wildlife. Such woodlands could well provide a template for more extensive tracts of urban fringe forest currently promoted by the Countryside Commission as Community Forests in the West Midlands, East London, and northeast England.

Many examples of ecological approaches to urban landscape design now exist (e.g., Ruff and Tregay 1982, Bradshaw et al. 1986) and radical changes in the use of open space in cities are becoming accepted. Even formal Victorian parks have been converted to naturalistic landscapes, as in the case of Spinney Hill Park in Leicester where colorful meadows have replaced the close mown lawns.

The tide has swept through horticulture too. When the creation of attractive grasslands using native species was first advocated, it was difficult to obtain sufficient seed. Now a wide variety of mixes are available, and wildflower gardens are championed annually by John Chambers and others at the Chelsea Flower Show, Britain's national festival for gardeners. But is there not a case for some cross-fertilization here? Few ecologists are good horticulturalists and many habitat creation schemes could benefit from sound horticultural practice. Fine examples of naturalistic landscapes in botanical gardens and arboreta in Berlin, Wisconsin, Wisley, or Groningen demonstrate what is possible.

Although techniques for habitat creation are widely available, there is still a long way to go in developing a satisfactory philosophy. Buckley (1989) explored some of the issues and provided a wealth of examples which illustrate just how far the subject has progressed in recent years. It is clear that habitat creation offers considerable opportunities in wildlife conservation. At the same time, we have to accept the fact that developers will use this to their advantage, arguing for the destruction of valuable habitats on the grounds that they can be recreated. Some have already claimed that ancient woodland can be recreated from scratch! Conservationists need to be very clear where the real advantages of habitat creation lie, and be prepared to defend that position.

Having the necessary ecological and horticultural skills and knowledge is not enough. Involvement of local people has been a key element in the success of many habitat creation schemes in Britain, as described below.

WILDLIFE AND PEOPLE

The relationship between people and wildlife is at the heart of urban nature conservation, but the fact that many people enjoy experiences of nature is nothing new. In Britain, we have a long and well established cultural heritage on which this is based. A social survey designed to evaluate the role of natural areas in the lives of people living in a city revealed that nature is valued for a wide spectrum of reasons that are deeply embedded in our culture (Harrison et al. 1987). The study emphasized the delight which many people have in direct experience of wildlife. Some conservation organizations have capitalized on this relationship. The late Sir Peter Scott based the whole ethos of the Wildfowl Trust on the attractiveness of wildfowl. So too, the Royal Society for the Protection of Birds has benefitted from the popularity of birds. Reserves such as Minsmere with its avocets (*Recurvirostra avosetta*) have proved extremely popular. But, as Richard Mabey (1980) and John Fowles (1984) have pointed out, the scientific credo of "official" nature conservation in Britain does not allow admission of this relationship. As a result, criteria for designation and protection of important wildlife areas do not, on the whole, take into account the value of places for people to enjoy wildlife. Instead, they are based on intrinsic biological features such as habitat quality or presence of rare species.

The philosophy developed in urban conservation is very different in that it caters directly for the needs of local people. Emphasis on "ordinary" wildlife and its value to people in places where they live or work is central to this philosophy (Goode 1986) and is an essential part of conservation value in an urban context (Barker 1986).

During the 1980s, there were many examples in Britain of local communities mounting campaigns to protect natural habitats within urban areas. Moseley Bog in Birmingham was successfully defended from development by local people, including children, who argued for its protection as a nature reserve. Another well publicized case is Gunnersbury Triangle, a small patch of birch and willow woodland in Chiswick, a part of west London. Proposals for warehouse development on this area in 1984 met with a vigorous campaign by local residents, who argued that it should be protected as a nature reserve even though the land was not accessible at that time to the public. A public inquiry was held to determine the future of this area at which local experts argued convincingly in favor of nature conservation. Over 200 residents attended the public hearing to voice their opposition to the proposed development.

Interestingly, the ecologists employed by the developers only used traditional nature conservation criteria in their arguments. They considered that the site had no value for nature conservation as it was too small, was lacking in diversity of species or habitats, was not a long established habitat, and contained no significant rarities. They did not recognize the one criterion which was paramount in this particular case, namely that it was the only area of relatively natural vegetation in a heavily built-up part of west London and that it therefore had considerable value to the local community.

The inspector decided in favor of nature conservation because of the local ecological value of the site, and the case set an important precedent for urban nature conservation. Many other sites have subsequently been defended in London and local communities have played a significant part in

most of these successes. Each inquiry has added to the caselaw of planning and has helped to establish wildlife conservation as a normal part of urban planning. The philosophy that ordinary wildlife has value to urban dwellers has thus become firmly established.

The decision by a Government Inspector following a public inquiry regarding a proposed housing development on railside land illustrates this very clearly (Department of the Environment 1989). In her decision letter, the Inspector stated, "My opinion is that although the appeal site may possess few if any very rare species, or unusual habitats, its real value is not to be assessed in those very specialised terms. I consider its true value lies in the social, educational and environmental contribution it makes to the lives of people living in the area." She went on to say that, "the virtue of the appeal site is that it is immediately adjacent to large residential areas and is potentially accessible to all members of those communities. The habitats . . . offer opportunities for the urban dweller to experience, learn and appreciate flora and fauna which they might otherwise not encounter." The appeal was dismissed, and I have no doubt that the Inspector's words will be quoted frequently at future inquiries.

Not only does urban wildlife have value for local people, but many urban wildlife projects depend on local residents for their success. Indeed active involvement of local people is a feature of urban conservation. The proliferation of urban wildlife groups in Britain during the 1980s illustrates the strength of this new movement. Over 60 such groups are now established within the Urban Wildlife Partnership and numerous other partnerships exist with the local community promoted by bodies such as the Trust for Urban Ecology, British Trust for Conservation Volunteers, UK 2000, and newly developing partnerships with industry (Industry and Nature Conservation Association).

The essence of urban wildlife conservation is that it brings nature conservation issues into the daily lives of thousands of people in all walks of life. In many cases, involvement of local people is built into official policies. A good example is the Policy for Nature in St. Helens (1986) which states that, "the Council will actively encourage voluntary groups and local communities to participate in the management of sites of existing and potential wildlife interest." Another example is the London Borough of Sutton, which promotes the involvement of local people in all its environmental activities, including the management of its local nature reserves.

The benefits to people of nature areas in cities, and criteria for success in establishing and running such projects in London, are reviewed by Johnston (1990) who clearly demonstrated the value of community involvement in successful projects. The personal benefits of participating in urban wildlife projects were investigated by Mostyn (1979) who found that the most common responses fell within four benefit classes; emotional, intellectual, social, and physical. More recent studies (Harrison et al. 1987) provide more detailed insight into how local communities regard nature and open space within the built environment, and studies are continuing in this field.

In *Nature Areas for City People,* Johnston (1990) identified 10 keys to success in the establishment and management of urban nature areas. These were identified following analysis of nine case studies in London including community gardens and nature reserves. The main issues are summarized as follows:

Key Person

Behind every successful nature area there is a driving force which keeps the project running smoothly: often it is one key person but can be a small group of individuals. Above all there must be someone (or several people) prepared to fight for all that a nature area requires: money, security, staffing, buildings, etc. Not only is an enthusiastic key individual needed to ensure successful development of a site, but also to provide a pivotal point and leadership for all those involved in the project.

Community Involvement

An urban nature area should provide local people with a facility that they will use and enjoy. People should be invited to share and help during each phase of a project's life. To maintain community interest, it is necessary to keep the nature area alive with new developments and projects and give local people responsibility for carrying out vital tasks. Everyone should be kept informed of events, progress, wildlife sightings, etc. The area should be promoted as an everyday place, not a nature reserve for specialists. Preferably it should be open to the public every day to encourage people to drop by at any time.

Balance Between Wildlife and People

The ideal site will have a range of habitats which support a wealth of wildlife while allowing maximum access to people who are able-bodied and those who have disabilities. Certain areas may be out of bounds to people (and dogs) to protect the wildlife. This can be accomplished through site design and location of fencing and natural barriers, such as water features and spiny shrubs. Nevertheless, pathways should allow people to see nature "in close-up" wherever possible.

Effective Management and Maintenance

Nature areas need long-term, caring management. A nature area that is looked after and well-maintained is attractive to visitors and can help to encourage volunteer involvement. One of the best ways to ensure successful management is to detail requirements in a management plan that is read and adhered to by all who take part in site maintenance. The intensity and frequency of management required varies greatly with the types of habitats on site.

Security of Tenure

Much nature conservation management requires a long-term commitment, and community involvement is built up slowly. Those who use a nature area regularly form emotional attachments to the site. Organizations responsible for running a site should aim to have a freehold interest, long leasehold, or licence. This also helps to build a sense of permanence and can be helpful if the use of the land is challenged.

Staffing

Many sites serve a useful community function without resident staff, but where the aim is for intensive use, especially for education, it is essential to have staffing. Nature parks and small nature reserves used for environmental education should have at least two full-time staff: one who can concentrate on site management and upkeep and one who oversees interpretation, teaching, and publicity. Ideally four full-time staff are needed to keep a medium size site (1 to 10 ha) with a nature center fully operational 7 days each week: two wardens (to undertake site management, publicity, and interpretation) and two teachers (for on-site studies, teaching materials, and outreach work in schools). More staff will be needed on larger sites. Staff should be appointed at an early stage in the development of the project. They can work from one site only or alternatively be part of a comprehensive ranger program dealing with several sites.

Nature Center

Staffed sites need a building on or near the area. A building on site provides a natural focus for visitors and a base for all activities. It acts as a magnet for volunteers and gives an impression of permanence to the landscape. Ideally the nature center should accommodate toilets, interpretation area, tool store, small kitchen, office, and classroom. Outside in the nature area there should be adequate seating for visitors. The center and all parts of the landscape open to visitors should be fully accessible to all members of the community.

Interpretation and Publicity

In urban areas, the emphasis in nature conservation is on human enjoyment. Information about objectives, flora and fauna, and events must be available to all visitors. Publicizing the project is vital in order to attract people from all sectors of the community throughout the year.

Funding

Successful nature areas cost money: facilities and fencing, staffing, and maintenance all require a significant financial commitment. Although it may be possible to offset costs by inviting volunteers to help with maintenance and interpretation, and through other avenues such as staff secondments and corporate donations, nature areas should be seen as a priority area for local authority spending. When compared with the cost of other leisure facilities and traditional landscaping and environmental improvements, the development and maintenance of nature areas is very cost-effective.

Partnership Approach

Several organizations and individuals are usually involved in the establishment and maintenance of an urban nature area. Partnerships can be formed among a local authority, voluntary organization, local residents, business and industry, central government, and national agencies. An effective method of coordinating involvement by several different sectors is to establish a management committee.

CAMLEY STREET NATURAL PARK

The detailed case studies described by Johnston include Camley Street Natural Park, which is a good example of a totally created nature area in central London. The park was developed during 1983–1985 by the Greater London Council on a derelict coal yard near King's Cross railway station. It was carefully designed to include a sizeable pond with fringing marsh grading into spinneys of birch and alder. The park was opened in May 1985 and within 2 years had a remarkably natural feel about it. It is now fully booked during term time by local schools for environmental education and is a very popular place with local people.

Part of its success lay in ensuring that local people knew all about the park right from the start. A warden was appointed by the London Wildlife Trust even during the construction phase and many of the local children enjoyed digging out Victorian bottles in the rubbish tip unearthed when the pond was excavated. At a meeting in the local community center when plans were first unveiled, one elderly resident said "This is the first beautiful thing that has ever happened to us here." Community involvement was crucial and has paid off. Camley Street Park has suffered virtually no vandalism.

The park's success also lies in the fact that it is adequately staffed with two wardens and a full-time teacher, and there is a purpose-built classroom and office facility. Like Alley Pond Marsh Center in New York, the John Inskeep Environmental Learning Center in Portland, Oregon, and the Indian Creek Nature Center in Cedar Rapids, Iowa, Camley Street Park depends on the dedication and enthusiasm of the full time staff and regular volunteers who ensure that local people, including children, really are able to re-establish their link with nature.

REFERENCES CITED

Association of County Councils et al. 1990. Environmental Practice in local government. Assoc. Co. Counc., Assoc. District Counc., and Assoc. Metro. Authorities, London, U.K.

Association of Metropolitan Authorities. 1989. Action for the future: priorities for the environment. Assoc. Metro. Authorities, London, U.K.

Baines, C., and J. Smart. 1984. A guide to habitat creation. Ecology Handbook 2. Greater London Counc., London, U.K. 44pp. (Reprinted London Ecol. Unit and Packard Publ. Ltd., 1991).

Barker, G.M.A., ed. 1986. Biological survey and evaluation in urban areas: methods and application to strategic planning. Nat. Conserv. Counc., Peterborough, U.K.

Bradshaw, A.D., D.A. Goode, and E.H.P. Thorp, eds. 1986. Ecology and design in landscape. British Ecol. Soc. Symp. 24. Blackwell Sci. Publ., Oxford, U.K.

Buckley, G.P. 1989. Biological habitat reconstruction. Belhaven Press, London, U.K.

Countryside Commission. 1991. Green capital: policies for London's open spaces. Countryside Comm., London, U.K.

Department of the Environment. 1987. Nature conservation. Circ. 27/87. H.M.S.O., London, U.K.

——— . 1989. Decision letter regarding land to the rear of Halsbury Road, London Borough of Ealing (APP/A5270/A/87/079021). 14 August.

Elkin T., D. McLaren, and M. Hillman. 1991. Reviving the city. Friends of the Earth, London, U.K.

Emery, M. 1986. Promoting nature in cities and towns: a practical guide. Ecol. Parks Trust and Croom Helm, London, U.K. 396pp.

Fowles, J. 1984. The blinded eye. Pages 77–89 in R. Mabey, ed. Second Nature. Jonathan Cape, London, U.K.

Goode, D.A. 1986. Wild in London. Michael Joseph, London, U.K.

——— . 1987a. Nature in the city. Urban Design Q. 24. Urban Design Group, London, U.K.

——— . 1987b. Creative conservation for public enjoyment. Pages 117-129 in H. Talbot-Ponsonby, ed. Recreation and wildlife working in partnership. Countryside Recreation Res. Advisory Group, Bristol, U.K.

——— . 1989. Urban nature conservation in Britain. J. Appl. Ecol. 26:859–873.

Greater London Council. 1984. Ecology and nature conservation in London. Ecology Handbook 1. Greater London Counc., London, U.K.

——— . 1985. Nature conservation guidelines for London. Ecology Handbook 3. Greater London Counc., London, U.K.

Greater Manchester Council. 1986. A nature conservation strategy for greater Manchester. Policies for the protection, development and enjoyment of wildlife resources. Greater Manchester Counc., Manchester, U.K.

Harrison, C., M. Limb, and J. Burgess. 1987. Nature in the city—popular values for a living world. J. Environ. Manage. 25:347–362.

Johnston, J.D. 1990. Nature areas for city people. Ecology Handbook 14. London Ecol. Unit, London, U.K.

Mabey, R. 1980. The common ground. Hutchinson, London, U.K.

Mostyn, B.J. 1979. Personal benefits and satisfactions derived from participation in urban wildlife projects: a qualitative evaluation. Nat. Conserv. Counc., London, U.K.

Nature Conservancy Council. 1987. Planning for wildlife in metropolitan areas: guidance for the preparation of unitary development plans. Nat. Conserv. Counc., Peterborough, U.K.

_____ .1988. Tyne and Wear Nature Conservation Strategy. Nat. Conserv. Counc., Peterborough, U.K.

Pape, D.P. 1989. A strategic view of nature conservation in London. Unpubl. rep., London Ecol. Unit, London, U.K.

Ruff, A., and R.J. Tregay, eds. 1982. An ecological approach to urban landscape design. Dep. Town and Country Planning, Univ. of Manchester, Manchester, U.K.

St. Helens Borough Council. 1986. A policy for nature. St. Helens Borough Counc., St. Helens, U.K.

Scott, D., R.D. Greenwood, J.D. Moffatt, and R.J. Tregay. 1986. Warrington New Town: an ecological approach to landscape design and management. Pages 143-160 *in* A.D. Bradshaw, D.A. Goode, and E.H.P. Thorp, eds. Ecology and Design in Landscape. British Ecol. Soc. Symp. 24. Blackwell Sci. Publ., Oxford, U.K.

Wells, T.C.E., S.A. Bell, and A. Frost. 1981. Creating attractive grasslands using native plant species. Nat. Conserv. Counc., Shrewsbury, U.K.

West Midlands County Council. 1984. The nature conservation strategy for the county of West Midlands. West Midlands Co. Counc., Birmingham, U.K.

The Role of Nature Centers in Wildlife Education

TRACY R. KAY, *Rye Nature Center, Post Office Box 435, Rye, NY 10580*

RICHARD PATTERSON, *Indian Creek Nature Center, 6665 Otis Road SE, Cedar Rapids, IA 52403*

An estimated 1,500 nature centers currently exist within the United States. As defined by the Association of Nature Center Administrators, a nature center is a facility that connects people with the natural environment under the guidance of trained professionals. The primary objective of these centers is to encourage the public to interact with, learn about, and enjoy nature. The essential components of a productive nature center are a natural site (or home base) at which to conduct educational programs, a paid professional staff, and an established environmental education program.

Nature centers vary in size and ownership or operation. A directory recently published by the Natural Science for Youth Foundation indicated that nearly 19% of all nature centers are situated on sites of 2 ha or less, whereas 31% are larger than 202 ha. Over half of the nature centers are operated by federal, state, county, or municipal governments; approximately 39% are private not-for-profits; and 9% are administered by educational institutions (colleges, universities, or school districts). An additional 3% are owned or operated by private for-profit, or industry organizations.

Regardless of size or type of ownership, nature centers are uniquely suited to educate the public about wildlife. Indeed, in many areas, these centers are the only local source for such assistance. Nature center staffs typically handle an array of information requests, from simple identification to providing a detailed description of the habits and characteristics of a particular species. Homeowners frequently request advice concerning wildlife "nuisance" problems. Many calls received by the Indian Creek Nature Center in Cedar Rapids, Iowa come from citizens who feel they are being victimized by a particular species: deer (*Odocoileus virginianus*) destroying shrubbery, raccoons (*Procyon lotor*) invading garbage cans, squirrels (Sciuridae) residing in an attic, skunks (Mephitinae) digging up a lawn, or mockingbirds (*Mimus polyglottos*) singing too late at night or too early in the morning. Such calls led to the publication of *There's a Bat in My Attic and a Woodchuck in My Garden*, a booklet addressing common situations in which humans confront wildlife.

Although nature center personnel often can provide tips for solving, preventing, or reducing wildlife problems, many situations create an opportunity for more in-depth education leading to a greater appreciation of nature. For example, people encountering fledgling birds for the first time usually assume that the birds have been abandoned; the traditional reaction is to rush the "orphans" to a local nature center for care (usually under vocal protest from the fledglings' parents). Center personnel then have the opportunity, and sometimes a challenge, to educate the rescuer concerning fledgling development. Many people are not aware that when a bird leaves its nest, it and its siblings are still under the watchful eye of parents. Recently, a coalition of nature centers in Westchester County, New York, worked with the State Department of Environmental Conservation on a publicity campaign concerning young wildlife. The resulting "Don't Be a Kidnapper" and "If You Care, You'll Leave Them There" programs have taught children to observe wildlife from a safe distance to determine when a young animal is really in trouble. Nature center wildlife education programs thus serve to inform the public and can reduce the potential adverse impact of humans on wildlife.

Nature centers also provide wildlife education through direct programming in the form of "weekend walks," evening lectures, and special events. In addition, nature centers often provide outstanding, specialized educational services to local school systems. Some, like the Rye Nature Center in southern New York State, have contracts with local school districts to provide environmental education services. As outdoor facilities, nature centers offer unique opportunities for field studies and their professional staffs can augment the efforts of classroom teachers. In fact, partnerships between nature centers and local school districts are quite common. In addition to school class programs, some centers provide in-service training for teachers. Such programs give teachers the knowledge and confidence to

Wildlife Conservation in Metropolitan Environments. NIUW Symp. Ser. 2, L.W. Adams and D.L. Leedy, eds. Published by Natl. Inst. for Urban Wildl., 10921 Trotting Ridge Way, Columbia, MD 21044, USA, 1991.

supplement their curriculum with important information about current wildlife and environmental issues.

In addition to education, nature centers can offer a variety of research opportunities and auxiliary wildlife services. Many centers participate in traditional bird banding programs, breeding bird censuses, species counts, and wildlife behavior studies. Several centers also operate wildlife rehabilitation programs. The Raptor Center at the Greenway and Nature Center of Pueblo, Colorado provides rehabilitative care for birds of prey to prepare them for release to the wild. The program's main focus is to ensure the protection of these birds by educating visitors about their natural history and the important role they play in the web of life. Moreover, the story associated with a particular animal can provide a unique and entertaining lesson in wildlife education.

The National Institute for Urban Wildlife (NIUW) long has recognized the important role that nature centers play in wildlife education. In 1988, with assistance from the Edison Electric Institute, NIUW established a program to assist nature center administrators. Known as the Association of Nature Center Administrators (ANCA), the organizational goals are to: (1) establish a national network for nature center administrators, (2) promote the identity and credibility of nature centers as educational facilities, and (3) provide nature center administrators with products and services to improve job performance. ANCA's membership currently represents nature centers from 38 states, and new members continue to join as word of the program spreads.

The need for environmental education is constantly increasing. Although 1-day events, such as Earth Day celebrations and festivals, may inform the public, it is local nature centers that provide this service on a reliable, long-term basis. Their facilities and programs are pivotal in educating the public about wildlife and their continued existence will significantly influence the ability of society to respect and grow in concert with nature.

Fostering Residential Participation in Urban Wildlife Management: Communication Strategies and Research Needs

CHARLOTTE YOUNG, *Social and Natural Resources Section, Argonne National Laboratory, 9700 S. Cass Ave., Argonne, IL 60439*

INTRODUCTION

Urban residents can be involved with wildlife near their homes in various ways, from watching wildlife to recreating to participating in management. Management includes providing food, water, shelter, and space for wildlife (Leedy and Adams 1984). Specifically, residents can plant vegetation that provides food or shelter for wildlife. They can install bird and wildlife feeders as well as provide water. Better habitats can be provided through manipulations of their yards such as planting ground cover and leaving brush piles. Participation in some of these activities is more common than others. Although a substantial proportion (approximately 40% urban residents) feed birds, only about 12% feed other wildlife, and about 6–7% maintain natural areas or plantings for wildlife (Shaw et al. 1985). This low rate of participation in wildlife management activities suggests that urban wildlife managers may fail to recognize that a significant portion of urban people could provide valuable wildlife habitat.

Although there are numerous approaches to promoting participation in residential wildlife management, including legal mandates and incentives, this paper focuses on communication strategies for fostering involvement. First, it describes communication techniques (interpersonal, print media, electronic media) that may be used. Second, benefits to, and barriers of, implementing these strategies are explored. The paper concludes with research needs for improving the effectiveness of various communication strategies and for reducing barriers to implementation. Due to the scarcity of urban wildlife literature dealing with residential participation, much of the paper will draw from research in other fields, such as urban forestry and environmental education.

COMMUNICATION STRATEGIES FOR ENCOURAGING INVOLVEMENT

Numerous communication strategies can be used to foster residents' involvement in urban wildlife management.

These techniques range from public information meetings to exhibits to workshops (Table 1). Each technique has specific advantages and disadvantages according to the situation (Fazio and Gilbert 1981, Propst and Roggenbuck 1981, Sharpe 1982). Interpersonal communication strategies are advantageous because they foster two-way communication, provide a feeling of informality, and can engender audience enthusiasm through the communicator's personality. On the other hand, personalized approaches require trained and skilled communicators, and properly managed programs.

Print and electronic media techniques also offer several advantages. They can reach audiences who may not attend

Table 1. Sample communication strategies for fostering participation in residential wildlife management.

Interpersonal strategies
- public meetings
- response to public inquiries
- hot lines
- workshops
- wildlife days at local educational institutions
- talks/lectures

Written strategies
- signs/labels leaflet and keyed signs (particularly relevant for demonstration areas)
- self-guided trails and auto-tours
- exhibits/displays, bulletin boards
- maps
- brochures/leaflets/pamphlets
- newsletters
- letter requests for comments

Electronically-based strategies
- audio recorded messages
- messages over portable cassette recorders
- messages over auto radio
- films/movies and videotapes
- slide shows

Media materials
- press releases, including those inviting comments
- public service announcements
- interviews
- press conferences
- television stories

Wildlife Conservation in Metropolitan Environments. NIUW Symp. Ser. 2, L.W. Adams and D.L. Leedy, eds. Published by Natl. Inst. for Urban Wildl., 10921 Trotting Ridge Way, Columbia, MD 21044, USA, 1991.

personal services, and can supplement personal communications. With print media, people may pace themselves; as a result, this material may be better remembered than verbal messages (Furnham and Gunter 1988).

Various factors influence the appropriateness of a particular technique in certain circumstances. These include characteristics and preferences of the audience, such as whether the audience is informed or uninformed, setting, length of presentation, amount of time that audience has, content of the message, resources available, amount of controversy regarding the issue (e.g., deer management), and the objective of the wildlife communication, such as information provision or solicitation.

Audiences

Audiences with whom wildlife managers may communicate urban wildlife information are diverse. They include: elected officials, organized groups such as school children, service groups, senior citizens, condominium and apartment groups, and special interest and community groups. Audiences also consist of the "average" urban resident, homeowner or private landowner. Each audience may have different needs and/or reasons for attending programs and obtaining wildlife information. The degree of organization of the group will also likely differ, which has implications for message design. Schools and service clubs, for instance, may want structured programs that fit within their larger agenda. Private landowners, on the other hand, may prefer more loosely structured programs that capitalize on individual differences and allow specific needs to be met.

Settings

Wildlife agencies are only one of numerous types of facilities from which materials about urban wildlife management might be communicated. Types of settings might be grouped into three somewhat overlapping categories: public, quasi-public, and private (Table 2). As urban residents may be uninformed about wildlife agencies and their purposes, taking advantage of these diverse settings is important for reaching urban audiences. Being aware of these diverse settings is also important for promoting inter-agency links with community groups.

Within these settings, participants may move through space or remain stationary. Personalized programs, where a speaker remains in one place, include talks, lectures, or programs; they may have variable formats (Table 3). Programs where the audience is mobile include: walks through demonstration areas or wildlife habitats, auto tours through demonstration areas or wildlife habitats, exhibits, and self-guiding trails. Audiences will have different experiences depending on whether they remain stationary or not, which should be considered during program design.

Types of Messages

Just as techniques used to communicate messages may vary, the content of the message may also vary. Many

Table 2. Settings from which wildlife management information may be provided for urbanites.[a]

Public settings
- wildlife agencies
- local community development departments
- public works units and urban forestry sections
- local governmental offices
- legislative offices and town halls
- Cooperative Extension Service offices
- parks
- nature centers/environmental education centers (with subsettings such as campfires, amphitheaters, auditoriums, visitor centers)
- local schools

Private settings
- nurseries and garden stores
- Christmas tree farms
- grocery stores
- local businesses such as hardware stores and other places where people get information about their communities

Quasi-public settings
- museums
- libraries
- community centers

[a]Demonstration areas, places that show actual wildlife management techniques, may fall into any of the three categories, depending on administration and ownership.

Table 3. Sample formats for meetings and talks.

Informal small group or community meetings

General public information meetings

Large group
- briefing/question and answer
- town meeting
- panel

Large group/small group format
- workshops
- coffee clutch/kitchen meeting
- walk-in information session (often combined with displays)
- combined television and discussion groups/participatory
- television (e.g. call in show, mail in responses)
- computer based participation (e.g. computer conferencing)

environmental messages focus on biological concepts. Although these are important and necessary, they may be insufficient, by themselves, for promoting urban wildlife participation. Other types of concepts include the role of wildlife in urban ecosystems, human interactions with wildlife, general descriptions of management concepts, and specifications of what urban residents can do to manage wildlife. The balance and emphasis of different types of content must be considered in designing effective communication strategies.

BENEFITS OF IMPLEMENTING STRATEGIES

Implementing these communications strategies yields benefits for both wildlife managers and urban residents. Managers may obtain assistance in implementing wildlife management projects, resulting in more comprehensive management with little monetary expenditure. The public may provide useful information (Canter 1977), such as locations of important tracts of uninventoried land suitable for wildlife habitat. Participation by the public also helps enhance public confidence and credibility in the wildlife agency. This is important because the public may view some wildlife management techniques as controversial. Another benefit could be improved inter-organizational coordination. This may manifest itself by agencies working with more diverse groups, such as private organizations and universities, as they obtain needed information.

Residential involvement also may provide benefits to people by improving quality of life. For instance, areas that are suitable for wildlife provide ideal places for children to play (Schicker 1988). Residential areas more suitable for wildlife as evidenced by "wooded" tracts are often considered more aesthetically appealing (Kaplan 1984, Schroeder 1982) and tend to have higher property values (Dwyer 1982, Reichenbach 1988, King et al. 1991).

Although very few studies have specifically examined benefits of residential wildlife management involvement, studies in related areas suggest that this type of involvement might be very satisfying. For instance, people enjoy spending time in their yards and use these areas frequently for gardening, relaxing, and similar activities (Palmer 1988, Talbot and Bardwell 1989). Moreover, urbanites like wildlife (Hronek 1989), have a strong affection for individual animals, and feel that ethical treatment of animals is important (Kellert 1984). They like common attractive vertebrates such as song birds (Kellert 1987, O'Donnell and Van-Druff 1987), and mammals such as squirrels and rabbits (Hastings and Hammitt 1986). Invertebrates with aesthetic or utilitarian appeal such as butterflies also are generally desirable (Kellert 1984). Together, these findings suggest that yards would be pleasant places for people to work with wildlife.

The final payoff for implementing these communication strategies will be increased participation in wildlife management activities. This, in turn, provides other benefits. Perhaps the most obvious is more contiguous habitat corridors for wildlife. If several homes provide habitat within a neighborhood, and numerous adjacent neighborhoods provide habitats, this matrix of "mini" habitats provides continuous links critical for the ranges of many wildlife species (Schicker 1988).

BARRIERS TO IMPLEMENTING STRATEGIES

Although the above described strategies appear sufficiently simple for wildlife managers to carry out, they have generally been haphazardously implemented, if at all. For communication strategies to promote widespread residential participation, they must be implemented systematically. Systematic implementation of these strategies, however, requires that several barriers be overcome.

Lack of Understanding of Urbanites

In general, wildlife managers do not understand who "residential wildlife managers" are or might be. More spe-

cifically, managers lack an understanding of urbanites' motives, satisfactions, and needs for participating or not participating in wildlife management activities, and the reasons for these orientations. Moreover, they are uncertain about factors that influence participation or non-participation in wildlife activities (Lyons 1987).

Urban residents are generally not knowledgeable about wildlife. Urbanites are often unaware of the names of all but the most common species (Penland 1987), and lack a general understanding of wildlife biology (Kellert 1984). They also are unaware of what to do, or management behaviors they might become involved in (O'Donnell and Van-Druff 1987). This lack of awareness may result in existing wildlife information being too complex for urbanites to understand.

The visual appearance of urban wildlife habitats may be viewed as less than desirable to urbanites. A large body of research has shown that people prefer savanna-like settings with open spaces and a few trees (Schroeder 1982, Kaplan and Kaplan 1989). Moreover, inner-city residents, in particular, tend to like settings that are more, rather than less, manicured (Talbot and Kaplan 1984). These findings would suggest that urbanites might view the "scruffy" appearance of wildlife habitat areas as less than aesthetically pleasing. This, in turn, might reduce their likelihood of providing such habitat.

Although urban residents are emotionally attached to many animals (O'Donnell and VanDruff 1987), many urbanites are fearful of certain types of wildlife. They dislike snakes (Hastings and Hammitt 1986), and find most invertebrates undesirable (Kellert 1987). These fears and perspectives may make people hesitant to be involved in activities that they feel would bring them closer to these animals.

Informational Barriers

Not only are urbanites generally unaware of wildlife management and biology, information may be a limiting factor. Technical information that managers need is often unavailable (Shaw and Supplee 1987), and information that is obtainable is generally not geared to lay audiences. For instance, much of the literature is often written or presented in a highly technical style, with jargon and ambiguous specifications about how the audience might become involved.

Moreover, the content of the information is not always relevant to urbanites. Urban wildlife programs frequently include protection, preservation, enhancement of wildlife resources, nuisance animal control, and control of diseases (Marion 1986). Although these concepts are important, urbanites also need explicit information on what to do, and how to do it (e.g., the National Wildlife Federation's Backyard Habitat package (Thomas et al. 1973)). In fact, the limited research suggests that most homeowners who had a wildlife problem indicated they did not try to solve the problem because they did not know how (O'Donnell and VanDruff 1987).

Institutional Barriers

Institutions and organizations involved in wildlife management are generally not created to serve urbanites. There are several subclasses of institutions and organizations that could support urban wildlife services: private organizations, local municipal institutions, and state and federal governments.

Private institutions involved in urban wildlife programs are sparse. For example, there are few equivalents to garden stores, which people may use for tree care and forestry-related information. Landscaping and engineering firms rarely include wildlife considerations in their operations for various reasons (Dunster 1987).

Local governmental structures, relatively well-established for urban forestry (e.g., urban forestry departments or units within public works), typically do not have parallel organizational entities for urban wildlife. Community-based nature centers, while often interested in wildlife issues, generally do not focus their programming efforts on such topics as residential participation.

Although some state natural resource and land management agencies have recently included non-consumptive wildlife in their mission, most wildlife agencies have not dealt with urban wildlife (Shaw and Supplee 1987). The forestry arrangement might provide some insight to establishing community-based wildlife programs. For instance, most states have community forestry programs within the state agency, and these are administered through Departments of Forestry (Casey and Miller 1988).

The paucity of institutional arrangements for urban wildlife results in other difficulties. Ordinances to promote habitat are generally lacking; widely-used street tree ordinances consider tree stress, rate of growth, and care required, but rarely encompass wildlife needs. Moreover, comprehensive inventories of wildlife habitats, which would be helpful to target neighborhoods for residential participation, are generally unavailable.

Wildlife Manager Backgrounds

Another barrier to fostering residential involvement in wildlife management may be the backgrounds of wildlife managers. Many wildlife managers feel that communication and involvement with the public is a low priority (Fazio 1987). Moreover, wildlife managers' training customarily emphasizes biology and habitat manipulation. As a result, their orientation to wildlife tends to be scientific and/or ecologistic as opposed to the humanistic and moralistic perspectives of much of the urban population (Kellert 1987). These differing orientations may hinder effective communication and understanding.

RESEARCH NEEDS

Whereas a substantial body of literature exists on wildlife recreation, research on residential participation in urban wildlife management is sparse. Research is needed to reduce barriers and obstacles to implementing communications strategies, to document and quantify benefits of carrying out these techniques, and to improve the effectiveness of such strategies. This research must draw from the social sciences and be applied to wildlife management. Relevant bodies of literature include: psychology (such as learning and memory, perception and motivation); marketing (such as consumer behavior and promotion); and communications (such as network analysis, persuasive communications and diffusion of innovations). Three broad categories of research needs are discussed below: needs and preferences of participants and non-participants, organizational analysis and information networks, and program effectiveness.

Needs and Preferences of Participants and Non-participants

Research under this category would focus on cultivating our understanding of the people who might and might not participate in urban wildlife management. Research is needed on the satisfactions, levels of knowledge, preferences (including fears and attractions), and perceptions of those who participate. Studies on the motivations for involvement and impediments to such involvement are also of value. These investigations might benefit from scrutinizing studies of residents already involved in some type of "land management" (defined broadly) such as non-industrial private forest owners (e.g., Bliss and Martin 1989), and gardeners (e.g., Kaplan 1973). The relationships between these variables should also be investigated. For instance, studies could investigate how, or if, levels of knowledge of wildlife influence people's perceptions, motives, and satisfactions.

A slightly different line of research would use a framework for exploring how information and technologies move through social systems (diffusion of innovations, e.g., Rogers 1983). This would be useful for identifying types of people who might be involved in urban wildlife management, those people likely to serve as role models for other community members, and expected rates at which people might engage in wildlife management.

Organizational Analysis and Information Networks

The above studies would focus on understanding individual behaviors and barriers to performing these behaviors such that one would be able to more effectively implement communications strategies. Research is needed in another area—focusing on community and organizational levels. One line of research would be to explore how and where lay people find out about wildlife issues. This is important for selecting appropriate communication channels so wildlife messages will reach their intended audiences. Communication network analysis (Littlejohn 1983) could provide a framework for understanding how people find out about wildlife information in their communities. (A communication network can be thought of as a network of individuals linked by information exchange through mass media or interpersonal communications.) Relatedly, studies should investigate communication networks that overlap with wild-life networks. This would include how networks such as Cooperative Extension Service, master gardeners, birders (Kent et al. 1987), nurseries, Christmas tree farms, and networks about composting, could be modified to include information about urban wildlife management.

The framework of network analysis could also apply to interagency communication and coordination. This would entail investigating the communication links between wild-life agencies and other organizations that have wildlife or wildlife-related missions or interests, such as nature centers, libraries, and private groups like Ducks Unlimited. A better understanding of inter-organizational communication chan-nels could improve interagency information sharing and program development. The literature on diffusion of inno-vation and marketing would provide additional frameworks for examining interagency communication links as well as how people find out about wildlife in their communities.

Another needed area of research is that of organizations themselves. As mentioned above, urban wildlife organiza-tions are poorly defined or nonexistent. This suggests that organizations need to be established and programs and ser-vices formulated. To do this, however, requires an under-standing of what organizational entities are most effective—should they be governmental bodies, non-profit groups, or other types of organizations? If governmental, what is the best level—federal, state, or local? There are also structural and arrangement issues. This includes whether the urban wildlife organizational entity belongs within an existing organizational unit like an urban forestry department, or whether it should stand as a separate unit. Structural and arrangement issues also include appropriate lines of author-ity and spans of control. Related questions are what types of staff are suitable and how should they be trained? Given that a large portion of urban resource managers' responsibili-ties involve interaction with people, traditionally-trained wildlife biologists may or may not fit the job requirements of urban wildlife managers. Training to help managers understand urbanites, among other topics, is likely to be needed (see above "Needs and preferences of participants and non-participants").

Along with investigating and testing the effectiveness of organizational arrangements and personnel needs, goals of the organization and required programs and services must be developed. It may be useful to draw upon the successes and failures of municipal forestry programs and special events (e.g., Tree City USA) for such program development (Duntemann et al. 1988, Hibberd 1989).

Program Effectiveness

Once the programs are implemented, they must be tested to determine how well they are working. Research in this area should begin with an inventory of the types of programs currently being carried out. This would then lead to an assessment of audience preferences for those programs. These assessments require managers to consider numerous factors when designing the evaluations. These include:

- types of audiences (e.g., children versus adults, and casual versus organized groups).
- resultant variables of interest (e.g., knowledge of residential management techniques, and actual par-ticipation in wildlife management).
- appropriateness of content (e.g., relative emphasis of biology, management techniques, role of humans in wildlife, wildlife diseases).
- trade-offs across strategies (e.g., brochures versus talks versus exhibits).
- different designs within a strategy (e.g., how bro-chure text should be written, what types of graphics are most useful).

The literature in environmental education, interpreta-tion, teacher education, science education, citizen involve-ment (e.g., forest planning), and persuasive communication could provide helpful guidance for developing studies in this area.

Related to examining the effectiveness of the programs are ascertaining circumstances that influence program suc-cess. This could include such factors as the role of manage-ment in participation (Lyons 1987), leadership abilities of managers, participants' previous exposure to wildlife issues, and amount of controversy surrounding the management technique. Identifying these factors is critical to producing a comprehensive picture of program effectiveness because simply providing wildlife information in and by itself may at times be inadequate for producing the desired participa-tion. It is necessary to recognize variables that may strengthen or weaken program success and to address factors that indirectly influence program accomplishments.

SUMMARY

Many people in urban areas have access to green space that could effectively be used for urban wildlife habitat. However, to foster urbanites' participation in such activities requires utilizing communications (and other) strategies in a planned and precise manner. Numerous communication strategies may be used to foster such participation. These range from formal talks to media materials to brochures to workshops. To choose the best technique, managers must assess the strengths and weaknesses of each approach as it relates to audience characteristics, the setting in which the program will take place, and the type of message.

Implementing these communications strategies to facil-itate participation reaps several benefits. Wildlife itself profits from more continuous habitat corridors. Urban resi-dents have more aesthetically appealing neighborhoods with places for children to play. Moreover, people seem to enjoy relaxing and spending time in their yards, so managing urban wildlife would most likely be psychologically rewarding.

On the other hand, there are several barriers to effectively carrying out communications strategies. Managers' poor understanding of urbanites revolves around urbanites' poor levels of knowledge, their aesthetic preferences, and their fears. Information to develop programs that are relevant to urbanites is often unavailable. In addition, institutional structures to operate and oversee urban wildlife programs are inadequate. Finally, wildlife managers' training and backgrounds are not always appropriate for extensively interacting with urban residents.

Given these barriers, research is needed that concentrates on three broad areas. Firstly, managers must understand urbanites' needs and preferences. A better understanding of the needs of urban residents provides a foundation for designing strategies that are relevant to the audience. Secondly, managers must assess the organizational arrangements and information networks to determine effective organizations from which to operate urban wildlife programs, and from where wildlife personnel, as well as the public, can obtain wildlife information. Finally, managers must evaluate how well communication strategies help urbanites become involved in wildlife management near their homes.

By addressing these research needs, managers can better communicate wildlife messages to urbanites. This, in turn, will help generate support and participation from urbanites, which is critical to habitat enhancement in urban centers.

REFERENCES CITED

Bliss, J.C., and A.J. Martin. 1989. Identifying NIPF management motivations with qualitative methods. For. Sci. 35:601–622.

Canter, L. W. 1977. Public participation in environmental decision making. Pages 220–232 in L. W. Canter, ed. Environmental impact assessment. McGraw Hill Book Co., New York, N.Y.

Casey, C.J., and R.W. Miller. 1988. State government involvement in community forestry: a survey. J. of Arboriculture 14:141–144.

Dunster, K. 1987. Designing for urban wildlife: results of a 1986 survey of the landscape architecture profession in Canada. Pages 92–97 in L.W. Adams and D.L. Leedy, eds. Integrating man and nature in the metropolitan environment. Natl. Inst. for Urban Wildlife, Columbia, Md.

Duntemann, M., T. Gargrave, and J. Andersen. 1988. Community forestry initiatives. J. Arboriculture 14:90–93.

Dwyer, J. F. 1982. Urban tree and forest pest management: an economic perspective. Pages 139–143 in B. Parks, F. Fear, M. Lambur, and G. Simmons, eds. Urban and suburban trees: pest problems, needs, prospects and solutions. Conference Proceedings. East Lansing, Mich.

Fazio, J. R. 1987. Priority needs for communication of wildlife values. Pages 296–304 in D. J. Decker and G. R. Goff, eds. Valuing wildlife: economic and social perspectives. Westview Press, Boulder, Colo.

———, and D. L. Gilbert. 1981. Public relations and communications for natural resource managers. Kendall/Hunt Publishing Co., Dubuque, Ia. 375 pp.

Furnham, A., and B. Gunter. 1988. The primacy of print: immediate cued recall of news as a function of channel of communication. J. of Gen. Psychol. 116:305–310.

Hastings, B. C., and W. E. Hammitt. 1986. Preferences of visitors for wildlife species. Pages 89–93 in D. G. Kulhavy and N. R. Conner, eds. Wilderness and natural areas in the eastern U.S.: a management challenge.

Hibberd, B. G., 1989. Involving the public. Pages 26–37 in B. G. Hibberd, ed. Urban forestry practice. For. Comm. Handbook 5. Her Majesty's Stationary Office, London, U.K.

Hronek, B. 1989. Some random thoughts. Soc. of Am. For. Rec. Group Newsl. December.

Kaplan, R. 1973. Some psychological benefits of gardening. Environ. and Behav. 5:145–162.

———. 1984. Dominant and variant values in environmental preference. Pages 8–11 in A.S. Devlin and S.L. Taylor, eds. Environmental preference and landscape preference. Conference Proceedings. Connecticut College, New London, Conn.

———, and S. Kaplan. 1989. The experience of nature: a psychological perspective. Cambridge University Press, Cambridge, Mass.

Kellert, S. R. 1984. Urban American perceptions of animals and the natural environment. Urban Ecol. 8:209–228.

———. 1987. The contributions of wildlife to human quality of life. Pages 222–231 in D. J. Decker and G. R. Goff, eds. Valuing wildlife: economic and social perspectives. Westview Press, Boulder, Colo.

Kent, R. J., R. Buerger, and T. Litwin. 1987. Training volunteer fish and wildlife educators for suburban programming. Pages 71–73 in L.W. Adams and D.L. Leedy, eds. Integrating man and nature in the metropolitan environment. Natl. Inst. for Urban Wildl., Columbia, Md.

King, D. A., J. L. White, and W. W. Shaw. 1991. Influence of urban wildlife habitats on the value of residential properties. (Published elsewhere in this volume.)

Leedy, D.L., and L.W. Adams. 1984. A guide to urban wildlife management. Natl. Inst. for Urban Wildl., Columbia, Md. 42 pp.

Littlejohn, S. W. 1983. Theories of human communication. Wadsworth Publ. Co., Belmont, Calif. 340 pp.

Lyons, J. R. 1987. Basic and applied social research needs in wildlife management. Pages 285–295 in D. J. Decker and G.R. Goff, eds. Valuing wildlife: economic and social perspectives. Westview Press, Boulder, Colo.

Marion, W. R. 1986. Developing an urban wildlife program. Proc. Natl. Urban For. Conf. 3:232–235.

O'Donnell, M. A., and L.W. VanDruff. 1987. Public attitudes and response to wildlife and wildlife problems in an urban-suburban area. Page 243 in L.W. Adams and D.L. Leedy, eds. Integrating man and nature in the metropolitan environment. Natl. Inst. for Urban Wildl., Columbia, Md.

Palmer, J.F. 1988. Residents' characterization of their residential greenspace resource. Pages 373–379 in Healthy Forests, Healthy World, Society of American Foresters Proceedings. Rochester, N.Y.

Penland, S. 1987. Attitudes of urban residents toward avian species and species' attributes. Pages 77–82 in L.W. Adams and D.L.

Leedy, eds. Integrating man and nature in the metropolitan environment. Natl. Inst. for Urban Wildl., Columbia, Md.

Propst, D., and J. Roggenbuck. 1981. A guide to cultural and environmental interpretation in the U.S. Army Corps of Engineers. Environ. Lab., U.S. Army Eng. Waterways Exp. Sta., Vicksburg, Miss. 150 pp.

Reichenbach, M. R. 1988. Perspective gained from the national urban forestry assessment: forestry a community tradition. Pages 392–395 in Healthy Forests, Healthy World, Society of American Foresters Proceedings. Rochester, N.Y.

Rogers, E. M. 1983. Diffusion of innovations. 3rd. ed. Free Press, New York, N.Y. 453 pp.

Schicker, L. 1988. Planning for children and wildlife begins at home. J. of Environ. Educ. 19:13–21.

Schroeder, H. W. 1982. Preferred features of urban parks and forest. J. of Arboriculture 8:317–322.

Sharpe, G. 1982. Interpreting the environment. 2nd ed. John Wiley and Sons, New York, N.Y. 649 pp.

Shaw, W.W., W. R. Mangun, and J. R. Lyons. 1985. Residential

enjoyment of wildlife resources by Americans. Leisure Sci. 7:361–375.

———, and V. Supplee. 1987. Wildlife conservation in rapidly expanding metropolitan areas: informational, institutional, and economic constraints and solutions. Pages 190–197 in L.W. Adams and D.L. Leedy, eds. Integrating man and nature in the metropolitan environment. Natl. Inst. for Urban Wildl., Columbia, Md.

Talbot, J. F., and L.V. Bardwell. 1989. Making "open spaces" that work: research and guidelines for natural areas in medium-density housing. Pages 110–115 in G. Hardie, R. Moore, and H. Sanoff, eds. Changing paradigms, proceedings of the annual EDRA conference. EDRA 20/1989, N.C. State University.

———, and R. Kaplan. 1984. Needs and fears: The response to trees and nature in the inner city. J. of Arboriculture 10:222–228.

Thomas, J.W., R. O. Brush, and R. M. DeGraaf. 1973. Invite wildlife to your backyard. National Wildlife 11:5–16.

Public Response to Bald Eagle Appreciation Days

LAURA SPESS JACKSON, *Iowa Department of Natural Resources, Nongame Program, Rural Route 1, Boone, IA 50036*

INTRODUCTION

Bald Eagle Appreciation Days (BEADs) is a cooperative educational event sponsored by the Nongame Programs of the Iowa Department of Natural Resources and Illinois Department of Conservation, plus the U.S. Army Corps of Engineers. Local businesses, tourism bureaus, county conservation boards, and conservation groups have become more involved in BEADs during recent years. The main goals of the event are to:

(1) enhance the public's understanding and appreciation of an endangered species, raptors, and natural resource management by highlighting the bald eagle (*Haliaeetus leucocephalus*); and
(2) promote the Nongame tax checkoffs.

BEADs has indoor and outdoor activities. Inside, visitors can attend a 45-minute program about bald eagles. The program includes an introduction to the event by agency personnel, an interactive "eagle facts and trends" preamble, a 15-minute audio-visual program, and a presentation of live eagles by a representative from a certified raptor education center. The presentation concludes with a question and answer session and instructions on what to see in the area. Visitors also can tour a variety of agency, raptor, and conservation displays while indoors. Outside, people can visit observation areas to view wild eagles. Biologists with spotting scopes staff the observation areas to help visitors view the eagles and to answer visitor questions. Biologists work in teams that rotate between the indoor program and outdoor observation areas.

The first Iowa-Illinois event was held in Keokuk, Iowa in 1985. It was formatted after the Missouri Department of Conservation events (Witter et al. 1980) and was assisted by James D. Wilson of that agency. In 1986, the event was expanded to include Fridays for school children, in addition to being open to the public during the weekend. Attendance soared from 600 visitors during 1985 to over 4,000 visitors in 1986. In 1987, another joint Iowa-Illinois-Corps event was initiated in the Quad Cities metropolitan region. A third Iowa-Corps event was started at Red Rock Reservoir in 1989.

Due to the popularity of the events and the sensitivity of working with an endangered species, visitor guidelines were established. Boyle and Samson (1985) noted that wildlife observers and photographers could be more disturbing to wildlife than other outdoor recreationalists because observers-photographers actively seek and approach wildlife. Higher frequency of encounters and longer duration of observation could be more disturbing than brief accidental human-wildlife encounters. Although Boyle and Samson (1985) noted it was difficult to show cause-and-effect relationships, they recommended limiting the effects of recreationalists by proper location and design of facilities and viewing areas. Stalmaster and Newman (1978) recommended winter buffer zones of 250 m between human activity and bald eagles in open areas and 75-m to 100-m buffers with vegetative screens between humans and eagles. Specific to the Mississippi River, where two of the BEADs events are held, Southern and Southern (1984a) found that peak eagle foraging occurred before 8 a.m., probably in response to increasing human activity after 8 a.m. To some extent, there also was an increase in feeding prior to sunset (Southern and Southern 1984a).

To reduce eagle disturbance during the winter, Southern and Southern (1984b) recommended restricting human activity near foraging areas prior to 10 a.m. and after 2 p.m. These authors also recommended developing winter eagle observation areas, educational programs, and guidelines to eagle watching.

To address potential problems with eagle viewing, an eagle brochure was developed that featured "eagle etiquette" (Jackson 1986). Eagle etiquette is taught at all events and is now regularly featured in various media stories about wintering eagles. Observation areas at BEADs are open from 9 a.m. until 4:30 p.m. Most visitation does not begin until 10 a.m (after the first indoor program) and visitors view the eagles from the width of the Mississippi River or a partially screened road >250 m from eagle perch sites. Observation points are at areas of regular human activity.

Due to the indoor and outdoor aspects of BEADs and the large crowds, the events require a large commitment in personnel. From 1985 to 1989, most events used 25 staff per day. The events were among the biggest winter nongame activities and had the highest potential media exposure during the time period when potential contributors were filing their income taxes. To evaluate the effectiveness of the personnel commitment, a survey was conducted at all three BEADs to:

(1) determine audience enjoyment of the programs;
(2) gather market information on visitor expenditures;
(3) test audience recognition of the sponsors; and
(4) document whether visitors contributed to their state's nongame tax checkoff.

The survey allowed the government agencies to assess the popularity of the events, determine the value of the events in agency and checkoff recognition, estimate government cost of the BEADs, and estimate a gross economic value of the events.

STUDY AREAS

Keokuk, Iowa is located in the extreme southeast corner of the state. The city is within 16 km of Missouri and is bordered on the south and east by the Mississippi River, which also serves as the state line between Iowa and Illinois. Keokuk has a population of 13,500 and is over 160 km from a metropolitan population center of >100,000. Most nearby towns have populations <30,000. Although the city does not draw on a large nearby metropolitan area, attendance at BEADs is good. Keokuk tends to offer the highest concentrations of wintering bald eagles (25 to >200 birds). Indoor programs are held in the Keosippi Mall, which provides visitors with ample pre- and post-event activities.

The Quad Cities include the Mississippi River towns of Davenport (Ia.), Bettendorf (Ia.), Rock Island (Ill.), and Moline (Ill.). The area has a population >200,000. Indoor programs have been held in a private business building (Modern Woodmen of America) and the Milan community center where display space has been limited. The indoor portion of the event will be moved in 1991 to a permanent site at the large Quad Cities Conservation Alliance Expo Center. Less than 25 eagles are normally in the area during the event.

The Red Rock event is held in central Iowa. Indoor programs are held at the Pella community center, and the outdoor observation area is about 16 km away at Red Rock Reservoir. Pella has a population <10,000. However, the city is within 72 km of the Des Moines metropolitan area, which has a population of >250,000. Up to 25 eagles at one time have been observed at the observation area and over 50 eagles are normally in the area.

METHODS

The attendance figure for a BEADs event was based on actual hourly counts of people attending the indoor live eagle program. This resulted in a minimum estimate of the total number of people "exposed" to the event because some people only visited the outside area or toured the displays without attending the live eagle program. However, the live eagle program was the highlight for most of the visitors and was where the main educational and agency messages were delivered.

The questionnaire used in the study consisted of 12 questions, 11 of which were close-ended (Babbie 1982). To avoid people selecting a socially desirable response (Babbie 1982), the checkoff question was worded, "were you *able* to contribute money on your income tax form to your state's Nongame program." The open-ended question asked visitors to list the sponsors of BEADs.

Because taxpayers were a primary focus group of the survey, questionnaires were distributed only to adults attending the live eagle program during the weekend. Most couples or two-parent families answered the questionnaire as a single unit. Free eagle buttons were given to individuals or families returning survey forms.

Response frequency tables were generated for each question by location (SAS Institute Inc. 1987). To test for significant differences between consumptive (purchased a hunting or fishing license) and nonconsumptive (did not purchase a license) users and contributors to the Nongame tax checkoffs, SAS general linear models (SAS Institute Inc. 1987) procedures were used.

Expenditure data for each location were calculated by multiplying the number of responses to each price range by the mid-point of the range. Expenditures over $100 were minimally estimated by using $101 as the multiplier. Expenditure estimates were calculated only for the respondents and were not expanded to represent the total weekend attendance.

Government costs were estimated by calculating the salary, lodging, food, postage, and eagle rental costs for each event. Keokuk and the Quad Cities each required 25 staff for 4 days of salary (included travel time and setup), 4 days of food, and 3 nights lodging per event. Red Rock only required 15 staff for 3 days salary, 3 days food, plus 2 nights lodging for seven people. Gross salary for an Iowa biologist II, with 5 years service, was $13.63/hour in 1989. This figure was used to calculate the costs of salaries, although salaries varied between agencies and personnel. State of Iowa food allowance ($15.25/day) and motel allowance ($30/day) were used to estimate food and lodging costs. Lodging cost represents a maximum value because a variable number of people had roommates and divided room costs. The eagles cost $1,626 per event and miscellaneous postage for notices to schools cost $50.

Throughout an event, media exposure was tracked by recording newspaper, newsletter, magazine, radio, and television interviews. Recorded coverage was less than actual exposure because materials from weekly newspapers, local conservation groups, business advertising, and tourism-chamber of commerce contacts were not recorded.

RESULTS

Since 1986, indoor attendance at BEADs has ranged from 2,000 to 5,500 people with an average of 3,370 people/event ($n = 11$) (Fig. 1). During 1989, 52% ($n = 3,242$) of the weekend visitors were surveyed in Keokuk, 41% ($n = 990$) at the Quad Cities, and 34% ($n = 1,396$) at Red Rock. Although response rates <50% should be questioned (Babbie 1982), response rates of the target audience (adults) were much higher than the rates indicated because the total attendance figures included children <18 years old who were not surveyed.

On average, 67% of the people attended an event in 1989 with their family, whereas 19% attended with friends (Table 1). At the Quad Cities, a higher percentage of people traveled with a tour group than with friends (Table 1).

Overall, 27% of the participants drove <16.1 km, whereas 18% drove >160.9 km (Table 2). Fifty-seven percent of the Quad Cities respondents drove <49.9 km, whereas 52% of the Red Rock and 38% of the Keokuk respondents drove the same distance. Keokuk drew the highest percentage of long-distance travelers (21%); Red Rock drew the fewest (8%). Most visitors attended a BEADs event as a day trip. Eighty-five percent of the respondents

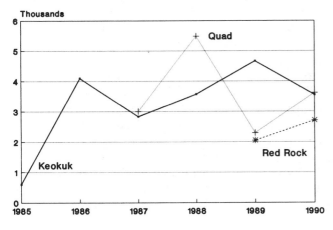

Fig. 1. Public attendance at three Iowa "Bald Eagle Appreciation Days" events, 1985–1990.

Table 1. Frequency (%) of social group attendance at three Iowa "Bald Eagle Appreciation Days" events in 1989.

Social group	Event location		
	Keokuk	Quad Cities	Red Rock
Family	70.5	50.0	69.8
Friends	19.5	18.4	18.2
Tour group	4.1	24.9	6.7
Alone	5.9	6.7	5.3
Total	100.0	100.0	100.0
n	1602	386	434

Table 2. Distribution (%) of driving distances for the attendees of three Iowa "Bald Eagle Appreciation Days" events in 1989.

Driving distance (km)	Event location		
	Keokuk	Quad Cities	Red Rock
0 – 16.1	21.8	43.7	34.0
17.7– 48.3	16.3	13.4	18.4
49.9– 80.4	24.6	9.9	23.4
82.1–160.9	15.9	15.6	16.5
> 160.9	21.3	17.4	7.8
Total	99.9	100.0	100.1
n	1684	403	474

at Keokuk ($n = 1674$), 91% at the Quad Cities ($n = 402$), and 98% at Red Rock ($n = 467$) did not spend the night while attending an event. At the two Iowa-Illinois BEADs, 920 (44%) of the participants were from Iowa, whereas 1033 (49%) were from Illinois. Only 127 respondents came from Missouri and 124 of those attended Keokuk. Only 17 respondents came from other states.

On a scale of 1 to 5, and averaged over all three locations, 76% of the respondents gave the event the highest (5) enjoyment rating, whereas 18% rated it a 4 (Table 3). Five percent felt the event was "ok" and <1% felt the event was less than okay or did not enjoy it at all. Enjoyment among areas was similar (Table 3). A majority of respondents (83%) indicated they would be willing to pay admission to the event. Although the three BEADs events were extremely popular, 52% of the respondents did not attempt to identify the sponsors and only 10% correctly listed all three agency sponsors ($n = 2,574$). Nineteen percent correctly identified one or two agencies and 11% of the participants listed local entities as the event's sponsor. Seven percent listed entities not even related to the event as sponsors.

Although BEADs is a "nonconsumptive" event, 50% of the total respondents indicated they, or a member of their group, had purchased a hunting or fishing license during the past year ($n = 2,464$). There was no significant difference ($P > 0.25$) between the attendance of consumptive and nonconsumptive respondents at any location. Likewise, there was no significant difference ($P > 0.25$) in enjoyment of the event between consumptive and nonconsumptive respondents.

Overall, 51% of the participants said they had been able to contribute to the Nongame checkoff ($n = 2,396$). Fifty-nine percent of the contributors donated less than $5,

Table 3. Attendee enjoyment (%) of three Iowa "Bald Eagle Appreciation Days" events in 1989.

Enjoyment category	Event location		
	Keokuk	Quad Cities	Red Rock
5 (Enjoyed very much)	76.4	71.8	76.8
4	17.5	19.3	18.5
3 (Average or OK)	5.2	6.8	4.5
2	0.5	1.3	0.0
1 (Did not enjoy)	0.3	0.8	0.2
Total	99.9	100.0	100.0
n	1639	383	426

26% donated $10, 7% donated $20, 4% donated over $30, and 5% could not remember the donation amount (n = 1,212). Of the contributors, consumptive users were significantly more apt to contribute to the Nongame checkoff than non-license buyers ($P = 0.02$). Contributors and non-contributors equally enjoyed the event ($P > 0.25$).

Relative cost-benefits of BEADs were determined for the government agencies, individuals, and regions involved with the events (Table 4). Government cost per person ranged from $3.51 at Keokuk to $7.13 at the Quad Cities, based on total attendance (school day and weekend). When cost was divided among sponsoring government agencies, the cost/person dropped to $1.17 to $2.37 per agency. Thus, to host the events, it cost the government agencies an estimated $16,355/event to sponsor BEADs at Keokuk and the Quad Cities, and $7,693 to host Red Rock. Participant expenditures for gas, food, lodging, and miscellaneous items ranged from $10 per respondent at Red Rock to $22 at Keokuk. Gross expenditures totalled $36,384 at Keokuk, $5,834 at the Quad Cities, and $4,580 at Red Rock.

Respondents learned of BEADs by a combination of media forms (38%), the newspaper (28%), word-of-mouth (15%), television (8%), newsletter (5%), radio (3%), and tourism bureau (2%) (n = 2,438). Media coverage of the events was good on local, statewide, and national levels. In 1989, statewide coverage included three magazine, three newsletter, and seven newspaper stories; local coverage included: 12 newspaper, 10 radio, and 10 television stories; and there were three stories written in national tourism-birding magazines.

DISCUSSION

Historically, state wildlife agencies have focused primarily on hunting and fishing activities. However, there is a need to expand beyond this traditional use and clientele of wildlife to include nonconsumptive uses and users (Kruckenberg 1988, Vickerman 1988). Recent estimates documented that over 60% of the U.S. population directly participate in nonconsumptive recreation (USFWS 1988a). In Iowa, the estimate was 90% (USFWS 1988b).

Although there is something inherently disturbing about considering wildlife in terms of dollars and cents (Powell 1980), the economic assets of wildlife need to be promoted (Kruckenberg 1988, Vickerman 1988) and added to its other values. Steinhoff (1980) noted that the true value of wildlife is the sum of multiple values: recreational,

aesthetic, educational, biological, social, and commercial. Natural resource managers also have to focus more on "customer satisfaction" to make wildlife conservation more competitive with other land uses (Salwasser et al. 1989). Strong, positive, customer-oriented programs can simultaneously preserve biological diversity and contribute to local, regional, and national economies (Salwasser et al. 1989).

Henderson (1986) recommended interfacing with the public through active educational programs and through working with the media to facilitate a progression of positive public awareness, appreciation, and action regarding natural resources and government agencies. BEADs fulfilled both interfacing methods and the results of the survey provided insight to customer satisfaction, government cost-benefits, and gross regional economic benefits.

Similar to Missouri's "Eagle Days" (Witter et al. 1980), the events in Iowa and Illinois were appealing to families (Table 1). BEADs also were attended equally by consumptive and nonconsumptive "units". Because only one member of a family had to purchase a hunting or fishing license to qualify the group as a consumptive unit, the data do not provide the actual number of consumptive users. Indeed, there might be more total nonconsumptive attendees than consumptive attendees if, in numerous families/groups, only one member had purchased a license. However, other members of such groups would have had at least some positive exposure to consumptive recreation compared to groups where no members participated in consumptive activities. Thus, although lumped as consumptive and nonconsumptive users, respondents might better be described as units with or without some consumptive exposure.

BEADs provided high customer satisfaction (Table 3). The events were equally enjoyed by consumptive and nonconsumptive units, as well as contributors and non-contributors to the checkoff. Although the survey did not measure whether enjoyment was perceived as a recreational, educational, aesthetic, biological, or social value to the respondent, it did illustrate that BEADs must have had some positive value. Measures of value also can be determined by a visitor's willingness to pay for an item (Steinhoff 1980). Although the survey did not measure "how much" visitors would have paid to attend a BEADs event, it clearly demonstrated that BEADs had a perceived dollar value, above the respondent's base expenditure to attend the event, to over 80% of the people.

Expenditure data can be used to estimate the gross economic value to a community (Bart et al. 1979), or to indicate customer "cost" of a "product" (Steinhoff 1980). Overall, respondents at Keokuk "paid more" to enjoy BEADs than respondents elsewhere (Table 4). This is logical because Keokuk had a higher percentage of long-distance travelers (Table 2) and 15% of the visitors spent the night. Red Rock and the Quad Cities were able to draw visitors from nearby metropolitan areas and had less than 2% and 9% overnight guests, respectively.

Gross expenditures indicate a minimum value of

Table 4. Relative costs and benefits ($) of three Iowa "Bald Eagle Appreciation Days" events in 1989.

Event cost and attendee expenditure	Event location		
	Keokuk	Quad Cities	Red Rock
Cost/person	3.51	7.13	3.76
n	4658	2293	2046
Expenditure/person	21.97	14.77	10.04
n	1656	395	456

BEADs at each location because expenses were not extrapolated to estimate the cumulative expenditures of all weekend visitors. Because the survey only asked for expenses incurred during the BEADs trip rather than at the specific BEADs site, gross economic benefits are probably spread across the region rather than directed to a particular community. However, in a small community with many long-distance travelers, direct economic benefits can be felt in the community. According to Keosippi Mall Marketing Manager, Jay Zetterlund, following the Keokuk event in 1989 "[Mall] traffic this year was estimated between 8,000 to 10,000 people. Merchants have recorded record breaking sales." (Jay Zetterlund, pers. comm.).

Government agencies also incurred costs and derived benefits from sponsoring BEADs. Total government cost per attendee appears high until the costs are divided among the cooperating agencies. Iowa-Illinois-Corps agencies divide personnel commitments fairly equally. Eagle costs are rotated between Iowa and Illinois, whereas the Corps pays production and duplication costs of audio-visual material. Government-agency cost/person varied widely among events (Table 4) because of differences in personnel needs and total number of visitors. Keokuk and the Quad Cities are farther from most personnel's home so required an extra day for travel and lodging. These two events also had two or three eagle observation areas so required additional staff to cover all stations. Red Rock was operated with more local personnel and more volunteers. In addition, Red Rock only had one observation area.

Weather was one of the most important factors affecting attendance of events during the weekend (Fig. 1). In 1985, temperatures were below zero; in 1986, they were above freezing. Keokuk had snow and ice in 1987, mild weather in 1988 and 1989, and one good and one bad day in 1990. After a mild weekend in 1988, blowing snow and sub-zero temperatures dramatically decreased attendance at the Quad Cities in 1989. If poor weather decreased attendance, the government cost/person increased because of personnel already present to conduct the event. However, even during poor visitations, agency cost/person has been low compared to what "consumer units" have been willing to pay to attend the event (Table 4). This suggests that the agencies are producing a valuable "commodity" at a relatively low cost. Unfortunately, direct cost-benefits could not be calculated because the number and size of family units is unknown.

Programs conducted on Fridays (with school children) were consistently well attended because all attendees were "committed" by advance reservations. No prior reservations were required for individuals during the weekend. Tour groups were "committed" by the originator who was asked to notify us that they were coming. Tour groups were encouraged to attend morning programs. If visitation started to exceed what the auditoriums could accommodate per hour, tickets were distributed so people did not have to wait in line 2 hours to attend the program.

According to the Iowa Department of Revenue, <3% of state taxpayers contributed to the Nongame checkoff in 1989; yet 51% of the BEADs respondents contributed. Although an even higher contribution rate had been expected for BEADs, this response documented that the Nongame program still has potential for attracting more contributors. Several respondents wrote that they would contribute in the future. The survey also noted that consumptive units were more apt to contribute than nonconsumptive units. Possible explanations for this observation are:

(1) consumptive units are more actively involved in wildlife and consequently more likely to attend a BEADs event, and
(2) consumptive users are more familiar with wildlife agencies so might have had more opportunity to learn about the Nongame checkoff.

Consumptive users must leave their home environment to pursue their sports. Consequently, they may be more accustomed and more willing to travel to wildlife events. In Iowa, 92% of consumptive users also enjoy nonconsumptive recreation (USFWS 1988b), so this type of an event would have been appealing.

Because consumptive users must purchase licenses to pursue their sport, they have had to establish at least some line of communication with wildlife agencies. Many state agency letters, envelopes, licenses, hunting regulations, magazines, brochures, and posters contain checkoff logos or explanations. Consequently, consumptive users may have more exposure to the checkoff and may, therefore, be more apt to contribute.

BEADs events are not necessarily providing agency recognition. It is unknown whether the 1,345 non-respondents did not know who the sponsors were or did not want to take an extra minute to list them. It was not encouraging that, even though the sponsors were mentioned during the indoor program at least twice, only 10% of the participants correctly listed the agencies. Because respondents did not recognize the sponsors, they might also be missing the checkoff message. As more businesses and groups assist BEADs events, and as the government agencies continue to thank and recognize these groups for their assistance, the public may become even more confused in the future because of multiple agency and group involvement.

Media coverage and the multiplier effect of the media have been very useful for announcing BEADs. Statewide, local, and national media have helped attract thousands of visitors to the events each year, although weather is a final determining factor for attendance. The media also has been very active in promoting eagle etiquette, which is a direct benefit to the eagles. However, good media coverage has not necessarily meant agency or checkoff recognition. Because of time and space constraints, agency sponsors and the fact that Nongame checkoff contributions have paid for the event are rarely mentioned by the media. The media further denies recognition by consistently shortening personnel titles from "Nongame biologist" to "DNR biologist." Lastly, improper sponsors ranging from "game wardens" to the eagle handlers (who get paid to come) have been frequently mentioned by the media as the sponsors of BEADs.

Unfortunately, lack of media credit to sponsors means that the multiplier effect is not working. Nonconsumptive citizens, who have no recognition of the agencies or checkoff, are not getting exposure to either one. Fortunately, people who do attend the event can pick up agency and nongame handouts. The handouts provide individuals unfamiliar with state programs an opportunity to start learning about wildlife agencies and programs that might interest them.

CONCLUSIONS

BEADs had high customer satisfaction and several factors which indicated a perceived economic value to consumers. The events were enjoyed by consumptive, nonconsumptive, contributing, and non-contributing respondents alike. Most people incurred travel expenses to attend BEADs yet would be willing to pay admission in addition. The events also generated some gross economic benefits to the region. BEADs had low costs/visitor when several agencies cooperatively sponsored the events. Government costs/visitor were affected by the number of personnel necessary to run the event and attendance. Weather was one of the biggest factors affecting attendance.

Although BEADs had positive customer value, gross regional economic value, and relatively low production costs, the events did not necessarily provide agency or checkoff recognition. Confusion caused by multiple agency-group involvement plus the failure of media to mention sponsors diminished the positive value of recognition to the agencies. Fortunately, people who attended the event were exposed to government personnel and handouts, which may have enlightened individual visitors. Unfortunately, this did not facilitate communication with unaware nonconsumptive recreationalists or use the multiplier effect of the media.

Since 1989, government agencies have continued to improve BEADs. To lower government costs, the number of observation areas and personnel have been decreased. Numerous staff members indicated they would rather overwork than underwork. Consequently, events are conducted with the fewest possible staff (8 to 16) and more volunteers. If weather hampers attendance, personnel are still busy. If attendance soars, personnel are more than busy.

To increase recognition, individual media and tourism personnel have been contacted. The response is generally very positive. Most of these people recognize that if agencies are not getting credit for the events, they cannot continue to justify the expenditure of sponsoring BEADs. Additionally, the Corps and assisting groups have been willing to

sacrifice their recognition to help the states promote the Nongame checkoff.

Local communities are clearly demonstrating their support of BEADs for 1991. Because budgetary difficulties are restricting normal activities of Iowa's Nongame Program, local entities are raising money to pay for the live indoor program and are publicizing the event above and beyond government news releases and publications.

Future improvements could be made by developing a bald eagle teacher's guide and more raptor materials. Governments need to continue to clarify their existence and duties and strive for correct representation from the media. Governments also need to recognize the economic and noneconomic values of both game and nongame wildlife and teach local communities and a variety of target audiences about the positive benefits of all wildlife. Governments must act, not only as stewards of wildlife, but also as wildlife's biggest promoter.

BEADs provide a valuable positive pubic service. They directly reach 8,000 to 12,000 people each year at a relatively low government cost. They provide some gross economic benefits at a regional level and have attracted increasing community support. BEADs also join consumptive and nonconsumptive users and can help states understand and promote a diversity of wildlife values.

Acknowledgments.—We are grateful to the following for their assistance with BEADs events: Sue Clevenstine, Steve Dinsmore, Bruce Ehresman, John Holt, Sandy Howell, DeWaine Jackson, Keosippi Mall, Sue Laue, Lee County Conservation Board, Jim Mergen, Modern Woodmen of America, Randy Nyboer, Marilyn Pohorsky, Raptor Rehabilitation Project, Pat Schlarbaum, Mike Sweet, Lester Wadzinski, Susan White, Jay Zetterlund, and all who have ever worked and attended an event.

REFERENCES CITED

Babbie, E. R. 1982. Social research for consumers. Wadsworth Publ. Co., Belmont, Calif. Pp. 139–164.

Bart, J., D. Allee, and M. Richmond. 1979. Using economics in defense of wildlife. Wildl. Soc. Bull. 7:139–144.

Boyle, S. A., and F. B. Samson. 1985. Effects of nonconsumptive recreation on wildlife: a review. Wildl. Soc. Bull. 13:110–116.

Henderson, C. L. 1986. Interfacing with the public. Pages 137–142 *in* Management of Nongame Wildlife in the Midwest: a developing art.

Jackson, L. S. 1986. The bald eagle: sea bird of the Midwest. Iowa Dep. Nat. Resour. brochure, Des Moines.

Kruckenberg, L. L. 1988. "Wyoming's wildlife—worth the watching": management in transition. Trans. North Am. Wildl. and Nat. Resour. Conf. 53:424–430.

Powell, R. A. 1980. Comments on using economics in defense of wildlife: the value of wildlife and wilderness. Wildl. Soc. Bull. 8:79.

Salwasser, H., G. Contreras, M. Dombeck, and K. Siderits. 1989. A marketing approach to fish and wildlife program management. Trans. North Am. Wildl. and Nat. Resour. Conf. 54:261–270.

SAS Institute Inc. 1987. SAS Manual. SAS/GRAPH guide for personal computers, Version 6 ed. SAS Institute Inc., Cary, N.C. 534 pp.

Southern, W. E., and L. K. Southern. 1984a. Bald eagle habitat use in the vicinity of oak valley refuge, Hampton, Il. Pages 23–76 *in* Proc. Midwest Workshop on Bald Eagle Research and Management.

———, and ———. 1984b. Bald eagle management concerns and recommendations for the Mississippi River, locks and dams 14–15. Pages 106–113 *in* Proc. Midwest Workshop on Bald Eagle Research and Management.

Stalmaster, M. V., and J. R. Newman. 1978. Behavioral responses of wintering bald eagles to human activity. J. Wildl. Manage. 42:506–513.

Steinhoff, H. W. 1980. Analysis of major conceptual systems for understanding and measuring wildlife values. Inst. Ser. Rep. 1:11–21, Cent. for Assessment of Noncommodity Nat. Resour. Values.

USFWS. 1988a. 1985 national survey of fishing, hunting, and wildlife-associated recreation. U.S. Dep. of the Interior, Fish and Wildl. Serv., Washington, D.C. 167 pp.

———. 1988b. 1985 national survey of fishing, hunting, and wildlife-associated recreation—Iowa. U.S. Dep. of the Interior, Fish and Wildl. Serv., Washington, D.C. 81 pp.

Vickerman, S. 1988. Stimulating tourism and economic growth by featuring new wildlife recreation opportunities. Trans. North Am. Wildl. and Nat. Resour. Conf. 53:414–423.

Witter, D. J., J. D. Wilson, and G. T. Maupin. 1980. "Eagle Days" in Missouri: characteristics and enjoyment ratings of participants. Wildl. Soc. Bull. 8:64–65.

Florida's Cooperative Urban Wildlife Program

CRAIG HUEGEL, *Pinellas County Extension Office, 12175 - 125 St. N., Largo, FL 34644*

FRANK MAZZOTTI, *Broward County Extension Office, 3245 College Ave., Davie, FL 33314*

JOE SCHAEFER, *118 Newins-Ziegler Hall, University of Florida, Gainesville, FL 32611*

BRIAN MILLSAP, *Florida Game and Fresh Water Fish Commission, 620 S. Meridian, Tallahassee, FL 32301*

PROGRAM ORGANIZATION

On 6 January 1986, the Florida Game and Fresh Water Fish Commission (GFC) and the University of Florida signed a Cooperative Agreement to develop and implement an urban wildlife management program. This Cooperative Urban Wildlife Program (CUWP) is administered through the Department of Wildlife and Range Sciences, School of Forest Resources and Conservation, within the Institute of Food and Agricultural Sciences (IFAS).

Funding for the CUWP comes largely from the GFC Nongame Wildlife Program. It was envisioned that CUWP direction would enhance and supplement the Nongame Wildlife Program, and that urban wildlife programs would be developed through the cooperative efforts of both agencies.

Florida's CUWP is a unique cooperative program between a state fish and wildlife agency and a state land-grant university. As such, it can serve as a model for other states seeking to develop an academically administered urban wildlife program.

Direction was given to the CUWP through a Cooperative Agreement written by staff of the GFC and the University of Florida. To quote from the Agreement, the purpose of the CUWP is "to provide for active cooperation in development and implementation of an urban wildlife program, a component of the Florida Nongame Wildlife Program, to increase the appreciation of and enhance urban wildlife resources in Florida's urban environments through management, education and applied research."

Objectives

The objectives for the CUWP also were stated clearly in the Cooperative Agreement. It states,

"Urban environments are to be viewed as unique ecological systems that are inhabited, from the human perspective, by both desirable and undesirable wildlife species. Consequently, programming efforts must consider enhancement (proactive) and control (reactive) measures. Proactive programming, however, should outweigh reactive programming. Program objectives are:

1. To develop cooperative planning, technology transfer and educational programs to enhance nongame wildlife resources and habitats in urban settings.

   This shall include, but not be limited to: (a) development and distribution of methods and materials necessary to enhance urban wildlife habitats in areas such as private residences, green belts, stormwater retention areas, neighborhoods and entire urban communities; (b) development and promotion of programs instructing citizens on ways to enhance urban habitats for wildlife; and (c) providing technical guidance and input on enhancing urban wildlife habitats and special wildlife planning considerations to local governments, planning units, recreation departments, developers, and civic groups.

2. To increase public awareness, appreciation and knowledge of urban wildlife, and increase recreational opportunities associated with urban wildlife.

   This shall include, but not be limited to: (a) development and distribution of materials and programs designed to educate the public about urban wildlife and its value; (b) development of programs that encourage and assist local governments, nature centers, natural history museums, civic groups, and private institutions in planning and implementing wildlife-related recreational opportunities such as wild-

Wildlife Conservation in Metropolitan Environments. NIUW Symp. Ser. 2, L.W. Adams and D.L. Leedy, eds. Published by Natl. Inst. for Urban Wildl., 10921 Trotting Ridge Way, Columbia, MD 21044, USA, 1991.

life tours, field trips, wildlife displays and exhibits, wildlife viewing and photography areas, interpretive nature centers and nature trails; and (c) development and distribution of materials that instruct property owners on methods to attract and observe wildlife near their homes or properties.

3. To develop and transfer information on nuisance wildlife and animal damage control in urban areas.

This shall include, but not be limited to: (a) development and distribution of materials and services to assist the public in reducing or avoiding problems caused by wildlife in urban areas; (b) development of materials and services that will educate the public about potentially dangerous wildlife and wildlife diseases, and problems associated with exotic plants and animals; (c) development of materials and services that reduce unreasonable public fears and misconceptions about wildlife; and (d) provide technical guidance to community planners and developers on design features that will minimize wildlife-related problems.

4. To provide liaison and cooperation in urban wildlife programming with local, state and federal governments and agencies, private businesses, academic institutions, conservation organizations and civic groups.

This shall include, but not be limited to: (a) programming to encourage public understanding of nongame wildlife in urban areas; (b) coordinating urban wildlife programs with local, state and federal governments and agencies, institutions, businesses, and conservation and civic groups, especially where volunteer participation is required to accomplish urban wildlife program objectives; and (c) coordinating urban wildlife programming with other agencies (especially the Department of Natural Resources) involved with the Nongame Wildlife Program.

5. To monitor selected urban wildlife species and habitats consistent with goals established by the GFC Nongame Wildlife Program.

This shall include, but not be limited to, providing support or organizing volunteer participation for surveys of selected wildlife species or taxa and their habitats within urban areas.

Achievement of program objectives will center on three major methodologies: cooperative planning, technology transfer, and education. These three methodologies are principal program elements of the Florida Cooperative Extension Service and are effected through

city and county commissions, planning commissions, developers, civic groups, conservation groups, educational institutions, and resource agencies."

Staffing

The CUWP became operational with the hiring of three urban wildlife specialists in the spring of 1987. One specialist is located in the Department of Wildlife and Range Sciences at Gainesville, and the other two are housed in County Cooperative Extension offices in different regions of the State. Because Florida's wildlife, wildlife habitats, and urban wildlife issues differ so greatly geographically, this arrangement allows the specialists to develop regional programs that are more responsive to the needs of the resource and local clientele, and also facilitates direct interaction between CUWP staff and local clientele. Coordination for statewide programming efforts is done through cooperative planning by all three specialists.

PROGRAM DIRECTION

Program direction for the CUWP was defined after the three urban wildlife specialists were hired. The nominative group technique was used with the GFC Nongame Program staff, the Nongame Wildlife Program Advisory Council, and the faculty of the Wildlife and Range Sciences Department. Each was asked to list, by major importance, the issues affecting wildlife in Florida. Results of these three exercises were then used to develop a Strategic Plan to guide the overall course of the CUWP.

The CUWP operates with many levels of supervision and coordination. As employees of the Department of Wildlife and Range Sciences, the three urban wildlife specialists are responsible directly to the Department Chair. The Chair oversees the overall direction of the program and meets with the specialists on a regular basis to review progress. Also, as principal investigator on the Cooperative Agreement, the Department Chair serves as liaison to the GFC through the Nongame Program Section Supervisor.

The three urban wildlife specialists essentially operate on two levels. At the regional level, extension and research programs are determined independently. Coordination among the specialists for these areas is made when warranted, but in most cases, regional extension activities and research emphases reflect individual expertise, interests, and client needs.

At the statewide level, programs are developed and implemented through coordinated planning efforts of all three specialists. Specialists meet annually to produce an operational plan for the coming fiscal year. Operational plans outline time budgets for all activities of the CUWP, including research and publications, and statewide and regional extension programs. Major responsibility for different statewide programs is assigned equally among the specialists. These programs include production of a wildlife resources handbook, wildlife habitat program, wildlife videos, news releases, and in-service training.

Coordination of the CUWP with GFC also is accomplished on several levels. The annual operational plan is sent by the CUWP to GFC for input and approval. Funding for the CUWP is contingent on GFC's approval of this plan. The operational plan allows GFC to critically review proposed programs. Through this procedure, the operational plan can become a meaningful and mutually acceptable guideline for the following year.

GFC reviews CUWP progress through quarterly and annual reports of CUWP activities. Quarterly reports provide detailed information on the activities of each urban wildlife specialist as they relate to the operational plan. Regional and statewide extension programs are reported, as are research programs that are urban-related. During the fourth quarter, an annual report is sent to GFC that summarizes the activities, progress, and achievements of the CUWP during the previous fiscal year. The annual report allows the GFC to compare actual progress and activities against those originally proposed in the operational plan. This provides a mechanism to objectively evaluate the program.

PROGRAM SUCCESSES AND PROBLEMS

The CUWP has had both successes and problems. We have tried to capitalize on the successes over the past 3 years and to resolve the problems. The process of making the CUWP satisfactory to all cooperating parties has taken time and effort.

Successes

The CUWP's structure is quite effective in responding to regional issues. By having the program based in three separate areas of the State, the urban wildlife specialists can better develop regional contacts, understand regional issues, and become involved in regional concerns that require their expertise. This is especially important in a diverse state like Florida where wildlife and growth management issues change dramatically on a regional basis.

The CUWP's location within IFAS and the Cooperative Extension Service allows the program to take advantage of an information dissemination system that is quite effective at reaching the public statewide. Because the Cooperative Extension Service has offices in each county, staffed by agents who work with public education, the CUWP has an established network to get timely information of local interest to the public.

The structure of the CUWP also is successful because it takes advantage of facilities and equipment available through both the University of Florida and the GFC. For example, monies for publications have been limited in the State University System, but less so at GFC. The CUWP has been able to print many publications for the public through the GFC that would have otherwise been impossi-

ble to print. Conversely, the GFC has not yet been able to take advantage of television as a major educational tool, although a marketing study (Montgomery Research Consultants 1988) funded by the Nongame Wildlife Program determined that this was the most effective educational outlet in Florida. Video studios located in IFAS have been used by the CUWP to produce numerous television programs, including seven, 30-minute videos that are aired in central Florida and available statewide by request.

Another advantage of our program structure is the ability of the CUWP and GFC to augment and complement each other's program efforts. Because the urban component is outside the structure of the state wildlife agency system, it can approach wildlife concerns differently and reach a different clientele. But, because of the cooperative nature of the program, the CUWP can take advantage of regional biologists and education specialists of GFC when this approach is warranted.

Problems

Although the CUWP has produced a number of significant results, problems have arisen because of differing philosophies between the CUWP and GFC regarding program direction and product expectations. Program objectives are defined by the Cooperative Agreement, but this document is broad-reaching in terms of direction-setting and does not weigh the relative importance of the five separate objectives. For example, GFC expected that CUWP efforts would significantly reduce their need to address urban nuisance wildlife issues. A reduction of GFC staff time addressing this issue was not apparent, although attention was given to nuisance wildlife programming by CUWP staff. Moreover, the CUWP staff spent a greater percentage of time working on habitat loss issues than GFC expected. These misunderstandings have caused tension in the early developmental stages of the CUWP, but are being resolved by better defining lines of communication, by increasing communication efforts, and by better defining the role of the annual operational plan in directing activities and evaluating program success.

Coordination of communication also has been a source of difficulty. The CUWP staff members are separated geographically, as is the University of Florida, from GFC headquarters. Communication between the groups was not well-coordinated initially and products produced by the CUWP staff were not always adequately routed among all parties. All of this made it difficult to determine the nature, number, and quality of the products produced by CUWP staff. Many of these problems are being resolved by very clearly defining lines of communication and establishing procedures to account for all products delivered to the GFC.

Problems in program direction have arisen because of differing definitions of "urban." To emphasize proactive programming, the CUWP staff interpreted urban as both urban *and* urbanizing, whereas GFC intended activities to be confined to urban areas and those publics within defined urban boundaries. Better understanding of these types of issues and the subtle differences that exist between organizations need to be resolved through continued communication for an urban wildlife program to achieve its goals.

Coordinating paperwork is another problem in such an arrangement. Besides the reports for GFC already discussed, the CUWP staff also has an equal number of reports required by IFAS and the University. Because every group wants information reported in its own style and format, this requires duplication of effort. Efforts to reduce this while maintaining adequate communication should be explored in the initial stages of program development.

A final concern is the potential for duplication of program effort. For example, the CUWP staff is very involved in public education, but the Nongame Wildlife Program also has nongame education specialists. The CUWP staff works extensively in wildlife and growth management concerns, but the GFC Office of Environmental Services also has staff to address these issues. Duplication of effort is sometimes difficult to avoid because there are no readily apparent lines dividing "urban" from "non-urban" wildlife issues. Better communication should enable us to avoid serious duplication of effort.

REFERENCES CITED

Montgomery Research Consultants, Inc. 1988. Specific educational strategies for Florida's nongame wildlife program. Final Rep. Fla. Game and Fresh Water Fish Comm., Tallahassee. 161 pp.

VI.

Planning for Natural Areas in the Portland, Oregon— Vancouver, Washington Metropolitan Region

Chair: JOSEPH PORACSKY, *Associate Professor, Portland State University, Portland, Oregon*

Cochair: MICHAEL C. HOUCK, *Urban Naturalist, Audubon Society of Portland, Portland, Oregon*

Metropolitan Wildlife Refuge System: A Strategy For Regional Natural Resource Planning

Michael C. Houck, *Audubon Society of Portland, 5151 NW Cornell Road, Portland, OR 97210*

INTRODUCTION

In 1982, the Audubon Society of Portland (PAS) initiated its "Urban Naturalist" program to encourage planning for urban wildlife and wildlife habitat in the Portland-Vancouver metropolitan region. Through this program PAS has worked with local elected officials, the planning community, and citizens to protect and manage rapidly diminishing urban wildlife habitats.

The transition of the Urban Naturalist program to a proposed region-wide Metropolitan Wildlife Refuge System has been prompted by a continued, and accelerated, loss of wildlife habitat and concern on the part of the public that these habitat losses have resulted in a decreased index of "livability" throughout the region.

It also has been recognized that several historic documents provide the basis for developing a local strategy to promote a regional natural areas program. The most notable proposals for local and regional planning were (Houck 1989):

1. A report to the Portland park board by Frederick Law Olmsted, Jr., and John Charles Olmsted.
2. Lewis Mumford's 1938 address to the City Club of Portland.
3. The Columbia Region Association of Governments (CRAG) 1971 open space and park planning document, "Proposals to the Portland-Vancouver Community for a Metropolitan Park and Open Space System."

Nationally, several conference proceedings also have provided invaluable technical and philosophical bases for proposing a Metropolitan Wildlife Refuge System (Noyes and Progulske 1974, Stenberg and Shaw 1986, and Adams and Leedy 1987).

International models also have been utilized to generate interest at the local level for regional natural resource planning. Of particular importance is Dr. David Goode, Director of the London Ecology Unit in London, England, who has participated in several key Portland area workshops and meetings. Dr. Goode's 1989 keynote address at the Country In The City II symposium "Parks and Natural Resources in the Urban Environment" was pivotal in garnering support within the political arena in Portland and Vancouver. Goode's book, *Wild In London*, and the London Ecology Unit's series of planning handbooks on inventory techniques, and habitat creation and management have provided an international context for systematizing a regional natural areas program.

HISTORICAL BACKGROUND

The Olmsted Vision

The Olmsted brothers, Frederick Law, Jr. and John Charles, first proposed a comprehensive and interconnected system of parks for Portland, Oregon in their report to the Portland Park Board. Although the Olmsteds never referred specifically to urban fish and wildlife habitat, it was clear that their intent was to incorporate natural areas and wildlife habitat as an integral component of the urban landscape.

The Olmsteds also presaged recent national trends toward a multiobjective management strategy for urban stream and river corridors and wetlands. They commented specifically on the preferred future for Johnson Creek in southeast Portland, and other urban stream corridors:

> "economy in municipal development may be effected by laying out parkways and parks, while land is cheap, so as to embrace streams . . . Thus streams which would otherwise become nuisances that would some day have to be put in large underground conduits at enormous expense, may be made the occasion for delightful pleasure grounds or attractive parkways. Such improvements add greatly to the value of adjoining properties . . ." (Olmsted and Olmsted 1903).

This statement anticipated current multi-agency efforts to address flooding and water quality initiatives throughout the Portland-Vancouver region.

Wildlife Conservation in Metropolitan Environments. NIUW Symp. Ser. 2, L.W. Adams and D.L. Leedy, eds. Published by Natl. Inst. for Urban Wildl., 10921 Trotting Ridge Way, Columbia, MD 21044, USA, 1991.

Lewis Mumford's Regional View

It was Lewis Mumford who first advocated a natural resource plan that would link the Portland and Vancouver metropolitan areas. In his address to the City Club of Portland, Mumford (1938) stated,

"People who pay more attention to abstract figures than to realities are accustomed to look upon a river (the Columbia River) as a dividing line . . . rivers are dividing lines from only one point of view: military attack. From every other point of view the river . . . as a whole is a unit."

Modern Day Regionalism, The Urban Outdoors

The Columbia Region Association of Governments (CRAG) produced the first modern proposal to establish a regional natural areas program. CRAG's 1971 report was the first government document that promoted the protection and management of wildlife habitat as an important planning objective in the urban and urbanizing environment (Columbia Region Association of Governments 1971).

Unfortunately, the Olmsteds, Mumford, and the CRAG study were largely ignored by local planners with respect to urban natural resources. The most notable exception is the Olmsteds' recommendation for an interconnected system of parks. A local group, the 40-Mile Loop Land Trust, and park planners expanded the original Olmsted vision into a 224-km hiking-bicycling trail that links the county's most significant natural areas.

It was not until the late 1980's, however, that serious attention was given to identifying, protecting, and managing urban wildlife habitat and natural areas. PAS's proposed Metropolitan Wildlife Refuge System has been one of several catalysts in the effort to focus on urban habitats.

KEY ELEMENTS OF THE REFUGE SYSTEM

The following are some of the key elements that the Metropolitan Wildlife Refuge System project has employed in advocating a comprehensive regional natural areas program.

Concept Map

Although no formalized system exists at this time, a Metropolitan Wildlife Refuge System concept map has been a primary basis for discussion of urban wildlife habitat management. It also has provided the context to promote the management of interconnected ecosystems and wildlife corridors.

Highly Publicized Animals

In some cases the project has focused on spectacular or highly publicized animals as a tool to achieve habitat protection strategies. Two successful efforts have involved the great blue heron (*Ardea herodias*) and Chinook salmon (*Oncorhynchus tshawytscha*).

Great Blue Heron.—PAS, working with local neighborhood groups, park bureau staff, and members of Portland's city council adopted the great blue heron as Portland's official city bird in 1986. The city council's proclamation read, in part:

"Whereas Portland is one of a select few cities that can boast two active Great Blue Heron rookeries . . . (and we) enjoy the opportunity to observe these Heron rookeries within minutes of downtown . . . ; in honor of its enormous contribution to our quality of life, the Great Blue Heron (*Ardea herodias*) is hereby honored with the title of Portland City Bird."

The publicity associated with this action has contributed to the protection of specific wetland sites through subsequent city council decisions—most notably wetlands adjacent to north Portland's West Delta Golf Course, which was later renamed Heron Lakes Golf Course.

Chinook Salmon.—Impacts on fall Chinook salmon spawning areas by fishing activities in the lower Sandy River (35 km east of downtown Portland) prompted an educational program that was initiated by Multnomah County Parks, Oregon Trout, and PAS in 1984. What began as an informal walk with 40 participants to educate the fishing and non-fishing public about salmon spawning beds in the Sandy River has grown to become a northwest environmental education event that attracted over 7500 participants at the 1989 weekend festival.

The festival also has resulted in Oregon Fish and Wildlife Commission action to close the lower Sandy River fall Chinook redds to fishing within the county park.

Threatened and Endangered Species

Wintering bald eagles (*Haliaeetus leucocephalus*) as well as flocks of dusky Canada goose (*Branta canadensis*) and mixed flocks of trumpeter swan (*Cygnus buccinator*) and tundra swan (*C. columbianus*) provide spectacular winter wildlife viewing opportunities for a burgeoning urban population 16 km from downtown Portland and immediately across the Columbia River from Vancouver, Washington. The increased interest in wildlife viewing and concomitant decline in hunting license applications is prompting the Oregon Department of Fish and Wildlife to address nonconsumptive wildlife interests and expand its non-game wildlife program.

Valuable Habitats

Wetlands.—PAS's primary focus for its land use planning efforts in the Portland metropolitan area has been on wetland habitats. Audubon and other conservation groups, such as The Wetlands Conservancy and 1000 Friends of Oregon, have chosen this focus, in large part, because existing federal and state regulations can be utilized to bolster local efforts to identify and afford wetlands some level of protection. The Metropolitan Wildlife Refuge System also has established wetlands and riparian habitats as a high priority due to their relative scarcity (Poracsky 1991) and tremendous historic losses (Oregon Natural Resources Council 1986–87).

Much attention has been focused on bringing wetland areas into public ownership and for development of management plans to ensure their long-term viability. Elements of the Metropolitan Wildlife Refuge System that fall into this category include Smith and Bybee Lakes, an 800-ha wetland-riparian-open water habitat, which will soon become Portland's newest natural park (City of Portland 1990a). In another city of Portland initiative, 64 ha Oaks Bottom Wildlife Refuge was dedicated as Portland's first official wildlife refuge in 1989.

Multnomah County dedicated Beggars Tick Marsh, named for the annual composite Bidens (*Bidens frondosa*), as an 8-ha urban wildlife refuge in April of 1990. This was the first officially designated wildlife refuge within the county park system and was specifically nominated as an element in the Metropolitan Wildlife Refuge System.

To the west of Portland, the City of Hillsboro and the Hillsboro Chamber of Commerce have begun plans for the 1200 ha Jackson Bottom Wildlife Preserve, which is situated on the Tualatin River floodplain. The city, Chamber of Commerce, Oregon Department of Fish and Wildlife, and a coalition of other interest groups have installed a wildlife viewing platform and developed plans for the Kingfisher Trail, a river and wetland access trail. The local Friends of Jackson Bottom have initiated a wetland education program.

Riparian Areas.—One of the most important objectives of the Metropolitan Wildlife Refuge System is the protection and management of urban stream and river corridors and greenways. The Refuge System project is promoting, and is itself being incorporated into, programs within the City of Portland's Clean Rivers Program (City of Portland 1990b) and Washington County's Tualatin River Surface Water Management Project (Unified Sewerage Agency 1990). Both of these projects are developing multi-objective management strategies that recognize the importance of wetland and riparian wildlife habitat in meeting clean water and flood abatement objectives. Wildlife viewing also will be an important element of these projects.

Corporate Amenity Values

Local corporations are recognizing the value of having wildlife in their immediate vicinity. Koll Creekside Marsh in Beaverton, Oregon is one example of wetland and stream protection that has led to the protection of significant urban wetland habitat. What was proposed to become wetland fill, through the land use and regulatory processes, was reduced significantly and the entire wetland area was then donated to the Tualatin Hills Park and Recreation District. Through this effort, a relatively pristine 8-ha emergent wetland was protected and recognized as an amenity for adjacent high

technology developments. Recently, Mentor Graphics, a local computer software firm, hired consultants to create similar habitat at their new corporate headquarters.

Citizen Amenity Values

Finally, the Metropolitan Wildlife Refuge System has sought to protect and enhance the sense of "livability" within the Portland-Vancouver metropolitan region. A recent poll indicated that 81% of the region's residents would be willing to "Support a bond measure to acquire and protect urban natural areas to achieve long-term environmental balance in the Portland metropolitan area" (Market Trends 1990).

This response is consistent with recent polls from other west coast communities and with passage of numerous regional bond measures such as the $225 million East Bay Regional Park District AAA measure in the fall of 1989. Several local levies, with funds earmarked for natural area and wildlife habitat acquisition and management, were passed by Portland metropolitan voters in the 6 November 1990 elections as well. This was the first time that funds have been specifically earmarked for urban wildlife habitat acquisition in the three county area in Oregon.

Citizens want to experience wildlife in their own backyards. The knowledge that native cutthroat trout (*Oncorhynchus clarki*) occur, even in degraded urban streams, has been a major factor in generating public support and work to protect streams in the Portland-Vancouver region.

The presence of black bear (*Ursus americanus*), pileated woodpecker (*Dryocopus pileatus*), and elk (*Cervus elaphus*) in 2000-ha Forest Park, immediately adjacent to Portland's densest residential neighborhood, is an amenity valued by all Portland-Vancouver metropolitan residents. Urbanites in the Portland-Vancouver region fear a loss of "sense of place," which is defined in large part by the existence of wildlife and wildlife habitat. The public's high regard for maintaining a sense of place (Hiss 1990) is a powerful factor in initiatives to protect urban wildlife habitat and open spaces.

A REGIONAL PLANNING APPROACH FOR URBAN WILDLIFE

Although Oregon enjoys a national reputation for its land use planning program and has become a model for other states, its state-wide land use program has focused primarily on protection of rural farm and forest land and coastal resources. Even though this program has been in existence since 1973, planning for protection of urban wildlife habitats was not aggressively pursued in the Portland metropolitan region until the late 1980's (Houck 1986, 1987).

There are several deficiencies in Oregon's planning process that have resulted in inadequate protection of individual habitat sites and fragmentation of wildlife corridors on a regional basis (Rogers and Houck 1984, Oregon Natural Resources Council 1986–87, Ketcham 1988, Lev and Houck 1988). Some contributing factors to a general lack of urban wildlife habitat protection include:

1. Lack of staff expertise and financial resources.
2. Refusal of some local jurisdictions to place a high priority on natural resource protection.
3. Inadequate natural resource management experience.
4. Lack of adequate inventories for wildlife habitat.
5. Lack of formal programs to manage natural resources that cross political boundaries.
6. Inconsistency among jurisdictions.

Recently, however, progress has been made within the Portland-Vancouver metropolitan region to remedy some of these deficiencies. For example, the City of Portland's Bureau of Planning has completed a comprehensive inventory of wetland and riparian habitats throughout the Columbia Corridor in north and northeast Portland (City of Portland 1989).

The Planning Bureau also has produced a model management plan for 800 ha of wetland and open water habitats in the Smith and Bybee Lakes region of north Portland (City of Portland 1990a). The most recent Portland Planning efforts include a management plan that protects an entire watershed within Forest Park (City of Portland 1990c) and along one of the metropolitan area's last free flowing streams, Johnson Creek (City of Portland 1990d).

Attempts to pass an effective state-wide land use program in the state of Washington failed during November, 1990 elections.

Metropolitan Greenspaces Program

Beginning in 1988, it was recognized that the Metropolitan Wildlife Refuge System was inadequate to address all of the issues of concern to the public—the loss of open space; lack of a coordinated recreational trails system; lack of an integrated, regional environmental education program; and the absence of a regional land acquisition strategy.

Coincidentally, the regional planning body for Oregon's three metropolitan counties, the Metropolitan Service District (Metro) had initiated a regional park study at this time (Metropolitan Service District 1989). Metro's study focused primarily on active recreation (swimming centers, tennis courts, soccer and ball fields). In early 1989, a critical mass of natural area and recreational trail advocates, Metro staff and a supportive Metropolitan Service District Council redefined the project as a regional natural areas program.

The institution of the Metropolitan Greenspaces Program through a regional planning entity holds promise to assist with the local planning process. However, even with improved local planning efforts, truly regional natural resources, especially riparian corridors and other large, multi-jurisdictional wildlife habitats, cannot be adequately protected and managed without cooperative, regional planning (Collins 1990).

The Metropolitan Greenspaces Program has already achieved several notable results (presented below) that are consistent with, and add to, the Metropolitan Wildlife Refuge System's objectives:

Comprehensive Regional Habitat Mapping.—The Metropolitan Greenspaces Program has produced consistent, uniform coverage of the four-county Portland-Vancouver metropolitan region through the use of color infrared photography. This has allowed, for the first time in the region, comprehensive mapping of all remaining natural areas (Poracsky 1991). The mapping and field inventory (Lev and Sharp 1991) have been coordinated through Portland State University's Geography Department. The involvement of Portland State University in the Metropolitan Greenspaces Program is an essential element of providing invaluable technical assistance to the program.

Interjurisdictional Cooperation.—The Metropolitan Greenspaces Program has generated unprecedented cooperation among local jurisdictions and has involved the public in greater numbers than in any previous planning effort. At this time, 16 cities, two counties, and numerous non-profit organizations, neighborhood groups, and special districts have passed a resolution calling for the institution of a regional natural areas project as embodied in the Metropolitan Greenspaces Program (Metropolitan Service District 1990).

Institutionalization of Urban Wildlife Habitat Protection.—There are many indications that concern for urban wildlife habitat is being institutionalized in new local, state, and federal programs. The Oregon Department of Fish and Wildlife (ODFW) has hired its first urban biologist for the state and the agency's Nongame Wildlife Management Plan specifically addresses urban wildlife habitat protection and management as a critical element of its nongame strategy (Marshall 1986). This action is due in large part to the increased public awareness about, and demand for, urban wildlife programs.

The Portland Bureau of Parks and Recreation recently created an urban natural resources position and Multnomah County has instituted a Trust Fund that dedicates 50% of the sale of unrestricted properties for the acquisition and management of urban natural areas.

CONCLUSION

It has taken 87 years for Portland-Vancouver metropolitan planning agencies to act on the Olmsted vision as outlined in their proposals for a comprehensive and interconnected park system. It has taken 52 years to begin incorporating the bi-state regional perspective espoused by Lewis Mumford in 1938 and it has been 19 since efforts to specifically incorporate concern for urban wildlife habitat was first recommended by the Columbia Region Association of Governments in 1971. Accelerated region-wide population growth and fears about loss of livability have brought these early visions to the fore. An increased sense of urgency, local initiatives such as the 40-Mile Loop and other regional trail projects, the Metropolitan Wildlife Refuge System, a proliferation of local neighborhood initiatives, and the newly emerging Metropolitan Greenspaces Program all contribute to a renewed dedication to ensure that plans for "A cooperative regional system of natural areas, open space trails and greenways for wildlife and people" are realized.

Acknowledgments.—Thanks go to the Oregon Department of Fish and Wildlife's nongame checkoff program for funding early (1982–1987) urban wildlife habitat inventories and to the Meyer Charitable Trust, which in 1989, provided a $116,000 3-year challenge grant to get the Metropolitan Wildlife Refuge System off and running. PAS deserves much credit for supporting an urban-oriented wildlife habitat program when so many pressing forest, coastal, and desert issues exist. The PAS board of directors has made a firm commitment to addressing important wildlife habitat issues in our own backyard, where we can provide environmental education to a growing urban population. It is difficult to imagine that we would have generated the local enthusiasm for the project without the unselfish support in the form of energy, expertise, and enthusiasm that we have received from Dr. David Goode, Director of the London Ecology Unit and from the East Bay Regional Park District board and staff.

REFERENCES CITED

Adams, L. W., and D. L. Leedy, eds. 1987. Integrating man and nature in the metropolitan environment. Natl. Inst. for Urban Wildl., Columbia, Md. 249 pp.

City of Portland. 1989. Columbia corridor: inventory of wetlands, water bodies, and wildlife habitat areas. Bur. of Planning, Portland, Oreg. 78 pp.

_____ . 1990a. Natural resources management plan for Smith and Bybee Lakes. Bur. of Planning, Portland, Oreg. 70 pp.

_____ . 1990b. Bureau of Environmental Service's clean rivers program. Bur. of Environ. Serv., Portland, Oreg. 12 pp.

_____ . 1990c. Balch Creek watershed protection plan: inventory, analysis and regulations for fish and wildlife habitats, natural areas, open space, water bodies and wetlands. Bur. of Planning, Portland, Oreg. 158 pp.

_____ . 1990d. Johnson Creek corridor plan district including: Johnson Creek, Reed Lake, Crystal Springs, Powell Butte, and Mt. Scott areas. Bur. of Planning, Portland, Oreg. 158 pp.

Collins, C. 1990. The greening of Portland, can nature survive the northwest's urban boom? The Sunday Oregonian, Northwest Magazine, August 26, pp. 10–17.

Columbia Region Association of Governments. 1971. Proposals

to the Portland-Vancouver community for a metropolitan park and open space system. The Urban Outdoors. 52 pp.

Hiss, T. 1990. The experience of place. Alfred A. Knopf, New York, N.Y. 226 pp.

Houck, M. C. 1986. Urban wildlife habitat inventory and urban wildlife education programs in Portland, Oregon. Pages 136–143 *in* K. Stenberg and W.W. Shaw, eds. Wildlife conservation and new residential developments. School of Renewable Nat. Resour., Univ. of Arizona, Tucson.

_____ . 1987. Urban wildlife habitat inventory: the Willamette River greenway, Portland, Oregon. Pages 47–51 *in* L.W. Adams and D.L. Leedy, eds. Integrating man and nature in the metropolitan environment. Natl. Inst. for Urban Wildl., Columbia, Md.

_____ . 1989. Protecting our urban wild lands: renewing a vision. City Club of Portland, Oreg., Unpub. Address, 14 pp. (Typescript).

Ketcham, P. K. 1988. Status of wetland planning in Oregon. Oregon Planning Inst., Bur. of Gov. Res. and Serv., Univ. of Oregon, Eugene. 21 pp.

Lev, E., and M. C. Houck 1988. Planning for urban wildlife in metropolitan Portland, Oregon. Women in Nat. Resour. 9:23–26.

Lev, E., and L. Sharp. 1991. The Portland-Vancouver natural areas inventory: field surveys and preliminary wildlife data. (Published elsewhere in this volume.)

Market Trends. 1990. Public opinion survey. Portland, Oreg.

Marshall, D. B. 1986. Oregon nongame wildlife management plan. Oreg. Dep. of Fish and Wildl., Portland. 334 pp.

Metropolitan Service District. 1989. Metro recreation resource study, Portland, Oreg., Feb., 51 pp.

_____ . 1990. Work plan, metropolitan greenspaces program, a cooperative regional system of natural areas, open spaces, trails and greenways for wildlife and people (Draft). Portland, Oreg. 17 pp.

Mumford, L. 1938. Regional planning in the Pacific Northwest. Northwest Reg. Counc., Portland, Oreg. Unpub. Rep.

Noyes, J. H., and D. R. Progulske, eds. 1974. Wildlife in an urbanizing environment. Planning and Resour. Dev. Ser. No. 28, Mass. Coop. Ext. Serv., Amherst. 182 pp.

Olmsted, F. L., Jr., and J. C. Olmsted. 1903. Report of the Park Board, Portland, Oregon. Unpub. Rep. 75 pp.

Oregon Natural Resources Council. 1986–87. Our vanishing wetlands. Wild Oreg., Vol. 13, 32 pp.

Poracsky, J. 1991. The Portland-Vancouver natural areas inventory: photo interpretation and mapping. (Published elsewhere in this volume.)

Rogers, R. T., and M. C. Houck. 1984. Wetlands: dirt cheap and disappearing. Landmark 1:12–19.

Stenberg, K., and W. Shaw, eds. 1986. Wildlife conservation and new residential developments. School of Renewable Nat. Resour., Univ. of Arizona, Tucson. 203 pp.

Unified Sewerage Agency. 1990. The urban area surface water management plan of Washington County. Unified Sewerage Agency, Hillsboro, Oreg. 350 pp.

The Portland-Vancouver Natural Areas Inventory: Photo Interpretation and Mapping

Joseph Poracsky, *Geography Department, Portland State University, Portland, OR 97207-0751*

INTRODUCTION

The key to maintaining and restoring populations of wildlife in urban areas is in retention and enhancement of the vegetated habitats necessary for their support. As interest in urban wildlife expands, there is a growing need for baseline data on urban natural areas. Without information on the extent and character of available habitat, efforts to identify areas for preservation or habitat enhancement run the risk of being haphazard and incomplete.

There have been natural areas inventories produced for a variety of places. In each case, the methodologies have differed, reflecting differences in goals, available data sources, budget constraints, and definitions of natural areas (e.g., CLEARS 1987, Matthews et al. 1988, Pryde 1988, Sukopp and Weiler 1988, Merchant and Dillworth 1989).

Early in 1989, a natural areas inventory and analysis project was initiated for the Portland, Oregon-Vancouver, Washington metropolitan region. The immediate goal of the project was completion of an inventory that would produce both a map of several categories of natural areas and a detailed set of field data about a sample of the areas. Through a subsequent process of analysis and evaluation, the inventory data will be used to identify a subset of the natural areas that constitutes an ecologically viable interconnected system. This paper presents a summary of the project background and goals, focussing on the inventory process and the details of the mapping portion.

BACKGROUND TO THE STUDY

Region Description

The Portland-Vancouver metropolitan region lies at the confluence of the Columbia and Willamette Rivers. Politically it includes parts of four counties in two states: Clackamas, Multnomah and Washington Counties in Oregon, and Clark County in Washington. Together these four counties encompass 9,580 km². The landscape varies from river valley and flood plain to steeply rising hills to rolling terrain broken by isolated hills. The region has a modified west coast marine climate, with wet, mild winters and clear, dry summers (Johnson 1987). The native vegetation in the higher elevations was western hemlock (*Tsuga heterophyla*) forest and, in the valley areas, a sub-climax community of *Pinus-Quercus-Pseudotsuga* that was heavily influenced by the activities of pre-settlement Indians (Franklin and Dyrness 1973).

During the past 150 years, the ecological character of the metropolitan region has undergone major transformations as a result of intensive agricultural development, timber harvesting, and urbanization. These transformations have included removal of native vegetation, introduction of alien vegetation species, stream modification, and wetland filling, all of which have contributed to the loss of wildlife habitat. The result is that wildlife abundance in the region is greatly reduced from former levels.

Recent Local Interest in Natural Areas

In 1989, the Metropolitan Service District (Metro), a regional government agency encompassing the urbanized portions of the three Oregon counties that comprise metropolitan Portland, completed a study of parks in the Metro region. One of the study's conclusions was identification of the need for the "cataloging and evaluation of existing natural areas throughout the metropolitan area" (Metro 1989a). To indicate the pattern of existing natural areas, the study produced a very generalized map of natural areas, using high altitude aerial photography taken in 1980 (Metro 1989b). Despite the relatively small scale of the source photography, the 9-year-old date of the photography, and the highly generalized character of the portrayal, the map succeeded in capturing the attention of a number of people.

The appearance of this natural areas map and the recommendation for further study of natural areas coincided with two other related activities. The first activity was the effort to develop a trail system in the metropolitan area. Originally proposed by the Olmsteds in 1903, the trail idea was revived several years ago and is being implemented by

Wildlife Conservation in Metropolitan Environments. NIUW Symp. Ser. 2, L.W. Adams and D.L. Leedy, eds. Published by Natl. Inst. for Urban Wildl., 10921 Trotting Ridge Way, Columbia, MD 21044, USA, 1991.

the 40 Mile Loop Land Trust, a local non-profit group. The second activity was a proposal to establish a Metropolitan Wildlife Refuge System, a composite of already-protected and as-yet-unprotected natural areas in the metropolitan region that would be connected by a system of greenways and riparian corridors (Houck 1988). The regional, rather than local, approach and the focus on wildlife and habitat potential as a means of gauging the quality of urban natural areas served to make the refuge system proposal an attractive idea.

The fortuitous combination of the regional parks study recommendations and map, the on-going 40 Mile Loop efforts, and the Metropolitan Wildlife Refuge System proposal, along with some strong public lobbying efforts, had the important effect of focussing interest on the viability of the concept of a regional system of natural areas. As a result, Metro's Park and Natural Areas Advisory Group decided to initiate a detailed study of natural areas and to refocus their activities from developed parks to natural areas and issues of natural areas protection.

The Metro-coordinated effort has been joined by several non-Metro jurisdictions in Oregon and by Clark County, Washington, bringing the total number of local and regional jurisdictions up to 26, plus several state and federal sponsors. This unique four-county, bi-state cooperative effort has come to be called the Metropolitan Greenspaces Project and includes 2,390 km² or 25% of the four-county region. The rest of this paper will deal with the details of the inventory process. Sample results will be presented for the 1,192 km² area within the Metro district boundaries because that portion of the inventory has been finished (Fig. 1). Identical procedures are being employed

to complete the rest of the Metropolitan Greenspaces Project area.

Definition of "Natural Areas"

Through the time that the inventory was initiated, the use of the term "natural area," by those concerned with the project, had been fairly loose. One of the first tasks, therefore, was to develop a definition of natural areas that clearly identified the kinds of areas the study was to deal with. The definition that was finally adopted was:

> a landscape unit (a) composed of plant and animal communities, water bodies, soil, and rock, (b) largely devoid of man-made structures, and (c) maintained and managed in such a way as to promote or enhance populations of wildlife.

This definition purposely dealt with area characteristics rather than attempting to list all the categories of areas to be included or not included. The intention was to provide enough information to clearly indicate the common attributes of natural areas, but to leave room for interpretation of individual cases. For example, golf courses and farms do not fit the definition of natural areas. This is not to say that these two kinds of areas may not serve as wildlife habitat, just that they are not managed to include wildlife habitat. On the other hand, a cemetery, depending on its particular design and management, might or might not fit the criteria for a natural area. Overall, this definition of natural areas is more conservative than that used in some other studies (e.g., Matthews et al. 1988), but it proved to be acceptable to all those concerned with the study.

THE INVENTORY PROCESS

The starting point for the inventory was the acquisition of a recent, uniform set of remotely sensed data for the entire region. This was accomplished during May and June of 1989, when specially-contracted 23 by 23 cm color infrared aerial photography was taken over the four-county area. In all, 598 photographs at a scale of 1:31,680 were taken.

The actual inventory process began in September, 1989 and involved both mapping and field survey. Though the ideal inventory would consist of on-site observations of every natural area, this was impossible in terms of both time and money. The resolution of this issue was to use a two-stage data collection approach (Lillesand and Kiefer 1987). The first stage was the systematic mapping of all natural areas in the region, considering four characteristics that were readily obtainable from the aerial photographs. The second stage was the selection of a small sample of all the mapped areas and the performance of field surveys, considering a large number of site characteristics. This two-stage approach to the inventory combined the speed and cost effectiveness of remote sensing with the detailed data that only field survey can provide.

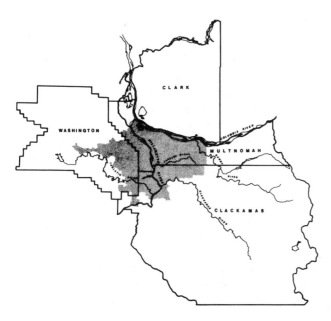

Fig. 1.   The shaded portion of this map is the Metropolitan Service District (Metro), which includes the City of Portland and the surrounding urbanized area in Oregon. It lies in the center of the Portland-Vancouver metropolitan region and covers 1,192 km².

Mapping

The mapping was based on air photo interpretation performed on 1:24,000 scale enlargements of the 23 by 23 cm color infrared aerial photographs. For the Metro area, this included approximately 115 photographs. The base for the interpretation was a 1:24,000 scale film positive map with all roads, railroads, and streams indicated. The base also included township-range grid information, which allowed referencing of the data to standard geographic coordinate systems. Registered to the film positive was a sheet of frosted acetate on which the natural areas were delineated.

Each natural area was assigned a code, consisting of a combination of letters and numbers to describe and classify the area. The first portion of the code referred to whether the site was upland or wetland, symbolized by the letters U and W respectively. It should be noted that because of the leaf-on date of the photographs, the vegetative canopy masked many wetland areas and resulted in an anticipated underestimation of this category. However, because wetland information was not the main thrust of the inventory, the underestimation was not considered a problem.

The second portion of the code referred to the cover type and included 11 classes (Table 1). The first three classes identified forest vegetation with different degrees of canopy closure. The second three classes did the same for shrub-scrub woodlands. The final five classes indicated other categories of natural area land cover. If an area did not include one of these cover types, it was not considered a natural area and was not mapped.

The third portion of the code applied only to the woody vegetation classes of Forest and Shrub-Scrub and indicated the mix of deciduous-to-conifer species within the delimited area. Visual estimates were made to the nearest 10% and recorded as the percent of the wooded area with deciduous vegetation. Values were recorded as two digits from 00 to 99, with 99 being used to represent 100%.

The fourth portion of the code was the letter R, for riparian, which was used for sites that were adjacent to water bodies (Table 2).

In performing the delineations, one of the basic questions that had to be addressed was that of minimum mapping size. As a practical matter, it was felt that attempting to

Table 1. Classification of cover types for natural areas inventory, Portland, Oregon-Vancouver, Washington metropolitan region, 1989.

Cover type	Code
Forest, Closed Canopy	FC
Forest, Open Canopy	FO
Forest, Scattered Canopy	FS
Shrub-Scrub, Closed Canopy	SC
Shrub-Scrub, Open Canopy	SO
Shrub-Scrub, Scattered Canopy	SS
Clearcut	CC
Meadow/Grassland/Emergent	M
Bare Ground	B
Rock Outcrop	R
Water Body	W

Table 2. Examples of mapping codes used in the study. Each natural area site was described by at least a two-letter code and at most a six-letter/number code. A total of 284 different codes was theoretically possible, although a number of these do not actually occur in the study area.

Code	Description
UFO30	Upland, forest, open canopy, 30% deciduous
WSC99	Wetland, shrub-scrub, closed canopy, 100% deciduous
UR	Upland, rock outcrop
WMR	Wetland, meadow/grassland, riparian
UFC90R	Upland, forest, closed canopy, 90% deciduous, on water body

delineate anything smaller than approximately 2.5 by 2.5 mm was not feasible. On the 1:24,000 scale photos employed for the interpretation, a square of this size represented approximately 0.4 ha. As an operational matter, it was felt that the regional nature of the inventory did not require identifying areas as small as 0.4 ha for the whole study area. With this in mind, a hierarchy of minimum sizes was used, depending on the class of feature. For example, standing water bodies and their adjacent vegetation areas had to be at least 0.4 ha to be delineated. Riparian vegetation along streams was mapped either as it was discernable on the photograph, or as a 60-m wide corridor (i.e., a 2.5-mm band on the photo) in areas where no boundary was apparent between riparian and non-riparian vegetation. On the other hand, upland natural areas had to be at least 4 ha, or approximately 8 by 8 mm in size, to be mapped. Overall, 2,342 different sites with a cumulative area of 244 km² were mapped within the 1,192 km² Metro district.

Data Entry

Once the photo interpretation portion of the inventory was completed, the resulting compilation map was digitized and entered into a geographic information system (GIS). The polygonal outline for each of the 2,342 natural areas was stored as a set of coordinates in the computer. This set of polygon outlines constitutes the basic spatial data of the inventory. Also stored in the computer were the codes for the categories into which each of the natural areas was classified by the photo interpretation process.

The entry of the data into the GIS format allows a great deal of flexibility in manipulating both the statistical and graphical outputs. The extraction of area statistics, counts, and locational information by category, sub-category, subarea, or other combinations of criteria is easily performed. Likewise, production of maps at various scales and portrayal of various themes or subsets of the data are facilitated. Illustrative of this flexibility are Table 3, a tabular summary of the 11 land cover categories (in this case aggregated into six categories), and Fig. 2, a map of all the natural areas in the Metro district. Both the data for Table 3 and the map (Fig. 2) were generated directly from the GIS.

Not only does the GIS format assist in the simple

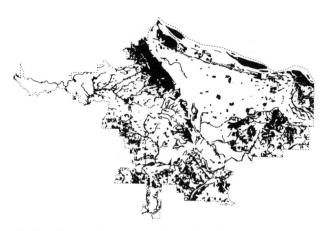

Fig. 2. The natural areas in the Metropolitan Service District area as of June, 1989. The various classes of land cover are not portrayed, nor are the boundaries between the areas. In the database these natural areas are differentiated as 2,342 distinct sites.

Table 3. Land cover types within natural areas of the Metropolitan Service District, 1989.

Cover type	Size (ha)	Composition (%)
Forest	19,945	81.9%
Meadow	2,869	11.8%
Water	754	3.1%
Shrub/Scrub	536	2.2%
Rock & Bare Soil	205	0.8%
Clearcut	45	0.2%
Total	24,354	100.0%

output of the natural areas data, but it will be invaluable in the subsequent analysis phase of the project.

Field Survey and Database

The mapping was followed by biological field inventories performed during the spring and summer of 1990. Ninety-seven sites were visited in the field. Their selection was guided by the results of the mapping to include a cross-section of the mapped natural area categories. Information was collected on an eight-page form that incorporated such items as the dominance of particular species, wetlands classification, habitat quality, and human impacts. In addition, the field work utilized a species checklist that included all the plant and vertebrate species commonly found in the metropolitan region. The methodologies and results of the field inventories are detailed in Lev and Sharp (1991).

The data collected by the field surveys also were entered into the GIS, forming the basis for a detailed natural areas database for the region. Although there are initially only 96 sites in the database, plans are to continually expand and update this database as new data are collected.

THE NEXT STEPS

Long-term Plans

The aerial photography acquisition and the inventory constitute Phases 1 and 2 of a planned six-phase project.

Phase 3 will utilize the inventory data to perform analyses of the pattern and character of the natural areas in the metropolitan region and to identify a proposed system of protected natural areas. Phase 4 will focus on the development of an acquisition and financing plan for the system, including a public education program to inform people about the importance of the system. Phase 5 will seek funding for a land acquisition program that will allow for the purchase of properties to be included in the region-wide system. Phase 6 will be the actual implementation and management of the system.

Analysis Phase

The analysis planned for Phase 3 is intended to examine the spatial patterns and biological characteristics of the natural areas, with the goal of identifying a formal system of interconnected natural areas for the metropolitan region. A major portion of this analysis will be performed using GIS technology, which will facilitate the use of additional mapped data about the landscape. The GIS approach will make a multi-factor approach possible, incorporating such items as land use plans, existing parks, other protected natural areas, utility rights-of-way, National Wetlands Inventory data, and soil/slope information. The incorporation of these multiple data sets means that more complex and, hopefully, more meaningful analyses can be performed.

Although all natural areas are of interest in the study, wetlands and riparian areas are of special concern because of the varied ecological functions that these areas serve. Stream corridors are doubly unique, due to their spatial function. These types of linear features potentially serve not simply as natural areas but as connectors between larger, more compactly-shaped patches of natural area.

This connector function is potentially important at two scales. First, at the local scale, connectors allow movement of species between individual patches of natural area. By allowing movement *within* the heavily urbanized area of a metropolitan region, these connectors can help prevent progressive degradation of wildlife diversity. Second, at the regional scale, the connectors provide a pathway for interaction between the natural areas *inside* the urbanized zone and those *outside* the urbanized zone. The connection to areas outside the urbanized portion is especially important because it prevents isolation of the species within the urbanized zone and assures a larger gene pool for maintaining diversity.

In more general systems analysis terminology, we may view a metropolitan region as either a closed system or as an open system. It is necessary to consider energy flows within the system at both levels, i.e., *within* the closed system and *between* the metropolitan area and outside areas. It is the ability to foster these energy flows that makes corridors especially important as an element in this study.

CONCLUSIONS AND IMPLICATIONS

The completion of an urban natural areas inventory such as outlined in this paper provides an important and often overlooked set of data for dealing with the human environment of the city. Too often, the data that are available about a city concern strictly economic and social factors, with no information concerning natural and people-nature interactions. Natural areas databases will become increasingly important as areas of urban growth continue to crowd fragile natural areas and difficult decisions need to be made concerning urban growth and the maintenance of quality of life.

In the present inventory, all natural areas were identified, regardless of whether they were protected or unprotected. The long-term goals of the project are to (a) identify an interconnected subset of the natural areas that constitutes a system, and (b) obtain protection for the natural areas in the identified system. Through the establishment of a regional system of natural areas and the development of an acquisition and management program, the urban region will be able to preserve its diverse natural habitats to support wildlife and to provide passive recreation for people.

One of the unique characteristics of the project is that it involves multiple levels of jurisdiction working together on a bi-state effort that is defined not by arbitrary political boundaries, but by a coherent ecological region. It is this unusual alliance between a broad group of jurisdictions and public constituencies that gives the Metropolitan Greenspaces Project a high probability of success. The completion of the inventory is an important initial step in the overall project and provides a valuable source of uniform data for the region. For public administrators, environmental professionals, planners, educators, and researchers, the study will provide a benchmark from which to assess future changes in the metropolitan region.

Acknowledgments.—Portland State University Geography students Karla Peters, A. Paul Newman, Maureen Smith, Scott Augustine, Gary Bishop and Manette Simpson assisted in performing the work on this inventory. Bob Abrams prepared the location map.

REFERENCES CITED

CLEARS. Undated (ca. 1987). City of New York, Bronx and citywide park projects: vegetative cover and land use classification. Cornell Lab. for Environ. Appl. of Remote Sensing, Ithaca, N.Y. 8pp.

Franklin, J. F., and C. T. Dyrness. 1973. Natural vegetation of Oregon and Washington. USDA For. Serv. Gen. Tech. Rep. PNW-8, Portland, Oreg. 417pp.

Houck, M. C. 1988. Metropolitan wildlife refuge system. Map at scale of 1:126,720. Audubon Soc. of Portland, Portland, Oreg.

Johnson, D. M. 1987. Weather and climate of Portland. Pages 20–37 *in* L. W. Price, ed. Portland's changing landscape. Dep. of Geogr., Portland State University, Portland, Oreg.

Lev, E., and L. Sharp. 1991. The Portland-Vancouver natural areas inventory: field surveys and preliminary wildlife data. (Published elsewhere in this volume.)

Lillesand, T. M., and R. W. Kiefer. 1987. Remote sensing and image interpretation, 2nd ed. John Wiley, New York, N.Y. 721pp.

Matthews, M. J., S. O'Connor, and R. S. Cole. 1988. Database for the New York State urban wildlife habitat inventory. Landscape and Urban Planning 15:23–37.

Merchant, J. W., and M. E. Dillworth. 1989. Automated techniques for wildlife habitat analysis in urban and urbanizing areas. Kansas Applied Remote Sensing Program, Univ. of Kansas, Lawrence. 63pp.

Metro. 1989a. Metro recreation resource study. Metropolitan Serv. Dist., Portland, Oreg. 51pp.

———. 1989b. Natural areas. Map at scale of 1:48,000. Metropolitan Serv. Dist., Portland, Oreg.

Pryde, P. R. 1988. An inventory and evaluation of natural areas in San Diego County. Yearbook of the Assoc. of Pacific Coast Geogr. 50:87–99.

Sukopp, H., and S. Weiler. 1988. Biotope mapping and nature conservation strategies in urban areas of the Federal Republic of Germany. Landscape and Urban Planning 15:39–58.

The Portland-Vancouver Natural Areas Inventory: Field Surveys and Preliminary Wildlife Data

ESTHER LEV, *Environmental Consultant, 729 SE 33rd, Portland, OR 97214*

LYNN SHARP, *Environmental Consultant, 10906 SE 54th Place, Milwaukie, OR 97222*

INTRODUCTION

Over the past several years, interest in urban growth management has grown in the Portland-Vancouver metropolitan region. The need for a comprehensive natural areas program, as part of this growth management, has been recognized. The region has enjoyed a high quality of life that is largely attributable to the vast green spaces and vegetated stream and river corridors within the area. As the population in this region continues to increase, the loss of natural areas, proportional to growth, continues.

Concern about fragmentation and loss of these natural areas, and the resulting decline of wildlife species, led The Metropolitan Service District (Metro) to coordinate a Natural Areas Inventory. It is anticipated that the inventory will evolve into a natural areas program including participation by every city, county, and park agency in the Portland-Vancouver metropolitan region.

The objectives of the program are to:

1. inventory, analyze, protect, acquire, and manage natural areas on a regional basis; and
2. develop an interconnected regional system of habitats, open space, and trails that maximizes ecological values while providing public access and appropriate passive recreational opportunities.

The inventory involves three major parts: a mapping effort, a biological survey of sample natural areas, and the entry of the survey data into a database. (See Poracsky 1991 for a definition of natural area used in the study.) This paper discusses the methodology and preliminary results of the 1990 biological survey.

Although "working landscapes" (Hiss 1989: 44) and golf courses provide habitat and travel corridors for some wildlife species, they were excluded from the inventory because they often also involve management practices that conflict with vegetative diversity and wildlife enhancement. However, these areas may have important positive ecological impacts on nearby natural areas and their relationship to natural areas should be considered in the future.

PHYSICAL SETTING

The Portland-Vancouver metropolitan region is located at the confluence of the Willamette and Columbia Rivers. In Oregon, to the west of the Willamette River are the Tualatin Mountains, which rise sharply from the west bank of the river. East of the Willamette, flatter terrain gently rises toward the foothills of the Cascade Range, broken by numerous volcanic, forested buttes. In Washington, a belt of wetlands, lakes, and stream corridors along the Columbia River are the dominant features of the remaining natural landscape. The combination of buttes, Tualatin Mountains, Cascade and Coast range foothills, river valleys, and flat lands dotted with numerous wetlands and riparian corridors provide a great diversity of green space and wildlife habitat in an urbanized setting.

In Oregon, west of the Tualatin Mountains lie the communities of Beaverton, Tigard, Hillsboro, and Forest Grove on a rapidly urbanizing landscape of farm and forest. To the east are the developing areas of Clackamas and East Multnomah Counties, and Gresham, Oregon's fourth largest city. The cities of Lake Oswego, Milwaukie, Oregon City, Gladstone, and West Linn, expanding residential communities bordered by agricultural and forest lands, form the southern edge of the metropolitan region. Increasing growth and development in the Vancouver, Washington metropolitan area is beginning to impact the Vancouver Lake lowlands and associated wetland systems.

Approximately 80% of the natural areas remaining in the Portland-Vancouver metropolitan region are forests (Poracsky 1991). The remaining 20% include successional shrublands and meadows created by logging, wetland shrub and meadow communities, emergent wetlands, bare ground, and rock outcrops. The logging of old-growth forests that accompanied European settlement has greatly altered the

Wildlife Conservation in Metropolitan Environments. NIUW Symp. Ser. 2, L.W. Adams and D.L. Leedy, eds. Published by Natl. Inst. for Urban Wildl., 10921 Trotting Ridge Way, Columbia, MD 21044, USA, 1991.

natural communities that remain in the area, and occurred so early and completely that the characteristics of some of the original communities in the Portland area are unknown (Franklin and Dyrness 1973).

Once common in old-growth forests in the Portland area, western hemlock (*Tsuga heterophylla*), grand fir (*Abies grandis*), and western yew (*Taxus brevifolia*), are now uncommon. Successional Douglas-fir (*Pseudotsuga menziesii*), red alder (*Alnus rubra*), and bigleaf maple (*Acer macrophyllum*) communities less than 100 years old have replaced the mature forests. Intensive agriculture, grazing, fire suppression, and urbanization have almost eradicated the few native prairies that existed in the Portland area. Many new grasslands have been created by agriculture, and are now dominated by tall fescue (*Festuca arundinacea*), velvetgrass (*Holcus lanatus*), and orchardgrass (*Dactylis glomerata*).

Wetlands have been filled or hydrologically altered since settlement began, and wetland loss continues today. Oregon ash (*Fraxinus latifolia*)-dominated wetlands were once common along stream courses, and are now becoming uncommon because of clearing and filling. Wetlands dominated by reed canarygrass (*Phalaris arundinacea*) are the prevalent palustrine emergent wetland type in the region. Shrub-dominated wetlands are uncommon. Remnant riparian communities dominated by black cottonwood (*Populus trichocarpa*), willows (*Salix lasiandra, S. fluviatilis, S. sessifolia*), and red alder can be found along stream corridors throughout the region.

METHODOLOGY

The purpose of the field inventory was to document wildlife and plant species found within each vegetative community throughout the metropolitan area. These data were used to: (1) investigate the role and significance of each vegetative community and its wildlife in relation to the larger regional ecosystem, and (2) begin to identify the effects of other variables, such as area, size, location, and adjacent land use on wildlife and plant species occurrence and diversity.

Survey Design and Data Form

The first step in designing the field inventory was development of a standardized survey method and field data form. Natural area inventory methodologies and classification systems from the City of New York's Natural Resources Group (1986), the London Ecology Unit (1985), and the City of Bellevue Washington (1988) were reviewed prior to designing the field survey methodology and data form for this study. As an early step in designing the field inventory, vegetation cover types were listed, which are a critical aspect of the entire project (Kuchler 1967: 54). Cover type classi-

fications used in the field were identical to those used in the aerial photo mapping effort (Table 1 of Poracsky 1991).

An eight-page data form was designed to record field observations in standardized form, and to facilitate data entry into a natural areas database. Table 1 summarizes the information collected in the field. A second form was also taken into the field. This form was a checklist of common plant, bird, mammal, amphibian, and reptile species of

Table 1. Information collected in the field for the natural areas inventory, Portland, Oregon-Vancouver, Washington metropolitan region, 1990.

Location (City, County, Watershed)

Date/Time

Land Classification Code (Cornell Laboratory for Environmental Applications of Remote Sensing, undated)

Cover Type (recorded in the field as ground truth)

Site Character: natural, disturbed, agricultural

Trees
    Density (Canopy; closed, open, scattered)
    Percent deciduous
    Dominant Species
    Old Growth Elements
    Snags (number of) (none, rare, uncommon, common, abundant)
    Dead Down Wood (none, rare, uncommon, common, abundant)

Shrubs
    Density (Canopy; closed, open, scattered)
    Percent deciduous
    Dominant Species

Ground Cover
    Density
    Mowed or Grazed
    Dominant Species
    Percent Bare Ground, Rock Outcrop

Vegetative Community Type (Franklin and Dyrness 1973)

Comments on Apparent History of Site

Wetland Classification (Cowardin et al. 1979)

Water
    springs, storm water drainages present
    stagnant, seasonally flushed
    appearance, stream bottom color, stream odor
    depth, stream width
    channel alterations
    barriers, obstructions; natural, manmade
    litter

Wildlife Species observed
    Insects
    Macroinvertebrates
    Fish
    Reptiles
    Amphibians
    Birds
    Mammals

Special/Unique Features (rare and threatened species)

Generalized adjacent Land uses (Cornell Laboratory for Environmental Applications of Remote Sensing, undated)

Adjacent Corridors

Human Uses
    Informal trails, formal trails, camps, debris/trash

the area. Each plant and wildlife species seen, heard, or otherwise identified by obvious sign was recorded on the list. This checklist was designed to facilitate entry of the data into the database. (Readers interested in a copy of the checklist may contact the authors.)

Site Selection

Time and budget constraints did not allow field visits and inventories to be conducted at each of the 3,680 natural areas identified by the aerial interpretation (Poracsky 1991). A random selection of sites in proportion to their abundance was made from the map of natural areas produced from the aerial interpretation. The sites selected represented a cross-section of habitat types, sizes, adjacent land uses, and geographic location throughout the metropolitan area (Fig. 1).

Several workshops with local professional field biologists were held prior to field survey site selection to gain an understanding of the existing state of knowledge of individual natural areas. The workshops indicated that pre-existing data were available for a large number of sites. The sites identified in the workshop were excluded from the random selection process, thereby avoiding duplication of effort during the surveys.

Field Surveys

Field surveys of 97 sites were conducted in the Portland metropolitan area from May through early July, 1990. Surveys took place between one-half hour before sunrise to 3 hours after sunrise on mornings without heavy rain or high winds to maximize detection of breeding birds. All species seen, heard, or leaving recognizable sign were recorded during a 45-minute to 75-minute period when two observers slowly walked a ground transect of measured length through each site. Identification was made with the aid of binoculars, field guides, and tape recordings. An additional 63 sites (23 in Oregon and 40 in Washington) were surveyed later during

the summer, but these were not included in the present analysis because they do not represent breeding season data.

RESULTS

The 120 sites inventoried in the Oregon portion of the study area represent 3.26% of the 3,680 polygons identified in the mapping effort. The 40 Washington sites inventoried represent 1.43% of the 2,800 sites mapped in that state. A preponderance of forested sites were sampled because forests represented approximately 80% of the polygons mapped in the study area (Poracsky 1991).

Common Wildlife Species

Table 2 summarizes information on the most common species found at each type of site. Species observations representing 2% or more of the total number of animals (or signs) observed during all surveys of that mapped habitat type (or combination of types) were included.

The most abundant wildlife species observed during these surveys included the bushtit, which tends to occur in flocks of up to 20 or more; the European starling, which tends to also occur in flocks; and mole sign, which was particularly common in upland habitats. Other common species included the American goldfinch, American robin, chickadees (*Parus atricapillus*, *P. rufescens*, and unidentified), rufous-sided towhee, and song sparrow, which were all over 2% of the total in at least six of the eight general habitat types distinguished. The American crow, Bewick's wren, brown-headed cowbird, European starling, and scrub jay comprised over 2% of the total in at least four habitat types.

Nearly all of these common species are permanent residents in the Portland area and are adapted to patchy habitats, edges, or open areas. This is consistent with observations elsewhere in both urban and rural areas where habitat patches become increasingly fragmented (Robbins 1980, Whitcomb et al. 1981, Lynch and Whigham 1984). As urbanization proceeds, the less common species with specific habitat affinities will continue to decline in abundance and the more common species will increase.

Wetland forests and upland shrub habitats were the areas where the average number of wildlife or signs observed were highest—over 40 per survey. These also were areas where relatively few sites were visited. The habitats with the greatest number of samples, upland closed forest and upland closed riparian forest, had an average of 32 and 25 observations per site, respectively. Other sites ranged from 20 to 43 observations per site.

Uncommon and Rare Species

A number of species we consider truly wonderful to have in our urban area were observed during these surveys (Table 3). Often only one or two observations were made, but these are still impressive considering the very small

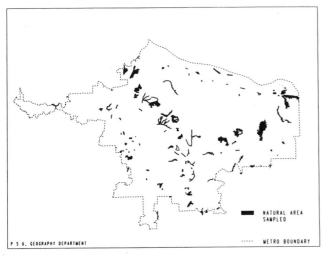

Fig. 1. Natural areas that were sampled in the Metropolitan Service District area. See Poracsky (1991) for a map of all natural areas in the metropolitan region.

Table 2. Common wildlife species in major habitats of the Portland metropolitan area, May through early July, 1990.[a]

Species	Upland forest 1[b]	2[c]	3[d]	4[e]	Upland Shrub	Meadow	Wetland Forest[f]	Meadow
Birds								
American crow (*Corvus brachyrhynchos*)	3.6	2.5	2.5	5.0			3.5	
American goldfinch (*Carduelis tristis*)	2.4	2.5	3.2	2.8	3.3	4.0	4.1	2.2
American robin (*Turdus migratorius*)	6.6		6.3	4.0	3.7	3.4	6.2	5.6
Barn swallow (*Hirundo rustica*)		2.5				4.6	2.9	
Bewick's wren (*Thryomanes bewickii*)		3.4	3.0	2.1	2.3		2.4	
Black-headed grosbeak (*Pheucticus melanocephalus*)	2.1		2.8					
Brown-headed cowbird (*Molothrus ater*)	2.3	4.2			2.3	4.6	3.2	
Bushtit (*Psaltriparus minimus*)	4.9	7.6	4.8	8.8	7.9		6.8	21.6
Cedar waxwing (*Bombycilla cedrorum*)				2.1			2.6	
Chickadees (*Parus* spp.)	7.6	4.2	7.2	3.1	5.1			2.2
Cliff swallow (*Hirundo pyrrhonota*)					2.3			
Common yellowthroat (*Geothlypis trichas*)		2.5			2.8	2.3		4.3
European starling (*Sturnus vulgaris*)			2.5	11.9	6.1		3.2	3.0
Golden-crowned kinglet (*Regulus satrapa*)	2.6							
House finch (*Carpodacus mexicanus*)						3.4		
House sparrow (*Passer domesticus*)				4.3				
Mallard (*Anas platyrhynchos*)				2.4				
Orange-crowned warbler (*Vermivora celata*)		3.4			2.8	2.3		
Pine siskin (*Carduelis pinus*)					14.0			
Red-breasted nuthatch (*Sitta canadensis*)	2.1							
Red-winged blackbird (*Agelaius phoeniceus*)							2.6	7.8
Rock dove (*Columba livia*)				2.6				
Rufous-sided towhee (*Pipilo erythrophthalmus*)	6.2	10.2	4.6	4.5	5.1	4.0	3.8	3.0
Scrub jay (*Aphelocoma coerulescens*)		3.4		2.4		2.3	2.1	
Song sparrow (*Melospiza melodia*)	4.0	7.6	8.6	6.9	5.1	5.2	7.9	8.2
Steller's jay (*Cyanocitta stelleri*)	2.9		3.0					
Swainson's thrush (*Catharus ustulatus*)	3.9	2.5	4.0					
Violet-green swallow (*Tachycineta thalassina*)							2.9	
Western wood pewee (*Contopus sordidulus*)	2.4						2.4	
White-crowned sparrow (*Zonotrichia leucophrys*)						4.0		
Willow flycatcher (*Empidonax traillii*)		2.5			3.3			2.2
Wilson's warbler (*Wilsonia pusilla*)	2.3							
Mammals								
Calif. ground squirrel (*Spermophilus beecheyi*)		2.5						
Mole sign (*Scapanus* spp.)	3.6	6.8	7.0			10.9	3.2	2.2
Mountain beaver sign (*Aplodontia rufa*)	2.1							
Pocket gopher sign (*Thomomys* spp.)						9.2		
Vole sign (*Microtus* spp.)		2.5						
Total percent of observations	62	71	60	63	66	60	60	62
No. observations	840	118	568	421	214	174	340	232
Mean	32	20	25	35	43	22	42	26
n	26	6	23	12	5	8	8	9

[a]Data represent percent of total observations. Only observations making up over 2% of the total for each habitat are shown.
[b]Closed canopy.
[c]Open to scattered canopy.
[d]Closed canopy, riparian.
[e]Open canopy, riparian.
[f]Closed to open canopy.

sample of the Portland-Vancouver metropolitan region we were able to visit in the field.

DISCUSSION

Urbanization fragments natural habitats into smaller and more isolated units. Development and continued growth destroy many natural habitats while modifying some and creating other new habitats for some species (Adams and Dove 1989). These alterations and disturbances increase the isolation of these habitat islands from one another and from the surrounding rural area. This isolation affects species diversity, and often encourages recruitment of alien plant and wildlife species.

A group of permanent resident species appears to dominate breeding bird communities in the urban natural areas that were surveyed. However, many less common species are still present in small numbers in our urbanizing area, primarily in less disturbed areas and in nature parks. Many of the less common species require large blocks of forest or special habitat features such as open water, snags, or large old trees. Snags were rarely observed during our surveys and their absence is reflected in the relatively low numbers of woodpeckers, swallows, and other secondary cavity users

Table 3. Uncommon and rare wildlife species in the Portland metropolitan area, 1990.

Birds

    Band-tailed pigeon (*Columba fasciata*)
    Barn owl (*Tyto alba*)
    Belted kingfisher (*Ceryle alcyon*)
    Black-crowned night heron (*Nycticorax nycticorax*)
    Brown creeper (*Certhia americana*)
    Common merganser (*Mergus merganser*)
    Lazuli bunting (*Passerina amoena*)
    Lesser goldfinch (*Carduelis psaltria*)
    Merlin (*Falco columbarius*)
    MaGillivray's warbler (*Oporornis tolmiei*)
    Northern harrier (*Circus cyaneus*)
    Olive-sided flycatcher (*Contopus borealis*)
    Osprey (*Pandion haliaetus*)
    Pileated woodpecker (*Dryocopus pileatus*)
    Red-eyed vireo (*Vireo olivaceus*)
    Solitary vireo (*V. solitarius*)
    Townsend's warbler (*Dendroica townsendi*)
    Vaux's swift (*Chaetura vauxi*)
    Varied thrush (*Ixoreus naevius*)
    Warbling vireo (*V. gilvus*)
    Western tanager (*Piranga ludoviciana*)
    Yellow warbler (*Dendroica petechia*)
    Yellow-breasted chat (*Icteria virens*)

Mammals

    Mountain beaver (*Aplodontia rufa*)
    Beaver (*Castor canadensis*)
    Porcupine (*Erethizon dorsatum*)
    Bobcat (*Lynx rufus*)

observed during the study. The aggressive, ubiquitous starling clearly dominates in the open riparian forests. These were the areas where snags were most frequently found, although snags were not common anywhere.

The information collected in this inventory is critical to understanding the regional ecological landscape and its individual habitat components. The next step is to identify the weak or missing linkages in this regional landscape. Identification of corridor fragmentation and declining plant and wildlife species will become the basis for a regional natural areas acquisition and restoration program. Critical corridor linkages, fragile habitats sensitive to adjacent development, and unique areas can be identified and acquired. We can then begin to create a habitat restoration program based on pre-settlement to the present records of plant and wildlife species and vegetative communities. Remnant native vegetation communities within the region can become models for future restoration efforts.

This inventory has attempted to stress both biocentric and anthropocentric landscape ecology, emphasizing the significance of landscape phenomena and processes. The "Metropolitan Greenspaces" program coordinated by Metro also is examining the importance of human relationships within the landscape through a strong program of public involvement. Short- and long-term human needs can then be emphasized, along with responsibilities of humans for the landscape and all its organisms (Vink 1983). Creation of a bi-state regional natural areas system is an action addressing both human needs and responsibilities. Our opportunities for providing maximum protection and enhancement of

wildlife habitat in the Portland metropolitan area appear to lie in maintaining interconnections among forest patches (primarily along streams where less development has taken place) and on increasing snag densities and enhancing other habitat features important to the wildlife species that are becoming rare in urban environments. This will provide people with an opportunity to observe and appreciate the "quality" wildlife species that are less common than many other successful urban species.

REFERENCES CITED

Adams, L. W., and L. E. Dove. 1989. Wildlife reserves and corridors in the urban environment: a guide to ecological landscape planning and resource conservation. Natl. Inst. for Urban Wildl., Columbia, Md. 91pp.

City of Bellevue Washington. 1988. Sensitive Areas Notebook.

City of New York's Natural Resources Group. 1986. Wildlife habitat appraisal manual. Dep. of Parks and Rec., New York, N.Y.

Cornell Laboratory for Environmental Applications of Remote Sensing. Undated. Vegetative cover and land use classification. Ithaca, N.Y.

Cowardin, L.M., V. Carter, F.C. Golet, and E.T. LaRoe. 1979. Classification of wetlands and deepwater habitats of the United States. Rep. No. FWS/OBS-79/31. U. S. Fish and Wildl. Serv., Washington, D.C. 103pp.

Franklin, J.F., and C.T. Dyrness, 1973. Natural vegetation of Oregon and Washington. For. Serv. Gen. Tech. Rep. PNW-8. USDA For. Serv., Washington, D.C. 417pp.

Hiss, T. 1989. "Encountering the Countryside- 1." The New Yorker, August 21, 40–69.

Kuchler, A.W. 1967. Vegetation mapping. The Ronald Press, New York, N.Y. 472 pp.

London Ecology Unit. 1985. Wildlife habitat survey specification and criteria. London, U.K.

Lynch, J.F., and D.F. Whigham. 1984. Effects of forest fragmentation on breeding bird communities in Maryland USA. Biol. Conserv. 28:287–324.

Poracsky, J. 1991. The Portland-Vancouver natural areas inventory: photo interpretation and mapping. (Published elsewhere in this volume.)

Robbins, C.S. 1980. Effect of forest fragmentation on breeding bird populations in the Piedmont of the Mid-Atlantic region. Atlantic Nat. 33:31–36.

Vink, A.P.A. 1983. Landscape ecology and land use. Longman Inc., New York, N.Y. 264 pp.

Whitcomb, R.F., et al. 1981. Effects of forest fragmentation on avifauna of the eastern deciduous forest. Pages 125–205 *in* R.L. Burgess and D.M. Sharpe, eds. Forest island dynamics in man-dominated landscapes. Springer-Verlag, New York, N.Y.

VII.
Poster Papers

Chair: LAURA S. JACKSON, *Iowa Chapter,
The Wildlife Society, Madrid*

Cochair: LOREN R. FORBES, *Iowa Chapter,
The Wildlife Society, Iowa City*

Influence of Proximal Land Use on Avian Utilization of Recent Clearcuts

AMY L. RICHERT AND SCOTT E. RICHERT, *Geography-Earth Science Department, Shippensburg University, Shippensburg, PA 17257*

Previous studies of avian responses to forest clearcutting have concentrated on *in situ* successional stages and habitat complexity. Preliminary research conducted by the authors suggested that knowledge of habitat characteristics and resources within clearcuts is insufficient for completely explaining avian community composition. The avian community within a logged area may be influenced by spatial components such as size of the clearcut and proximity to different land areas.

The present study examined the influence of proximal urban and agricultural land use on avian utilization of clearcuts. Bird communities were compared between forest edge clearcuts and interior clearcuts. Bird censusing was conducted on eight recent clearcuts within Michaux State Forest, Southcentral Pennsylvania, which is located on the fringe of megalopolis. Proximity of the clearcuts to urban or agricultural land areas ranged from 0.5 km (for forest edge) to 5.0 km (for interior forest).

Proximity of land uses affected species composition and species richness. House finches (*Carpodacus mexicanus*) and purple martins (*Progne subis*) were observed only on clearcuts close to agricultural land. Highest densities of field sparrows (*Spizella pusilla*) and eastern kingbirds (*Tyrannus tyrannus*) were on clearcuts close to agricultural land. Highest densities of common grackles (*Quiscalus quiscula*), American robins (*Turdus migratorius*), European starlings (*Sturnus vulgaris*), and brown-headed cowbirds (*Molothrus ater*) were attained on clearcuts close to urban-agricultural land.

The immigration of some urban bird species (e.g., European starlings, brown-headed cowbirds) onto clearcuts has important implications regarding nest site competition and nest parasitism. Forest management practices should be designed to minimize negative avian impacts caused by changes in land use surrounding the forest.

Breeding Bird Density and Diversity in Residential Areas of Metropolitan Toronto

JEAN-PIERRE L. SAVARD, *Canadian Wildlife Service, P.O. Box 340, Delta, British Columbia V4K 3Y3, Canada*

J. BRUCE FALLS, *Department of Zoology, University of Toronto, Toronto, Ontario M5S 1A1, Canada*

We studied bird-habitat relationships in seven residential areas of Metropolitan Toronto and correlated species abundance with characteristics of entire survey plots that ranged from 13 to 17 ha in size.

Breeding bird density varied from 200 pairs/km^2 in a new residential development to 824 pairs/km^2 in an old and poorly vegetated residential area. Species diversity and densities of mourning dove (*Zenaida macroura*), American robin (*Turdus migratorius*), common grackle (*Quiscalus quiscula*), and northern cardinal (*Cardinalis cardinalis*) were positively correlated with foliage volume below 9 m and with the surface of the ground covered by lawns and gardens. Densities of rock dove (*Columbia livia*) and European starling (*Sturnus vulgaris*) were positively correlated with high canopies (probably reflecting the presence of two-storey houses) and with house area, and negatively correlated with lawn area. Blue jay (*Cyanocitta cristata*) density was positively associated with volume of coniferous foliage. Chipping sparrow (*Spizella passerina*) density was negatively correlated with high canopies. Song sparrow (*Melospiza melodia*) density was positively associated with extent of lawn and gardens and negatively with house area and extent of paved areas. No strong relationships were found between house sparrow (*Passer domesticus*) density and the habitat features measured. Results indicated that landscaping patterns in residential areas determine the abundance and diversity of native avifauna.

Wildlife Conservation in Metropolitan Environments. NIUW Symp. Ser. 2, L.W. Adams and D.L. Leedy, eds. Published by Natl. Inst. for Urban Wildl., 10921 Trotting Ridge Way, Columbia, MD 21044, USA, 1991.

Use of Strip Censuses for Measuring the Breeding Bird Population in Urban Residential Areas in Toronto

JEAN-PIERRE L. SAVARD, *Canadian Wildlife Service, P.O. Box 340, Delta, British Columbia V4K 3Y3, Canada*

J. BRUCE FALLS, *Department of Zoology, University of Toronto, Toronto, Ontario M5S 1A1, Canada*

A crucial point in bird population studies is the technique used to estimate the abundance of each species. Strip censuses have been widely used in urban areas but little work has been done on their efficiency and accuracy in such environments. We compared the results of strip censuses carried out in several types of urban residential areas with estimates of breeding bird populations derived from a combination of the spot mapping method and nest searches.

Strip censuses underestimated the breeding densities of nearly all species. The technique provided estimates that were proportional to the size of the breeding populations for the American robin (*Turdus migratorius*) and the house sparrow (*Passer domesticus*) but not for the common grackle (*Quiscalus quiscula*) and the European starling (*Sturnus vulgaris*). Relationships between the results of strip censuses and the size of the breeding population varied according to species and habitats, suggesting caution when using strip censuses for relative comparison purposes. Strip censuses mainly provided a measure of the likelihood of seeing birds in a given habitat, taking into account their density and conspicuousness.

Distribution and Relative Abundance of Fall Migrating Birds in Relation to Urbanization in Metropolitan Toronto

JEAN-PIERRE L. SAVARD, *Canadian Wildlife Service, P.O. Box 340, Delta, British Columbia V4K 3Y3, Canada*

J. BRUCE FALLS, *Department of Zoology, University of Toronto, Toronto, Ontario M5S 1A1, Canada*

The abundance of fall migrants was determined in urban habitats ranging from a naturally vegetated park to a poorly vegetated downtown area. Three types of residential areas were sampled with two survey routes (1.3 to 4.4 km in length) per type.

Fall migrants were composed mostly of warblers and other canopy-associated birds. Migrants averaged 8 ± 8 ($\bar{x} \pm$ S.E.) ($n = 2$) birds per 10 km of transects in the downtown area and accounted for only 1% of all birds observed there. The urban park had the highest density of migrants with 638 ± 66 ($n = 3$) birds per 10 km, which represented 73% of all birds. Residential areas with high density 2-storey houses and limited vegetation had slightly lower migrant densities (105–122 birds/10 km) than residential areas with bungalows and moderate vegetation (167–175 birds/10 km). Migrants represented from 11% to 14% of all birds observed in these habitats. Two residential areas with a continuous canopy of high ornamental trees had migrant densities of 295 and 270 birds per 10 km, which represented respectively, 37% and 29% of the total avifauna observed. The abundance of migrants was related to the volume of foliage present in the various residential areas. This suggests that migrants distributed themselves in proportion to the amount of foliage present.

Winter Bird Density and Diversity in Metropolitan Toronto

JEAN-PIERRE L. SAVARD, *Canadian Wildlife Service, P.O. Box 340, Delta, British Columbia V4K 3Y3, Canada*

J. BRUCE FALLS, *Department of Zoology, University of Toronto, Toronto, Ontario M5S 1A1, Canada*

We determined winter bird density and diversity in six urban habitats ranging from a downtown area to a natural park. Plots (17–34 ha) were surveyed (4–11 times) by walking from one side of the street to the other and visiting every third backyard.

Differences were noted in the bird populations of these habitats. Species richness ranged from four species in the downtown area to 17 in the most heavily vegetated residential area. Winter bird density was higher in the downtown area (592 ± 79 birds/km²) ($\bar{x} \pm$ SE) than in the natural park (204 ± 24 birds/km²). In residential areas, winter bird density was positively correlated with house density and negatively with the relative abundance of conifers. Winter bird density ranged from 1942 ± 110 birds/km² in the poorly vegetated residential area to 883 ± 47 birds/km² in the heav-

Wildlife Conservation in Metropolitan Environments. NIUW Symp. Ser. 2, L.W. Adams and D.L. Leedy, eds. Published by Natl. Inst. for Urban Wildl., 10921 Trotting Ridge Way, Columbia, MD 21044, USA, 1991.

ily vegetated one. As expected with increased levels of urbanization, the percentage of introduced species in the wintering avifauna increased from 39% in the natural park to 100% in the downtown area. The three most abundant species were house sparrow (*Passer domesticus*), European starling (*Sturnus vulgaris*), and rock dove (*Columbia livia*). Density of birds in the natural park was higher in summer (540/km²) than in winter (205/km²). The reverse was true in the poorly vegetated residential area (1206/km² in summer vs. 1942/km² in winter). Winter bird distribution was clumped due to concentrations around bird feeders. The abundance and diversity of native species in winter were influenced by landscaping patterns and by the presence of bird feeders.

Nesting of the American Crow in Urban Areas

Louis J. Laux, Jr., *Wittenberg University, Box 720, Springfield, OH 45501*

John F. Gallagher, *Ohio State Audubon Council, 121 Larchmont Rd., Springfield, OH 45503*

Stephanie Dubs, *3613 Northcliffe Rd., University Heights, OH 44118*

Nesting of the American crow (*Corvus brachyrhynchos*) in urban areas is being widely observed, but hard data are scarce. Such nesting is a significant departure from the historic description of the crow in Ohio as a rural species most frequently associated with woods interspersed with agricultural activities.

During the spring and summer of 1990, 19 nests were located throughout Springfield, Ohio, (pop., 70,000+), and observed through fledgling. Eleven nests were in deciduous trees (eight species), eight in conifers (three species), with the eight nests in conifers somewhat clustered (average distance apart being 663 m as compared to 1180 m for all nests) in one quadrant of the city. Habitat settings ranged from "typical" (tall deciduous trees, usually oak, in a woods) to relatively isolated deciduous or conifer trees frequently within 15 m of human habitation. Seven nests were relatively low (8.5–12.5 m); nests in conifers averaged 14 m, in deciduous trees 17 m, and in all trees 16 m. At least nine nests fledged young (1–4) and at least 11 nests had "helpers." Some rural nesting data were collected and compared, and questions regarding the ecological role of the American crow in the urban setting were raised.

The Clayton County Kestrel Corridor

Mary Ford and M.J. Smith, *Ingleside Study Club, 103 Hayden Street, Guttenberg, IA 52052*

In the springs of 1988 and 1989, nesting boxes for bluebirds were erected at the Guttenberg Golf and Country Club in Clayton County, Iowa. This effort was a huge success as 95 bluebirds were fledged.

Because of the positive response of bluebirds, interest grew in establishing similar nesting boxes for the American kestrel (*Falco sparverius*), which had been observed on utility wires along Highway 52 between Guttenberg and Garnavillo. In May 1989, Interstate Power Company of Elkader, Iowa was contacted and permission was secured to use existing utility poles for placement of the kestrel boxes. Furthermore, the company agreed to place the boxes at the required 6.1-m height with its own truck. Nest box specifications were received, and a budget of $87.00 was established. Ten utility poles along Highway 52 were tagged with a red ribbon as kestrel box sites. Pole selection was based on the needs of this prairie bird, including locations at sufficient distance from farm driveways and the presence of potential perches for fledglings, and on easy access for the utility truck. Nest box construction was completed, using cedar wood. Wood chips used as nesting material inside the boxes were donated by Livingston Lumber of Guttenberg and Interstate Power Company mounted the boxes.

Kestrel response to the nest boxes has been positive. In May, 1990, male kestrels were observed at eight of the 10 sites bringing food to the nesting females. Three of these females were driven out by starlings, leaving five successful nestings. The first bird fledged on 6 June 1990. A late nesting occurred in one of the boxes and eight kestrels near this nest box were observed in early September. On 20 September 1990, Interstate Power Company removed the old nest material and replaced it with new wood chips to prepare for the spring 1991 nesting season.

To educate local residents about the American kestrel and its need for habitat, discussion of the project took place with local Kiwannis and Rotary members. In addition, it was featured in two newspapers in the county and the project coordinator served as a resource person to the local school on conservation issues. A videotape documenting the various steps in this project was created.

The bluebird and kestrel projects have been very successful and have served as impetus for other conservation efforts by Ingleside Study Club, including the master-minding of a community effort to establish Guttenberg as a

Wildlife Conservation in Metropolitan Environments. NIUW Symp. Ser. 2, L.W. Adams and D.L. Leedy, eds. Published by Natl. Inst. for Urban Wildl., 10921 Trotting Ridge Way, Columbia, MD 21044, USA, 1991.

National Urban Wildlife Sanctuary. Guttenberg is an attractive area for tourists, with the Mississippi River and limestone bluffs, and there is a need to enhance these natural attractions with wildlife.

Using Geographic Information Systems to Determine Nest Box Placement for the American Kestrel

CHRIS J. DIETRICH AND DANIEL S. LEKIE, *Kansas Department of Wildlife and Parks, 9539 Alden, Lenexa, KS 66215*

CHARLES NILON, *The School of Natural Resources, University of Missouri, Columbia, MO 65211*

We tested a geographic information system-based habitat suitability model for the American kestrel (*Falco sparverius*) by comparing kestrel use of nest boxes located in sites predicted by the model to have high habitat suitability with use of nest boxes located randomly. The model, developed by the Department of Geography at the University of Kansas, was designed for use in Kansas City, Kansas, an urban area where rapid changes in land use and land cover are occurring. Measures of land cover type and landscape pattern were used to determine habitat suitability. Our objectives in the project were to determine the accuracy of the model in predicting kestrel use. This assessment is the first step in a high-profile program to place nest boxes in suitable sites throughout the Kansas City area.

Twenty kestrel nest boxes were placed in sites with high habitat suitability scores. An additional 18 boxes were placed at randomly located sites with similar land uses to those selected by the model. Roadside counts were used as indices of kestrel abundance. Nest box use was determined by visiting each box in the two areas during the nesting season.

Kestrel use of nest boxes at the two sites was similar. During the first nesting season following placement of boxes, four of 20 boxes at optimal sites had active kestrel nests with at least one egg. Four of 18 randomly located boxes had kestrel nests with at least one egg.

Control of Ring-billed Gull Colonies on Urban and Industrial Sites in Ontario

HANS BLOKPOEL AND GASTON D. TESSIER, *Canadian Wildlife Service, 49 Camelot Drive, Nepean, Ontario K1A 0H3, Canada*

During 1984–1990 at 11 urban and/or industrial sites in southern Ontario, colonies of ground-nesting ring-billed gull (*Larus delawarensis*) were controlled to ameliorate problems caused by the adults, their nests, and their young. All control operations were carried out by the affected landowners under special permits issued by the Canadian Wildlife Service. At DOW Chemical Canada Inc., on the St. Clair River near Sarnia, nesting of gulls was first discouraged by scaring, and later eliminated by installing overhead monofilament lines. At the Nanticoke Generating Station on Lake Erie, a growing colony was eliminated by collecting eggs and subsequent harassment of adults. At the Lakeview Generating Station on Lake Ontario, attempts were made to discourage gulls by installing a gull exclosure over part of the colony and by scaring. One colony at the Stelco Yards in Hamilton Harbour was eliminated by installing a gull exclosure and collecting eggs from nests outside the exclosure, and another was controlled by frequently destroying nests and eggs. At Toronto Island Airport, an incipient colony was controlled by collecting eggs and harassing adults. At Mugg's Island, Toronto Harbour, control efforts included construction of a large gull exclosure and repeated egg collection. Large-scale gull-scaring operations at the Eastern Headland, Toronto Harbour, included the successful use of tethered raptors, distress cries, and pyrotechnical devices. A new colony in the center of the Greenwood Racetrack, Toronto, was discouraged by scaring the adults, using tethered birds of prey. A new colony at Bluffer's Park, just east of Toronto on Lake Ontario, was eliminated by collecting eggs repeatedly. A colony on the yards of the St. Mary's Cement Company in Bowmanville was reduced by alteration of habitat and harassment of the adults.

Iowa Bird Feeder Survey

LAURA SPESS JACKSON, *Iowa Department of Natural Resources, Nongame Program, Rural Route 1, Boone, IA 50036*

RICK J. HOLLIS, *Iowa Ornithologists Union, 3351 Lower West Branch Road, Iowa City, IA 52245*

The Iowa Ornithologists Union and the Nongame Program of the Iowa Department of Natural Resources have jointly sponsored a winter bird feeder survey for the past 7 years. The purpose of the survey is to: (1) document gross population trends of Iowa's winter birds that commonly use bird feeders; and (2) encourage public participation in bird watching.

The survey is conducted during 4 days in late January. Participants watch their feeders for 2 consecutive days during the survey period and record the highest number of each bird species that uses the feeders. Participants also record whether they live in a town or rural area, and classify their neighborhood by habitat types described on the survey form. In addition, the type of seeds offered and the date that feeding began for the season are noted. A standard form has been used since 1986.

The survey is promoted through state-wide news releases, newsletters, media interviews, and by distributing the actual survey form to some bird feeding stores. Response has ranged from 840 to 1,754 participants during the past 7 years and averaged 1,096 people/winter. Participation rates between town and country observers have remained fairly constant with approximately 60% and 40% reporting from urban and rural areas, respectively. Downtown areas and farm houses bordered by row crops tend to have the lowest participation.

Percent occurrence (percent of households reporting a species) and means (average number of birds observed at one time) are documented by the survey. This provides information on the most frequently observed birds and flock size. Between-year comparisons are made to document overall statistical differences in occurrence and differences by region. Comparisons also are made between habitat and frequency of occurrence.

The survey has been very useful in gathering information about "winter invasions" of cyclic species. It also has shown increases or decreases of certain species or feeding guilds. For example, the survey documented the movement of house finches into Iowa.

Overall, the survey has provided good information about Iowa's winter birds at a very low cost. It also has attracted a high number of participants each year.

Movement and Behavior of Relocated Urban Raccoons

DAVID J. HAGEN AND LARRY W. VANDRUFF, *State University of New York, College of Environmental Science and Forestry, Syracuse, NY 13210*

GORDON R. BATCHELLER, *New York State Department of Environmental Conservation, Wildlife Resources Center, Delmar, NY 12054*

Numerous individuals associated with a diversity of organizations receive calls from homeowners seeking relief from troublesome raccoons in the urban-suburban environment. Problems range from the simple annoyance of an overturned garbage can to destruction in dwellings by denning raccoons. Nuisance control personnel and private homeowners face a dilemma when a raccoon is captured. Euthanasia of the offending animal is one option, but commonly the animal is moved some distance and released. This poster presented the movements and behaviors of two of over 20 relocated nuisance raccoons in a field study conducted in Islip (Long Island), New York. Radio-collared animals were released either in the middle of a 81-ha refuge or at street-side in an adjacent residential area.

A male raccoon (RM5) captured in Bayport on 4 June 1990 was released at a residential site in Islip approximately 11.6 km west of its original home. This raccoon showed the greatest and fastest movement of any study animal thus far. RM5 wandered back and forth covering a total of at least 80 km in the first 14 nights following release. He travelled at least 12.4 km on Night 11 with sustained speeds ranging from 30-50 m/min. Although RM5 followed the same routes on several occasions, he did not settle in one area for over 1 month post-release.

Raccoon SM6 was captured in West Bay Shore on 7 June 1990 and released on the 81-ha Seatuck National Wildlife Refuge about 5.0 km to the southeast. SM6's first movement was to the east and by Night 6 he was over 14.5 km east of the capture site. At the end of the ninth night, he was found within what was later estimated to be a part of his original home range. This was the most extensive display of homing that we had seen. Unfortunately, SM6 was killed by a car on the Sagtikos Parkway on Night 11. Several hours of searching along the road revealed that the animal, still transmitting the mortality signal, had been buried by a motorist or a member of a road crew in the median strip of the parkway.

The movements and behaviors of these and other relocated individuals are in sharp contrast to the restricted

Wildlife Conservation in Metropolitan Environments. NIUW Symp. Ser. 2, L.W. Adams and D.L. Leedy, eds. Published by Natl. Inst. for Urban Wildl., 10921 Trotting Ridge Way, Columbia, MD 21044, USA, 1991.

movements and secretive behavior of refuge-inhabiting and residential-inhabiting raccoons monitored on the same study area concurrently and during the previous 2 years. We conclude that relocated raccoons move extensively before settling in a new activity area (home range), which is rarely at the area of release, be it an urban greenspace or a residential neighborhood site.

Tree Squirrel Research in Urban Environments

JOHN L. KOPROWSKI, *Department of Systematics and Ecology, University of Kansas, Lawrence, KS 66045*

Traditionally, urban wildlife research has been ignored in field studies. The primary value of urban species frequently was believed to be their aesthetic value to wildlife observers and photographers. However, many species may have additional nonconsumptive value as educational tools that link the lay and scientific communities, environmental health monitors, and subjects of basic and applied ecological research.

Since 1983, I have researched the population and behavioral ecology of fox squirrels (*Sciurus niger*) and eastern gray squirrels (*S. carolinensis*) in small urban woodlots. A review of my research and that of others suggests urban tree squirrels have considerable nonconsumptive value in addition to their aesthetic value. However, the value of urban tree squirrels in ecological research is largely unexploited.

Urban tree squirrels are well suited for studies on population and behavioral ecology because such squirrels habituate to human presence, facilitating trapping and observation. My studies of uniquely marked individuals of known age, sex, and relatedness permit social interactions, time budgets, and survivorship to be monitored. Two major findings have resulted from this methodology. Firstly, a critical period for squirrel populations occurs during late spring-early summer prior to the ripening of mast crops. Foraging efficiencies, weights, and survival (especially of juveniles) can be markedly lower because squirrels rely on only a few species of late-spring fruiting trees for food. Secondly, the social organization of fox squirrels and gray squirrels differs in significant ways. Female-biased natal philopatry results in the formation of clusters of related females within a gray squirrel population. Both sexes of fox squirrels disperse from their natal areas, and this results in solitary social organization. Differences in social organization likely account for

the differential response of gray (positive) and fox (neutral) squirrels to the addition of artificial nests.

Some of the most intriguing research investigates the impact of the fragmented urban landscape on wildlife populations. Urban landscapes frequently include high-quality woodlot "islands." Squirrel densities and woodlot size are negatively related, suggesting that fragmentation may have significant demographic consequences for squirrel populations. Research on urban wildlife species can provide crucial data on many important, timely issues in biology. Urban wildlife should not be viewed merely as having aesthetic value but also as a valuable resource in "cutting-edge" basic and applied research.

A Management Plan for Creating and Maintaining a Fishery Resource in an Urban Lake

SUSAN D. BITTER, *Biohabitats, Inc, 303 Allegheny Avenue, Towson, MD 21204*

ROBERT DANEHY, *Syracuse University, Syracuse, NY 13210*

An environmental management program was created to accompany a new development under construction in Montgomery County, Maryland. The proposed Town of Kentlands, located approximately 32.2 km northwest of Washington, D.C., was formerly a 142.6-ha country estate and working farm that also was managed for wildlife.

Outstanding features of the property include three man-made lakes. The largest impoundment, Inspiration Lake, covers 4.5 ha and is approximately 6.7 m deep. As a condition of a Corps of Engineers wetland permit, the developer must establish a naturally reproducing fisheries resource in the waters of Inspiration Lake. In order to fulfill the terms of the permit, a lake management plan was developed to evaluate the current and post-construction ability of Inspiration Lake to support a balanced fishery resource. Several competing uses are slated for the impoundment, including stormwater quality and quantity management, recreational boating, and recreational fishing.

The Inspiration Lake Management Plan consists of four phases. Phase I is attempting to balance the existing overpopulation of stunted bluegill sunfish (*Lepomis machrochirus*) through the introduction of a predator, the largemouth bass (*Micropterus salmoides*). Phase II will enhance the shore and bottom conditions of the lake in the spring

Wildlife Conservation in Metropolitan Environments. NIUW Symp. Ser. 2, L.W. Adams and D.L. Leedy, eds. Published by Natl. Inst. for Urban Wildl., 10921 Trotting Ridge Way, Columbia, MD 21044, USA, 1991.

of 1991 using vegetation and structures (boulders, artificial reefs, debris piles) to provide optimal largemouth bass habitat. Phase III will involve quarterly and annual sampling of water chemistry (DO, pH, TSS, TDS, nutrients, and metals) and aquatic life (zooplankton, macroinvertebrates, fish) for a period of 5 years. Conditions within the lake will be analyzed and compared with predevelopment baseline conditions to identify population and community trends, and any potential water quality problems that may affect the establishment of a naturally reproducing fishery. Phase IV of the plan will include the development of finalized long-term fish stocking, monitoring, and habitat maintenance programs based upon the results of Phase III sampling. Phase IV also will develop public sport fishing regulations.

Quality Urban Fisheries Management: More Than Just Trophy-Sized Fish

DONALD R. GOBER, GREGORY J. LANGER, AND LISA LANGELIER, *U.S. Fish and Wildlife Service, Rocky Mountain Arsenal, Building 111, Commerce City, CO 80022-2180*

The Rocky Mountain Arsenal is a 70-km² site located 16.1 km northeast of Denver, Colorado. The Arsenal supports three self-maintained, trophy, catch and release warm and coolwater fisheries totaling 60.8 ha in size. Arsenal anglers were surveyed to determine average catch rates, satisfaction level, angling expertise, and why they fish at the Arsenal. Average catch rates (number of fish per angler hour) and length of fish caught do not appear to differ significantly from Yellowstone Park fisheries or nearby urban military fisheries. Angler satisfaction levels are not significantly higher than other selected fisheries. Arsenal anglers considered themselves to be more experienced on the average than anglers using other premiere catch and release fisheries such as the Yellowstone River. Arsenal anglers reported that closeness to home, fewer people, and the aesthetics of fishing at this de facto wildlife refuge were important qualities of the site. By maintaining high quality catch and release fishing and emphasizing other aesthetically pleasing aspects of the site, we can influence angler profile. We are currently evaluating the potential to organize and manage Arsenal anglers so they may assist in the preservation of Arsenal resources.

Acknowledgments.—We would like to acknowledge the following in preparation of this poster: Program Manager Rocky Mountain Arsenal—U.S. Army; Colorado Fishery Assistance Office—U.S. Fish and Wildlife Service; and the Department of Recreation Resources and Landscape Architecture—Colorado State University.

The Value of Urban Parks for Education and Research: Examples from North Carolina and Florida

AL KINLAW, *Wekiwa Springs State Park, 1800 Wekiwa Circle, Apopka, FL 32712*

JOHN CONNORS, *Raleigh Parks and Recreation, P.O. Box 590, Raleigh, NC 27602*

WILLIAM KENDALL, DAVID ADAMS, PHILLIP DOERR, AND PHILLIP MANOR, *Departments of Statistics, Forestry, and Zoology, North Carolina State University, Raleigh, NC 27695*

Urban nature parks provide semi-isolated areas where ecological impacts on natural systems from adjoining human developments can be studied. Often these areas can be utilized as small-scale empirical "testing grounds" and outdoor teaching laboratories for ecological theories such as island biogeography or succession. Naturalists can capitalize on the existence of nearby large human populations by providing interpretive programs that demonstrate the ecological value of park experiments, allow "hands on" participation, and teach local residents how to minimize the adverse effects of development.

Because development density patterns are the result of both ecological constraints as well as the politics of the marketplace, we believe it is important for urban scientists to understand the patterns of wildlife distribution by using development density as a key factor in habitat analysis. Often, areas adjacent to parks are zoned for high residential development, yet the impacts of this development remain largely unknown. We collected data on breeding birds from 1985–1990 in an established urban park and an adjoining woodland tract under development. We observed declines in populations of some woodland passerines and increases in house finches (*Carpodacus mexicanus*), mockingbirds (*Mimus polyglottos*), and house sparrows (*Passer domesticus*) in the developed tract. Other data have been collected on aquatic invertebrates, macrophytic plants, and butterflies that could be used as baseline data to evaluate effects of future development.

We developed a baseline database of the flora and fauna at Dorothea Dix Farmlands, a park about to be developed as a campus extension of North Carolina State University and prepared an environmental impact statement to evaluate impact of three likely types of development. The research and educational value of this approach was discussed, as well as results of a 13-year student sampling exercise at the Yates Pond Biological Area that documented a reciprocal relationship between *Oxydendron* and *Cornus*.

We presented results of a questionnaire sent to urban naturalists to determine how they capitalize on their urban setting for research and education. Lastly, we provided statistical protocols for studies to determine impact of trampling terrestrial and streambed vegetation by people, horses, canoeists, and waders in Florida parks.

Prairie Propagation and Environmental Education in Metropolitan Environments

NEIL P. BERNSTEIN, *Department of Biology, Mount Mercy College, Cedar Rapids, IA 52402*

This project combined two important concepts: prairie propagation and environmental education. Iowa has lost over 99% of its original prairie. To counter this loss, organizations such as the Indian Creek Nature Center (ICNC) of Cedar Rapids, Iowa, have attempted to re-establish prairies. The ICNC also conducts environmental education for the city's public schools.

In spring, 1989, when president of the Cedar Rapids Audubon Society, I became convinced that we needed to increase our efforts in promoting a "hands-on" approach to environmental education. Therefore, the chapter purchased prairie plants for all second grade classrooms to plant in a brome meadow at ICNC designated for prairie propagation. Students were told about Iowa's prairie, given their plant with a description of its natural history, and then allowed to plant it as a class project. This allowed the students to identify with conservation concerns, and it also helped the ICNC re-establish a prairie.

During the first year (under drought conditions), deer browsed most of the plants because they were some of the few green plants present. More spring rains in the second year enhanced survival of the plants. The project, sponsored by the Cedar Rapids Audubon Society and ICNC, is receiving praise from ICNC staff, teachers, and conservationists, and is continuing.

The Ecology of Colorado's Urban Wildlife: An Illustrated Book and Teacher's Guide

CAROL ANN MOORHEAD[1], AND GENE DECKER, *Department of Fishery and Wildlife Biology, Colorado State University, Fort Collins, CO 80523*

Approximately 80% of Colorado's residents live along the eastern edge of the Rocky Mountains in a 240-km urbanized corridor between Fort Collins and Pueblo. Educational materials entitled *The Ecology of Colorado's Urban Wildlife* were developed specifically for these urban residents with the purpose of increasing their understanding about Colorado's wildlife. This paper outlined why these materials are needed in an urbanized state like Colorado and the justification for their content and curricular design.

Specifically, *The Ecology of Colorado's Urban Wildlife* is a color-illustrated book (70–80 pages) with a separate teacher's guide. The subject was chosen on the premise that the best place to teach urbanites about wildlife is in their daily environment. The book introduces students and lay-persons to basic ecological principles using Colorado's urban wildlife and habitats as illustrations. In addition, the book discusses the history of urbanization in Colorado, the benefits of urban wildlife, and the importance of cooperative planning to the conservation and establishment of wildlife habitats in urban areas.

The teacher's guide is designed for use in grades six through eight. To promote the book's integration into existing school curricula, the teacher's guide features inter- and multi-disciplinary activities. In addition, it emphasizes field projects that can be conducted in school yards and other local habitats.

The development of *The Ecology of Colorado's Urban Wildlife* was made possible by financial support from the Colorado Division of Wildlife (CDOW). Publication of these materials, by Roberts Rinehart Publishers of Boulder, Colorado, is anticipated in September, 1991. The book and teacher's guide will be sold to school districts and other educational organizations throughout urban Colorado, as well as to the general public. Posters of the artwork will also be available.

[1]Present address: U.S. Fish and Wildlife Service, Rocky Mountain Arsenal, Building 111, Commerce City, CO 80022-2180.

Support for Wildlife Restoration and Habitat Protection Programs: The Case of Recreational Users of an Urban River Corridor

ROBERT A. ROBERTSON, *Recreation Management Program, 202 Beyer Hall, Iowa State University, Ames, IA 50011*

JOANNE M. GRADY, *Department of Animal Ecology, 124 Science II, Iowa State University, Ames, IA 50011*

RABEL J. BURDGE, *Institute for Environmental Studies, 101 West Peabody Drive, University of Illinois at Urbana-Champaign, Urbana, IL 61801*

Waterways and associated lands within close proximity to urban population centers serve as habitat for many different species of wildlife. As such, urban river corridors provide the opportunity for millions of people to see wildlife and experience nature first hand. Unfortunately, commercial, industrial, and municipal uses of urban river corridors receive top priority, and only within the past decade has wildlife restoration and habitat protection become a policy-related concern.

Local, state, and federal monies are currently being utilized to enhance both economic development and wildlife restoration-habitat protection programs adjacent to urban waterways. Different interest groups usually have very different ideas about the future of a particular stretch of river. The goal of achieving balance between economic growth and the protection of wildlife values creates a critical need for better understanding of the level of public support for wildlife restoration and habitat protection programs. The objectives of this research were to determine whether recreation visitors to an urban river corridor favor "more," "the same," or "less" tax support for wildlife restoration and habitat protection programs, and to identify variables that are important for distinguishing among the various recreational user groups.

The resource setting for this study was the Upper Illinois Waterway-Illinois and Michigan Canal National Heritage Corridor, which stretches 161 km across Illinois and includes the southern portion of the Greater Chicago Metropolitan Area. The corridor provides opportunities for water-based and water-enhanced recreation for persons from both urban and rural areas. Data for this study were collected from May to September of 1988. One thousand sixty-seven parties were contacted as they arrived or departed various recreation sites, access points, and campgrounds within the study area. Individuals were asked if they would be willing to complete an eight-page questionnaire about various issues associated with the corridor and its resources. Of those initially contacted, 1024 (96%) agreed to participate and were given a mail-back questionnaire; 757 questionnaires were completed, for a response rate of 71%.

A support of wildlife restoration-habitat protection score was computed by adding and averaging the response score from three of the tax preference items (wildlife restoration, wetland preservation, and protection of natural areas, alpha = 0.83). Based on these averages, the respondents were assigned membership in one of three groups (less support, same support, and more support). Initial examination of the frequencies indicated that over 57% of the sample favored increased tax support for wildlife restoration-habitat protection programs, whereas 20% favored maintaining current support, and 23% favored decreased support.

Discriminant analysis was used to examine the relationship between level of support group (less, same, and more) and various independent variables (age, income, education, place of residence, and four attitude variables). The results provide a better understanding of the level of public support for wildlife restoration and habitat protection. For example, attitude towards a continued decline in wildlife populations, attitude toward commercial development, and years of formal education had the most distinguishing power among the three groups, whereas income, place of residence, and the lack of encounters with wildlife had the least. Overall, the model had two significant discriminant functions and correctly classified 63% of the respondents.

Motivations Associated with Urban Pest Management Activities[1]

CHARLOTTE F. YOUNG, *Social and Natural Resources Section, Building 301, Argonne National Laboratory, 9700 S. Cass Ave., Argonne, IL 60439*

Although some homeowners have begun adopting wildlife management type activities, these behaviors are not widely practiced. Many factors influence people's level of participation in such activities, including their skill and knowledge levels, feelings of efficacy, and their motivation.

---

[1]Work not funded or sponsored by Argonne National Laboratory or Department of Energy.

Wildlife Conservation in Metropolitan Environments. NIUW Symp. Ser. 2, L.W. Adams and D.L. Leedy, eds. Published by Natl. Inst. for Urban Wildl., 10921 Trotting Ridge Way, Columbia, MD 21044, USA, 1991.

This paper examines types of motivations associated with urban residents' involvement in gypsy moth management activities for communities with and without gypsy moth infestations.

Information on types of motives potentially applicable to gypsy moth management behaviors was gathered from studies in areas such as recreation, hazardous materials management, recycling, environmental education, and pest management. Research in these broad areas suggested many applicable motives. These included: yard care providing social opportunities, the problem being too removed, concern about using hazardous chemicals, spraying as the easiest form of gypsy moth control, and being afraid of insects. Based on these expected types of motivations, multiple statements for the different types were included in a questionnaire that was sent to a random sample of homeowners in two urban areas. One of these communities currently has a gypsy moth infestation and management program; the other does not. The types of motives suggested by the literature were then compared with respondents' patterns of answers, using cluster and factor analyses. Responses from the two cities were analyzed separately, given the differences in gypsy moth infestation levels.

Study results suggested that several types of motives may be salient for participation in gypsy moth management activities. Seven types of motives emerged from respondents who lived in the city with a gypsy moth problem. Five of the same motives and two different ones were found for respondents who lived in the city with no gypsy moth infestation.

For both cities, a scale named LAWN CARE ENJOYABLE included the notion that "puttering around in one's yard" is enjoyable, the social component of doing lawn care, and intrinsic aspects of beautifying one's neighborhood and learning about the gypsy moth. Again, for both cities, the grouping called TREE DAMAGE addressed people's concern about the potential damage that the gypsy moth might do to their trees. It also contained one item on the economic aspects of tree damage, as well as an intrinsic aspect that "tree care seems like the right thing to do."

For both cities, two items grouped together, named concern about GYPSY MOTHS causing SKIN RASHES. One item, focusing on people's entomphobia, and grouping by itself, was termed AFRAID OF INSECTS.

Another type of motive that emerged for both cities, but in somewhat different form, was called USING INSECTICIDES. This motive included the ease of using sprays to manage the gypsy moth and concerns about the harmful effects of insecticides. However, it did not include the item that insecticides harm people for respondents who lived in the city with the gypsy moth infestation.

Another grouping, termed CONTROL TOO COM-

PLEX, emerged for both cities, although again, it varied slightly across cities. It contained two items about knowing how to manage the gypsy moth for both cities. It also included the effort needed to protect one's trees and concerns about the expense of management for respondents from the uninfested city.

Two additional dimensions emerged from the analysis, although these differed by city. For respondents who did not live in the city with a gypsy moth problem, a motive type called TOO REMOVED was found. This motive addressed the notion that the gypsy moth problem was irrelevant to people's current lives. For respondents in the infested city only, a grouping called BURLAP BAND HASSLE emerged. This motive tapped the notion that using burlap bands (for managing the gypsy moth) may be cumbersome.

The results suggested that multiple motives are important for homeowners' participation in urban pest management activities. Implications for understanding these motives and for facilitating such participation were discussed.

Categorizing and Mapping Urban Habitats with a Geographic Information System

GEORGIA G. BRYAN AND JAMES J. DINSMORE, *Department of Animal Ecology, Iowa State University, Ames, IA 50011*

LAURA S. JACKSON, *Iowa Department of Natural Resources, RR 1, Boone, IA 50036*

PAUL A. VOHS, *Cooperative Fish and Wildlife Research Unit, Iowa State University, Ames, IA 50011*

Beginning in 1989, a study of avian species composition and abundance patterns in urban areas was conducted in Ames, Iowa. The project's goals were to develop methods of inventorying urban birds and their habitats and to use those methods to better understand how various species respond to different habitat types. MIPS (Map Image Processing System), a GIS system, was used to categorize and map habitats within the city limits of Ames. Infra-red air photos were used for the initial habitat mapping and were field-updated for areas where recent land use changes had occurred.

Five habitat types representative of urban areas were identified from the initial habitat mapping on the basis of the proportions of certain habitat features (i.e., herbaceous

Wildlife Conservation in Metropolitan Environments. NIUW Symp. Ser. 2, L.W. Adams and D.L. Leedy, eds. Published by Natl. Inst. for Urban Wildl., 10921 Trotting Ridge Way, Columbia, MD 21044, USA, 1991.

vegetation, trees, shrubs, and buildings and roads). MIPS allowed us to rapidly determine the location and area of each of the habitat types. It also facilitated stratified random selection of 40 points (eight in each of the five habitat types) as starting points for the bird censuses. Additionally, MIPS was used to map the habitat within each of the individual bird census areas by using airborne video images taken at 915 m. Such a system has great utility to urban planners and others in identifying habitats, mapping their location, decreasing the amount of field work necessary, and increasing our understanding of the value of various habitats for wildlife in an urban environment.

A Design for Urban Wildlife and Affordable Elderly Housing

RICHARD C. PAIS AND ZOLNA RUSSELL[1], *Daft-McCune-Walker, Inc., 200 East Pennsylvania Avenue, Towson, MD 21204*

Preservation and enhancement of wildlife habitat was a primary concern in the design of a site plan for 104 units of affordable elderly housing at Maiden Choice Terrace Apartments in Baltimore County, Maryland. A habitat inventory and an analysis of vegetation were conducted, and the building, parking, stormwater management, and sediment and erosion control facilities were located to provide maximum preservation of existing vegetation and habitat. Final design plans retained 40% of existing vegetation and detailed locations for a nature trail, nest boxes, bird feeders, water features, and emergent aquatic vegetation within a stormwater pond.

The planting plan incorporated plants attractive to songbirds, hummingbirds, and butterflies. The cost of wildlife-sensitive landscaping compared favorably with the cost of traditional landscaping and met Baltimore County landscape requirements. Landscape maintenance costs after construction will be significantly less than for a traditional landscape.

A program of wildlife studies with a local nature center will be initiated following construction, and we believe significant therapeutic and recreational benefits will be obtained by residents through wildlife-associated recreation.

[1]Present address: William F. Kirwin, 28 East Susquehanna Avenue, Towson, MD 21204.

Management of Powerline Rights-of-way for Botanical and Wildlife Value in Metropolitan Areas

H.H. OBRECHT, III, *U.S. Fish and Wildlife Service, Patuxent Wildlife Research Center, Laurel, MD 20708*

W.J. FLEMING, *U.S. Fish and Wildlife Service, North Carolina Cooperative Fish and Wildlife Research Unit, Box 7617, North Carolina State University, Raleigh, NC 27695-7617*

J.H. PARSONS, *Potomac Electric Power Company, Washington, DC 20068-0001*

Powerline rights-of-way (ROWs) are common features of metropolitan landscapes. These ROWs are often >76 m wide and extend for many km through urban environments. They include thousands of ha in population centers where the demand for land is high and costs for acquiring new conservation areas often are prohibitive. Cooperative ventures between power companies and state, federal, and private conservation groups can yield unique plant communities and wildlife habitats in these urban ROW properties.

In 1960, the U.S. Fish and Wildlife Service entered into a partnership with the Potomac Electric Power Company (PEPCO) to manage vegetation on a newly constructed ROW transecting the Patuxent Wildlife Research Center, Laurel, Md. To minimize arching potential, it was agreed that vegetation was to be limited to <3.5 m in height. The vegetation was to be managed in a fashion consistent with the mission of the wildlife center. Native vegetation was allowed to revegetate the soils that were denuded of plants during the construction phase. The vegetation was then managed by periodic removal of all tall-growing tree species. This was accomplished by selectively applying a small amount of herbicide to the stems of each unwanted species. There was no mowing or indiscriminate use of herbicides. Now, 30 years after the powerline was constructed, the ROW is dominated by an artificially maintained shrub community that is rich in botanical diversity and is heavily used by wildlife. The success of this pilot study has led PEPCO to adopt this vegetation management system on half of the 3200 ha of ROW that they own in the Washington, D.C. metropolitan area. Techniques and results of vegetation management on the ROW at the Patuxent Wildlife Research Center and their application to the creation of conservation habitats along urban powerline ROWs were described.

Wildlife Conservation in Metropolitan Environments. NIUW Symp. Ser. 2, L.W. Adams and D.L. Leedy, eds. Published by Natl. Inst. for Urban Wildl., 10921 Trotting Ridge Way, Columbia, MD 21044, USA, 1991.

Development of a Private Firm Specializing in Urban Wildlife Management

KEVIN D. CLARK, *Critter Control Inc., 640 Starkweather, Plymouth, MI 48170*

LYNN BRABAND, *Critter Control Inc., P.O. Box 19389, Rochester, NY 14619*

Critter Control Inc. developed from a single office in 1982 handling nuisance wildlife problems to a nationwide firm (over 50 offices in 20 states as of 1990) involved with diverse wildlife-related services. The company started in response to the need for responsible, reasonably priced nuisance wildlife control in suburban Detroit.

By 1987, branch offices were opened in nine other cities in Michigan and Ohio. With plans to go nationwide, the firm concentrated on hiring well-informed and articulate professionals as managers. Today, the company has one manager with a Ph.D. in wildlife ecology, seven with Master's degrees, and over 20 with Bachelor's degrees in wildlife-related fields. To facilitate expansion, the company compiled data on population, per capita income, and housing starts (an indicator of urbanization) to determine potential markets. In 1988, Critter Control franchised, with approximately one half of the offices now manager owned.

As a result of a June 1989 strategic planning meeting, the company began the development of wildlife-related services in addition to nuisance control. "Wildlife Management Services" provides consulting and in-field services for backyard habitat, land development, and municipal wetland-woodland ordinances. "Critter Country" (five stores currently located in Michigan, Ohio, Maryland, and Virginia) sells wild bird supplies and nature-related gift items and promotes conservation and appreciation of wildlife. A mail-order business, "Wildlife Management Supplies," offers such items as live traps and rodent control supplies to the pest control industry, animal control departments, and nuisance wildlife control operators.

Social trends, such as urbanization, decreasing government funding, and heightened environmental awareness point toward an increasing role for the private sector in wildlife management. In order to develop an effective, long-term urban wildlife management strategy, the current schism between wildlife conservation and wildlife damage control needs to be replaced with a more integrative approach.

An argument can be made that a schism exists between the promotion of wildlife and wildlife damage control. Illustrations include separate federal government agencies for the two functions, the frequently minimal attention given to damage control in wildlife education and literature, and the tension that sometimes occurs among natural resource professionals over damage control. Wildlife management needs an integrated approach that recognizes the need for both wildlife conservation and effective damage control. Such an approach will be particularly important in urban areas where any increase in wildlife habitat and populations will result in an increased likelihood of wildlife nuisance and damage situations. Accurate, effective information and services on preventing and alleviating such situations will be important in any long-term approach to urban wildlife management.

Wildlife Conservation in Metropolitan Environments. NIUW Symp. Ser. 2, L.W. Adams and D.L. Leedy, eds. Published by Natl. Inst. for Urban Wildl., 10921 Trotting Ridge Way, Columbia, MD 21044, USA, 1991.

VIII.

Symposium Summary

Eric G. Bolen, *University of North Carolina at Wilmington, Wilmington*

Urban Wildlife: The End of the Beginning

ERIC G. BOLEN, *Dean, The Graduate School, and Department of Biological Sciences, University of North Carolina at Wilmington, Wilmington, NC 28403*

Let me begin with a pronouncement: urban wildlife has emerged as a vigorous and exciting new dimension to the theory and practice of wildlife management—a view that is amply reinforced by the sizable audience at this conference. I thus have entitled my summary—with due credit to the wartime observations of Winston Churchill—as The End of the Beginning in recognition of the steady evolution of urban wildlife into a solid subdiscipline, to wit:

- this is at least the sixth symposium devoted to urban wildlife—the first being held in 1968—and more are sure to follow;
- the United States is represented by the National Institute for Urban Wildlife and at least two companion centers exist elsewhere in the world (i.e., urban wildlife is an international movement), each publishing enlightening newsletters and management information;
- the revised (in 1973) North American Wildlife Policy specifically mentions urban wildlife management;
- an urban wildlife policy statement was approved by The Wildlife Society in 1983;
- relevant journals regularly publish papers addressing the management and research of urban wildlife;
- a growing number of state conservation agencies have urban wildlife biologists and programs; and
- the forthcoming edition of the Wildlife Techniques Manual, published by The Wildlife Society, will include a chapter dedicated to urban wildlife.

The task before me involves the delivery of a review—in an allotment of 20 minutes—of 33 papers. Of these, three concerned the Portland-Vancouver metropolitan area, six each addressed ecological subjects, management issues, and public and resources needs, seven considered planning and design, and another five appraised public participation and education. An additional 23 papers were offered in the poster session. Hence, for a college professor who, on the occasion of the last class of the semester, has covered perforce entire units on population dynamics, animal behavior, and wildlife diseases, I nonetheless remain both numbed and humbled by my assignment.

MEETING PUBLIC AND RESOURCE NEEDS

Wilson, on behalf of the Iowa Department of Natural Resources, opened the symposium by noting the growing importance of urban wildlife to the citizens of what generally is regarded as a rural state. Iowa and its sister states on the plains and prairies of North America have experienced two significant transformations, the second of which continues today. First came the plow, and with it wildlife habitat rapidly diminished as crop monocultures replaced the vast sea of native grasses and prairie wetlands. For decades thereafter, a prairie empire of farms and small towns flourished, but a second transformation—urbanization—continues its spread across the midwest. Since its passage in 1988, Iowa's Resource Enhancement and Protection Act (REAP) began funding activities devoted to the state's natural and cultural resources, including such urban-oriented activities as the development of bird-feeding stations at retirement and nursing homes and the city-based release of peregrine falcons. All told, urban wildlife increasingly represents the primary contact with nature for many of Iowa's citizens, hence REAP's growing importance to the management of urban wildlife.

The importance of urban parks, as well as job opportunities in outdoor activities, may be ascending for African-Americans (Daniel). Unlike their own experiences as teenagers, black college students indicated that, as adults, they and their families expect to spend more time engaged in outdoor activities. Hence, largely because of advances in their education and economic status, African-Americans in the near future will represent a greater population of "users" and exert greater bearing on the resolution of environmental issues.

Hester viewed urban wildlife from the vantage point of lands managed by the National Park Service (NPS) where, for most citizens, elk, bison, grizzlies, and bighorn sheep normally form the image of wildlife in the American wilder-

Wildlife Conservation in Metropolitan Environments. NIUW Symp. Ser. 2, L.W. Adams and D.L. Leedy, eds. Published by Natl. Inst. for Urban Wildl., 10921 Trotting Ridge Way, Columbia, MD 21044, USA, 1991.

ness. However, in recent years, desires for improving the quality of life in the nation's cities led to the creation of urban parks within the NPS system. Despite some concerns about just how much "naturalness" might be preserved, Rock Creek Park in Washington, D.C. harbors 1,200 species of plants, muskrats, red and gray foxes, deer, beaver, about two dozen species of fishes, and a host of birds, including pileated woodpeckers and great horned owls. Indeed, raccoons already are unwelcome in nearby residential areas, and deer soon may become troublesome. Other urban parks provide visitors with such "hands-on" experiences as banding raptors or restoring native vegetation in addition to nature trails and other educational programs—one of the latter, a mock trial of a developer threatening an endangered species certainly is an imaginative learning device. Finally, urban parks are laboratories where thoughtful research might forewarn us about the threats of human encroachment on parks in more pristine areas.

Blanchard outlined the U.S. Fish and Wildlife Service's view of our urbanizing nation—a nation in which 90% of its citizens will live in urban areas within 10 years! Indeed, third and fourth-generation urbanites are already among us, and their view of the "natural world" surely differs from the visions of John Muir. Hence, the development and effective delivery of educational programs emerges as a special thrust within the more traditional programs of wildlife management (e.g., migratory bird management). The attitudes of minorities toward wildlife are also of concern; 85% of all African-Americans live in cities, and surveys indicate that this group is not well informed about wildlife. Fortunately, several federal refuges (e.g., San Francisco Bay National Wildlife Refuge) are advantageously situated for the transfer of knowledge to large numbers of urban citizens.

Liu spoke on behalf of industry's concern for improving the quality of life across both urban and exurban landscapes. Corporate America thus must be involved in seeking solutions to environmental issues instead of being part of the problem, and science, as a tool in problem-solving, must not yield to ill-founded perceptions and unbridled emotions.

Fish and Wildlife 2000 is a blueprint for managing the wildlife resources on the 109 million ha administered by the Bureau of Land Management (Almand). More than 3,000 species of animals and some 900 species of plants with special status fall under BLM's stewardship. Most of the BLM land lies in the West, where urbanization is progressing rapidly (e.g., 85% of the population in Utah is concentrated along the Wasatch Front). Hence, because of urbanization, wildlife habitats in the West will receive more stress than otherwise expected, and thus greater pressures for resource management will befall state and federal agencies.

Session Summary

Urbanization has transformed much of North America, including Iowa and other geopolitical units once regarded as rural and sylvan. Moreover, new constituencies (e.g., African-Americans) as well as dynamic new wildlife pro-

grams can develop concurrently with urbanization. In urban settings, parks and wildlife refuges uniquely enrich the lives of city dwellers, and industry, following the leadership of public-land agencies, also can share a part in providing urban citizens with outdoor recreation and an exposure to nature.

ECOLOGY OF URBAN WILDLIFE

Most studies of urban wildlife feature native species that somehow cope in a highly modified environment (e.g., peregrine falcons nesting in downtown Baltimore), but Haspel and Calhoon studied the behavior of a species that is not alien to the urban setting: they contrasted the behavior of free-ranging house cats at two sites where the patterns of human occupancy were dissimilar. This study, conducted in Brooklyn, clearly indicated that human life-styles produce major influences on the structure and behavior of cat populations.

Deer continue to plague human settlements. In metropolitan Milwaukee, Bryant and Ishmael determined that translocated deer "do not lead idealized lives" (e.g., high mortality), and the program costs increased nearly twofold ($17,600 to $32,760) in 3 years despite decreased costs per translocated animal. More disheartening is the finding that the translocated deer retain their urban behavior and again frequent gardens, roadways, yards, and bird feeders, thereby continuing their troublesome ways. Thus, like the proverbial bad penney, nuisance deer were simply passed on from the backyards of one community to those of another.

Zoonoses rightly produce concerns for public health, but perhaps more so when rabies and cities are involved. Hence, dense populations of skunks, raccoons, and foxes warrant special attention in Toronto, where 40% of the rabies cases in urban Ontario occurred (Rosatte et al.). Indeed, high turnover rates suggest that rabies and distemper represent the factor limiting skunk and raccoon populations in Toronto; nonetheless, both species continue increasing in numbers and spreading into a larger variety of urban habitats.

The effect of urbanization on foraging strategy of birds offers a test of competitive exclusion theory (Moulton and Adams). That is, as urbanization progresses, do species face increasing competition, perhaps to the point where some are extirpated? In this case, six coexisting species of woodpeckers were studied in relation to their foraging behavior at sites where, because of development, natural environments were increasingly more limited. The results indicated that niche overlap was avoided, but that the strength of resource partitioning followed a gradient of urbanization (i.e., most intense at the urbanized site and less so where the habitat was undisturbed). Nonetheless, at least under conditions of this study, woodpeckers showed enough plasticity in their foraging behavior to continue their coexistence in the same relative abundance at all sites, irrespective of urbanization.

Hadidian et al. determined the daytime dens of radio-collared raccoons frequenting residential areas surrounding an urban park in metropolitan Washington, D.C. Trees accounted for most (69%) of the sites, but raccoons also rested in residences (15%) and ground dens (11%) in such places as storm sewers. Almost all (90%) of the locations in residential buildings were in houses occupied year-round by humans; chimneys and attics were commonplace dens, but preferences for such sites in winter were not evident. Raccoons changed their daytime dens in trees more often than those located in buildings, but it remains unclear whether these findings indicate preferences or reflect a more limited selection of adequate sites.

Habitat within the city of Cheyenne, Wyoming, represents an oasis of diversity otherwise absent in the surrounding exurban prairie (Sears and Anderson). As might be expected, vegetative structure is related to the age of neighborhoods within the city, which in turn influences the nature of the avian communities in each stratum. Thus, birds were both more abundant and more diverse where plant cover was greatest, especially where the landscaping included native plants.

Session Summary

Research continues to reveal the absorbing world of urban environments in which ecological phenomena once attracted only occasional attention (e.g., the remarkable circumstances in which titmice learned to open milk bottles in England). Thus, the study of cats should make us wonder how raccoons, blue jays, and other wildlife might be similarly influenced by the character of human neighborhoods and if such "ecotypic variation" might affect the scale and grain of our management goals. We also see again how ecological studies may shape management; the dynamics of denning raccoons in urban environments clearly indicate that structural modifications are the long-term remedy for troublesome wildlife. Finally, urbanization offers structured environments where competitive exclusion and other ecological theories might be tested, as demonstrated by the work with woodpeckers. In short, the studies in this session clearly indicate that, for creative minds, the city becomes a dynamic laboratory for a broad range of valuable ecological research.

PLANNING AND DESIGN

As biologists, we have learned much about the effects of small islands in terms of extinction rates and colonization, but Dawson called our attention to the insidious hazards of "human predation"—the outright theft or vandalism of unique materials from nature reserves. As a sad case in point, fully 6 of 17 (35%) species of orchids were extirpated by plant poachers at a small reserve in the hammock communities of southern Florida. Hence, future considerations for the establishment of natural areas cannot overlook what I shall dub the "biogeography of social influences," which

requires buffer areas, zoning, or other measures for the fullest protection of a site's biological resources.

Concerns for "island effect" occurred in Tucson where Evans described the city's efforts for managing, by ordinance, the biotic communities associated with saguaro cacti. Specifically, that effort concerned protecting the biotic integrity of the riparian vegetation bordering ephemeral river beds ("washes," in the lexicon of westerners); the washes extend from Saguaro National Monument into urban areas subject to development. This report provides further evidence of the national commitment for preserving riparian environments—whether in a southwestern desert, deciduous forest or prairie system—and underscores the necessity for comprehensive planning if vital resources are to exist as a continuum in our cities *and* adjacent nature preserves.

Indeed, Hilliard has attempted just such planning—in this instance, the reestablishment in Syracuse, New York, of natural areas where selected species of mammals might thrive. Using a series of biological screens (e.g., dietary information and home-range data), a planning scheme emerged whereby sites might be designed for selected species of mammals. In addition to the educational and aesthetic values resulting from such a program, the restored sites—as recognized natural areas—will reduce the maintenance load presently borne by the city budget.

Klem calls our attention to a staggering source of avian mortality: collisions with glass. His *lowest* estimate is that nearly 100 million birds, representing 25% of all species north of Mexico, die each year when they fly into windows reflecting an image of safe passage through vegetation or open sky. However, the toll goes on with little fanfare visa-a-vis catastrophes such as the Exxon Valdez oil spill, of which more than 300 spills of the same magnitude would be required to produce the same number of bird victims. Klem's field studies dispel the notion that decoys or silhouettes of predators might mitigate collisions. Ultimately, new designs (e.g., angled windows) or materials (e.g., nonreflecting glass) offer the best remedies, again illustrating the unique interdisciplinary character of urban issues (i.e., dilemmas for which answers require the expertise of such disparate professions as structural engineers, glass manufacturers and, of course, wildlife biologists).

In the 1880s, after the arrival of railroads, urban sprawl became a reality in southern California. Early plans for an urban park system linked by corridors failed to materialize in Los Angeles, and most sites where green spaces might have been saved were lost as development spread. Nonetheless, at least one arroyo and a chain of hilltops in southern California serve as exemplary sites where topography favors the restoration and establishment of corridors suitable for wildlife (Lyle and Quinn).

The Roanoke River flows through a highly urbanized zone, but its drainage still harbors one of the richest faunas on the Atlantic seaboard. Because of periodic flooding, the river system will be modified, but not until planning elements consistent with the protection of wildlife habitat have been incorporated (Lardner). Both the city of Roanoke and the Army Corps of Engineers agreed to actions that will benefit wildlife habitat (e.g., management of riparian vegetation). Uniquely, citizen groups were given boat tours so that the plans became a living experience and not just lines on a blueprint. The result will be a linear park system, replete with wildlife resources, and lessened risk of flooding.

Endangered species often face hazards associated with urban growth and development (e.g., land clearance), thus invoking strictures of the Endangered Species Act. However, Beatley describes how an amendment to the act enables development to proceed under the guidance of an acceptable Habitat Conservation Plan (HCP). Whereas some HCPs have protected large parcels of habitat, development may continue at the expense of sensitive species. Moreover, HCPs give birth to crucial policy issues, among them the adequacy of biological knowledge on which land-planning is based and the preservation of biodiversity for communities instead of single species.

Session Summary

The necessity of appropriate planning scarcely needs repeating here, but environmental disasters in urban settings are too often magnified because of the intensity of land use. Hence, immense numbers of birds collide with windows—and will continue to do so—unless changes are made in the construction of buildings. And, in addition to preserving the remnants of riparian zones, I hope we might find efficient ways of restoring the biological integrity of riparian zones already destroyed by thoughtless urban expansion, a topic that seems a fertile area for the teamwork of landscape and wildlife ecologists. Fortunately, the fruits of farsighted planning are apparent in case studies from urban areas as far-flung as Roanoke, Virginia and Los Angeles, California, including the well-taken lesson gained from involving the public (e.g., boat trips for citizen groups). Lest we believe all is well, however, Habitat Conservation Plans, despite their good intentions, nonetheless beg additional concerns for the integration of land-use planning with biodiversity and conservation strategies for endangered species.

MANAGEMENT ISSUES AND SUCCESSES

Alcatraz once was the epitome of "hard time" for unrepentant criminals—almost 40% of the island's habitat is concrete!—but today "The Rock" is managed by the National Park Service as a historic landmark where 950,000 visitors step ashore each year. Howell and Pollak thus examined the compatibility of cultural landscapes with the wildlife resources on Alcatraz. The latter includes an avifauna numbering 108 species, of which seven breed on the island, including significant colonies of black-crowned night-herons and western gulls. Recommendations focus not only on traditional methods (e.g., modifying human trespass and intensive habitat improvements), but also an educational

component that describes the dynamic ecological processes at work on an island's biota. The proposal clearly illustrates the potential for a responsible measure of multiple use on public lands.

Traditional wisdom suggests that the proximity of wildlife resources may enhance property values, but little empirical work is at hand to support the concept. King et al. have helped fill that void with an econometric study in which the values of single-family residential properties were assessed in terms of various outdoor amenities (e.g., parks). The results were complex, but among the findings was a relationship indicating that the proximity of certain types of wildlife habitat outranked (in terms of implicit price) private golf courses, the supposed "amenity deluxe" for modern lifestyles. More research is needed before we can state unequivocally that the proximity of urban wildlife habitat enhances the property value of residential homes—which in turn yields a community value via an increased tax base—but this study narrows the gap.

Our conference theme stresses the accommodation of wildlife management to the urbanization of America, and DeBruyckere and Garr noted how such a response has occurred in metropolitan St. Louis. Whereas hunting and fishing are permitted on state-owned wildlife areas near the city, exit surveys indicated that other activities (e.g., hiking) are enjoyed by more than half of the visitors. Maintenance changed to incorporate an "urban perspective" (e.g., roadways managed for two-wheel-drive vehicles). Regulations and habitat also were modified in ways that provided recreational opportunities for all users (e.g., special seasons for hunting with primitive weapons, food patches scattered to disperse hunting pressure, and wetland drawdowns for migratory waterbirds). A far-reaching effort at conservation education caps the program, including not only the activities (e.g., Day on the Marsh) of two resident naturalists, but also a Family Fishing Fair, a butterfly garden, a chalkboard where birders can list their discoveries, and the involvement of volunteers. By combining traditional and urban-oriented outdoor activities on single parcels of land, this project represents another fine example of the innovative conservation work for which Missouri has gained well-deserved recognition.

Because of urban sprawl, Schaefer et al. developed a management plan for Orlando, Florida, where a relatively intact river basin is at risk. Major components of the plan, much of which was endorsed by local governments, call for protection of critical habitat elements associated with the Econlockhatchee River system, including 335-m-wide setback Conservation Zones on either side of the river, restrictions on land-use practices (i.e., no activities that permanently alter vegetation), establishment of corridor linkages with other sites (e.g., xeric scrub communities), and acquisition of key parcels not otherwise protected by regulatory authority.

As urbanization steadily advances, humans often feed birds to fulfill their aspirations for lingering contact with nature. Today, some 82 million people annually dispense more than 454 million kg of birdseed, but what effect does this have on bird populations? Brittingham's study indicated that winter survival rates may increase almost twofold for chickadees having access to feeders when compared with those that do not; such differences are pronounced during long periods of cold weather. Feeders also may influence the abundance and distribution of certain birds (e.g., blue jays), which in turn may affect other species (e.g., increased egg predation). Disease, accidents, and predation are other factors often associated with feeding stations, but comparative data are wanting. Delayed migration probably is not an important aftermath of supplemental feeding.

The attraction of birds also concerned the safe operation of a busy urban airport in Minnesota, where Canada geese frequent the mowed borders of runways and thereby pose serious hazards for landing and departing aircraft. Of the various management options potentially available (e.g., harassment; shooting), Cooper determined that trapping and translocation offered the best results (i.e., fewer geese crossing the runways), largely because subflocks exist within the locally breeding goose populations. However, more must be learned about this form of management before the threat of airstrikes is completely eliminated, especially how to keep new birds from visiting airport locations.

Session Summary

The management of wildlife resources in urban systems is maturing as rapidly as any facet of natural resource conservation. This is evident in a highly structured site—Alcatraz by name—in neighborhoods where the proximity of wildlife habitat may influence real estate values, and in the ways that bird populations respond to feeding stations. A solid base of research spawns these and other management opportunities, as was pointed out in the important studies of goose behavior at an urban airport. We must, I believe, continue to champion the necessity of research as the foundation of wildlife management, and I know of few places where we face greater management challenges than in city environments.

PUBLIC PARTICIPATION AND EDUCATION

Nature centers, numbering some 1,500 across the United States, connect people with natural environments (Kay and Patterson). The primary focus is on public interaction and education at a natural site under the guidance of a professional staff. Programs involve an array of subjects, including advice about nuisance wildlife, care of injured or "orphaned" animals, public lectures, nature walks, and such auxiliary services as bird banding, censuses, and research services.

Urban wildlife management has not profited fully from the array of communication strategies currently available (e.g., newsletters), nor has research focused on ways to improve and assess these methods in urban environments

(Young). Better communication offers clear benefits for gaining public cooperation and involvement in wildlife programs, but the type of audience, setting, and nature of the message are important variables to consider when developing effective delivery systems (e.g., school children visiting a tree farm; slide shows for residents of rest homes; semitechnical presentations for city officials).

Bald Eagle Appreciation Days in Iowa combines the sponsorship of private enterprises and state and federal agencies to enhance the public's awareness of an endangered species, raptors, and the management of natural resources (Jackson). The program also aspires to promote tax check-offs for wildlife, although that goal has not yet been fully realized. Indoor (e.g., TV video and live eagles) and outdoor segments (e.g., observation in the company of biologists) comprise each event. After attracting an initial audience of 600, each weekend presentation now attracts an average of nearly 3,500 people—most in family groups—who, not incidently, contribute $25,000 to $75,000 to the local economy.

A partnership between the University of Florida and Florida's Game and Freshwater Fish Commission produced a highly functional Cooperative Urban Wildlife Program staffed by three professional biologists (Huegel et al.). The program's objectives focus on both the positive and negative values of wildlife, which are realized in management, educational, and research efforts; however, enhancement activities outweigh those concerned with nuisance wildlife. Association of the program with the state extension service enhances the delivery of information. Also, certain activities (e.g., printing costs and TV programs) can be assumed by one or the other partner that is better able to handle the task at hand.

Session Summary

The session highlights what has been, and remains to be, accomplished in the area of partnerships, communication, and sponsorships in the realm of urban wildlife management. Nature centers are focal points in such an infrastructure, and some types of special events (e.g., "Eagle Days") offer a welcome spinoff of adding hard dollars to local economy. Cooperative efforts include various configurations (i.e., combinations of local, state, and federal governments, as well as private and collegiate agencies), yet better methods of communication with the lay public are needed to improve the development of wildlife programs within urban environments.

POSTER SESSION

Kestrels attracted the attention of Dietrich et al. who tested a habitat suitability model by placing nest boxes in prime habitat in Kansas City, Kansas, vis-a-vis randomly placed boxes; the birds used both sets of boxes with about the same frequency. Nest boxes on utility poles established a successful "kestrel corridor" along a highway in Iowa (Ford and Smith). Also in Iowa, Jackson and Hollis described the utility of the winter bird-feeder survey, which yields various sorts of population data (e.g., invasions of cyclic species). Common crows no longer sustain their historical image as exclusively rural birds, as they now regularly nest near human habitations in urban settings, including Springfield, Ohio (Laux et al.).

In Ontario, nuisance ring-billed gulls were discouraged by various methods including harassment, overhead monofilament lines, collecting eggs, tethered raptors, distress calls, fire works, and habitat alteration (Blokpoel and Tessier). Savard and Falls presented a four-part package for birds occurring in Toronto: (a) breeding bird density and habitat features, (b) the underestimation of breeding bird populations using transects, (c) the abundance of fall migrants in relation to foliage, and (d) the density and diversity of birds in relation to the degree of urbanization. Clearcuts in forests near urban environments promoted the influx of urban birds, which may increase competition with forest birds (Richert and Richert).

Tree squirrels (two species) offer useful tools for studies of basic and applied biology in addition to their aesthetic values as urban wildlife. For example, Koprowski found a negative relationship between squirrel densities and the size of urban woodlots—an example of island biogeography theory and the impacts of fragmented landscapes. Urban parks also may be testing grounds for island biogeography and other ecological concepts (e.g., community succession) as well as sites for demonstration projects designed for public education (Kinlaw et al.). Nuisance raccoons wander for considerable distances following their relocation—one traveled at least 82 km in the first 14 days after its release—leading Hagen et al. to conclude that relocated raccoons seldom remain at release sites located in either residential areas or urban green spaces.

Cooling ponds at the Rocky Mountain Arsenal provide an unique urban fishery; bass, pike, and catfish are managed as a catch-and-release trophy operation, which also offers opportunities for studying hooking mortality and resource economics (Gober et al.). Management of a 4.5-ha lake associated with an urban development included four phases: releasing bass to control a stunted bluegill population; improving bottom and shoreline habitats; sampling water quality and aquatic communities; and long-term management of the bass fishery (Bitter and Danehy).

Powerline rights-of-way in urban landscapes are readily available for conservation uses (i.e., expensive land is already at hand for wildlife management, given the availability of suitable techniques). Obrecht et al. thus selectively managed a right-of-way crossing Patuxent Wildlife Research Center for vegetation that did not compromise the powerline yet enhanced the habitat for wildlife; because of the positive results, the power company adopted the management program for much of its rights-of-way elsewhere in the Washington, D.C., area.

Bernstein thoughtfully combined prairie restoration and environmental education into a hands-on program for second-graders; the students planted prairie vegetation after learning about the natural history of each species and its role in Iowa's grasslands. This is conservation at the "grassroots level"—twice over! The urbanization of the Front Range (Fort Collins to Pueblo) provided the impetus for *The Ecology of Colorado's Urban Wildlife*, an educational book and teacher's guide that uses urban wildlife and habitats to describe ecological ideas for school children and the lay public (Moorhead and Decker).

In Iowa, Bryan et al. used a GIS strategy for spatially determining urban habitats; in addition to its value as a land-use map, the system facilitates research by locating random points for transects (e.g., bird census). A wetland, nature trails, and other wildlife considerations were included in the design for a rest home for senior citizens at a cost comparing favorably with traditional landscaping, and maintenance costs will be significantly less (Pais and Russell).

Motivation for participating in urban wildlife activities may be complex, as determined from the attitudes of homeowners toward pest management for gypsy moths (Young). Based on a user's exit survey, education and income emerged as useful variables for models that assess public support for the protection of urban river corridors; the urban or rural residence of the respondents was of lesser importance (Robertson et al.). Urban wildlife now is marketed by private enterprise; Clark and Braband trace the evolution of their firm into the realm of habitat analysis, animal damage control, and retails sales.

SPECIAL SESSION: A TALE OF TWO CITIES

PLANNING FOR NATURAL AREAS IN THE PORTLAND, OREGON—VANCOUVER, WASHINGTON METROPOLITAN REGION

Portland, Oregon, and Vancouver, Washington, are sister cities whose ties now include the preservation of natural areas within the metropolitan area. This ambitious project includes multiphased inventories, including photointerpretation and mapping (Poracsky), and field surveys that described major habitat types and wildlife communities (Lev and Sharp). Nested within the larger venture is the creation of an urban wildlife refuge system guided by FAUNA—Friends & Advocates of Urban Natural Areas—whose 2,000 + members were instrumental in securing a funding base for the acquisition and management of urban natural areas (Houck).

Let us hope that similar projects arise in Minneapolis and St. Paul, Dallas and Fort Worth, Detroit and Windsor and, indeed, in sister cities everywhere.